To Barbara with my warmest regards and best wishes — Spurdwood Marion
AKA Captain Bernard W. Peterson USMCR Ret
and Corporal Marion G. Peterson USMCR
20 March '96
Scottsdale AZ.

SHORT STRAW

MEMOIRS OF KOREA
By a Fighter Pilot/Forward Air Controller

Captain Bernard W. Peterson USMCR (Ret)

Published by:

Chuckwalla Publishing
27015 N. 92nd Street
Scottsdale, AZ 85255
U.S.A.
(602) 585-4868

SHORT STRAW

MEMOIRS OF KOREA
By a Fighter Pilot/Forward Air Controller

Captain Bernard W. Peterson USMCR (Ret)

Published by:

Chuckwalla Publishing
27015 N. 92nd Street
Scottsdale, AZ 85255
U.S.A.
(602) 585-4868

All rights reserved. No part of this book may be reproduced in any form or by any means, except for the inclusion of brief quotations in a review, without permission in writing from the author.

Copyright © 1996 by Bernard W. Peterson
First Printing 1996

SAN: 297-5874

Printed in the United States of America

Library of Congress Catalog Card Number 95-83262

Senior Editor: Marion Gleason Peterson,
Associate Editors: Marcia Greene Peterson and Randall Rhoads Peterson
Maps: Elaine Marion Averitt
Typesetting: Beverly Peterson Dulaney and Elaine Marion Averitt

Photos courtesy USN, USMC, National Archives, Dept. of Defense, except where noted. Special Photo Credit to Captain James Van Ry USMCR (Ret) for front dust cover, Jim flying his AU-1 Corsair in Korea, 1953.

ISBN 0-9631875-3-8

Other books by author:

BRINY to the BLUE, Memoirs of WWII, by a Sailor/Marine Fighter Pilot

AIR FORCE Journal, Official Service Journal of the U.S. Army Air Forces, Facsimilies of Six Months, January 1943 through June 1943

Refer to Book Reorder Form on back page

CONTENTS

COPYRIGHT PAGE
CONTENTS PAGES
DEDICATION I
ASIAN MAP II
KOREAN MAP III
A MESSAGE FROM THE COMMANDER IV
DESIDERATA V
PREFACE VI

CHAPTER 1 KOREA
MY FIRST ENCOUNTER WITH THE WILY MIG 1
THE DREADED RUSSIAN COMMUNIST MIG-15 FIGHTER IN KOREA 4
TWO YEARS OF MIG ACTIVITY 5
FRIENDLY VS ENEMY CLAIMS 1 NOV 1950 TO 31 OCT 1952 5
OUR SITUATION AS CORSAIR PILOTS 6
THE U.S. MILITARY OCCUPATION OF KOREA
 IMMEDIATELY FOLLOWING WWII 7

CHAPTER 2 THE POST WORLD WAR TWO YEARS 10
ABOUT AIRESEARCH AND THE GARRETT CORPORATION 12
THE STORK VISITS 13
OUR FIRST MOVE 14
TRYING OUR HAND AT AGRICULTURE IN OUR SPARE TIME 14
THE COLD WAR HEATS UP/THE RESERVIST IS TWICE THE CITIZEN 15
OUR SECOND SON ARRIVES 16
RUSSIA EXPLODES HER FIRST NUCLEAR BOMB 16
SOUNDS OF WAR IN KOREA 17
PUSAN PERIMETER "STAND OR DIE" ORDER 20
AIR WAR IN KOREA 21
THE FLEET MARINE FORCE (FMF) AND READINESS POSTURE 24
POOR OPERATIONAL LOGISTICS PLANNING 25
THINKING ABOUT VOLUNTEERING 25
THE INCHON LANDING, OPERATION CHROMITE 25
THE ONSET OF THE CHINESE ENTERING THE WAR 27
CALLED TO ACTIVE DUTY AS PILOT OF FIGHTER AIRCRAFT 29

CONTENTS cont'd

CHAPTER 3   **GETTING RETREADED**   31
- THIS DEADLY GAME OF JOUSTING   32
- AN ENCOUNTER WITH CHESTY   33
- EL CENTRO BOUND   33
- WE LOSE TWO FINE MEN   34
- CHRONOGRAPH   35
- ANOTHER CLOSE CALL   35
- MARINE FIGHTER SQUADRON VMF-232 GETS A NEW PILOT   36
- TESTING THE STRATEGIC AIR COMMAND   36
- LESSONS ONCE LEARNED   36
- UNDERGOING TRAINING AT FALLON, NEVADA   37
- MAKING LIKE GROUND MARINES   38

CHAPTER 4   **DADDY IS LEAVING YOU FOR A LITTLE WHILE**   40
- REFLECTIONS   40
- A DISTORTED IMAGE   42
- MARTIN JRM-2 CAROLINA MARS   44
- I STEP ON JAPANESE SOIL FOR FIRST TIME   47

CHAPTER 5   **IN KOREA AT LAST, WITH VMF-212**   51
- THE MISSIONS OF MARINE CORPS AVIATION IN KOREA   53
- MANNING THE MOTHBALLED CARRIER FLEET   53
- AVIATION SHIPS AND CARRIERS   56
- SEARCH FOR GEN MATT RIDGWAY'S SON'S DOWNED B-26   60
- MAJOR DEXTER DIES   61
- THE HISTORIANS   63
- PITTMAN'S PLANE STRUCK BY 90MM AA   63
- COMMUNIST CAMOUFLAGE AND DECEPTION   64
- COMMUNIST VS UN AIR ACTIVITY   64
- CAPT BEAUMONT COOLEY USMCR RECALLS KOREA TOUR OF DUTY   66
- GOSS TAKES A HIT ON HIS PROP   68
- AIRFIELDS AND MILITARY INSTALLATIONS   69
- A MULE KICK OF A 1000-LB BOMB   71
- DEADLY MIG-15 VAPOR TRAILS SIGHTED INK BOTTLES SHAKING AT PEACE TABLE   71
- VMFA-312 HISTORY   75

CONTENTS cont'd

CHAPTER 6   REDEPLOYED   77
- THE FIRST MARINE DIVISION   77
- TULK'S CHUTE FAILS TO OPEN   78
- COMMUNIST TRANSPORTATION   79
- VMF-323 PILOT SURVIVES WHEELS-UP LANDING
  ILLINOIS SENATOR BREWSTER PROPOSES FLIGHT PAY CUT   80
- REPUBLIC OF KOREA AIR FORCE (ROK)   82
- AN UNBELIEVABLE SCENARIO   83
- BEWARE OF THE SWORD HIDDEN BEHIND THE SMILE   84
- THE MAJOR ISSUE THAT PROLONGED THE WAR   86
- WORKING WITH THE COMMONWEALTH BRIGADE   89
- BOB BARBOUR MAKES IT HOME WITH HIS DAMAGED PLANE   89
- HILLS OF KOREA   90
- MY ENGINE QUITS COLD OVER ENEMY TERRITORY
  FATHER BURKE'S WHISKEY BREATH   93
- WON'T FLY OFFICER GETS PRISON TERM   98

CHAPTER 7   WE FLY TO OUR NEW BASE, PYONGTAEK, TUNP O RI   99
- CAMERON'S CRASH   99
- THE PEACE NEGOTIATORS   100
- COMMUNIST ATROCITIES   101
- EXPLAINING MY NEAR ACCIDENT TO ST. PETER
  CAPT FELITON ESCAPES DEATH WHEN HIS BRAKES FAIL   101
- ONE HAIRY MISSION AS RECALLED BY CAPT BILL SHANKS USMC   103
- TRAGIC LOSS OF A SIX-PLANE FLIGHT OF F9F PANTHER JETS   104
- ROSTER OF MARINE FIGHTER SQUADRON VMA-212,
    KOREA, MARCH-JULY 1952   106
- APRIL AIR OPERATIONS FOR MARINES HELPED SET ONE-DAY WAR RECORD   107
- HOT WATER--HAVA NO!   108
- VMA-212 SQUADRON PILOTS HIT COMMUNIST TANKS   111
- SERENADING GENERAL "HOWLING MAD" SMITH/CIVILIANS INJURED   113
- LT JACK'S PLANE HITS ENEMY CABLE/
  RYAN BLOWS UP TANK, THEN HITS DEBRIS/
  EIGHT PLANES GROUNDED IN TWO DAYS   115

CHAPTER 8   MY FIRST R&R IN JAPAN   118
- CONVERSATION WITH THE F-86 SABERJET PILOTS   122
- TEN OR MORE VICTORIES IN KOREA (39 TOTAL ACES)   123
- ACES IN TWO WARS/ACES OF WORLD WAR II AND KOREA   124

CONTENTS cont'd

	UNITED STATES, JAPANESE PEACE TREATY SIGNED	129
	GERM WARFARE PROPAGANDA	129
	SUPPORT AND SERVICES PRISONER OF WAR RIOT AND CHANGE OF COMMAND PUTTING A FOUR-ENGINED R5D TRANSPORT INTO A STALL	130
	A WORD ABOUT G.W. PARKER	132
	MY FRIEND, WILBUR PICKERING	133
	OUR FLIGHT COVERS DOWNED AD-1 SKYRAIDER PILOT	134
	TASK FORCE SMITH	137
	HUGH HOLLAND AND I BRIEFED FOR SPECIAL MISSION	138
	MPQ, RADAR BOMBING	140
CHAPTER 9	**FLAK AND OUR MISSIONS**	145
	SOME RULES THAT I FOLLOWED	145
	DAVE KENNEDY'S ROCKETS EXPLODE PREMATURELY UNDER MY PLANE	150
	AN EVENING AT THE SNIVELER'S BAR	155
	ATTACKED BY A MIG-15	158
	BRITISH METEOR JETS MAKE THREATENING RUNS ON OUR FLIGHT	159
	BOMB DROPS FROM MY PLANE UPON LANDING	162
	ALLIED BOMBERS BLAST HUGE RED INDUSTRIAL AREA	163
	CAPTAIN LARSON'S CLOSE SHAVE/LOTS OF PROBLEMS WITH MY PLANE	163
	PICKED TO LEAD A DIVISION	165
CHAPTER 10	**FAMILIARIZATION VISIT TO THE FRONT**	168
	THE SPIRIT OF THE RED CROSS	171
	MY SECOND SECTION ATTACKS COMMUNIST TANKS	175
	JAPAN'S NEW GOVERNMENT	180
	HOME GROWN JAPANESE COMMUNISTS GIVE US A SCARE	181
	JET ACE SAYS MIGS BETTER; PILOTS SKILLED	182
	CRASH ON RUNWAY DELAYS LANDING	186
	A VERY CLOSE CALL	189
CHAPTER 11	**BRAND NEW AU-1 CORSAIRS**	191
	COLONEL GALER MAKES IT BACK	192
	MY PLANE IS HIT BY ENEMY GROUND FIRE	193
	TREADING ON THIN ICE	194
	COMBAT AIR SUPPORT FOR A BRITISH CRUISER	196

CONTENTS cont'd

          LARGEST SINGLE AIR EFFORT OF THE KOREAN WAR   201

          THE HYDROELECTRIC STRIKES OF 23 JUNE 1952   206

CHAPTER 12   **THE SHORT STRAW**   215

          CAPTAIN BIBEE CRASHES ON TAKEOFF
          I FLY MY LAST COMBAT MISSION IN A CORSAIR   216

          NORTH KOREAN CAPITAL OF P'YONGYANG HIT   223

          MY FIRST DAY AT FAC SCHOOL   224

CHAPTER 13   **UP FRONT--BUNKER HILL**   238

          OP2 (OUTPOST DUTY)   240

          FORWARD AIR CONTROL AND CLOSE AIR SUPPORT
          MY FRIEND, CAPTAIN ROBERT B. ROBINSON USMC   242

          A BIRD'S EYE VIEW--FROM THE GROUND UP
             BY LTCOL ROBERT B. ROBINSON USMC (RET)   243

          FROM THE FRYING PAN INTO THE FIRE   249

          AN OVERVIEW OF THE GENERAL SITUATION AT THE FRONT   254

          OPERATION RIPPLE   256

          THE BATTLE FOR BUNKER HILL BEGINS IN EARNEST   256

          STRAYED FRIENDLY BOMB ALMOST HITS US   258

          MARINES DIG IN TO DRIVE REDS OFF BUNKER HILL   261

          PURPLE HEART TIME FOR YOURS TRULY   263

CHAPTER 14   **HELLFIRE**   264

          MARINES CUT REDS DOWN
          HILL 122 (BUNKER HILL)   265

          CHANGING THE GUARD   268

          THE MAKEUP OF THE UNITED NATIONS COMMAND   271

          CREEPING TACTICS BY SHOVEL   274

          "OPERATION SNATCH"   280

          JACK CRAM, MARINE HERO IN WWII   281

CHAPTER 15   **THE DEATH OF A TRUE HERO**   288

          THE DIVISION SPECIAL RECONNAISSANCE COMPANY   289

          A RECORD MONTH FOR CLOSE AIR SUPPORT   292

          NORTH KOREAN MP SURRENDERS AT PANMUNJOM   299

          OUR BRAVE YOUNG MARINES ARE STILL DYING
          THREE AIRMEN SHOT DOWN--FATE UNKNOWN   300

CONTENTS cont'd

          A SALUTE TO THE NAVY CORPSMEN
          LTGEN JAMES VAN FLEET VISITS MY BUNKER   301

          CORSAIR PILOT DOWNS MIG-15   302

          LAWS OF COMBAT (MURPHY'S LAW)   304

CHAPTER 16   **GUS AND THE WHIRLY-BIRD**   **307**

          WE MOVE TO BATTALION RESERVE   308

          A VISIT FROM THE COMMANDANT OF THE MARINE CORPS   312

          FIRST REGIMENT GETS NEW AIR OFFICER   316

          TWO FRIENDS SHOT DOWN FLYING AN OE OBSERVATION PLANE
          CORSAIR EXPLODES AND CRASHES NEAR OUR POSITION ON THE LINE   322

CHAPTER 17   **1ST MARINE REGIMENT IS RELIEVED ON THE
MAIN LINE OF RESISTANCE (IN THE REAR WITH THE GEAR)**   **329**

          A CONFIRMATION FROM A SURRENDERED NORTH KOREAN SECURITY OFFICER
          (I SAW HIM THE NIGHT HE GAVE UP)   331

          THE FESTIVAL OF THE HONEY BUCKETS   333

          HELICOPTER QUALIFIED AT LAST   337

          COMMUNIST FORCES OVERRUN THE CANADIANS ON OUR RIGHT FLANK   341

          PLAYING TIPPY TOE WITH LAND MINES   342

          MEMORIAL SERVICES FOR OUR FALLEN COMRADES   343

          THE BATTLE TO REGAIN THE OUTPOST CALLED THE HOOK   345

CHAPTER 18   **INN OF THE OPEN DOOR**   **350**

          THIRTY THOUSAND ROUNDS OF COMMUNIST ARTILLERY IN ONE DAY   352

          A TRUCKLOAD OF UNEXPLODED ENEMY SHELLS GIVES US A SCARE   353

CHAPTER 19   **177TH BIRTHDAY OF THE UNITED STATES MARINES**   **361**

          1ST REGIMENT TAKES UP FORWARD POSITION AGAIN   365

          FOLLOW-UP TO LOST KOREAN LETTERS   371

          PEACE TALKS AND PRISONERS   373

          FOLLOWING THE CESSATION OF HOSTILITIES   374

APPENDIXES   1.   **MESSAGES FROM THE MEMORIAL**   **375**

                      2.   **HEMORRHAGIC FEVER--A FATAL VIRUS**   **377**

                      3.   **MY FRIEND, COLONEL BILL SHANKS USMC (RET)**   **380**

                      4.   **RIDING THE RANGE AT MACH 2.5,**
                              By World's fastest--LtCol R.B. Robinson, USMC   **381**

CONTENTS cont'd

5. KOREAN REFUGEES AND RESIDENTS IN THE 1ST MARINE DIVISION SECTOR   384

6. SAFE CONDUCT PASS   385

7. MEMORIAL SERVICE IN THE FIELD--26 OCT 52   386

8. VMF-214 MARINE FIGHTER SQUADRON--FIRST IN KOREAN ACTION   389

9. LIEUTENANT COLONEL BEAUMONT COOLEY, USMCR (RET), EXPLAINS DEATH OF SON'S FATHER 43 YEARS LATER   391

10. MARINE PILOTS AND ENEMY AIRCRAFT DOWNED IN KOREAN WAR   394

11. MARINE CORPS CASUALTIES (GROUND AND AIR)   396

12. GLOSSARY OF TECHNICAL TERMS AND ABBREVIATIONS   397

DEDICATION

To my life's partner, Marion, and our progeny: Eric, Randall, Elaine, Beverly and their children: Bodhi, Lura, Ansel, Cody, Gregory, Austin, Benjamin, Zane and Dylan--in answer to the grandchildren's question, "What did you do in the war, Grandpa?"

and

To all of my shipmates and squadron mates, living and dead, in the Navy, Marine Corps, Air Force, Army and Coast Guard. Bless each and every one of you. Hail Heroes! Rest with God.

SPECIAL THANKS to the following for their contributions of stories, photos and support:

   Brigadier General Jay W. Hubbard USMC (Ret), Orange California
   Colonel Stu F. Nelson USMCR (Ret), Palos Verdes, California
   Colonel William Shanks, USMC (Ret), Sun City Center, Florida
   Colonel Robert R. Van Dalsem, USMC (Ret), Loveland, Colorado
   Lieutenant Colonel Beaumont B. Cooley, USMCR (Ret), Austin, Texas
   Lieutenant Colonel Wilbur W. Pickering, USMCR (Ret), Port Orchard, Washington
   Lieutenant Colonel John S. Perrin, USMC (Ret), La Conner, Washington
   Lieutenant Colonel Robert B. Robinson USMC (Ret), St. Louis, Missouri
   Major Merlin L. Dake, USMC (Ret), Bend, Oregon (Deceased)
   Major George W. Parker, USMC (Ret), Sebring, Florida
   Captain Robert O. Barnum, USMCR (Ret), Morehead City, North Carolina
   Captain James Q. Van Ry, USMCR (Ret), Rohnert Park, California
   Sergeant Charles Aubrey Buser, USMC, Frederick, Maryland

A VOTE OF GRATITUDE to my faithful enlisted companions, all radio operators and wiremen in the Tactical Air Control Party (TACP:) of the 3rd Battalion, 1st Regiment, 1st Marine Division: (rank held in 1952)

   Sergeant Koch, USMC
   Sergeant C. J. Walwood, USMC
   Corporal A. Skinner, USMC
   Corporal D. Evans, USMC
   Corporal M. Stamps, USMC
   Corporal R. M. Boone, USMC
   Corporal Casey, USMC
   Corporal H. O'Gara, USMC
   Private First Class E.J. Bowman, USMC

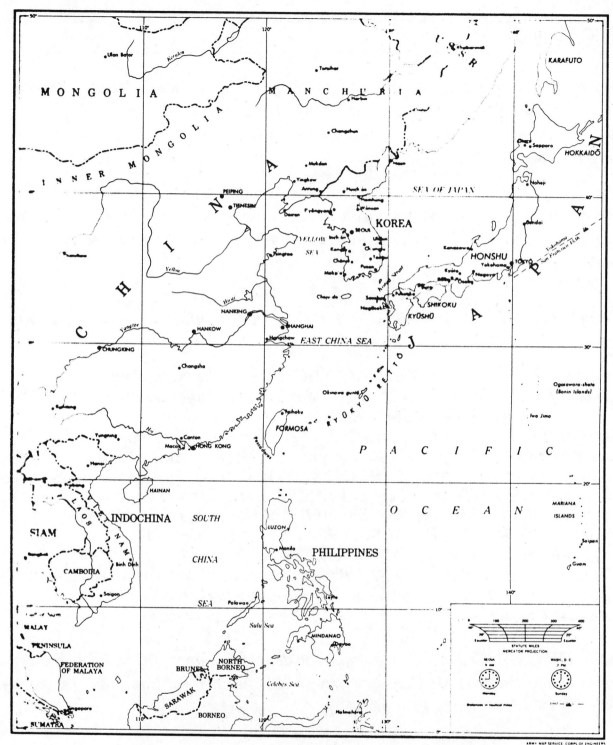

KOREA, ROUGHLY THE SIZE OF UTAH, IS A PENINSULA HANGING OFF THE NORTHEASTERN COAST OF CHINA AND FACING THE JAPANESE ISLANDS ACROSS THE SEA OF JAPAN.

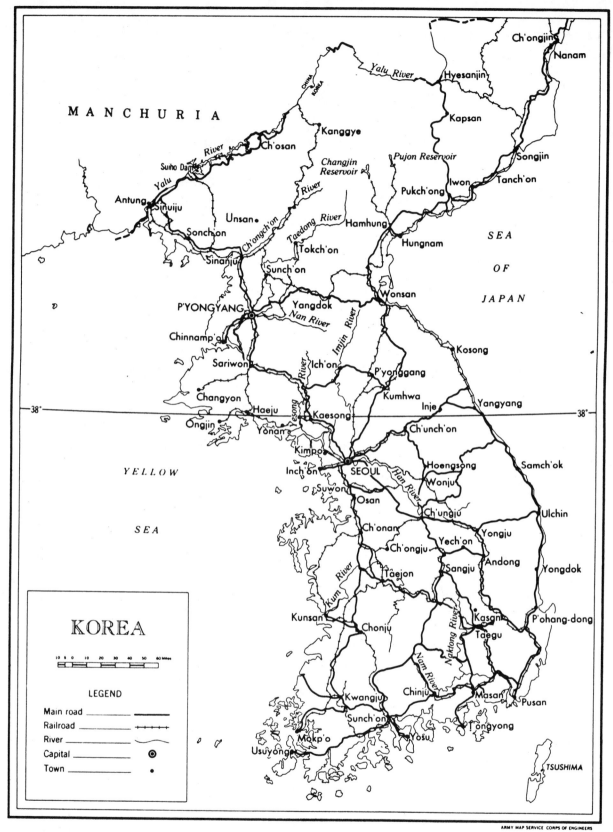

On 8 Sep 1945 the vanguard of the U.S. 7th Infantry Division arrived at the Korean port of Inch'on and began to disembark. The following day elements of the division moved on to the capital city of Seoul, where the Japanese officially surrendered their authority in Korea. With the conclusion of WWII, the U.S. occupation forces turned to the dual task of disarming and repatriating Japanese nationals and preserving law and order until such time as the Koreans themselves could once again take over the responsibilities of government.

To the majority of the occupation troops, Korea was little more than a blip on the map—a temporary stopover before they returned home.

A MESSAGE FROM THE COMMANDER

WHAT ARE WE FIGHTING FOR?

To me the issues are clear. It is not a question of this or that Korean town or village. Real estate is, here, incidental. It is not restricted to the issue of freedom for our South Korean Allies, whose fidelity and valor under the severest stresses of battle we recognize; though that freedom is a symbol of the wider issues, and included among them.

The real issues are whether the power of Western civilization, as God has permitted it to flower in our own beloved lands, shall defy and defeat Communism; whether the rule of men who shoot their prisoners, enslave their citizens, and deride the dignity of man, shall displace the rule of those to whom the individual and his individual rights are sacred; whether we are to survive with God's hand to guide and lead us, or to perish in the dead existence of a Godless world.

If these be true, and to me they are, beyond any possibility of challenge, then this has long since ceased to be a fight for freedom, for our own survival, in an honorable, independent national existence.

The sacrifices we have made, and those we shall yet support, are not offered vicariously for others, but in our own direct defense.

In final analysis, the issue now joined right here in Korea is whether Communism or individual freedom shall prevail; whether the flight of fear-driven people we have witnessed here shall be checked, or shall at some future time, however distant, engulf our own loved one in all its misery and despair.

These are the things for which we fight. Never have members of any military command had a greater challenge than we, or a finer opportunity to show ourselves and our people at their best--and thus to do honor to the profession of arms, and to those brave men who bred us.

This message was delivered to all the troops in Korea 21 Jan 51, by Gen Matthew B. Ridgway, U.S. Army, shortly after taking over command of the 8th Army.

DESIDERATA   Found in old Saint Paul's Church, Baltimore, dated 1692

Go placidly amid the noise and the haste, and remember what peace there may be in silence. As far as possible without surrender be on good terms with all persons. Speak your truth quietly and clearly; and listen to others, even the dull and ignorant; they too have their story. Avoid loud and aggressive persons, they are vexations to the spirit. If you compare yourself with others you may become vain and bitter; for always there will be greater and lesser persons than yourself. Enjoy your achievements as well as your plans. Keep interested in your own career, however humble; it is a real possession in the changing fortunes of time. Exercise caution in your business affairs; for the world is full of trickery. But let this not blind you to what virtue there is; many persons strive for high ideals; and everywhere life is full of heroism. Be yourself. Especially do not feign affection. Neither be cynical about love; for in the face of all aridity and disenchantment it is as perennial as the grass. Take kindly the counsel of the years, gracefully surrendering the things of youth. Nurture strength of spirit to shield you in sudden misfortune. But do not distress yourself with imaginings. Many fears are born of fatigue and loneliness. Beyond a wholesome discipline, be gentle with yourself. You are a child of the universe no less than the trees and the stars; you have a right to be here. And whether or not it is clear to you, no doubt the universe is unfolding as it should. Therefore be at peace with God, whatever you conceive Him to be, and whatever your labors and aspirations, in the noisy confusion of life keep peace with your soul. With all its sham, drudgery and broken dreams, it is still a beautiful world. Be careful. Strive to be happy.

PREFACE

I'm not a professional writer, nor a historian for that matter, but just one ex-marine among thousands who wants to tell of his small part during a tragic and dramatic period of our country's history. Numerous books on the Korean War have been written by professional historians who have only gleaned their stories *from* active participants rather than relating their own first-hand experience, probably lacking in many cases. It is therefore my intention to preserve as many of my first-hand, on-the-spot personal accounts as possible, and to try to put the reader right there beside me, whether it be in the cockpit of my F4U Corsair or in a slit trench with the 1stMarDiv calling in air strikes.

The Korean War commands little more than a a footnote in history books, when in fact it was a long drawn-out campaign during which nearly six million men and women served in the armed forces under the UN (United Nations) banner, fighting three times as long as they did in World War One, "the war to end all wars." Actually, the war in Korea lasted almost as long as WWII, and ironically, all of Korea, China and Russia had been our allies back then and Japan our common enemy. Talk about reversals and the vagaries of politics!

The purpose of our entrance into this conflict was to rescue the newly established Republic of Korea (ROK) from the invading communist hordes, first the North Koreans and then the Chinese communists, all marching to the drum beat of Joe Stalin's International Communism.

The state of our country in 1950 was one of prosperity even though defense industries had been severely cut back along with our standing military establishments. We were ill-prepared for another war. Communism was winning many hearts and minds the world over, and it was the fear of its spread here which fostered the hysteria of the McCarthy Era. Most now feel that McCarthy's crusade was an exaggerated reflection of Americans' fear of another tyrannical power grasping for world domination; still it caused the un-seating of the Democratic Party by Dwight D. Eisenhower. Americans would not tolerate another bid for tyranny. Many of us began to feel that the western world couldn't find the strength or the courage to stand up to communism, but we did find that courage and ultimately the strength, even though it cost thousands of lives in the process.

It all began with our peaceful ally, South Korea, being attacked by its neighbors to the north. This was unprovoked, raw aggression, first by the North Koreans and then by massive Chinese armies. Unfortunately, nobody had really explained to us why we were expected to fight, and, yes, die for an Asian country of which most of us had never heard. However, a defeat would have been a national disgrace and Japan, not yet recovered from WWII, would have fallen next.

As the early stages of the war began to go against us, once the most powerful nation on earth, we all felt the ugly guilt and shame of losing and realized how ill-prepared we actually had become since the end of WWII, only five years previous. This had a profound impact upon me personally. Like so many vets of WWII, I felt I had done my share and paid my taxes for a strong military. In those dark, early days of the war we were asking ourselves of the Koreans, "Where are they? Why can't they stand up to a fellow Asian aggressor? Where did all of those defense dollars go?" Most people during this period simply watched accounts of the war on television, and became more depressed with each setback the communists dealt our meager forces in that deadly Asian corridor from one brutal assault after another.

I could stand it no longer. This was my primary reason for writing to the Commandant of the Marine Corps, volunteering my services, an act profoundly difficult considering my wonderful family, comfortable home and the fine job I had at that time, as my story will relate. My re-training as a

PREFACE cont'd

Marine fighter pilot and later assignment in Korea to Marine Fighter Squadron (VMF-212), flying F4U Corsairs, are covered in this book, including my tour as a forward air controller with the 1stMarDiv.

The war delayed normal relations with the People's Republic of China for over a decade, as well as causing increased hostilities between the West and all of the Communist-bloc nations. It really kicked into high gear the massive nuclear and even the conventional arms race between Russia and the United States, which did not stop until the Berlin Wall came tumbling down and the "evil empire" finally collapsed. In fact, the Korean conflict came within a blink of an eye of starting WWIII, which undoubtedly would have caused a nuclear holocaust worldwide. On the other hand, the war brought an unswervingly good relationship between the U.S. and South Korea, as well as our UN allies, which still endures today.

A deeper study of the Korean conflict could have prevented us from making the same mistakes less than ten years later in Vietnam; in fact, it could still do this in the future by causing us to rethink our foreign policies.

My letters home to my wife, Marion, weren't always complimentary to the South Koreans nor their "honey bucket" way of life, but this was normal for most GIs, many still battle-scarred from WWII, away from home in far off battlefields. Some historians have done a credible job of picturing the human side of the war--the mud, the frost, gallantry and sacrifice, but few have portrayed the day-to-day thoughts and gut-wrenching reality of the conflict as it unfolded from an eye-witness standpoint, which I have endeavored to do, calling upon my letters home.

In the final analysis, Korean vets can stand tall and be proud in spite of all the old clichés, such as 'The Forgotten War," "Uncertain Victory," etc., even though there were no welcome home marching bands or keys to the city handed out. The satisfaction of having been a part of a united effort to stop communism wherever it threatened the free world is enough.

A thousand volumes couldn't begin to portray the chaos, drama, meanness, frenzy and cold terror that took place over the three years of fighting, which resulted in nearly the same number of deaths as the Vietnam War did over a *ten year* period. The number of Americans killed during the Korean War was 54,246. Approximately 92,970 UN troops had fallen into communist hands--7140 of them Americans, 84,715 Korean, and some 1115 members of other UN units. The communists admitted to holding only 11,500 UN POWs. Two thirds of them--Americans held in communist prison camps--were destined never to return. I can only hope *my* book will provide fresh insight into this devastating military exercise. Refer to Appendix numbers 1 and 11 for a further statistical accounting.

Most military planners and historians are now looking back and saying that the Korean War was the decisive action that turned the tide of World Communism and will be so noted when the ultimate definitive history is written. My book, then, will by no means be the last word on the valor and heroism that was shown by our American servicemen and women, as well as our allies. The significance of this little "footnote in history" may finally be understood.

'Behold the work of the old. . .
Let your Heritage not be lost,
But bequeath it as a memory,
Treasure and Blessing. . .
Gather the lost and the hidden
and preserve it for thy Children.'

CHAPTER 1

KOREA

MY FIRST ENCOUNTER WITH THE WILY MIG

The regular evening intelligence briefing was anything but cheerful as we assembled in the makeshift ready room a few hundred feet from the edge of our Korean airstrip. The intelligence officer grimaced as he spoke of the fate of a four-plane division of F-51 Mustangs which had been jumped by MIGs the day before--one shot down in target area of BS 108649. He broke off reading and turned to the large briefing map behind him, his map pointer sliding to the very top, indicating the position to be pitifully close to the Yalu River and only a few minutes' striking distance from the Communist MIG base at An-tung, in China, just west of the Yalu River. A muffled sardonic remark escaped someone's lips in the background, "He had about as much chance as a snowball in Hell." The briefing continued along the same morbid lines and I comforted myself with the hope that tomorrow's schedule would place me somewhere along the 38th parallel on a close air support mission where MIGs seldom venture, for my old Corsair was no match for a MIG-15.

Long after the briefing broke up, my thoughts wandered back to the ill-fated F-51, and I wondered how soon it would be before we too would be embroiled in the same unevenly matched contest, in our World War II vintage Corsairs. I didn't have to wonder long, for shortly after I arrived back in my Quonset the normal calm was broken by Snapper's shocking exclamation, "Looks like it's our turn to get our name in the papers!"

"Yeah, it's Baker Sugar 108649 in the obituaries for *us* tomorrow!" added "the sniveler", Dave Kennedy.

After nudging my way up to the bulletin board I caught a glimpse of the flight schedule, and wouldn't you know it, I had drawn not one, but two of those Baker Sugar hops! Walking back to my bunk I couldn't help looking over at the personal effects of Johnson whom we had lost just a few days before, and as I hit the sack for the night, I kept telling myself that everything would be OK up there with us tomorrow.

In the morning Snapper led the first division with four planes and I led the second with two. A few minutes brought us near Seoul as we winged our way north toward our objective. The fact that we would have F-86 Sabre escorts somewhat reassured us, although we didn't know whether they would be there when we needed them. We were to contact them on channel 8 ten minutes from target to let them know that we were over our IP (initial point). It seemed as though we had flown for hours and my fuel pressure kept fluctuating nervously because I was drawing from my belly tank. The MSR (main supply route) could be seen winding its way along the North Korean coastline and before long the enemy had spotted us, and an uncomfortably large number of 90mm could be seen exploding among us. We'd been informed that the 90mm antiaircraft batteries were manned by Russians, and they were deadly accurate. Quickly spreading out, we went into our change of heading and altitude to throw the Communist radar off our tails. Their AA intensity doubled as our flight came directly over the MSR, and we all worked at a fever pitch--climbing, turning, diving, but always trying to make good our northerly heading toward our objective.

Try as I may, I couldn't see the Sabre escort, although we had established radio communications with them a few minutes earlier. Snapper was doing a beautiful job of leading our group of six Corsairs over that unfamiliar North Korean terrain. Our approach at an altitude of 11,000 feet was taking us just over the tops of some fast-building cumulus clouds, and as we proceeded north, the terrain became obscure. We had left the 90mm fire behind us and were over an apparently unstrategic sector, judging from the letup in ack-ack.

I had been timing Snapper ever since we passed the MSR, and from my calculations I knew he was accurate when he gave the signal over his radio, "Thirty seconds from pushover." My ordnance switches had been on for the last ten minutes, in preparation for this signal. Fortunately, our target could be seen through a broken cloud layer just off our right wing tips. Snapper rolled in, as did each member of the flight behind him. From what I could see, the preceding planes were getting beautiful target coverage. It was as though we were chained together as our bombs and rockets bore home on the enemy marshaling yard. Dozens of trains and a large number of boxcars went flying into the air. These supplies coming into North Korea from China and Russia (which they would have used to kill our boys) would now never reach their troops on the front lines.

We looked around and, as far as we could tell, our flight had received only meager ground fire while immediately over our target. Elated with the success of our mission thus far, we headed south and were climbing to regain our lost altitude for our join-up. Due to the cloud buildup south of the target area, we were forced to vary our heading in and out of the clouds in a somewhat spread out formation.

Suddenly, right off my cockpit and right wingtip, basketball-sized fireballs with six-foot tails shot by. "Jesus, where the hell is that ground fire coming from?" I wondered. Then, like a shot, a Communist MIG, with that familiar swept-wing and tail, blue nose, and red star on the fuselage, went streaking by and I knew it had come from his 37mm cannon fire. My altitude was 3000 feet, speed 175 knots, and we were approaching that hot spot in their MSR where we had earlier encountered the 90s. The clouds made it difficult to tell how many MIGs were playing with us, but it seemed to me like maybe four, and each made about three runs through our formation. Our course south had fortunately taken us over a rather sparsely protected antiaircraft zone and I don't know whether it was because we were approaching the MSR and the 90mm fire, or because the MIGs figured we had had time to call in our Sabre escort that they broke away.

During the confusion, none of us had jettisoned our two belly tanks, which now added to the drag and slowed us down just that much more. Somehow we slipped through the 90s, winged our way out over the Yellow Sea, and I could still count six noses.

The Sabres, at 15,000 feet awaiting our call, could not have given us any assistance during the initial dogfight because the MIGs had jumped us at too low an altitude. All strung out in altitude--Snapper at approximately 6000 feet and our last member at about 2000 feet--we were too low and slow to regroup for our tactical weave, for which we had trained ever since our cadet days for just such occasions. However, at Snapper's radio signal, we found ourselves working into the weave in order to set ourselves up for firing shots at the enemy on a buddy's tail. Obviously, these particular MIGs had been scrambled just to intercept our flight because their 90mm ground-fire crews had given them a full ten minutes early warning from the time we received the first 90s over the MSR and had done little in the way of changing course. Our proximity to the MIG base had allowed the Communist pilots ample time to intercept our flight during that period.

We monitored the Sabre radio transmission as they chased the Red planes back to their Yalu River sanctuary. "Strange," I mused, "here I am in the jet age, in another war, still flying a Corsair, but with my role now switched from a fighter to a bomber, and being dependent on our jet fighters for our support. Nothing stays the same for long."

25 May 1952
Tunp o ri, Korea
Sunday, 2030

Hello baby girl,
Honey, I can tell you this because I came out smelling like a rose. I was up at 0300, had a cup of coffee, went over and got briefed and stood by on ready alert until 0700. We weren't scrambled by JOC, so I came on back and had a full breakfast, then went over to the Group and briefed on this special railcut up near the Yalu. After that we briefed at the Squadron for quite a while, then took off--all six of us. It was over 250 miles up there and only 24 miles from the Yalu. The target was at Taegwan-dong, which you can find on your map at home, honey, if you'll look at An-tung on the Chinese side of the Yalu and bring a line straight across to the right until it intersects the main road and rail line that goes north from the town of Chongju. It's a little above that line. Well, anyway, as we crossed the east-west road network near Songhon, we got clobbered with the heaviest barrage of 90mm AA that I have ever seen. We dove and climbed and turned violently from left to right to throw their radar directed antiaircraft batteries off as much as possible. After we crossed over it wasn't too bad.
We were at an altitude of 11,000 feet. As we approached the target we got in a left echelon and peeled off at the target in a screaming 360-knot dive. We covered the target and really got a lot of cuts. I was the second from the last one to go in and, as we were retiring south, climbing to join the rest, I immediately made a tight left turn and looked back over my right shoulder just in time to see two swept-back MIGs go swooping by. The rest of the division was being jumped from head on and to the left. Everyone was turning and diving and climbing. I turned back to the right again hard and gave them a spraying from my four 20mm cannons. Pieces were flying off of one of the MIGs I shot at. I came awfully close to getting myself a MIG with a Corsair. I was so confused and shook I hardly knew what to do, as were the others in the flight. They were doing everything they could do. Our leader, John Snapper, called the F-86 Sabres in from 15,000 feet. They came on over, but the MIGs made another sweep on us and then were seen heading west, climbing back to their side of the Yalu which was a safe haven for them because we had orders against hot pursuit across the Yalu. The Sabres had to break it off even before they got in position for a shot.
Now that I've had time to think about it, we were just up there as MIG bait for the F-86s, I'm positive. Fortunately, we had the Group's new tactical officer along with us, Colonel Axtell, who was working with me in our protective weave--turning in on each other and firing at anything on the other's tail. He congratulated me on my good sense during the attack, and I told him he did a fine job covering my tail. Everybody on the mission was visibly shook, and probably I was the worst shook of any of the group because I was jumped from the tail by two MIGs, both firing at me.
My whole life passed before me, darling. I thought of you, my precious girl, and my little guys, and honestly figured I had had it. Even after they broke it off and retired we figured it was only a few minutes breathing spell for us and they'd be back on us again. By that time we were all joined up and over the main east-west road network and they started throwing 37mm and 90mm at us all the way along the road. By then we had 9000 feet, and after we got over the water area to the south we were out of their fire. We held our breath all the way home, hoping and praying they wouldn't attack us again. Oh, how I wished I were flying a F-86 Sabre jet at this moment!
After we landed three hours later, I went over and had a sandwich which I gobbled down in five minutes, then dashed over to the Group and briefed on another railcut to the same area. I began praying that JOC would divert us, but knowing full well in my own mind they wouldn't do it. We moved on over to the squadron, got into our gear and were walking out the

Above: A reminiscent scene of typical destruction wrought by our flight over the marshaling yard we hit at Taeguan-dong, 24 miles from the Yalu River border with China.

Left: A group of Communist Pilots, dressed in their black leather jackets receiving their briefing for a mission over Korea.

Lower Left: Several sleek Communist MIG-15s being readied for a flight into Korea from their Chinese sanctuary across the Yalu River.

Above: North American F-86 Sabre Jets, a welcome sight for a WWII propeller-driven fighter/bomber pilot in the skies of North Korea.

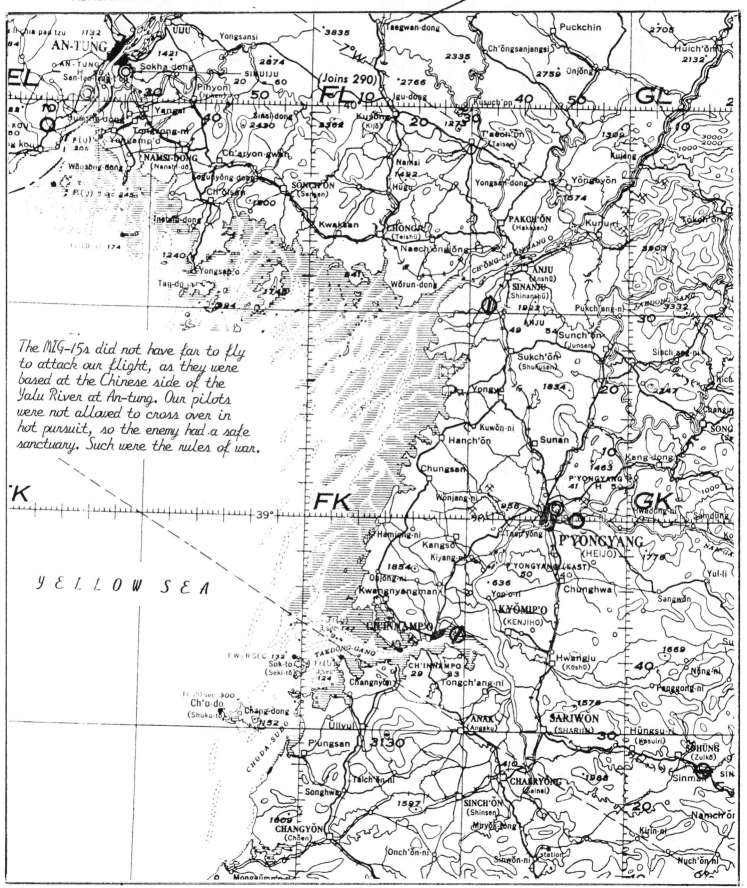

OUR FLIGHT'S ASSIGNED TARGET AREA FOR THE 25 MAY '52 STRIKE WAS TAEGWAN DONG. THIS WAS ABOUT AS FAR INTO NORTH KOREA AS ANY WWII VINTAGE FIGHTER/BOMBER AIRCRAFT EVER PENETRATED DURING THE KOREAN WAR.

The MIG-15s did not have far to fly to attack our flight, as they were based at the Chinese side of the Yalu River at An-tung. Our pilots were not allowed to cross over in hot pursuit, so the enemy had a safe sanctuary. Such were the rules of war.

NORTH AMERICAN F-86 SABRE

Fifth Air Force North American F-86 jet fighter. This was our best fighter and a major threat to the sleek Communist MIG-15, which was powered by the British Rolls Royce jet engine.

The Air Force had done a superb job in writing their specifications for their future fighter plane. The Air Force/North American Aviation team conceived the F-86 in 1945 and first flew it in 1947. It was supplied to their squadrons by April 1949. The fighter actually achieved its published speeds of between 610 and 679 mph at altitudes of 48,300 and 54,600 feet. The 4th and 51st U.S. Air Force Fighter Wings flew the F-86 Sabrejet and achieved the remarkable 10 to 1 kill ratio over the MIG-15. The General Electric J-47 jet engine which powered the fighter had a thrust of 5910 pounds.

LGen George C. Stratemeyer's Far East Air Force depended on the Douglas B-26 Invader as the principal light bomber of his eight and a half combat groups, while the B-29 Superfortress comprised his medium bomb group.

The Douglas B-26 Invader, which first saw combat service in Europe on 19Nov44, was available in ample quantity for the Korean War. Powered by two R-2800-27 or -71 engines, it was capable of carrying 4000 lbs of bombs and up to eight .50 calibre machine guns. External pick-up points on each wing allowed for 2000 lbs of bombs, 16 rockets or extra fuel tanks. U.S. Air Force pilots flew deep missions against North Korea—bombing bridges and railroad junctions, closing tunnels and destroying other key transport facilities—thus bringing most of the enemy's ground transportation to a grinding halt.

A member of our Strategic Air Force, the Boeing B-29 Superfortress, having proven itself during WWII in bombing raids over Japan in 1944 and 1945, was still available in large numbers during the opening days of the Korean War. They bombed big marshalling yards at Chonan, Seoul, and as far north as Pyongyang, destroying railroad and highway bridges at Seoul, Chongju, Ich'on, Kongju, Pyongtaek and dozens of other crucial points.

The MIG-15 (named after its Russian designers, Mikoyan and Gurevich) made its combat debut over Korea on 1Nov50. Its 6000 HP engine, copied from the 1948 Rolls Royce "Nene" centrifugal-type turbojet, had been acquired from the British. Armament consisted of one 37mm automatic cannon and two 23mm automatic aircraft guns which were aimed by a lead computing optical gun sight. The MIG-15 was superior to the F-86 in climb and maneuverability at high altitudes but inferior in range, dive speed, and most important, pilot skill.

ready room door to man our planes when the "hot" phone rang and we were informed that, due to weather conditions over our pre-briefed target area, we were being diverted to a locomotive marshalling yard, rail bridges and tunnel area which was located in a "hot" spot--but to me it was my answer to my prayer. I had been on missions near the area, knew where some of their guns were located, and knew what to expect of them.

Look on your map, darling, on the west coast of Korea at Chinnampo. There's a big inlet bay there. Now bring your eyeballs across the map to the town of Kyomipo, follow the river down to the southeast to the road and rail net and you'll find the town of Hwangju. It's a big build-up area. We clobbered it, recovered west, and returned home just before dark. I led the second division of four planes and after we landed Denny Clyde crashed into Hugh Holland's tail on their landing. Denny's prop chewed Hugh's tail nearly off and came awfully close to Hugh. Denny's plane nosed up then and his prop came to a dead halt when it hit the steel runway. Nobody got hurt, thank God. This was all I needed to round out my day--two of my buddies in the division I was leading crashing just behind me as I led them in for a landing.

I walked over to chow and sat down to eat at 8:00 PM: hamburger patties, mashed spuds, gravy, coffee. Then as I walked out of the mess hall past the outdoor movie, I saw Humphrey Bogart, so I sat down for about an hour. I was dead from exhaustion, but awfully glad *to be alive, somehow.*

Now I'm writing my baby girl whom I love and adore. I miss you so very very much, darling. I'll be so happy when this nightmare is all over. I've got 37 missions in now, darling. As I was eating my supper I recounted how long I had been on the go today--seventeen hours. Only actually flew a little over six hours, but so much time is consumed in briefing, getting maps together and studying flack maps and mosaic photographs of the target areas. Needless to say, dearest, I'm bushed and I'm turning in right now.

Kiss my precious, darling little boys for me, honeygirl, and tell them their daddy loves them.

Your very own, Daddy

P.S. *I believe we have been the first Corsairs to have been jumped by MIGs. They haven't sent any flights that far up before. Wouldn't you know I'd get it! They didn't hit any of us (the MIGs that is).*

THE DREADED RUSSIAN COMMUNIST MIG-15 FIGHTER IN KOREA

The MIG-15 (named after its Russian designers Mikoyan and Gurevich) made its combat debut over Korea on 1 Nov 1950. This swept-wing fighter, developed after World War II in answer to the threat of United States Air Force strategic bombing, had a conventional semi-monocoque, stressed-metal-skin fuselage. Its 6000-horsepower engine had been copied from the 1948 Rolls Royce Nene centrifugal-type turbojet acquired from the British. Weighing 12,500 pounds, the MIG-15 measured 33-by-33 feet. Two 23mm automatic aircraft guns were mounted on the lower left side of the nose, with one 37mm automatic cannon on the lower right side. Guns were aimed by a lead-computing optical gun sight. Underneath the wing panels were attachments for external fuel load or bombs. USAF pilots considered the combat capabilities of the MIG to be superior to the F-86 in climb and maneuverability at high altitudes, but inferior in range and dive speed. Its armament had been effective against slower aircraft but less so in high-speed aerial combat.

Night activity on the part of the MIG-15 was extremely limited and ineffective. Six MIGs *did* jump four F-51s (redesignated P-51s) returning from a dusk raid at 1945 hours on 28 Jun 1951, but this first engagement by enemy jets at so late an hour can hardly be considered night activity because of the visibility that prevailed. Other reports of enemy jet sorties at night were predicated upon observations of a glowing light moving at speeds characteristic of jets. However, piston aircraft were predominant in enemy night action. The Sabrejet's superior kill ratio over the MIG has been attributed to USAF pilot skill and to constant analysis of MIG tactics.

In spite of sporadic indications of improvement, over-all enemy pilot proficiency seemed to be greatly inferior to the MIG performance characteristics and capabilities. While the enemy pilot had been spurred on to greater efforts with the December 1950 appearance of Sabrejets, he had found his pilot-aircraft combination to be a poor match for that of USAF pilots flying F-86s. The enemy was far less reluctant to oppose F-80, F-84, and B-29 aircraft, and especially WWII piston fighters such as I was flying, over which there was a decided advantage.

TWO YEARS OF MIG ACTIVITY

On 1 Nov 1950 Russian-built jet fighters of the CCAF (Chinese Communist Air Force) made their initial appearance in the Korean air war when six MIG-15s attacked four F-51s over Namsidong. Eight days later the first MIG was destroyed, knocked from the skies by an RB-29 tail gunner. Thus a new force, the CCAF, and new equipment, the MIG-15, had entered the Korean conflict.

That the Communists had failed to produce a fighter-interceptor which had a pilot-and-plane combination equal to that of the USAF is particularly evidenced by the results of MIG-15 and F-86 engagements over the two years of MIG activity from 1 Nov 1950 through 31 Oct 1952 (approximately the end of my tour).

Friendly vs Enemy Claims: 1 Nov 1950 to 31 Oct 1952

Type of USAF Aircraft	USAF Claims: MIG-15s destroyed or damaged			Enemy Claims: USAF aircraft destroyed
	Destroyed	Probably Destroyed	Damaged	Destroyed by MIG-15s
F-86	447	57	511	59
F-84	8	11	83	18
F-80	6	8	32	14
F-51	0	0	9	10
RF-80	0	0	0	1
B-26	3	0	1	0
B-29	16	7	11	13
Totals	*480	*83	*647	*115

*By war's end the kill ratio had climbed to a ten-to-one advantage for us.

MIG activity over the past two years had fallen into four rather distinct phases of operations, each apparently resulting from a change in the enemy's operational concept.

(1) The first ten months, November 1950 to August 1951, was one of buildup--a period of acquiring aircraft and operational experience.

(2) The next eight months, September 1951 through April 1952, saw the enemy send large numbers of aircraft over North Korea. The nature of the tactics then employed by the enemy indicated that this was a phase of mass training and familiarization.

(3) Throughout May, June and July 1952 activity was diminished. It appeared that the enemy had, for the time being, settled on a concept of operations under which UN forces were engaged by the more proficient enemy pilots in a more or less token effort, while the majority of Red fighters were carrying out their training over Manchuria rather than over Korea.

(4) August 1952 marked the beginning of the fourth distinct phase of MIG operations. It was believed that MIG pilots were now engaged in another training program over North Korea. While the mass characteristic of the second phase of operations had not been observed, later displays of pilot inexperience and lack of aggressiveness indicated a program of combat orientation and indoctrination of new pilots.

OUR SITUATION AS CORSAIR PILOTS

Much like the slower and larger AD-1 Douglas Skyraiders, our F4U-4B Corsairs, equipped with four 20mm cannons, had now become classified as strictly ground support aircraft. That's why it perplexed us whenever the Fifth Air Force would send us slow-prop jobs up north into MIG Alley on deep interdiction targets. On these missions we referred to ourselves as "MIG bait," since our mere presence near the Yalu invariably brought out the dreaded MIG-15s. The Corsair had hit the scene in 1938, with first combat experiences occurring in February 1943 in the Pacific. Flying fighters developed 14 years previously had put us at a decided disadvantage.

The three specific targets that struck terror in our hearts (not unlike the WWII bomber pilots over Schweinfurt, Germany) were Sinuiju, at the Yalu River, Sinanju, 75 miles to the southeast; and Taegwan-dong, 24 miles from the Yalu, due to the fact that these objectives lay farthest to the north, in the dreaded MIG territory, and along the MSR, heavily defended by Russian 90mm radar-controlled antiaircraft guns. There were numerous alternatives open to the Fifth Air Force mission planners, such as using all jet aircraft, like the F9F, P-80, F3D, F-84 and the Gloucester Meteor. They could have made the long flight up north with extra fuel drop tanks, albeit carrying a much smaller bomb load, but could have fought their way back more effectively than we could if jumped by MIGs. It was never explained to us why they didn't use jet aircraft exclusively in these critical areas. I'll have to admit, there were times when we felt like sitting ducks up there. The Navy/Marine Corps soon recognized the superiority of the F-86 Sabre, and by 8 Mar 51 the Navy ordered the prototype of the USAF's F-86, with minimum necessary modifications for carrier operations. This Navy version, designated the FJ-2 Fury, was equipped with four 20mm canons but came too late for the Korean War.

The Corsair, however, remained a far superior close support aircraft, since we could stay over our target area up to an hour with a multitude of lethal ordnance, and we could be selective in our use of ordnance while making up to a dozen runs on the various targets, as the FAC directed. This wasn't the case for aircraft such as the F9F Panther, which could barely get airborne in temperatures over 90° while carrying a couple of 500-pound bombs, continue up to the bomb line, make a run, then get the hell out of there back to K3 in the southern part of Korea because of low fuel. On these short missions they didn't carry drop tanks.

No doubt about it, the only really effective fighter interceptor the Allies had was the North American F-86 Sabre jet. The Air Force had done their homework on this one and had left the Navy and the Marines way behind, since we had absolutely nothing comparable. The Air Force had the right plane for the job, so they naturally were assigned that mission and they performed admirably.

The F-86 was used by the 4th and 51st Fighter Groups in Korea starting in December 1950, as an interceptor. I could never figure out why one service was able to write their specifications for a fighter, obtain their appropriations, and select a superior aircraft over another service. There should have been more inter-service planning. In the case of the F-86 vs the F9F, the Air Force and North American first conceived the F-86 in 1945 and had flown it by August 1947. They'd supplied it to their squadrons by April 1949. Using the General Electric J-47 with 5910 pounds thrust, this achieved published speeds of between 610-679 MPH at altitudes of 48,300 and 54,600 feet, certainly not very dramatic by today's standards.

The F9F Panther, on the other hand, first flew 4 Dec 1947, using the Rolls Royce 5000-pound thrust Nene engine. VF-51 was the first Navy squadron assigned to fly the F9F, in May 1949, but this version came equipped with the Nene engine, built by Pratt and Whitney. F9F-3 and -4 had Allison J33-A-8 and -C-6 engines. The swept wing version F9F-6, called the Cougar, equipped with a J48-P-8 engine, was first used by VF-32 in December 1951. These early versions of the Panther were rated at around 526 MPH at 22,000 feet, increasing to 690 MPH at 40,000 feet in the later F9F-8 versions by December 1953 when the 7200-pound thrust J48-P-8 engine was installed, but the -8 came too late to see combat in Korea. They had a dual role, one as a fighter and the other as an attack aircraft capable of carrying several 1000-pound bombs. Any Navy or Marine aircraft was saddled from the very beginning with the added burden of being slower and heavier than an Air Force land

Left: The jet age had arrived but the WWII "Whistling Death" F4U Corsair, still considered one of the premier fighter/bombers for supporting front line troops, could also deliver heavy ordnance to all enemy installations. Hundreds pulled from mothballed storage in the deserts of Arizona and from reserve-based squadrons around the country were pressed into service in Korea. The Corsair in the photo is delivering a salvo of 5" HIVAR rockets, which have just been fired from their wing racks and the trailing white exhaust can be seen ahead of the plane.

VOUGHT F4U CORSAIR

Below: The Corsair pilot's instrument panel. Note right hand floor's heavy wear and the scuffed-off critical warning notice, as well as white caution notice on upper instrument panel—so much for the pristine maintenance.

VOUGHT F4U CORSAIR

Vought F4U Corsair single-seat fighter leaving the deck of a U.S. carrier; note rockets under wing of craft. On 4-5 August 1950, Navy planes attacked targets in the Suwon-Seoul area and provided support for troops fighting in the Chinju area. B-29s, B-26s and fighter planes were active at this time, attacking the Seoul marshaling yards and enemy shipping, as well as rendering support to ground troops. On 3 Aug 1950 eight VMF-214 Marine Corsairs, led by Squadron Executive Officer Major Robert P. Keller USMC, catapulted from the deck of the USS Sicily (not shown here) to launch the first air strikes in the Korean action. My friend, LtCol John S. Perrin USMC Ret, was Keller's wingman at the time.
See Appendix 8 for further exploits of VMF-214 and other units of the 1st Marine Aircraft Wing in Korea.

MCDONNELL F2H-2 BANSHEE

McDonnell F2H-2 Banshee - Made its appearance in 1949, having a longer fuselage than earlier versions in order to accommodate more fuel in the fuselage as well as fixed-wingtip tanks. They produced 334 under two contracts between Aug '49 and Sep '52, making this the most popular of all Banshee variants used by the U.S. Navy and Marines. Two J34-WE-34, 3150 lb thrust jet engines powered this fighter. It was equipped with four 20mm cannons, and some variants had refueling probes and cameras. I personally remember the Marine Banshee squadrons in Korea being used for photographic missions.

DOUGLAS F3D-2 SKYNIGHT

Douglas F3D-2 Skynight - Used exclusively by a U.S. Marine Corps squadron in Korea, primarily as a night fighter, taking advantage of its radar. This fine VMF(N)-513 night fighter squadron was flying out of a west coast field called K-8, near the village of Kunsan.
The Skynight was powered by two 3400 lb thrust J34-WE-36 engines. During my re-training phase at El Toro in 1951, I had a few flights in this plane, since it was a two-seat side-by-side aircraft, making it ideal as an instrument checkout plane. Each one of us re-treaded Marine pilots was required to have his full instrument ticket before being put on an overseas draft for Korea.

LOCKHEED F-80 SHOOTING STAR

Lockheed F-80 Shooting Star, based in Japan, leaving on a mission against the North Koreans, passes over Japanese workers in a rice paddy. This was necessary during the early 1950s fighting, but after the Eighth Army breakout from Pusan, many airfields became available for operations in Korea proper. F-51's later replaced the F-80s.

based fighter, by the simple fact that they had to be more ruggedly stressed in their design in order to withstand the punishing landings on an aircraft carrier's deck. For all these reasons the Air Force dueled with MIGs in their F-86 fighter interceptors, while the Navy and Marines were relegated rolls as attack squadrons. Only when a lucky few Marines were assigned to the Air Force 4th Fighter Group on an exchange basis, were they fortunate in knocking down the MIG-15. From this observation, I think even the Air Force F-86 pilots would concede that, given an equal fighter plane, either an Air Force or a Navy/Marine fighter pilot would have performed better against a MIG-15. Air Force pilots did report that their Chinese counterparts generally lacked overall combat proficiency, but at times their aggressiveness, sheer weight in numbers, and utter disregard for losses counterbalanced any apparent deficiencies. No doubt their individual aggression was directly related to the amount of training and previous combat they had experienced.

THE U.S. MILITARY OCCUPATION OF KOREA IMMEDIATELY FOLLOWING WWII

On 8 Sep 1945 the vanguard of the U.S. 7th Infantry Division arrived at the Korean port of Inch'on and began to disembark. The following day elements of the division moved on to the capital city of Seoul, where the Japanese officially surrendered their authority in Korea. With the conclusion of WWII, the U.S. occupation forces turned to the dual task of disarming and repatriating Japanese nationals and preserving law and order until such time as the Koreans themselves could once again take over the responsibilities of government.

To the great majority of the occupation troops, Korea was little more than a blip on the map--a temporary stopover before they returned home. With the dramatic collapse of Japan after the atom bombs had been dropped and with the entrance of the USSR into the war, little time had been allotted for the occupation troops to prepare properly for the problems that lay before them. With the Russians moving south into Korea from Manchuria and the U.S. forces hundreds of miles distant from the peninsula, a quick and supposedly temporary arrangement on the occupation areas had to be worked out with the USSR. Under the agreement, the Russian troops would accept the surrender of Japanese forces north of the 38th Parallel and the U.S. units would perform the same function to the south of the Parallel. To ensure against any long delay in the arrival of the U.S. forces, General of the Army Douglas MacArthur, Commander, United States Army Forces, Pacific, had been forced to select the units to be assigned for occupation duties on the basis of availability of troops and transport. Thus the first arrivals had little knowledge of the land and the people they were destined to control.

Although Korea had undergone troublesome times in the twentieth century, it was one of the earliest of the modern national states to emerge with essentially the same language, boundaries, and ethnic composition that it has at the present. During the seventh century the kingdom of Silla had emerged triumphant from the petty wars that had plagued the peninsula. With Chinese help, Silla was able to consolidate its gains and to introduce a golden period in Korean art and literature. Chinese influences in government, law and ethics soon became prevalent, and the Koreans adopted the Confucian system of social relationships. Under this system the Korean rulers assumed the role of sons or younger brothers to the Chinese emperors. Despite later barbarian attacks from the north and a devastating Japanese invasion in the late sixteenth century, Korea remained faithful to its tenuous relationship with China.

In the nineteenth century Korea became an unwilling pawn in the power struggles among China, Japan, and Russia for the dominant position in the Far East. By applying pressure upon the declining Chinese empire, Japan secured a commercial treaty with Korea in 1876 that fostered Japanese economic penetration. To counter Japanese ambitions, China proceeded to encourage other nations to seek similar privileges.

In 1882 the United States concluded a treaty of peace, amity, commerce and navigation with Korea. When the treaty was ratified the following year, the Korean king asked the United States to send military advisors to train his army. Five years later--in 1888--the United States finally dispatched three officers as its first military advisory group to Korea. The long delay and the insignificance of the mission did little to sustain Korean confidence in the value of U.S. friendship.

The Japanese began to move more aggressively toward control of Korea in the closing years of the century. In the Sino-Japanese War of 1894-95 they effectively eliminated China as a rival, but then proceeded to underestimate the Korean people. Japanese involvement in the murder of the Korean queen in 1896 led to a wave of popular indignation, and the Korean king brought in the Russians as a counterweight. The respite was only temporary, however, for the jealousy between Japan and Russia came to a head in 1904-05. The Russo-Japanese War resulted in a decisive victory for the Japanese and *this* time they were determined not to forfeit the spoils. During the next five years they strengthened their hold on Korea and won recognition from Great Britain and the United States for their special interests in that area. In 1910 Japan formally annexed Korea to the Japanese empire.

The ensuing forty years of Japanese occupation witnessed the transformation of Korea into a Japanese colony. Japanese administrators, officials and police descended en masse upon the peninsula and assumed complete control of all important phases of Korean activity. Japanese became the official language of the government and courts, and the Shinto religion was given a favored place. Through the use of spies, police and the army, the Japanese governors were able to exercise a tight rein over the political scene and to curb quickly and ruthlessly any signs of nationalistic unrest.

To provide for the needs of Japan, the Korean economy was reshaped. Korea became the rice bowl of Japan and essentially a one-crop country insofar as exports were concerned. Natural resources necessary to complement, but not to compete with, Japanese production were developed, usually under Japanese ownership and management. Industry and communications facilities were built up to promote Japanese exploitation of Korea and to support the Japanese war machine.

Until the end of WWII, the Japanese kept an iron grip on the positions of political, economic and military importance on the peninsula, and few Koreans were given an opportunity to gain high-level experience in responsible jobs. In the few cases where Koreans did rise to important positions in government, industry and the army, they were usually regarded with disdain as collaborators by their own people. Thus, trained native administrators, technicians and military leaders, untainted by association with the Japanese, were extremely difficult to find in postwar Korea.

Despite forty years of repression, most Korean people had not lost their national self-consciousness. After a revolution in 1919, an independent Korean Provisional Government had been established in Shanghai with Dr. Syngman Rhee as president and, although it had undergone many trials, it was still in existence in 1945. Numerous splinter groups also existed, both within and outside the country, whose aim purportedly was independence. Extreme factionalism, however, appeared to be an inherent Korean trait and the Japanese had carefully nurtured this destructive tendency of Korean political parties to fragment themselves into warring groups at the slightest provocation.

The disposition toward internecine strife came to the fore when Japan surrendered in 1945. A plethora of political organizations, approximately 70 in number, sprang up overnight, each claiming popular support as *the* party that would lead Korea out of the political wilderness. Since the Allied leaders had promised at the wartime conferences in Cairo in 1943, and Potsdam in 1945, that Korea would in due course become free and independent, the Koreans assumed that independence would come almost immediately. The misconception was abetted by the fact that the Korean language had no expression that conveyed the meaning of the words "in due course."

Thus, when the first U.S. forces landed in Korea in 1945, the situation was hardly encouraging. The Korean people expected quick liberation and independence although they were not adequately prepared for self-government and lacked trained administrators. The Korean economy had fallen into a state of deterioration. The dislocation of the close economic ties with Japan could not fail to have a tremendous effect upon the entire nation until new markets could be established and industry rehabilitated and reoriented toward Korean rather than Japanese requirements. In addition, the Japanese had resorted to the use of the printing press during the closing days of the war and had paved the way for a tidal wave of inflation.

With an unbalanced economic structure, a nation divided physically by the Russo-American occupation agreement, and politically by the internal factional groups on the other, the U.S. troops began their untenable mission in Korea. The task of establishing a viable and stable economy and enforcing internal order until Korea attained full independence promised to be a challenge demanding the highest degree of effort, skill, and tact.

General MacArthur selected LtGen John R. Hodge as the Commanding General, U.S. Army Forces in Korea (USAFIK), and assigned the U.S. XXIV Corps, composed of the 6th, 7th, and 40th Infantry Divisions, as the occupation force. To handle civil affairs, Hodge appointed MGen Archibald V. Arnold, Commanding General of the 7th Division, as the head of the United States Army Military Government in Korea (USAMGIK).

CREDIT: Maj Robert K. Sawyer, *USA Military Advisors in Korea: KMAG in Peace and War.*

Chapter 1 showed that many war-weary GIs, just trying to put the war behind them, had again been caught up in the snare. Seven years previously, we would never have imagined such a future. The horrors of WWII had cost America alone 405,399 dead and 670,846 wounded. We, the survivors, had counted ourselves fortunate and were eagerly pressing on with our young lives as civilians when the clarion call sounded once again. But first, Chapter II describes the period immediately following WWII. . .

CHAPTER 2

THE POST WORLD WAR TWO YEARS

Having served as an enlisted man in the Navy on three of Uncle Sam's aircraft carriers, *Saratoga, Yorktown* and *Enterprise*, from September 1941 until early 1943, when our country was definitely the underdog in the Pacific, I had witnessed firsthand the early defeat and feeling of hopelessness as we lost one carrier after another. Returning in late 1944 to the Pacific as a Marine fighter pilot, my ensuing 80 missions allowed me to observe personally the unbelievable growth of our armed forces as we finally took the upper hand. My overseas tours amounted to 24 months of combat and provided me with the opportunity to see this war both through the eyes of an enlisted sailor and as an officer and fighter pilot in the United States Marine Corps with VMF-223.

Many of my pilot buddies stayed in the Marine Corps after the war and retired after 20 or 30 years, but there were those such as myself who loved to fly but didn't care to pursue a military career. So, along with millions of my fellow WWII servicemen, I was relieved of active duty (discharged) in November 1945 and returned to my hometown, Huntington Park, CA, to pick up the pieces and begin my life again as a civilian.

On VJ-Day there were 2538 aircraft at North Island awaiting transportation to combat zones. More would flow in for disposition. Airplanes comprised only a small part of the material tide that had to be reversed before normal peacetime activity aboard the Station would be possible. Returning ships unloaded mountains of aviation material. Meanwhile, surplus items from deactivated auxiliary air stations soon reached alarming proportions. That was not all. The flow of new supplies from manufacturers continued for several months. Moving that gigantic stockpile of war materials and disposing of it in an orderly way was the major job facing the Supply Department for several months following the war. Somehow the pile slowly disappeared.

The aircraft were disposed of in various ways, but the flyable ones during the early months were ferried to storage. Between VJ-Day and the end of December, 1945, 1700 planes were flown to Clinton, OK, for storage. That represented the equivalent of almost one-third of the entire Navy inventory of 5233 aircraft which had existed at the beginning of WWII.

By the end of the war most of the defense contracts had been cancelled and workers let go until they could tool up for peacetime production. The debilitating effects on the industrial base of our country caused by the rapid demobilization after WWII had a profound effect upon the nation. To stimulate the civilian economy, the government sold most of the industrial plants whose construction had been federally financed during the war. A huge surplus of equipment and ammunition made industrial preparedness seem to many an item of low priority. Those plants not sold began to deteriorate because of inadequate appropriations for maintenance. One estimate cites that an expenditure of only $50 million for plant maintenance from 1945 to 1950 would have saved $200 to $300 million in rehabilitation costs expended during the upcoming Korean War, but our planners had not foreseen this. Hindsight is, of course, 20/20.

Defense workers headed back east with their pockets bulging from their high paying defense jobs and severance pay, only to return to California in a few months with their kin, as did thousands of GIs who had trained or passed through the state during the war. There had been nothing like it in California since the Gold Rush days. Housing was of an absolute premium because nothing had been built during the war, building materials having been diverted to the war effort.

Marion and I were among this new wave of California pioneers, solely devoting the next few weeks to house hunting. (We stayed, for awhile, with my mother and stepfather, Scotty. They were really good about it, but we wanted our own homestead.)

One evening, after spending the entire day looking with a real estate agent, we came upon this little 35-year-old frame bungalow on Beck Avenue in Bell. The agent knocked and asked if it was OK to bring us in, right at dinner time. The Garretsons said yes, so in we went. Mrs. Garretson was cooking hotcakes on a grill on top of her stove and the smell was absolutely tantalizing, especially since we were starving hungry. One look at their cozy back yard with its huge pepper tree, dichondra lawn and beautiful flower garden full of blooming chrysanthemums did it.

"Let's buy it," I whispered to Marion. She agreed. Mind you, this all took place within five minutes. The sale price was $5,750, with $3,000 down and $27.50 per month on the balance. However, there was one catch; due to the poor condition of the outside paint the loan company wouldn't give us the $2,750 loan unless the house was scraped, and painted with two coats of paint. Thus, with the Garretsons still living in the house, Marion and I scraped, wire brushed and sanded the old place, including the garage out back, and applied two coats of paint in the next two weeks. We then called the loan company people over for the inspection and they approved the loan. We had ourselves our first home.

Since we didn't have a stick of furniture, we investigated a sale ad at Singer's in North Hollywood and came home with a houseful for $325. No refrigerator included, nor a washing machine, we put our names on a waiting list and bought an old fashioned ice box which sufficed while we waited for our name to come up. I always forgot to dump the ice box drain pan so, after a half dozen evenings spent mopping up the floor when we came home after going out, I became convinced that I should drill a hole through the wooden floor just under the drip.

Marion had just become pregnant with our first child, Eric. She had taken a secretarial job at the Calavo Avocado Company in Vernon, an industrial town a few miles away, near Los Angeles, but the bus ride through the stockyards to get there, plus the diesel fumes of the old bus, proved too much for her, so she quit and took another secretarial job about a block away from home at a small venetian blind manufacturing place, making $32 a week. I started college at Curtiss Wright Aeronautical Institute located 25 miles away in Burbank. Under the GI Bill I received $99 a month; together with what Marion brought home we just made it from one month to the next.

Since I had Saturdays off and Marion didn't, I did all the washing, by hand, in the laundry tub. Later, when our name came up on the priority list because of the forthcoming blessed event, we bought a washing machine. Hallelujah! Fortunately, we had great neighbors. An older couple, Fred and Paula Gregory, lived on one side of us. Fred, an old gravel-voiced ice man, would peer over the fence and tease me when he saw me hanging up Marion's lingerie behind a sheet I'd deliberately hung first to screen the filmy stuff from his view.

On the other side, Chuck and Martha Swan, a young couple about our age, lived with her mother. Chuck, also an ex-GI, had enrolled at Northrup Aeronautical Institute. We'd get together and burn the midnight oil on calculus and stress problems and, on several occasions, we all had picnics at the beach together on weekends.

Upon returning to the U.S. from Okinawa, I had bought a 1940 Chevy which I then sold to a friend, Harold Colwell, because we needed the money. Then I purchased a 1927 four-door Chevy from Scotty's son-in-law, Bud James. It was a real cream puff.

Marion's mom and dad drove out to California from Boston when Dad's company, the General Electric, went on strike. Answering an ad in the newspaper, they paid their share of the ride with some Mormons driving to California via Utah (Mom Ruby entertained them all as they were going through the capital city with her rendition of "Salt Lake City, Holy Gee!") The folks had no car but wanted to be on hand when our first-born arrived. While visiting with us they decided to remain after Eric was born because G.E. was still on strike and Marion's dad had gotten a good job as a turbine hand finisher at AiResearch Mfg. Co. at the Los Angeles International Airport. He had extensive experience on turbine blades, having been a wartime inspector at the G.E. Lynn works in Massachusetts. They just instructed their son, Arthur, to sell off the things they didn't want and ship the rest to them in Bell. Dad loved his new job and his newly adopted state of California.

ABOUT AIRESEARCH AND THE GARRETT CORPORATION

Nine years after Charles A. Lindbergh flew the Atlantic, our founder, Cliff Garrett, opened the doors of his infant aviation industry. The date was May, 1936. Initially, he called his new company Aircraft Tool and Supply, changing it later to The Garrett Supply Company. His first 11 people there in Los Angeles busied themselves with heat exchangers and other related sheet metal items, under the watchful eye of his Chief Engineer, Walt Ramsaur, a pure genius in his field. They counted up the receipts after the first year in business and found that they had sold $284,683 worth of their new products.

With the advent of World War II, our government called on Cliff and Walt to expand their facilities, which they did. The huge facility at the Los Angeles International Airport was built and the Phoenix facility at Sky Harbor, operating under a Defense Plant Corporation classification, was established from 1942 to 1946. These two manufacturing facilities, called AiResearch Manufacturing Company of Los Angeles and Phoenix respectively, produced vital equipment for B-17 and B-29 bombers, including intercoolers for cooling engine oil and preheating fuel, and cabin pressure regulators for the B-29. The B-29 became the first production aircraft to be pressurized, a major advancement for aviation, largely Garrett's development which came along only 10 years after the formation of the infant aviation company.

I think it's interesting just how I came to work at AiResearch Mfg. Co. in the first place. After the war ended and Marion and I began visiting with my old friends, it seemed natural that Mike and Terry LaScala would be our favorites among them. Mike, having quit the shipyards at the close of the war, rented an apartment in Compton, CA, not far from Bell, where we purchased our first home. Mike had come from Buffalo, NY, around 1934 during the height of the Depression. He couldn't find work anywhere, so wound up on the Grand Canal where thousands labored. Assigned to a survey crew, he told of killing hundreds of big old coontail rattlesnakes as they tramped the desert area around Yuma, AZ. Later he became a cement inspector.

During the war Mike and Terry had lived and worked in San Diego. I would stop off to visit them and their newborn son, Dale. (Lord, that was a long time ago. Dale is now an executive with a large computer company in Southern California. Mike and Terry are retired, living in Newport Beach, CA). After the war, Joe Wilber, a close friend of Mike's, knew I was attending college and talked up AiResearch as a great place to work. He had recently quit AiResearch and taken a large severance check along with him, having worked there most of the war years as a manufacturing engineer setting up their experimental turbine blade welding machine program.

Upon Joe's insistence, I went along with him one day to meet his old friend, Joe Rosales, the shop superintendent at AiResearch. The plant tour proved extremely interesting and their laboratory experimental projects covering a new gas turbine engine intrigued me. Mr. Rosales suggested that both Joe and I hire in. Joe rehired immediately but I continued looking at companies I was still considering.

Through my math professor, Mr. Evans, I got a great tour of Menasco Aircraft Company in Burbank. They had been manufacturing aircraft landing gear systems for many years and had an opening in their stress department which I could have had if I'd cared to sign up with them that day. I was very impressed with the people I met at Menasco and especially with their experimental laboratory, which had been selected by our government to be the recipient of captured German aircraft engines and rocket components. I had almost made my decision to accept their job offer but, while on the plant tour, they showed me a corner of their vast production assembly floor where, lo and behold, they were assembling washing machines! I decided then and there that I didn't want any part of an aircraft oriented company that had to resort to building washing machines as a sideline to survive the post-war slump. I rushed back to AiResearch and signed up August 6th, 1946 as a mechanical assembler in the Production Assembly Department, working for $1.16 per hour--half the pay I could have received at Menasco--but remember--I wanted to build planes, not appliances. Menasco, by the way, did very well without me.

My boss, Royal Peterson, a prince of a person, showed real patience and understanding to all who worked for him. He put me in charge of the balance room where all of the high speed rotating components we were building received their balance. I also ran a small overspeed tank where many of those components would be run to a speed above their normal operating speed prior to acceptance. Royal later placed me with Chris Olsen, the technician in charge of assembling AiResearch's first gas turbine, which they simply referred to as the Black Box. That special privilege afforded me the opportunity to meet and work with numerous AiResearch engineers and top management people, such as Cliff Garrett himself, president of the Garrett Corporation and AiResearch Mfg. Co. The Black Box turned out to be an unqualified failure and, after they shelved it, Russ Walker and I set up the first AiResearch overhaul department in an abandoned two-car garage to the rear of the main plant on Sepulveda Blvd., adjacent to the Los Angeles International Airport. From its humble beginning that department grew into one of the major money-making divisions in our corporation, involving hundreds of skilled workers.

THE STORK VISITS

The Baby Boom of 1946 loomed upon us. Marion woke me up just past midnight on September 17th saying, "I think this is it; better call the doctor." I immediately called Griffith Park Maternity Home where we had earlier made reservations and they replied, "Sorry, we're all filled up. You'll have to make some other arrangements." I then called the local hospital in Maywood, next to Bell, and they said they could take us. But when I called Marion's physician, Dr. Schoenfeld, who lived in North Hollywood, he told us to come on over to Griffith Park and he would work us in somehow.

Marion's mom, Ruby, and I helped Marion into the old '27 Chevy and the three of us headed full blast toward the hospital, which was a good 25 miles away bulleting right through the city of Los Angeles. By this time it was three AM and Marion's contractions were coming closer together. The roads deserted at those wee hours, I didn't stop at a single red light. Upon arrival the nurses made a place for her on a cot in the aisle, behind some swinging doors which divided the lobby from the working area, explaining that the first baby usually takes quite a while and that Ruby and I would be better off to go home, and they'd call us as soon as anything happened. So we stopped for some breakfast and I drove Ruby home before going to work. On the way to work I stopped off to buy some cigars labeled "It's a Boy." What confidence!

Ruby called me at about 8:30 AM, announcing, "It's a boy! He's big enough to start school--weighs almost ten pounds!" He had been born only about an hour after we'd left the hospital. The only delivery room in the small maternity home had been occupied when we'd arrived, so they had put Marion on the small cot just outside in the hall awaiting her turn, but the patient in the delivery room dallied too long and Eric was eager to see the world, so the birth took place right there in the hall at 6:40 AM on September the 17th, 1946.

I wasn't the least bit surprised that it was a boy as I went around passing out cigars to all of my co-workers. Marion had to stay ten days before I could bring her home, with Eric (Ricky) wrapped in the baby blanket I had purchased at the Marine PX in Seattle. I'd known what I was doing when I'd bought that baby blanket!! (Unbeknownst to me, Marion had also been doing some planning, having bought a silver baby spoon while visiting Yellowstone Park on her trip south after the war's end.)

OUR FIRST MOVE

Our home in Bell was simply too far for my father-in-law, Art Gleason, and I to drive every day, so Marion and I sold it in 1947 for $8750, making a cool $3000 profit on our one year occupancy. Of course it looked like a picture book doll house from all of our fix-up efforts. We purchased a home in Hawthorne, CA, right on El Segundo Blvd. for $7900. Our good neighbors, the McCrarys, had three children. The eldest, Julia Ann, spent a lot of time chatting with us and playing with our baby. Mrs. McCrary was divorced and worked every day, while her mother kept house and cared for the children, so I had the opportunity to provide the father image to her kids along with our own little guy, Eric, who was just one year old. All of our spare time was spent painting and fixing up the place. We all knew it was an interim move and felt that we might pick up a few bucks for our efforts.

A highlight of the Hawthorne house stands out in my mind. My brother Ben was visiting Marion and her mother one day while Dad and I were away at work. Marion had just picked up Eric from his crib in the bedroom and brought him into the livingroom to see his Uncle Ben, when an explosion shook the whole house. Ben immediately checked the water heater, but it was intact. The front bedroom, however, was a disaster scene; broken pieces of plaster and shards of glass had showered the room, including the baby's crib. Intruding through the broken window stuck the tongue of a hauling trailer which had broken loose from a car while traveling at a high rate of speed on the boulevard in front of us, careening down between the eucalyptus trees and smashing through the bedroom wall. What a blessing Eric hadn't been in there or he'd surely have been severely injured, if not killed. The trailer owner's insurance handled all repairs; in fact, even compensated us for cracks in the living room, which I repaired myself.

Meanwhile, Northrup Aircraft Company, located just to our north about a block away, was busy running up the engines on its new Flying Wing night and day. We witnessed its first flight and wondered if it would ever be a success.

On weekends we had driven to Palos Verde Hills and along the beach towns of Manhattan, El Segundo, Hermosa and Redondo, and had become particularly attracted to Manhattan Beach. An old German realtor persuaded us to invest in four small lots up on the hill about a mile in from the beach, assuring us that $900 apiece was a good buy, even though utilities were not yet that far out. We purchased them and immediately contacted a local contractor, Joe DeFlavio, who designed and built our redwood-sided shake-roofed ranch house for us. After we had been turned down by the local Bank of America for having selected our lots in a "frontier area," we found a loan company in Los Angeles that would give us up to $5500 on a $10,000 home. We could hardly believe we were actually building our own dream home, which we finally occupied in May 1948 after selling the Hawthorne house for several thousand dollars profit in just a year. We were happy to leave Hawthorne, but not our beautiful neighbors, the McCrary family. Julie would continue to visit us over the years.

TRYING OUR HAND AT AGRICULTURE IN OUR SPARE TIME

For recreation during those years we drove down to Vista, 100 miles to the south of Manhattan Beach and about 40 miles north of San Diego, and worked with my brother Ben on his six-acre avocado ranch nestled among the hills 12 miles inland from the Pacific. It was great fun with our various little family groups converging on Ben's small ranch. His old gang, Harold and Millie Wassel, Harry Ringer, Harlan Hansen, Jack Wanzer, Bob Dale, Irv Day, and even my mom and Scotty would join us for pot-luck and overnights in his old

20x20 army tent. Pack rats would come in and raid the trash can at night, frightening the girls, but the clear clean air and beautiful country more that made up for that.

Ben hired a big cat tractor to rip up the soil four feet deep, breaking up the caliche and rocks--this after we found that it was taking us on the average of three sticks of dynamite to blow a hole deep enough to plant the Fuerte avocado, budded to a Mexican seedling as root stock. The government surplus pipe carried the drip irrigation water to a well around each little tree and we had dutifully prepared the wells with mulching straw and horse manure. The trees grew rapidly and Ben was pleased with the whole operation. As the years passed we built a frame cabin and things began to take on all the comforts of home.

One year, between the avocado tree rows, we planted six acres of beefsteak tomatoes. Since Ben and I were working 100 miles north all through the week, there was no one around to watch over things but all seemed to be in order whenever we went down. Ben felt that one particular weekend appeared just right for picking the huge juicy crop, so he procured plenty of tomato boxes and a flat bed truck and we headed south to reap our bountiful harvest. But cruel fate greeted us with a horrifying discovery when we arrived; some thief had also been waiting for the tomatoes to ripen and had stolen about ninety percent of our crop. Undaunted, Ben hung onto the ranch for about eight years, finally selling it at a good profit. The avocado trees were all bearing a cash crop when he sold, particularly the ones closest to the cabin, having been the recipients of special attention (where we had all relieved ourselves until Ben had gotten a regular privy installed).

THE COLD WAR HEATS UP/THE RESERVIST IS TWICE THE CITIZEN

I missed the flying I had loved so very much over those prior five years. Being a member of the Marine Aviation Reserves, as were all WWII Navy and Marine pilots from the old V5 program, I tried on many occasions to find a slot with an active Marine Reserve squadron at Los Alamitos Naval Air Station. Unfortunately, they had been snatched up by my fellow Marine reservists, who had found that the extra pay was really helpful during those years immediately following the war. This reserve pay supplemented the GI Bill money they were receiving and helped put them through college. I still went down on an occasional Sunday and checked out an SNJ trainer just to keep my hand in, but very infrequently. Soon I grew weary of not being able to get a plane when I'd driven down there and waited all day. Such was the budget situation during those years. This more or less reinforced the old cliche, "When the regular Navy or Marine Corps catches a cold, their reserve forces catch pneumonia." Nevertheless, I felt that sooner or later our country would be tangling with Russia and I certainly wanted to be somewhat prepared if that should occur. I always felt that Winston Churchill was probably right when he'd said, 'The reservist is twice the citizen." I would have been more than happy to have been accepted into an organized Marine squadron, but they were filled solid.

To absolutely nobody's surprise, the Cold War began to heat up. In early 1946 the Russians pressed Turkey for the control of the Dardanelles. Back in the pre-war years our presidents had practiced a policy of non-involvement, but President Truman in those post-WWII years broke with the past and established a firm policy to support the cause of Freedom whenever it was threatened. Although indeed noble, it hardly jibed with our country's headlong rush for almost complete disarmament.

Convinced that strategic bombing had won the war and would be the means of delivering nuclear as well as conventional weapons during this dangerous period, our nation concentrated almost completely on development of strategic bombers; meanwhile the poor Army, Navy and Marine Corps had to take "hind tit" until the Admirals Revolt in the late '40s and the start of the Berlin Airlift in 1948. Many of my ex-Air Force pilot friends at AiResearch had been recalled to active duty to maintain a life-line to West Berlin for one year, flying in food and other supplies. The Navy flew about 25 percent of those supply missions, but few Navy or Marine reserves had been called up. The times remained tense, ominous, and the possibility of our returning to a hot war loomed large. I closely watched the nightly news on our recently purchased 1948 Zenith model television set with its ten-inch screen.

OUR SECOND SON ARRIVES

As the months marched into 1949 Randall Rhoads Peterson, our second son, was born on June 23rd at the Stork's Nest in Inglewood, CA--4 lbs., 13 oz., soaking wet. They kept him in a warming device for a few days, until he reached five pounds of weight and then we were able to bring him home. A proud mother and dad brought him out to the car to his almost-three-year-old brother, Ricky (as we called Eric) who fully expected him to join him in fun and games, and seemed somewhat disappointed when we told him it would be a couple of years yet for that. However, when Randy was three months old, Marion left him lying on the bed on the south porch for a sun bath. Checking on him a short time later, she found him missing and, upon searching the house, found him propped up next to Ricky in a red leather chair, both staring bug-eyed at the TV. Ricky had apparently carried him from the bed across the concrete porch floor and up a step into the living room, then stuffed him into the corner of the chair beside him, and Randy wasn't making a peep. In defense of his actions, Ricky declared, "He wanted to watch TV with me, Mama."

RUSSIA EXPLODES HER FIRST NUCLEAR BOMB

The world stood still when in October of this same year, 1949, Ricky and I were sitting in the famous red leather chair and heard that Russia had exploded a nuclear device. Their efforts had been speeded by the help of several Russian spies in our own country. With the explosion of that nuclear device, it was universally expected that the next conflict would be an atomic war and that fighting even a limited war ever again was extremely remote. In March of 1949 our new Secretary of Defense, Louis A. Johnson, a political appointee of President Truman, brought about the Admirals Revolt by his almost total lack of knowledge of defense matters. He saw the Navy's fast carrier task force as obsolete in the atomic age.

Following Russia's exploding of her own nuclear device, we only partially changed our country's headlong drive into total disarmament, at least along the lines of ever fighting a non-nuclear limited war again. I could feel this attitude whenever I visited the Marine Reserve base at Los Alamitos. Those guys were getting the crumbs left over from the regular armed service's meager budget. I never received ten cents for any reserve time served.

Life on the Hill, as we referred to our home at Manhattan Beach, was a warm and pleasant experience. We had fine neighbors nearby, Carl and Beck Satzky and their charming little daughter, Mary, who practically adopted us along with Ricky and Randy. Next door, Marion's folks, Art and Ruby, had begun construction on their small home, and next to them the same company was building another place for my old friends, Peggy and Trooper Kilday, to whom I'd sold one of the lots I had purchased, at my cost. How great it was, having that gang on the Hill! Peggy was still working in town at the Broadway Department Store, while Trooper took care of the house. They treated Ricky and Randy the same way they had treated my brother Ben and me back in Huntington Park in 1929 when we'd lived next door to them. It was history repeating itself.

Down the hill lived the Oviatt family, consisting of Berenice and Keith, their daughters Michele and Laura, and Berenice's mother, a sweet old Norwegian lady. Across from them, the Colton family were building their own home out of adobe bricks mixed right on the property. The walls were so thick we all referred to it as Fort Colton.

The Keating family had just moved into a new home south of us--Al, an ex-Marine, Lorana, an ex-Wave, and their two adorable daughters, Helen and Mona, about the same ages as our boys. Northwest of us lived the Rices, with son Butchie, Ricky's constant companion and Randy's idol because he would read him comic books and pull him in his wagon.

By 1949 my AiResearch job had taken me into the Experimental Development Lab where I became more deeply involved in the company's latest gas turbine engines. These had turned out to be very successful and I accepted ever increasing responsibility. My immediate supervisor, Eddie Butler, was as fine a fellow as I would ever meet. Among others I worked with were Bob Calvert, Andy Boucher, Jim Bennett, Glenn Basore, Dick Frey, Roy Nelson, John Miles, Ernie Hall, Maynard Chaney, Bob Bancroft, Perry Sebring and Vern Smith. I found my work very interesting and challenging.

AiResearch, being a pioneer in the field of aircraft pressurization dating back to the B-29, was naturally led into building engine-driven compressors to pressurize the airplane, and secondary equipment such as the gas turbine engine, considered an essential auxiliary power source for on-board electrical and hydraulics. When they recognized the need for both pressurization and/or cooling, the industry's first approach was to take compressed air from somewhere in the power plant such as out of the engine's supercharger or the turbocharger. With the introduction of the jet engine as prime mover, there suddenly became available more than enough compressed air and the so-called air-cycle air conditioning system was adapted. It simply fit hand-in-glove with AiResearch's product expertise. They were soon being produced for nearly all our fighters and would become known as a "tempest in a teapot," since the main compressor and turbine were in fact about the size of a teapot. The tiny turbine wheel, driven by bleed air from the jet engine, passed through an interstage cooler first, to reduce its high temperature, then drove the rotating group to speeds in excess of 100,000 RPM. When air is compressed it's heated and, conversely, when it's expanded, it cools very rapidly. This is the principle known as air cycle refrigeration. We watched with amazement the tests performed where engine bleed air at 550-600°F was cooled to 350°F to drive the turbine, and the discharge of the turbine spewed out snow particles. We've often laughed at our early company slogan, "We were founded on hot air," but that was an absolute fact. We would say of our company that we built our reputation out of "thin air."

SOUNDS OF WAR IN KOREA

The Chinese Nationalists fled to Formosa (Taiwan) after they lost their struggle with the Communists in 1949. Then containment of further Communist expansion became our country's policy. The seeds of trouble with Russia had been sown immediately after Japan capitulated in 1945, with the Russians accepting the surrender of all Japanese forces north of the 38th parallel in Korea and with the U.S. accepting the surrender of their forces south of the 38th. Russia refused to permit a United Nations observation team to enter their zone to conduct free elections. The Korean peninsula was divided by two rival nations, the north supported by Russia and the south supported by the United States.

Then, inevitably, it happened--on June 25, 1950 the North Koreans crossed over the 38th parallel, claiming to be combatting an invasion, which of course was a trumped up charge. Being driven far to the south and outclassed militarily, it looked like all of South Korea would soon be overrun.

Those prominent names we kept hearing on the nightly news, such as Syngman Rhee, head of the South Korean government, came into our living rooms with commentary that sounded less than reassuring: "The unpopularity of the Syngman Rhee government and the questionable political and military reliability of the army and the police force," wrote Hanson Baldwin in *The New York Times* on June 27, 1950, filling us with doubts about the South Korean government's stability.

We all knew that Communist aggression had to be checked, as it appeared to be gaining strength everywhere--in Europe, Asia, the Middle East and Latin America, nourished and financed by Stalin's Russia. To the frightened dismay of everyone in the free world Eastern Europe, a particularly troubling area, seemed to be disappearing into an abyss of totalitarianism.

In Korea, frightening as it was, many felt that Kim Il Sung, the Communist leader of North Korea, had made a huge miscalculation by starting his invasion, since, if left alone, South Korea might have gradually fallen into his hands anyway, as a result of the aggressive Communist agents in the south and the unpopularity of Syngman Rhee and his government.

Dean Acheson, then our Secretary of State, perhaps unintentionally invited the Communist invasion of South Korea when, in January 1950, six months prior to the invasion, he had carelessly excluded South Korea from the defined area of American primary interests in the Far East. Listed as having more interest were

Berlin (East Germany), Greece, Turkey and Iran. Later he was quoted with a much revised statement of our intentions after the invasion:

> . . . *this attack did not amount to a* casus belli *against the Soviet Union. Equally plainly, it was an open, undisguised challenge to our internationally accepted position as the protector of South Korea, an area of great importance to the security of American-occupied Japan. To back away from this challenge, in view of our capacity for meeting it, would be highly destructive of the power and prestige of the United States.*

For many months prior to the invasion, our Ambassador Muccio had been sending warnings from his station in Seoul, the capital of South Korea, that there existed serious dangers in excluding South Korea from our stated interests, and the situation worsened when the president's opposition, the right-wing Republicans, steadfastly refused any financial aid. Further, by the summer of 1950 our armed forces had reached their lowest ebb, having dropped from 12 million men in 1945 to 1.6 million. Spending had gone from $82 billion to $13 billion. Practically every unit in the Army was understrengthed, undertrained, and poorly equipped. As the Supreme Commander there in Japan, it appeared that General of the Army Douglas MacArthur had let that happen right under his nose. Four divisions of his occupational army had been permitted to be stripped of a battalion here, a battery there, a platoon next. Their training for any war contingency had become practically nonexistent, but MacArthur blamed everyone but himself for the miserable conditions and gave little credence to any possible threat coming from Kim Il Sung's ragged rabble of Communist troops up north of the 38th parallel.

Following the North Korean Communist aggression, our CIA reported on 28 Jun 1950:

> *The invasion of the Republic of Korea by the North Korean Army was undoubtedly undertaken at Soviet direction, and Soviet material support is unquestionably being provided. The Soviet objective is the elimination of the last remaining anti-Communist bridgehead on the mainland of northern Asia, thereby undermining the position of the United States and the Western Powers throughout the Far east.*

President Harry Truman and his Administration were doggedly determined to meet this naked aggression head on, and every other Communist encroachment henceforth. With this decision, they plainly drew the line in the sand; thus far and no farther!

The U.S. went before the United Nations Security Council on 26 Jun 1950 with a resolution branding the invasion a breach of international peace, and demanded that the North Koreans withdraw. The Russians had boycotted the organization that day and were not present, so the resolution was passed. Several days later, acting on another U.S. resolution, the UN directed the member states of the UN, "to furnish such assistance to the Republic of Korea as may be necessary to repel the armed attack."

Our country was extremely ill-prepared to take up arms, having become a mere shadow of our dynamic military organization at the end of WWII. A *New York Times* editorial of July 16, 1950, after the conflict began, said it all:

> *Our emotions as we watched our outnumbered, outweaponed soldiers in Korea must be a mingling of pity, sorrow and admiration. This is the sacrifice we asked of them, justified only by the hope that what they are now doing will help to keep this war a small war, and that the death of a small number will prevent the slaughter of millions. The choice has been a terrible one. We cannot be cheerful about it, or even serene. But we need not accept as inevitable a greater war and the collapse of civilization.*

Above: Joe Stalin's international communism had brought about this terrible scene of human misery--hundreds of thousands of refugees fleeing war on clogged roads, going they knew not where. Their plight gave us G.I.s raison d'être, smothering our own desire to be at home with our loved ones.

Below: Army Chief of Staff J. Lawton Collins (right) meeting in Korea with his army commanders, 25th Infantry Division C.O., William B. (Bill) Kean (left) and Eighth Army Commander Johnnie Walker (center) with polished helmet and G.I. pistol casually stuck under his belt.

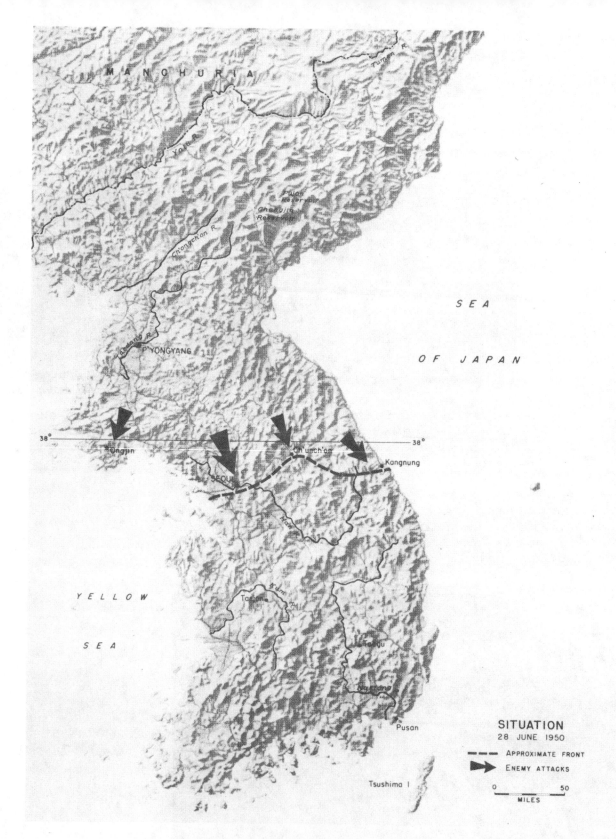

PRELUDE TO NORTH KOREAN AGGRESSION... In the early morning hours of 25 June 1950 when the North Koreans launched their powerful offensive across the 38th parallel against the Republic of Korea, the attention of the entire world was suddenly focused upon that little, mountainous Asiatic nation. Since the Republic of Korea was not a member of the United Nations, the United States Government immediately brought the aggression to the attention of the United Nations Security Council, branding the assault across the 38th parallel by the hostile forces as a breach of the peace, an act of aggression, and a clear threat to international peace and security... CREDIT: Department of the Army, KOREA 1950.

Above: An army infantry battalion shown assembling near the front lines during 50's fighting.

Left: Front line fighting; note fixed bayonets. At first contact with the invading Communist army, our combat forces could not stop the Russian T-34 tanks with our 2.3-inch rockets until the newer, more powerful 3.5-inch bazookas arrived later in the fighting. The Communists would outflank the American soldiers, kill their rear fire support teams, sever their radio and munitions support, isolate them into small pockets and cut them to ribbons.

Below: Moving out to engage the well equipped and tenacious enemy.

Left to Right: President Harry S. Truman, tough-as-nails ex-artillery officer in WWI, with his new Secretary of Defense George C. Marshall, former general and architect of the post WWII Marshall Plan to save Europe; his deputy secretary, Robert A. Lovett. Marshall took over after Louis Johnson was fired.

Left to Right: Chairman of the Joint Chiefs of Staff Omar N. Bradley, the president's chief military advisor, famous in WWII for his handling of the St.-Lô breakout in Europe; Secretary of Defense Louis A. Johnson, who earned so much hatred in his postwar handling of our armed forces unification efforts. But some say he was merely the hatchet man for President Harry S. Truman; Commander in Chief, Far East, Douglas MacArthur. Picture taken in Tokyo on the eve of the Korean War.

Left to Right: Adm Forrest P. Sherman, Gen Bradley, Air Force Gen Hoyt S. Vandenberg and Army Gen Joseph Lawton Collins. This group of military experts constituted The Joint Chiefs of Staff in 1950-51. They unanimously advised President Truman to sack Gen MacArthur because he was not in sympathy with their decision to try to limit the conflict in Korea in order to avoid a third World War.

Below: Gen Walton Harris (Johnnie) Walker, Eighth Army commander in the heroic stand at Pusan. Passed over by MacArthur to command the X Corps and the amphibious landing at Inchon in favor of his Chief of Staff Edward M. (Ned) Almond, the most controversial senior commander in Korea. Walker later died in a jeep accident, here shown standing in his jeep holding the grab bar—the siren and flashing red light on the right fender are Pattonesque touches.

NORTH AMERICAN F-51 MUSTANG

Briefing South Korean pilots on the performance of the North American F-51 Mustang, 27 June 1950. On 26 June ten Mustangs were transferred to the Republic of Korea by the United States. By 2 July a U.S. volunteer force of 11 officers and 150 enlisted men arrived at a small air base in South Korea to fly these ships.

By the time I arrived in Korea in March 1952, our forward base at K18 Kangnung was shared with a ROK squadron of F-51 Mustangs. Throughout Korea the Korean pilots flew hundreds of this popular WWII fighter, and sustained the greatest losses as well. This close association with the ROK air force is discussed under sub-title REPUBLIC OF KOREA AIR FORCE (ROK).

Above, Left and Right: The frail and aging Gen John Church who assumed the command of the 24th Division following the capture of William F. Dean during the early fighting in the 1950's; and Gen Walton Harris (Johnnie) Walker, Eighth Army Commander.

Defense Secretary Marshall and Secretary of State Dean G. Acheson. Acheson had been assured by his Korea-based experts, Muccio and Roberts, that the South Korean army in the spring of 1950 could defend themselves from a North Korean invasion, especially if they were given an air force to defend against the almost one hundred Russian aircraft of the North Korean forces. This was denied by Washington for fear that South Korean President Rhee would invade North Korea.

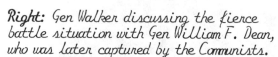

Right: Gen Walker discussing the fierce battle situation with Gen William F. Dean, who was later captured by the Communists.

Left: Controversial Gen Edward M. Almond (Ned), MacArthur's former chief of staff and later commander of X Corps.

Following the daily news accounts really tore me up, especially when we heard of the humiliating retreats our small handful of military advisors were experiencing in their heroic but futile town-by-town holding actions. Quoting from the *Air University Quarterly Review*, Vol. 6, No. 1, (Spring 1953):

> *In April and May 1950 large shipments of military hardware flowed from the U.S.S.R. into North Korea: heavy artillery, trucks, tanks, and automatic weapons for the North Korean People's Army (NKPA) and some outdated aircraft for the North Korean Air Force (NKAF). The NKPA was fat; supplementing the Soviet deliveries, North Korea itself provided light arms, ammunition, and food. For its basic combat strength the NKPA had nine fully equipped and trained infantry divisions and one armored division on the line on 25 June, augmented to approximately 13 divisions during the first two months of the war. The NKAF's strength at the outbreak of hostilities was approximately 150 obsolete Russian planes, mainly YAK-7's YAK-11's, and IL-10's. In comparison, the Republic of Korea ground forces (ROKA) comprised six infantry divisions, organized primarily for border and internal security. The largest weapon at their disposal was the 81mm mortar. For all practical purposes, the Republic of Korea Air Force (ROKAF) was nonexistent, although there was an Air Force organization with ten T-6 trainer aircraft.*
>
> *The North Korean Communists and their Russian advisers apparently anticipated no resistance from the U.S., or from other nations. Furthermore the Reds probably felt that intervention by others could not be effective before they accomplished their military objectives.*

The South Korean Army, numbering a little over a hundred thousand, evaporated in the face of the advancing North Koreans. Made up of farmers and peasants, the South Korean Army had really been organized only about ten months previously, when our government finally decided that we would in fact support South Korea and train her army. Although officially the U.S. Military Advisory Group's (KMAG) history begins 1 Jul 1949 when the group was formally established, the genesis of its mission can be found in the immediate post-WWII period. During the 1945-48 period, the seeds were planted and the area of development laid out. Thus, the story of the formation of the Republic of Korea's armed forces must properly start at the close of WWII when the nucleus for the future ROK Army came into being and American military advisors first were assigned to the task of organizing and training security forces. Insufficient time had ensued, however, to train her officer corps; also poor discipline, along with outdated arms, were the main troubles with the South Korean Army, not the will nor lack of courage to fight for their country.

Troop strength and readiness were two large problems that faced the U.S. Army when the surprise invasion of South Korea demanded action in the summer of 1950. Assigned strength of the Regular Army on 26 June, worldwide, was 630,201, of whom 360,063 were in the continental United States. Of the remainder, 108,550 were in the Far East Command (nearly 10,000 below authorized strength) and 80,018 in Europe, with the rest scattered about the globe. The strength ceiling of the National Guard was 350,000, and the Organized Reserve Corps had a strength of 255,000. Approximately 185,000 students were enrolled in the Reserve Officer's Training Corps. General MacArthur's Far East Command was in its worst condition since the end of WWII.

It consisted of four divisions in Japan, the 24th, 25th, and 7th Infantry Divisions and the 1st Cavalry Division, and one Regimental Combat Team (RCT) in Okinawa. Unfortunately, all of those divisions had demobilized their medium tank battalions because they were too heavy for the Japanese bridges. Although each had an authorized wartime strength of nearly 19,000 men, in June of 1950 they actually had only two-thirds of that number. Manpower cuts had forced MacArthur to reduce his infantry regiments to two battalions instead of the authorized three. Similarly, his artillery battalions had been cut to two batteries instead of the usual three. (It is my personal opinion that the Supreme Commander on the Asian scene could have prevented that from happening if he had made a more forceful case against it.) That meant the commanders would find it difficult, if not impossible, to maintain a tactical reserve in combat, nor could they rotate units out of the front line to rest them in the usual way.

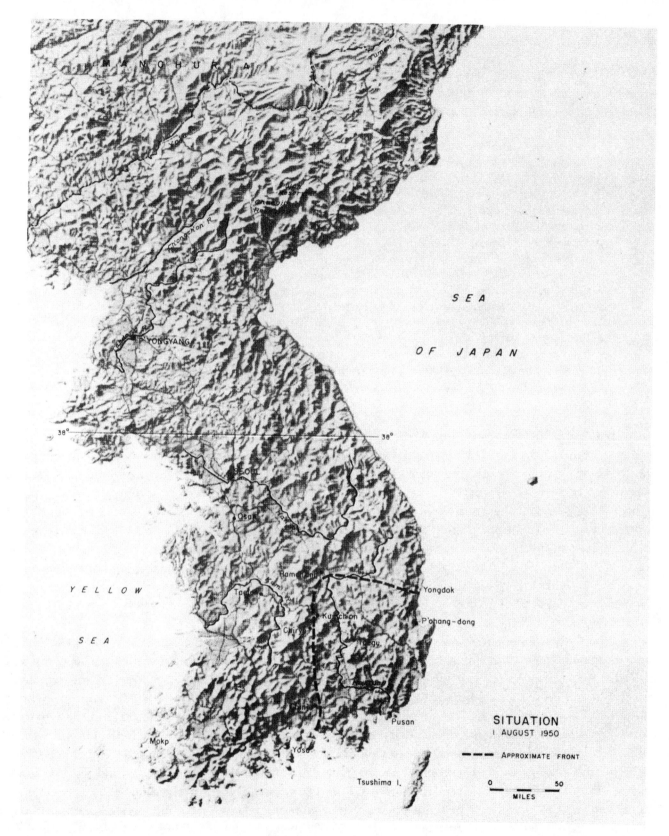

DEFENSE OF THE PUSAN PERIMETER, 1 August – 14 September... During the first week of August three large contingents of U.S. reinforcements began to disembark in Korea. Sailing directly from the United States, advance elements of the 2d Division, commanded by Maj. Gen. Laurence B. Keiser, landed to prepare for the arrival of the rest of the division which followed in the middle of the month. On 3 August the 5th Regimental Combat Team (Separate) reached Korea from Hawaii and was committed quickly on the Chinju front. At about the same time, Brig. Gen. Edward A. Craig's 1st Provisional Marine Brigade, a heavily armed advance component of the 1st Marine Division, reached Pusan after a sea voyage from Camp Pendleton, California.

CREDIT: Department of the Army, KOREA 1950.

At the start of the Korean offensive on 25 Jun 1950, the FEAF (Far East Air Forces) under LGen George E. Stratemeyer, were made up of some eight and a half combat groups, charged with the defense of Japan, Okinawa, Guam and the Philippines, comprising three fighter-bomber groups, two fighter intercept groups, one all-weather fighter group, two light bomb squadrons, one medium bomb group, and a troop-carrier group. The all-weather fighter groups had F-82s, and were credited with making the first enemy kill of the war, a Russian YAK-3 fighter.

NORTH AMERICAN F-82 TWIN MUSTANG

North American F-82 Twin Mustangs – Available in Japan and used with much success during the early fighting. Left over from a batch of 250 ordered in 1946, they were powered by two Allison V-1710-143/145 inline engines. They had replaced the P-61 Black Widow in service with the Air Defense Command.

GRUMMAN F7F-3 TIGERCAT

The Grumman F7F-3 Tigercat, too late for WWII, postwar Marine squadrons used them extensively until our entry into the Korean War and beyond. Some variants, equipped with radar and cameras, served dual roles as night fighters and photographic planes. Powered by two R-2800-34 engines, they carried four .50 caliber guns in the nose and four 20mm cannons in the wings. They were capable of carrying two 1000 lb bombs, six rockets or a standard naval torpedo.

Our air wing had F7Fs at the K6 airfield, where my VMF-212 squadron was based, and the Tigercats' night-long noisy operations were a great source of disturbance to a good night's sleep. Our living quarters were much too close to the active runway. So much for planning! On several occasions they accidentally dropped a bomb or two, which _really_ got our attention.

The units largely consisted of young and inexperienced soldiers, armed with police-type weapons. By mid-July three of MacArthur's divisions were in Korea; the 7th Division, which remained in Japan, had to be skeletonized to make the other units deployable. The 29th Regimental Combat Team, reduced to two full battalions, went to Korea as a replacement unit for the divisions. General MacArthur's efforts to fill out combat units included a sweep of every U.S. military nook in Japan to find general service personnel with combat experience or potential.

PUSAN PERIMETER "STAND OR DIE" ORDER

Our forces retreated south from June until August, when additional Army and Marine troops were brought in to form a defense perimeter around Pusan, and the "Stand or die" orders went out to all of our forces holding the perimeter, and "hold" they damn well did. Men pulled from desk jobs in Japan's occupation force became the primary fighting force that carried out the delaying action until LtGen Walton Walker's Eighth Army could be gathered up and landed at Pusan. In those initial days of the war, with mere rifle fire, our forces were in no way mentally prepared to stand up to the 35-ton Soviet T-34 tanks. Falling back, giving up ground, buying time at a terrible sacrifice of their young lives was all that they could do.

On 27 Jun 1950, President Harry Truman announced that he had ordered sea and air forces in the Far East to give support and cover to Republic of Korea forces and had directed the Seventh Fleet to take steps to prevent the invasion of Formosa. The North Koreans continued to pour into the south. With the situation becoming more critical by the hour, President Truman announced on June 30th that he had ordered the Air Force to bomb military targets in North Korea, the Army to go into action to support the Republic of Korea forces and the Navy to blockade the entire Korean coast immediately.

Carrier aircraft swept into action in Korea 3 Jul 1950. *USS Valley Forge,* with Air Group Five aboard, and *HMS Triumph,* operating in the Yellow Sea, launched strikes on airfields, supply lines and transportation facilities around P'yongyang, northwest of Seoul. The first combat tests of the F9F Panther and Douglas AD Skyraider were made in the initial engagement with North Korea.

Almost from the moment the North Koreans marched across the border, there was a rapid expansion of workload at North Island, San Diego, CA. The highest initial emphasis was on the immediate modernization and preparations for service of aircraft stored locally in cans or in the open at Litchfield Park, AZ. I always felt that the first Corsairs I flew in Korea came from that lot. During the final six months of 1950, 301 F4Us, 21 PB4Ys, and 113 TBMs were made ready by North Island forces for use in Korea. Delivery dates in many cases were close, the work pace very rapid and the pressure great.

The Commanding Officer, Captain Erdmann, on 21 July, expressed his approval of the manner in which the North Island personnel had met the challenge of sudden war:

> *The primary mission of the Naval Air Station, San Diego, CA, is to provide service to the Fleet. That means not only service to the ships and units of Air Force Pacific Fleet attached, but to all Fleet activities.*
>
> *Since June 28, 1950, when the international situation in Korea became acute, this Station has been involved in performing its mission on a 24-hour per day, seven-day a week basis. The* **Philippine Sea, Boxer, Sicily** *and* **Badoeng Straight** *have been loaded with ammunition, fuel, stores of all descriptions and their full aircraft and pilot complements. In addition, nearly a dozen attack transports and cargo vessels of the Amphibious Force, Pacific Fleet, have been loaded at our docks.*
>
> *All hands have been involved in one way or another in accomplishing these feats and all ships have been loaded on time. This has been accomplished in addition to more stringent security measures involved, and in addition to routine operations.*
>
> *To all hands in general and to the Supply, Public Works, Operations, Transportation and Security Departments, including the Police Force and Fire Departments in particular, I desire to express my gratitude for the manner in which you have performed your duties; WELL DONE.*

Fourteen squadrons of the organized reserves were activated 20 Jul 1950, for Navy duty: eight carrier-fighter, two carrier-attack, one ASW, two patrol and one Fleet Aircraft Service. Of that number, 11 reported to North Island for transfer to the fighting fleet.

Five new squadrons reported aboard North Island during the first week in August and more were expected. The five new squadrons were: VA-702 from Dallas, TX; VF-721 from Glenview, IL; VF-791 from Memphis, TN; VF-821 from New Orleans and VF-884 from Olathe, KS. The middle of August found six more squadrons reporting to the Station as the Navy's response to the crisis increased in tempo. The new North Island based units were: VS-892 from Seattle, WA; VA-823 from St. Louis, MO; VF-871 and VF-874 from Oakland, CA; and VF-781 and VF-783 from Los Alamitos, CA. Meanwhile, ships were being brought out of the mothball fleet and returned to service.

The Blue Angels, the Navy's famed precision flight team, went to war via North Island. After their last flight demonstration at the National Model Airplane Meet in Dallas, TX, on 30 July, they reported for duty with the Pacific Fleet Naval Air Force. They would prove in combat they were skilled performers, both in peacetime and in war.

As the summer moved on, the increased tempo of aviation activities and the support of fleet operations made it necessary to activate and redesignate Auxiliary Landing Field, Ream Field, and Auxiliary Landing Field, Brown Field.

Many planning conferences were held at NAV-AIRPAC headquarters during 1950 when the Navy was mustering its forces for the Korean conflict. On 21 July, Admiral F.P. Sherman, Vice Admiral J.D. Price, Vice Admiral J.H. Cassidy and Rear Admiral H.M. Martin arrived from Memphis to confer with Admiral A.W. Radford who had come from Barbers Point for a Reserve Officers conference with Vice Admiral Thomas L. Sprague.

By August, the output of aircraft from the mothball fleet was moving rapidly. An all-time high was claimed by personnel of the Overhaul and Repair Department test line when they ground checked, flight tested and corrected discrepancies in 264 aircraft during the month of July. Employees worked seven days a week to keep the airplanes moving out and meeting deployment dates.

Supply Department, too, was feeling the pinch for time. During the July-December period, 13 ships plus 18 squadrons and other aviation units were outfitted. This represented 38,000 items for allowance lists. During that period, Supply loaded 21 ships and unloaded five. The Operations Department logged 89,668 landings and takeoffs, an average of one every three minutes.

During an action-packed two-week period beginning 11 Nov, North Island helped the Air Force move 75 F-84 and 49 F-86 jet aircraft overseas. Part of a mass movement, the planes included the XC-99, prototype of the B-36, C-47s and other transport aircraft which arrived aboard the Station where the Air Force and Navy worked together to ready the fighter aircraft for surface shipment to forward areas.

AIR WAR IN KOREA

Charged with the air defense of Japan, Okinawa, Guam, and the Philippines at the start of the Korean offensive on 25 Jun 1950, the Far East Air Forces, under LtGen George E. Stratemeyer, were made up of some eight and a half combat groups, comprising three fighter-bomber groups, two fighter intercept groups, one all-weather fighter group, two light bomb squadrons, one medium bomb group, and a troop-carrier group.

To meet the threat of Russian jet fighter opposition, FEAF fighter groups had just been converted from F-51 to F-80C aircraft. A few F-51s remained in that area, awaiting shipment back to the U.S. The light bomb squadrons had been equipped with B-26s, the medium bomb group had B-29s, the all-weather fighter group--whose squadrons were dispersed throughout the FEAF area--had F-82s and the troop-carrier group had C-54s and some C-82s.

LOCKHEED F-80 SHOOTING STAR

Loading .50-caliber ammunition for machine guns of an F-80 jet fighter. On 7 August 1950 enemy units crossed the Naktong River near Waegwan; others drove south from Yonggi-dong against U.N. forces. Later in the war the Air Force ordered more F-51 Mustangs to Korea, as a superior ground support aircraft over the F-80.

NORTH AMERICAN F-86 SABRE

REPUBLIC F-84 THUNDERJET

LOCKHEED F-80 SHOOTING STAR

Three types of U.S. Air Force jet planes used in Korea. The F-86 Sabre, which first appeared in combat in Korea on 18 December 1950 (top); The F-84 Thunderjet (center); and the F-80 Shooting Star (bottom). Later in the Korean War the Air Force pulled the F-80s and replaced them with F-51 Mustangs.

As soon as word reached FEAF bases that the North Koreans had attacked, General Stratemeyer ordered a maximum effort in air support of South Korean forces, an effort which would continue without a day's let-up throughout the entire campaign. First to go into action, the troop carrier group was assigned to evacuate key government officials and civilians from Seoul via Kimpo airfield. Fighters provided cover for the C-54s, and before the first day came to a close a pair of F-82s made the first enemy fighter kill, a YAK-3 threatening the evacuation operations.

During the first weeks all missions against North Koreans had to be flown from bases in Japan since no fuel reserves or maintenance facilities were available for our aircraft at South Korean airfields. Combat lines being some 400 miles from U.S. fighter bases, this distance taxed the range of the F-80s and permitted them to spend only a few minutes at low altitude over the combat zone. F-51s, though slower and somewhat more vulnerable to ground fire, had much greater range and, fortunately, proved capable of outfighting the YAK-3s, YAK-9s and YAK-15s, the only challenges the North Koreans had put up against them. All-weather F-82s had a range well beyond that of the F-51s, plus greatly superior fire power. The lethal Russian MIG-15s wouldn't arrive until much later in the year.

Restriction from attacking enemy airfields above the 38th parallel hampered attempts to keep North Korean fighters out of the air during the first few days. As a result, some YAKs eluded the air defense, strafed South Koreans and attacked Suwon airfield in the first week of fighting. That restriction was soon lifted, however, and by 28 June the USAF began pummeling North Korean air bases in the short campaign to gain air superiority.

By 30 June 331 close-support and 103 interdiction sorties had been flown despite two days of bad weather. Although plenty of targets presented themselves as North Koreans pushed UN troops back all along the front, the lack of radio communications among the front-line defenders on the ground prevented adequate close-support operations. Air Force fighters struck at targets of opportunity wherever they came upon them, strafing and rocketing tanks, locomotives, trucks and troop concentrations. Weather frequently became an inhibiting factor during the early summer, but it never stopped the regularity of attacks. By 10 July Air Force daily sorties topped the three hundred mark. Many aircraft flew two and three sorties a day as maintenance crews worked around the clock to rearm and service them. Desk pilots in FEAF administrative jobs took turns flying missions while regular pilots snatched a few hours' sleep. Squadrons at outlying bases of the FEAF area were brought into Honshu and Kyushu to reduce their flight radius, leaving only skeleton air defense units at their home bases.

The Army rushed aviation engineers and fuel supplies into Korea to prepare airfields. In mid-July, within three days after they'd begun work, operations began from one such steel-matted airstrip. Aircraft flew from Japan to combat zones and landed at the improvised strip to refuel and rearm as often as possible before returning to their Japanese bases.

Within two weeks after fighting began, North Korean air opposition had been virtually eliminated, and FEAF was able to devote itself almost exclusively to operations in support of ground troops. Under the existing conditions, the F-51 Mustang, with longer range and the ability to operate from short, improvised airstrips, clearly surpassed the F-80 in overall performance. Consequently, FEAF called for more Mustangs so the Air Force began reconditioning several hundred from storage in the U.S. During that process, they borrowed Mustangs from the Air National Guard for emergency use. They managed to gather up 145, loaded them aboard the Navy carrier *Boxer* and ferried them across the Pacific in the record time of eight days and seven hours.

The additions to FEAF's fighter force enabled it to fly more than 400 sorties a day by the end of July while the battle lines were being driven back toward the Naktong. The July-end figures showed more than 4300 sorties in close support, 2555 in interdiction, 57 in two strategic bomb strikes and some 1600 reconnaissance and cargo sorties, for a total of more than 8600. Also, ground-to-air communications improved steadily, and the Air Force assigned fighter pilots to controller duties with forward ground units, as it had in WWII.

The Naktong River to the west of Pusan became their holding line. Within that defensive box eight divisions had now assembled, consisting of the ROK 3rd, Capitol, 8th, 6th and 1st, plus ROK manpower, consisting of stragglers who had joined with the battered American 1st Cavalry, 24th and 25th Infantry Divisions and a fresh 5th Regimental Combat Team from Hawaii.

The Provisional Marine Brigade, newly arrived from the States, also became a part of this Pusan Perimeter defense. They were 5000 strong and under the command of General Craig USMC. LtGen Walton Walker used them as his principal reserve force in mid-August against the enemy breakthrough at the bulge, east of the Naktong River. The marines were pulled out of the Perimeter at Pusan on 6 Sep 1950 to be used in the landing at Inchon on September 15th. The old Korean College which our forces took over as a headquarters building, was referred to as Pusan U.

PUSAN "U" (Sioux City Sue)

I was roaming 'round the countryside, t'was down near Pusan Bay.
I stepped into a local bar to pass the time away.
I met a girl who said, "How do." She hailed from old Chin-ju.
I asked her what her school was. She said, "Oh Pusan U."

CHORUS:

Oh Pusan U, Oh Pusan U,
I hail my alma mater, to you, Oh Pusan U.

I enrolled in that great college, founded by Kim Pac Su.
'Twas built of honey buckets, so they named it Pusan U.
The smell it was terrific, somehow I struggled through,
So now I lift this glass to the school of Pusan U.

Chorus:

I saw a girl most beautiful, she was a sight to view.
She won a beauty contest and was crowned Miss Pusan U.
They spotted her in Hollywood; now she's a star there too.
When asked to what she owes her fame, she says, "Oh Pusan U."

Chorus:

Oh Pusan U, Oh Pusan U, your course is good for engineers.
"A" frames and ox-carts pulled by steers.
Oh Pusan U, Oh Pusan U,
I hail my alma mater, to you, Oh Pusan U.

LtGen Walton Walker's fighting team, such as it was, had for the first time a chance to defend their flanks. The Communist forces had previously been able to outflank the Americans, encircling them with their T-34 tanks, killing their rear fire support teams, severing their radio and munitions support, and finally cutting them to ribbons after isolating them into small pockets. The T-34s could not be stopped until some 3.5-inch bazookas capable of penetrating the thick armor were flown in from the States. Our 2.3-inch rockets would simply bounce off the T-34s, as would the shells fired from our 105mm. A few American M-26 Pershing tanks finally arrived, along with other types of tanks, and their 90mm cannon did prove effective against the Russian T-34, as did our aircraft.

The allies experienced much anguish and frustration in meeting this terrible threat from Communism. Millions of Koreans, whose lives had been a struggle for a meager existence *before* the war, now had to flee for the southern part of their country by foot and oxcart, embarking on a three-year odyssey, barely subsisting on

American milk powder and herbs picked along the way until after the war ended. Scarcely a family in that unhappy land would be spared.

It was terribly disturbing to see what appeared to be a large group of refugees coming toward the first American troops to meet the Communist threat, only to find them swept aside at the last moment to reveal North Korean infantrymen sheltered among them. The enemy did not consider it treachery or a breach of the rules of war in their use of soldiers wearing civilian clothes, or even faking surrender in order to mask their attacks. Equally horrible, Americans shuddered with revulsion and rage at the shocking discovery of the first group of American prisoners in Korea, shot dead along the roadside, their hands tied behind their backs with barbed wire.

The makeup of the UN Command consisted of the United States, United Kingdom, Canada, Turkey, Australia, Thailand, Philippines, France, Greece, New Zealand, Netherlands, Colombia, Belgium, Ethiopia, South Africa and Luxembourg; in addition the Scandinavian nations and Italy furnished hospital units. India, who stayed neutral, sent a field ambulance unit. Other nations furnished food or money in limited amounts; the U.S. contribution amounted to ten times that of all other nations combined, excepting, of course, the Republic of Korea, which suffered a terrible loss of manpower. She would lose during the course of the conflict 1,312,836 men, women and children, as well as the almost complete destruction of her towns and cities. Contributions from the other countries ranged from a company to a brigade, with South Africa sending a fighter squadron. Almost all troops sent by other countries were professional and came from units of long history and proud tradition.

Back here at home we were encouraged by the first positive sign in this cruel war, after so many setbacks during the first few months. More and more reserves were called up to fill the ranks of the dead and wounded we had incurred in that far off oriental land of Korea. Not everyone in our country was gung ho for this war; in fact, unlike the situation at the onset of WWII, in this conflict there remained a noticeable lack of a mad rush to the recruiter's office.

THE FLEET MARINE FORCE (FMF) AND READINESS POSTURE

The flexibility and readiness capability inherent in the Marine Corps FMF structure provided a strong foundation in its swift response to the Korean crisis. In June 1950 the Marine Corps had 74,279 officers and men on active duty. Its Fleet Marine Force, consisting of FMFPac and FMFLant, numbered 27,656. The 11,853 personnel of FMFPac included 7,779 men in General Smith's 1st Marine Division at Camp Pendleton and 3,733 in General Harris' 1st Marine Aircraft Wing at El Toro. On the East Coast, FMFLant numbered 15,803 with approximately 8,973 Marines in the 2d Division at Camp Lejeune and 5,297 air personnel attached to the 2d Wing at Cherry Point.

The outbreak of Korean hostilities presented the Marine Corps with the tasks of organizing and deploying for combat, first a brigade and then a full war-strength reinforced division, each with supporting aviation elements. Despite the low strength to which FMFPac had shrunk due to stringent national defense economy measures, the heavy demands placed upon it were met. Both missions were accomplished quickly and effectively.

Manpower potential of the Marine Corps Reserve was 128,959, nearly twice that of the regular establishment. In June 1950 the Organized Marine Corps Reserve (Ground) numbered 1,879 officers and 31,648 enlisted personnel being trained in 138 OMCR units of battalion size or less. Membership of the ground reserve consisted of approximately 76 percent of its authorized strength. At the same time, the Organized Reserve (Aviation) had 30 fighter and 12 ground control intercept squadrons attached to the Marine Air Reserve Training Command organized at Glenview, IL in 1946. They were spread out over the various states.

These MARTCOM squadrons numbered 1,588 officers and 4,753 enlisted, or approximately 95 percent of authorized strength. In addition to nearly 40,000 members of the OMCR, the Marine Volunteer (non-drill, non-pay status) Reserve carried approximately 90,000 on its rolls. Only a fraction of the latter number were pilots. I fit into this small fraction.

While the organized ground reserve was being mobilized, the first of the 42 MARTCOM fighter and intercept squadrons began arriving at El Toro. Personnel of six reserve VMF and three MGCI squadrons were ordered to duty on 23 July as replacements in the 1st MAW which had furnished units and men for the MAG-33 component of the brigade and by October of 1950 all of the reserve squadrons had been called to active duty. Of the 6,341 organized air reservists, 5,240 received orders; 4,893 or 93.4 percent, reported in. Buildup of Marine Corps personnel during the Korean War from the June 1950 base of 74,279 grew to 249,219 Marines on active duty by June 1953. Altogether an estimated 424,000 Marines served during the period of hostilities.

POOR OPERATIONAL LOGISTICS PLANNING

As for operational logistics planning--how to get supplies and equipment, once produced, from the United States to the troops in the theater--the failure of war planners to foresee the possibility of a North Korean invasion of South Korea meant that there was no war plan to form a basis for logistical planners. Presumably, then, there were no logistical plans for operations in Korea, and the literature reflects this presumption. However, in a letter to the editor of *Army*, July 1985, Col Donald McB. Curtis (USA, Ret.) claims that the plans division of G-4, Army General Staff, in the fall of 1948 initiated a series of strategic logistic studies that included one for an invasion of South Korea across the 38th Parallel. According to Curtis, he, as a member of the division's strategic plans section, prepared a strategic concept that called for, "a retreat to and defense of the Pusan perimeter, buildup and breakout, and *an amphibious landing at Inchon* to cut enemy supply lines." The purpose of these strategic logistics studies, Curtis states, was to, "ascertain in advance what unusual logistic requirements could be expected in various potential theaters of operation." Although he also states that other sections of the General Staff concurred in his strategic concept, he does not make clear whether special logistical support requirements were ever computed in conjunction with it. (His main concern is to challenge General MacArthur's parentage of the idea for the Inchon invasion.): A revision of the accepted wisdom that there were no logistical plans for the Korean War awaits a testing of Curtis' claim through thorough archival research.

THINKING ABOUT VOLUNTEERING

Shortly after the war started I felt that sooner or later I would be called back to active duty and therefore wrote a letter to the Commandant of the Marine Corps asking for an active duty assignment. Since I had not flown actively in the organized reserves for almost six years, I felt that they would not let me fly, but I could qualify for at least a dozen or more ground jobs, such as squadron engineering officer. Months went by with no response from Washington. The pitiful sight of the Korean refugees, particularly the children, we were seeing nightly on our TV screen was jerking at my heartstrings, not unlike what we all had to witness for the people of Somalia and Bosnia in recent times. My own little guys were tucked away safe and sound in their beds at night, thank God, and would not have to face the fear of death or starvation. I know what was tearing at my insides. My first duty as a father and husband was with my family, and yet, I felt a powerful force tugging at me saying, "You should be over there doing what you were trained to do, along with your buddies."

THE INCHON LANDING, OPERATION CHROMITE

Army LtGen Walton (Bulldog) Walker had conducted a superb defense of the Pusan perimeter with his battered troops in Korea, earning himself the status of folk hero here in the U.S. MacArthur thought otherwise and gave the Inchon operation to his old protégé, Gen Edward M. Almond, a former divisional commander in Italy during WWII.

Almond, now commander of what was to be called the X Corps, did not inspire a great deal of affection among his subordinates, but was a driver of men. He least inspired the very professional 1stMarDiv's commander, Gen Oliver P. Smith, a slim, white-haired Texan of 57 years. Smith expressed concern about the tremendous 23-foot tides and the mud flats during low tide which the 20,000 men in his division would encounter, but he and other worried commanders were ignored by Almond who mirrored MacArthur's optimism. Gen Smith was more than adequately staffed with Col Ray Murray of the 5th Marines, Col Homer Litzenburg of the 7th Marines, and especially the bombastic folk hero with the 1st Marines, Col Lewis B. (Chesty) Puller, who would lead the first landing assault during this risky operation.

Vice Adm Arthur D. Struble's 260-ship armada shoved off from Yokohama, Japan, on 5 Sep 1950 with his makeshift transport fleet carrying 70,000 Army and Marine troops in the 37 LSTs, which had been transferred to the Japanese at the end of WWII. Among the troops were many hastily recruited and untrained Koreans of mixed ages. The LSTs had been used as fishing boats and still smelled to high heaven. Piloted by their Japanese skippers and crewed by American sailors lately flown in from various Pacific naval bases, they headed for Inchon, Korea, in the eye of brewing typhoon *Kezia*, whose 125 mph winds wrought havoc with all those aboard, especially those hapless troops crammed below in her stinking compartments.

Hardened marines with WWII island-hopping experience were later quoted as saying that they had been ferried to Inchon by a Japanese who had been an admiral at Midway and that the whole trip had been a rusty, stinking travesty of a WWII amphibious operation, especially after numerous breakdowns of the old LST's equipment. One had to remember, however, that at no time had there been any doubt as to the importance of the landing, not just for the cause of the UN but for the Marine Corps' very survival, which at that time period was under tremendous pressure from Congress and had shrunk to a shadow of its wartime strength.

The Supreme Commander, General of the Army MacArthur, sailed from Sasebo, Japan, on 13 September on his command ship, *Mount McKinley*. Then, on 15 September, at 0633, following a heavy naval barrage, the marines of Litzenburg's 5th assaulted Wolmi-Do Island with very little opposition, sweeping ashore at Green Beach. By noon nearly half the Inchon landing, dubbed Operation Chromite, had been expertly executed, aided by fighter bombers of the 5th Air Force. Due to the fact that early in the opening days of the war our carrier aircraft had almost completely neutralized the some 200 Communist old propeller-driven Russian aircraft, both in the air and on the numerous airfields in the North, North Korean air and naval action against *our* invasion forces had amounted to nothing. Their navy hadn't shown any inclination for action since July 2nd, when four Communist torpedo boats had attacked our *Juneau* and the British cruiser *Jamaica*, but three of the enemy torpedo boats had been promptly sunk or put out of action.

Under the command of RAdm James H. Koyle, the U.S. Naval attack forces, known as TASK FORCE 7, pounded Wolmi-Do and the Inchon beaches prior to the early morning invasion of Wolmi-Do, where a 400-man garrison and elaborate fortifications existed. At 1731, the tide reaching its maximum, the remainder of the troops and landing craft assaulted the sea wall, scrambling up their makeshift ladders brought along for that purpose. The Army's contribution to the Inchon landing consisted of the 7th Infantry Division, 32nd Infantry Regiment and 3rd Battalion, 187th Regiment. A ROK Marine regiment also participated.

Inchon was in American hands by midnight with fairly light casualties, 22 men killed and 174 wounded. Major house-to-house fighting took place for Kimpo Airfield and the town of Seoul in the following days. General MacArthur declared, "The Navy and the Marines have never shone more brightly."

The remaining Communists fled back across the 38th parallel as the two prongs of the trap closed on them, the 8th Army coming up from Pusan and the Inchon landing forces approaching from the other direction. With this operation so successful, MacArthur, in spite of warnings that the Chinese Communists would possibly intervene if he moved north of the 38th, chose to make another amphibious landing 115 miles northeast of Seoul at Wonsan, a harbor bristling with 3000 Communist mines. Over 200 transports and supply ships waited eight days for the harbor to be cleared before landing the troops, suffering 200 casualties in the clearing, according to Admiral Sherman, chief of naval operations. In the meantime, ROK forces had moved north and were there to greet the marines as they came ashore.

MAG-33 was joined by three MAG-12 fighter squadrons during the Inchon-Seoul operation--VMF-212, VMF-312 and VMF(N)-542. After the capture of Kimpo Airfield, 212's Devilcats and 542's night fighters

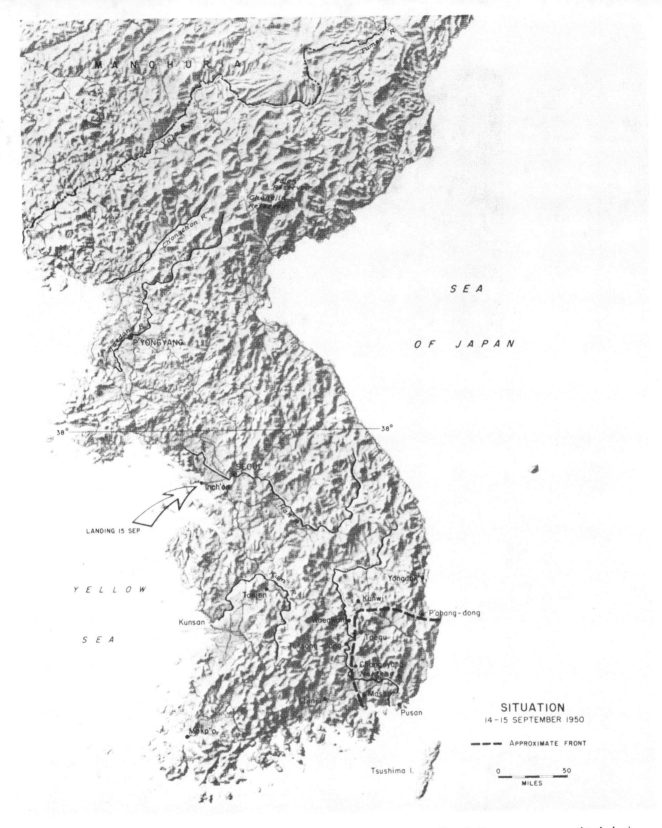

SITUATION
14-15 SEPTEMBER 1950
- - - - APPROXIMATE FRONT

UNITED NATIONS COUNTEROFFENSIVE, 15 September - 24 November... The North Korean regime, which had counted on a quick and overwhelming conquest, was given a stunning shock during the last two weeks of September: the U.S. X Corps swept into Inch'on from the Yellow Sea and the Eighth Army drove north from the Pusan perimeter. This gratifying turn of events, which led to the defeat of the North Korean divisions in South Korea, was the culmination of General MacArthur's plan to cling to southeast Korea until sufficient reinforcements were concentrated in the Far East to permit an amphibious landing behind enemy lines. While the U.N. army fought along the Naktong and Nam Rivers, the X Corps had been activated in Japan. Commanded by Maj. Gen. Edward M. Almond, the new organization in mid-August was given the mission of making an amphibious landing on Korea's west coast, and seizing Seoul and the communication routes over which enemy troops and supplies were traveling south... CREDIT: Department of the Army, KOREA 1950.

Right: (Not in photo) VAdm Arthur D. Struble and his 260-ship armada approach Inchon. MacArthur (with binoculars), on his command ship MOUNT McKINLEY, views the proceedings with his senior assistants, (left to right): Courtney Whitney, the GHQ G-3; Edwin K. (Pinky) Wright; and (pointing) the GHQ chief of staff and X Corps commander, Ned Almond.

Left: The Inchon amphibious landing completed. The 31-foot tidal swings were negotiated by those 37 LSTs carrying 70,000 Army and Marine troops. At 5:31 PM, when the tide reached its maximum, the remainder of the troops and landing craft assaulted the sea wall, scrambling up their makeshift ladders brought along for this purpose.

Left: With Inchon in U.N. hands by midnight of the landing day, suffering fairly light casualties (22 killed and 174 wounded), major house-to-house fighting took place for Kimpo airfield and the town of Seoul during the following days. MacArthur declared, "The Navy and the Marines have never shone more brightly." The liberation of Seoul and all of South Korea was celebrated by --

Left to Right: South Korean President Syngman Rhee, Douglas MacArthur, American Ambassador John J. Muccio, Ned Almond and guests.

Below: MacArthur at Wake Island, assuring President Harry S. Truman and his senior advisers that the Chinese Communists would not enter the Korean War if his U.N. Army continued to push north into North Korea all the way to the Yalu River. With the North Korean forces now in complete disarray, MacArthur sent his forces into North Korea on 11 October despite numerous threats from the Chinese that if he did, they would enter the Korean War in force.

This Wake Island visit, 15 October 1950, was Truman's first and last meeting with MacArthur.

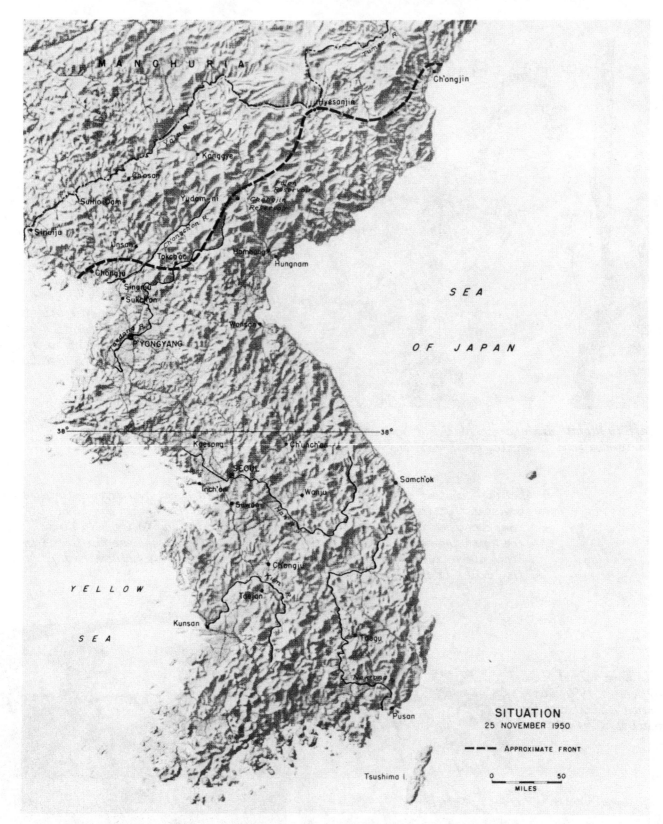

SITUATION
25 NOVEMBER 1950

– – – APPROXIMATE FRONT

0 50
MILES

WITHDRAWAL FROM THE YALU, 25 November - 31 December... The conflict in Korea entered a new phase during the fourth week of November. Elements of the American 7th Division, after a swift advance through the bitter-cold mountain area of northeast Korea, had reached and occupied the town of Hyesanjin, the most northerly point to be reached by American forces during 1950. Here troops of the 17th Infantry Regiment of the 7th Division could look across the Yalu River at the rugged Manchurian countryside. ROK troops had reached the border of Manchuria at Ch'osan nearly a month earlier, but were forced to retire. Now, for the first time, the U.S. Army stood at the international boundary.

Gen. Almond's X Corps, operating in the east, was composed of the U.S. 7th and 3d Divisions, the 1st Marine Division, the ROK 3d and Capital Divisions, and a commando group of British Royal Marines.

..CREDIT: *Department of the Army, KOREA 1950.*

transferred from Itami in Japan, to Kimpo in Korea. (At this point in my story, I'll interject the fact that VMF-212 Devilcat squadron was the one I would be joining in March 1952 there in Korea.) Flying out of 2d MAW headquarters, Cherry Point, NC, on 18 Aug 1950, the Devilcats had made a hurried dash halfway around the world to get into the action and had flown their first combat mission from Kimpo a month after their departure from the East Coast. At the conclusion of the Inchon operation on 8 October they'd shifted to the Korean east coast in preparation for the Wonsan landings.

THE ONSET OF THE CHINESE ENTERING THE WAR

With the North Korean forces now in complete disarray, General MacArthur sent his forces into North Korea on 11 Oct 1950, despite numerous threats from the Chinese Communists that if we did, they would enter the Korean War in force. True to their word, the Chinese forces began crossing the Yalu River from China into Korea three days later. Several weeks went by before they hit forward elements of our Eighth Army, which was in hot pursuit of the remnants of the North Korean Army and was nearing the Yalu.

The conflict in Korea entered a new phase during the fourth week of November. Elements of the American 7th Division, after a swift advance through the bitter-cold mountain area of northeast Korea, had reached and occupied the town of Hyesanjin, the most northerly point to be occupied by American forces during 1950. There troops of the 17th Infantry Regiment of the 7th Division could look across the Yalu River at the rugged Manchurian countryside. ROK troops had reached the border of Manchuria at Ch'osan nearly a month earlier, but were forced to retire. Now, for the first time, the U.S. Army stood at the international boundary.

Paralleling the 17th Infantry's success in reaching the Manchurian border, the ROK Capital Division progressed rapidly up the east coast to the Naman-So-dong area. By 24 November the UN positions extended from So-dong in the northeast to Hyesanjin on the Yalu, and thence in a southwesterly direction through the areas around Sang-ni, Handae, Yudam-ni, Yongwen, Ipsok, Pak-ch'on, and south of Chongju to the Yellow Sea. The UN forces continued their northward movement, slowly in the west, swiftly in the east. There had been an ominous address over the Moscow radio on 19 November, which asserted that withdrawals by North Korean and Chinese forces were only a prelude to a counteroffensive that would result ultimately in communist victory. General MacArthur, in the meantime, ordered a final offensive idealistically designed to defeat the North Koreans south of the Yalu River, end the war and restore peace and unity to Korea. MacArthur planned to advance the Eighth Army on a broad front northward through western and central Korea to the Manchurian border regions. At the same time the X Corps was to carry out an enveloping movement to the northwest to cut the supply lines of the remnants of the North Korean Army.

Subfreezing temperatures had already reached Korea. Despite the glazed roads and the rugged and barren terrain, there still existed an atmosphere of optimism on Friday morning, 24 November, when General MacArthur announced from Korea that a major offensive had been launched. At that time there were two distinct major commands in Korea, separated by the country's mountainous spine. General Walker's Eighth Army, operating in the west, consisted of the U.S. 1st Cavalry, 2d, 24th and 25th Infantry Divisions, the ROK 1st, 6th, 7th and 8th Divisions, the British 27th Commonwealth Brigade, the 29th Independent Infantry Brigade, a Turkish brigade, as well as a battalion each of troops from the Philippines and Thailand. Gen Almond's X Corps, operating in the east, was composed of the U.S. 7th and 3d Divisions, the 1stMarDiv, the ROK 3d and Capital Divisions plus a commando group of British Royal Marines.

For more than 24 hours the offensive to end the conflict did not encounter serious enemy opposition. Troops of the ROK Capital Division fought their way into the steel center of Chongjin, about 60 miles from the Siberian border. This was the northernmost penetration by UN forces during the year. Although high mountains prevented physical contact between the Eighth Army and the X Corps, Generals Walker and Almond exercised direct communication by radio, aircraft and courier. On 25 November, however, in the mountainous territory surrounding the central Korean town of Tokch'on, hostile troops initiated a violent counteroffensive. There, the ROK II Corps, forming the right flank of the Eighth Army, was crushed. Two

Above: Gen Matthew B. Ridgway took over the Eighth Army upon the untimely death of Johnnie Walker in a jeep accident. Ridgway's reputation was built upon his performance in Europe, where he actually jumped with his troops during WWII, as Commander of the XVIII Airborne Corps. Soon after taking over his new command, he began a major housecleaning, especially in the American artillery units, which had suffered disgraceful losses to the enemy. He demanded and got immediate replacements and results, including the activation of ten National Guard and Army Reserve artillery battalions sent to South Korea. He asked for and received additional air support from the Navy and Marines, which supplied a carrier task force consisting of the SICILY and BADOENG STRAIT, with two Marine Corps close support squadrons and a Marine Corps jet squadron based at Pusan. He wore his everpresent grenade on the right parachute strap of a parachute chest harness and a first aid kit. Ridgway was loved and respected by all, and really turned the war around to our favor in the months to follow.

Left: Among the many changes Ridgway ordered was the leadership of the Eighth Army. Bryant E. Moore (right) was brought to Korea to replace John Coulter as commander of X Corps. However, he kept Leven C. (Lev) Allen (left) in the job of Eighth Army chief of staff.

Right: Moore suddenly died of a heart attack and Ridgway chose William M. Hoge to replace Moore as IX Corps commander.

Marines march in a direction opposite that of the signpost indicating the advanced CP of the U.S. X Corps, in a photo that captures the cold, melancholy, and resilience of men of the Chosin campaign.

A unit of Company C, 7th Marines, led by senior regimental commander Col Homer L. Litzenberg, Jr., moves out to repair a downed bridge south of Koto-ri during the 1st Division's "attack in a different direction" of early December 1950.

Ordered by X Corps to withdraw to Hamhung, 1st Division Marines begin their fighting five-day march down mountain trails 40 miles from Hagaru-ri to the sea. MajGen Oliver P. Smith insisted on also bringing out all of the division's supplies and equipment.

Left: For more than 24 hours the offensive to end the conflict did not encounter serious enemy opposition. Troops of the ROK Capital Division fought their way into the steel center of Chongjin, about 60 miles from the Siberian border, the northernmost penetration of U.N. forces during the year. In the space of hours the Chinese snatched the initiative. Two Chinese Communist field armies pushed south, engaging our forces as the Siberian cold enveloped our U.N. troops with numbing temperatures of minus thirty degrees.

Right: Korean refugees by the thousands suffered from the bitter cold and lack of food and shelter.

Left: This narrow, frigid road was the only passage from Hagaru at the Chosin Reservoir to the seacoast town of Hungnam and the escape route to Pusan by sea. Under the worst possible conditions, 15,000 Americans escaped encirclement by Chinese forces. Weapons, food and medicine froze. The troops resorted to all possible means to keep from freezing.

Above: This pitiful scene of the cruel plight of two Korean mothers shown pushing a cart carrying their precious brood, in my belief, would soften even the hearts of our home grown communist sympathizers, which during the Korean War had infiltrated many of our labor unions. We GI's fighting in Korea at that time could not understand how they could support such an evil cause.

Korean refugees on the move during the winter, 1950.

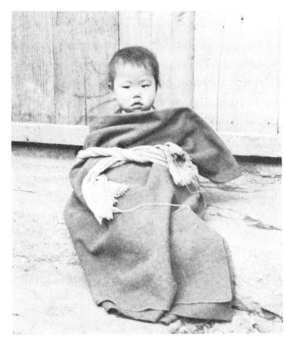

Baby-san waiting for parents to arrange passage out of Inch'on.

days later, a second enemy force struck along both sides of the Changjin Reservoir at elements of the X Corps' U.S. 1st Marine and 7th Infantry Divisions.

Snatching the initiative from the UN command in a space of hours, a new enemy, in the form of two Chinese communist field armies, had driven down from the north. The 4th Field Army engaged General Walker's Eighth Army while the 3d Field Army sought to destroy the X Corps. The objective of the twin Chinese offensive was to pin the UN commands against the coast while advancing additional communist divisions southward where they would be free to contact large concentrations of guerrillas and bypassed North Korean regulars who had remained to the rear of the Eighth Army zone. For a time, there was a definite danger that thousands of UN troops would be encircled and annihilated before they were able to protect their main lines of supply and reinforcement.

As people in the United States prepared for the holiday season, the UN troops turned their backs to the arctic winds and grimly regrouped for a winter withdrawal. To the accompaniment of exhaustion, heroism, pain, and death, the drama of retreat was played on a double stage of ice and fire. The thrusts by the enemy against the two UN forces necessitated an entirely different plan for the salvation of each. In the west, the Eighth Army elected to retire by land, while the withdrawal of the X Corps from the northeast was accomplished by land and sea with the co-operation of the Navy and Air Force. Credit: Paraphrased from the Center of Military History, Dept. of the Army--Korea, 1950.

Our 10th Corps, consisting of Army and Marine units, operated in the northeast, from Wonson on the coast to the Changjin Reservoir. Our forces, spread too thin--as were our supply lines--had no fall back defensive positions, so the guerrillas struck their rear bases. The vicious Korean winter closed in and the weight of two full Chinese armies descended heavily on our meager troops, who fell back in an honorable retreat to Hungnam on the northeast Korean coast. The Army and Marines brought out their wounded and most of their supplies, suffering huge losses equal to Tarawa and Iwo Jima. For the U.S. Marines, a rearward march had been unknown in their glorious history. Their pride was hurt, as well as our nation's pride, but they still held their heads high and never gave up.

The grim news reports spoke of the dead and the wounded. The 25° below zero temperatures had frozen the ground so tanks and blasting was required to dig the graves for the hundred or more dead, frozen marines, stacked like so much cordwood. The Chinese continued to throw mortar shells in and among the retreating troops causing additional casualties. A more miserable predicament couldn't be imagined. In spite of their situation, the young marines kept up their spirits in song. They sang as they marched down the frozen roads on their retreat to Hungnam this parody of the old British Indian Army song, "Bless 'em All":

> *Bless 'em all, bless 'em all,*
> *The Commies, the UN and all:*
> *Those slant-eye Chink soldiers*
> *Struck Hagaru-ri*
> *And now know the meaning of U.S.M.C.*
> *But we're saying goodbye to them all,*
> *We're Harry's police force on call.*
> *So put back your pack on,*
> *Next step is Saigon,*
> *Cheer up, me lads, bless 'em all!*

All available vessels, including the battleship *Missouri*, were dispatched to the evacuation port of Hungnam and, as planes and ships established a curtain of fire around the crowded port town, Adm Doyle carried out the immensely complicated evacuation. After they set off their cleverly planted explosives, the engineers were the last to depart, leaving practically nothing of value to the advancing Chinese armies. By

Christmas Eve, some 105,000 American and Korean troops, as well as other mixed UN forces, along with their supplies and 91,000 civilians, had been sea-lifted to the South Korean port of Pusan.

Things began to settle down roughly along a defense line considerably south of the 38th parallel as January 1951 rolled up on the calendar. General Matt Ridgway had ordered the UN to the offensive against the Chinese 4th Phase offensive. The UN line was approximately 90 miles south of the 38th parallel and was pushing again steadily north toward the Korean capitol of Seoul. We had been at war just over six months.

President Truman and General Douglas MacArthur seemed to clash constantly on the conduct of the war. Since President Truman was his Commander in Chief, many of MacArthur's statements as the local theater commander bordered on outright insubordination. He did not advocate putting American soldiers on mainland China, as reported, but *did* advocate the use of our bombers and naval blockade of Chinese ports, blocking off the source of war supplies to their forces fighting in North Korea. Our allies, as well as our President and Congress, were fearful that MacArthur would overstep his authority as the local theater commander and embroil us in WWIII, which none of us could condone.

Not surprisingly, on 11 Apr 1951 General MacArthur was relieved as Supreme Commander and replaced by General Matthew Ridgway, the famous WWII 82nd Airborne Division commander, who had jumped into Normandy with his troops. Ridgway had succeeded General Walker in Korea in December 1950 after General Walker had been killed in a jeep accident.

On June 23rd Jacob Malik, then Deputy Commissioner of the Soviet Union, proposed a cease fire, and a week later Gen Ridgway broadcast to the Chinese the United Nations' readiness to discuss an armistice everyone wanted so desperately. It finally appeared that things were really beginning to settle down when negotiations started at the little North Korean-held town of Kaesong on 10 Jul 1951. Nobody could have possibly known then what terrible bloody infighting would take place for the following two years, since both sides agreed that hostilities should continue. The enemy had 460,000 men facing us across the existing front at that time along with a large reserve force. Our forces built up to 600,000 across the 140-mile front by year's end, with 230,000 of them Americans.

CALLED TO ACTIVE DUTY AS PILOT OF FIGHTER AIRCRAFT

In early June of 1951 our mail brought me a very fancy letter and certificate signed by Secretary of the Navy Francis P. Matthews on 13 April 1950, denoting the fact I had been promoted from First Lieutenant (a rank I had held since the end of WWII) to Captain. The letter contained no reference to my previous correspondence volunteering my services.

Later the same month I received my second letter from Marine Headquarters, Washington D.C., stating in very terse terms:

Captain Bernard W. Peterson 033284
United States Marine Corps Reserve

You are hereby directed to active duty as Pilot of fighter aircraft. You will report for duty at the Marine Corps Air Station, El Toro, California, not later than 15 Jul 1951.
Signed,
Commandant Marine Corps

My heart skipped a few beats and my throat got very dry as the stark realization of what I had probably brought on myself hit me. Had I actually placed myself at the disposal of my country--*again*--to do as they saw fit with me? Looking around at my comfortable home, wonderful wife and precious little boys, I broke out in a cold sweat when the full impact finally hit me that I had inextricably done just that, and I had no way of foreseeing what was about to change my life and theirs over the next couple of uncertain years. All of my previous fighting skills had been blunted over the past six years. It would take a great deal of training to hone those skills again.

The gang at AiResearch took me out to a farewell dinner in Hollywood and the company gave me a military leave of absence, paying me off with some $800 in severance pay. That act in itself seemed awfully final and I began wondering if I would ever return to AiResearch and the many co-workers and friends I had become so very close to over the years.

Since I had 30 days before I had to report to active duty, we took off in our little Terry Rambler camp trailer and our 1950 Chevy for Montana, Wyoming and Idaho, visiting Yellowstone National Park, my mother's Montana relatives, Aunt Edna and Uncle Charlie, Uncle Roy and Aunt Maude and their daughters Roberta and Vera, Uncle Ray and Aunt Mary and daughter Louise. We stayed with Uncle Charlie and Aunt Edna at their rustic cabin, Silver Run Chalet, up in the Bear Tooth Mountains. Silver Run was an icy little stream that gurgled down the side of the mountain right next to the cabin and served as a natural refrigerator as it ran through the cooler house built over it.

On our return we traveled along the Snake River in Idaho, celebrating Randy's second birthday on the road, eating his birthday cake in our trailer. He was still wearing the head bandages the doctor had applied after taking a few stitches a few days before, when he had fallen off a small playground merry-go-round. We all knew this was to be the last time for an indefinite period that we would be completely together as a family, and we all tried to forget the hard reality that Daddy was going to be leaving soon for a strange land, and for a fate unknown.

VOUGHT F4U CORSAIR

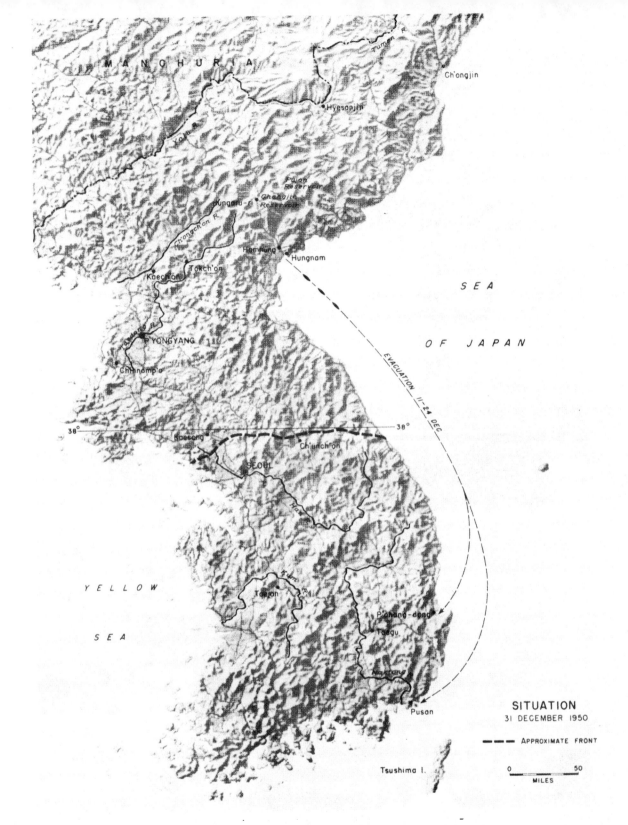

EVACUATION OF X CORPS FROM HUNGNAM TO PUSAN, 11 - 24 Dec 1950... Carrier based planes showered the hostile areas beyond the tiny perimeter with rockets, bombs, jellied gasoline and machine gun fire. Warships of the Seventh Fleet executed harassing, interdiction and called fire over the heads of the withdrawing units which climbed into waiting landing craft and amphibian tractors. From the carrier **Philippine Sea** a message relayed the information that at 1436 hours on 24 Dec 1950 the last soldier, marine and sailor of the U.N. forces in northeast Korea was safely on board ship, headed for Pusan. Hours before, Army engineers had blasted buildings, bridges and rail lines as large forces of the enemy renewed their persistent attempts to penetrate Hungnam's defense perimeter. On 23 Dec LtGen Walton H. Walker was killed in a jeep accident. LtGen Matthew B. Ridgway was selected to command the Eighth Army and on 26 Dec took full command of all U.N. ground forces in Korea. CREDIT: Condensed from Department of the Army, KOREA 1950.

Left: LtGen Matthew B. Ridgway and LtGen James Alward Van Fleet (right). On 26 Dec 1950 Matt Ridgway replaced Johnnie Walker as Eighth Army Commander following Walker's sudden death. President Truman sacked Gen MacArthur and Ridgway was made Commander in Chief Far East, headquartered in Japan. Ridgway appointed Van Fleet to command the Eighth Army.
Note Ridgway's trademark hand grenade on his right-hand chest strap; also Van Fleet is wearing his trademark pearl-handled .45 pistol.

Below: Sickening sight of thousands of Korean refugees fleeing the communist hordes on clogged highways, creating unbelievable hardships for our forces. Chinese troops disguised themselves as Korean refugees and infiltrated the areas.

Left, L to R: Van Fleet, Eighth Army commander, and his West Point football buddy, "Shrimp" Milburn, I Corps commander, petting his dog, Ebbo; "Lev" Allen, Van Fleet's chief of staff, and "Shorty" Soule, 3rd Division commander.

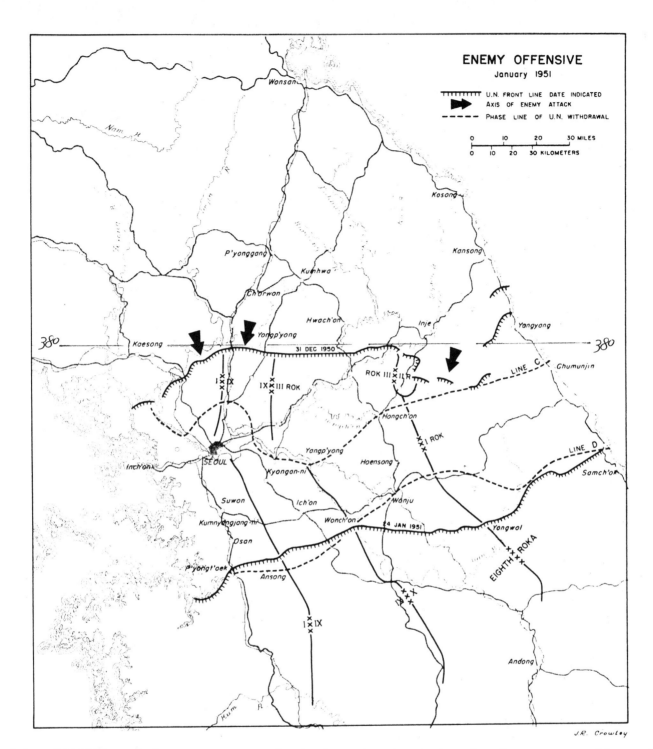

THE ENEMY HIGH TIDE, 1-24 January 1951 . . . As the first day of 1951 dawned in Korea, weary soldiers of the United Nations braced themselves to withstand the expected onslaught of North Korean and Chinese armies. The outlook for the United Nations, though not hopeless, was far from promising, for the unpredictable history of the fighting in Korea seemed only to be repeating itself. Since the initial North Korean invasion across the 38th parallel into the Republic of Korea on 25 June 1950, the months had been filled with bitter reverses, gallant defenses, spectacular advances, sudden blows and more withdrawals for the U.N. forces. . .

LtGen Matthew Ridgway commanded about 365,000 men. The largest single contingent was the Army of the Republic of Korea, which was under his control but not part of the Eighth Army. The next largest was the Eighth Army, to which certain U.S. Air Force, U.S. Marine Corps and several United Nations units, including Koreans, were attached. The U.N. command estimated that about 486,000 enemy troops, or twenty-one Chinese and twelve North Korean divisions, were committed to the Korean front and that reserves totalling over one million men were stationed near the Yalu, in Manchuria, or on the way to Manchuria. . . CREDIT: Condensed from Department of the Army, *KOREA 1951-1953*.

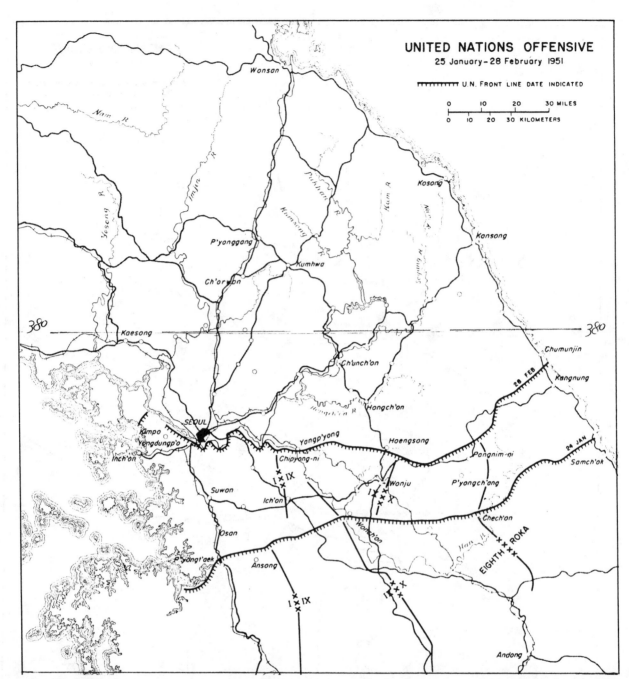

ATTACK AND COUNTERATTACK, 25 January – 28 February 1951... On the first day of Thunderbolt (25 January) six of the seven participating columns proceeded against scattered resistance. Only the Turkish Brigade east of Osan encountered stiff opposition. By nightfall elements of the U.S. 35th Infantry, 25th Division, were on the south edge of Suwon, and in the U.S. IX Corps zone a column reached Ich'on and took up positions north and east of the town. U.N. air units meanwhile co-ordinated their close support missions, armed reconnaissance, and interdictory attacks with the fire and movement of the advancing ground elements. Gen Ridgway requested U.N. naval forces to intensify their offshore patrolling along the west coast in order to prevent any amphibious infiltration of the army's left flank.

The support furnished by the air forces was most effective during this period. When the Eighth Army foot elements flushed elusive enemy soldiers into the open, U.N. aircraft closed in to destroy them. Air strikes softened up points of resistance almost as fast as they developed. Most important was the damage being inflicted upon Communist supply lines by air power, which, according to air intelligence estimates, kept as much as 80 percent of the enemy's supplies from reaching his front lines. The enemy now had to move not only ammunition but food down from the north, for local rice stockpiles had been removed or destroyed by the withdrawing U.N. forces or burned during the fighting, and he could no longer live off the countryside.

CREDIT: Condensed from Department of the Army, *KOREA 1951-53.*

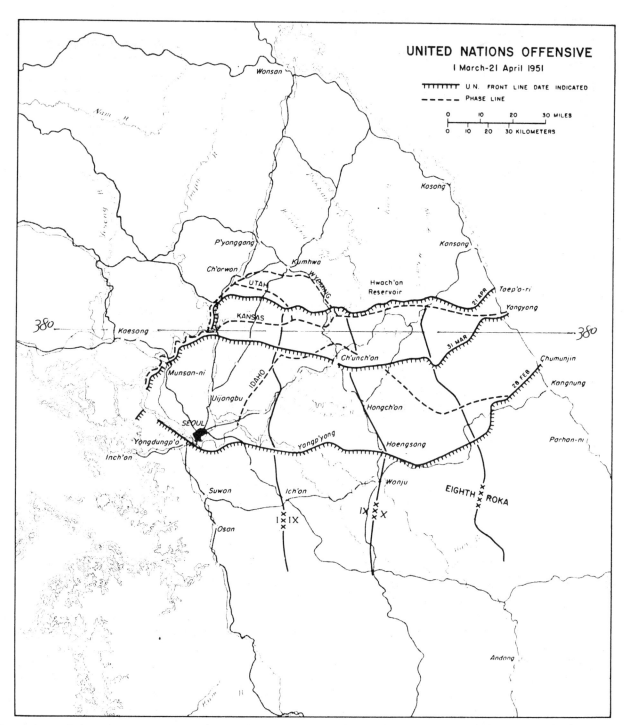

CROSSING THE 38th PARALLEL, 1 March–21 April 1951 . . . Operation Killer—the advance by the IX Corps—had not fulfilled all of General Ridgway's hopes for it, for the enemy had managed to withdraw while wretched weather was disrupting Allied road and rail movement. But in large part the recent losses had been recouped and the geographical objectives were attained by 1 March. The U.N. line, situated about halfway between the 37th and 38th parallels, swung in a concave arc from south of the Han River in the west through Yangp'yong and Hoengsong, then curved gently northeast to Kangnung.

With MacArthur's approval, Ridgway determined to continue the offensive with a new attack, Operation Ripper. He planned to attack northward in the central and eastern zones to capture Hongch'on and Ch'unch'on and seize a line, designated Idaho, just south of the 38th parallel. Ripper's purpose was, again, to destroy enemy soldiers and equipment, to keep up pressure that would prevent the mounting of a counteroffensive, and to split the Chinese from the North Korean forces, most of which were posted on the eastern front. The U.S. IX and X Corps were to advance in the center through successive phase lines to Idaho while the ROK units in the east covered the right flank with local attacks and the I Corps in the west maintained its positions south and east of Seoul. The drive by the IX and X Corps would create a bulge east of the capital city from which U.N. forces could envelop it. . . . CREDIT: Condensed from Department of the Army, *KOREA 1951–1953*.

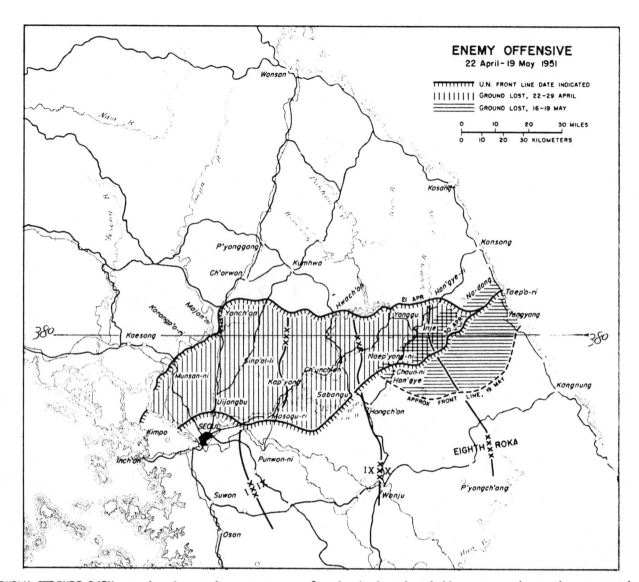

THE ENEMY STRIKES BACK, 22 April - 19 May 1951 . . . By the light of a full moon in the early evening hours of 22 April, three Chinese Communist armies attacked the U.N. forces following four hours of artillery bombardment. The initial attack, a secondary one, was delivered through the Kwandok Mountains in the Yonch'on-Hwach'on area of central Korea. By daybreak the enemy was in motion across the whole peninsula.

Delivering his main effort against the U.S. I and IX Corps, the enemy attempted a double envelopment against the west sector to isolate Seoul, coupled with the secondary thrust in the Yonch'on-Hwach'on area and a push against the eastern part of the line near Inje. Radio P'yongyang announced that the ultimate objective—destruction of the U.N. command—would be readily accomplished. Of an estimated total of 700,000 available troops in Korea, the enemy commanders employed about half in the offensive, but they used little artillery, few tanks (contrary to U.N. expectations), and no close air support. Their tactics—assaults by a "human sea" of massed infantry—were the same as before, and again bugle calls and flares co-ordinated night attacks in which small units infiltrated the U.N. lines. When dawn came the enemy broke contact and, using camouflage and natural and man-made features, sought cover and concealment against artillery fire.

The U.N. lines held firm against the first assaults everywhere except in the central sector held by the IX Corps, where the ROK 6th Division was defending the center with the U.S. 24th Division on the left and the 1st Marine Division on the right. Here the enemy struck the ROK division in the Namdae River valley south of Kumhwa and drove it back. As the division withdrew in confusion south of the Utah Line, the enemy attempted to exploit his advantage by moving into the gap between the 24th Division and 1st Marine Division but they held on in spite of their exposed flanks.

With his line cracked, General Van Fleet ordered the I and IX Corps to retire step by step to Kansas while the infantry, supported by artillery and aircraft, slowed the enemy. Thus was lost the ground gained in the recent U.N. offensives. . . . CREDIT: Condensed from Department of the Army, *KOREA 1951-1953.*

Left: This tea house was the first meeting place for the June 1951 armistice talks, in response to overtures from Washington. It was located in the town of Kaesong, near the 38th parallel, reached by crossing the Imjin River over the Freedom Gate Bridge. Later in the war the site would be moved a few miles to the southeast to Panmunjom near the 1stMarDiv. This date coincided with the month I received my call to active duty with the Marines.

In the twelve months of war ending 25 Jun 1951, Army statisticians determined that there had been a total of 1,960,354 battle casualties. The figures were as follows--CCF: 600,000 (dead, wounded and captured), NKPA: 600,000 (d,w,c) ROK civilians: 469,000 (170,000 dead), ROK Army: 212,554 (21,625 dead), and U.S.: 78,800 (21,300 dead). Two more years of intense fighting still remained.

Right: The Chinese and North Korean Communist negotiating team was led by North Korean General Nam Il (center), during the truce sessions.

Left: Our U.N. team was led by VAdm C. Turner Joy (center). The team membership would be changed over the next two years as the fierce fighting continued, to the disgust and consternation of everyone.

NORTH AMERICAN F-51 MUSTANG

Top: F-51 (P-51) receives a load of fragmentation bombs for its next mission. *Bottom:* Pile of empty .50-caliber ammunition boxes accumulated after loading two jet fighter planes with enough ammunition for two days of fighting. The North American P-51D Mustang had already earned an enviable reputation in Europe, starting in December 1943 with the U.S. Eighth Air Force. Britain had named it the Mustang when they first received their early versions in Nov '41 and the name stuck. From an early prototype built to British specifications in only 120 days, it evolved into the best fighter in Europe, escorting bomber formations. Its top speed reached 441 mph at 30,000 ft. With the loss of 2520 P-51s in combat in Europe, the USAAF claimed destruction of 4950 enemy aircraft in the air and 4131 on the ground—a better ratio than any other U.S. fighter. The 1200-hp V-1710-81 Merlin in-line engine could be distinguished from the noisier radial engines of the Corsairs we flew. The ROK air force had a squadron of F-51s at our base at Kangnung (K18) while I was there.

Above: June 1951. AiResearch Mfg. Co. Gas Turbine Laboratory members gathered together to say good-bye to former lab technician, Capt. B.W. (Spud) Peterson. From L to R: Glenn Basore, Roy Nelson, Jim Bennett, Bob Bancroft, John Miles, Perry Sebring, Maynard Cheney, Bob Calvert, Eddie Butler, and Ernie Hall.

Above: Spud's AiResearch gang at a going-away bash in Hollywood. "Good luck and safe return" toast.

Left: Capt Peterson, Marion and sons. The uniform still fits after six years in the closet.

Left: Randy's second birthday, on the road in Cody, Wyo. 23 June 1951, with Ricky and Mom Marion.

Above: June '51, and the Bear Tooth Hwy. is still covered with snow.

Left: Randy now a big two-year-old, traveling in our little Terry Rambler trailer.

Left: Our little family group on the road, for the last outing together before Spud reports for active duty with the Marines the following July 1951 at El Toro, CA.

Above: Randy and Ricky, Xmas 1951 at our Manhattan Beach, CA, home.

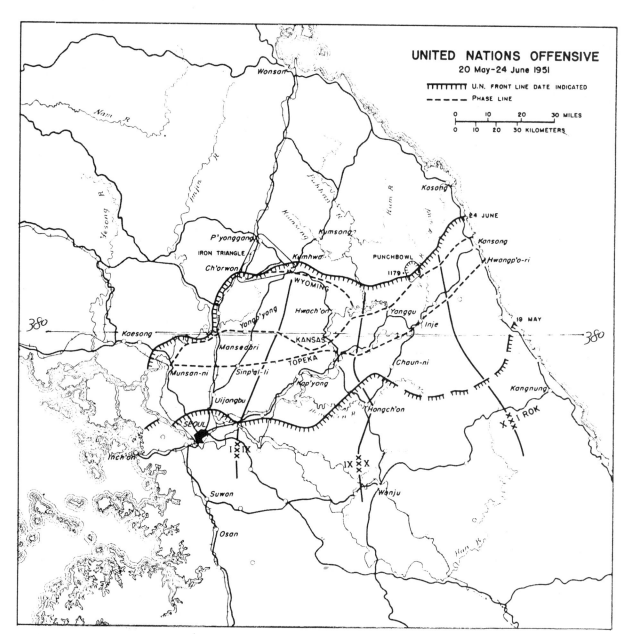

THE UNITED NATIONS RESUME THE ADVANCE, 20 May-24 June 1951 . . . General Van Fleet opened his new offensive with a series of local attacks designed to relieve enemy pressure on the U.S. X Corps. On 18 May he ordered the U.S. I and IX Corps, and the U.S. 1st Marine Division, the left flank element of the X Corps, to send out strong patrols and prepare to attack a phase line (Topeka) about halfway between No-Name-Line and Kansas. The next day, after bolstering the U.S. 3d Division by attaching to it the newly arrived Canadian 25th Brigade, he enlarged the goals of his offensive by directing the I, IX, and X Corps to advance to enemy supply and communications areas near Mansedari, Hwach'on, and Inje. The ROK I Corps, on the east, was to advance and conform to the movements of the X Corps' right flank. The ROK III Corps, which had recently broken under enemy attack, was deactivated. Together with part of the old ROK III Corps front, the ROK 9th Division was given to the X Corps, and the ROK 3d Division and its front were given to the ROK I Corps.

The new offensive, Van Fleet hoped, would deny the enemy any chance to gather himself for another counterstroke, threaten the enemy supply route in the Hwach'on Reservoir area and eventually result in the capture of the Iron Triangle. He shifted boundaries to place the western third of the Hwach'on Reservoir in the IX Corps zone, leaving the remaining two thirds the responsibility of the X Corps. Once the X Corps had taken its objectives, he hoped to send it in an enveloping move northeastward to the coast to block the enemy while the ROK I Corps attacked northwestward. As he put it, "The 38th Parallel has no significance in the present tactical situation. . . . The Eighth Army will go wherever the situation dictates in hot pursuit of the enemy."

Once more, as the enemy pulled back, the United Nations forces rolled forward against generally light resistance. . . . CREDIT: Condensed from Department of the Army, *KOREA 1951-1953*.

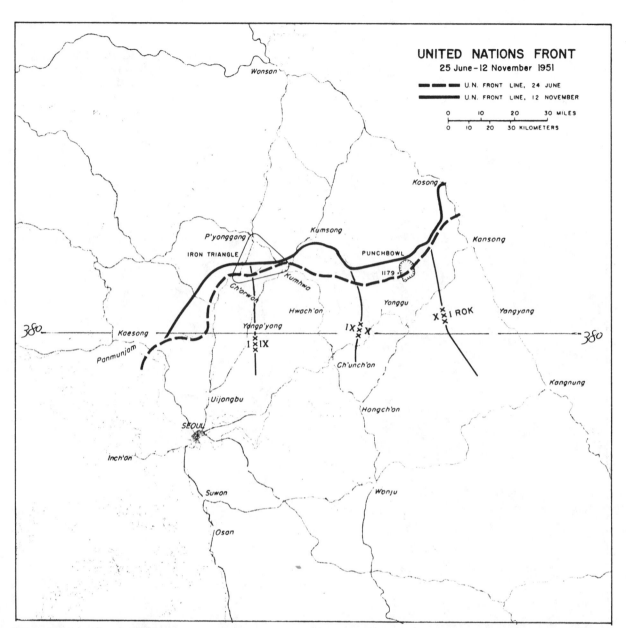

LULL AND FLARE-UP, 25 June-12 November 1951 . . . After Mr. Malik made his proposal, the Peiping radio followed his lead and indicated that the rulers of Communist China favored a truce. President Truman then authorized General Ridgway to conduct negotiations with the enemy generals. The U.N. commander at once sent radio messages to his opposite numbers in the enemy camp and, after some argument, both sides agreed to meet in Kaesong, a town near Korea's west coast about three miles south of the 38th parallel and between the opposing armies' front lines. After liaison officers had made preliminary arrangements, the negotiations opened on 10 July with Vice Adm. C. Turner Joy, the Far East naval commander, acting as chief delegate for the United Nations. Lt. Gen. Nam Il led the enemy delegation.

Both sides agreed that hostilities would continue until a truce was signed, but neither side was willing to start any large-scale offensives while the peace talks were in progress. All along the front—which now extended from the Imjin River to Ch'orwon, paralleled the base of the Iron Triangle, swung southeast to the lower edge of the Punchbowl and then ran north and east to the Sea of Japan above Kansong—the fighting died down. U.N. troops busied themselves improving their positions and consolidating the ground they had just won. Action was characterized by artillery fire and air strikes, plus a continuing bombardment of Wonsan. Combat patrols went out regularly; enemy attacks were repulsed. Offensive action consisted chiefly of limited regimental or battalion attacks designed to seize more favorable terrain, capture prisoners and keep the enemy from nosing too close to the U.N. lines. With the exception of the flare-up in the fall of 1951 that followed the breaking off of the truce negotiations in August, this general pattern was to prevail until just before the signing of the truce in 1953. . . . CREDIT: Condensed from Department of the Army, KOREA 1951-1953.

CHAPTER 3

GETTING RETREADED

In the middle of July 1951 I reported to the Marine Corps Air Station at El Toro, CA, near Santa Ana, for active duty. After going through a briefing session with a major at Headquarters, it was decided that I would be assigned to a Corsair squadron as a fighter pilot. My total flight time breakdown, he noted, according to my WWII Naval Aviators Flight Log Book, consisted of the following: 74 hours N2S Stearman and Timm Trainers, 60 hours SNV Vultee Aircraft, 231 hours SNJ, 125 hours SBD Dauntless Dive Bomber and 450 hours F4U Corsair, for a rather unimpressive 881.9 hours as a pilot in command. He indicated by a sort of sardonic chuckle that I was going to need a little brushing up before they sent me off in the big bird to Korea to tangle with the best of the North Korean, Chinese and Soviet fighter pilots, especially when he noted the last entry date of 18 Sep 1945, when I had last crawled out of the bent-wing bird at Okinawa and hung up my goggles. I remembered back when I was flying regularly in WWII that even a few weeks out of the Corsair caused a thrill upon resuming daily flying. But now almost six full years had slipped by and I was certainly not the same 22-year-old daredevil, come-what-may, do-or-die, devil-may-care fighter jock--I was a 28-year-old husband, father and family man. It was a big deal to park by the breakwater at high tide and watch the waves beat against the seawall at Redondo Beach on our Friday night family outing and enjoy a fish dinner on the pier.

After my first day at El Toro I was inclined to think that the old French Army saying from before World War I, "Les Reserves, c'est zero!", now discredited, nevertheless described my situation to a tee. I had so far to go to catch up after all those years away from a cockpit, to say nothing of the fact that the jet age had slipped in during the interim.

The good major assigned me to VMT-2, VF, a training squadron there at El Toro, and on the 16th of July I began my long way back to becoming a "retreaded" fighter pilot, flying 9.5 hours in seven flights in my old friend, the North American SNJ-4, -5, -6 during the month of July (the Air Force called theirs the T-6). By 3 August I finally got behind the controls of an F4U Corsair, and at that moment all my inhibitions were thrust aside. A feeling of euphoria nourished my being and the old self-confidence was back to stay. By the end of August and nine training flights later it seemed like old home week in the bent-wing bird--with the familiar aroma of hot oil and the ever-present oily windshield, the faded blue paint job, the masking tape at the top seams of the forward centerline fuel tank, the fumes from the high octane fuel permeating the cockpit, the scratchy intermittent radio reception and the hurricane-like howl coming from air leaks at the pilot's poor-fitting cockpit canopy drowning out almost all radio communication. For an instant it was as if the past six years had been a dream from which I had just awakened.

I was amazed at how fast the art of flying actually came back to me. The most difficult things for me were catching on to the radio chatter, regulations and procedures which had taken a giant leap forward from the prop age to the subsonic jet age during those years I had been a civilian. Easing back into the cockpit of the famous Corsair once again thrilled me beyond belief. Feeling comfortable flying it after those many years on the ground surprised me even more. Almost as if time had stood still, it seemed nothing had really changed since my first flight back in Congaree, SC, with VMF-524 around June of 1944. Being one with the bird once again gave me a sense of invincibility and power to do almost anything in the air that came to mind. I was shaking hands with an old friend after many years of separation.

THIS DEADLY GAME OF JOUSTING

Since most of my early flights in the Corsair took place without another plane flying next to me, and were programmed to familiarize me with my plane, I remained free to fly wherever I chose, within reason. Usually I wound up over San Diego, San Clemente Island or Catalina Island, Edwards Air Force Base or the Salton Sea area. Locating another fighter plane somewhere along the way, we pilots would join up for a few minutes while we discussed the time of day, where we were from, how we liked our type of fighter, and then we'd challenge one another to a dogfight.

These friendly duels varied. Some days I'd be fighting another Corsair, then an F-86, F-84, P-51, T-33, F9F, AD-1--even an SNJ-5. I found that I hadn't lost any of my previous flying ability and held my own in these dogfights that carried us from 30,000 feet to sea level, lasting up to an hour or more. Naturally, the jet fighters had a tremendous speed advantage and could climb away from me as they chose; however, as they returned and came down on me, they allowed me (in my prop-driven Corsair) to turn toward them much as we had learned back in WWII, using the Thach Weave. Then, with my gun switches always on SAFE but my illuminating gun sight on, I had them bore-sighted every time they made a run on me. This was quite a revelation. (The jet pilots, wearing G-suits, could pull more Gs than I. G-suits had not been retrofitted to Corsairs. That being the case, whenever we attained G-forces of five or more, I usually blacked out. After an hour at this deadly game of jousting, I would be drained, but strangely uplifted and assured that I indeed might have a fighting chance in the unfriendly skies of North Korea.)

I concluded that if the jet fighter pilots didn't shoot me down on their first pass, I'd have a good opportunity to nail them on our next head-on maneuver. These head-on runs against a stranger in another plane were tantamount to playing chicken as we passed each other with closing speeds of the equivalent of 800 MPH, often missing one another by a mere 15 to 20 feet. The jets wouldn't twist and turn with me a la the typical dogfight method which was *my* game, so I had to play theirs. My confidence level tremendously bolstered, I eagerly continued to prepare myself for eventual combat with the Communist MIG-15s over North Korea.

The Marine Air Base there at El Toro, a well organized complex, was a beehive of activity. Tactical fighter squadrons flew the Grumman F9F-2 Panther subsonic jet fighter, as well as the F3D-1 Douglas Skynight, a radar equipped two-seat night fighter. An occasional McDonnell F2H-2 Banshee jet could be seen. The other prop plane, besides the Corsair, being flown was the Douglas AD-1 Skyraider, a real work horse of an attack bomber.

On non-flying days I received ground school, navigation and Link Trainer. Our instructors insisted, since we flew in a very congested civil corridor around Los Angeles, Long Beach and Riverside areas, and occasionally over Edwards Air Force Base, that we learn the very important FAA regulations. I held a commercial pilots license and had memorized all of the FAA regulations in order to attain it, which helped to speed my transition along somewhat.

1. Our family group just prior to reporting for active duty with the Marines.

2. Spud in the cockpit of his F4U Corsair fighter, retraining at El Toro, CA. Six years is a long time to be out of flying completely.

3. Ground crew gassing up the Lockheed T-33 jet trainer Spud is being introduced to.

4. Beside the T-33. A marvelous experience, my first jet flight.

5. Spud beside his favorite bent-wing bird, the F4U Corsair.

1. L to R: Marion, Spud and his cousin, Vera Ross, from Montana. The Marine C-46 military transport is seen in the background. Oct 1951, El Toro MCAS.

2. The squadron flew from El Toro to the Marine base at El Centro, CA, for rocket and gunnery practice. I brought the family along and we stayed in our camp trailer.

3. Marion and boys in the trailer park at El Centro, while Daddy is flying.

4. Ricky and Randy trying on Daddy's heavy winter flight gear. Jan 1952.

5. Randy, ready to take off in his dad's hard hat, goggles and oxygen mask.

AN ENCOUNTER WITH CHESTY

In order for us to receive as much training as possible involving survival procedures and close air support work with our ground marine brothers, we participated in joint exercises with the newly formed Third Brigade, which was undergoing ground training at nearby Camp Pendleton in preparation to move overseas to Korea momentarily. I'd never seen such gung-ho spirit as was evident at that base, which had just received a new commander, Brigadier General Lewis B. (Chesty) Puller USMC. Chesty was the colorful marine general who had won fame and glory in Haiti, Nicaragua, Shanghai, Pearl Harbor, Guadalcanal, Peleliu, and Korea's Inchon landing as well as the Chosin Reservoir actions. He had been the last officer to leave Koto-ri on 10 Dec '50 on their march to Hungnam, in Korea, giving encouragement to his bedraggled half-frozen troops, which had won for him everlasting gratitude and near hero worship. Besides being the only Marine in history to have won five Navy Crosses, he was the toughest commander the Marines ever had. The adjectives they used for Chesty were "ferocious," "arrogant," and the "bravest of the brave." And above all, he loved the non-coms more than he did the junior officers, and therefore earned a reputation as an enlisted man's general, often in hot water with his fellow officers and the higher command for his outspoken feelings, especially during the Korean War. He called it as he saw it and this was too often an embarrassment to his superiors.

Chesty was to the ground marine as Pappy Boyington was to the air marine. Chesty Puller had been Pappy's instructor in 1936 back at Basic School in Philadelphia, where all young marine officers of the time were trained. It was there Pappy formed his early opinion that Chesty was the greatest marine of them all. I had first followed Chesty's achievements in September 1942 at Guadalcanal, where he bloodied the Japanese as commander of the First Battalion of the 7th Regiment on Henderson Field's perimeter. His name was already a household word to everyone who had served at Guadalcanal.

I saw Chesty in action at Pendleton, while I was training for Korea, when we jeeped over from El Toro to receive survivor training. We were to be picked up at a helicopter pad next to the drill field, where Chesty had just finished reviewing the troops. Never better, the Marine base band sent chills through all of us as the young recruits marched smartly past in review. The stirring sounds of a John Philip Sousa march filled the air, and we stood there, proud to be marines, as Old Glory came by. He came over and chatted with us pilots for a few minutes, and asked us what we were doing there at Pendleton in our full pilot's flight gear on the parade grounds. We explained that we were waiting to be picked up by a helicopter, taken back into the hills and dropped off. We would take only the basic items that we would need if we bailed out of our Corsairs. We would signal our search planes with a small mirror. They would fly down to give us strafing support and call in the helicopter for our rescue. Chesty said something like, "Old man [his favorite expression], our boys will really need your support when you get to Korea, so learn your lessons well." This was a special treat for me and the rest of my group, just to have talked briefly with this great man who had led a portion of the 1stMarDiv along the narrow frigid road from Hagaru at the Chosin Reservoir to the seacoast town of Hangnam and the escape route to Pusan by sea only a few months prior to this assignment. A few minutes later our little chopper arrived and individually we were carried off on our training exercise.

EL CENTRO BOUND

Our squadron was dispatched south to El Centro, CA, for rockets and gunnery training in the latter part of August. I hauled Marion and the boys along with me, leaving them in our camp trailer at a park just outside the base. I wanted them near me as long as I could possibly manage it.

A lot of guys in my squadron, like myself, hadn't flown actively since the last war. We had all matured, ranging in age from 27 to 32, and most had attended college after the war, married and had had a family. Most of the younger pilots just out of flight school had been sent directly to Korea along with the balance of the regulars and those pulled in from selected organized reserve squadrons at the start of the Korean War.

In WWII we had been high school and college age, 17 through 23; now considerably older, we represented a strange cross section of civilian professions, such as contractors, cattlemen, farmers, morticians, druggists, airline pilots, geologists, shop keepers, engineers, salesmen, cowboys--you name it, we had it in our re-tread squadron. Actually, it made for a very interesting group since, for the most part, we had long since lost any semblance of military discipline. We'd regularly break out into songs like "Call Out the Reserves."

CALL OUT THE RESERVES
(My Bonny Lies Over the Ocean)

In peacetime the regulars are happy,
In peacetime they're willing to serve,
But let them get into a fracas
And they call out the goddamned reserves

> *CHORUS:*
> *Call out, call out, they call out the goddamned reserves.*

I'm sure we must have been a trial and a challenge to the Regular Marine officers trying to whip us into a first class fighting unit.

Captain Ted (Hopalong) Cassidy, our squadron cowboy, drove his Cadillac convertible, pulling his horse and trailer all the way from Amarillo, TX. His horse went everywhere with him. He stabled him at a ranch while at El Toro, and when we moved down to El Centro he hauled him along and tethered him by the trailer out in a grassy area at a corner of the Base. Hopalong was quite a showman and loved to take bets, so we bet him he couldn't jump the hood of his Cadillac on his horse. He tried it and lost. The horse cleared it with his front legs nicely, but his rear hooves slammed into the hood of that beautiful car and left a great big dent halfway across. Hopalong just laughed along with us and paid us off good naturedly. We all liked his free spirit. He wasn't going to let an old war mess him up and deter him from his one and only pleasure in life-- having his horse with him at all times.

The mountains and canyons of Carrizo, west of El Centro, had been prepared as our target areas. Old tanks, amphibious tractors, trucks etc. had been scattered around, duplicating the terrain and targets we would be encountering in Korea. Diving from 10,000 feet, firing our rockets or releasing our bombs proved quite challenging, especially with the fantastic sink rate the Corsair had on pullout in that 100° plus temperature at El Centro, located right next to the Mexican border.

WE LOSE TWO FINE MEN

Marion had made friends with several of the other pilots' wives while we were training there at El Centro. One particular afternoon she waited with the wives of Capt Jones and Capt Javoronick for our flight to land. The three of us were out on a bombing practice run at a target west of the base, with three other pilots. We positioned ourselves in a spaced-out loose racetrack pattern at 10,000 feet, peeling off into our dive when we were due south of the target, in single file. The sun's intense glare that day interfered with our visibility. Suddenly I saw Jones and Jav peel off, making a simultaneous run on the same target. We got on the radio and tried to get them to break it off, to no avail. When their two Corsairs collided, pieces flew everywhere, as their propellers knifed into each other. They crashed nose-down doing over 500 MPH, making deep craters in the desolate brown desert landscape below. The other members of our flight broke it off for the day and solemnly returned to our base. Our three wives watched us land and knew immediately that something had happened as we crawled out of our planes, walked dejectedly back to the ready room and broke the news of the terrible tragedy to Mrs. Jones and Mrs. Javoronick. Marion took them both in hand to comfort them. Their husbands' deaths were no doubt the direct result of being out of active flying practice for so long.

Capt Jones and I had worked together at AiResearch Mfg. Co. and had both been recalled. His untimely death made me even more aware that if I was to return to my little gang in one piece, I would have to do a lot of heads-up flying.

THE CHRONOGRAPH

About two months after I had left AiResearch to go on active duty a very nice thing happened. One night upon returning home late after a full day of flying, I found our Manhattan Beach house had been cleaned spic and span from stem to stern. Furniture had been rearranged and a few borrowed throw rugs were lying here and there. I asked Marion what was going on. She said, "Oh, my old girlfriend, Peggy Patchett from Marblehead, Massachusetts, is coming out for a visit."

I made a crack, half in jest, "Boy, nobody would go to that much trouble for one of *my* friends." I would live to regret that cutting remark, for then the doorbell rang and there standing on the porch were 25 of my buddies from AiResearch, headed by Eddie Butler, Andy Boucher and Cedric (Dutch) Leinbach. They had planned a wonderful surprise party for *me* and presented me with a beautiful LeCoultre Chronograph pilot's watch, which they had special ordered as a going-away present. Deeply touched, I used it all through the Korean War, and still treasure it.

Several years after the war someone entered our house and stole my watch. We reported the theft to the local Manhattan Beach police. I especially regretted the loss of the Chronograph, but had written it off and figured I would never see it again. However, one evening about a year after its theft a knock on our door brought a very distraught father and his teenage son with a large box in hand. The father said, "My son has been caught burglarizing homes in this area and we are going around house-to-house contacting everyone whose home he entered." The valuables he had stolen had been placed in a coffee can and buried for over a year. Now transferred to a shallow box so one could inspect the contents, to my great surprise, I spotted my precious Chronograph among jewelry of every description. Thanking the father and his son, I told them it was a fine thing they were doing. As a father myself, I could imagine the embarrassment of the highly principled father and the shame of his son, to have to face every one of his victims. Although moisture condensation had badly corroded the works in the watch, I sent it to the factory and they returned it like new.

Now, back to the comment I had made to Marion earlier; the next day after the AiResearch gang had been to our house I bought a Dormeyer electric mixer at the PX and gave it to Marion as a peace offering. It took a while for her to get over that one. I don't think I have ever uttered anything so stupid or lived to regret anything as much as that comment and would never do it again.

ANOTHER CLOSE CALL

The Marines were trying desperately to familiarize all pilots with every type of ordnance we would be using in Korea. Unbeknown to me I was soon to become a guinea pig for them.

One late afternoon, near dusk, the ground crew loaded my plane with the giant 11.75-inch Tiny Tim rocket, the largest air-to-ground rocket in our armed forces at that time and weighing about 1800 lbs. They were commonly used as dam busters. After takeoff I flew west of the El Centro base at 10,000 feet to the "B" target range. Sizing up the target below, I put the Corsair into a 30° dive and released the rocket at about 2500 feet. It fell loose from the belly rack, dropped about 10 feet from the plane and, upon reaching the end of the release cable, the rocket fired. The purpose of having the monstrous rocket fall clear of the plane was to assure that it would clear the propeller arc when it was fired.

Upon ignition, however, the rocket's tremendous glare totally blinded me in dusk's last light. As I plummeted earthward at about 450 MPH, I pulled back on the stick with all my strength. Pulling about 5.5 Gs added a blacked-out condition, dulling my consciousness until I was flying by the seat of my pants, literally. Then, as the Gs decreased and the blood returned from my butt to my upper extremities, my body told me I was now in a climbing attitude and not digging a big hole in the ground. My vision coming back very slowly, I climbed to about 15,000 feet, where I made a right wingover, then leveled the plane's flight and, still shaken but relieved, headed back to the base.

A full hour passed before my vision completely returned. That was as close a shave as I had ever had, or ever would have, with death: I had almost become a statistic. After reporting my experience to the squadron commander, he passed the word that future firings of the Tiny Tim would take place only during full daylight conditions when the blinding effects would be minimized.

MARINE FIGHTER SQUADRON VMF-232 GETS A NEW PILOT

The months of October through March found me in another, more advanced fighter squadron, VMF-232, with Col Gray commanding. Here we would do section and division tactics, fighter intercept, gunnery, and field carrier landing practice--an all-out effort to get us an instrument ticket before we could be put on an overseas draft; there had been too many operational losses in Korea from the poor training of recalled inactive reserve pilots, as well as just plain bad weather, to leave anything to chance.

TESTING THE STRATEGIC AIR COMMAND

Our squadron left El Centro 11 December on a cross country flight. Upon reaching El Paso, TX, we hit a blinding snowstorm, forcing us to make instrument let downs at Biggs Air Force Base. Biggs, a SAC (Strategic Air Command) base, was actually off limits to the likes of us because this was the home of the 97th Bombardment Wing, the most secretive and highly strategic arm of our national defense. At that time they were flying the Boeing B-50, an improved version of the famous B-29 which had leveled Japan in 1945. A follow-me jeep ushered us out to a parking area where, as we cut our engines, a bus load of military police rushed up, guns drawn, and ordered us all to line up while they checked our IDs and interrogated us, shining their flashlights in our faces to check us out. Having apparently passed this test, they herded us into a waiting bus, and off we went to the base security office where we were interrogated once again. Wow! We were absolutely amazed at the security at that SAC base.

The base security police bused us to the transient officer quarters where we changed into our uniforms and went into Juarez, Mexico, for a little R&R before we flew home the next day. None of us had had the slightest idea just *how* tight security was on a SAC base until that episode. Of course the obvious reason for all the zealous watchfulness was the presence of nuclear devices, used only by the SAC. Admittedly, it was a wise procedure, since it seemed that the Communists had ways of knowing almost everything our country did.

LESSONS ONCE LEARNED

In December of 1950, when the Chinese hordes pushed the Army and the Marines from North Korea, the frozen fields of Hagaru and the Changjin reservoir, many sad lessons had been learned about fighting in frigid weather, something that this generation of Marines had never had to do before. They also recognized the need for protective body armor.

> *To a large extent, U.S. forces fought the early part of the Korean War with weapons from the preceding war--only five years removed. Three tactical innovations employed by the Marine Corps during the Korean War, however, were highly successful and largely adopted by the other services. These were the thermal boot, individual body armor, and the helicopter. All were first combat tested in 1951.*
>
> *Frostbite casualties during the first winter in Korea resulting from inadequate footwear made it necessary to provide combat troops with specially insulated footwear. The new thermal boot virtually eliminated frostbite for both Marine infantrymen and aviators. Armored utility jackets had been developed toward the end of World War II but were not*

actually battle tested. The Marine Corps had renewed the experimentation in 1947. First combat use of the plastic light-weight body armor was made in July 1951 by Marines while fighting in the Punchbowl and Inje areas of X Corps. Improvements were made to the prototypes and by the following summer the Marine Corps, following a request made by the Army Quartermaster General, furnished some 4,000 vests to frontline Army troops. By 1951 the 1stMarDiv had received its authorized quota of 24,000 vests and the new lower torso body armor had also been put into production by 1953.

Medical experts reported that the effectiveness of enemy low-velocity missile weapons striking a man wearing body armor was reduced from 30-80 percent. Chest and abdominal wounds decreased from 90-95 percent after issuance of the armored vests. Overall battle casualties were estimated to have been cut by 30 percent. By the time of the cease-fire, the protection offered by the Marine body armor had been extended to some 93,000 Marine and Army wearers. Hardly anywhere would the U.S. taxpayer or fighting man have found a better buy for the money: mass production had reduced the per unit cost of the Marine armored vest to just $37.50. Credit USMC in Korea.

Those officers and men who survived the five long days and nights fighting their way out of the Communist trap at Yudamni (the Marines' Korean Valley Forge), to a man, were determined that the lessons learned there would be passed on to all future Marine recruits, and pilots as well. Accordingly, a Marine Corps cold weather survival school was established in the High Sierras at a base camp called Pickle Meadow. The camp, located 90 miles west of Reno and 107 miles north of Bishop, CA, off Highway 108 and only 25 miles from Bridgeport, was sometimes called the coldest part of the United States. The peaks were sharper there than those in Korea, and the valleys wider, elevation higher and the temperatures colder. It proved ideal for a cold weather camp. Every raw recruit, as well as ground officer or pilot, scheduled to go to Korea on an overseas draft, had to go through the cold weather survival training before he could be shipped out. Some 850 Marines from Camp Pendleton were flown into Fallon, NV, then bused to the camp.

With our cold weather survival gear issue (identical to that of the marine infantry foot soldier) stashed away in our parachute bags and nestled behind us in the radio compartment to the rear of the pilot seat in our Corsairs, all of the pilots of VMF-232 took off for Fallon on 21 Jan 52 from El Toro. Our flight path took us near the top-secret Naval Test Station at Inyokern, China Lake, CA, where a Navy AD-1 Skyraider flew alongside our formation to notify us that we were under report for violating their restricted air zone. They were right; we had wandered off course just a smidgen when we had become distracted by a flight of P-51G Mustangs from the San Fernando Air National Guard, who had tried to jump us for a little mock fighter duel. We had had to decline, however, because our fuel reserves simply would not have allowed it on our long flight to Fallon. (I would, however, return at a later date and pick up their challenge.)

The air got extremely rough as we skimmed along the very peaks of Mount Whitney, whose rocky crest reached 14,496 feet. First we'd hit tremendous up-drafts, pushing us crazily upward a thousand feet, followed by equally severe down-drafts, hurling us downward the same distance. Our hard-hat crash helmets kept banging the top of the cockpit enclosure, rattling our brains. We had spread out in a very loose formation by that time, and all realized that we had better fly farther to the east of the highest mountain ranges, or else face the possibility of making physical contact with terra firma.

This is the area where so many soaring records have been achieved, due to the tremendous air currents over these mountains. The slopes of the High Sierras are dotted with the skeletal remains of airplanes whose pilots misjudged the intensity of the air around and over their majestic heights.

UNDERGOING TRAINING AT FALLON, NEVADA

The facilities at Fallon, NV, were crude by any standard. Barracks were tar paper covered and conveniences meager, basically what you would expect of an overseas facility, but adequate for the purpose. Like El Centro in southern California, Fallon provided for Navy and Marine pilots good experience in rockets, bombing and gunnery. Strewn with old tanks, amphibious tractors, trucks and bunkers, Fallon afforded excellent practice for what we would meet in North Korea.

Our squadron also provided the close air support training for our Marine infantry buddies, dug in on the snowy slopes of Pickle Meadow. We made simulated bombing and strafing runs on the troops, giving them all the realism of battle. Our pull-ups in that 6,900 foot elevation seemed unreal, for our Corsairs would mush hundreds of feet more than they did in the denser air of the lower altitudes. Several of us barely made it out of the box canyons, missing the edge of the craggy mountain ridges by less margin than I care to remember. Captain George Murphy wasn't so fortunate, as his Corsair mushed and hit pancake-fashion in a thick snowy blanket on the side of a mountain range about three miles from the troops on whom we had been making runs. Thankfully, he survived the crash and Baldie Owens dropped him a cold weather survival pack which provided him with all of the necessities to carry him through that 11° below zero night. The ground patrol found him the next morning, none the worse for his ordeal. He owed his life to the quick thinking of Colonel D.B. Hubbard, who was in charge of the base camp and who organized the ground rescue team.

MAKING LIKE GROUND MARINES

Our turn arrived for the ground survival training and we were trucked up to Pickle Meadow from our airfield at Fallon, joining the ground troops for a solid week of cold weather survival. The wind chill factor made it closer to 35° below, we were told. In snow over three feet deep on the ground, with drifts up to 25 feet, we moved about only with snow shoes. Our warm clothing, well engineered for the minus 11° nights, kept us comfortable all the time we were there.

Our little group made a shelter among three pine trees with a parachute and we tried to keep the fire going all night with wood we'd gathered during the day. Conditions there would have been almost tolerable thanks to our pup tents, mummy-style sleeping bags and long johns, but midnight "aggressor forces" made ridiculous attacks on us, forcing us out into that bone-chilling cold to dress hurriedly and arm ourselves in order to run off our would-be enemy.

We joined the infantry, making rope ladders and bridges to ford streams and rocky canyons. When the week finally ground to an end I was more than happy to return to the squadron at Fallon and resume flying my Corsair, making runs on those poor unfortunates who took my place at Pickle Meadow.

Upon returning home from Fallon, our little boys got a real blast out of dressing up in my cold weather gear and trudging around the house. Our photo album is full of pictures of Eric and Randy decked out in Daddy's funny clothes, including my flight gear.

Thirty-three years later, when we visited the Marine Corps Air Museum in Quantico, Virginia, I jotted down the serial numbers of the two Corsairs there on display: an F4U-4, serial number 97369, and an FG-1, serial number 13486. Immediately upon arriving home, I checked by old Aviators Flight Log Book and, to my great surprise and delight, I found that I had flown the very same F4U-4, S/N 97369 on several occasions while attached to Marine Fighter Squadron VMF-232 at El Toro and El Centro. Quite a coincidence! The list below logs my flying time in this very plane:

Sept. 26, 1951, El Centro, Calif. Bureau No. 97369. F4U-4 2.3 hours, Bombs and Rockets type flight.

Sept. 26, 1951, Same as above, 1.5 hours duration.

Oct. 16, 1951, El Toro MCAS, 1.3 hours, Instrument check out.

Nov. 2, 1951, El Toro MCAS, 2.0 hours, Ground Control Approach, instrument landing.

Dec. 3, 1951, El Toro MCAS, 1.0 hours, Field Carrier Landing practice.

Dec. 20, 1951, El Toro MCAS, 1.3 hours, Fighter Tactics.

The log is certified by Captain W.L. MacQuarrie, VMF-232 Asst. Operations Officer. March 4, 1952.

(As of this writing, VMF-232 is still an active Marine fighter squadron flying F-18s in Hawaii. Now designated VMFA-232, they still proudly wear the famous Red Devil patch on their flight jackets.)

I had received all of the mandatory flight and survival training required of an inactive reserve pilot and now awaited my orders for Korea. In February I had the opportunity to get a checkout ride in a Lockheed T-33 two seater jet trainer, and in an F3D-1 Douglas Skynight as part of my instrument training. I shall never forget the thrill of flying those subsonic jet fighters. On several occasions I would land in a jet and then race over to our Corsair squadron for a scheduled training flight. The roughness and noise of the old Corsair's reciprocating engine and prop compared to the smoothness and noise-free operation of the jet made it appear that you were, sure as shooting, having engine trouble. It was a rare comparison and an impressive one. The jet age had arrived and I wanted the opportunity to get into a jet squadron, but such was not to be. Fate had me scheduled for an overseas draft as a replacement pilot, much as I had been in December 1944.

The thought had frequently crossed my mind that perhaps I should have stayed in the Marines after WWII, for I would have had a coveted seat in one of those jet fighter cockpits (which, I must admit, I often longed for). Several of my best friends, G.W. (George W. Parker), Gus (Merlin Dake), big Robby (James W. Robinson), Bill Shanks, and little Robby (Robert B. Robinson) had all become qualified as jet pilots and decided to stay with the Corps. Most of them retired as majors after 20 years, or colonels, after 30 years of devoted and exemplary service to their country.

*At Hagaru-ri, U.S. Marines of the 1st Division, **left**, welcome members of Royal Marine LtCol Douglas B. Drysdale's Task Force Drysdale, which included both U.S. units and the British 41 Independent Commando. Sgt Ralph Schofield sketched the encounter.*

Above: Being a fighter pilot wasn't excuse enough to get you out of the full week of cold weather survival training at nearby Pickle Meadow in the high Sierras, Midwinter.

Upper Left: My fighter squadron VMF-232 flew from El Toro, CA, to Fallon, NV, for a two week training exercise. Fallon was the Navy/Marine Corps gunnery, bombing and fighter tactics training range for the west coast. It has grown considerably from the crude tent officers quarters of Jan 1952 into a major base today.

Left: Our squadron pilots arrived in the middle of a major snow storm and nothing was moving.

Below Left: Our cold weather survival training included making a bridge to span this stream.

Above: Try 35°F below 0 with wind chill factor, while trying to keep warm and sleep in these pup tents for a full week.

Left: March 1952. Following receipt of my Korea overseas notice, I boarded a Marine air transport at El Toro and said my good-byes to the family. First stop was here at Moffett Field, near San Francisco. The air transport was part of a 7-plane squadron VMR-152 (Detached), flying Douglas 4-engine R5Ds. They were home based in Itami, Japan.

Right: I separated from the main group of pilots who continued on to Barbers Point in Hawaii, while I tried out the JRM *Caroline Mars* flying boat. Here I am rejoining my original group at Barbers Pt.

Left: The Navy's *Caroline Mars* flying boat Spud flew in from San Francisco to Pearl Harbor, later rejoining his original pilot replacement passengers at Barbers Point, HI, for the remainder of the trip to Japan.

CHAPTER 4

DADDY IS LEAVING YOU FOR A LITTLE WHILE

As for my family, they had all entertained thoughts that the war might end and I wouldn't have to go to Korea. They held that thought until the very day Marion and my brother Ben drove me from our home in Manhattan Beach to El Toro Marine Corps Air Station, where I kissed Marion goodbye and squeezed Ben's hand as I crawled on board the Marine R5D troop transport for the first leg of my long journey to Korea. It seemed inconceivable that day, that I should be leaving my little family. I had hugged my little boys for the last time and left them at home with their grandparents, a heart-wrenching emotional experience.

During WWII Marion and I had written to each other every day, but with all of our moving around some of our letters became misplaced. During my tour in Korea we also wrote every day and have managed, over the years, to maintain my complete letter file to her. Since the military did not censor letters during the Korean War, I gave a fairly good account of my daily activities, much like one would in keeping a diary. To spare Marion some of the more gruesome details, I held back quite a bit from my letters, but for the most part I told it like it was.

For the balance of this accounting I will draw from my personal letters to Marion, and from other background material, just as it happened.

REFLECTIONS

Every one of us, on one occasion or another, has reflected back on his life and asked himself, "What am I doing here on this planet? What's my purpose? Where do I as a single, solitary individual fit into the master plan or scheme of things? What is expected of me, and by whom? For whom do I have to perform? What or who is keeping the Great Log Book in the Sky on me or my activities? Where and on what singular event will the final report card grade be filled out on me? What particular event or happening in my life will change me forever from a boy, or at least from thoughts of a boy, into the next metamorphosis for us male homo sapiens, that of manhood?"

For me the place would be Korea, pure and simple. The "who" in my hypothetical interrogation turned out to be myself. Nobody but me could feel my hurt, my loneliness for my loved ones, my heartache, my joys, my fears, my compassion, my disgust, my sorrow, my pride, my fulfillment or lack of same. Nobody but myself could know my thoughts, feel the warm tender friendship I felt for a buddy, or the compassion I felt for a displaced ragged, cold, hungry Korean child--homeless, scared and confused. Nobody but myself could tell the story many years after it had happened.

No event before or since would ever compare with it. Yet, after it was over and I returned home safely to my wife and boys, picking up where I had left off, no event was so quickly forgotten by the general public, the press, the historians, and the politicians. It seemed almost as though somebody had only told me about it, or that I'd read about it someplace, or maybe like I'd just had a bad dream and it had never really happened at all.

But it *was* real. It *did* happen. Just ask the mothers, dads, and wives of those boys who didn't make it home. And if you look deeply enough into the reasons for the Korean conflict you will see that America tried to prevent the first overt Soviet Communist grab for world power. Sadly, it would not be their last attempt. But in retrospect, this makes the Korean War all that more important.

The Korean War was a traumatic and momentous chapter in American history. To save South Korea from Communism, U.S. airmen, soldiers, sailors and marines fought nearly three times as long as they had in WWI, and nearly as long as they had in WWII.

During the *first year* of combat, the total American casualties amounted to 33,629 killed and 103,284 wounded. Following the start of the peace talks many more Americans would die, for a grand total of 52,246. During the three-year period of the Korean War (Police Action), nearly six million men and women of the USA served in the armed forces.

I firmly believe that taking a stand against Communism and our participation in the Korean War marked the beginning of the end of Communist aggression, the tearing down of the Berlin Wall many years later and the coming apart of the "Evil Empire."

Naval Air Station, Moffett Field
San Francisco, Calif.
Wed., 26 Mar 52

Dearest Marion and boys,
As our R5D taxied out to take off from El Toro it seemed to me that I was being separated into two parts. I know, sweetheart, I left my heart and soul with you. I felt sort of weak in my stomach too--the same kind of feeling I had when I left you in San Diego in Dec. of 1944. After this last farewell, honey, nothing will seem difficult to me again in my whole lifetime.

We took off at about 1330 and climbed up over El Toro and Santa Ana. I looked down at the road I had instructed you to take home, wondering if I could get just one peek at the car as you and Ben headed for home, but I couldn't see any cars down there. I was seated on the port side right in the middle of the wing, and I think you saw me looking through the window because every time I'd wave you seemed to also, until we got airborne.

Climbing up and over Los Angeles we could hardly make anything out because of the haze. However, as we flew farther north the visibility cleared considerably and the mountains were beautiful all the way up.

After landing yesterday they unloaded our plane and brought our gear into a huge new modern terminal building, built right into the side of a blimp hangar--just as big or bigger than at LTA in Santa Ana. A huge luxurious snack bar and luggage check stand--everyone on the ball doing their part. The Red Cross had a library of pocket editions with well over 500 books. Clean modern heads--efficiency itself.

They told us they had ten seats available on the Navy's old flying boat Mars, so I volunteered and made the team. We will take off at 1900 this evening and some 14 or 15 hours and about 2400 miles later we'll land in Pearl Harbor, where I will have to arrange transportation of my gear over to Barbers Point Marine Air Base on Oahu, Hawaii, where I will join the original flight that I started with in the very same plane, and probably proceed on to

Japan with them. I thought it would be more interesting to fly the Mars rather than the R5D bucket all the way over.

After we landed last night I got my foot locker and hand bag and rearranged everything. I checked my foot locker at the Navy terminal and proceeded to the BOQ. Checked in and had a nice shower (I felt crummy because of the heat). I dressed and walked over to the Senior BOQ across the court yard, where I had a nice chicken dinner for $1.25. Then I had an hour to burn before the eight o'clock movie, so I went down to the basement of the ship's service and watched the sailors bowl.

Caught the movie, "An American in Paris" and thought it was excellent--all color and the dancing and singing were out of this world. Gene Kelly was wonderful.

Hit the rack at 2230 and only had a sheet and a light spread over me all night--window open too--hot night. Everybody is talking about how muggy it is.

Tell Ricky and Randy how very much their daddy loves them and misses them, and tell Ricky to remember he's the man of the house while Daddy is away. Have the boys draw something or try and write something for me once in a while.

Your ever lovin' hubby, Spud

A DISTORTED IMAGE

The typical American view of its combat pilot, embellished by movie and television, is that of a fierce, stern-eyed, square-jawed youth who fights by day, drinks and loves by night. But for those of us who had become happily married men, deeply family oriented, the picture changed. Being jerked away from hearth and home, brushing off the somewhat tighter fitting uniform resplendent with tarnished wings and battle ribbons, and being stuffed into the cockpit of a venerable, somewhat tired and balky war-bird to do battle in far off Asia filled many of us with doubt. Not so, however, with some of my squadron mates, who viewed this experience as possibly the last fling of their vanishing youth or an opportunity to put distance between themselves and a faltering marriage, a nagging spouse, or a lackluster job.

Naval Air Station, Barbers Point
Oahu, Hawaii
27 Mar 52
0900 HST (11:00 AM PST)

My dearest family,
Well, here I am safe and sound at Barbers Point Naval Air Station, and to bring you up to date I'll have to go back to Moffett Field in San Francisco. Yesterday at about 1000, while still at Moffett Field, I went over to a huge aeronautical development laboratory which belongs to the National Advisory Committee on Aeronautics (NACA). They have named it the Ames Aeronautical Laboratory in honor of their past committee head, Joseph Ames, who retired a few years ago. They wouldn't let me go through the lab because of restrictions, so I just looked it over from the outside and studied the scale model of the entire lab in the administration building. You could probably loop a Piper Cub in their huge wind tunnels and hangars. I went out on the flight line where they were readying an F86 Sabre for a special test. Someday, if I ever get up that way again and I have a little more spare time, I'm going to really give it the once over. I went over to the Navy hangar, which used to be a blimp hangar, and saw a bunch of new jets being readied for flight, the FH1-2H Banshee for one--boy, what an aircraft!

All the other fellows had gone to San Francisco the night before, so I arranged to have all the footlockers and gear belonging to the ten of us going on the Mars taken to the Mars terminal at NAS Alameda. After all the gear had been unloaded and tagged, I had a malt at a little snack bar there in the terminal and decided to see NAS Alameda because it was only 1500 and the rest of the guys weren't going to show up until 1800, and the plane wasn't to depart until 2000.

First I went over to the Assembly and Repair section and contacted the supervisor, a Mr. Lucas, and along with his foreman, Mr. Reynolds, they showed me the whole jet overhaul building--how they balance the big babies and rebuild the J33 and J35 Allisons--very interesting. They quit at 1600, so I walked down to a pier about a mile away and went aboard an aircraft carrier, the CVE, **Cape Esperance.** *It is only a troop and aircraft carrier now--no actual aircraft operations are conducted from her. She just came back from Korea, and on her way over carried the two Marine Fighter Squadrons going to Kaneohe, Hawaii, VMF-235 and -241. The chief who was assisting the Officer of the Day took me on an hour's tour of the ship. He was interested when I told him I had been on the* **Saratoga, Yorktown** *and* **Enterprise** *during the war. They were loaded to the brim with new F-84 Thunderjets, F-86 Sabres, F-80 Shooting Stars--every one of them wrapped in a cocoon and sprayed with a real heavy grey goop for preservation against salt spray from heavy seas in transit.*

I shoved off at 1730 and walked back to the Mars terminal, which of course faces the bay, and the Mars lies right in a slip, with two floating wharfs alongside her. At 1800 the rest of the gang arrived, and they gave us 41 passengers a briefing on the emergency equipment they have aboard in the event they had to ditch or abandon ship at sea. We all listened, of course: 2200 or more miles of nothing is a lot of nothing, and if they ever had to go down a fellow could get awfully wet. We finally boarded the plane at 1945 and were airborne by 2010. It was rather odd taking off in a huge seaplane in the middle of San Francisco Bay with all the lights around us and the boats going this way and that, but we finally got airborne with no hitches, although I swore we were never going to leave the water with all our weight. The Mars grossed out at--get this--77 tons! After he poured the coal to her it took a full minute and a half before we were finally airborne. This particular Mars (they have four of them) had four Pratt & Whitney 4360 engines on it, which is the same engine as the B36 has. Boy, what a noise on takeoff when they give it full power! I was sitting in the bottom deck in a very comfortable reclining chair near a window. The window was only a few inches above the waterline when we were taking off, so I couldn't see anything for the water and the darkness. The pilot made a wide circle of S.F. and we could see the lights, which seemed to reach out for miles.

We finally headed out on course and I watched the lighted shoreline grow dimmer and dimmer and then fade into the ocean. Then I reclined my chair, put a blanket over my legs, a pillow over my face and slept off and on, only to be awakened every 10 minutes by a guy in the seat next to mine. Every time he'd move he'd toss his arm over and hit mine and I'd wake up. However, at around 0530 Pacific time the crew woke us up and told us we were going to have breakfast. They served everything in disposable cups and dishes. We had two sweet buns with butter, coffee, milk, tomato juice, an orange and some cold cereal. Then we cleared up the trays and settled back to another hour and a half of flying.

We landed just as day was breaking, exactly 12 hours from the time we took off. They hustled our gear off the plane, took the gear and us to a terminal where we claimed it--then threw the gear on another truck while we boarded a bus and drove 21 miles around the island to Barbers Point, a Naval Air Station that was really booming during the War, but about 50% of it is unused. Barracks and hangars are covered with jungle vines, and it really seems queer--just the same as Livermore was, remember, dear? Navy Air Transports operate out of here mostly. Some PV2 and a few F6F Hellcats and TBFs. We separated our gear and here we are in the BOQ, all shaved and showered. The word just came in that we'll be leaving tonight at 2000.

The ride over here from Honolulu to Barbers brought us through Pearl Harbor, the Sub Base near Hickam Field Air Force Base, then out through sugar cane fields and papaya. They are sure funny looking trees, with only a couple of little leaves at the top and the trunk almost solid with fruit which looks exactly like avocado. They grow and bear from 6' to 20'. This place certainly has undergone some changes since I was last here in 1945, and looking back to 1941 you'd hardly know the Island. We were on the road during the morning rush hour, and boy, were the cars thick--the Hawaiians all have new cars. Never in all my born days have I seen so many new cars.

It had just stopped raining when we landed this morning--all the roads, trees and flowers showing the results of it--real green and lush looking. The Hawaiians out here near

Barbers Point live in shacks and old lean-tos, or whatever they can get their pineapple-picking hands on, to keep the water off them. However, their city cousins fare much better--fairly modern clean dwellings, not unlike those of So. Calif.

How's everything there at home? I suppose Freddie the Frog is getting his fly-a-day. Have you cut down Lady's dog chow? Keep me posted on Ricky's new tooth. Honey, you had better replant those pole beans and some more peas and carrots and beets because that last garden is a complete fizzle.

Pick Ricky and Randy up and give them a big hug and kiss and tell them that it's from their daddy who loves them very much. Here's a couple for you too, honey.

Bye, bye,
Spud

MARTIN JRM-2 CAROLINA MARS

As the 1940s drew to a close, the Lockheed P2V "Neptune" and the Martin JRM-2 "Mars" made many headlines. The P2V, out to prove it was keen competition for seaplanes, earned a reputation for distance which has become almost a legend. North Island was involved in one flight which helped carve out a very special place in the Navy Hall of Fame for the trudging work horse "Neptune". The P2V-3, piloted by Commander L.F. Ashworth, landed at Naval Air Station, North Island, after a 4800-mile non-stop, non-refueling flight of 25 hours, 40 minutes. The plane took off from the carrier MIDWAY at sea off Norfolk, Virginia, flew to the Panama Canal, northward over Corpus Christi, Texas, then on to San Diego.

The "Carolina Mars" began a series of flights which would set and break records for the total number of people airlifted from one place to another. In February, it transported 202 men from Alameda to San Diego, then broke the record the same day by returning with 218 aboard, not including the four-man crew. Two weeks later the "Mars" reached a new high by transporting 263 passengers and a crew of six on a Fleet Logistics Air Wing flight from San Diego to Alameda. In May, the "Mars" continued to assault its own record when 301 passengers and a crew of seven were air-lifted from Alameda to San Diego.

The JRM "Carolina Mars" broke the news again in 1950 when it completed the 2609 mile flight from Honolulu to San Diego with 144 men aboard, for the largest passenger lift over the Pacific on record at that time.

Another plane to make news during 1949 was the Lockheed R-60 "Constitution" which landed at North Island July 15 with 98 midshipmen on board. This was the first time a plane of such mammoth size had landed at the Station. The field proved adequate for the landing and takeoff. **(Credit: Sudsbury,** *Jackrabbits to Jets,* **The History of North Island, San Diego, California.)**

Eleven years after my flight to Hawaii the following news article appeared in *Newsweek* concerning the old flying boats:

SIDNEY, BRITISH COLUMBIA--One of the largest airplanes to ferry freight in the '40s is still logging flight time over Canada--fighting forest fires. It is a huge (200-foot wingspread) Martin Mars "winged battleship," the only survivor from a fleet of five Pacific-hopping flying boats developed (for about $5 million each) during the closing days of World War II. In their heyday the four-engine giants broke all kinds of flight records (one flew 4,848 miles non-stop). In 1958 four flying boats (the fifth sank off Honolulu) were sold as surplus for $23,243 to lumber firms which fitted two of them with hull tanks, then used them to saturate flaming forest areas. (Since then one has crashed.) The other two contribute hard-to-get spare parts for the plane still flying.

DADDY IS LEAVING YOU FOR A LITTLE WHILE

Between Guam and Kwajalein
Sat. 1045
29 Mar 52

Dearest Family,

Hope this letter finds each and every one of my darlings healthy and happy. I hope Randy is keeping relatively quiet--that double hernia worries me.

We left Barbers Point at 2000 in the very same R5D as I flew up to Moffett Field in. I believe I'll stay with this same plane all the way to Japan now. We flew at 10,000 feet, hitting rough air and thunder storms occasionally. I grabbed a litter that was hung from the top and side of the plane and rested for a few hours. Talked mostly, though, to an enlisted Sgt. pilot and navigator who is being transferred to Korea as a navigator for some general's plane. He gave me a short course in celestial navigation, pointing out the various stars and the like (I'd long since forgotten, having taken celestial navigation way back in 1943).

We arrived at Johnston Island, which lies 731 miles southwest of Honolulu, at midnight, and promptly set our watches back one hour again. Johnston Island is maintained by the Air Force and they have a terminal building where we had coffee, and some had chow. It was real warm and muggy at Johnston and all the island personnel were wearing T-shirts at midnight. It is strictly a way station--nothing else. They gassed us up and we were airborne again in an hour, headed for Kwajalein Island, which is one of the Marshall Islands. Bikini is in the same group, the Atomic Bomb testing island. Johnston Island is real small. The runway, 8000 feet long, utilized the entire length of the island. It looked like a carrier deck as we approached it in the night.

When we arrived at 0630 Kwajalein time we had lost an hour but gained a day. We lost Friday the 28th completely. It had just finished raining as we set down after eight hours flying time, having left Johnston Island some 1425 miles behind us. There was a warm moistness to the air as we got off the plane for breakfast and refueling.

For breakfast we had coffee, toast, and gravy over fried potatoes for 40 cents. In the terminal building (which wasn't much) they had a tropical garden planted with two giant clamshells measuring 24" and 15" and a Bikini native canoe, made from coconut log bark which had belonged to a Bikini chief. Also a huge outrigger with an 18' mast; no nails were used at all. They used the canoe to move from island to island and for fishing. It held 15 passengers. Kwajalein is in the form of a horseshoe which forms a slight lagoon. It has two runways and quite a few buildings and hangars. There were a lot of B26s and B29s there. All of the flight crews were there having chow at the same time we were. They were on their way to Okinawa and Japan. We are a pretty crummy lot of Marines, but it can't be helped, traveling as we have been without any layover.

We departed Kwajalein at 0800 for Guam, which is 1382 miles distant. It will take about 8 hours and then we'll have a 12-hour layover in Guam while they pull engine checks on the plane prior to our 1352-mile hop to Japan. I figured it up and my total hours flown will be 42, and the total miles flown will be 7090 to Japan. Then I'll have the additional flight to Korea. To compare the hours flown with that of a Constellation, for instance, would be the equivalent of 7 hops across the U.S., averaging 6 hours per trip; however, in miles flown it is only 3 crossings of the U.S. If time permits, and there aren't any changes in our plans I'm going to look Guam over better than I did in 1945. There was just some talk of turning back to Kwajalein due to heavy winds which have cut our speed down. We are just slightly short of a line of no return, which means the halfway mark, but which changes due to headwinds. For instance, the miles distant is the same, but due to the stronger winds and the fuel remaining it might mean we will have to turn back, because we wouldn't have fuel enough to buck the headwinds which lie ahead of us.

Well, I'm going to knock off and have a box lunch, which I purchased at Barbers Point last night before taking off.

Great! They just announced that instrument weather prevails at Guam, which means a blind landing in a storm that's raging over Guam.

1.

2.

1. Looking back at Agana, Guam, just after takeoff from our first refueling stop.

2. Coming in for a second refueling stop at Kwajalein Atoll, not far from the A-Bomb blast site.

3.

4.

3. Our R5D Douglas transport at Kwajalein Atoll following a heavy tropical storm.

4. The main passenger terminal at Kwajalein, a very hot and sticky place.

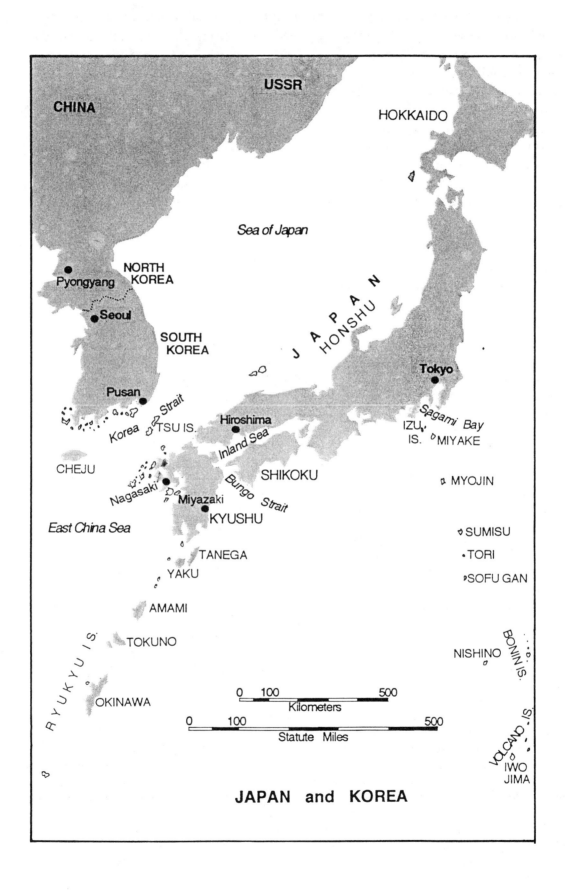

Following WWI, the League of Nations mandated the Marshall Islands, including Eniwetok, to Japan. Early in WWII, the commanding generals of our armed forces recognized the strategic position of this island group for any Pacific drive toward Japan.

Kwajalein, 60 miles long and 20 miles wide, the largest atoll in the world, lay in the heart of the Marshalls' cluster of 32 atolls, more than 1000 islands and 867 reefs. Surrounded by a semi-enclosed series of 80 reefs and islets around a huge lagoon of some 800 square miles, Kwajalein was the prize. Roi and Namur, a pair of connected islands shaped Kwajalein at the south.

Previously, in 1942, our forces had occupied Guadalcanal in the Solomons, then Tarawa in the Gilberts in November of 1943. Kwajalein came next in the long chain of events. After heavy fighting from 31 Jan '44 to the end of February, the 4th Marine Division and the Army 7th Division, transported by 380 ships carrying 85,000 men, Kwajalein and its surrounding islands yielded. The Army's 7th Division had won Kwajalein and the Marines' 4th Division had taken Roi-Namur and Eniwetok.

Much later on Guam
1800 Guam time (12:00 midnight Calif.)

Hi again, Honey,

We finally got into Guam and boy, is it hot here. It's all of 100° and awfully sultry (and I was griping about 85° in S.F.). We were only a little late arriving here at Guam. Fortunately, the weather wasn't as severe as it was earlier predicted. There is hardly anything here to speak of at Agana Naval Air Station. We circled the island prior to landing and could only see WWII installations that were practically eaten to the ground by termites, wrecked by hurricanes and overgrown by jungle. Here at Agana there's nothing but a couple of hangars and a mess of Quonset huts. It was 1430 Guam time when we landed, and they took us over and we had a swell chow--pork chops, French fried spuds, corn, chocolate milk and ice cream (which is peddled by an international creamery company out of Oakland, Calif. They distribute milk, chocolate milk and ice cream all over the Pacific islands.)

Here's news for you--I decided to write on only one side of this stationery after I tried to read one of the first pages of this letter--I couldn't do it.

This place is practically nothing, honey. As far as a defense establishment goes, it's nothing. None of the facilities I have seen amount to a hill of beans. The town of Agana from the air looks like a Mexican village--nothing but old weather-beaten buildings. Every one of the permanent establishment personnel here on the island looks like they're ready to give up the ghost, what with the awful heat. Everyone is dressed for this tropical weather. They have an O'Club that I had to go to to get my room assignment for the night. I had a nice shower and shave, and I'm sitting on the edge of my sack writing. It sure feels good to have had the opportunity to clean up after that long flight from Barbers Point. I'm not going to have any chow tonight because I ate at 1430, immediately after landing. However, I am going to try to catch a movie.

Boy, that over-water flying gets old, believe me. You see nothing but water hour after hour. Tell Trooper that the harbor in Guam is practically naked. He probably remembers it as a bustling harbor, with hundreds of ships coming and going during WWII.

I haven't written to anyone else as yet and guess I won't until I hit Japan tomorrow. We're laying over here until 0700 tomorrow morning. We'll have an 0400 reveille, eat, then muster for the briefing for the hop to Japan. They say that more often than not they have the same rugged weather as we experienced yesterday on our flight to Guam. Right now the weather is nice, except for the heat, only scattered alto-cumulus clouds are about. They had us all shook up on the way into Guam, on account of the instrument flying.

I sure miss you, precious girl, and my two darling boys. Do they miss their daddy, Honey?

Gosh, I'll be glad to get to my destination, if only go get some mail. The farther west we come the lousier and dirtier and crummier everything seems to become. Looks like they lost their paint brush. I'm wondering what Korea will be like.

Bye, bye until tomorrow, dearest ones.

Your loving Daddy, Spud

Guam, an island in the Marianas chain, brought back memories. On my way home from the Pacific following the end of WWII, our Douglas R5D transport had landed on Guam for refueling.

The principal islands targeted by our forces in mid 1944 had been Saipan, Tinian and Guam. This had been a daring decision, for Saipan was 1344 miles from the Marshalls, 3226 miles from Hawaii and only 1250 miles from Japan, but that decision made it possible four months after the islands were secured to launch 100 B-29 Superfortress Bombers on their raids over Tokyo. Having performed magnificently at Guadalcanal and at Tarawa in 1942 and 1943, the famous 2nd Marine Division also carried out this daring operation. D-Day was 15 Jun 44, just nine days after the Allies' invasion on France. Saipan was declared secured on 9 Jul 44, and the militaristic Japanese General Tojo, the Premier, and his entire cabinet fell from power on 18 Jul 44, nine days later.

The Japanese Navy sent the remainder of their operational aircraft carriers into the battle, where they suffered unbelievable losses of their aircraft and carriers in the battle action known as "The Great Marianas Turkey Shoot."

I STEP ON JAPANESE SOIL FOR FIRST TIME

Atsugi, Japan
30 Mar 52
Sunday, 1530

Hi little family,
Well, I set foot on Japanese soil for the first time about an hour ago. Atsugi is a U.S. Naval Fleet Logistics airfield with Privateers, PV2s, TBFs, Corsairs, R5Ds, etc. It's just 20 miles from Tokyo.

The sun is shining and it is very nice weather so far; temperature is about 75° F. We had to exchange our money into Japanese currency and also go through customs. There are a bunch of old hangars and unused buildings all around and there are about a dozen Japanese helping load planes and clean the terminal. The trip from Guam was smooth and very clear. It took eight hours, just as we planned.

I mailed your last letter at Guam at 0500 this morning, had breakfast at 0530 and we were on our way by 0700. Guam is almost covered by forests and hills, and the coastline on the south is rugged, like Palos Verdes. Agana Air Field was situated on high ground, 300' elevation. I had a box lunch at around noon--airborne--chicken sandwich, beef sandwich, hard boiled egg, candy, pickle, apple and 3 olives.

We're all loaded up again and I just found out the reason we stopped here rather than going to Itami was because this is the only Japanese customs airfield in the area. We're taxiing out as I'm writing so it's a little rough writing--got to blame it on something.

While I was hanging around the terminal building just a few minutes ago I saw a bulletin board on the wall with pictures of the Navy personnel on it who were in this command. Under one of the names I read "Tillman," so I looked real close and sure enough the face looked like Dick Tillman of AiResearch, so on a hunch I called up the chief's quarters and asked for Tillman and got him. He sure enough was Dick Tillman's brother. We talked for 10 minutes and he would have come down to see me except that we were going to shove off immediately. Tell your dad, Marion, to tell Dick at work that I talked to his brother on Atsugi, Japan. He's sending for his family because he's going to be here 2 years. We saw a lot of industrial buildings and double railroads, bridges etc. from the air on our approach to the field here.

The country is green and hilly, with truck gardens everywhere you look. Everything is planted with something. I didn't see any snow on any of the mountains coming south from Guam up here to Japan. Tokyo, you know is on Honshu. The weather here is just about the same as Manhattan Beach was when I left. Same old sun shining up there, while it's night time where you are. Boy, I am far away from home and still going farther.

We just took off and we're turning now, and I can see all the little farms below, and there's a power line with big towers going for miles in one direction. Guess they have plenty of electricity. I've taken my 12th picture and can't get to my trunk where my other film is, or I'd take some more. Believe it or not, we're over an area of homes that looks like a tract, but they are very small. Boy, this is a great bird's eye view of Japan. We're high now--about 5000'. Everything looks the same now, as in the States, except there are a million little streams and rivers going every which way. I've been trying to see Fujiyama, but it's a little too hazy. Here go the boys again. Every time we level out to cruising altitude out comes a foot locker--they put a blanket over it and a game of hearts is in the making. Most everyone else is reading. The cards they are using all have naked women on them except the joker and that's a picture of a wolf with his tongue hanging out. We are over a big bay now and I can't see land in either direction. We're flying SW now toward Itami. The bay is very calm, not a whitecap anywhere. We fared a little better than a preceding R5D full of Marines that landed ahead of us at Atsugi. They were unloaded and their plane was taken for some special cargo, so I guess they'll be hanging around Atsugi until another ride comes along. I'm about all written out for now but I'll pick it up again after we sight Itami. Out.

Monday, 31 March, 0600

Hi again Darling,

Well, after we landed at Itami we boarded a rickety old Japanese bus with a young Jap driver. He took us to the BOQ office where we checked in and got our assignment in an old beat-up one-story barracks, with bunk beds. The head is Japanese also, and I'd wager it's all of 30 years old. The fixtures in the bath and toilet are all old Japanese makes. While I was standing at the urinal I happened to look down at the manufacturer's trade mark, and when I read it I thought I'd keel over laughing to myself. It was made by the TAKASHITA Plumbing Mfg. Co. How about that!

The hop over here from Atsugi finally took us within sight of Fujiyama, which was snow covered. The distance from Atsugi to Itami is around 300 miles or the same as from San Francisco to Los Angeles by air miles, that is. It took us almost 2 hours, landing here at 1630 Sunday afternoon. The island of Honshu is really huge. We flew over Nagoya, which is a monstrous city. The country is very mountainous and the little farms crawl right up to the mountainside. Saw a fleet of fishing boats in the bay with all their little white sails set.

Itami is an old civil airport, then taken over by the Japanese military and now us. However, a Japanese airline is operating out of here now, flying Convairs, serving all of Japan. They land here because Osaka is a large city only 20 miles from this base.

I had a shower, shaved and put on all clean clothes, then had chow at the officers' mess (Marine mess, that is). You know this is an Air Force base and the Marines are just using part of it. The Marine officers' mess is run completely by Japanese, with men cooks and women waitresses. I got there late--7:00 PM and they were just closing; however, they let me in. They served a nice vegetable soup with little pieces of toast in it, in a delicate Japanese soup dish. Then I had a plate of delicious cold cuts with potato salad, bread and butter, coffee, donuts (Japanese style). They looked like real old greasy raised donuts, but when I bit into one it was delicious and fresh, honestly the best donut I ever had. Oh yes, then I topped that off with ice cream--it all cost me 50 cents in military scrip. Then I walked over to the Officers Club, which is a beat-up building. However, it has been very nice in its time. I just looked in and saw about 20 officers who were sitting around the bar, some writing letters at the tables in the lounge. A sign over the bar said, "He who covered enters here buys the boys a round of cheer." I checked the movie schedule and saw "Fabiola" was showing, so shoved off to the station theater. It was fair--about early Roman-Christian troubles. I hit the sack at 2200 and woke up at 0400 and just lay there listening to the rain on the metal roof and thinking of my 44 hours of flying it took to get this far. Mainly I thought of my precious little family and how much I love and miss you all.

Bye darlings, Daddy

P.S. Will write tonight. Wrote Mother yesterday.

Itami Air Base, Japan
31 Mar 52, 8:00 PM

Hi Darlings,
Just came back from Kobe, the big Japanese seaport. Sit down a minute and I'll tell you how I stole the Colonel's staff car and shoved off. It all happened like this. Ray Villareal, Bill Higgins and myself wanted a ride from the BOQ office to the electric train depot outside the main gate, because it was raining cats and dogs. Bill Higgins phoned up transportation and asked them to send a man over with some wheels to take us to the depot. Well, I stuck my head out the door just as a brand new Chevrolet staff car with driver rolled up, so I yelled in to the boys, "Our wheels are here!" So they all came piling out and we all crawled into the staff car and the driver drove off. I told him to take us to the depot and asked him instructions of Osaka.

He came back with, "Oh, do you want me to drive you to Osaka, sir?" and I said it would sure beat riding the electric train, so he said he would. I began thinking to myself as we drove out the main gate and the sentry saluted us, and I asked the driver if they didn't usually reserve staff cars for colonels and above. He said, "Yes sir, they do, Colonel." In our rain gear the driver hadn't seen our rank and he thought I, or one of us, was Col Ullman, the executive officer of Marine Air Group 33 in Korea. It seems the good colonel had called for transportation at about the same time as Bill had. I told him to turn around and go back because we had stolen the colonel's car by mistake. When we got back the Colonel was waiting in the rain, and as we piled out I explained to him what had happened. He was a good egg and asked us to accompany him to Kobe, 20 miles away, while he ordered some china for his wife.

We went on into Kobe and boy, the roads are horrible. You drive on the left hand side of the road, the roads are bumpy and in horrible condition, and real narrow. Millions of Japanese riding bicycles every which way, carrying huge loads on the back of the bikes, their backs, and even on their heads--produce especially. Women are carrying their babies on their backs, dressed in kimonos and wearing wooden shoes, shuffling along as only Japanese women can do. Taxies, trains, bikes, pedestrians, horns, horns horns and cops everywhere. Everybody has all the goods they own on little stands out on the street under a shelter, selling everything and anything. It was raining like mad, but they had everything out. Pedestrians were carrying umbrellas and they won't move for cars, either.

My eyes were sticking out of my head two inches, Honey. I've never seen anything in my life to compare with it. Some modern buildings, mostly old dirty, crummy ones, with a slight odor of human you-know-what filling the air. After much inquiring of Japanese "boysan" cops we finally found the honorable Nippon Kanko Shohin Co. Ltd. of Kobe, Japan. What traffic! No curbs on many of the streets and even narrower than Boston's. We went in and they showed us his catalog and opened up all the showcases, brought out cups and saucers and plates by the score. He bowed and was very amusing to me. A 20-year-old who seemed like a very small boy in years waited on me and sold me a beautiful set of Satsuma, a special Cobalt Blue Satsuma Demitasse set. 3500 yen ($10.00); they packed it and I brought the box back with me and Ray Villareal is going to send it on to you by 3rd class freight. I marked it etc. and you'll be getting it in a couple of weeks. Wash it and clean it up real good. It would sell for about $25.00 in the United States. Satsuma is the crackly looking china, completely unlike bone china. I bought you a tiny little demitasse cup and saucer in bone china too. It will come along by itself maybe a little bit later. They gave me the little ash tray coming with the cup and saucer. I'd

49

have sent them all together, only I picked it out at the last minute and they already had the tea set packed.

I had a long talk with the Japanese boy. He's in his second year of college. He's going to be an economist. He told me they start school at 8 years and finish junior high at 12 years. They export to all parts of the world. Not too much to America, however, because there is a 55 percent import fee in America on such items. I'll not have to pay any tax on anything I buy over here for my own personal goods. A huge fine is imposed, however, if you fudge on that. I can send anything of unlimited value home custom free, as long as each box is limited to $50.00 maximum value (not really unlimited), because I am in the armed forces. They investigate, however, sometimes and if the goods are given away or sold after reaching the U.S. they are confiscated and the party is fined $5,000. The Colonel also bought a tea set. Hope you like what I got, Honey. It's not as delicate as bone, but it's more expensive than some bone they had. I preferred it to any other they had. Now you and Nanna can have your tea parties in style.

Got my greens all packed away and I have my dungarees out with my billed hat. Reveille at 0430 in the morning and takeoff for Korea, and the Lord knows what. I have my little family's picture out in front of me while I'm writing. I love you all very much and miss you more than you'll ever know.

Your ever loving,
Daddy

1. Former Japanese kamikaze pilot BOQ, our quarters until we received assignment in Korea. Itami Air Force Base was shared equally by Marine and the local Japanese commercial air lines (JAL).

2. Itami PX, laundry and storage area. We left our foot lockers here, since we had to travel light as we progressed toward our squadron assignments in Korea.

3. The big bird, R5D Douglas transport that carried us here from Hawaii.

4. View of nearby town from our BOQ quarters here at Itami.

5. Merchants just outside Itami's main gate, set to separate us from our hard earned cash.

3.

4. 5.

JAPANESE TO ENGLISH LANGUAGE GUIDE

A partial list of words we used on our R & R's while in Japan. Some are Japanese, some English, some both, and some are neither. Many of these same words we used in conversation with our hut boys back in Korea, since the Japanese language had been mandatory for many years during the Japanese occupation of that country.

ARIGATO (ah ree gah toh)—Thank you.

A SO DESU (ah so dess)—That is so; that's right.

A SO DESUKA (ah so desskah)—Is that so? The "ka" shows that it is a question.

BUTTERFLY—English, meaning to flit from romance to romance even when one has a "steady" love interest.

CHICHI (chee chee)—Jane Russell has 'em, Marie Wilson has 'em . . .

CHISAI (chee sah ee)—Small. In many cases this is most unfortunate.

CHOTTO MATTE (cho toh mah teh)—Just a minute.

DAI JOBU (di joh bee)—Okay.

DAME (dah mee)—All wrong; no good; lousy.

DESHO (deh shaw)—I suppose, I guess, maybe, I expect.

DOMO ARIGATO (doh moh ah ree gah toh)—Thank you very much.

EAT MONEY—It's the "yen" that buys the chow.

FUJI (foo jee)—Japan's world-famous sacred mountain, often called Fujiyama by the Americans, or by the Japanese, Fuji-san.

GEISHA (gay shah)—A professional female entertainer schooled from childhood in the social graces and fine arts.

GETA (gay tah)—Wooden clogs, one of several types of footwear used by the Japanese.

GOHAN (goh hahn)—Although literally meaning boiled rice, the word serves for meals.

GOMEN NASAI (goh man nah sah ee)—Pardon me; I beg your pardon.

HIBACHI (hee bah chee)—A charcoal burner, usually referred to by servicemen as the "hibachi pot."

ICHI BAN (ee chee bahn)—The best; the most, or literally, number one.

KATA KANA (kah tah kah nah)—The simplest or more formal of Japanese "alphabets" of syllabic sound.

KIMONO (kee moh noh)—Clothes, generally speaking.

KONBAN WA (kohn bahn wah)—Good evening. A greeting, never as a farewell.

KONNICHI WA (koh nee chee wah)—Good afternoon.

KUDASAI (koo dah sah ee)—Give me.

MAMASAN (mah mah sahn)—Mother; lady of the house, or an elderly lady.

NANJI DESUKA (nahn gee dess kah)—What time is it?

NE (neh)—Undoubtedly the most overworked word in conversational Japanese. Means—Isn't that right; see what I mean, etc. Seemingly it is used after every statement, either for emphasis or to keep the listener awake.

NEVAH HOPPEN—It will never happen. Want to bet?
NEVER HATCHEE—Sailor-English meaning same as above.

NOBODY HOME UPSTAIRS—English slanguage meaning dumbness or no brains.

OBI (oh bee)—The broad waistband of the traditional feminine kimono attire.

OHAYO GOZAIMASU (oh hah yoh gohz eye mahs)—Good morning. Often shortened to just "Ohio."

OKANE (oh kah neh)—Money, brother, and you'll need it!

PAPASAN (pah pah sahn)—The landlord, the old man.

PRESENTO (pre sent oh)—With or without the "o" it means a gift.

SAKE (sah keh)—Wine, a beverage of intoxicating delight.

SAMUI (sah moo ee)—Cold.

SAN (sahn)—A suffix that literally seems to mean honorable; it is a title of respect comparable to our Miss, Missus, Mister, or Master.

JAPANESE TO ENGLISH LANGUAGE GUIDE

SAYONARA (Usually slurred to sah ah nah dah)—Goodbye, or good night. A farewell greeting. Also used to mean "gone." For instance, "he speak sayonara (is gone)."

SHOOK—Slanguage for angry or irritated.

SOROBAN—A calculating device, speedy and efficient in the hands of the Japanese. Sometimes the Americans, not the Japanese, erroneously call it an abacus because of its similarity to the ancient Greek calculator.

SPEAK—English, serving to mean tell me, told me, will tell me; say, said, will say, are saying; like "what does newspaper speak?" or "you speak (tell) your friend . . ." or "what (did) your friend speak (say)?"

SUKIYAKI (Skee yak kee)—Thinly sliced beef a la Japonaise, and it's good!

SUKOSHE (sko shee)—A little. Refers to amount, not size.

SWABBIE—A sailor.

TABI (tah bee)—Sock or socks (Japanese use no plurals) with the divided toe.

TAKUSAN (tock sahn)—Many or much, or a large amount.

TATAMI (tah tah mee)—A mat or matting. A woven rice-straw floor covering.

TESUTO (tess toh)—Testo, testo, is the signal to test or try something. A slight corruption of the English word taken into the Japanese language years ago.

TORII (toh ree)—The gateway to Shinto shrines.

YEN—It can by Japanese money or an urge. It's nice to have both!

Street merchant on Itami side street.

Japanese children near our base. They were all adorable and well mannered.

The standard uniformed policeman, circa 1952, Japan.

Main street outside Itami Air Base.

1.

2.

3.

1. Kangnung, K18, home for my newly joined Marine Fighter Squadron VMF-212 Devil Cats.

2. The Koreans did not have sewers; they saved everything to put on their crops. The "Honey Bucket Brigade" came by daily to retrieve it.

3. Kim Jin Kook (Chipmunk), age 17 and truly a fine young man, was my assigned hut boy while here at Kangnung, K18.

4. Marine Fighter Squadron VMF-212 Devil Cats, F4U-4B Corsair flight line.

5. K18 officers quarters. Congress was investigating reports of lavish overseas officers quarters at the time.

4.

5.

CHAPTER 5

IN KOREA AT LAST, WITH VMF-212

VMF-212, MAG-12
Kangnung, K18 Korea
2 April 1952

Hi precious family,

    Finally, I have arrived and my assignment is with Marine Fighter Squadron 212, flying F4U-4B Corsairs, a little different from the ones I flew in the past. The "B" stands for 20mm cannon (4 of them--2 in each wing), whereas the Corsair I flew before had six .50 cal. machine guns, three mounted in each wing.
    I'm living in a tent city and our tent has had many previous occupants who have displayed some very clever initiative. We have a wooden deck and sides, a parachute overhead, a chair similar to one of our backyard chairs at home, a writing desk and a wash basin mounted on a wooden frame that drains into a bucket below, which has to be emptied. I have a sleeping bag and a mattress on a folding G.I. cot. There are shelves etc. around to put clothing, stationery, flight gear etc. We have electricity--however, the generator is broken down temporarily and we are using candles. The head, about 600' away, has hot showers for one or two hours in the late afternoon. A regular two-holer with hot and cold running water, it's in an old Japanese shanty, one of the very few existing buildings on the field. Nearly everything here is temporary and built of rusty black sheet metal. The lousy field has only one runway, metal Marston matting laid on sand, and when it rains it just settles into it.
    Right now I'm waiting for our group lecture that they are going to give to all the new pilots.

We had a 0430 reveille yesterday at Itami, dressed, ate, carried our gear to the plane, an R5D 4-engine transport like the one we flew across in, loaded and took off from Itami for the southern part of Korea, where we landed at K3 Pohang after flying on instruments for an hour and a half. They took us to the 1st MAW headquarters, where BGen Lamont Scribner USMC gave all of us a sincere and heartfelt, but gruesome, welcome. As he spoke, an occasional tear came to his eye, for he was very concerned about all the casualties our Infantry has been sustaining. He spoke about the young kids getting hit and how it was up to us to give the Commies everything we could, as often as we could. He told us why we were here, and it sounded like myself talking. The situation is very very grave, and worldwide, and this is only the beginning. No one could help feeling excited and I for one had butterflies in my stomach after seeing all the jets taking off and everyone running around double time. Now I really knew this was war, and in a day or two I would be part of the team, doing what I could to help.

We secured for lunch, so I looked up G.W. Parker and found him over at a Marine Radar control center. He had been on duty all night and had just retired to his sack. I called him up and he came over in a beat-up truck to get me. We had an hour's talk and I looked at his log book on his writing table. Boy oh boy, he's really had some experiences in F9F Panther jets. He's practically grounded now, however, and is running this radar control center. He looked fair, except of course quite tired from working all night. He's coming home around May sometime and doesn't know whether or not he'll get as far south as El Toro. So if he doesn't come south you will have to pack his suit and laundry in his foot locker that he left with us (your dad and Troop could help) and take it to the railway express in Hawthorne and ship it to him. G.W. will write you and let you know whether or not it will be necessary. After we had lunch at his unit's very nice officers mess, he drove me back to Wing H.Q. and dropped me off. I got my assignment at the Wing and they flew six of us north to this field, K18, about an hour's hop. We turned our orders in to the Group (MAG-12) and secured to the tents, where I found I needed a sleeping bag, so I drew one from the QM.

The movie theater here is enclosed and equipped with rough benches--and the building is very crude. I went in the late afternoon after chow--saw Donald Duck and some oldie named "Million Dollar Pursuit." Had a looksee at the O'Club, made of logs, but didn't see anybody I knew so I hit the sack.

This morning I arose, shaved and went looking for my flight jacket which I missed this morning. I don't think it was stolen, but believe I took it off at the head last night and forgot to put it back on. I had my wool sweater on also and for that reason didn't notice the cold as I left the head. It's not there this morning anyway and I'm without a flight jacket. I believe I can draw one though. I had to buy a pair of boondockers for $6.25 this morning. It's muddy around here, but not too bad--sort of hard-packed on the roads. This whole field is laid on a rice paddy.

Attended the Group briefing from 0800-1130 on all the activities here in Korea--bomb lines, rescue facilities, friendly and enemy positions. This afternoon at 1300 they are going to lecture us on flak.

I know quite a few boys in 212, so it will not be too lonesome here. They sure are glad to see me because they have a terrific shortage of fighter pilots. They are all flying two and three strikes a day, then getting a day off in between--however, nothing organized. Tomorrow or the next day I will fly my first strike with the squadron, and be one of them before long. I was talking to Gibson (Ramon). He left on the 1st plane out here and he's really been flying thick and heavy--had lunch with his flight, which had just returned from a three-hour railcut almost up to the Yalu. They said the flak was coming at them thick, heavy and accurate. A plane from another squadron was hit, but landed back here OK. He had a hole in his wing 18" in diameter. I've been listening to all these flying tales and to say I'm a little shaken up is putting it mildly, but I know when I get with it it won't seem so bad--I hope.

The ROK (Republic of Korea) Air Force has a half dozen P-51's here. Outside of that, it's mostly Corsairs. One of the ROK's is an ex-Japanese fighter pilot with over a half dozen Corsairs to his credit around Okinawa. Strange business, politics. I had dinner with him and chatted about old times.

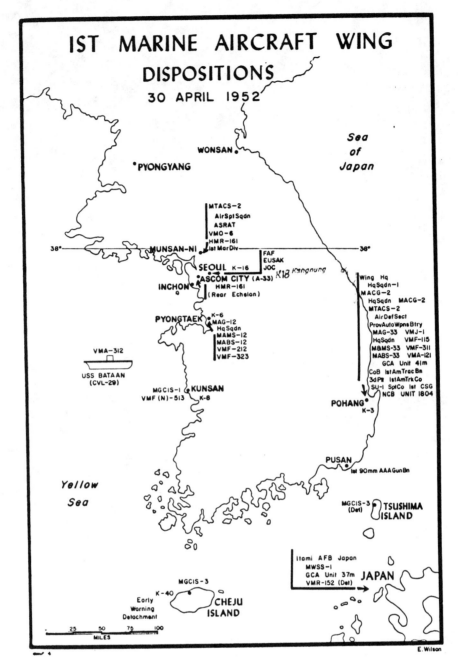

When the 1st Marine Division moved to western Korea in March 1952, the two 1st Marine Aircraft Wing units that had been in direct support of the ground Marines also relocated. Marine Observation Squadron 6 (VMO-6) and Marine Helicopter Transport Squadron 161 (HMR-161) completed their displacements by 24 March from their eastern airfield (X-83) to sites in the vicinity of the new division CP. About two and a half miles south of the helicopter forward site was an old landing strip (A-9), which LtCol William T. Henning's observation squadron used as home field for its fixed and rotary wing aircraft. In west Korea, VMO-6 and HMR-161 continued to provide air transport for tactical and logistical missions. Both squadrons were under operational control of the division, but administered by the wing.

Commanding General of the 1st MAW since 27 July 1951, Gen Christian F. Schilt, a Marine airman, had brought to Korea a vast amount of experience as a flying officer. During World War II Gen Schilt had served as 1st MAW Assistant Chief of Staff at Guadalcanal, later became CO of Marine Aircraft Group 11, and participated in the consolidation of the Southern Solomons and air defense of Peleliu and Okinawa.

The USS LEYTE being refueled at sea by the USS CIMARRON as the USS HENDERSON stands fire watch off the coast of Korea. Continued support was given by jet fighters, fighter bombers and dive bombers from the carriers off the coast of North Korea, sending down tons of bombs and rockets on military targets in support of the rapidly advancing U.N. units.

The glistening upright wings clearly identify the deck load of aircraft as being the F4U Corsair, Vought's most successful and longlived aircraft in naval aviation history. From its inception it set records, some of which still stand today. Of the 12,570 examples produced (7,829 by Vought, 4,006 by Goodyear, and 735 by Brewster), the Corsair still remains the most manufactured tailhook aircraft of all time. Fortunately, with the advent of the Korean War, the Navy possessed 846 F4Us and -4Bs.

Nearly everyone around here has a cold because the weather is so changeable. It's noon and the sky is clear with the temperature around 55°F. It froze last night. We don't have a hut boy yet, but we may get one. I'm writing by candle light at the desk--it's dark here in the tent.

Received your letter of 25 March when I landed at Wing HQ yesterday. It was sure swell hearing from my little family. I love you, my precious Marion, and my little boys, too. Tell them their daddy loves them and misses them very much.

Better I should secure this letter and mail it so it'll be picked up. Tell everyone I miss them too, and think of them real often. My head will be full of flying info. for the next couple of days, but not so full that I won't be able to think of my precious family.

I love you, darling,
Daddy

THE MISSION OF MARINE CORPS AVIATION IN KOREA

As in past months, the majority of Gen Schilt's Marine aircraft in Korea during March 1952 remained under operational control of Fifth Air Force. In turn, FAF operated the largest subordinate command of Far East Air Forces (FEAF), headquartered at Tokyo, the latter being the U.S. Air Force component of the Far East. The FAF-EUSAK Joint Operations Center (JOC) at Seoul coordinated and controlled all Allied air operations in Korea. Marine fighter and attack squadrons were employed by FAF to:

Maintain air superiority
Furnish close support for ground units
Provide escort (for attack aircraft)
Conduct day and night reconnaissance and fulfill requests
Affect the complete interdiction of North Korean and Chinese Communist forces and other military targets that had an immediate effect upon the tactical situation at that time.

Squadrons carrying out these assignments were attached to Marine Aircraft Groups (MAGs) 12 and 33. MAG-12 and its two day-attack squadrons, VMF-212 (to which I was assigned) and VMF-323 stayed at K18 Kangnung until 21 April, 1952, then moved to K6 Pyongtaek (Tunp o ri) on the west coast of Korea, 30 miles south of Seoul. The home base of VMF(N)-513 was situated farther to the south at K8 Kunsan.

MAG-33 was located in southeast Korea at K3 Pohang, with active squadrons VMJ-1, VMF-311, VMF-115, and VMA-121, plus support units of the Wing headquarters. Over in Japan, at Itami AFB, we had our VMR-152 Transport Squadron with seven R5D four-engine Douglas transports. Corsair squadron VMF-312, which my good friend, Jim Van Ry, would join later, was operating off the light carrier *Bataan* (CVL-29) in the Yellow Sea.

MANNING THE MOTHBALLED CARRIER FLEET

In order to give the reader a glimpse of the situation the Marine Corps faced regarding the lack of experienced pilots at this time, I have selected Jim Van Ry, a well-seasoned combat fighter pilot of WWII, as perhaps a typical example of the inactive reserve aviators now being called back into action.

Born in Holland, Michigan, 17 Jun 1922, to Ruth and Jim Van Ry, Jim finished high school and one year of business college prior to fulfilling his patriotic duty by swearing allegiance the 4th of July, 1942, in Detroit, MI, and joining the then popular CPT (Civilian Pilot Training) program. His naval aviation cadet training took place in Minneapolis April through June 1943, then July through November 1943 at Pensacola, FL, where he received his Wings of Gold as 2nd Lieutenant USMCR. Cecil Field, FL, saw him flying the fabled SBD Dauntless divebombers of Midway fame December 1943 through February 1944. F4U Corsairs came next at El Toro, CA, March through August 1944, then on 16 Aug 1944 he was finally sent overseas, where he joined Marine Fighter Squadron VMF-212 at Bougainville, in the Solomon Islands, transferring to VMF-223, 13 Oct 1944 with 12 other pilots (It was here that Jim and I had first met and completed 80 missions together in the Philippines and Okinawa until war's end).

Marine Fighter Squadron VMF-223 Bulldogs had gained its fame from the early days of the war at Guadalcanal, Bougainville, Philippines, Okinawa, and finally Japan. At the close of WWII, like thousands of other Marine pilots, both of us had elected to leave the Marine Corps, go to college, get married and raise a family (Jim was not yet married).

Jim had stayed in the flying industry between wars as a civilian flight instructor, along with aerial spraying and dusting all over Oklahoma, Kansas and Texas during the years 1947-1950. Then, in 1950, he had joined Tulsa's largest department store as an assistant buyer in men's wear until being recalled for "Truman's Korean police action."

Fully converted into their civilian professions after WWII, many former military pilots were now being retrieved and thrust back into the service of their country once again. Their valuable expertise gained through those years of conflict would quickly return to these combat-proven warriors of the sky. Some, however, would have to learn new techniques. Desperate for carrier pilots to man the previously inactive or mothballed carrier fleet, the Marine Corps was forced to recall inactive reserve pilots of WWII vintage with no previous experience on aircraft carriers. Van Ry, recalled to active duty in early 1952, received his re-training in Corsairs at NAS Kaneohe, Hawaii, and although he had never made a carrier landing before, he qualified as a carrier pilot on the *Valley Forge* with only eight landings and catapult shots.

The famous VMF-312 Checkerboard Squadron had been operating on and off carriers ever since they had departed California for Japan on 14 Aug 1950. On 11 Apr 1953 Jim joined that squadron aboard the USS *Bataan* (CVL-29) in the Yellow Sea, which lies between China and Korea. After performing two landings and one catapult shot, he subsequently flew 22 combat missions from the *Bataan* in F4U-4B Corsairs. During rough seas, the top-heavy *Bataan*, built from a cruiser's hull, rolled and pitched terribly, making every landing a real experience. Jim related one typical incident he well remembered:

> *On 2 May 53 we four Corsairs were catapulted off the* Bataan *led by our VMF-312 executive officer, Maj Grover R. Betzer, who perished when his plane, struck by heavy antiaircraft fire, burst into flames and crashed.*
>
> *This was one snake-bit mission. I was leading the 2nd section as we worked over some trenches. Maj Betzer wanted to go in for a 2nd run and really got nailed, plus his wing man had some wounds in his right arm.*
>
> *I requested a vector to the nearest air base. The three of us landed at an F-86 base. The wing man was taken care of and kept there for several days.*
>
> *My wing man and I decided to go back to our carrier,* Bataan. *My wing man took off first (or tried to). Not being used to take-off runs vs catapults, by the time he had full power he was way out in the boondocks and with an upside-down F4U-4.*
>
> *With three pilots/planes out of commission, I said 'The hell with this,' turned off of the runway, taxied back to the parking area and shut it down. Then I headed for the O'Club for some quick refreshment.*

Jim flew 20 more combat missions from the deck of the *Bairoko* (CVE), a Kaiser built carrier, from 9 May until 16 Jun 1953, when they left the *Bairoko*. VMF-312 was then sent to Miami, FL, (paper-wise) but most of her pilots, including Jim, went to Pyongtaek, Tunp o ri, K6, in Korea, to join VMA-212, which had been my old squadron from March to July 1952. They took over our old AU-1 Corsairs and Jim flew 18 missions from there, finally completing his 17 months of active duty time. He then flew home to go on inactive duty status once again, having flown a total of 60 missions in Korea. This coincided with exactly the same number of missions I had flown, but mine had all been land-based.

Following Jim's Korean tour, he returned to department store retailing in Tulsa, Sacramento, Oakland and Phoenix. As division manager, his duties also took him to Europe and Asia. Then, feeling the need of change, he decided to try real estate sales in Phoenix, where we met once again after some 35 years, when, as a real estate agent, he stopped by my home to solicit a listing (We had a sign, "For Sale by Owner" outside). Entering my den, he spotted a picture of me seated in the cockpit of my Corsair, and exclaimed, "I know that guy--isn't that Pete Peterson? I flew with him in VMF-223!" We have maintained a close relationship ever since.

Jim and his wife, Billie, have now retired in the Santa Rosa area of California's wine country, close to their daughter, son and granddaughter. Firmly in place now, puttering in their flower garden and taking an occasional vacation trip, they are enjoying their loving family, but Jim still has moments when he recalls his considerable contribution to his nation's defense.

It was the policy of the 1st Marine Air Wing to have at least one Marine fighter squadron operational aboard an aircraft carrier at all times. VMF-212 had gone aboard the aircraft carrier *Rendova* in October 1951, carried out numerous missions against North Korea, then had finally become land based again at K18 Kangnung a short time before I joined the squadron there. With the wintertime water temperature in the 30's, our pilots were tickled to death to be land based once again.

The Navy saw to it that there were never more than four aircraft carriers in action at the same time around Korea. Some of the 17 listed here were mainly used for transporting replacement aircraft to the war theater and returning other aircraft back to the U.S. for major repair and/or upgrading. Usually these were the smaller escort carriers.

North Island NAS, San Diego, was the home port for many of the following active American carriers: *Philippine Sea, Boxer, Sicily, Badoeng Strait, Valley Forge, Leyte, Antietam, Essex, Rendova, Bataan, Cape Esperance, Midway* (mostly in the Atlantic). The British supplied the HMS *Triumph* and the HMS *Ocean*. The Australian aircraft carriers *Sidney* and *Melbourne* also participated off the Korean coasts.

This was a far cry from those dark days in 1942, when the *Saratoga* and the *Enterprise* were all we had left in the Pacific. The carrier construction program had been in high gear and the Navy had converted nine light cruiser hulls to light carriers (10,000 tons). It had built new escort carriers called Jeeps and had converted merchant hulls into additional Jeeps. Ninety-nine escort carriers were in various stages of construction by mid-1942. New, fast carriers of the *Essex* class (27,000 tons) had been built; also, larger *Midway* class ships (45,000 tons) supplemented the existing fast carrier force. By war's end the Navy had 28 fast carriers and approximately 50 Jeep carriers, with many additional going to our British friends. At the start of WWII our country had only 12 recognized private shipbuilding firms, but by late 1942 there were over 300. The Japanese had indeed awakened us.

The Korean war was totally different from World War II. Yet in three years of war, Navy and Marine aircraft flew 276,000 offensive sorties, dropped 177,000 tons of bombs and fired 272,000 rockets. The Korean War came within 7000 sorties of WWII totals in all theaters. It bettered the bomb tonnage of WWII by 74,000 tons and the number of rockets by 60,000. Some may still refer to it as the "Korean Conflict," but it was a full-blown war.

CAPTAIN JAMES VAN RY USMCR

Jim and I flew together during WWII in the Philippines and Okinawa with Marine Fighter Squadron VMF-223.
Recalled to active duty during the Korean War, Jim flew with the famous VMF-312 Checkerboard Squadron aboard the carriers USS BATAAN (CVL-29) and the USS BAIROKO (CVE-115).
He finally joined my old Korean squadron VMF-212 at Tunp o ri, K6 Korea, but not until after I had departed for good ole Uncle Sugar and out. He flew 60 combat missions during the Korean War.
The muzzles of the long-barrelled Hispano cannons protruded well forward of the wing's leading edge, immediately identifying Jim's Corsair as the F4U-4B, of which 1685 had been produced, ending 2 Feb 1945. Four 20mm M-2 automatic cannons in place of the standard six 50 caliber machine guns were on the F4U-4B. Four ammunition boxes were carried in each wing panel, supplying 220 rounds of ammunition to each cannon.

USS BAIROKO (CVE-115) was one of 19 CVE carriers built to the Commencement class configuration. The BAIROKO, commissioned 16 July 45, displaced 21,397 tons (deep load), length 525 ft, beam 75 ft. With top speed of 19 kts, powered by 16,000 SHP, it could operate 33 aircraft.

Flight conditions were slightly different on the USS BATAAN (CVL-29), which had a smaller displacement but a longer deck and greater speed than the BAIROKO. The BATAAN (CVL-29) was an Independence class CVL, commissioned 17 Nov 43. With a displacement of 14,750 tons (deep load), length 600 ft and a 71 ft beam, 100,000 SHP gave it a speed of 31 kts. Thirty aircraft could be carried operationally. It was laid up on a Cleveland class cruiser hull. As a transport carrier it could carry 40 aircraft in its hangar deck and up to 70 topside. Nine ships in her class were built.

Jim VanRy, aboard carrier BAIROKO in the Yellow Sea, off Korea, June 1953.

SOME MARINE CORSAIR CARRIER PILOT HUMOR DURING THE KOREAN WAR --- Courtesy Captain James Van Ry USMCR

Yea, he waveth off the angel Donald saying, "Landeth ye not on a pass which is so long in the groove." Make him thy friend. When thou engagest in a game of chance, calleth not his lowly two pair with thy full house for he prizeth the winning hand above all things and he will love thee. Angereth him not else he bringeth thee in low and slow and spinneth thee into the potato locker.

Verily I say unto all ye who wouldst fain operate the great bent wing bird from the tilting airdrome: for it requireth technique that cometh to no man naturally and is acquired only by great diligence and perseverance and great faith in the father almighty.

Hell hath no fury like the catapult officer scorned. Therefore treat him with great kindness and speak unto him in tender tones, for whosoever arouseth the wrath of the catapult officer receiveth a cold shot and the next of kin knoweth great anguish.

Left: Capt Jim VanRy, 4th from left, with his VMF-312 Checkerboard Squadron buddies, off the carrier for a change.

Right: VMF-312 Corsairs on forward portion of the deck, being readied for another mission over North Korea. 1953.

Left: VMF-312 Corsairs.

Above: Capt Jim VanRy and his VMF-312 Checkerboard Squadron buddies sitting on the wing of one of their F4U-4B Corsairs, aboard carrier **USS BAIROKO (CVE)** in the Yellow Sea, off Korea.

Above: VanRy caught a cable.

Right: **USS BAIROKO (CVE)** with VMF-312 aboard.

AVIATION SHIPS--CARRIERS (Completed through 1947)

LANGLEY (CV-1)
Displacement: 12,700 tons STD
Commissioned 20 Mar 22

LEXINGTON CLASS

Ship	Commissioned
Lexington CV-2	14 Dec 27
Saratoga CV-3	16 Nov 27

Displacement: 38,500 tons STD; 47,700 Deep Load

RANGER (CV-4)
Displacement: 14,000 tons STD; 17,577 Deep Load
Commissioned 4 Jul 34

YORKTOWN CLASS

Ship	Commissioned
Yorktown (CV-5)	30 Sept 37
Enterprise (CV-6)	12 May 38
Hornet (CV-8)	20 Oct 41

Displacement: 19,872 tons STD; 25,500 Deep Load

WASP (CV-7)
Commissioned 25 Apr 40
Displacement: 14,700 tons STD; 18,500 Deep Load

LONG ISLAND (CVE-1)
Displacement 7880 tons STD; 14,050 Deep Load
Commissioned 2 Jun 41

CHARGER (CVE-30)
Displacement: 11,800 tons STD
Commissioned 3 Mar 42

SANGAMON CLASS

Ship	Commissioned
Sangamon (CVE-26)	25 Aug 42
Suwannee (CVE-27)	24 Sep 42
Chenango (CVE-28)	19 Sep 42
Santee (CVE-29)	24 Aug 42

Displacement 10,500 tons STD; 23,875 Deep Load

BOGUE CLASS

Ship	Commissioned
Bogue (CVE-9)	26 Sep 42
Card (CVE-11)	8 Nov 42
Copahee (CVE-12)	15 Jun 42
Core (CVE-13)	10 Dec 42
Nassau (CVE-16)	20 Aug 42
Altamaha (CVE-18)	15 Sep 42
Barnes (CVE-20)	20 Feb 43

BOGUE CLASS continued

Ship	Commissioned
Block Island (CVE-21)	8 Mar 43
Breton (CVE-23)	12 Apr 43
Croatan (CVE-25)	28 Apr 43
Prince Wm. (CVE-31)	9 Apr 43

Displacement: 8,390 tons STD; 13,980 Deep Load

WOLVERINE (IX-64)
Displacement: 7,200 tons STD
Commissioned 12 Aug 42

ESSEX CLASS

Ship	Commissioned
Essex (CV-9)	31 Dec 42
Yorktown (CV-10)	15 Apr 43
Intrepid (CV-11)	16 Aug 43
Hornet (CV-12)	29 Nov 43
Franklin (CV-13)	31 Jan 44
Ticonderoga (CV-14)	8 May 44
Randolph (CV-15)	9 Oct 44
Lexington (CV-16)	17 Feb 43
Bunker Hill (CV-17)	25 May 43
Wasp (CV-18)	24 Nov 43
Hancock (CV-19)	15 Apr 44
Bennington (CV-20)	6 Aug 44
Boxer (CV-21)	16 Apr 45
Bon Homme Richard (CV-31)	26 Nov 44
Leyte (CV-32)	11 Apr 46
Kearsarge (CV-33)	2 Mar 46
Oriskany (CV-34)	25 Sep 50
Antietam (CV-36)	28 Jan 45
Princeton (CV-37)	18 Nov 45
Shangri-La (CV-38)	15 Sep 44
Lake Champlain (CV-39)	3 Jun 45
Tarawa (CV-40)	8 Dec 45
Valley Forge (CV-45)	3 Nov 46
Philippine Sea (CV-47)	11 May 46

Displacement 27,200 tons STD; 34,880 Deep Load

INDEPENDENCE CLASS

Ship	Commissioned
Independence (CVL-22)	1 Jan 43
Princeton (CVL-23)	25 Feb 43
Belleau Wood (CVL-24)	31 Mar 43
Coupens (CVL-25)	28 May 43
Monterey (CVL-26)	17 Jun 43
Langley (CVL-27)	31 Aug 43
Cabot (CVL-28)	24 Jul 43
Bataan (CVL-29)	17 Nov 43
San Jacinto (CVL-30)	15 Dec 43

Displacement 10,662 tons STD; 14,750 Deep Load

NAME & HULL NUMBER
SABLE (IX-81)
Displacement: 8,000 tons STD; Commissioned 8 Mar 43

CASABLANCA CLASS
Ship	Commissioned
Casablanca (CVE-55)	8 Jul 43
Liscombe Bay (CVE-56)	7 Aug 43
Anzio (CVE-57)	27 Aug 43
Corregidor (CVE-58)	31 Aug 43
Mission Bay (CVE-59)	13 Sep 43
Guadalcanal (CVE-60)	25 Sep 43
Manila Bay (CVE-61)	5 Oct 43
Natoma Bay (CVE-62)	14 Oct 43
St Lo (CVE-63)	23 Oct 43
Tripoli (CVE-64)	31 Oct 43
Wake Island (CVE-65)	7 Nov 43
White Plains (CVE-66)	15 Nov 43
Solomons (CVE-67)	21 Nov 43
Kalinin Bay (CVE-68)	27 Nov 43
Kasaan Bay (CVE-69)	4 Dec 43
Fanshaw Bay (CVE-70)	9 Dec 43
Kitkun Bay (CVE-71)	15 Dec 43
Tulagi (CVE-72)	21 Dec 43
Gambier Bay (CVE-73)	28 Dec 43
Nehenta Bay (CVE-74)	3 Jan 44
Hoggatt Bay (CVE-75)	11 Jan 44
Kadashan Bay (CVE-76)	18 Jan 44
Marcus Island (CVE-77)	26 Jan 44
Savo Island (CVE-78)	3 Feb 44
Ommaney Bay (CVE-79)	11 Feb 44
Petrof Bay (CVE-80)	18 Feb 44
Rudyerd Bay (CVE-81)	25 Feb 44
Saginaw Bay (CVE-82)	2 Mar 44
Sargent Bay (CVE-83)	9 Mar 44
Shamrock Bay (CVE-84)	15 Mar 44
Shipley Bay (CVE-85)	21 Mar 44
Sitkoh Bay (CVE-86)	28 Mar 44
Steamer Bay (CVE-87)	4 Apr 44
Cape Esperance (CVE-88)	9 Apr 44
Takanis Bay (CVE-89)	15 Apr 44
Thetis Bay (CVE-90)	21 Apr 44
Makassar Strait (CVE-91)	29 Apr 44
Windham Bay (CVE-92)	3 May 44
Makin Island (CVE-93)	9 May 44
Lunga Point (CVE-94)	14 May 44
Bismarck Sea (CVE-95)	20 May 44
Salamaua (CVE-96)	26 May 44
Hollandia (CVE-97)	1 Jun 44
Kwajalein (CVE-98)	7 Jun 44
Admiralty Islands (CVE-99)	13 Jun 44
Bougainville (CVE-100)	18 Jun 44

CASABLANCA CLASS (continued)
Ship	Commissioned
Matanikau (CVE-101)	24 Jun 44
Attu (CVE-102)	30 Jun 44
Roi (CVE-103)	6 Jul 44
Munda (CVE-104)	8 Jul 44

Displacement 8,200 tons STD: 11,074 Deep Load

COMMENCEMENT BAY CLASS
Ship	Commissioned
Commencement Bay (CVE-105)	27 Nov 44
Block Island (CVE-106)	30 Dec 44
Gilbert Islands (CVE-107)	5 Feb 45
Kula Gulf (CVE-108)	12 May 45
Cape Gloucester (CVE-109)	5 Mar 45
Salerno Bay (CVE-110)	19 May 45
Vella Gulf (CVE-111)	9 Apr 45
Siboney (CVE-112)	14 May 45
Puget Sound (CVE-113)	18 Jun 45
Rendova (CVE-114)	22 Oct 45
Bairoko (CVE-115)	16 Jul 45
Badoeng Strait (CVE-116)	14 Nov 45
Saidor (CVE-117)	4 Sep 45
Sicily (CVE-118)	27 Feb 46
Point Cruz (CVE-119)	16 Oct 45
Mindoro (CVE-120)	4 Dec 45
Rabaul (CVE-121)	15 Jan 46
Palau (CVE-122)	15 Jan 46
Tinian (CVE-123)	15 Jan 46

Displacement 18,908 tons STD; 21,397 Deep Load

MIDWAY CLASS
Ship	Commissioned
Midway (CVB-41)	10 Sep 45
Franklin D. Roosevelt (CVB-42)	27 Oct 45
Coral Sea (CVB-43)	1 Oct 47

Displacement: 47,387 tons STD; 59,901 Deep Load

SAIPAN CLASS
Ship	Commissioned
Saipan (CVL-48)	14 Jul 46
Wright (CVL-49)	9 Feb 47

Displacement: 14,500 tons STD; 18,750 Deep Load

NOTE: The carrier ship building program did not commence again until October of 1955 with 4 ships of the *Forrestal* class, displacing 60,000 tons.

CURTISS TYPE BIPLANE AND
GRUMMAN F9F-2 PANTHER

GRUMMAN F9F-2 PANTHER

DOUGLAS AD-1 SKYRAIDER

Above: Grumman F9F-2 Panther jet fighter over North Island, San Diego, during the Korean War, first introduced there in 1949. The later version of the F9F, with swept wings, was called the Cougar.

Upper Left: This 1951 photo shows the Curtiss-type biplane flown to North Island by Billy Parker from Lindbergh Field, San Diego. The F9F Panther is alongside for comparison.

Left: A right echelon formation of AD Skyraiders flown by pilots of VC-35 over San Diego Bay, with Coronado in the background. 1953.

Lower Left: Lockheed TV-2 Shooting Star jet trainer. It had been identified as the TO-1 when assigned to North Island-based Squadron VF-52 back in 1948. It is now called the T-33 most commonly. I had my first jet indoctrination in the T-33 at El Toro MCAS in 1951.

Lower Right: Sikorsky HO-3S-1, used extensively by the Navy and Marines during the Korean War. It performed numerous missions on and off carriers, such as life guard duty.

LOCKHEED SHOOTING STAR TRAINER

SIKORSKY HO-3S-1

Above: Naval Air Station, North Island, San Diego, CA, in the mid 50's. A real hub of activity, her runways were extended to accommodate the heavier attack aircraft, as well as the increased volume.
Upper Left: USS VALLEY FORGE, recently returned to San Diego from a tour in Korean waters, for a short-lived rest for her deserving crew.
Left: Several ESSEX class carriers shown "mothballed" here at naval shipyard, Puget Sound, WA. After WWII mass decommissioning of ships and air squadrons took place.
Lower Left: BODOENG STRAIT, an escort carrier, loaded with F4U Corsairs in 1951, during the Korean War.

The USS BOXER during the Korean War.

Shipload of Grumman F9F Panther jets off-loading at North Island Naval Air Base quay wall, after the Korean War ended.

Thursday, 3 Apr 52
Kangnung, Korea (K18)
(Don't tell anyone what town our airfield is in.
Keep this strictly quiet.)

Dearest family,
    Yesterday we were briefed on everything under the sun in Korea by the group. Then last night until late the VMF-212 squadron operations officer, Major Richard Elliott, talked to the three new pilots and gave us SOP (Standard operating procedure) for VMF-212 and how to beat the enemy at his own game. He scheduled me for a familiarization hop for today. All morning and part of this afternoon I prepared all of my maps, marking bomb lines, friendly positions, enemy positions, escape and survival routes, rescue helicopter positions, and their call signs and radio channels, flak map of North Korea, and also the area around Kaesong, where the peace talks are going on. Then finally this afternoon I got a plane, between strikes, flew it all around the area about 50 miles north and south, dove it and got the feel of it generally. I called up the radar director and got radar steers from him, which gave me my heading home and I also practiced with my radio direction finding gear and found the field every time.
    Honey, I have flown over rugged country, but look at your map at the country west of Kangnung on the east coast; that's the area I was over. Well, it's nothing, and I mean nothing, but one darn mountain after another, and the peninsula is over 100 miles across. They are sending our squadron up to Sinanju, just below the Yalu River. Between 550 and 600 miles round trip, it's too long a hop for Corsairs, and everyone is pretty put out about it. The boys are getting two hops a day and they sometimes run over three hours each--the bulk of the time over enemy territory. It's right up in MIG Alley, but they try to coordinate the F-86s to be up there at the same time. The MIGs aren't bothering the boys yet (in Corsairs, that is). It's the thick concentration of antiaircraft fire of every type of caliber imaginable that's the problem. They won't even send B-29s up there in the daytime because of the MIGs and heavy flak from the ground. I had a good look at things and got the butterflies out of my stomach, and now I guess I'm all ready to go.
    My takeoff was bumpy on this lousy metal matting strip of ours and I thought I was on a Manhattan Beach road as I landed. Boy, is the taxi strip ever horrible! Honest, honey, you can't taxi over two miles an hour or you'll tip the plane over. It's bumpy all around, even the roads are awful. The chow is still good, however. This morning we had fried eggs, biscuits and jelly, bacon, coffee and figs. This noon, boiled potatoes and beef stew with cake and coffee, cocoa or water; and for supper tonight ham with raisin sauce, lima beans, vegetable soup, coffee and bread and butter. We go through a cafeteria line after picking up our plates and silverware, then we're seated at a four-place table, which has a red oilcloth on it. The men are helped by Koreans, young boys about 12 years, maybe older. The Koreans do about 50 percent of the work, it appears. Chow is served in a beat-up old quonset hut--two of them stuck together, one for the mess hall and one for the galley.
    The base looks mighty good, though, I'll tell you, after flying over that rugged country. By just looking at the map you have no conception of the ruggedness of the area. I was at 10,000' and some of those peaks were really close, and it was cold up there too (The heater wasn't working in my plane). Most of the mountains were snow-covered, unlike these around here. Today was very spring-like, temp. around 75°. However, I'll bet it was around 35° in those mountains north of us and inland a few miles.
    I have my two nice pictures before me, the ones of Ricky and Randy on the stool before the fireplace and of our whole wonderful little family altogether out on the front lawn. Hi, darling Marion. I love you, precious girl. Hi, Ricky. How's the big brother and man of the house? Fine, I hope. Say, Ricky, are you eating all your food like you should, and are you being a real good boy while Daddy is away? Hello, Randy darling, and how's my little baby boy tonight? Listen, Randy, you remember to take it easy and don't play hard with brother or jump on the tricycle hard or do anything that will strain yourself, will you Randy?
    Have you played the record we made at the airport that time? I'll bet the kids would enjoy hearing Daddy once in a while. You know, sweetheart, the next time I get to Japan I'm going to make a record and send it to you. I won't have any way of playing one here, however.

Next time I go to Japan I'm going to go into a department store and see if they have anything worth buying and sending home to you.

Did I tell you that they are only going to deduct $30.00 a month from my pay for board and room? That will help some. I'm working on a deal to get per diem for six days while traveling via government transportation out here. I haven't spent but $6.25 (for my boondockers) since I arrived in Korea. As I see it, I won't be spending any either, because they give you nearly all your PX needs, including stationery, free mailing privileges, free movies etc.; however, I've been too busy to take in a movie.

The darn night fighters are taking off and landing at all hours during the night and early morning and the wind blows and shakes the tent, but I still get my rest off and on. The officers' tents are only about 500' from the strip.

So long, dearest little family that I love and miss so very much. Will write again tomorrow.

Love, Daddy

P.S. Have only received one letter to date.
P.P.S. I was just thinking, if you do all the lawn work while I'm gone you'll be more rugged than I am when I get back.

The Marine pilots who flew off of the CVE's came up with this little ditty:

CUTS AND GUTS (My Bonnie Lies Over the Ocean)

Navy pilots fly off of the big ones,
Air Force pilots aren't seen over the seas,
But we're in the goddamn Marine Corps
So we get these damn CVE's.

> *CHORUS:*
> *Cuts and guts, cuts and guts,*
> *The guys that made carriers are nuts, are nuts.*

The MIDWAY has thousand-foot runways,
The LEYTE eight hundred and ten,
But we'd not have much of a carrier
With two of ours tied end-to-end.
The name of our carrier's Bairoko,
A harbor down in the South Sea.
If the harbor's as small as this carrier,
It won't hold a goddamn P.T.

Our LSO's never give rogers,
We don't even know they can see.
They say as we crash thru the barriers,
"He was O.K. when he went by me."

Our catapult shots are quite hairy,
Our catapult gear is red hot.
It never goes off when you're ready
And always goes off when you're not.
The air boss stands up on the island,
His hand on the yodel and flag.
We're cut and the goddamn hook bounces,
So he grabs good old paddles and wags.

We're back from a reccy at Sinmak.
We're ready to smoke and to spout.
That goddamn O.D. saw us pancake,
So he turned all the smoking lamps out.

We envy the boys on the big ones.
We'd trade in a minute or two
'Cause we'd like to see those poor bastards
Try doing the things that we do.

Some day when this fracas is over
And back at El Toro we'll be,
We'll load up with rockets and napalm
And sink all these damn CVE's.

SEARCH FOR GEN MATT RIDGWAY'S SON'S DOWNED B-26

Korea
Friday, 4th of April, 1700

Hi little family,

  Just got down from a familiarization hop. Three of us new guys went up with (6) 100-lb bombs each and dropped them in the ocean. They wanted us to get the feel of the plane again in a high speed dive, as we will do on railcuts up near the Yalu, or at least to Sinanju, as the squadron has been doing lately.
  Ramon Gibson came back today from a search mission, looking for a B-26 crew that was lost up near P'yongyang last night. He and seven other Corsairs from our squadron went. While searching (sweeping back and forth fairly low) they opened up on him, and boy, that Corsair looked like a sieve. They got a direct hit on his left aileron control and knocked it off, blasted a huge hole in his left wing, splattered his whole port side through the canopy, but the good Lord had his arms around Gibby and he didn't get hurt. He flew it back home the 200 miles and landed OK. Just to look at it gives ya the creeps. I found myself walking away (after seeing the shape of his plane) talking to myself.
  During my bombing hop this afternoon I found that my neck was being rubbed raw from my wool sweater and the weight of my shoulder harness for my pistol, and also my life jacket which is real heavy and weights you down, especially around your neck. I made up my mind today, after getting down, that I was going to get me a silk scarf and a leather jacket, a wool shirt and wool pants--which I did. Now I'll be a lot more comfortable flying and not so hot either. I can take my wool sweater and wool undershirt off now, and just wear a cotton undershirt and my flight jacket and flight suit with my Air Force survival vest, which has a compass, knife, medical kit, mirror for signalling and some rations, some wound tablets, morphine shots, bandages, Atebrin, water purification tablet, wool and leather gloves, fish hooks, matches, blood chit (which has a number on it that you give to a North Korean civilian which guarantees him $50.00 if he sees to it that you get back to friendly lines); and it even has a new cheap Japanese wrist watch, a fountain pen, cigarette paper (for trading your life with the Korean). Of course you're only guessing he won't turn you in. It's got an English to Korean language sheet and directions on how to survive if shot down behind enemy lines. Then on top of that I wear my Mae West, which has a mirror, shark chaser, dye marker, and two signal flares; I sit on my life boat which, when inflated, also supplies smoke flares, signal mirror, two colored signalling cloths, and a water making outfit which makes fresh water from sea water with chemical additives. Besides that, I carry a knife and a bunch of spare 38 amo. for the pistol. So you see, I'm a one-man army, whether in the air or on the ground. I'm going to watch

out for myself though, honey, and not take any foolish chances. I'll do my job; that they can be sure.

I don't get any word here about the peace talks. Nobody seems to have a radio because of our darned power generator. I'll have to go over to Group Intelligence and ask. I checked the mail room and no letters--still received only that one. I'm sure they'll start arriving before too long--as soon as they get my address squared away.

How do you like the stationery? I found it in my tent. It must have been left by an ex-occupant. Bill Higgins, my tent mate, is in another squadron and the other fellow is a mess officer of the Group--a young, carefree, happy-go-lucky guy named Bob Ferguson. No troubles on his mind--nobody's shooting at him. He says, "You guys can have your $120.00 a month extra. I'm staying on the deck."

I hadn't as yet become completely comfortable on my familiarization flights when Ramon Gibson took this terrible hit. This was the second major hit he had received in two days. Small groups of us green pilot replacements strolled out to examine the antiaircraft damage inflicted on his plane and marveled at how he had ever managed to fly that thing home. We didn't take it lightly and, personally, I spent a very uncomfortable night dreaming about it and wondering if this was what I could expect during the remaining months of flying my own combat missions here in Korea.

A suave, handsome individual with a very slight Latin accent, Ramon had an aristocratic air and probably came from a diplomatic family background. Like me, he had flown in WWII and had been released to inactive duty at war's end. Coming from Lima, Peru, where he was the Traffic office manager for Braniff Airways, Inc., we understood that he held a dual citizenship, having spent half of his life growing up there and half in the U.S. Under these conditions, he could have refused when he was recalled to active duty for the Korean conflict, since he had returned to Lima to live and work at the end of WWII, but evidently he had chosen to serve.

MAJOR DEXTER DIES

Back again, honey. Just grabbed chow--roast beef, mashed spuds, peas, coffee and cookies--served in a dirty mess hall, however, which takes away from the food somewhat.

Went to an early movie at 1800 and saw "Mystery Submarine," an old rehashed deal which was fair.

Shaved and washed, brushed my teeth. The head is funny, and I don't think I mentioned it to you before but they only have hot water for a couple of hours in the morning and from seven to ten at night. There's a little room inside the head with a big 100 or 200 gallon water tank and a Korean sits in there feeding little pieces of wood to it all the while. He sits on his haunches like most of them do--sure looks funny. There's no light in the room; all you can see is the fire and the outline of the Korean and he's usually quietly chanting a little tune.

Just went over and checked the flight schedule. I'm on it for one strike tomorrow. It's a close air support. I'll be carrying (1) 1000-lb gas napalm bomb, and 200 rounds of 20mm cannon in 4 guns, 800 rounds. We'll fly up to the front lines on either the west or the east side of Korea and check in with a controller, who will direct us into our targets. I'll give you the lowdown tomorrow night.

Hope everything at home is fine, honey. Keep the home fires burning, precious girl, and keep cheerful and happy and don't worry about the daddy, because I'm going to be very, very careful. Give Nanna and Gramp, Peggy and Trooper my love, and tell Ricky he's the man of the house and has to watch out for my things in the garage and help keep the kids out of the flowers, and has to take is easy with little Randy. Gosh, darling, I miss you. I suppose I've asked a lot of questions in my past letters that you probably have supplied answers to; however, I won't know until I begin getting more letters. I could ask you what kind of weather you have been having and by the time you answered and I got your letter it would be altogether changed.

I just signed as witness to Bill Higgins' power of attorney. He's sending it to his wife so she can sell his car.

I turned my itinerary in to the paymaster today, so I will be getting my travel pay soon.
I'm going to close and write to some others about my trip over. Honey, when you tuck the darlings in at night, tell them their daddy loves them and says a little prayer for both of them each night.

Night darling, Daddy

P.S. They told me Major "Herman the Hat" Dexter was killed a day or two before I arrived. He was flying an old beat-up Corsair back to Japan for a major overhaul. His right wing folded just after takeoff and he crashed and was killed when it hit the water. He had been executive officer in VMF-223 in Okinawa in 1945. I remember him as being a good man, but misunderstood by many because of his quiet nature as being aloof. Just the night before he was killed the pilots of VMF-323 sang "Early Abort," one of the squadron's most popular songs. Even Major Dexter chimed in good naturedly, I was told by Bill Higgins.

EARLY ABORT (MAC NAMARA'S BAND)

My name is Pete McGlothlin and I'm the leader of the group.
If you will step into my tent I'll give you all the poop.
I'll tell you where the commies are and where the flak is black.
I'll be the first one off the deck and I'll be the first one back.
    CHORUS:

Early abort, avoid the rush; early abort, avoid the rush;
Early abort, avoid the rush; oh the raggedy-ass Marines are on parade.

My name is Major Dexter and I lead 323,
And if we go on railcuts, my boys will follow me.
But if you say P'yongyang, I'll tell you what I will do,
Get in your plane and go ahead, and I'll wait here for you.
    CHORUS:

I'm sure you've heard of Checkerboard and the things they do
But if you'll come down to the line, you'll see they're far from true.
The pilots they are ready, but let their skipper shout
And all those bastards yell at once "My mags, they won't check out!"
    CHORUS:

And then I'm sure you know of the leaders in the wing.
Any night in the O'Club you can hear how well they sing.
With words they fight a hell of a war; they say they wanta go too,
But just you give them a half a chance and here's what they will do.
    CHORUS:

Now when this war is over and we're back in the U.S.A.
We'll fly the planes in all war games and do what the generals say,
But if we have another war and they give us the F4U,
To hell with all the generals' staffs, here's what we're gonna do:
    CHORUS:

Upper Left: Spud being strapped into his #5 F4U-4B Corsair, which is loaded with two napalm and 5" wing rockets. This is a common load.

Upper Right: Same plane from another angle.

Left: This AD-1 Skyraider crash-landed on a road near Seoul after being hit by enemy AA during a close air support mission with the 1stMarDiv.

Below: Cluster bomb. When released the metal straps came off and the small anti-personnel bombs fall over a wide area.

Above: The Douglas AD-1 Skyraider was a huge plane, capable of carrying 10,000 pounds of mixed ordnance and could stay over the sector for up to three hours. They would engage in up to 10 separate divebombing, rocket or napalm runs, as directed by the FAC. This subjected them to an unusual amount of flak and numerous hits were taken, with the resultant crashes such as the one pictured here. The AD-1s were located in Pohangdong, K3, in the southern part of Korea and were known as VMA-121. Their CO was LtCol Philip L. Crawford from 20 Jun 52, relieved by LtCol Wayne M. Cargill on 11 Sep 52.

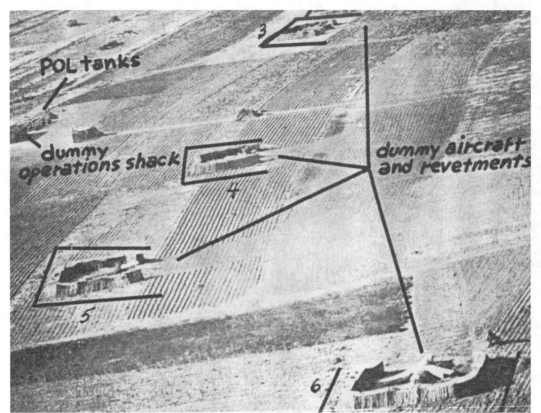

Left: This elaborate dummy Communist airfield is complete down to a dummy antiaircraft battery, six revetments with a fake MIG in each, an operations shack, and a small petroleum, oil, and lubrication dump. The oblique photograph shows the care lavished on the dummy aircraft. They are even raised off the ground so they cast shadows. The entire purpose is to lure us down low enough to shoot us out of the sky.

Left: F4U Corsairs, flown by Navy and Marine pilots during the Korean War. Both services flew off aircraft carriers but only the Marines were also land-based in Korea with other U.N. air forces. Powered by the 2000 HP Pratt & Whitney R2800 radial engine, the Corsair was an ideal ground support aircraft.

Lower Left: Douglas AD-1 Skyraider loaded with a mix of rockets and bombs. Its capability of carrying up to 10,000 pounds made it a formidable bomber for its size.

Below: The USS ESSEX (CVA-9), recalled to active duty April 1951 during the Korean War, sails out of San Diego, having been recently pulled out of the "Mothball" fleet and modernized with strengthened flight deck, personnel escalators, and streamlined island superstructure. During WWII she earned a proud record of 1531 enemy planes destroyed by her air groups.

1. My faithful house boy, Chipmunk, at K18.

2. My great hutmates at K18, Capt Bill Higgins, pilot with VMF-323, the other Corsair squadron here, and 1stLt Bob Ferguson of MABS-12. Bob handled all food services on the base. Nobody was shooting at him, and he was satisfied with the whole deal.

3. Spud. Just landed from a long "butt buster" over enemy lines. I lived with the map case, trying to get myself oriented here in this strange land. (I still have the map case and maps.)

4. Capt Ramon Gibson just landed, with his Corsair riddled from antiaircraft fire. He was flying low and slow on a search mission for Gen Matt Ridgeway's downed son.

5. Korean laborers loading an engine on plane for Itami overhaul.

KOREAN POINTIE TALKIE

We were given this English-to-Korean (phonetic) translation guide to aid us in case we were forced down in North Korea. The escape and evasion training officer also informed us that our chances of survival would be improved if we could find a Christian. The guide would also be helpful in South Korea.

ENGLISH	KOREAN – PHONETIC
1. Is there someone here who can speak English?	1. Mikuk mal (Yongo, yongkuk mal) ahnun sarami issumnikka?
2. Please get me someone who speaks English.	2. Mikuk mal (Yongo, yongkuk mal) ahnun saramul iri poneyo chusiyo.
3. Is there anyone here who can help me?	3. Nugutundi narul tawa chul sarami issumnikka?
4. Please hurry back.	4. Sokki tora osipsiyo.
5. Thank you.	5. Komapsumnida.
6. Thank you for all of your help.	6. Sugo hessumnida.
7. I will see that you are rewarded.	7. Tangshin unhairul kapkessumnida.
8. Please write down your name.	8. Tangshin ilhomul soh chusiyo.
9. I am hungry.	9. Paega kopmnida.
10. Please give me some boiled water.	10. Gurin mul chom chusiyo.
11. Please give me some hot food.	11. Tohun umsik chom chusiyo.
12. I am very grateful to you. Please accept this money.	12. Shinseh mahni chossumnida. Ii tonrul padayo.
13. Thank you, but I am not hungry.	13. Komapsumnida paega kopujiansumnida.
14. Thank you, but I am not thirsty.	14. Komapsumnida, mulun shiryoyo.
15. My airplane is destroyed.	15. Nae pihengiga puhsojossumnida.
16. I am a Christian.	16. Nanun kitokkyoinimnida.
17. I came to help the Korean people.	17. Nanun hanguk saramul tawa churyo wassumnida.
18. Please hide me. (us)	18. Nah (uri) rul kamchuo chusiyo.
19. Do not tell anyone I am here.	19. Nugutunji naega yohgeh ittago mal hojimasiyo.
20. I am an American aviator.	20. Nanun mikuk pihengssimnida.
21. Are you a Christian?	21. Tangshini kitokkyoinisimnikka?
22. Have you heard of any other aviators downed here?	22. Tahrun mikuk pigengsaga yohgeh dorojossumnikka?
23. Please help me find them.	23. Ku saramdul chajo chusikirul pahramnida.
24. Where are they?	24. Ku saramduli ohdeg issumnikka?

1 미국말(영우말, 영국말) 아는 사람이 잇습닛가
2 미국말(영우, 영국말) 아는 사람을 이리 보버여주시오
3 누구든지 나를 도와줄 사람이 잇습닛가
4 속히 도라오십시오
5 고맙습니다
6 수고 햇습니다
7 당신 은헤를 갑겟습니다
8 당신 일홈을 써주시요
9 배가 곱홈니다
10 꿀인물 좀 주시요
11 더운음식 좀 주시요
12 신세 만히 젓습니다. 이돈을 밧아요
13 고맙습니다. 배가 곱흐지안슴니다
14 고맙슴니다. 물은 실혀요
15 내비행기가 부서젓슴니다
16 나는 기독교인입니다
17 나는 한국사람을 도와주려왓슴니다
18 나(우리)를 감추어주시요
19 누구든지 나가 여게 잇다고 말하지마시오
20 나는 미국비행사입니다
21 당신이 기독교인이십닛가
22 다른 미국비행사가 여게 떠러저젓슴닛가
23 그사람들 차저주시기를 바랍니다
24 그 사람들이 어데 잇습닛가

THE HISTORIANS

When you're flying your combat missions in lousy weather and dodging flak, or taking protective cover down in your bunker or trench day and night trying to avoid a shower of hot shrapnel falling on you, it's easy to lose sight of the big picture. Thank God for the historians. My letters home to Marion reflect the situation as I perceived it at that moment. However, the Historical Division Headquarters, U.S. Marine Corps, put together a truly fine piece of work entitled, U.S. Marine Operations in Korea Vol. V, Operations in West Korea," by LtCol Pat Meid, USMCR and Maj James M. Yingling USMC. I have drawn upon much of this history throughout, often paraphrased and interspersed with my personal thoughts and letters, to put things in their proper perspective and to try and help the reader grasp a more accurate feel for the real "poop from the group." I had, in fact, contributed to these historical works through my many combat missions, debriefings and unit diaries when I was later attached to the 1st MarDiv, so, in effect, I drew upon some of my own reports when writing this book.

PITTMAN'S PLANE STRUCK BY 90MM AA

5 April 1952 - 1925

Hi precious little family,

I have your pictures up on the desk ahead of me, and now we'll have a little chat. This morning I attended lectures and briefings, and this afternoon at 1600 I took off with three other boys, Smith, Pittman and Barbours. The flight was led by Captain Barbours and I was his wing man. We were loaded with two 1000-lb napalm and eight 5" high velocity aircraft rockets; that was the loading of each plane, besides 800 rounds of 20mm cannon. We flew up the east coast of Korea and cut inland just below Wonsan Harbor, about 50 miles to the front lines. There we contacted a controller in a liaison plane, and he directed us to the target. I could look up and see the tops of the ridge lines as I swooped down and let go with my 1000-lb napalm and strafed with my four 20mm cannons. The ridge lines are honeycombed with tunnels, slit trenches and bunkers, and you can see the Commies crawling around in them. We filled them with flaming jelly gas, though, and the controller gave us a high estimate of casualties inflicted. We were under their fire as we made our attacks and one of our boys (Pittman) got a slug through his tail. Nobody picked up any more. Just as we arrived over their positions they let go with a burst of 90mm which fell far short of us, and was about 100' high. That was all they fired of the 90mm stuff, but you could see the small arms winking at you and a few tracers as we swept down low on our passes. They were just trying to scare us off and their accuracy was very poor.

Looking down at the ridges, we could see a serpentine line of trenches just at the ridge line. We were over the target area for about an hour and I made about six runs altogether. Then we retired to the east coast and flew back home over water, landing just at 6:00 PM.

I grabbed chow which was very good--steak, onions, mashed spuds, gravy, string beans, hot biscuits, bread and butter, jam, coffee and apricots. Then I came over and got out of my hot, sweaty flight gear, showered and shaved, and I believe I'm going to take in a flicker tonight at 2000.

How's the garden progressing? Are my little poppies coming along OK near the geraniums in the front yard?

How is Randy's hernia bulge, honey? Keep a real close lookout for my little darling, won't you, honey? Is Ricky helping you while I'm away? I hope he is because I've told him he's the man of the house while Daddy is away.

No mail plane came in today. Still have only received one letter that I've read a dozen times.

I took some pictures of the Corsairs in our squadron today, with their full loads. Took some of the strip too.

I miss you, angel girl. Kiss the little guys for me, darling.

Love, Daddy

COMMUNIST CAMOUFLAGE AND DECEPTION

Air University Quarterly Review (Spring 1953) describes camouflage and deception tactics used by the communists in North Korea:

> *A little publicized but extremely effective Communist device to circumvent the USAF interdiction campaign has been expert, extensive use of camouflage, deception, and dispersal of military targets. Laboriously repaired runways are dotted with dummy bomb craters to look as if they are still inoperative. In daytime, trains and truck convoys hide in tunnels and roadside shelters, then scuttle out after dark. Damaged bridges, railroad tracks, and highways are repaired and the repairs camouflaged with straw or dirt. Troop concentrations, vehicles, aircraft, or huge supply dumps are spread over several square miles, protected from effective air attack by dispersal and by a phenomenal amount of "rat-holing"--excavating caves and revetments out of cliffs and digging thousands of large trenches along mountain slopes or in open fields, to be filled with supplies and covered over. Such extremes of passive defense testify to the impact of UN aerial interdiction. They also decisively exhibit several important enemy characteristics. Although deficient in engineering equipment, he has expert engineering assistance. He has inexhaustible hordes of laborers, and the speed and general quality of their work in large measure counterbalances their lack of modern machinery. His long, varied experience in limited and guerrilla warfare pays off in cunning, skills, and disciplines peculiarly suited to operations in rugged and primitive Korea. Like any shrewd soldier, he has squandered his most plentiful resource--man power--to protect his weak point--modern equipment and supplies. Reconnaissance photography has recorded his methods. He has not defeated our interdiction campaign, but he has made it more difficult and has limited its results, even though it has cost him heavily to achieve this.*

― ― ― ― ―

Just came back from the flicker--"The Tougher They Come."

Tell Ricky I use his flashlight every night and don't know what I'd do without it. There are lots of big drainage ditches here and there, and if you're not careful you could fall in up to your neck.

By the way, it hasn't rained a drop since I arrived; in fact there hasn't been a cloud in the sky since after the day I arrived. We've had beautiful weather. Today was just as warm and comfortable as could be--a tee shirt was all a guy needed. The thing I hate is to have to dress for cold weather survival up in the northern Korean mountains, in the event you get shot down. While you're on the deck you're roasting, and also when you're flying below 5000'. However, if a guy had to get out of his plane and crawl around on a mountain top it would really be cold, so you dress to survive the worst weather. The mountain tops are covered with snow. I just checked the schedule and I see I have a briefing at 0600 and a standby until scrambled for a close air support or a railcut up north. Then in the afternoon I have a 1745 brief, 1800 takeoff on a ready alert, which means that there is a possibility I won't get off if nothing hot comes up. I'll write you tomorrow and give you the "hot skinny" as they call it, or "the poop from the Group."

I love you, darling, Daddy

COMMUNIST VS UN AIR ACTIONS

As our retreating army, fighting its delaying action and buying precious time, made its way south during the opening days of the war, the North Koreans were striking them with old Soviet propeller-driven aircraft such as the YAK-9 and the YAK-15. Our fighters were being flown from Japan some 150 miles away and off carriers. The P-80s, P-51s and F-84s, all land based in Japan, were finally supplemented by F4Us, ADs and F9Fs from aircraft carriers, who performed close air support for the Pusan perimeter and the amphibious landing at Inchon. Carrier based Corsairs and AD Skyraiders hit communist airfields and installations in North Korea eight days after the initial outbreak, flying off the USS *Valley Forge*. British airplanes--the Navy Hawker, Sea Fury and Fairey Firefly, flew off the HMS *Triumph* and HMS *Ocean*. The Royal Australian Navy's carriers, *Sidney* and *Melbourne*, arrived with Sea Furies and Fairey Fireflys. The first Russian MIG-15 jets entered the fighting arena around 1 Nov 1950 and had a field day shooting down our outclassed fighters until the North American F-86 Sabrejets arrived from the U.S. mainland on 17 Dec 1950 and began a field day of their own, destroying 841 Soviet built MIG-15s while losing only 78 of our F-86 Sabrejets during the entire war.

A third of those victories were scored by two percent of the 1700 Air Force Sabrejet pilots, making numerous jet aces and providing the trial battle arena for the then untested second generation jet fighters on both sides.

The jet air war corridor known worldwide as "MIG Alley," extended from high over the Yalu River to the very north of Korea, marking the separation point between it and the Chinese Manchuria borders. Then it continued down south to the N. Korean river of Chongchon, near Anju, a very wide area.

Besides the superior flying skills provided by our Sabre pilots, their 10 to 1 kill ratio was aided by the F-86's APG-30 radar ranging gun sights, which the MIG didn't have. Even though the MIG-15 flew faster than the Sabrejet and had superior maneuverability above 30,000 feet, some of our jet pilots showed their superiority, such as cigar-smoking James (Jabby) Jabara from Oklahoma, of Lebanese ancestry, who became a triple jet ace with 15 kills. (Jabby had taken first blood in Europe in WWII.) He and Capt Joseph McConnell of Apple Valley, California, both USAF pilots, had a running duel over the skies of N. Korea to see who would emerge as the Free World's top jet ace. Joe won the duel with 16 kills.

While flying over the Yalu, Joe and Jabby reported seeing enemy pilots walking to their MIGs at their fields at Antung, Manchuria, safely within their privileged sanctuary, which we could not violate under the UN rules that prevailed all during the Korean War. A very frustrating kind of war. Ironically, after his harrowing wartime experiences, Jabby would be killed in 1960 in a tragic car wreck, along with his daughter, in the States.

Some other leading USAF aces of the Korean War were Col Royal H. Baker (13), Maj Frederick C. Blesse (10), Lt Harold E. Fisher (10), LtCol Vermont Garrison (10), Col James K. Johnson (10), Capt Lonnie R. Moore (10) and Capt Ralph S. Parr (10).

Capt Manuel J. Fernandez, flying Sabrejets with the 4th Wing in Korea, ended the war with 14.5 kills to his credit. Just behind Fernandez was Maj George A. Davis with 14 kills, who was himself shot down and killed 10 Feb 1952. He received the Medal of Honor posthumously.

Joseph Connell, the top MIG killer of them all, died, not from wartime injury, but after the Korean War had come to a halt when, on 25 Aug 1954, he crashed while test flying a newly modified F-86 Sabrejet.

There were 40 new American aces created in the Korean War: 38 USAF, one Marine (Maj John Bolt) and one Naval pilot (Lt Guy P. Bordelon). Eleven pilots stacked up ten or more victories. Numerous other pilots became aces after combining their Korean scores with WWII credits.

The Navy had their one and only one ace in Lt Guy P. Bordelon, a night fighter, flying my favorite bent-wing bird, a vintage F4U Corsair. His kills were not MIG-15 jets but he was a true ace for eliminating two Russian made YAK-18s and three LA-11s, all propeller-driven aircraft that intruded near Seoul between 29 June and 16 July 1953.

The Marines had only one jet ace during the Korean War, Maj John F. Bolt, who left VMF-115 and flew F-86 Sabrejets with the Air Force on exchange duty. He shot down six MIG-15s. Marine pilot John Glenn shot down three MIG-15s on exchange duty with the Air Force.

In Korea during 1952 the air war was going hot and heavy. September would prove to be our best month when our 5th Air Force shot down 64 MIG-15s while losing 7 Sabrejets. So, while the air war raged overhead in MIG Alley, men died defending hills on the battle line with strange sounding names like Porkchop, Little

Gibralter, Bunker Hill, Old Baldy, Heartbreak Ridge, Charlton Hill #543 (named after a black soldier who won the Medal of Honor), Punchbowl, Reno, Carson, Vegas, Hill 983, Bloody Ridge and Iron Triangle.

Back home the loss of our men brought anguish and suffering to thousands of families who were wondering just exactly where Korea was located. But the men staggering up and down the treacherous slopes with the "thousand-yard-stare" knew where it was, and wished to God they were home and out of it on their "Big R" (rotation).

Numerous stories have emerged from the Korean War concerning the makeup of the MIG fighter pilots. The majority were Chinese and North Korean, but one story that I find very interesting is as follows: A Russian Major General Kojedub (sometimes spelled Kozhedub) is reported to have commanded an air division in North Korea equipped with MIG-15 jets. It is possible that he added to his WWII victory record there, but it is also reported that his unit was given such a mauling by the Americans that he was recalled to the USSR. He had 62 kills in WWII flying LAGG-5 and LAGG-7 Russian built fighters against the Germans.

CAPT BEAUMONT COOLEY USMCR RECALLS KOREA TOUR OF DUTY

Texas-bred Beaumont B. Cooley and I had flown with Marine Fighter Squadron VMF-223 in the Philippines and Okinawa during WWII. Prior to that Beau had been with the same squadron in Bougainville, Solomons, flying missions against Rabaul, an island infested with Japanese Zero fighters. A seasoned division leader, he gave comforting assurance to anyone in his flight. He related two stories of his harrowing experiences in Korea, both of which nearly landed him in the "Who's Who" of very brave, but very dead Marines:

* * * Story One * * *

On 1 October 51 while flying in Korea out of K-18 in the Blacksheep squadron, VMF-214, in a F4U-4B Corsair on a rail interdiction mission, I had a MIG 15 make a pass at someone in my division. We never did figure out who he had zeroed in on. The first I knew of his presence was when he came out from under my left wing climbing away, a good hundred knots faster than me. My division had just completed a dive bombing attack on the rail yards at Kuni-ri north of Sun'chon, North Korea. Because this was a real hot spot for anti-aircraft fire, we had come in from about 17,000 feet. On the recovery, I was clipping along in a full throttle, sixty degree climb doing at least "reeptie-torque" knots.

This MIG pilot had to be the dumbest person in the North Korean Air Force, as he pulled right out in front of me. Having spent eighteen months instructing in the Operational Training Command and having at the time over 3000 hours of flight time, I knew what it took to nail this fellow. There was no "buck" fever for me, I was calm and collected. I very carefully put the pipper just ahead of him and squeezed the trigger. There was no question I had him. When I fired he was about 1000 feet to my front, in the ideal position for the bore sighting of my guns. I thought, "At the speed he is traveling, my four 20 mm canons will shred his plane at this range. This is like shooting fish in a barrel!"

When I fired, I had one gun respond--I fired <u>one</u> stinking round! My guns were either frozen or I had just experienced a three-gun jam. I quickly leaned forward and hit the charging knobs, but by the time I completed this and looked up, he was well out of range. My single shot did him no harm.

It wasn't until 10 September, 1952, almost a year later, that Jess Folmar shot down a MIG off the west Coast of Korea to become the first Marine to down a jet airplane in aerial combat while flying a Corsair. Except for the 20 mm malfunction, that could have been me--I could have been famous.

* * * Story Two * * *

In December 1951 while flying a Cessna OE-1 Bird Dog with VMO-6 in the Tenth Corps area of Korea, I had my second close encounter with immortality in the Marine Corps. The day was one of those beautiful late autumn days with bright sunshine and very little breeze. The ground temperature probably was in the high forties, perhaps the low fifties. Al Pollock, my Observer, and I were on a reconnaissance mission in the vicinity of Musan, just north of the Soyang Gang (river), when Al spotted a group of enemy soldiers sunning themselves on top of a dugout. Their area was just on the back side of a ridge which was in defile from our artillery, so we could not undertake firing at them. We watched for a while, but soon tired of this and left to find something more of interest.

About forty minutes later, we chanced by this area again, and they were still out there enjoying the autumn sunshine. Al watched them through his glasses, but was unable to discern anything because of our height. To go lower would have invited a shoot-the-Yankee melee--and we certainly did not want that. Again we left.

We chanced by again about thirty minutes later. Al began to mumble in his beard as he again scanned these troops with his glasses. He was saying, "If I could only make out those uniforms. . .!" He then elaborated when he said this would be a valuable bit of intelligence, as it would let our folks know who they are facing.

I asked, "Do you really want to see people up close?"

He responded, "It sure would be nice."

"Okay--we are on our way down."

As you could imagine, just peeling-off in a dive at this time would not be very smart, so I told Al, "We're leaving for now, but we'll be back in about fifteen minutes, and you can have your look."

We left and spent the next fifteen minutes away. As time passed I slowly worked us back toward the ridge with the troops, but I kept us on the other side of the mountain mass from where they were. I wanted to make sure they could not see or hear us. At the last possible minute, I dove for the ground near the top of the mountain, passed over and settled down, flying just below the ridge line, but on the opposite side from the soldiers.

When I judged we were close, I popped us over the ridge and down on the other side. We were on top of them in a flash as I shouted to Al, "There they are--start looking!"

We were moving along about 120-30 knots, no more than twenty feet from the ground. The slope was steep and artillery fire had long since reduced what had been a tree-covered slope to stumps. Our surprise was complete--well almost. They were still just lazing around still engaged, no doubt, in reorganizing Communism and grousing about the war--all but one smart-ass. This guy just happened to be facing in our direction and saw our approach when we were about one hundred feet out.

He shouted something to his buddies and immediately stooped down and picked up a stone about the size of a brick, cocked his arm and let fly. When I saw the pitching motion, I tightened up at both ends, and watched him throw--how could he miss? Well, miss he did! The stone passed close behind us. We continued on down the ridge, jumping back to the other side as soon as we could, and held course until we hit the Soyang Gang. We were in and out without a shot being fired, but there had been one brick thrown. Once in the river bed, I turned left, dropped as low as I could and wound toward friendly lines about two miles away. Once on our side, we slowly climbed back to altitude and returned to see what the group was doing now. When we got back, they were all gone. We had broken up the "bull session"--that's for sure. I guess they were all inside the dugout telling their latest war story.

Had that soldier taken the stone and thrown or simply tossed it at us underhanded, there was no doubt it would have hit our propeller. What would have happened after this is problematical, but it unquestionably would not have been good for our side. His action, of attempting to throw overhanded, delayed his throw just enough that the stone missed. Had he made the underhand toss, Al Pollock and I would have been famous for having been "shot down" by a rock.

Between wars Beau instructed flying in both fixed wing powered aircraft and gliders, achieving near records in the latter during U.S. soaring meets, and he kept up this interest for over 20 years. He also became involved with a boat charter company serving the U.S. Virgin Islands and Florida, while also teaching sailing and power boat navigation as a member of the U.S. Power Squadron.

WELCOME TO KOREA - TRANS-KOREAN AIRLINES - ANYTHING-ANYWHERE-ANYTIME
SMALL FIELDS A SPECIALTY - A NON-PROFIT ORGANIZATION

Beau in front of a quonset at K-50, on the east coast of Korea about 15 miles north of the 38th Parallel. K-50 was a 6000' gravel air strip, where all replacements to the 1stMarDiv came and went. One of his daily chores at VMO-6 was to pick up mail and bring back one and sometimes two passengers to X-83 and the Division. Beau flew the single-engine OE-1 observation plane for the Marines, with a variety of assignments, such as airborne forward air control, observation, photo recon, weather, liaison, as well as transport.

Captain Beaumont (Beau) Cooley in the snow Christmas day 1951. Beau was flying with Marine Observation Squadron VMO-6 at a small airfield called X-83, located at Sunchon, Korea, attached to the 1stMarDiv as part of the Tenth Corps. The field was in a valley called Soyoy, near the Gang River just east of the Punchbowl, scene of some ferocious fighting.

Beau in front of his tent, his home with VMO-6. The temperature was -15 F. when this shot was taken.

Beau in Japan, in the town of Kyoto, on a well-earned R & R. Beau and I flew together during WWII, as fighter pilots with VMF-223 at Bougainville, Philippines and Okinawa. He was my flight leader upon occasion, and a darn good one.

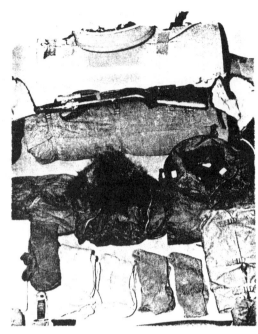

Above Left: Debriefing—Marine pilots of MAG-33 report to BGen Clayton C. Jerome, 1st MAW CG, upon return from June 1952 Air strike, biggest to date.

Above Right: Clothing and equipment packed in a "survival bomb" dropped to Marine pilots awaiting rescue.

Middle Left: Pilots of VMJ-1 are briefed on the day's mission over North Korea.

Below: MSgt Theodore H. Hughes, 1st MAW, presents 900,000 won (equivalent to $150,000) to Bishop Mousset, of Little Flower's Orphanage in Pohang. Money was donated by MAG-33 Staff NCO Club.

Photo credit USMC.

Upon receiving his master's degree at the University of Texas in 1955, Beaumont Cooley's civilian pursuits in his chosen field of Petroleum Geology, mostly with CHEVRON, involved an amazing variety of outstanding work experiences both in the U.S. and in the far reaching depths of foreign lands around the world, totalling 46 years in the petroleum industry. After retiring in 1988, he is still professionally affiliated with the Society of Professional Well Log Analysts, the Society of Petroleum Engineers (SPE of AIME), and the American Arbitration Association. During many of those busy years he still maintained his active participation in the Marine Corps Reserves, finally retiring from the Corps in 1970 as a LtCol, having accumulated 28 years of active and reserve service.

Beau's story came to mind because he had been recalled to active duty from an organized reserve squadron during the Korean War and his experiences somewhat paralleled my own. Forty-seven years had passed before we got together at our VMF-223 reunion and we have remained in close communication ever since.

(Note: Refer to Appenidx Number 9 for additional reflections by Beau Cooley.)

GOSS TAKES A HIT IN HIS PROP

Kangnung, Korea (K18)
Sunday, 6 April 1952

Hi little family o'mine,

Today has been long and filled with many things, which I will attempt to enumerate forthwith.

Reveille went at 0445, had breakfast and then went over to the Group briefing at 0600. J.O.C. (Joint Operation Command - 5th Air Force), from whom we get all our mission assignments, had some priority target for us and as a consequence we never got airborne to conduct our strike until after an artillery bombardment of the local area had subsided. Finally, got airborne, 16 of us from our squadron, splitting up into (4) four plane divisions and going to the four different corps sectors along the 145 mile front to work with the airborne controller. We were loaded with two 1000-lb four- to five-second delay (general purpose) bombs, and eight 5" hi-velocity aircraft rockets, with 800 rounds of 20mm cannon.

We flew north along the east coast to below Wonsan and cut inland about 10 miles to the battle line, where we were directed on some gun positions that had been holding our boys up for some time. We made repeated runs down to very low altitudes, strafing and dropping either bombs or firing rockets on each run. One of my hits landed on a gun position and another caused a secondary explosion; on several of my strafing passes (which I brought down very low) I could see the Commies firing at me with everything they had. I banked up, swung on around and let them have it with a 1000-lb on my third pass. I strafed and took a damage assessment pass and there was nothing there but a huge hole in the ground about 30' in diameter. Needless to say, I got the enemy and their artillery. The other planes of the division did equally as well and the air controller gave us credit for 80 percent destruction on the target area. He was quite happy with our work.

Only one of us picked up any flak, and that was Captain Goss who got a slug in his prop, which bit a great big chunk out of it and caused terrific engine vibration due to the unbalance. He throttled back and we nursed him home some 75 miles or so--all landed safely.

I grabbed lunch, then went back to the squadron and had to stand by for the squadron duty officer until 1600. I had quite a session getting an 11-plane strike out; seeing to it that I got plane number assignment made and seeing if the aircraft were all armed, gassed and raring to go, herding the pilots out to the planes and informing the group of their departure. I also had to call across the peninsula to another field to try and find out about Jack Ryan from our squadron, who had had to make a forced landing at K14 near Seoul. I had to go through three operators and after about five minutes I made contact. He'd gotten his plane squared away and flown it back here this afternoon. This 11-plane strike from our squadron went to within 15 miles of the mouth of the Yalu, deep in MIG Alley. They hit railroad bridges and other targets of opportunity. They saw vapor trails way up above them, but they never came down on them. They all came back unhurt and really did a good job.

I have the same strike tomorrow, taking off at 0900--it's a three hour hop, 600 miles.

After I finished standing the duty I had supper, which was very delicious--fried chicken, sweet spuds, creamed corn, coffee, and pineapple slices for dessert. After dinner I went back to the squadron, got all my gear on and stood by on a ready alert until 1900 (dark), but they never scrambled us. It's 2000 now and I'm seriously thinking of taking in the cinema. It's been warm today--I wore the tee shirt nearly all afternoon and was plenty comfortable.

AIRFIELDS AND MILITARY INSTALLATIONS

Since sprawling airfields and other large military installations cannot be completely hidden from the prying eye of visual or photographic reconnaissance, the Communists contented themselves with basic camouflage of buildings, deceptive devices, and dispersal. Their airfields seldom had hangars. Aircraft were maintained and protected in thick-walled earth revetments frequently two or three miles from the airfield. Wherever possible revetments were built into cliff faces. Dummy bomb craters were dotted on runways to make the airfield appear inoperative. Elaborate dummy airfields were constructed to draw bomb loads destined for real airfields. The Communists were very skillful in their use of local natural materials--brush, dirt, rock--to camouflage buildings and gun positions. Their discipline in minimizing tell-tale track activity around installations was excellent, a high achievement for any army.

2145

Hi again,

Just came back from the movie, "The Whistle at Eden Falls, New Hampshire." It was all about a shoe factory that went broke and then a plastic factory went broke. Then they got a new president with a lot of new ideas and he bought a bunch of automatics and put on three shifts and everyone got their old job back and didn't have to leave Eden Falls because they all loved the little town so very much--very touching, to say the least.

Still no mail from my baby girl. There's only one guy that came out with us that's getting any, and his family is in Long Beach. Pittman was the guy who received the letter and he says it's been 85° in Long Beach. Can't understand it. I even made out another address card and sent it down to the Wing P.O. in hopes they'd rush things a little.

Several boys have dropped into the tent, saw my pictures of my precious family and have complimented me on my selection of a very lovely looking wife. They weren't telling me anything I didn't know, however. I sure do miss you, darling, and would give anything to be home again with my wonderful family. I need every one of you more than I can tell you.

This part of Korea is a land of nothing--nothing much will grow here, most of the mountains are barren, and we're burning what they do have growing on them with our fire power. As you approach the battle line, even on a clear day, there's a haze, and visibility is very limited due to all the fighting, bombs, and napalm, causing brush and timber fires for miles and miles. Oh well, so goes it, I guess.

Will write again tomorrow. When you tuck the babies in tonight, kiss them for me and tell them their daddy loves them very much.

Love, Daddy

Kangnung, Korea
7 April 1952

Hi little family,

Here I am in my flight gear standing by for my railcut mission. However, I don't believe it will go out because there's a cold front moving up from an occlusion over our airfield, which means a thunder burst. The visibility is rather poor, the sky is overcast and it's generally a very poor, gray day.

My stomach has been very good, honey, ever since leaving the States. The chow isn't too greasy and I try not to eat too much at any one meal.

It's raining now. I haven't had a drink of anything since leaving the States, nor have I even had one little old cigar. All this clean living will pay big dividends, though, in keeping my general health at a fairly high peak because there are so many confounded diseases over here one needs a rugged constitution. They give free candy and cigarettes to the boys once a day and, as a consequence, some of them who didn't smoke before they came over here have now taken up smoking as a pastime.

I sent along an Easter card to you, precious darling, and one to Nanna, and Mom. I don't have any more and can't get any, so I guess I'll just have to write to Peggy for Easter. As long as it's raining I guess I'll write Peggy and Aunt May today because I haven't written to them since I left.

I hope you're comfortable there at home, darling, and are getting along OK with the kids. I guess you can handle the situation OK though, honey--you've done all right practically by yourself up to now, anyway. Do Ricky and Randy ask about their Daddy and do you read them my letters? Knowing Ricky as I do, I almost guess that he would want to have my letters read to him. Each and every one of you are on my mind and in my prayers constantly, dearest. I want nothing more from this life but to return home to my little family and resume our happy home life that we all enjoyed so much before the 25th of March. Never you mind, dearest, that day will come, and when it does we'll enjoy each other even more than we have in the past. I get a lot of strength just looking back on the past eight wonderful years we have been married and I know the remaining years that we will be together will be given even more significance by this absence (although no absence was needed to spur my love for you, dearest, or our two little darlings).

There are a few things I'd like to hear about in your letters to me, honey. How is Ricky progressing in school? What has he learned for the day? How is he doing with his dancing lessons? and Sunday School? How are you doing with the car? How's the garden, the cat, the dog, and everything else around the place? To you it's everyday commonplace and you'd probably avoid mentioning them for fear of repeating yourself.

Here's something else I want done, and just as fast as you can manage it. I want a full length picture of you in one of your smooth dresses--no skirts--and one of you in your bathing suit. Get them blown up to 4x8 with a little cardboard frame to keep them in shape. I'd like one of you and the boys close up; also send those colored pictures of you Bob took in 1945--I've got to have a little cheesecake, haven't I? Do this just as soon as you can, darling, because I sure would like to have them.

Will secure for now but will resume a little later. I sure enjoy these little chats, honey. It's second best to talking with you firsthand, but then, there's nothing that can be done about that.

1400 Monday afternoon (same day)

Well, the weather got foul and I didn't fly today. I wrote Mama, Ben, Vera and Don, Peggy, Aunt May--guess that will hold them for a while. My hand is about tired out, but there's nothing else to do on a day like this so I might as well write on. If you don't keep yourself occupied with something it gives you too much time to think of home and then you become gloom itself.

Will close for now, darling.

Bye bye, Daddy

IN KOREA AT LAST, WITH VMF-212

THE MULE KICK OF A 1000-LB BOMB

Kangnung, Korea
8 April 1952, 2100

Hi precious family,
   Well, I just finished reading the April 5th edition of the Stars and Stripes, a service newspaper that is published daily in Japan for all service personnel, but doesn't find its way over here until about three or four days after it's published. The peace talks are still dragging on. I don't get any other word from any source other than the Stars and Stripes, and I haven't heard a radio since leaving the States. Some of the fellows have radios here, but haven't been able to use them since our AC generator burned out and we're using a DC generator that was used to operate a search light on the field prior to our snatching hold of it.
   Still no mail! I'm not worried though, dearest, because I know that you are writing to me. When it does begin arriving this delay won't even matter. It's hard to figure out how I got that one letter from you when I first landed at South Korea at the Wing.
   Today I was scheduled for a railcut way up by MIG Alley, but the weather was bad so they delayed it a while, then finally scrambled us up to a forward air controller in a Mosquito plane south of Wonsan, who had a good target for us. He said that a group of about 15 Commies had several bunkers and field pieces on a piece of land (high ground) jutting out into the water and that they had been harassing our front lines for days. He warned us that they would shoot back with plenty because they had many times in the past, with 50 caliber machine gun and smaller weapons. They had their position well camouflaged, but we spotted it and gave them the full treatment with 20mm cannon, 1000-lb bombs and 100-lb bombs. They were on this point of land, as I said before, and they commanded this open plain, and nothing could get past them.
   The air controller buzzed down after we each made six separate passes at them, and said we had made 100 percent target coverage and destruction. Then he asked, "Did you bring any aspirin? Better throw some out--thy'll need it after all that pounding!" He gave us credit for 15 KIAs. They were firing at us from the time we went into our runs until the time we recovered--until we silenced them. They won't bother our front line buddies with any more fire. When those 1000 pounders go off it feels like a mule kicking the tail of my plane. Boy, those things sure pack a wallop!
   Tomorrow, if the weather clears up north, I will go on that MIG Alley railcut. A long ride up there. It's estimated it will take a total of about three hours for the round trip.
   In the morning I have to get up at 0430, brief at 0530, sit in my plane for the early morning ready alert until 0730; then, if we're not scrambled, I'll have an 0800 briefing with an 0900 takeoff and a 1200 return. Then I have a 1400 briefing and a standby status until scrambled, which will probably become a close air support hop. So you see I'll have a busy day tomorrow.
   I love you, darling, and miss you very, very much.
   Give my two little boys a big hug and kiss for me, won't you, darling.

Bye bye 'til tomorrow, Daddy

DEADLY MIG-15 VAPOR TRAILS SIGHTED
INK BOTTLES SHAKING AT THE PEACE TABLES

Kangnung, Korea
Wed., 9 April 1952

Hi darlings.
   I really have had it today. My tailboard is dragging.
   Reveille at 0430, breakfast a 0500, briefed at 0530, stood by my plane until 0730, but we weren't scrambled. Then I dashed over and attended the 0800 briefing at the Group for our railcut hop up to within 25 miles of the Yalu River, dead center in MIG Alley; in fact we would

71

have been in the MIGs' traffic circle on one of their long fast approaches. We could see vapor trails above us as we dove down and made seven out of nine perfect cuts (direct hits) on the railroad with 1000 pounders and 100-lb bombs. Colonel Bryson followed me in and he said they were on my tail with 37mm and what-have-you, but I made a bull's eye, recovered dead ahead and never got more than 100' off the deck until I was 10 miles from the rail center. I was doing nearly 400 mph when I came out of my dive and every time I saw a burst come at me I'd push the throttle a little further, but it wouldn't go any further because it was all the way up there already.

There was a very bad haze all the way up there and visibility was very poor. We had a tough time finding our assigned target. We flew about 600 miles round trip across the peninsula west from Kangnung over Seoul up across Chinnanpo Peninsula, hit them, and returned the same way. It took us three hours and fifteen minutes of hard pushing.

We landed at 1230 and I grabbed lunch, then went over and briefed for a JOC alert, hoping we wouldn't get scrambled because I was tired. But the 'hot line' from JOC (5th AirForce) was buzzing when we got to the Group and I knew it was asking for our four-plane standby. Sure enough, they wanted us to get up to the First Marine Division and work over a heavy concentration of Commies on a hill which was giving our boys a bad time.

In an hour we were up there and contacted a controller on the ground. He smoked our target for us with a round of what we call Willie Peter, which stands for W.P., which is short for White Phosphorous Smoke Shell. Together with the forward air controller and an airborne Mosquito plane that wouldn't come within a mile of the target because they were shooting at him, we managed to clobber the Commies again. We hit them just a few seconds after they lobbed the Willie Peter on them and they knew we were coming in to get them. You could see them leaving their bunkers on the crest of the hill for lower ground, but we were on them in seconds, got five machine gun positions and caused a huge secondary explosion, which wrecked four or five deep bunkers. It's going to be rough for them to replace them too, because we practically ploughed their mountain post under.

The friendly troops (Marines) were only 600 yards away and we had to be extremely careful in our drops for fear of hitting our friendlies. We were working--get this--just six miles southeast of the Peace Talks, and I'll bet the ink bottles on their tables were jumping when those 1000 pounders went off. We each made about six runs on the target. We had to be careful not to hit our friendlies or to recover in such a direction as to carry us over near Panmunjom.

Look at your map, honey, and find the Imjin River southeast of Kaesong. We were wondering if they brought us in close like that so the Chinese at the peace talks would know we meant business. We were glad to get out of there safely and head for home. My windshield was covered with oil and the haze made landing tough on this horrible runway. The close air support hop lasted 2.3 hours, which, with the railcut this morning gave me 5.6 hours in the bent-winged monster. We were on the deck by 1700, got debriefed, turned in our damage assessment for forwarding to the 5th AirForce (JOC).

Had roast beef, mashed spuds, gravy, tomatoes, soup, apricots, and coffee, for supper. I showered, shaved, went to the 1800 movie and saw a corny picture, "Variety Review," a bunch of second rate talent that couldn't make TV. I almost got up and left, but didn't because I needed something to get my mind off of flying just for a little while.

Ray Vilareal sent my pictures back from Itami, Japan, and also my little cup and saucer and ash tray I had forgotten to pick up when I went shopping for your tea set in Kobe, Japan. I'll mail it home right away, dearest. I'll send the pictures along too. The two pictures I have of you are really the most important of all my possessions over in this godforsaken land. (Our generator keeps dying and the lights go out, then come back on again.) I sit here and study every little detail of my precious family. I love you all so very much, precious girl, and we'll make up for this separation, sweetheart, during the many years we'll have together after I come home.

I certainly miss seeing the boys every day because I know how the little rascals change. I guess you have plenty of company, don't you sweetie?

No mail today! Give my love to Pappy, Nanna, Peg, Troop, and above all, tell my little guys their daddy loves them and misses them very much.

Does Randy ask for me, honey? I know Ricky would, but Randy is smaller and his little head gets full of ideas that may not allow him to think of Daddy.
Kiss them goodnight for me, honey, and tuck them in warm.

Bye bye, Daddy

P.S. I was left off the schedule tomorrow, but we lost one of our boys today and I'm going out at 0600 tomorrow and search for him if I can get a plane. He's somewhere in South Korea.

All of our Marine airwing bases throughout Korea had O'Clubs of sorts. Most of us pilots would frequent them in our off-duty hours, especially in the evenings. Without exception we all loved to sing. The songs we sang were a definite relief to us all for it let us get off our chests the things that we faced every day, and it helped develop the camaraderie that held us together.

NO FLAPS AT ALL

Come listen, my children. Come listen to me.
I'll tell you a story, that will fill you with glee.
It tells of a pilot, so handsome and tall,
Who tried to take off with no flaps at all.
    CHORUS:

    No flaps at all, no flaps at all,
    Wide open throttle, but no flaps at all.

He went to his "U" bird to look at his load,
Two napalm with wing bombs, 'bout all it would hold.
He said to himself, "I've got lots on the ball."
"I'm sure I can take off with no flaps at all."
    CHORUS:

He moved his plane out to the end of the strip,
Four thousand foot runway with never a dip.
He checked with the tower and heard the voice drawl,
"No wind, you can't take off with no flaps at all."
    CHORUS:

Our hero was cocky, his ego was hurt,
For what was the word of an ignorant squirt?
"He's probably a corporal, knows nothing at all.
He thinks he can take off with no flaps at all."
    CHORUS:

He poured on the throttle and lined up with care,
Gave the flap handle an arrogant glare,
Then on the radio we heard him call,
"14-1 scrambling with no flaps at all."
    CHORUS:

At the end of the runway with no speed to spare
He pulled back the stick, staggered into the air,
About fifty feet up he went into a stall
And when he hit the deck he had no flaps at all.
    CHORUS:

The pilot was handsome, but now he is dead.
It must have been stuffy where he had his head,
But he should be happy that his time had come;
He might have been sent to 161.
     CHORUS:

The following letters are about my sister squadron, the Checkerboards, VMFA-312, submitted to me by my friend Col Stuart Nelson USMCR Ret, who can't resist a good war story. Stu's executive officer, BGen Jay Hubbard USMC Ret, wrote the first letter in response to the daughter of their flying buddy, Bill Deeds. Jay's and Stu's interesting letters reflect the camaraderie between the reserve and the regular Marine officers. The descriptive condensation of our missions as fighter pilots put the situation into proper perspective, including the hazards and the humor.

I am grateful to Stu for the many surviving Marine ballads from the Korean War era appearing within these pages. (Incidentally, Stu must hold the all-time record of being hit by communist ground fire--17 times out of the 33 combat missions he flew--and he's still around to talk about it!)

                                                    21 July 1986
Dear Catherine:

This responds to your letter regarding VMFA-312 and the wives' newsletter. First of all, what a treat it is to hear of Bill Deeds, even if it is roundabout. Your dad is one super officer, aviator and friend. I hope that life is pushing perfect for him these days and I would appreciate being remembered to him.

Now, as to my experience with the Checkerboards. I joined the Squadron in early September 1951 as Executive Officer. We were in Korea, as a part of MAG-12 [Marine Air Group], flying F4U-4B Corsairs out of K-18 at Kangnung, about thirty kilometers south of the 38th Parallel. Put another way, we were only about ten minutes from the bombline. This made us truly responsive to frantic calls for air support.

Although, then Captain, Phil DeLong made like a fighter and nailed two YAKs in April 1951 (his wingman Lt Daigh also got one) and, then Captain, Jesse Folmar downed a MIG-15 in September 1952, the squadron's basic mission was ground attack, even though we retained the VMF designation.

Except for occasional "specials," our schedule alternated between pre-planned or on-call close air support anywhere along the front on one day and interdiction strikes on rails, roads, bridges, tunnels and supply sites on the next day. The latter were deep efforts all the way to the Yalu in some cases. There were also occasional armed recce opportunities. Legalized flathatting best describes those. In Korea, as in VietNam later, you really had to get down on the deck and literally blow the cover off to find any real targets. Nothing worthwhile moved on the ground, at least during daylight, when we were overhead.

The Squadron was loaded with spirit and competed with the sister VMFs 212-214 and 323 without letup. We made our TOTs [Time On Targets], always scored respectable, sometimes remarkable, BDA [Bomb Damage Assessment] and put on awesome winter rain danced when snowed in at our "tinkertoy" (pierced steel planking, also known as Marston Matting) expeditionary airfield.

During my tour, which lasted into mid-January 1952, 312's pilots were principally recalled reserves who made it clear, by both word and deed, that they didn't uproot from their civilian pursuits and their families to come out there and pussyfoot around. They wanted to hit it hard and get it over with. Collectively, these guys were tigers and smart tactical aviators. As a WWII "grunt," experiencing combat as an aviator for the first time, they taught me one helluva lot--for which I have long been grateful. A few weeks before I joined, there was only one "reggie" pilot in 312. The reserves built a cage for him where he "served time" when operations were socked in, until reinforcements finally arrived.

Thanks to our allowing the Communists to play their usual game of using the promise of truce talks to buy time and rebuild their forces, the lines became stabilized during this period and the air defense system in the North increased to a point which many highly experienced combat pilots considered to have become more intense and accurate than Truk or Berlin at the height of their capability. Against that background, it seems worthy of not that all of the MAG-12 squadrons of that period could walk among any mix of combat pilots with heads high, knowing that they had carried more than their proportionate share of loads to all of the most heavily defended targets on a daily basis. While there was frequent disagreement with weight of effort, target selection and timing of strikes by 5th Air Force, who ran the air show in Korea, there was no question as to the full application of our airpower. In sharp contrast to the failure to turn the firepower of MAG-12 loose with its four A4 squadrons in VietNam where it would have done the most good. But I digress.

MAG-12 in Korea was also committed to rotating one squadron aboard the CVE (sometimes we would luck into a CVL) operating in the Yellow Sea. Each time its turn came up, old Checkerboard handled the cruise with characteristic spirit and professionalism. Again, heavily dependent upon those outstanding recalled reservists--many of whom had never flown aboard before.

Although sparsely equipped, we flew some instrument patterns that would turn the entire FAA pale. The friendly part of the peninsula was dotted with low frequency homing beacons--which were fine, if you had a "bird dog" to receive with. We had four aircraft with the ARN-6 Bendix directional receivers when I joined the squadron. The next three aircraft shot down were among those. But, we practiced some bootleg procedures which I won't even try to describe. They worked, because we had only one operational accident during my five-month squadron tour and that was not weather-related.

Everything I have said about the pilots, applied to the troops and then some. From hot and constant dust to freezing and numb hands, always without any real shelter on the line, those rascals worked day and night...and never missed a turnaround that I know of. They considered "above and beyond" as pure routine.

As in any war, maintaining your sense of humor in Korea ranked closely with knowing your weapons and how to take on a target. The Checkerboards demonstrated all three characteristics, IN ABUNDANCE! Although we envied the jets, particularly as you pulled off a hot target and immediately slowed to your 140-knot retirement, I doubt that you would find many who would retroactively trade places. It was a great bunch, a sturdy old bird and an honor to be part of that particular time and place.

Judging from the purpose of your letter--to dig up material for the wives' newsletter--it is obvious that the Checkerboard spirit is alive and well, to include the wives and that is just great. As you well know, the call to duty isn't just for the husbands.

This is about all that comes to mind without going into the history books, so I'll close with best wishes to you and your gang.

Most sincerely,

BGen Jay Hubbard USMC Ret

VMFA-312 HISTORY

The end of January 1952, VMF-312 moved from K-18 at Kangnung, Korea to Itami (city of S. Honshu Japan on Osaka Bay near Osaka). The squadron began FCLPs [Field Carrier Landing Practice] in preparation for shipboard duty. On February 11, 1952 the squadron began operations from the USS *BAIROKO* (CVE115). On February 25, while the mission capability remained the same as in the past, the unit's designation was changed to Marine Attack Squadron (VMA) 312.

In a letter from Col Stuart F. Nelson, we learned first hand about the Checkerboards during that time:

"I served with Jay (BGen Jay Hubbard) when the squadron was land-based at K-18, and later transferred to the carrier USS BAIROKO. It was our mission to neutralize the Communist effort in the Western part of North Korea near the capital, P'yongyang. This was the first combat tour for the BAIROKO, and having acquired the most colorful of the MAG squadrons, The Fabulous Checkerboards, the Navy officers were delighted, and outdid themselves in supporting VMF-312.

The cowling of our F4Us were painted in the checkerboard design; we soon surreptitiously painted a large checkerboard band under the ship's CVE 115 on the sea side of the island. This remained for sometime; this and their rather mild response almost implied tacit approval. We experienced the usual Navy-Marine rivalry exacerbated by occasional use of non Naval terminology such as requesting 'Thumbtack'(code name for the carrier) to get the boat into the wind so we could land. The hangar deck was the basement, and we would climb up the stairs to fly the planes off the roof.

All was not fun and games, however; in one 12-day period 312 lost 11 of its 24 aircraft, all but one to enemy ground fire. During that particular cruise my plane was hit at least once on every mission. There were lots of arrows out there! Perhaps that would explain the Navy's tolerance of our needling.

Every pilot was assigned an ancillary responsibility; mine was PIO officer. On a tip from a young correspondent, Bob Pierpont, I routed the press releases through COMNAVFE (the military is great with acronyms) rather than the 5th Air Force. The net result was that VMF 312, 'The Fabulous Checkerboards' received more publicity than the entire 1st Marine Air Wing. This was a great morale boost for the pilots and the troops, and the cause of some concern from the Wing. We loved it!

I was one of the 'Raggedy A--ed Reserves' Jay referred to; our relationship with the 'Reggies' was, in my opinion, highly complementary.

Upon completion of my combat tour, I returned to the U.S., was released from active duty, and joined TWA from which I recently retired. I remained in the Reserves and flew F4Us, F8Fs, T-33s, F9Fs and A4s in several VMF and VMA squadrons, but with the possible exception of an outfit I commanded, my fondest memories are with VMF 312!"

Col Stuart F. Nelson, USMCR Ret

3/20/87

Dear Jay,

Found the log book! VMF-312 landed aboard the "Bairoko CVE-115" on 11 February 1952. I shot seven more landings on the 13th (needed eight carrier landings to be legal for combat!)

My first mission was flown in F4U-4 Buno. 96973. On 7 March flying the same aircraft, the hydraulic system was shot up; with no flaps and inadequate wind across the deck, I landed at K-13. On 10 March again in good old Number 9 (96973, that is), I was fairly well shot up, but managed to get aboard. This should be an authentic, representative number to use.

If you prefer another choice, during that same cruise, I was hit while flying Buno. 91558 (twice) and Buno. 96869. One of these resulted in another trip to K-13.

During the period the "Bairoko" was home for VMF 312, 11 February to 19 April, I flew 22 different aircraft on 33 combat missions, and picked up arrows on 17 of them. I guess I wasn't much of a pilot; couldn't keep out of the way!

This is more than you asked for; just can't resist a War story.

Stu Nelson

CHAPTER 6

REDEPLOYED

THE FIRST MARINE DIVISION

Just mention the Korean War and almost immediately it evokes the memory of Marines at Pusan, Inchon, Chosin Reservoir or the Punchbowl. Marine Corps combat readiness, courage and military skills, along with those of our gallant allies, were largely responsible for the success of these early operations in 1950-1951. Not as dramatic, or as well known, are the important accomplishments of the Marines during the latter part of the Korean War.

In March 1952, the month I arrived in Korea, the 1stMarDiv redeployed from the East-Central Front to West Korea. This new sector, nearly 35 miles in length, anchored the far western end of I Corps and was one of the most critical of the entire Eighth Army line. Here the Marines blocked the enemy's goal--to penetrate all the way to Seoul, the South Korean capitol. Northwest of the Marine Main Line of Resistance, less than five miles distant, lay Panmunjom, the site of the sporadic truce negotiations.

During the move to this new Western Front position, the 1stMarDiv struggled more than 140 miles over mud-clogged, mountainous roads. The weather was miserable with generous doses of rain, snow and sleet. The move involved realignment of the United Nations Command across the entire Korean front. Some 200,000 men and their combat equipment had to be relocated as part of the overall exercise called Operation Mixmaster.

The Marines employed 5800 truckloads to move most of the Division personnel gear and supplies. Sixty-three flatbed trailers, 83 railroad cars, 14 landing ships, two transport aircraft, the vehicles of four Army truck companies, as well as hundreds of smaller jeeps and trailers, were needed to accomplish this ambitious goal. Over 50,000 tons were redeployed by the Marine Division alone.

Although Seoul was not actually within the area of Marine Corps responsibility, the capital city lay only 33 air miles to the south.

Marine Gen Selden's 1stMarDiv's forces consisted of 1364 Marine officers and 24,846 enlisted Marines, 1100 Naval personnel and 4400 Koreans from the attached 1st KMC Regiment.

The 1st KMC (Korean Marine Corps), the 5th in the center, and the 1st Marine regiments, with the 7th in reserve, composed the fighting force on the west; the 25th Canadian Infantry Brigade of the 1st Commonwealth Division occupied the east.

The Marines had moved to an area situated in the western coastal lowlands and highlands of northwestern South Korea. On the left flank the Division MLR hooked around the northwest tip of the Kimpo Peninsula, moved east across high ground overlooking the Han River, and bent around the northeast cap of the peninsula. At a point opposite the mouth of the Kangnung River, the MLR traversed the Han to the mainland, proceeding north alongside that river to its confluence with the Imjin River. Crossing over the Imjin, the line followed the high ground on the east bank of the Sami-Ch'on River for nearly two miles to where the river valley widened. There the MLR turned abruptly to the northeast and generally pursued that direction to the end of the Marine sector.

Panmunjom had been designated as the center of a circular neutral zone of 1000-yards radius. A three-mile radius around Munsan and Kaesong had also been neutralized, as well as 200 meters on either side of the Kaesong-Munsan road.

Defense of their strategic area exposed the Marines to continuous and deadly Communist probes and limited objective attacks. These bitter and costly contests for key outposts bore such notorious names as Bunker Hill, the Hook, the Nevadas (Carson, Reno, Vegas), and Boulder City. For the ground Marines, supported by 1st Marine Air Wing aircraft, the fighting dragged on until the last day of the war, 27 Jul 53.

The Korean War marked the first real test of Free World solidarity in the face of Communist force. In repulsing this attempted aggression, the United Nations, led by the United States, served notice that it would not hesitate to aid those nations whose freedom and independence were under attack.

TULK'S CHUTE FAILS TO OPEN

10 April 1952
Kangnung, Korea

Hi folks,

Today I wasn't on the schedule for a mission, but I was awakened at 0430 and told I had been selected for a search mission. I was more than happy to accept because we were to search for a very good friend of mine, a Captain Tulk, one of the few men that I had gotten to know very well (William A. Tulk, a VMF-223 buddy of mine in 1945).

We got airborne a short time later, but I had to return to the base because my generator burned out. I got another plane, took off and had no sooner joined up with the flight when my radio burned out, so I had to return to the field again. I asked for another plane and they told me I could have No. 7, so I crawled in and was just getting ready to start it when the line chief told me I couldn't have it because it was a standby plane on the JOC alert. I gave up and figured it just wasn't my day. They found the crashed plane, but Tulk had attempted a bailout too close to the deck. He didn't make it.

No mail yet, darling. However, a couple of guys got mail today with a 19th replacement draft address, so it's beginning to arrive.

I've been meaning to tell you about the dogs around here. Originally, as all things must have their beginning, there were two varieties here at the base, so they tell me. One was a husky and the other an airdale. There are pups that look like huskies and others that look like airdales. Some have airdale heads with fat husky bodies, while others have husky heads and airdale bodies. Anyway, you can tell the original breeds have only been mixed up by two generations. The dogs came here with the Korean workers. They scrounge around and get chow here on the base--fellows feed them.

Our houseboy, Chipmunk, whose real name is Kim Jin Kook, was telling me how to speak Chosan or Korean today. I picked up quite a few lines. He's no bigger than a 12 year old, but he thinks he is 17. In Korea a child is one year old at birth. His father is a laborer and his sister is a teacher in Kangnung. He can't join the Korean army until he is 20. He wants to join, too. A Korean major draws 38,000 wan a month, which is $6.33. Chipmunk gets $2.00 a week or $8.00 a month.

Bob Ferguson is getting ready to go back to the States. (He's one of my roommates). The other roommate is Bill Higgins. We're all in different squadrons. Anyway, Bob was packing *some of his gear today and Chipmunk was cleaning up the tent. Bob would come across some article of beat-up clothing and throw it at Chipmunk. His face would light up and a great big grin would come over it. Bob would say, "Presento!" Finally Bob gave him a harmonica which must have cost him $10.00 anyway, and Chipmunk's face fairly shown. I do believe it must have been the finest present he had ever received. Bob wrote a note so that he could take it home with him tonight and off the base. Chipmunk played the Korean national anthem for us and did a good job. By the way, it's a real nice tune. Bob sometimes calls him Itshiban, which means No. 1--he likes that. For a joke, he calls him 89 or some other high number and Chip laughs.*

I sure have had my troubles writing this letter. My pens aren't putting out anymore and this pencil doesn't have any point to it. I'm going to secure this operation now, honey girl. It's been nice talking to you.

Hope everything is fine at home. At least, I know in my mind you have everything you need there.

Don't worry about the daddy, honey, and tell them their daddy loves them and misses them very much. I love and miss you, dearest girl, with all my heart and soul.

Good night, dear,
Daddy

P.S. *The clear, quiet night was just broken by a terrific explosion just off the end of the strip. An F7F night fighter had to make an emergency landing and jettisoned his load of flares and bombs. Boy, this place really came alive. Everyone figured the Commies were coming in to get us. What a noise! Wow!!*

COMMUNIST TRANSPORTATION

Transportation is a sensitive chink in the enemy's armor. To protect key points on his railroads and highways and to hide his vehicles he has been forced to resort to numerous and varied devices. Both highway and rail bridges are strenuously kept in repair.

By-pass bridges are constructed, often before the permanent bridge has been bombed, so that one of the two or three alternate bridges can keep traffic moving. Sections of repaired bridges are placed in position at night when the traffic moves, then removed in the daylight to make the bridge appear inoperative. Repaired bridges are covered with patches of debris to simulate disrupted roadbed, or their sides are covered with foliage to make the underpinnings look like earth fill. Some bridges are completely camouflaged; others are built under water. Trains hide under camouflage or in tunnels by day. Special shelters have been built along the highways for trucks to hide in while they wait for darkness. Trucks disguised as small houses pull off the road into the fields when aircraft are sighted. Oxen are driven in front of a truck or a tank covered with straw to disguise it as a farm cart. Vehicle dispersal areas are provided near large supply areas and bivouacs, the type varying with the terrain. Often they are tunnels dug into hillsides. Wooded areas, orchards, and hedgerows frequently conceal rows of vehicles. In the winter canvas shelters are erected and covered with snow for effective camouflage. When all other means of moving supplies fail, the enemy has recourse again to his tremendous manpower. Thousands of coolies are loaded with packs of ammunition, gasoline, or other supplies. Like streams of ants, they crawl over the mountain where the tunnel has been blasted and ford the river beside the broken bridge. Flexible, invisible, and unending, these human supply trains constitute one of the major breaks in the wall which UN aerial interdiction has thrown up between Communist front lines and their supply areas back in Manchuria.

Credit: "Enemy Bridging Techniques," Air University Quarterly Review V, No. 4 (Winter 1952), 49-52.

VMF-323 PILOT SURVIVES WHEELS-UP BEACH LANDING/
ILLINOIS SENATOR BREWSTER PROPOSES FLIGHT PAY CUT

11 April 1952
Kangnung, Korea

Hello sweetheart,

I've sure missed my little family today. I've been thinking of each one of you and looking at your pictures and talking with you. I'd give a month's salary right now to be home for one hour with you, my precious darlings. Each one of you plays a definite role in my life and without any one of you my life is incomplete.

I was scheduled for big things today--a railcut up in Korea; then because the target got weathered in we were briefed again on a close air support, and have been standing by in the ready room in all our gear waiting to be scrambled since 1300. It is now 1700. The weather has been horrible lately, what with this cold snap we've been having lately--fog and haze. It's raining right now and I'm sitting here in my tent with the fire going and it's very comfortable. We have the regular Marine issue oil burning space heater.

Lots of mail came in today, but none for me. I know I'll feel a lot better when I do get some mail.

A Corsair pilot from VMF-323, the other fighter outfit here with us, was shot down on a close air support mission working over the Commies at the same, or nearly the same location that I was working on two days ago. They hit him with 20mm in the oil system and he just made it to a stretch of enemy held beach south of Wonsan, making a wheels-up landing on the sand. A helicopter snatched him a little while later. He's OK. He's back with us none the worse for his experience. It happened this afternoon. Those Commies really throw up the antiaircraft flak at you when you're working on them. They are fairly sharp too.

I showed Chipmunk the family picture and he thought it was real nice. I told him all your names and he said them after me. He asked me what your names meant, and I said they didn't mean anything; not like Korean or Japanese names do. He was surprised.

There go the night fighters off. Those poor devils have to go regardless of the weather, day or night. They are equipped with special devices, however, to do it, where we can't.

This Brewster from Illinois (senator) wants to cut out special pay allowances such as flight pay. The darn fool doesn't know anything about it. They ought to send him out on a combat mission over enemy held territory day in and day out--I bet he'd change his tune.

Well, dearest, until I get some mail I'll just have to carry on like I have been. It will arrive soon, though, I know.

Kiss my precious little guys good night for me, dearest, and tell them their daddy loves them and misses them very, very much.

Bye bye dearest, Your own Daddy

12 April 1952
Kangnung, Korea, 2000

Dear Marion and boys,

It's been raining and blowing ever since yesterday afternoon. No flying for me today, although I was scheduled for a railcut and briefed this morning on the target. We stood by the Group operations waiting to go at a minute's notice until Aerology got word that the target area was cloud covered, raining, and winds to 60 mph. They decided to call it off. I spent most of my day planning my escape and evasion procedure and studying my maps.

Read part of the Cornet, but have a hard time concentrating on anything with my mind so full of flying and related matters.

I think of my little family constantly, and hope and pray everything is OK with everyone. I know you're careful with the boys, honey, but whenever you entrust anyone else

Above: Dick Francisco, My workout partner, great flyer, and squadron comedian. A boxer in civilian life, as well as coach.

Above: Capt Brauning

Below: Capt "Swede" Larson

Below: Capt J. P. "Jocko" Sutherland

Capt Thomas J. Burnham, VMA-212

Capt Malcolm P. "Stretch" Evans and his flying dog, Scoshie, VMA-212

Capt Luther T. Terrell, Jr., VMA-212

Capt Terrell, from my hometown, a race driver before being called up.

Capt Patrick McGinnis, VMA-212

with them be sure to insist they look out for our little guys. They're so preoccupied with other matters they don't look where they're going, and after all, they are still only a little more than babies.

You be careful driving too, darling. You're a good driver and so am I, but it's those other darn fools you've got to be on guard against. Think way ahead when you cross blind intersections and when you are on busy streets. Keep your head on a swivel constantly. I'm not worried about your driving, dearest, honestly I'm not. I want you to go out and use the car all you want to. I'm just pointing out a few things that I needed pointing out when I was just getting started, and if I mention them once in a while to you maybe it'll stay with you, just as it did me.

Today being Saturday, they had a matinee for the Koreans who work here on the base. "Captain Fabian," with Errol Flynn was playing, and I asked Chipmunk how he liked it, and he answered, "No. 89," (No. 1 being tops). They're funny about American pictures. Sometimes they go for the darndest pictures. Bob Ferguson tries to kid him about a girlfriend and Chipmunk clams up and stalks out of the tent without a word. Bob, who handles Koreans all day and really knows them, says they're all like that. None of them will talk about their women.

Bob is still packing to go home and keeps kidding Bill Higgins and myself about our eight months remaining. He says we'll really love the summer here in Korea. He's got an ice box that he's going to give us when he leaves, which we can fill with ice if we can find any ice, and we can fill with cokes if we can find any cokes. I haven't heard a radio or seen a soft drink or had any milk (fresh milk) since arriving here. They have powdered milk available every morning for cold and sometimes hot cereal. Chow is one thing I can't find any fault with. Fresh eggs for breakfast, canned beef stew for lunch, fried chicken for supper. No complaints. Bob Ferguson being mess officer, has had to supply chow for over 2000 men and officers. He only feeds 250 officers. All the nonperishables come by LST from Pusan to Kangnung port, then by truck to here. The perishables are flown in here and placed under refrigeration. He is only required to maintain a 15-day overhead; however, he maintains a 60-day overhead because of weather and storms that might prevent ships from unloading at Pusan and the LST from coming up here to Kangnung.

No mail today--the weather kept the mail plane from coming in. Don't you give up writing, dearest, just because I'm not getting any mail. This letter will probably be a week old by the time you get it and I'll have had oodles of mail by that time. I read your one and only letter nearly every night and I believe I can repeat it word for word by now. They have just dropped the ball down at headquarters down south, because they know perfectly well where I've been sent by now.

I saw another one of those crazy looking dogs today--airdale head and husky body. The mud has been terrible since the rain started. I forgot to take my flashlight to the movie tonight and on the way back to the tent I had several narrow escapes with deep mud holes. The soil is very heavy clay and you can imagine what sort of mud that becomes. They have sand around our tents, however, which helps matters somewhat.

Tomorrow I have the early early, which means an 0430 reveille. It's only a standby in the plane, in case some Commies send something down here at us we'll be ready for them. Then in the afternoon, weather permitting, I'm going up on a close air support.

I came upon this song in the song sheet they put out here at the Marine's request. It's called "Evening in October."

EVENING IN OCTOBER

'Twas an evening in October and I was far from sober,
I was walking down the street with manly pride
When my feet began to flutter, I fell down into the gutter
And a pig came up and lay down by my side.

*And he warbled, "It's fair weather when good friends get together,"
And a lady passing by was heard to say,
"You can tell a man who boozes by the company he chooses,"
So the pig got up and slowly walked away.*

The other verses I wouldn't repeat.

I've about run down for tonight, lover, except to tell you that you're my favorite sweetheart. I look at your picture and the boys' picture every day and have my little chat with you. I hope you're not working too hard, darling, what with the outside work too. Don't worry too much about it, dear, because it isn't worth it. Don't knock yourself out, do you hear me?!! I know you, when you get going there's no stopping you. Let it go until next Nov. or Dec., then give it hell.

Bob just came bursting in and says he just got word from the Wing that he will have to stay until the end of May now, which is getting into his cutting date. He's a ground officer and they have to stay here a year. He'll have been here a year the end of May. He was married a month before leaving for Korea. His home is in Chicago and that's where his wife is. He's 6'5", a graduate with a master's degree from Princeton. Bill Higgins is a civil engineer, and graduate from Cal. Tech. They say a college degree isn't worth fighting for. I had a better job than either one of them, they think. Bill was working for Bethlehem Steel in Texas, and Bob was a salesman for a large paper concern. Bill is married and his wife is working in Texas. She put him through school. No kids. It isn't worth it--kids and family are the most important thing in the whole world. I wouldn't care if I had to live like a Jap or a Korean if only I had my precious family by my side. It's a sad state of affairs when a guy has to up and leave his family and go 8000 miles away and help some Korean farmer keep his family together.

I hope the United States will some day evaluate the situation more deeply and offer aid where aid is needed, but in the form of supplies and not the lives of her own men. Korea has plenty of capable men.

Many a night at home I used to walk out of the house and stand on our front lawn, face west and pray I'd never have to leave my home and family. Then I'd look in the window and see you sitting there on the couch, not knowing I was looking in at you. I'd say to myself, You're a lucky guy to have such a precious wife as that. You've borne me two precious boys, dearest, and they have only helped to weld our love closer. No man could be more grateful for the love of a precious family than I am for mine. Come out on the lawn sometime, honey, and face west, as I often face east, and say hello, darling--and feel that maybe you're hearing me across these thousands of miles.

Kiss the little darlings for me, and tell them their daddy loves them and misses them, and is just existing until the day he comes home to them again. Tell them I'll make it up to them for being away so long, and we'll have some wonderful times again.

Good night, dearest. I love you and miss you with all my heart and soul.

Maybe the mail will come in tomorrow.

Bye bye, Daddy

P.S. I'll bet Ricky's new tooth is all the way in by now, isn't it? Don't forget my pictures, honey--I need them. Enclose drawings and scribbling from Ricky and Randy, won't you?

REPUBLIC OF KOREA AIR FORCE (ROK)

While our squadron was still based at Kangnung K18 on the east coast of Korea, we had the privilege of sharing the base with a squadron of ROK Air Force pilots. (When I started writing this manuscript I wrote to the ROK Air Force Headquarters in Seoul, Korea, requesting some background information to put into my story, but unfortunately I never heard anything from them.)

I referred to the ROK's only once, in my 2 Apr 1952 letter to Marion, but have thought about them and our discussions on numerous occasions since. I had been on several missions with them where our squadron and the ROK's hit the same target area; they were heard to converse both in English with their ground controller, and, among themselves, in Korean. We had a minor complaint, that they would hog the VHF channels with their unnecessary chatter, making it difficult for other flights to carry out their necessary radio communications. I regret that I did not keep a diary so I would have been able to retain some of their names. As it is, the only Korean names I did retain were Kim Il Sung, the Communist leader of North Korea, Dr. Syngman Rhee, the leader of South Korea (Republic of Korea), and my house boy, Kim Jin Kook, whom we called Chipmunk because he resembled that little animal.

We weren't quartered together with the ROK pilots, but we shared a common mess, and we purposely tried to sit at their table in order to become better acquainted. They flew the North American F-51D model Mustangs with the 1200 hp liquid cooled Merlin inline engines, which emitted their characteristic whine.

The ROK Air Force operated hundreds of F-51Ds (formerly P-51) throughout Korea, and accounted for the largest number of Mustangs lost. The U.S. Air Force flew F-51s in the 67th Fighter-Bomber Squadron, 18th F/B Wing at Wonju, Korea in September 1952 when I was there. These old WWII fighters were still deadly in their ground support role.

AN UNBELIEVABLE SCENARIO

Sitting there in that little Quonset mess hall in far off Korea, Colonel Kim and I put our heads together one night and realized something which blew our minds. My former allies had been China and Russia, to whom we had supplied P-51 Mustangs during WWII. My former enemy, Japan, had occupied Korea for many years and had inducted many of their finest young men into their armed forces. Colonel Kim had been one of those Koreans who'd received some of the finest pilot training Japan was able to give. He had flown Japanese Zeros from Kyushu against U.S. Navy, Air Force and Marine Corsairs during the war, and counted a number of Corsairs among his total of 12 kills. Now we two were sitting next to each other, friends and allies and fellow fighter pilots fighting my former allies, and flying with our former enemy--only seven short years having elapsed. Incredible!! Ah, the ironies of war!

Colonel Kim spoke English fluently and we discussed our strange fellowship openly. I admit I had a weird feeling about the fact that the Colonel had killed 12 of my countrymen, and I suspect he felt the same about me and my fellow squadron mates. He spoke of the many top Japanese aces who'd flown during the late unpleasantness (some of whom I recalled while doing research for my book), including Nishizama, Ota, Sasai and NAP 1/c Shoichi Sugita, who claimed 124 air kills himself. Other aces we discussed were Lt S/G Naoshi Kanno, with 52 victories, and Muto, with 35 victories. According to Kim, when Lt(jg) Teimei Akamatsu had been drinking sake he claimed 300 victories, but 50 appears closer to the real facts. Saburo Sakai, Japan's greatest fighter pilot to survive the war, had 64 aerial kills to his credit in over 200 aerial dogfights. Japanese Navy ace Shoji Matsumara survived the war to go on to fly F-86 Sabrejets as part of Japan's Air Defense Force years later, but of course not in Korea. He could claim six Navy Hellcats and Corsairs in his bag. I say again, incredible!

(In March 1979 the company where I worked, Garrett Turbine Engine Co., of Phoenix, Arizona, now renamed Allied Signal Co., was producing the gas turbine starting equipment on board the McDonald Douglas F-15 Eagle fighter. A contingent of Japanese engineers from Mitsubishi visited our plant off and on for several months studying our hardware, since they were building the F-15 in Japan for their Air Defense Force. Iwo Jima would become the training base for their F-15 fighters! Isn't it a full-circle world we're living in?)

BEWARE OF THE SWORD HIDDEN BEHIND A SMILE

During the short time I served in Korea I carried on long conversations with my friendly little hut boy, Kim Jin Kook, "Chipmunk." Also a good source of interesting information was 1stLt Bob Ferguson of MABS-12, who worked with dozens of Koreans there on our base at K18 Kangnung handling all of the food services. Bob was visited frequently by the local Catholic priests, usually Father Burke, who told us about his observations of the people with whom he was associated in his church. He loved them all. I developed most of my knowledge and opinions about Korea through these contacts.

Korea, roughly the size of Utah, is a peninsula hanging off the northeastern coast of China and facing the Japanese islands across the Sea of Japan. The climate is somewhat like our middle Atlantic states, but the rains are heaviest in July.

At the outbreak of the Korean War 20 million people lived south of the 38th Parallel and 10 million north of it. To me, they resembled the Chinese, except they appeared less bowlegged; more graceful than the Japanese and very rugged--a five and a half foot male Korean porter could carry 400 pounds!

Koreans practiced several religions; mainly Christianity, Buddhism, Confucianism and Animism. At that time, some 600,000 had been converted to Christianity, more than any other Oriental country.

White, the color of mourning, had been adopted by the older Korean gentlemen. According to legend, originally they had mourned members of the royal family; but gradually the white apparel worn by the elders began to signify age and wisdom, commanding respect. Married men wore horsehair hats and bachelors went hatless.

Historical records go back before Christ. Koreans claim to have invented the spinning wheel in 1376, moveable type in 1392 and surveying instruments in 1467. They built the suspension bridge 300 years before the Brooklyn Bridge.

Korea had been invaded by Mongols and Manchus among others. They had no Independence Day, but instead observed National Humiliation Day, recalling the sorrow of their subjugation by the Japanese in 1910. Too weak to throw their conquerors out and too stubborn to be assimilated, they had been thoroughly exploited, but their headstrong patriotism kept alive their reputation as "the Irish of the Orient."

During the time I was there the natives' simple diet consisted mainly of rice, fish and raw sea slugs. They were very fond of music and, strangely, one of the two Korean national anthems was sung to the tune of "Auld Lang Syne."

The language of the Korean people, uniquely their own, consisted of a 25 letter alphabet. Their philosophy contained many fine proverbs, mostly with a sad or apprehensive cast, such as, "Beware of a sword hidden behind a smile," "The flower that blooms in the morning is withered by noon," "A dead premier is worth less than a live dog" and, "Pinch yourself and you will know the pain when another feels pinched."

Most of us GIs would have agreed with the general observation that Korea was indeed a strange land with a bracing climate and depressing proverbs and needed defending to give it a fresh start.

13 April 1952
Easter Sunday
Kangnung, Korea

Dearest little family,
It's raining as per usual, and the mud is over my boondockers. The rain clouds are hanging very low and there isn't any flying being done at all.
What I am about to tell you is top secret, *so don't even hint of it to anyone, not even to your folks, Ricky, or anyone, because it affects the safety of many men. Our Air Group is in the process of moving to another field, which is more operational than this one here at K18 Kangnung. We're moving to the west coast to a place called Tunp'o ri. It is about 30 miles south of Seoul and 20 miles south of Suwon (or Suigen). We are packing up everything; tents, mess hall, squadron gear etc. and we hope to be over there and to have completely evacuated this*

base by next Sunday, 20 April. It's a mammoth job and everyone is pitching in. If the weather clears we will resume our missions just as though nothing has happened, so since this spell of bad weather, even though it has brought the mud (and it's very rough to get anything done with the mud everywhere), we're taking advantage of the situation and packing gear. You have no idea how much gear a fighter squadron of 25 planes has to carry!

I was offered squadron flight officer, but I turned it down because I don't want to get involved in operations and scheduling work. Everyone is always sore at an operations officer because they think he's showing partiality in his assignments, or something like that. It's a very important assignment because you practically run the squadron, along with all your missions besides.

Tunp'o ri is already occupied by the Air Force, and it is said that it will be a much nicer base all the way around. Remember, not a word. I'll keep you posted after we get squared away. No mail as yet.

This morning I had the early early--up at 0430, down to the squadron, stood by to man the plane, in case of an attack, but they would have needed radar to cut through this overcast. After 0800 I worked around the squadron packing gear.

Afternoon meal consisted of ham, sweet potatoes, etc.

I went to church and heard all about the Easter story. There were 200 men there, at least, many of them standing. A mixed choir of Korean men and women from the Kangnung Methodist church were there to sing for us. They were _very_ good. The women look so much alike to me--you'd swear they were all sisters. The men's looks vary quite a bit. They are all very small people. I asked Chipmunk today if he belonged to any church and he said no. They have a Catholic church in Kangnung also.

Kangnung wasn't damaged in this war, so Bob Ferguson tells me. I've flown over it and it's not much. Seoul, from the air, is terrific, though--it's huge. You can see by your map how the inland water way comes into town. Well, there are thousands of small boats on that water way, and the river that feeds it with fresh water is quite wide and swift. Fifty miles inland there is a huge hydro-electric dam harnessing that river. Most of the buildings appear to be straw roofed or else gave me that impression. We were at 8000', but the visibility was 30 or 40 miles. There are two huge Air Force bases in and around Seoul and I could see the aircraft (jets) taking off. I switched to their tower frequency for just a minute to hear the traffic clearance going on. It was busier than Los Angeles International.

I've been feeling fine, dearest. Stomach is 100 percent and my cold is getting better too. I'm disgustingly healthy this trip. At least the weather has come to my aid in holding the number of my missions down, but you know how I am when the weather is like this. The boys up on the front get it, weather or not.

I sure miss my radio programs. I had become almost a slave to the new programs. I swear the only news we get here is two and three days old from the Stars and Stripes. We get it after it's dead and buried.

Took in the cinema tonight, "Submarine Patrol,"--fair. Had steak for dinner. For a place as muddy and crummy and filthy as this, it's a wonder they can put out such good clean chow, but it's been very good--not always served as you might like it, but good anyway. Everyone gripes about everything around here except the chow.

There's one thing about the rain in Korea, and that's that it hits the Commies too, and slows up their supply trucks because their roads aren't better than ours, and ours can hardly be considered roads at all.

I haven't been off the base as yet, except to fly off. They say Kangnung isn't worth seeing, and I'm going to go along with them on that because nothing I've seen in Korea has done anything for me.

Bill Higgins loaned me an extra pen he had but it's lousy. I'd rather use a pencil.

They have me up for two close air support missions tomorrow, one at 1000 and the other at 1500. If the weather clears I'll get them, and from the looks of things tonight it will clear. The stars can be seen through the broken cloud layer.

Do you and Nanna and Trooper still get together on your coffee and donut sprees in the morning? I can see you all now gathered around the table confabbing about this and that. I *think of you all constantly and of what good times we've had in the past and the good times we'll have again when I come home to you, dear.*

The old cot and pad I've got get pretty hard. The sleeping bag is sort of hard to roll over in and sometimes at night I get all tangled up. Feels like a straight jacket. One night after I got here I had a nightmare--I dreamed I ditched my plane in the water and I was in the plane going down, and all the time I was tangled up with my sleeping bag, trying to find the face opening.

The following are the words to the Korean national song:

> Ahredong, ahredong, ahraw de yo
> Ahredong Co Gay Ro Noma abuda
> Na lul body go cawseenoun nemoun
> Mo kaw yo, paal puong nahnda
> Semneda.

It is called "Ahredong." Chipmunk wrote the words out for me and has sung the song a couple of times. He plays it on the harmonica Bob gave him as a "presento" because he was his "Itshiban"--No. 1 boy. He's so small he seems like a boy of 10 or 12. I can hardly believe he's 17. He's a real nice little guy. He calls me Captain Pete. Hope Randy boy has kept relatively quiet, altho' I know it will be impossible to regulate his actions. Miss you all very much, lost without you.

Your own, Daddy

THE MAJOR ISSUE THAT PROLONGED THE WAR

Since the battlefield could not be separated from the political scene, the Communists were bound to make great capital on the issue of screening the Chinese and North Korean prisoners that the UN held in POW camps, such as on Koje-do, an island off South Korea. They were obviously embarrassed when the UN POW screening showed that of the 135,000 captures, only fifty percent of the 70,000 POWs and civilian internees screened would voluntarily return to Red China or North Korea. While this was undoubtedly the greatest propaganda blow against world Communism, it brought nothing but pure misery to the UN Command, who wanted nothing but to end this senseless killing and go back home. The talks finally recessed in October 1952 over this issue, and wouldn't resume again until the following year, after I was home and once again trying to pick up the loose ends of my civilian life.

Monday, 14 April 1952
Kangnung, Korea

Hi precious little family,
How is everyone today? Fine, I hope.
The weather has kept us down again today. However, we've kept busy packing gear--squadron gear, because our own personal gear will only take 30 minutes. Tomorrow the weather should clear because tonight I saw a couple of holes up there in the sky, but that's not a very good sign either because last night was almost completely clear and today was lousy.
Still no mail, although some of the boys are getting it. I honestly don't understand what it's all about. They surely know my new address at the Wing by now. I hope my letters are getting through to you, honey.
They have closed up the club as of last night. They gave away free drinks and most of the guys got their fill. I went over to check the schedule and sat by the wood fireplace for 30 minutes and decided I preferred the quiet of my tent. I haven't had a drop of anything or a smoke since leaving the U.S., and what's more, I'm not going to. The club is made of logs with

beamed (cross beamed) ceiling, with a huge fireplace on either end. The boys shoot craps till all hours of the night.

I'm glad the club is far enough away from the tents so we can't hear them or nobody could get any sleep. Some guys would be absolutely lost without a club. That's all they're talking about regarding our move--what about the club over there? They can have it as far as I'm concerned. I guess I've changed quite a bit. I used to enjoy going over to the club last war, but now I wouldn't walk across the street to go to it, if it weren't for taking a look at the schedule and singing a few songs and seeing a few friends.

Tomorrow I'm scheduled for an 0630 brief, 0730 takeoff, for a close air support hop. Then in the afternoon I'm scheduled for a JOC alert at 1400. Reveille will go at around 0530 for me.

The plane brought 13 "Stars and Stripes" in, so I got the news only 24 hours after it happened.

I started a book on Barnum the Great--he's the "there's a sucker born every minute" guy. It's very good and it's given me lots of laughs. I can't think of anything but coming home, darling. Every time I begin thinking of something else, somehow or other home and you and the kids get into my thoughts and I can hardly think of anything but that. I've been sitting here trying to think of something new to tell you, but my life is so simple lately that it is very difficult. Besides, like I said, the only thing I want to think or talk about anyway is home and my precious little family that I love and miss so very much.

Kiss the little boys for me, honey, and tell them their daddy adores them and misses them.

Night, Daddy

I'VE BEEN WORKING ON THE RAILCUTS
(I've Been Working on the Railroad)

*I've been working on the railcuts
Up by Sinanju
With all the MIGs and all the ack-ack,
I hope they don't get you.
Can't you hear the skipper saying,
"One more pass, then home."
Can't you hear the others shouting,
"You do and you go alone!"*
    CHORUS:
    Skipper take us home, Skipper take us home,
    Take us back to K18.
    Skipper take us home, Skipper take us home,
    Take us back to K18.

*Back at the bar they're drinking,
They're drinking them right up,
But you can't blame those fly boys
'Cause they've been all shook up,
And they're singing - - -*
    CHORUS:

*Take me back to Laguna,
The Laguna girls we know
Would like to have us back there
And help us spend our dough.*

Kangnung, Korea
Tuesday 1430
15 April 1952

Hi precious family,
Today has been a windy, stormy day. Winds in gusts up to 60 mph have almost taken our tent and every other tent clear down. No rain with it. Our tent has been flapping in the breeze and I've tightened the tent ropes up about three times to keep it taut. Nothing has been flying except transports, and they sometimes look as though they are hardly going to make it into the field, the wind is so strong.

I've taken advantage of the flying lull, and have scribbled off notes to the Dakes, Perrys, Boles, Ritchies, and G.W. Parker. I asked G.W. to go over to the Wing Post Office for me and see if I had any mail over there. <u>Still no mail!</u> I'm going nuts not hearing from anyone. I'd give a hundred dollars for a letter from you right now, darling. By the time you get this, though, I'll probably have received all of it.

During the height of the storm Chipmunk and I went out and crawled on top of the tent to secure a piece of canvas near the top opening which had blown loose, and the cold wind was really streaming in the tent. Chipmunk is very clever, and between the two of us we managed to secure it. I told him he was Itshiban No. 1, and he says, "No, Kim 89, Captain Pete Itshiban for holding Kim." I asked him to give me his address and also to write my name in Korean for me:

캅 (CAP) 븓 (TAN) 피로ㄸ (Peterson)

His address is 449 Chung Yang, Kangnung, Korea. However, they don't have any mail service over here, so he doesn't think he'd get a letter if I sent him one.

The chow has been good. The mud is still bad.

I'm writing with the new ball point insert I bought at El Toro. It was too small for the pen, so I jammed paper up in there and it's OK now. Those pencil letters were getting to me, as I know they must have been getting you. Better a pencil letter than no letter at all, though, eh darling?

The wind has subsided somewhat, thank goodness. I was afraid we would honest to goodness blow away.

How are Ricky's love affairs coming along? Is he still our little Casanova? Has he asked for any more special dress up clothes lately? I sure thought he was cute when he asked for and got his white shirt and tie. I don't think he's crazy about the color of that tie. Why don't you get him another one, darling. Has either one of the boys come up with any cute sayings? Have you had them draw anything for me?

I took a couple of pictures of Chipmunk, Bill Higgins and Bob Ferguson today. I only have one more left; then I'll be ready for another roll. When I get to Itami I'll have it developed and send them home to you air mail. Everything is so crummy and muddy and beat up around here, I don't feel like wasting a roll, but I did anyway because I thought you might get a kick out of seeing it.

Forgive the incongruity of my letters, but I have a tough time thinking of anything to say.

Bob Barbours told me today that the PX run by the Navy in Akuska, which is near Hanada, Tokyo, Japan, has a wonderful assortment of things (Japanese) to buy. The trouble with buying things on the open market is that you never can be sure you're not being taken for a ride as to quality and price. The PX knows the Japanese market and probably gets it at a rakeoff, buying in quantity. Tokyo is a long way off though from Itami, so I don't know if I'll make it or not. If you'd like anything special, honey, name it and I'll shop around when I get over there and see what I can find.

Say goodnight to the little darlings for me. I love you, darling.

Daddy

WORKING WITH THE COMMONWEALTH BRIGADE

We would be working with an airborne air controller, or forward ground controller who spoke English, usually an American, except of course when we were over the Commonwealth 25th Brigade on the 1stMarDiv's right flank; and then it was an Englishman with a heavy English accent or a Canadian.

The main line of resistance in 1952 consisted of 16 divisions. Those manning the front were 11 divisions of South Koreans, three U.S. Army, one U.S. Marine Corps and one British Commonwealth division. Some ROK forces were scattered within the U.S. divisions and on the Marines' left flank we had a South Korean Marine regiment which I helped train. With a total strength of 768,000 men in the Eighth and ROK armies at the end of 1952, we faced nearly a million Communists--seven Chinese armies and a North Korean corps of 531,000 troops in reserve. A formidable foe.

BOB BARBOUR MAKES IT HOME WITH HIS DAMAGED PLANE

Kangnung, Korea
16 April 1952
2000

Hi precious family,

Joyous day, I got your letter of the 8th of April (No. 15). Gosh, it was swell hearing from my little family. I've read it over about three times, and I'll bet I read it again before I hit the basket tonight. Oh, I guess I haven't told you the new term for bed--well, it's "basket" now. Yeah, "sack" and "rack" are obsolete over here, so you'd better bring Ricky up to date.

This is a secret, so don't mention it. Yesterday, down at the Wing, where they assemble the mail and other items of gear to be flown up here to us, they had a big fire. Altogether, ten sacks of mail ready to come up here to our MAG were destroyed in the fire. The letter I received this afternoon must have come in down there after the fire. Maybe all the other letters you have written to me were destroyed, or maybe they hadn't got around to it yet and I still may get them. At any rate, honey, when you receive this letter assume all the others were destroyed and think back between March 26th and April 7th and tell me all the highlights even though I may get the rest of the mail at a later time if it wasn't destroyed.

Good girl--Nanna taking Mrs. Griffin up on that TV singing deal. I'd sure like to see her. Tell her I'm proud of her and I know she'd make good.

Glad you and Peg had an evening out. That's the picture she had spoken to me about wanting to see just before I left.

How about cutting out the picture in the AiReporter of me. I'd like to see it. I'll send it back. So you'd go for the old man even now, eh?

I can see Ricky and Randy gathered around you while you read my letters. Bless Ricky's little heart--he loves his daddy, doesn't he? So does Randy, but he's still a little young to know what's going on.

Nice to know you're enjoying your new automatic washer and not knocking yourself out on the wash any more.

The tentmates enjoyed the clipping of the F-86.

Today the weather cleared for us and I went up on a close air support mission supporting the 8th ROK Corps. For almost a week now the Commies have had freedom from air attack on their front line positions, but today we caught them with their trenches down and had a field day. We were directed onto the target by an airborne controller who gave us a hot spot. It was a command post and had four deeply entrenched bunkers with mortar and machine gun positions and a communication network.

The flight was led by Captain Bob Barbour. I was on his wing and Lieutenant Bill Bizzell made the third. Our fourth man had to return to base due to engine trouble. We hit them with rockets and 20 mm strafing first, then cut loose with our two 1000-lb napalms each on the command post. There were five runs apiece, and through heavy ground fire we destroyed everything. The observation plane flew down after we finished and counted 16 dead and gave us credit for destroying the command post--100 percent effectiveness. Bob Barbour was hit in the tail, but got home OK.

This afternoon I ate lunch at 1400 because of the morning mission getting back late, and right after that I took a plane up on an hour's test hop. Secured at 1700, ate and took in the 1800 movie, "Barefoot Postman." We saw it at El Centro, remember? When I got back to the tent your letter was on my bed. Hugh Holland had picked it up for me at the Squadron. It sure did pick me up because I just knew every one of your letters must have gone up in the fire.

Tomorrow I'm squadron duty officer, which means a big day for me. However, I don't have to get shot at, so that's some help. Don't pass this on--Secret. During the move across Korea our squadron and group trucks are carrying everything not classified as No. 1 priority (which will be flown across). The trip takes about 12 hours to do--a little over 200 miles. Those who have gone look like negroes when they come back. Honestly, they are just black; the only thing white is their eyes. It's a miserable trip and the guys are doing a good job. They even get shot at by Communist guerrillas on the way. Most of the roads are one way and 90 percent of it is mountainous. Some of the trucks are huge semis, which must stick out over the roads at some of the mountain switchbacks. They are doing a thankless job and deserve a lot of credit.

They've closed the officers' mess and we're eating with the enlisted men now, for the time being. The chow is every bit as good.

Tell Ricky to study hard in school because I want him to be Itshiban in his class. Tell him he's my No. 1 boysan. Everything in Korean ends in SAN--Mamasan, Papasan, Josan (means sister, girl or baby).

Did you ever wonder what flies look like in other countries? Well, I have wondered about it and they are just exactly like the ones back home. They have a mess of huge black crows around here. I've had duels with them in the air when I've been flying but haven't collided with one as yet.

Glad you have managed your housework so that you can find time to get out in the garden. How are my poppies coming along?

We had strong gusts of wind today and about 15 or 20 knots crosswind. It was rough landing and I never came so close to ground looping in my life as I did today. The Lord must have had his arm around me this morning--if not all day. The more I fly the Corsair the less I feel I know about it.

Miss you something terrible, darling. Kiss my darling little boys for me and tuck them into beddie bye and tell them their daddy loves them and says a little prayer for each one of you every night.

Your own Daddy

HILLS OF KOREA

Like so many of the hills in Korea for which so many men had died, the one that stood out from the air the best was the Punchbowl. Twenty-five miles from the east coast and the same distance north of the town of Inje, formed the zone boundary between the U.S. X Corps and the ROK I Corps. The rim, left over from an old volcano, rose knife-sharp from the ground several hundred feet from the crater floor, its sides thickly wooded. Although we spilled an incredible amount of blood there, we never gave it up because it had such a commanding view and prevented surprise attack from the enemy. Flying numerous close air support missions in support of our troops on the Punchbowl, I know every feature of its craggy slopes and every zig-zag of its extensive trench system. It was from this position that the First Marine Division moved out during their big march to the west in March '52, with the ROK 8th Division moving in to fill the gap. Most of my close air support missions in that area were with the ROK 8th. We had to come to their rescue on many occasions.

As the battle lines began to consolidate and the peace talks wore on, the South Korean ROK forces began to take over more and more of the battle line. Unlike the earlier ill-trained and ill-equipped ROK forces in 1950 and 1951, they had developed into a real fighting force and gave up very little ground to the enemy. The battle line looked for all the world like the trench warfare we had seen in the old WWI movies; and the artillery rounds fired by the enemy were unbelievable. The UN Command reported for one day that more than 45,000 rounds fell on our positions across the 8th Army front, and a few weeks later they recorded the all-time record of 93,000 rounds on UN lines in one day.

17 April 1952
Kangnung, Korea

Dearest Marion and boys,

I hit the jackpot today. I received five letters all at one time--4th, 5th, 6th, 9th and 11th of April and the AiReporter. I was so excited about it I didn't know which one to open first. I read every word time and again, and I'll read them all over again many times. Your visit to Mother was interesting to me in as much as you drove over. I'm proud of you, honey.

Gosh, darling, you really knocked yourself out on the polishing job on the Chevy. You didn't have to go all the way, dear. Golly, I've only used the Mac's Cleaner on the car, once myself. I'll bet it's a gleaming beauty.

Glad Lady dog is coming around to seeing things our way and letting you comb her.

So Randy is coming into his own, is he? I've always known he'd be a little terror and he's shown he was going to be determined ever since he was born. I thought that was sweet where you told me Randy says, "Daddy overseas," and where Ricky says a prayer for me. I miss you all so very much, dearest. The little "Ike" jacket must look cute on Ricky. He wears everything so well and he's getting to be a regular little man.

I enjoyed the AiReporter. I just asked you yesterday to send it. You're going to have to disregard a lot of my requests because of time delay.

I'll be only too happy to get home and take over my old duties and let you live like a queen, honey, that's my intent as long as I'm still King. You forgot I was still home when you bought Ricky the U.S jigsaw puzzle. I'm glad he's on the ball and is getting to know where all the states are located. Explain to him about the difference between California and Korea by locating the time disc on the tip of his globe. I believe there is 8 1/2 or 9 hours difference. Tell Ricky I felt awfully bad about him saying those bad things to you when you wanted him to take his nap the other day. Don't ever let me hear of you doing that again, Ricky. Don't forget, everything Mama has you do is for your own good.

Today we had a near-hurricane, with gusts up to 75 mph. All planes were grounded and every man was busy tying down gear and planes, and securing our tents against the terrific blow. It rained for an hour--the first rain in several days, but within an hour after the rain the dust was flying, and if you stepped outside you'd be sand blasted and nearly blinded. It was awful. Many tents and rickety buildings got torn down. This is the most miserable place on the face of the earth. It's little wonder the mountains are nearly bald and the natives are all weather beaten by the time they reach 20. They are small but they have hardened faces, due to the rough elements of nature I guess. My hands look all dried up from the wind.

During a slight lull in the blow the mail plane from K3, 100 miles south of us, came up with the mail. Thank God, I don't know what I would have done if the mail had been destroyed in the fire. There are still a number of outstanding letters, though, and some of them still may have been lost--we'll see.

My letters won't be as interesting as they were when I was traveling or when I first got here because the newness has worn off now and some of the things I see and hear I wouldn't mention to you. We've never had a blow at Manhattan Beach as we've had today. The wind is still blowing strong and it's 1930 PM. It has hardly let up for a minute today. Even the mail plane hit winds of 104 mph at 7000' coming up from the Wing (K3). Fortunately it was parallel of the runway (we have only one runway) when he arrived today, and at that it was blowing around 35 mph on the deck when he got here.

Our planes are filthy. The test hop I had yesterday afternoon was to check a new engine they had installed in the plane a couple of days ago at Itami, Japan. The plane and engine looked like it had a thousand hours on it. It was oily, dirty, dusty and just as crummy as any of the others.

Oh, what I wouldn't give for a nice warm bath and then to get into one of my nice soft flannel shirts with my slacks and my brown woven shoes, and to spend this evening with my very own precious little family that I love and miss with all my heart. A trip across the ocean, and then to be dumped off at a hole like this certainly drives home to a person the plush easy life we've all grown accustomed to enjoying. Even the most prosperous Korean family couldn't come up to one of our poorest class in the U.S. None of them have any cars and their clothes are all tattered and torn with patchwork all over them. They wear them rain or shine, mud or what else.

Bob Ferguson was invited to the Catholic missionary's home in Kangnung tonight for dinner. Father Nelican and Father Burke, both from the Irish Catholic Mission, have been here in Korea 19 years. Both were prisoners of the Japanese and both were forced to come south when the Communists came down. The Communists killed many of the Catholic priests and sisters. Bob put on his clean khaki shirt and pants he'd been saving for some special occasion and looked quite respectable, almost stateside in appearance. The fathers have servants and teachers, and run an orphanage besides the church. Bob says he's been there before and their cook is out of this world (not looks, but food). He's the mess officer, you know, so it's my idea they have him over every once in a while to fill their larder, although this is his first (and will be his last visit) since April 1st when we got here.

The Korean laborers all have a lost look about them, not knowing what's to become of them now that we're leaving here. Guess they'll all go back to the city of Kangnung and eke out an existence.

Bob Ferguson, the mess officer, had a Korean mess cook who adopted a seven or eight year old Korean boy who was helping him in the kitchen. Bob sent them over to our new base on a plane. They were very happy until they had to separate them due to staggering the weight in loading one of the planes. The foster father, a man of only about 30 years, went on the first transport, and the boy, who didn't speak any English, thought he was being left behind. He cried for a solid hour, tears bigger than a crocodile's coming down his face. Finally the other plane came and they loaded him on. It was all too much for the little guy. He was completely bewildered. They'll be together, as before, at our new base.

Knocked off for the movie, "Too Young to Kiss," with Van Johnson. It was real cute. You know, darling, I honestly believe I'll stop going to movies because when I'm watching them I get taken back to the States and throw myself into the story. Then when it's over and I step out into the black night and realize I'm over here in Korea and not back home in the States it's an awful letdown. Then I go over and check the flight schedule for the next day and see I'm up for a railcut or close air support, and I realize again it's war and I have a job to do.

I just read the letters all over again and I had to laugh at the part where you had to spank Randy three times in one evening. It's not funny, I know, and he's not to get away with it, but remember, darling, take it easy on account of his bulges, won't you?

Since when has Ricky been sleeping on the porch? Maybe you mentioned it in a letter I haven't received. I thought you were going to sleep on the porch and save washing all those double sheets. What's with you deciding to send Ricky to school for the Easter party? Has he been home sick, or something? I'll bet Randy is awfully cute on his little wagon and with his new fuzzy bunny. I'd give anything to see him zipping down the driveway, and to see Ricky riding his tryke like sixty.

Don't worry about phoning Mom. I've written her at least once a week and will continue to do so.

Felix the cat must have scared Troop in the car the other night like Lady scared me when I was under the house fixing the heater in the dark, and she licked my face.

Ricky will have to be shown how to use his compass. Tell him it points to the magnetic north pole, which is a magnetized field of metal southwest of the true North Pole. The needle of the compass is attracted to the magnetic pole and navigators and pilots have to make corrections to compensate for this error. In Manhattan Beach the error is about 6° East. So just swing to the left 6°, or west, and you'll be pointing toward the North Pole. Santa Claus lives there, you know, Ricky, and when he comes down to Manhattan Beach he uses a compass too, only he uses the back side of the needle instead of the pointer. Daddy uses his compass nearly every time he flies. I have a magnetic compass, an electric compass, and a gyro-compass to help me navigate. I use all of them together to get my answers.

I guess you'll just have to wait until the daddy gets home before you can get back into the pie and cake baking routine again. Don't lose your touch, though, dear.

Glad to hear Bem has a chance to settle his estate for cash. Maybe he won't have to go to work right away now. Hope he sells his trailer to the folks that are renting it. Are they on his property?

Troop's really wasting away to a shadow, isn't he? I've kept about the same--can't tell, though, no scales.

No radio news as yet.

I really have enjoyed the letters today, honey.

Love, Daddy

During our daily flight briefings our squadron intelligence officer would remind us pilots of the camouflage and dispersal means the Communists were having to take in North Korea. According to *Air University Quarterly Review* (Spring 1953), numerous devices were utilized in attempting to deceive aerial offensive campaigns:

Communists go to extremes in dispersing and hiding supplies. In every kind of terrain, reconnaissance photographs reveal scattered rows of trenches filled with supplies and covered. Cellars of bombed houses are stocked and roofed over. Villages are evacuated and the houses used for storage. Ruins offer good cover for odd-shaped piles of supplies. Drainage ditches along roads become huge trenches filled with camouflaged supplies. In open fields irregular stacks of supplies resemble boulders from the air. Regular stacks covered with rice straw take on the normal pattern of the farmer's gathered crop. In wooded areas, boxes or crates are scattered under the trees and in the underbrush, along the edges of orchards, and in hedgerows. In the mountains bombed-out railroad tunnels are used for storage. Caves are dug in hillsides, or roads running through deep cuts are roofed over. Only a profligate use of manpower provides this radical dislocation of supply centers. Its military disadvantages are enormous, underscoring the plight of a land force without air protection in the face of a well-organized, persistent aerial offensive.

MY ENGINE QUITS COLD OVER ENEMY TERRITORY/ FATHER BURKE'S WHISKEY BREATH

18 April 1952
Friday afternoon, 1500
Kangnung, Korea

Precious family,

I just now came down from a close air support hop, and the good Lord must have had both arms around me. We flew north up the coast (east coast) to a point 20 miles below Wonsan. We cut in about 10 miles and contacted our air controller. He gave us our target which was a command post and bunkers in a hidden valley--very inaccessible for our artillery. However, they had been pumping mortars into the area but couldn't pinpoint it.

We went over, analyzed the situation, located it and had to make very steep dives and rapid pullouts, due to the very high mountains surrounding the position. We had to take our planes down to as low as the water tank across from our house (in Manhattan Beach) in order to spot it and release our napalms. We cleaned them out for fair, the whole outfit. There were four of us on the hop--Feliton, McGinnis, Griffins and I. We all carried two 1000-lb napalms apiece and eight 5" hi-velocity rockets each, with 800 rounds of 20 mm cannon.

You get so keyed up on those hops when you're being directed and you have to dive and climb and put the old nose down toward the target, when you know full well they are throwing everything but the kitchen sink at you--they want to hit you just as bad as you're trying to hit them. The wind was as high as 45 kts in the area where we were working and the plane would buffet and jump around something crazy. We made about five runs on the target each, and on one of my runs I strafed up the side of a mountain on my pullout and got a whole column of the enemy with my 20's. I got one direct hit with my napalm and eight direct hits with my rockets.

On my last pass (the 5th) I dove from 8000' to the deck and at a very steep angle (60°) I had plenty of airspeed, which was a good thing because after I pulled up and was regaining my altitude to rejoin the division MY MOTOR QUIT COLD! I was over enemy territory and I didn't have a prayer left in me. As the plane continued to climb, and I used all of my airspeed I had built up in my dive, it carried me up to about 6000'; then I leveled off and put it into a shallow glide, using my airspeed very cautiously because my altitude and airspeed were the only things that would get me over to the friendly side of the battle line. Mountains everywhere, all around me, and no place to set it down. I called to my flight leader, "26 - 1 leader from 26 - 4, I'm going in with my plane. I've lost my engine. I'm trying to make friendly lines. Out."

The other three planes had made their runs before me and had long since climbed to 8000' and were headed south away from me at an ever increasing speed. I didn't know what I was going to do. Normally I'd have jumped, only I had to hold off because I wanted to make the friendlies if I could. Just when I figured all was lost and my life passed before me in a flash, my engine started running just as sweet as you please with nothing more than an occasional cough. I figured this was too good to last so I watched it very closely and nursed it back over the friendly positions, then out to sea, where I jettisoned a hung napalm bomb by manual release because my electrical circuit hadn't worked. Held my 8000' until I reached home base and corkscrewed down over it, maintaining my altitude in the event it conked on me again I could glide into a landing. To say I was shook is putting it mildly. I had to come back and lie down for a few minutes after that one. The whole trouble had been water in the fuel, and possibly a dirty carburetor.

After I came back down I went over to the officers' head for a minute and a field officer from one of the antiaircraft companies was taking a shower. All of a sudden I heard a thud that sounded like a body falling and then I heard a gasping sound. I got up from the can and ran into the shower section, where this guy, bare as a newborn baby, lay on his side gasping with his hands and legs twitching like a last dying quiver. I felt his pulse and couldn't find any. His eyes were rolled back in his head and he had swallowed his tongue. Two other fellows taking showers said he fell and it looked like he may have hit his spine on the cement floor, and was either dying or was in a state of shock. I ran for the doctor and got two corpsmen who brought the ambulance along. We picked him up and they took him to the sickbay. The corpsman pulled his tongue back out of his throat and he looked like he was regaining consciousness as we laid him and the stretcher in the ambulance.

What a day! I still have to go back down this afternoon at 1745 and stand by in my plane until 1930. Maybe we'll be scrambled, maybe not--depends on the Commies. I'll be glad when this day is over.

I haven't checked the mail yet, dearest, but after yesterday's good luck I'm afraid to hope for any.

This war flying is enough to drive a guy to drink, but I'm not going to, don't worry. I've packed almost all the gear I think we'll need and cut the legs off the desk in order to get it out of the tent. We're giving the tent to the Koreans. Knocked the arms off the chair to get it out, and I thought I had a supply of books until about 15 minutes ago. Father Burke from the Kangnung village, with whisky breath and an Irish brogue you could cut with a knife, comes in and says, "Is Fergy around? He promised me a box of books."

"They're on the floor in the box," says I. "You're welcome to them."

He says, "I've never had the pleasure to make your acquaintance," as he holds out his hand and I catch it. He's a big bull of a blond Irishman. Nice sort of guy. His Korean boy was asked to come in and he loaded the box on a new jeep--civilian jeep--light green in color with special side curtains. It was purchased in Japan for Father Burke. Boy, you'd be lost in this country without a jeep. He was feeling no pain. He said he'd been saying his goodbyes to his friends in the Group prior to our departure tomorrow. He's making out OK. They are leaving a bunch of junk behind here--pans, beat-up furniture, old lumber, canvas, tires, parts of stoves etc. The Koreans are all sorting over it and I'm quite sure they have given Father Burke first crack at it. If he doesn't get it now he never will, unless the Army comes in here.

Tomorrow morning (secret) we're leaving. It's been rough operating even on a 50 percent basis during this move. Everything is all fouled up--nothing is the same as when I got here. I have to have all my gear ready to go by 7:00 AM tomorrow morning and then I'm going to fly a plane on a mission and come back here to pick up some belly tanks and carry them over to our new base. I hope my gear will catch up to me tomorrow night. I'd much rather escort it and be sure it gets there, instead of wishing it will had hoping to luck. Oh well, my luck's been pretty good of late. I think I'll take the chance and not worry about it.

The other day I sat down and figured out about what I'm making in this overseas status:

INCOME		OUTGO			
Base	$370	Chow & Qts.	$30		
Subs	42	Taxes about	25		
Quarters	90		$55		
Flight	120				
	$622		$622		
		Less	55		
			$567	Monthly total	
		Less	405	Your monthly allotment	
			162	Amt I think I'll receive per mo. while I'm overseas	

I'll have no other expenses while I'm in Korea. I'll spend some on R&R in Japan, though, because I have to pay for my BOQ and chow on a pay-as-you-go basis and they still take the money out for the chow you're not eating in Korea.

I checked with the squadron adjutant and he says I'm down in the book to go to Japan on the 8th of May. I had figured the 5th for some reason.

I love you, precious little family of mine, and don't worry about the daddy because it seems I'm a cinch to come home to my loved ones, judging from the way my luck in the air has been running. Kiss the boys goodnight and tuck them in tight and give them my blessings. I love you all very, very much.

Your Daddy

P.S. Jack Ryan just brought me a letter from Ben mailed 10 April. Tells of trailer, ranch, job hunting, your visit to Mother.

P.P.S. Enclosed find Korean tooth picks--untouched by human hands--they use monkeys to make them--ha, ha!

LET'S GET THE HELL OUT OF HERE
(This is Worth Fighting For)

I saw a flak-covered valley,
With divisions of MIGs flying near,
And I heard a voice within me whisper,
Let's get the hell out of here.

And there is the town of Sinanju,
And those black clouds begin to appear,
And again that voice within me whispers,
Let's get the hell out of here.

Why do I fly these railcuts?
Won't somebody tell the brass
Those bastards that run those railroads
Aren't friendly, they're after my ass.

So when the ack-ack gets heavy
And my wingmen they all disappear
I'm going to take that whispered warning
And get the hell out of here.

19 April 1952
Kangnung, Korea

Hi precious family,

    I was up and at 'em at 0500, got my gear all packed up, folded cot, rolled up my bedroll and carried it out to the assembly area where it was to be picked up and trucked over to the field, loaded on a transport and flown to our new location.

    I had breakfast and went down to the squadron. The weather was growing darker and darker and all our gear was piled outside. A storm was about to break on us at any minute. We couldn't find a canvas tarp to throw over the gear, so we hailed down a truck and made several trips with it to an empty tent about 100 yards from where our gear had been stacked. About five of us handled every bit of gear for about 40 officers. and we just made it when the rain hit. It rained like a cow p---ing on a flat rock for about two hours. Then the low ceiling came rolling in and all our hops were cancelled for the day at around 1500. We intended to go up to North Korea and hit a bridge, with the whole squadron then proceeding on over to our new field from there. Now half of our squadron enlisted men have gone, and half of them are here. Some of our gear went and some didn't. Some will have cots and bedrolls tonight but most of them won't. I will--I saw to that. Bill Higgins loaned me his shaving gear and I'm all set. What a mess! And all on account of the weather! A good share of the squadron gear has left by LST to go clear around the peninsula; another good share has been air lifted over. Not a word about this to anyone until I tell you it's OK.

    I'm using Bill's Parker pen and it's real nice. Got a kick out of Bem's letter yesterday. He was his usual colorful self. He can't say anything without working it over a little bit. What a guy! No mail today from my darling.

    I've been kind of nervous all day from my experience yesterday. I guess as I get older it's harder to shake, or forget things as when you were younger.

    During the height of the storm this morning, nine of us piled into a jeep and went over to the squadron ready room. As we crawled out (the jeep had side curtains) an enlisted man was standing holding the door open and his eyes kept getting bigger and bigger; he couldn't believe what he was seeing. We like a little "grab ass," as we call it, every now and then. In the Navy they call it "skylarking;" in the Army it's "horseplay," but in the Marines it's "grab ass." You've got to play around and joke and have a little fun over here or I swear you'd go absolutely <u>A</u>ble <u>S</u>ugar.

    The Koreans have what we call an "A" frame. I don't know what the Koreans call it. Anyway, they hang it on their backs and strap gear onto it. In some of our escape and evasion lectures they recommended to us, in the event we should be forced down, to make ourselves an "A" frame for carrying articles we'd need for survival, such as a parachute, lifeboat, rations, etc. Somebody has come up with a song called, "I've got my 'A' frame on upside down," to a tune they play in the circus bands. I don't know any other words except, "And my ass is dragging on the ground." I'll have to pick up the rest of the words. It's really quite a touching little tune.

    I wish I were home with my little family instead of 8000 miles away. There just isn't any justice in this world, darling. It just doesn't seem fair somehow, to me, that a man who has fought one war, and has family responsibilities and an essential defense job, should have to sweat it out all over again--how far can a guy stretch his luck? I hope this situation will be corrected, and I suppose it will be to a certain extent. Our 3,500,000-man army should help correct the situation somewhat. To some men it doesn't matter whether or not they are in Tokyo, Berlin or New Orleans--it's just one big party after another with them. But I'm not a party boy and the only place I care to be for the rest of my life is right with my wonderful little family. A good majority of the fellows are of the same thought. There's definitely a need for us over here, but it really hurts when it has to be you (or me, if you know what I mean). Just like the people who were saying, "Let's go into China and carry out General MacArthur's idea." Fine, let's go into China with the people who support MacArthur. If they want to see a war, let them risk their own necks. People are always too ready to shout, "Here! Here!" when it doesn't mean even a tiny little piece of skin off their respective noses. Let that same person sit out here under the constant threat of death and make such a statement. I have one resolute purpose out here, and that is to fly my hops, killing as many Commies as I can, and to try to end this thing as fast as possible so I can return to my loved ones.

However, the signing of a peace treaty won't solve the Communist threat to the world. They are out to get us by any underhanded means possible---by commerce, small wars, and eventually WWIII. They have trade missions all over the world, and because of their slave labor they can out-produce us and undersell us. You wait and see. They'll try to break our economy by war or trade, or just threat of war, knowing we'll spend millions to counter their every move. Inflation at home could wreck us as quickly as WWIII could. In fact, inflation is the one thing we have to be more careful of than possibly the home front Communists. What I can't understand is how this country of ours can spend five billion dollars in Korea, with a loss of thousands of men fighting Communists, when right at home in our midst they are running stark free, doing far more damage than a Communist up on the front lines killing our boys. A Communist is a Communist wherever you find him. These people who have gone along with the Communists and have agreed with them at every turn and supported their ideals, and yet when they were asked if they were a Communist they deny it fervently, are as guilty for the murder of our boys over here as if they fired the shot that hit the lad on the front line.

This thing is world-wide, and Korea is just a passing episode in a long, bitter struggle for everything right and decent left in this world. Unions at home are doing the Communists' bidding, what with their strikes and threats of strike. They have it all planned--a round of price increases and government's war material costs go up because the cost of material to build them goes up, along with wages to produce them. The government is forced to raise the taxes to absorb this increase and Joe Blow, who struck for his union henchmen, has been duped by his own enemies; while the union says Uncle Sam is responsible.

Russia is ahead of us in men and equipment by several years. She may have had this angle figured out a long time back, figuring that sooner or later we'd go all out in defense spending to counter her, and in the process drag our own economy down to the very doorstep of depression and disaster. This world-wide trade thing Russia is sponsoring goes along with that now.

I'm going to knock off for chow.

Back from chow. We had ham, fresh cooked cabbage, beans, chocolate cake, coffee and chopped carrot and raisin salad. Very nice. For luncheon we had chicken fricassee (or stewed hen) with potatoes and carrots, gravy, coffee, apricots. For breakfast, scrambled eggs and sausages. I'm telling you, this chow is terrific. I haven't had a poor meal since I arrived. If what Ferguson says is so, and he being the mess officer ought to know, every man in Korea is eating the same. However, he says the quality is the same originally, but the quantity and the preparation vary from unit to unit. (Your preparation and service, though, darling, can't be compared with this.) They have to throw it at you as you walk by, and the feeling that you've got to get it eaten and make room for another guy to sit down is always with you. (Your cooking, dear, is the finest.)

Tonight, coming back from chow, I saw two Korean laborers struggling over a power generator which supplies the officers' tents with electricity. I stopped and watched them, and they were having a heck of a time getting it started. I looked in the gas tank and it was empty, so they went and got a 56-gallon drum of gas and a hand pump and filled up the gas tank. They tried to start it, but failed to choke it enough, so I stepped over again and started it for them, set the voltage output regulator and speed adjustment, told them it was OK now and to leave it alone unless they saw the voltage drop off to below 90. I had never seen one before but was *familiar with each individual phase of it from past experience. They were dumbfounded when I walked off back to my tent, and I heard them jabbering to themselves in Korean a mile a minute. They use their hands in talking more than the Italians and the Jews do.*

How have the TV programs been lately? I read over here in the "Stars and Stripes" that the quality has improved.

I also read that an Air Force pilot recently called back in from inactive duty, refused to fly, down in Texas somewhere. They court martialed him, gave him two years in prison and discharged him from the service. We've all been talking about it here and believe that he should have been given the opportunity to choose whether he wanted to fly or not. If he didn't choose to, he should have been reclassified in a ground job and had his flight pay and duty involving flying revoked. I believe a man should have the prerogative in choosing whether he should be a flyer or not. There are many things that enter into such a decision--nervousness, adaptability, mental outlook, alertness, proficiency, balance, etc. Many things change over a period of years, and who is to be a better judge of such a change than the individual himself?

I've rambled along enough, dearest, so guess I'll close this one by saying that I love you all very much and need you, each and every one, to make my life complete. Tuck the precious boys into bed with my blessing, dear, and tell them that I love them.

Your very own, Daddy

The article which was enclosed and mentioned in the above letter read as follows:

'WON'T FLY OFFICER GETS PRISON TERM'

EL PASO, Tex. (UP)--First Lt. Verne Goodwin of Peabody, Mass., has been sentenced to two years in prison and dismissed from the Air Force for refusing to fly, it was disclosed Wednesday.

Goodwin was the first of 22 reserve officers charged with disobedience to be court-martialed for their part in a "staydown" strike which has hit three Air Force bases.

Goodwin's father-in-law, Parker Cullom, an auto dealer at Las Cruces, N.M., disclosed that the 30-year old veteran had been sentenced. Col. James Y. Parker, commandant of Biggs Air Force base here, earlier had announced that Goodwin's case was heard by a court martial Tuesday night but he refused to reveal the court's verdict.

SIX RESERVE OFFICERS at Randolph AFB, San Antonio, Tex., and six at Mather AFB, Calif., also have been charged with wilful disobedience of a superior officer for refusing to accept flight duty. Nine others at Traux AFB are under investigation.

Eight nonvolunteer reserve officers met Tuesday night at Randolph, the Air Force's West Point, and drafted a statement explaining their stand against being sent back into combat by regular Air Force officers who have never seen action.

The next day would be one of our busiest since I had arrived in Korea. Since we were packed and ready to fly off to our new base of operation. Unfortunately we would be saying goodbye to all the ROK P-51 Mustang pilots and a number of our house boys whom we had grown to love and respect during the short time we had been there at Kangnung by the sea.

CHAPTER 7

WE FLY TO OUR NEW BASE P'YONGT'AEK, TUNP O RI

CAMERON'S CRASH

21 April 1952 (Sunday)
at our new airbase,
P'yongt'aek (K6)

Hello little gang I love,
    Today had been very hectic. Right from 0500 on it's been just one big confused mess after another. Today we decided we were going to take off for our new base, even if we had to go instruments all the way over. Well, we made several futile attempts to clear with operations, but they kept putting the kibosh on us. Finally at 1000, even though our field was socked in, we took off because the aerologist had reports that the weather at our destination was breaking up and we could probably find a hole near there to come down through. He was right. All 25 of us got off together and we were a very impressive formation of fighter bombers. We climbed to 8000' and cruised over a layer that hung at anywhere from 4000' to 5000', with only the highest mountain peaks protruding from the layer, and the peaks were all snow covered, but you could distinguish mountain peak from clouds. As far as the eye could see in any direction the same view met our eyes. It was beautiful, if such a thing is possible in Korea.
    As my old Corsair pounded and wheezed along I couldn't help but wonder what happens when this thing stops turning over and I read "Hamilton Standard" on the back of the propeller blades. Nothing did happen, though, and we flew "birddog" (radio compass) into Seoul, then switched to this field and flew radio compass down here, timing our flight until we estimated we were over or near our point of intended landing, where we spotted a hole in the cloud cover and came screaming down through right over our home field--a nice piece of blind navigating.
    Captain Cameron had engine trouble and just made it back to K18 Kangnung. However, he was excited about the condition of his engine, came in too fast and crashed on the far end of the runway, damaging a wing and the landing gear. He was OK and flew another plane over here later this afternoon. Can't keep a good man down.

Our field here, as I've told you, has been operated by the Air Force. They still have some units here, but in the main there is just one SeaBee Navy outfit coming in building their area now, and we Marines. The camp is laid out sort of nice, with one exception--the quonset huts are only about 700' from the VMF-323 Corsair flight line and we'll hear every plane turned up by the mechanics and pilots on the early, early hops every morning.

VMF-323 flew a 20-plane railcut and then followed us on in here to our new base. Then, during all the confusion of moving and what-have-you, they called on us for a 9-plane railcut at 1600. I wasn't on the schedule, fortunately, and had a chance to round up some squadron gear. At around 1700 our gear followed us in here on a Marine transport plane, and with much fuss and confusion we all managed to get our individual gear and laid it out in the quonset huts. We have 10 men in each quonset. As for me, I'd rather be in a tent, but they already had these things up, so we took them. They'll be OK, I believe, after we get some partitions in them. However, there are too many conversations going on and I can't concentrate on my letters to you. I'd like to be in a tent by myself, but it's not possible. Right now I'm hearing a story from Rainbow Jackson clear at the other end of the quonset. He's telling about a bar and restaurant he owned on the side when he was a cop back home. Boy, what a tale!

Well, we were tired, dirty, unshaven and generally disgruntled this afternoon until we got the Korean caretaker at the head and showers to heat up some water, by feeding it fire wood just like the other Korean at Kangnung did. The head and showers are a lot better here than they were at Kangnung. And for the first time in weeks we had ice cream for lunch. It was wonderful. The chow hall is very well managed and it's much cleaner that Kangnung. I'll have to hand it to the Air Force, they really get things well organized. The chow is delicious, so I'm all set here. Don't worry about me, honey, I'll get along fine.

The mud is awfully bad--red mud. The Air Force had to buy gold ore from a Korean gold mine in order to get hard gravel to make this runway. $250,000 worth! When we run out of things to do we can go out by the side of the runway and pan gold! There are a lot of Korean laborers here too. Lt Ryan brought his houseboy along with him from Kangnung, and he's going to be our houseboy.

No mail today. I have an early morning mission tomorrow. Guess it will be a close air support, possibly near Kaesong again.

I hope everyone at home is fine. I miss you all so very much. Kiss the darling little boys for me, dearest, and tell them I love them very much.

Your very own,
Daddy

THE PEACE NEGOTIATORS

A small village on the edge of the Imjin River some fourteen miles from Panmunjom was the permanent base camp for our negotiators. It was set up in an apple orchard. The newsmen were put up in a press train on a siding about a mile away. Adm C. Turner Joy USN headed our first peace negotiating team and LtGen William K. Harrison Jr., USA, relieved him in May 1952. During the ten months that Admiral Joy had sat with the Communists the talks had proven fruitless, dreary, repetitious, tedious and exasperating. The truce negotiations had been used to the hilt by the Communists as a propaganda platform and the POW issue had become perhaps the most vexing non-tactical issue of them all.

The Communist truce delegation, based at Kaesong, was made up of MGen Hsieh-Fang, LtGen Teng Hua, Chinese Army, North Korean LtGen Nam Il, Chief Delegate, who finally signed for the Communists, along with Gen William K. Harrison for the UN. Other North Korean delegates were MGen Lee Sang Cho and MGen Chang Pyong San. The actual signing and cessation of hostilities didn't take place until July 1953, however.

COMMUNIST ATROCITIES

Japanese cruelty had been revealed in the Philippines in 1945 when our forces reached Manila and freed our first POWs. And so it was in North Korea in October of 1950 during MacArthur's offensive which took our forces to the Yalu. The commander of the 23rd Infantry Regiment of the 2nd Division came to hate the North Koreans. He reported:

> *This was the first time we had really encountered Communist cruelty. When we first met some of these North Korean attacks they were driving civilians, elderly people, in front of them as a shield. We had a very difficult time making our men fire into them because if we didn't, we were dead. This was a very hard thing to do.*

In another incident, north of P'yongyang in a tunnel near Sunchon, our forces found the emaciated bodies of five Americans lying on a grass mat. They had either starved to death or died of wounds. Just outside the tunnel a young, thin, wounded American private staggered from behind some bushes with his horrible story. Nearby they discovered 15 more POWs sitting in a semi-circle, all dead, shot as they held their rice bowls in hand, apparently anticipating some food. Tales such as these made it a little bit easier to press our attacks to the limit.

EXPLAINING MY NEAR ACCIDENT TO ST. PETER / CAPT FELITON ESCAPES DEATH WHEN HIS BRAKES FAIL

21 April 1952
New Base

Hi little family,
I received three letters today, honey, the 11th, 12th and 13th, one telling me all about the kids' Easter hunt. It sounded wonderful to me, darling. I'd have given anything to have been there with you and the two darling little fellows. The Easter Bunny was sure good to the boys, wasn't he?
I was surprised to hear that you wouldn't receive your allotment until the last of April. Yes, I guess you will have to draw money out of the bank. Gosh, if you can save $165.00 a month, darling, you'll really be doing fine. I'll do my share over here, honey, you can be sure of that.
Today was one of my earliest reveilles since coming overseas, 0400. Ate breakfast, although I could hardly go it at such an early hour. I was tired from moving, flying and getting settled yesterday and the boys talked until late with the lights on, so I guess I really didn't get to sleep until about midnight. It was cold last night and this morning--brrrrrr. After the briefing this morning at about 0545 they called in from up north saying the weather was socked in near our target area, so they cancelled our hop. I dashed back to my warm sleeping bag, jumped in and slept until 0800.
I got up and had a haircut over at a real small building they'd built for the barber shop. There were two Korean barbers in there with only boxes for us to sit on, no running water or anything you usually associate with a barber shop, even in Korea, since it was here on the base. A little boy about six or seven years old warmed our water on the space heater in the middle of the room. He swept the floor five times while I was there--45 minutes. The barber had electric clippers, however, and they had wash rags with which they rubbed our heads and cleaned the shaving soap off. He gave me the best haircut I ever had in my life, massaging my head, shoulders and back for about two minutes with a rhythmic motion using both hands in a clapping movement. He stood erect and I watched him in the mirror. Honestly, I almost burst out laughing he was so funny. It's a ritual with them, believed to bring you healthy hair and body. The barber in Korea is a very important man, just as in America. The boys tell me I'll really enjoy my haircut in Japan. They say you can get a haircut, shampoo, manicure, back rub, and the works for less than a dollar. This haircut cost me 1000 wan, which is 15¢.

Maj Richard B. Elliott, former executive officer of VMA-212 up to 29 Feb 52, relieved by Maj Roy A. (Shorty) Thorson, followed by Maj Leslie C. Reed from 10 Jun 52.

Capt Glenn Smith

Capt McClure, our helicopter pilot attached. It was a reassuring comfort to have him and his chopper around to snatch us if ever required.

Capt Bernard W. (Pete) Peterson

1.

2.

3.

4.

5.

1. Capt Dave Kennedy--my hutmate, flying mate and R&R buddy. In jest, he was a regular Marine officer posing as a reserve, to deflect all the barbs he would otherwise get from all of us reserves. A thousand laughs, a true blue guy all the way.

2. Our dedicated VMF-212 line crew, hardworking professionals we all respected.

3. L to R: Ted Pittman, "Stretch" Evans and his flying dog, "Scoshie," and Peterson at K6, Korea.

4. L to R: Lew Bass, Dick Francisco and Gene Cameron. Lew and Dick were our squadron comedians--a laugh a minute. Cameron and I were close buddies.

5. A happy bunch of going-home pilots of VMF-212.

Dave Kennedy, who sleeps right next to me, helped me make furniture this morning. We went out stealing and came up with some 2x4's and some Korean-made plywood that looks like oak. We made a table or desk 30" x 5' and then a chair. Tomorrow we'll make another chair. We knocked off for chow (meat loaf, and macaroni and cheese), then went and got briefed at the group and briefed again at the squadron.

We finally took off at 1430, flew to a corps sector northeast of Kaesong about 30 miles or so, and hit the Communists' positions on a close air support mission. Each of us made about five passes and were drawing fire from them on every one. We creamed them and got credit for 100 percent effectiveness on troops and bunkers.

We flew over Seoul coming and going, and as we hit some mountainous country the wind was almost as rough as we'd encountered over the Sierras, but not quite. We would be shot up 500', then down 500' in only a few seconds. However, after we got north and over our target area, it smoothed out.

This field has a 5000' metal runway (Marston matting) and, when you land on it, the tires scream so loudly when you touch down at about 110 to 120 kts, that it almost scares the pants off you. It's smoother and much nicer than Kangnung, however.

I believe I'll like this place a lot more as time goes on. We returned from our hop at 1615, started looking for mail, and found some. Boy, I get a warm feeling all over when I get mail from my precious family. I got a letter from my mother mailed the 13th of April and one from Aunt Edna. They were nice newsy letters and it was good hearing from them.

We got some pilots in today from the 20th replacement draft. I'm not a boot anymore. Lt Jacks, Nellie Sharp, and Capt Shanks were among the newcomers. Jacks and Sharp you've met. They are both young 2nd Lts--jet pilots--and Shanks is a regular. We flew together in VMF-223 in WWII in the Philippines and Okinawa. He's one of "T" Walling's best friends. It's hard for me to believe the new draft has come out. Thank God there's one month almost shot and I'm still breathing and kicking just as before.

Jacks is the only one who got VMF-212; the rest got VMF-323, the other squadron in our Group 12. The only other planes here are some of the service squadrons, TBFs--Turkeys. It makes it nice in that respect, we're not crowded.

Our stove is on the far end of our hut and it's so darn cold up on this end I'm almost shaking. I have my shoes on and padded wool socks, wool pants, shirt, undershirt and leather flight jacket, and I'm still cold. I'm near the end, so when everyone comes in and out I catch the cold blast.

Every time you tell me what Ricky and Randy say I hold it in my thoughts and laugh at their little sayings time and time again. I thought I'd die when I heard about the baby sister routine, and also Grandpa Peterson. How did Randy get into the Grandpa Peterson act? You must have told him that when the back door comes open by itself it must be Grandpa Peterson, visiting from the next world. I know that Ricky has pulled the act several times, but that Randy guy! We've sure got a lot of laughs and good times ahead of us.

Our squadron area is clear across the field from all other activity. There's a Korean farm that comes right smack up against the fence only a few feet from some of our squadron tents. I watched an old Korean plowing a field with a beat-up old white ox, and another one following behind raking the earth. There are always about a dozen little Korean kids hanging on the fence watching our activities. They all have their heads shaved, and honest to Pete, every last one of them looks just exactly the same, mostly like Japanese.

The ordnance sergeant brought us back to the area here after our hop this afternoon, and as he rounded the corner I was sitting on the jeep hood reading your letter with one hand and hanging on with the other. I was slipping off as he went around and I came so darn near falling off it wasn't even funny. It would have been awfully embarrassing getting killed or even injured falling off a jeep after what I've already been through. I couldn't have explained that one to St. Peter if I'd tried!

Capt Foster (Bob) married a Wave Lt (jg), his navigation instructor when he was a cadet at Pensacola. He married her after he was commissioned, however. They were in the same squadron for four months. They have two boys now and a third on the way. Capt Dave Kennedy (a regular) led our section--I was on his wing. He's a character if I ever met one-- always singing and cracking jokes about the regulars and reserves. However, if nobody knew better they'd think he was a reserve. He must figure he had better make the first wisecrack about the reg's because he's always knocking them. I always toss it right back to Dave "the sniveler" with some appropriate wisecrack befitting his comment about the reserves, such as, "RESERVISTS FIGHT THE WARS. IN BETWEEN, THE REGULARS KEEP THE GUNS POLISHED." *He wasn't fooling me.*

Dave's sister just won a scholarship to some English university. She's 22 years old and already has a doctor's degree from an American university. He says it's a shame to waste so much talent on a woman. He has a two year old boy, a three year old girl, and another boy about eight.

Capt Jackson, a helicopter pilot, went with Jerry Lewis's ex-wife when he was in the States and she writes him all the time.

Capt Jim Feliton's brakes went out on him today and he wiped out a wing, nosed up and busted the prop--needs an engine change too. He's OK though. He's got three children and told us tonight he's going to have another in two weeks.

(Jim had a fine record as an F4F Wildcat fighter pilot in WWII, during the early fighting around Guadalcanal. His story of being shot down by a Jap Zero and his miraculous escape and survival is a classic. Friendly natives found him in the jungle, nursed him back to health and brought him back to Henderson Field).

Three of our boys got lost today but landed, nearly out of gas, 120 miles south of here. We flew some gasoline down to them after we found out where they were. They will come back tomorrow I guess. We have a railcut way up north tomorrow.

I love you all very much and miss you more and more every day. Kiss my precious boys for me.

Your very own, Daddy

ONE HAIRY MISSION AS RECALLED BY CAPT BILL SHANKS USMC

Forty years passed before I gave any serious thought to writing my memoirs of Korea. In order to reconnect with the past, I found it necessary to make contact with some of my VMF-212 Korean War buddies, and also a few fellow pilots who had flown with me in VMF-223 (during WWII) and who had also served with me, or near me, during the Korean conflict. Through the efforts of our VMF-223 squadron historian, Rex Hamilton, of Glenview, IL, we have been able to reconnect at several reunions I've attended, and also through Rex's newsletters.

In my letter of 21 April 1952 written from Korea I mentioned that we had finally received some pilots from the 20th replacement draft, one of them being my old friend, Capt Bill Shanks. Unfortunately he was assigned to VMF-323, our sister squadron.

William Shanks, was born 2 Jun 1924 at Rexford, Kansas, the son of a cattle breeding family. After finishing high school and one year of college in Santa Rosa, CA, he decided to enlist in the military service, entering the Navy V5 cadet program through his college CPT on 22 Jun 1942. He received his wings of gold 11 Sep 1943 at NAS Corpus Christi, TX.

Bill and I first met at Bougainville, in the Solomon Islands, around Jan 1945, and flew combat missions together throughout the Philippines and Okinawa until WWII ended.

He applied for and received a regular commission in the peacetime Marine Corps, serving as an operational flight and instrument instructor from Sep 1945 through Aug 1947 at naval air bases at Opa Locka, Fl, Fort Lauderdale, FL, and Cecil Field, FL. In 1947 he joined VMF-451, a designated carrier squadron, land-based at MCAS El Toro, CA. He made 63 carrier landings on the Jeep carrier USS *Bairoko* (CVE-115), the USS *Boxer* (CV-21) and the USS *Valley Forge* (CV-45). He also was afforded jet transitional training in the TO-1 (Navy version of the F-80 Shooting Star--the Air Force called theirs the T-33) during April and May of 1949. He completed the Marine Corps Amphibious Warfare School at Quantico, VA, during Jan 1951 and was transferred to MCB Camp Lejeune, NC, where he served as a Forward Air Controller.

Capt William Shanks, boarding his F9F Grumman Panther jet fighter in Korea, July 1952. Attached to the famous Able Eagle Squadron, VMF-115, he flew out of K3 strip at Pohang dong.

Bill and I flew together in WWII, both attached to VMF-223 in Bougainville, Philippines and Okinawa. Bill stayed in the Marine Corps, completing an action-packed flying career, including Viet Nam, prior to retiring as a full colonel in July 1974. Refer to his biography in the text for his full and interesting story. Few fighter pilots are still around to talk about surviving three major wars in their lifetimes—WWII, Korea and Viet Nam. Well done, Bill!!

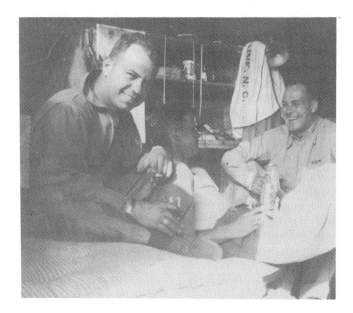

Above, L to R: *Denny Clyde and Dave Kennedy having a laugh in our quonset hut, K6, Korea.*

Upper Left, L to R: *Dave Kennedy, Peterson, Gene Cameron. We took the day off to jeep up to the walled city of Suwon, scene of the early 1950 fighting.*

Left: *One of our sister squadron's F4U-4B Corsairs which crashed as a result of taking heavy enemy flak. "WS" on plane's tail and VMF-323 under MARINES identifies it.*

Left: *Peterson returning from a long combat mission over North Korea.*

Right: *Lt Pierce, our ordnance officer.*

Above: 1000-lb bombs on carts preparatory to being loaded onto our VMA-212 F4U-4B Corsairs at K18, Kangnung, Korea.

Right: Korean civilians at our field, K18, Kangnung, coming to do their thing with the "honey bucket" cart.

Below: Control tower at K18, Kangnung, field.

Photos on this page courtesy of Robert "Van" Van Dalsem.

Right: Peterson about to climb aboard the "mount" for a combat mission up north in old #14.

Upper Left: Maj "Shorty" Thorson, executive officer of VMF-212.

Left: Capt Robert R. Van Dalsem. Van and I flew together in VMF-212 Mar-May '52, when he transferred to the air wing at K3 to fly the TBM. His missions were passenger and cargo on and off American and British carriers, including the HMS OCEAN when Col George Axtell rode as passenger in the rear compartment. Van had a few beers with the Brits in their wardroom while the Col conducted business on the bridge. The Col later qualified in his Corsair on an American carrier before becoming C.O. of VMA-312. Van retired from the USMC as a colonel and now resides in Loveland, CO.

Lower Left: One of our "LOVE DOG" Corsairs considerably worse for wear, flown by Capt Bibee.

Right; Bobby Foster, a fine person, well liked by all. He died in his Corsair while taking off on a sandy beach on Yo-Do Island, a small island east of Wonsan in North Korea. In WWII he had married his navigation instructor. They had two sons and a third child on the way.

Left: Peterson awaiting a mission at our new base, Tunp o ri, K6.

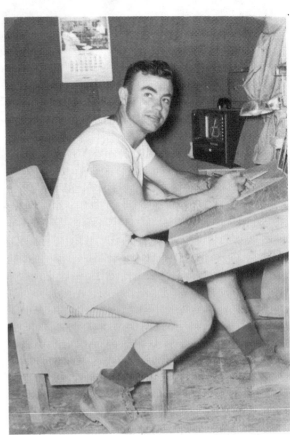

Right: Peterson at his homemade desk, writing home to Marion.

Above: VMF-212 fellow pilots in front of our squadron ready room, K6. **Back row, on R:** "Nellie" Sharp.

Front Row, R to L: Browning and Harry Perkowski. Harry is in VMF-323.

Above: Peterson in front of VMF-212 Devil Cats squadron sign. K6.

Left: VMA-212 "Devilcat" Marine ordnance ground crew loading deadly 5" Hivar rockets on F4U-4B Vought Corsair in preparation for day's mission.

Right: Navy corpsman displays armored jacket worn by infantryman who survived blast of 5 lbs of TNT accidentally exploded at close range. Author experienced similar damage to several of his flak jackets as a result of enemy mortar fire.

Left: Protective screen on dozer tank of 1st Tank Battalion is designed to explode 5.5-inch rockets before they hit armored vehicle. The wire fence turns with the turret.

Photo credit USMC

In Apr 1952 Bill reported to "VMF-323 at K6 Korea, where he flew 34 combat missions in the F4U-4B Corsair. He flew an additional 31 missions in the F9F Grumman Panther jet while serving with VMF-115 at K3 in Korea.

I asked Bill to recount for me one of his most interesting missions while flying in Korea. He offered the following hair-raising episode, which would shake up the most stout hearted.

> *In July or August of 1952, while flying F9F Grumman Panther jets with VMF-115, the Able Eagle Squadron, I was a member of either an 8- or 12-plane flight launched from K-3 toward an important target complex in North Korea. All aircraft were armed with 2-1000 lb bombs equipped with VT (proximity) fuses. This was the first time that our squadron had used the VT fusing in combat. Capt "Soupy" Campbell was leading the first four plane division, and I was flying in the second division about 10 minutes behind. We had flown about half way to the target area, when we overheard transmissions indicating that Capt Campbell's aircraft had blown up in mid-air prior to reaching the target area, and that his wingman suffered aircraft damage from the explosion and was heading out to sea in preparation for either an ejection or ditching of the aircraft, as it was too difficult to control to contemplate a landing.*
>
> *Of course we were all shocked, but had no idea, at that point, that the event would have far reaching consequences and would soon cause our own blood pressure to rise in fear. Minutes later we received an emergency transmission from MAG-33 Operations (on guard channel) directing that all aircraft armed with the VT fused bombs to immediately separate and proceed seaward to drop the bombs unarmed in a safe area, as it was highly likely that the bombs had been improperly wired. Our flight complied at once and I recall looking out at the bombs loaded on my aircraft (In the F9F we could see the nose of the bomb protruding beyond the leading edge of each wing) and was unable to detect anything out of the ordinary. However, my heart was racing until I jettisoned them and breathed a sigh of relief when I felt the jolt as they departed the aircraft.*
>
> *After returning to the base, I recall some pilots saying that they could see that the small propeller on the nose of each bomb was turning. This was not supposed to occur until the bomb had been dropped and the arming wire separated from the bomb, allowing the propeller to turn and arm the proximity fuse. As it turned out, the wire, in some cases, had not been fed through the proper channel and the propellers had been allowed to turn freely in the slipstream of the aircraft. We pilots had not detected this discrepancy during our preflight inspection, and at least some of the ordnance personnel were apparently not aware of the proper procedure for wiring the bombs. I'll never know for certain whether or not my bombs had been properly loaded and armed, but you can be sure that from that point forward, every last member of the squadron knew the proper procedure and what to look for when the aircraft was pre-flighted. To the best of my recollection Capt Campbell's wingman ejected successfully from his disabled aircraft but "Soupy," unfortunately, had been killed instantly.*

It has been my desire to introduce as many of my old friends in my memoirs as possible, and Bill's biography is one of the most interesting I have read. It shows how one person's decision to make the Marine Air Corps his profession worked out for him. Bill's career took him through three of our country's wars in which he served with distinction and honor.

(Note: Refer to Appenidx Number 3 for additional background on Bill's combat experience.)

TRAGIC LOSS OF A SIX-PLANE FLIGHT OF F9F MARINE PANTHER JETS

One of the Marine Corps' best known fighter squadrons, VMF-115 was activated 1 July 1943 and played a prominent role in the Pacific during World War II (earning a Presidential Unit Citation for its participation in the Philippines Campaign). At the start of the Korean War, the squadron was located at Cherry Point, North Carolina, but was deployed during January and February 1952 to Korea and assigned to Marine Aircraft Group 33, 1st Marine Aircraft Wing.

WE FLY TO OUR NEW BASE P'YONGT'AEK, TUNP O RI

During the month of September 1952, VMF-115 was located at K-3 air base, Pohang, Korea. The commanding officer of the squadron was LtCol Royce W. Coln, USMC, and as noted, VMF-115 was attached at this time to MAG-33, 1st MAW. Among its assigned missions were the destruction of enemy air power, close support of United Nations ground forces, armed reconnaissance and offensive strikes, interdiction of enemy ground lines of communication, escort/ cover for United Nations air, sea, or land forces, and air defense of military installations.

The official operation reports submitted by the squadron indicate that on 10 September, 23 F9F Panther jets from VMF-115 and VMF-311 set out on an interdiction mission to attack reported enemy troop and supply targets near Sariwon, about 35 miles directly south of P'yongyang. Following a successful strike, the 21 aircraft that completed the mission were returning to their K-3 home base when they were diverted by MAG-33 operations to land at K-2 airbase, Taegu, because of bad weather in the K-3 sector. Shortly after this message had been radioed to all the pilots, word was received from the K-2 base that 15 of the F9F Panthers had safely landed at that field. The remaining six planes, all from VMF-115, were in radio contact over K-2 and reported their fuel condition, but contact was not made again. As darkness fell over the area, there still was no word from the overdue Panthers. Telephone and radio calls were placed to operating airstrips in all of South Korea, but to no avail.

On the following day (11 September), all aircraft were made ready to search VMF-115's assigned sector for the six missing aircraft, but continued bad weather throughout the day curtailed hopes for conducting a search operation. However, on 12 September, MAG-33 operations received a terse message from K-2 base, which was forwarded to the VMF-115 Duty Officer. Despite poor weather, a search helicopter had discovered the wreckage of the aircraft strewn about a mountainous area southeast of Taegu. The scene was located by the search helicopter at approximately 23 nautical miles southeast of K-2 and 27 nautical miles southwest of K-3, in the vicinity of Unmun-San, a mountain peak that rises to 4,068 feet. An investigating party was immediately organized which examined, on 13 and 14 September, all six crash sites (with the last site physically located by Republic of Korea units operating in the area) and positively identified both aircraft and pilots. From dog tags, bureau numbers of the aircraft, and other material evidence, the identities of the six Marine pilots were confirmed to be Maj Raymond E. De Mers, Maj Donald F. Givens, 1stLt Alvin R. Bourgeois, 2ndLt John W. Hill, Jr., 2ndLt Carl R. LaFleur, and 2ndLt Richard L. Roth.

From examination of the crash sites, it was determined that the six aircraft, flying in formation in poor weather, crashed into the side of the mountain while descending towards K-2. Ironically, the aircraft would have required only an additional 600 feet of altitude to clear the summit. It is noteworthy that Marine intelligence sources estimated that the physical location and disintegration of the aircraft were such that all pilots had no forewarning of the impending disaster, and thus had been unable to avert the subsequent crashes. By order of the Commanding Officer of MAG-33, a minute review of operations SOP was made to guard against any possible future disaster. Air facilities charts were clarified and prepared for wider distribution covering all "K"-type fields in Korea.

In conducting the research for this article, the Reference Section was able to speak directly with the investigating officer of the air crash, who filed an official report on the tragedy to the Commanding General, 1st MAW. The officer recalled the substance of this report, which included under opinions, the following:

The lead pilot of the formation, a qualified flight leader, may have departed from the instrument let-down procedure upon seeing what appeared to be a "hole" in the overcast. This would not have been unusual, as the previous flights landing at K-2 immediately before had reported large holes occasionally seen during their approaches. The hole may have closed quickly after the flight left the minimum altitude, however, causing the six aircraft to re-enter the overcast. Under these conditions, the flight hit the Unmun-San mountain peak.

The crucial role played by the 1st MAW during the Korean War was recognized following the armistice when it was awarded the Navy Unit Commendation. Marine Fighter Squadron 115 shared in this award, and also received the Korean Service Streamer with four bronze stars, and the Korean Presidential Unit Citation Streamer. The "Able Eagles" of VMF-

115 flew 9,250 combat sorties, and logged more than 15,350 combat hours during their participation in the war.
   As noted earlier, allied air superiority in Korea was not achieved at an easy price, a fact made manifest by the 10 September 1952 loss.
(Credit: Robert V. Aquilina, Assistant Head Reference Section of the Marine Corps Historical Center. Note: only a portion of the complete report appears here.)

Roster of Marine Fighter Squadron VMA-212, Korea, March-July 1952
(This is the writer's best guess and is only a partial listing.)

LtCol Robert L. Bryson, Sqd CO Mar-Jun '52
LtCol Graham H. Benson, Sqd CO from 10 Jun
LtCol George C. Axtell
   (flew with VMA-212 but was Group Officer)
Maj Richard B. Elliott, former EO to 29 Feb
Maj Roy A. (Shorty) Thorson, Sqd EO from 8 Mar
Maj Leslie C. Reed, Sqd EO from 10 Jun
Maj. Frey
Maj MacMahon
Maj. Frank Mick
Maj Phillips--killed
Maj Richard "Dick" Webster
Capt Stan Adams
Capt Alexander
Capt. Robert Barbours
Capt Robert O. Barnum
Capt Lewis N. Bass
Capt Bibee
Capt Browning
Capt Budd
Capt Thomas J. Burnham
Capt Call
Capt Gene Cameron
Capt "Denny" Clyde
Capt George "Skee" Codding
Capt Robert W. "Cozy" Cole
Capt Eddens
Capt Malcolm P. "Stretch" Evans and his
   flying dog, "Scoshie"
Capt Jim Feliton (of Guadalcanal fame)
Capt Tony Foltz
Capt "Bobby" Foster--killed
Capt Fox
Capt Richard "Dick" Francisco
Capt Ramon Gibson (recalled from Peru)
Capt Guy M. Gipple
Capt Goss
Capt Griffith
Capt Hawkins
Capt Paul B. Henley
Capt Hugh Holland

Capt Holmes
Capt Ivy
Capt "Rainbow" Jackson (helicopter
   pilot attached)
Capt John Johnson--killed
Capt Dave "The Sniveler" Kennedy
Capt Merle A. Kime
Capt "Swede" Larson
Capt John Lawler
Capt McArdle
Capt McClure (helicopter pilot attached)
Capt McCullough
Capt McDonald
Capt Patrick McGinnis
Capt Bernard W. "Pete" Peterson
Capt Teddy L. Pittman
Capt. Perry Porter--killed
Capt Jack Ryan
Capt Fred Sells--killed
Capt Glen Smith
Capt John Snapper
Capt Harry Soladay--killed
Capt Soreide--killed
Capt Strom
Capt J.P. "Jocko" Sutherland
Capt Luther T. Terrell, Jr.
Capt William A. Tulk--killed
Capt Robert R. "Van" Van Dalsem
Capt Waters
Capt Watson
Capt Whitmore
Capt "Duke" Williams--shot down,
   taken prisoner (fate unknown)
Capt Woods
Lt William H. "Billie" Bizzell
Lt Ken Jacks
Lt Pierce--ordnance officer
Lt. Thompson
Lt. Welch

- - - - -

WE FLY TO OUR NEW BASE P'YONGT'AEK, TUNP O RI

22 April 1952
Tunp o ri

Precious family,
What a day! No mail. I was scheduled for a railcut way up by the Yalu for this afternoon, so I was taking advantage of my few free hours this morning, working like a beaver making a chair so we'd have something to sit on here in our hut. Well, while cutting on a piece of plywood, the saw slipped and came across my left thumb nail, cutting down very deep into the quick and removing a chunk of nail and about 1/16" deep. I ran over to sick bay where they dressed it right away and gave me some APC pills which I've been taking, two every four hours. It hurt when I did it, then tapered off until this evening when it started hurting again, I guess because I got cold. Anyway, needless to say, I was grounded by the flight surgeon for a few days because it would be too painful to manipulate the plane controls, and also needs time to heal. They were short on pilots so I volunteered to take the Group duty over, thus relieving Capt Harry Soladay to fly the railcut. Well, I've had a very busy day running the whole base as duty officer for the Group. I'm standing the duty now, but there's a little lag right now so I'm taking advantage of the situation. I have to be available all night, meet the midnight courier plane, and inspect the guards all during the night and early morning. I'm on 24 hr. call. So much for that.
Tomorrow I'm going to be the squadron duty officer and will be on another 24 hr. duty status. Boy, if you're not available to fly they use you for everything else. However, that's the way it should be because they need every man they can get out here.
Don't worry about me or my thumb, dearest--it'll be OK.
I'm going to cut this one short, honey, because something has to be taken care of right away in the line of duty.

Night, Daddy

APRIL AIR OPERATIONS FOR MARINES HELPED SET ONE-DAY WAR RECORD

By 20 April the three tactical squadrons of MAG-12--VMF(N)-513, VMF-212, and VMF-323--had completed their relocations on the Korean west coast. Two days later, combined MAG-12 attack and MAG-33 jet aircraft participated in what was a 5th Air Force one-day combat record: 1,049 sorties. Unfortunately I had sustained a hand injury and was grounded.

During April, Marine squadrons operating under the 5th Air Force put a total of 2708 planes into the air despite restrictive or prohibitive weather on 20 days. Continuing its emphasis on attacking the North Korean transportation system, the Air Force command dispatched 1397 Marine planes on interdiction missions. Marine-piloted close air support sorties flown to assist the 1stMarDiv numbered only 56 throughout April; those piloted by Marines for 16 other UN divisions totaled 547.

The month of April also marked change of command ceremonies for the 1st Marine Aircraft Wing. On 11 April at K-3, Gen Schilt turned over wing responsibility to BGen Clayton C. Jerome. Among the numerous civilian and military dignitaries attending the ceremony at the Pohang 1st MAW headquarters were the Hon John J. Muccio, U.S. Ambassador to Korea; Air Force LGens Otto P. Weyland and Frank F. Everest, commanders of FEAF and FAF respectively; and the Marine division CG, MGen Selden.

The new wing commander, Gen Jerome, like his predecessor, had a distinguished flight career. A 1922 graduate of the Naval Academy, he had served in various foreign and U.S. aviation billets and was a veteran of five World War II campaigns. Col Jerome had been operations officer for Commander, Aircraft, Solomon Islands in 1943. Later he was named Chief of Staff, Commander, Aircraft, Northern Solomons and Commander, Aircraft and Island Commander, Emirau, in the northern Solomons. Before returning to the States, Col Jerome had participated in the recapture of the Philippines, commanding MAG-32 and directing all Marine air support in the Luzon fighting. BGen Jerome became Director of Aviation and Assistant Commandant of the

Marine Corps for Air in September 1950 and served in that capacity until taking command of the 1st Marine Aircraft Wing in Korea.

During the command ceremonies the outgoing 1st MAW commander, Gen Schilt, received the Distinguished Service Medal for his outstanding leadership of the wing. LGen Weyland presented him with the award. Shortly before his Korean tour ended, Gen Schilt had also received from ROK President Syngman Rhee the Order of Military Merit Taiguk, for his courageous contribution to the military defense of South Korea.

HOT WATER--HAVA NO!

23 April 1952
Tunp o ri

Hello loved ones,
Just got relieved after having stood almost 48 continuous hours as squadron duty officer. I was on call all that time; however, I caught a few hours sleep during the period.
I uncovered a Korean rip-off during my tour as Group duty officer yesterday, last night and early this morning. The lumber situation here on the base is very critical and even the tiny little pieces that can be used to feed the hot water heater have been disappearing. I traced it down to the native civilians who were taking it home with them each night out one of the bases five gates. There's a garbage gate, quarry gate, bomb dump gate, main gate (to the main road up north to Seoul), and Korean labor gate. They were going out a sixth gate. I nipped that in the bud, and recovered a lot of firewood. I saw the Group commanding officer this morning and we went over to the Provost Marshall and got him on the ball, contacted the utilities section and arranged with them to police the base with a truck and a bunch of workers to corral all this loose lumber, have it cut up into short pieces, stacked and delivered to the various boiler rooms daily. The thing that burned me up was when I went into the officers' head last night real late to take a badly needed shower and shave only to find, as the Korean on watch so ably put it, "Hot water hava no, burn wood hava no." His countrymen were streaming out the hole in the gate with wood "to burn," to coin the expression. This afternoon "wood hava yes" and "hot water hava yes." Oh, the trials and tribulations I have to endure! Ha!
I was just listening to Radio Moscow on John Johnson's short wave radio. They told of finding a bomb case that germs were dropped in up in North Korea. Then they read so-called letters from American pilots to their families in the U.S. telling of how they dislike killing innocent women and children on their missions and how the politicians are forcing them to do this horrible thing, blah, blah, blah. This woman talking has a very nice honey-toned voice and speaks perfect English. She stops her chatter every now and then and plays some Russian songs and a few famous arias of German origin. Reminded me of Japan's Tokyo Rose we listened to in the Pacific during WWII.
I had the dressing changed on my thumb and it looked good. It's feeling a lot better now and it isn't nearly as tender as it was yesterday. I'll probably start flying again on the 25th. The doc left it up to me.
They have about 200 Korean laborers working here on the base and I snapped a picture of one the other day carrying half of a 56 gallon drum on his back, mounted on an "A" frame. I've told you about "A" frames, so I thought I'd better get his picture so you'd know what I meant. A 56 gallon drum is the size of Trooper's incinerator. Boy, you sure do see some funny sights.
Good news, 12 new pilots just reported into the squadron, and among them Perry Porter. I trained with Perry. That's going to take a lot of pressure off of us guys who were doing double duty. Maybe it will even shorten our tour, I hope, I hope, I hope.
Precious little family of mine, I miss you all so very much and love you all with all my heart and soul. You are forever on my mind.
No mail today.

WE FLY TO OUR NEW BASE P'YONGT'AEK, TUNP O RI

I forgot to mention to you, dearest, that there is another breed of dog over here which resembles the white Alaskan husky, not interbred either. There's just an occasional off-breed every now and then running around. Capt Evans, a new replacement who joined today, brought along his Chihuahua. He's a little tiny dog, awfully cute. This cold over here on the west coast doesn't agree with the little guy, though--me either. The Korean hut boys have named the little dog Scoshie, meaning little in Korean. I've been cold ever since we moved from Kangnung.

Three of our pilots who got lost and landed at a field 120 miles to the south of ours and were stranded because they didn't have any fuel at the base, finally got home yesterday. They were handed a letter from the members of our squadron informing them of the fact that they were picking up the check at the officers' club tonight for a squadron party they were giving. I was Group duty officer and couldn't go. It wasn't much of a party, though, and everyone secured early because most of them had the early early railcut up near the Yalu River this morning (shades of MIG-15's).

There aren't any drunks in the squadron to speak of. In fact, I haven't seen anybody drunk since I joined the squadron. That's quite a statement if you take into consideration that they are all flyboys, most of whom drink, and this place would drive anyone to drink anyway, but somehow they just don't take to it. It must be because of the pressing daily situation that every one of us knows he's to face the next day. These days really require a sober mind and a daily prayer if we're to succeed.

Night, night, dearest. Kiss the darlings goodnight for their daddy and tell them I love them and miss them very much.

*Love ya,
Daddy*

A MAN WITHOUT A WOMAN

*A man without a woman is like a ship without a sail,
Just like a boat without a rudder, a kite without a tail.
A man without a woman is like a wreck cast on the sand,
But if there's one thing worse in this universe,
It's a woman, I said a woman, it's a woman without a man.*

*Now you can roll a silver dollar on the ground
And it'll roll because it's round.
A woman never knows what a good man she's got until she turns him down.
Now my honey, oh won't you listen to me, I want you to understand,
Just as a silver dollar goes from hand to hand,
A woman goes from man to man, in a taxi,
A woman goes from man to man.*

24 April 1952
Tunp o ri, Korea

Hi little family,
Golly, it was swell getting three letters in one crack. I've read them all about three times and they'll be read many times more, you can be sure.
Today is quite clear and the air is brisk. There is only a light wind blowing. Our squadron is trying desperately to indoctrinate the new boys with map reading, intelligence reports, familiarization hops etc. Confidential statements, issuing emergency survival equipment and, due to our recent move from Kangnung to Tunp o ri, we're having quite a time. I've been helping out in as many ways as I can along those lines.

I have requested to be assigned as assistant engineering officer. However, I'm not sure that I really want the assignment because I've never done any other squadron job and perhaps I should change and get more familiar with some of the other squadron jobs during my non-flying hours. With the addition to the squadron of almost a third the total complement, I will not be flying as heavily as I was at Kangnung (K18).

Dave Kennedy, my neighbor who bunks right next to me here in the hut, was assistant flight officer and did all of the scheduling, while Capt Barbour went on R&R. Dave is really a nice guy and he and I have hit it off as well as any two in the squadron. Poor Dave just loves flying. He's a regular, and he was selected along with three others from our squadron to go up with the division as forward air controller. He had only been with the squadron since early March and had only acquired about 25 missions. Now he'll have to go to the division for three or four months, then have to return to flying. Most everybody, including myself, desires to get their missions in and over with and then get a ground job of some nature.

Radio Moscow was very kind to the American Communists in their comments today. They said, "Al least our fellow Communists in America are doing everything in their power to thwart the militarists and war mongers." Thank God I'm sharing in some way to fight Communism--the lying, conniving traitors. It makes me burn when I read how the Communist-inspired labor unions are threatening a strike or this or that in the U.S. and Australia, Japan, Philippines. They ought to grab them all and put them in a concentration camp along with all their sympathizers. It's a disease worse than the plague because it affects the minds and the very souls of the persons it hits. I had better get it all out of my system before I come home because I'm afraid I'd be a one-man underground if I came back right away.

Our little houseboy we brought along with us from Kangnung, Jack Ryan's boy, has proven to be a very good little worker. He sweeps and makes all our beds, and washes all our clothes under very crude circumstances--bucket and board style. "hot water hava no" about half the time and he heats some up somehow. He takes a couple of hours off during the day to get acquainted with his countrymen. I guess it's all new and exciting for him. I don't know his name. We just call him Kim like all the others, unless they're old, then we call them papasan.

I'm sending you some of the different kinds of money I'm using over here. The 1000 WON note is the legal tender off of military establishments in Korea. It's worth about 15¢ The 100 YEN note is Japanese, used only in Japan by both Japanese civilian and military personnel. 360 YEN makes a dollar ($1.00), so that would make this 100 YEN note worth about 35¢. The Military Payment Certificate is used on military establishments in Korea and Japan. It's very confusing, to say the least, except that you can get it changed at the pay office at any time, back and forth, as the situation dictates. Give it to Ricky and let him take it to school with him and show the kids. Maybe they would get a kick out of it. I'll send picture postcards in Japan and he can take them in to school and show them around.

I was forever dragging something in to school with me to show the other kids, even my white rats. The teachers would send me home with them sometimes. I remember one day I had my rat with me in my shirt and a girl sitting in the seat next to me screamed bloody murder when she saw the rat climb up my back inside my shirt and look over at her and wiggle his nose. She was deathly afraid of rats or mice. So was the teacher. She called the principal, but he was a good Joe and let me take him home. I saw him smile as I turned to go and I knew he must have done the same thing when he was a kid. I hope Ricky doesn't take the suggestion, however, because there would be no stopping that kid. I'll bet he's going to be a little devil and show-off. So is his little brother too. Golly, I miss those little darlings, and it goes without saying that I miss you, dearest, with all my heart. I'm counting the days until we'll be together again, precious girl. We'll have wonderful times again, sweetheart.

I'll close this out now, dear. Kiss the darlings for me.

Love, Daddy

VMF-212 SQUADRON PILOTS HIT COMMUNIST TANKS

25 April 1952
Tunp o ri, Korea
Friday afternoon

Hi Baby Girl and precious Ricky and Randy,
Tomorrow I'm on the schedule again and my thumb is feeling fine. It gave me considerable pain for several days, but it's looking fine and feeling real good now.
Today was a beautiful cloudless day over Tunp o ri. However, several flights were diverted due to bad weather over North Korea. Yesterday our sqd. clobbered four Commie tanks up on the battle line, and several trucks, gun positions etc. Then today they went in on a target and did so well the 5th Air Force called them up after and congratulated them with a "Well done." Tomorrow, I just heard, will be railcuts all day for the sqd. Nobody cares for the railcuts because they encounter so much flak on them.
Today the P.I.O. (Public Information Officer) took pictures of all of us in the Corsair for propaganda back home. I had to fill out a form for him, giving the names of the newspapers I desired to have my picture and story appear in. I gave him the name of the Huntington Park Signal, Daily Breeze, and the AiReporter, so keep your eyeballs peeled because before long my smiling face will be appearing on the Who's Who in Korea page of your favorite newspaper. It's just as before, only they took it from the other side of the plane, and they had a plane captain helping me into my parachute and shoulder harness.
I saw Harry Perkowski, my El Toro friend. Yes, he's arrived out here finally. Anyway, he was on the Marine transport that developed engine trouble in Texas last March and had to bail out. He said he had quite an experience. A LtCmdr in the Navy was killed in the jump. Harry is in VMF-323. Porter is in our hut and squadron.
In seven or ten days we'll be getting our brand new F4U Corsairs, only they've renamed these AU-1s because they have a higher powered engine and will carry a much heavier load. They've made it an attack fighter-bomber, and it was designed as a close air support plane. The pilot controls and cockpit arrangement are completely different. The Chance Vought aircraft service representative, Jim Barber, a former Chance Vought test pilot, is here already and is going to break us in on the beast. He gave me three new Corsair pictures, nicer than the ones we had. I'll send them home as soon as I can get a container to send them in.
Well, guess I'll close this out, honey, and tell you I love you and my little boys.

Daddy

26 April 1952

Hi Ricky,
Daddy just had breakfast, so he thought he'd have a few minutes to spend with you. I have a railcut that is going out at 1145 this morning and I have a little while to burn before I have to go brief for the mission and then get in my plane and take off and fly up to North Korea and bomb some railroads so the bad Communists can't use them to bring their trains down to carry the supplies, and then they can't fight anymore. Then maybe Daddy and his friends can come home.
Nearly all the pilots in our hut are married and have little boys and girls at home waiting for their daddy. Daddies don't like to leave their precious little families, but when our country is threatened by an enemy that would take over our freedom and the way of life we want to live, daddies have to go and fight for it.

Somebody said one time, "Freedom is reserved for those who are willing to fight and die for it." But let's not talk of fighting anymore. Let's just talk of how wonderful it will be when Daddy comes back home to his wonderful family and we can take up where we left off. They say that "absence makes the heart grow fonder," but our little family didn't need to have anybody go away just to find out how much every one of us needs and loves each other.

I hope, Ricky, that you will always be a loving little guy all your life, because you are one of the growing, coming generation which will take its place in this hectic but wonderful world, and yours is a rugged job. You'll have to bear the burden of taxes of past generations and it will be your job to piece together as best you can all the broken promises the governments of the world have made and broken almost in the same breath. Don't ever lose faith in your fellow man though, darling, because in spite of the way things appear to be going at times you have to look around you and if your eyes are opened to the truth you will see many other brave, sincere men with the same unshakeable ideals as you will possess, and you can regain all the strength and courage you'll ever need to carry out any task that confronts you. You can start building your character and personality right now by living every day of your life the way Mama and Daddy have always taught you. Always show that you love Mamma and Daddy by doing everything we ask you to do, and not getting mad when you're asked to do something you don't want to do.

Ricky, how are you getting along in school now? Are you making anything like a boat or train, like you did at one time? Are you doing any more finger painting? Gosh, I'll bet you're going to be a smart little guy when I get home. You can show me everything you've made in school and tell me everything you've learned. I'll really be interested in hearing all the nice songs you'll have learned while I was away.

Do you help Mama in the yard? You can do a lot to help her by always picking up all your toys and picking up rocks and sticks and papers and leaves that are on the grounds. You could load the garbage can and barrel in your wagon on the days they have to be put out. And you can bring the paper in and the mail in every day. During the summer when the yard will need watering a lot you can turn the sprinkler on and off, and move it around and help Mama a whole lot that way. Poor Mama has to do all the washing, ironing, cooking, housework, shopping, lawn watering and mowing. She has to pay all the bills and dress and wash you kids and see that you get plenty of good, healthy food to eat so you'll grow big and strong. Never give Mama a bad time about your food, Ricky, will you, because Mama only gives you what she knows you need to build big, strong muscles and strong legs so you'll be able to run faster than any kid on the block. We don't want a boy that can't beat the other kids in running games just because he wouldn't eat this or that and he cried or made a bad black face when he was asked to eat his food.

Mama has never written to me and told me anything that you have done that was naughty, so I guess you've been a very good boy and have done everything Mama has asked you to do. Thank you, Ricky darling, you're helping Daddy a lot by being a good boy, because Daddy would worry a lot if he thought you were being a naughty boy. Daddy is real proud of you, Ricky boy. I show everyone your picture and tell them what a fine big boy I have at home helping his mama while I'm in Korea. They all say you are a fine big boy and they all say,"He's going to be a handsome lad when he grows up."

How are you and Trooper getting along these days? Stay out of Trooper's garden, darling, because he works awfully hard and he oftentimes has tiny little plants growing where you'd least expect to find them.

I'm going to write Randy a letter now.
Daddy loves you and misses you, Ricky boy.

Daddy

WE FLY TO OUR NEW BASE P'YONGT'AEK, TUNP O RI

SERENADING GENERAL "HOWLING MAD" SMITH/CIVILIANS INJURED

26 April 1952
Tunp o ri, Korea

Hi Angel Girl and boys,

It's 1335 and I'm standing by in Group Operations waiting word on the weather up over North Korea and whether we will go on our railcut or no. It's up in Flak Alley, so I'm not particularly hoping for good weather. At any rate, I'll use this time to good advantage and write a few well chosen words to my little crew on the home front. This morning I greeted the Korean sunrise, in fact, I was up almost two hours before it was, standing by on the end of the strip on a fighter alert. There were four from our sqd. and four from VMF-323. We had to get up at 0400, eat and taxi out at 0530 and stand by, checking our engines every hour until 0800. Then we secured and another flight took our planes up north and cut some rails. The weather was terrible, however, and they couldn't reach their primary target, so Joint Operations Command (JOC) diverted them to a secondary target on Chinnampo, West Korea. I believe the secondary target is obscured now, so maybe they won't have a target for us this afternoon.

The wood situation is coming along well since we put the skids on them from taking away our firewood and taking it home with them.

A truckload of native civilians who were riding home last night (they were still on the base) went off a ledge and tipped over. About six were injured, none seriously. A marine was driving and they couldn't get them back in the truck after they'd righted it. They changed drivers and climbed back in. I guess they must be superstitious or something or wiser than we think.

They have unskilled Koreans working in the bomb dump doing various chores. They cut through our area going home at night, and you see some real characters among the group! Real long hair and beards, dirty, grimy, crummy, filthy, lousy, mangey are good adjectives, but don't even begin to do them justice. They have hardly any whiskers on their cheeks, but they have long sideburns and chin whiskers. Half of them are barefoot and their clothes are tattered and torn. The afternoon I was Group duty officer I went over to the labor gate where they come for jobs on the base and the line was a mile long. Little tiny guys six and seven years old standing in line waiting to be interviewed. They'll never hire them though. Those that do make it are really good workers because they know how many others are waiting in line outside to take their place. The "papasans" are really "king" because they have picked up a little English and, as they are a little older, they are the lead men and they really dish out the orders to their underlings.

The Korean guards we utilize around the base's interior posts are really on the ball. They'll toss you a salute 200' away and hold it until you return it. They had been trained and uniformed by the Air Force when they had this field.

I had a nice long talk with Jim Barber, the Chance Vought (Ft. Worth, Texas) field representative with our group. He was very interested in what I had done and was all ears. He said, "I'd like to get you into Chance Vought if you want a good job in the next couple of years. Just let me know." Who knows?

This afternoon "Howling Mad" Smith, a Marine general, and some other general of lesser rank (one star) were here on an inspection tour. Smith is a 4-star general about Trooper's age. While we were eating lunch Col Bryson, our CO, said it was too bad he wouldn't be around for tonight's get-together at the O'Club, so we could all get together and sing some of our Marine Flyers' Korean war songs. He said, "How about right here and now in the mess hall?" So Col Bryson and Col Gray (old VMF-232 CO at El Toro) got the boys (me included) and we sang the old man a mess of Marine songs: "Flak Valley," "Early Abort," "Let's get the hell out of here," "When the Reserves all go Home," "I got my 'A' Frame on upside down," and a couple of others, including "On top of Old P'yongyang to the tune of "On Top of Old Smoky."

ON TOP OF OLD P'YONGYANG (ON TOP OF OLD SMOKY)

On top of old P'yongyang
All covered with flak,
I lost my poor wingman
He never came back

For flying is pleasure
And crashing is grief,
But a quick triggered commie
Is worst than a thief

A thief will just rob you
And take what you save,
But a quick triggered commie
Will lead you to the grave.

The grave will decay you
And turn you to dust;
Not one MIG in a thousand
A Corsair can trust.

They'll chase you and kill you
And give you more lead
Than bomb-cuts on a railroad
Or MIGs overhead.

The planes they will shatter,
The pilots will die,
And we'll all be forsaken
And never know why.

So come all you pilots
And listen to me.
Never fly to Sinanju
Or old Kun-ir-ri.

Now the moral of my story
As I've told you before:
Never join the Marine Corps
Or you'll fight every war.

RESERVES LAMENT
(Mr. and Mississippi Make Me Feel at Home)

I won't forget Korea, I can't forget ol' Guam,
For Syngman Rhee and Joe Stalin have made me feel at home.
I flew across the bomb-line and I got a hole or two,
But all I get is a bunch of crap from you and you and you.
    CHORUS:
        Oh I was called to risk my life and save the UN too,
        But all I get is a bunch of crap from you and you and you.

The AA was terrific, the small arms were intense,
While fly boys bombed the front lines the division did the rest.
While the regulars held their desk jobs,
The reserves were called en masse,
For the UN knew that the Marine Reserves were the ones to save their ass.
    CHORUS:

I love you, dear old U.S.A., with all my aching heart.
If I hadn't joined the damn reserves we'd never had to part.
But we won't cry and we won't squawk, for we are not alone,
For one of these days the regulars will come and we can all go home.
    CHORUS:

Now we don't mind the hardships, we've faced 'em in the past
But we wonder if our congressmen have had 40's, what a blast.
We have to fight to save the peace, that's what the bastards said,
But when you check the casualties, you'll find few senators dead.
    CHORUS:

WE FLY TO OUR NEW BASE P'YONGT'AEK, TUNP O RI

I'm going to raise a family when this war is through.
I hope to have a bouncin' boy to tell my stories to.
But someday when he grows up, if he joins the Marine Reserve,
I'll kick his butt from dawn to dusk, for that's what he'll deserve.
    CHORUS:

The old boy just loved them and wanted more. I've never heard the songs sung with such gusto, and the colonels were all knocking themselves out. It was fun and it reflected the spirit I like about the Marine Air Corps--unity and comradeship, which can only be acquired in war times, it seems, when the chips are down. I'd trade it in a second, though, to be with my little family. The O'Club is nothing more than a quonset with one side opened up, and it is on a knoll overlooking the field. It has a big open circular fireplace in the middle of the room. They haven't a stick of furniture in it and won't have until the LST comes around the peninsula. I've begun to worry a little about the LST. It's been a week already.

Tell Ricky I have already taken a picture of "Chipmunk" and I'll be sending it along soon. I won't be seeing Chipmunk any more because he stayed behind at Kangnung because his mother and father were there. Our new boy is conspicuous by his absence here of late. We never know where he is. Usually, though, he is washing clothes or something like that.

There's a long haired rabbit that runs wild around here too, and the other day I saw a huge rat run under the hut. We haven't been bothered by them.

We boys in our spare time have undertaken to section off our hut into separate areas, which will give us a lot more privacy.

Kiss the darlings for me, honey.

                                        Daddy.

LT JACK'S PLANE HITS ENEMY CABLE/
RYAN BLOWS UP TANK, THEN HITS DEBRIS/
EIGHT PLANES GROUNDED IN TWO DAYS

Sunday evening
27 April 1952
Tunp o ri, Korea

Dearest girl,

Just returned from dinner at the mess hall. We had a very nice steak dinner, mashed potatoes, gravy, creamed corn, fried onions, cake and coffee. They had run out of ice cream when I got there, darn it. I'll get some ice cream tomorrow when I get to Itami, Japan.

After I wrote Ricky his letter our hop went out as scheduled and we made railcuts way up north near Sinanju. Look on your map. It's a large town near the west coast of North Korea. The F-86s were up there giving us cover and we thought we could see some MIGs coming after us on our way home over enemy territory. We were all set for a scrap when they turned out to be British Gloucester Meteor jets coming in after us for an identification run. We were a little shook, to say the least, especially after having been fired at over our target. We dove from 9000' and let her fly at about 2500' (released our bombs), diving for the deck and staying there right on the deck, jumping over buildings, strafing etc, on our way out to sea before we started *climbing. By staying on the deck as long as you can you give the Communist gunners a very low deflection. In fact, if we get low enough and stay there they'll shoot their own troops in the process. None of us got hit and we all returned safely. It was a long hop and we covered about as many miles as three trips to San Diego, or one way from San Francisco to our house--2 hrs. 15 min. at 200 mph.*

Our old Corsairs are really beginning to show their years. Yesterday the squadron had five planes AOG (aircraft on the ground) from battle damage. Today they had three more added to the heap. Lt Jacks creamed one when he recovered from a railcut hop, flying low, and hit a cable the Commies had raised for us. He smashed the whole front of his left wing in, dented his belly tank and nicked his propeller. He got back OK, though. It was his first hop.

Jack Ryan blew up a tank with four direct rocket hits. When the tank blew up he flew through the debris and creamed the whole front of his plane--engine nacelle, leading edges of both wings, and even his tail. He got home OK. I could go on and on, only the others in the squadron are less spectacular. The daddy has yet to be scratched (Knock, Knock).

Although I haven't detailed the battle damage for each of the eight planes I mentioned above, all flown by my squadron buddies, they all looked like sieves. Pierced by hundreds of small and large caliber bullets, one could peer clear through the planes in some places. Somehow these brave men flew their planes right to the edge of destruction in order to achieve their goal, making repeated runs until their targets had been completely obliterated, and then, miraculously, they managed to limp home. Every one of my squadron mates has shown conspicuous gallantry, mission after mission, against intense enemy fire. What great men they are!

2145

Just returned to the hut after seeing a technicolor movie called "The Highwayman." During the whole movie the power all over the base went out and we sat there in our open air theater for five minutes waiting for the lights or power to come back on. Last night we saw Bette Davis in her new movie, "Another Man's Poison," a creepy, dark, dull, dreary thing that gave her a chance to go into her dramatic role. I didn't care for it until the end where she finally took the poison and cashed out.

So you went and joined the daddy in getting a ticket. Now I've got a wife who's wanted by the law.

We all chipped in $10.00 and gave it to Jack Ryan, who is going to buy a record player and some records for our hut. It will be fine except I suppose Jack will have his ideas about what to get. We'll have a nice pool of records and we can buy them off the various fellows as they are transferred or leave for the States. Right now we only have one radio and nobody plays it, or when they do it's until real late at night. I was going to buy a radio in Japan but may reconsider what with the record player deal.

I learned today the chaplain here on the base has a record player and can make records. I'm going to look into it, honey, and I'll cut a disc if he'll let me.

I'm awfully tired tonight, baby girl, so guess I'll "sayonara" (sign off, or leave, or get lost--in Korean).

You asked about the time difference. Well, when it's 2230 Sun. night in California it would be 1530 Mon. afternoon in Korea. Your letters mean everything to me, darling. I really live for them now, honey. I write every day because it's a highlight in my day. It's the only way of chatting with you, although I'd give anything for a few words first hand with my little family. Kiss my precious darlings for me, honey.

Love, Daddy

WE FLY TO OUR NEW BASE P'YONGT'AEK, TUNP O RI

LOG FOR APRIL 1952

Date	Aircraft Type	Aircraft Number	Flight Duration	Type of Mission
3	F4U-4B	97437	1.2	Fam
4	F4U-4B	97489	1.0	Bombing & Fam
5	F4U-4B	62997	1.8	CAS - Troops & Bunkers, Sohuir-ri
6	F4U-4B	63040	1.3	CAS - Troops & Gun Pos, Ando-ri
8	F4U-4B	97399	0.9	CAS - Troops & Bunkers, Suwon-dan
9	F4U-4B	97420	3.3	Railcut, Kwaksan
9	F4U-4B	97420	2.1	CAS - Troops, Dokchuwon-ni
10	F4U-4B	63040	0.3	Search Abort
16	F4U-4B	62993	1.6	CAS - Command Post, 12 KIA, Mu-san
16	F4U-4B	97518	0.8	Slow Time
18	F4U-4B	62994	1.6	CAS
20	F4U-4B	97461	1.2	K-18 to K-6
21	F4U-4B	63060	1.8	CAS - Troops, Shelters & 3 Troops KIA Osong-san
27	F4U-4B	63023	2.4	Railcut, Sinanju

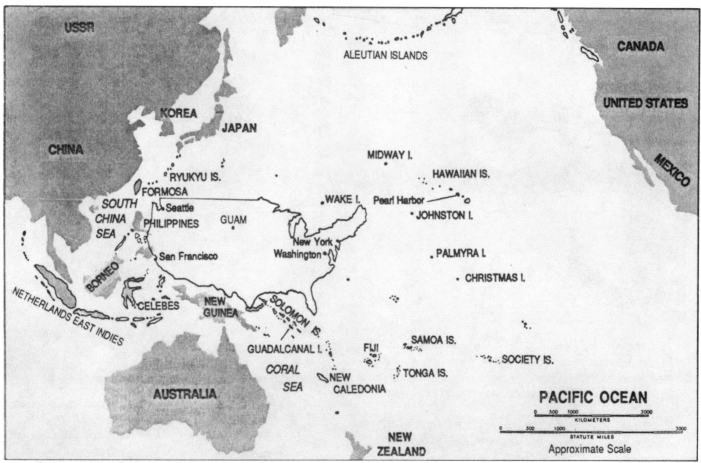

Note: Outline of United States superimposed for comparison.

1.

2.

3.

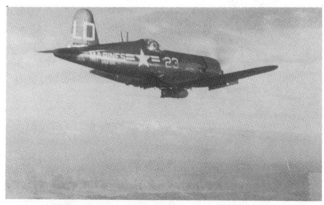

4.

5.

1. L to R: Maj Reed (S5) VMF-212 and civilian Field Service Rep. Bill Barber from Chance Vaught.

2. Korean laborers digging our protective bunkers.

3. Peterson at his desk, fabricated from discarded ammo boxes, writing his proverbial letter home. See family photos in front.

4. Corsair crashed at K6 while returning home damaged from heavy Communist AA fire. This was a common sight for us all.

5. Peterson returning from a combat mission in "LD" LOVE DOG # 23, with a hung 1000 lb bomb still on plane. I had the choice of bailing out or landing. I made a very smooth "soft" landing and it didn't come off. Not so a few days later when a 100 lb bomb fell off on landing and floated and bounced alongside my plane--but didn't explode.

Left: Aerial view of Seoul, capital of South Korea.

Middle Left: Capt Gene Cameron, Kim Jin Kil, our hut boy, and writer. K6.

Middle Right: 5" Hivar rockets.

Lower Right: 100 lb wing bombs with safety wire in nose fuses. Two 20mm cannon barrel tips can be seen protruding from wing's leading edge.

Lower Left: Battle damage claims another Corsair. If this keeps up, I can go home when all the planes are used up.

CHAPTER 8

MY FIRST R&R IN JAPAN

28 April 1952
Itami, Air Force Base, Japan
1730

Precious little family,
    I'm writing from Itami, Japan, the same spot that I landed in on the way over to Korea. This morning it rained and the wind blew something terrific, and I felt as though we would never get out of Korea.
    I was up at 0700, had breakfast, packed my gear in my little green navy issue suitcase, threw my raincoat over my freshly pressed green uniform I had carried on a hanger. Then I walked on down to the airfreight office with my orders to get my name on the cargo manifest. They told me an R5D would be in at about 1100 from Itami, so I was down there waiting for it at 1030. The storm grew worse, however, and we had to wait for them to load two Corsair engines on the plane, besides waiting for a clearing in the soup. The pilot figured it would not clear, so off we went into the blinding rainstorm. The wind was blowing at about 30 kts crosswind from our runway and the plane tail cocked around as the wheels left the deck, but off we climbed, bumping and jumping from one side to the other. We never broke through the stuff until we were about an hour and a half out of Korea towards Japan over the Sea of Japan. We took off at 1300 and landed at Itami at 1520. The weather was clear here and the sun is shining through the window onto my letter as I write. The plane made a slow let-down towards Itami and we flew over many Japanese villages, farms and forests, so I took pictures from the plane's dirty window.
    After we landed, the very first thing I did was to go over to the PX and order a giant vanilla malted milk. It was watery, but it tasted delicious to me. It was my first in a month. I have a bottom bunk in a big open dormitory, the same one I was in on the way through here last time. I showered and shaved, put on clean shorts, undershirt, socks and khaki shirt, greens and my brown oxfords for the first time in a month. I've grown so used to my heavy old boondockers that my oxfords feel like I'm almost barefoot, they are so light on my feet.
    After I finish writing to you, honey, I'm going to go into Osaka to the restaurant called "The Valley of the Moon," a place used exclusively by the Marine Corps. Nobody else is allowed in the place unless they're guests of a marine. I'm going with Capt Van Dalsem,

another 212 pilot who was on the 18th draft. He has been there once before and says the steaks at the "Valley" are out of this world. We'll see. I'll give you a full report either tonight or in the morning. If I'm back by 2000, I'm going to the movie here on the base, "Hong Kong."

I'm sitting on the edge of my bunk writing on a little low table with my brand new $2.00 "Parkerette" pen I just bought at the PX. I turned two rolls of film in for developing and will pick them up Wed. the 30th and airmail them on to you.

I wish you and the boys were here now because Japan, from what I've seen of it, is most interesting. If my pictures turn out any good you'll have a perfect idea of what Japan is like. They were taken from 5000' and again at about 1000'.

Give the little darlings a hug and a kiss for me, sweetheart. Bye bye for now, honey.

Love, Daddy

29 April 1952
Itami, Japan
0930 Tuesday

Hi little family that I love,

Yesterday evening I walked out the main gate for about a half mile to the electric train station and bought a ticket to Takaraska, which was about a 25 minute ride from the Hotarikaike station, where I boarded the train. It stops at many towns on its way to Takaraska, the names of which would tie your tongue trying to pronounce them. The fare was 50 yen (360 yen to the dollar). There were three cars hooked together, maybe 25 years old, but comfortable and clean.

Japanese from all walks of life jam-packed the cars--from farmers and peasants to women in slacks with sport coats and hair done up American style. Ninety percent of them wore wooden shoes. Many women wore kimonos, with their hair high on their head like buns, or braided. Some men wore modern sport clothes and good looking ties with windsor knots; others wore black kimonos and wooden shoes. Most of the people carried umbrellas, although it was a clear, mild spring evening and had been a warm, comfortable day. The majority were returning home from work, I guess. Many were busily engaged in reading their newspapers. I sat next to a man, looking over his shoulder, but of course couldn't read a thing. However, pictures covered 75 percent of the paper, so I was kept amused.

We were slightly elevated as we passed through the towns and we could look right down into the houses. Every house had a light in it for electricity is plentiful here. They all had a flower and vegetable garden, some only a patch of ground about 25 ft. square, but in it they would have a stand of wheat three feet high. You could see farmers carrying "honey buckets" (fertilizer) and spreading the contents on their gardens. Little kids were playing only a few feet from the train tracks, in the back yards of their homes. The Japanese children are adorable with their little inquisitive expressions, the crew haircuts on the boys and Dutch bob on the little girls. Some of the mothers dressed them in the oriental style, others had modern little dresses on the girls and cute little suits on the boys.

As the car stopped at the various stations, little pedestrian crossing bars would slide electrically across the foot paths about 200 feet ahead of the train. Children with books under their arms could be seen waiting for the signal bridge to be raised as the train proceeded ahead, and an all-clear bell was heard to ring behind us as we pulled away. The train's conductor would make a pass through the train about a minute prior to arriving at the next station, and he muttered the name in slow, guttural voice, although he walked very fast through the three cars. He operated an electric button at his station to the rear of the train, which controlled sliding doors, two on each car. They opened and closed in great haste, and more than once I saw some Japanese got their kimono tails caught as they attempted to board the train. It would come to a speedy stop, the doors would open, and people would just stream in and out; then the doors would slam shut and the train would be scooting ahead again, all in a matter of seconds. I was amazed and amused at the whole situation and wouldn't have missed the ride on the train for anything in the world.

I arrived at my destination. Takaraska is a little town of hotels, small shops, bath houses, parks with shade trees covering the foot paths, green lawns and flowers everywhere. The streets are only about 25 ft. wide and two cars have trouble passing each other. All the streets wind up and down hill, with hairpin turns and the like everywhere you go. Every inch of streetfront is covered with some sort of establishment, very small, crude little places, mostly opened in front. It was growing late, I was getting hungry, and I felt a little bit lost and confused as I wandered along the little cobblestoned streets, seeing the Japanese people as they lived and worked in this little unspoiled town. There were friendly smiles and bows from the storekeepers, half of their happy smiles disclosing a mouth full of gold-capped teeth. Little black perfect-circle horn-rimmed glasses were seen in abundance. Dried fish hung in the market areas, and other strange assortments of edible (I suppose they were anyway) offerings.

After about 15 or 20 minutes of roaming I finally came upon an Air Force sergeant and asked for the hotel called "The Valley of the Moon." He informed me that I had come one prefecture too far, and should reboard the train and return to the next town up the line. I had a rough time at the ticket office trying to purchase a ticket to a town I couldn't pronounce, but through gestures, motions and pidgin English I wound up with a ticket that cost me 25 yen, so I figured I had made my point. I got off at the first stop, about a five minutes' ride from Takaraska. Again bewildered as I walked the narrow little streets, I finally found an American sign directing me to the Air Force officers billet of the Takaraska Hotel, where I came upon Capt Jack Ryan standing in the lobby getting verbal directions from an Air Force captain as to the best place in town to eat. The hotel restaurant was closed and we were both starving.

On foot we set out for an Italian cafe called "Abelas," which we found only by sheer determination and perseverance. We walked about two miles over mountain passes, bridges, crossed rivers, and hiked up dark, spooky alleys. Finally we came upon "Abelas" after a nice piece of navigating. There were only five small tables in there. They had a radio and both gas and electric lights, but as we entered, only the gas light was going, and very dimly at that. We looked at each other and shrugged in bewilderment, wondering whether or not we should go in. It had been highly recommended by the Air Force captain at the hotel, so we figured we couldn't miss. The menu was handed to us and it was all in English. We both ordered spaghetti with steak, coffee and garlic bread. It tasted out of this world and we enjoyed it tremendously. Our bill was 1280 yen, or about $3.25 for the both of us. A group of people kept streaming in through the cafe and upstairs, so we questioned the waitress who informed us, "No waitress--Jo san, please." We asked what was upstairs and she replied "Geisha girls." Jack and I paid our bill and left, wondering who had prepared our food, etc.

We walked back all the way and never encountered a single car on the narrow little road, only an occasional bike. Upon arriving at the Takaraska Hotel we asked where the Marines congregated in this town. The Air Force captain said, "The Valley of the Moon" in Mefujinja, so we called a cab, and ten minutes later and 300 yen poorer we arrived at a private home, a mansion nestled up on a hill overlooking a beautiful lake surrounded by pines and many other types of trees. The gardens were beautiful. What a place! We were greeted at the door by a Japanese woman in a kimono, and saw about ten pairs of Marine oxfords lined up at the edge of the main entrance hall (this is a Japanese custom everywhere). We took ours off, put on some slippers, and were conducted into a large den with lounge chairs, fireplace, rugs, pictures all over the walls, and soft music playing. We found Bobby Foster and Bill Higgins feeding their faces with the biggest, thickest steaks I have ever seen--1 1/2" thick, mushroom sauce etc., coffee, bread and butter--500 yen. We informed them that we had already eaten but were sorry for it because even though we had had steak it couldn't have compared with what those guys were eating. They were having beer with their meal. We all left in about an hour and caught the train home. The train was loaded with servicemen and Japanese, all returning home. About 2330 we arrived at the Hotarikaike station (Itami Air Base) where a Marine truck met us and drove us to the base and BOQ. Tired from my day's gallivanting and my flight over here from Korea, I slept like a baby until 0700 this morning, got up, had breakfast and went over to try and locate my seabags. They believe they were lost; however, they are rechecking and will let me know by next Sunday, when I'm due to return to Korea. It's raining crocodile tears outside now, darling, so I'm afraid I'll be confined to Itami Air Base today. I

ABELA'S. A FABULOUS ITALIAN RESTAURANT. STEAK AND SPAGETTI. JAPAN

Upper Left and Right: Sign on left lured us to the famous Italian restaurant, Abela, a half hour train ride to the town of Takarazuka, where we feasted on fabulous food— steak, spaghetti and pizza.

Middle Left: Capts Terrell and Peterson waiting for our train to Takarazuka.

Middle Right and Lower Left: The great opera house at Takarazuka, where we saw "Les Chansons de Paris," an exact copy of the Parisian "Les Folies Bergère." Tunes, gowns, scenery, all exact duplicates of the show I would see in 1960 in Paris, but actually the Japanese version in 1952 was much better.

Top Left: My friends, Johnson and Terrell. Johnson was officer-in-charge at Los Alamitos Naval/Marine Reserve Air Station in Long Beach, CA, when I visited there several times immediately after WWII. In Korea, he was a jet pilot flying F9F Panthers. Terrell, an ex-race driver from my hometown, turned out to be a great friend and combat flying buddy. They are standing on the electric train platform and we are on our way to an opera.

Top Right: Two friends from our Air Group, having done some heavy shopping at Kyoto's KIGYO CO. LTD., a fine store for purchasing silk cloth.

Right: Peterson in front of silk factory, having purchased some silk goods for Marion. See packages beside me.

After flying any number of combat missions with your life on the line nearly every day, it was such a wonderful relief to be able to jump on an R5D Douglas transport and within a little over an hour be in a totally different environment—comfortable hotels, great food, rapid electric trains to any town you might wish to visit. Plays, theater, movies, and above all, the knowledge that nobody was shooting at you.

Left: The Japanese fly the fish flag for various holidays, and these typical signs are an eyesore littering the train route for miles.

transferred to another BOQ and have a room with another captain from a Marine night fighter squadron who returns to Korea tomorrow.

Miss my precious family more than I can possibly tell you. I want nothing more from this world than to return home to you all, never to leave you again. I'll not get any mail until I return to Korea, which will be my only incentive for returning to that hole.

Love, Daddy

A good bit of advice, which everyone can use during times of adversity:

PRESS ON!

"Nothing in the world can take the place of persistence.

Talent will not; nothing is more common than unsuccessful men with talent. Genius will not; unrewarded genius is almost a proverb. Education will not; the world is full of educated derelicts.

Persistence and determination alone are all powerful. The slogan 'Press on!' has solved and always will solve the problems of the human race."

Calvin Coolidge

29 April 1952
Itami, Japan

Dearest family of mine,

Today I visited Kyoto. When I boarded the train the sliding door slammed closed and, believe it or not, it was so packed when we got to Kyoto the people's noses were pushed against the door; when it opened it bent them. Due to its being the emperor's birthday yesterday many of the houses had the red meatball and fish kites flying, which must have been an oriental custom. The fish were mostly all black and six feet long, but some were all red. They were hollow inside and the wind blew them out horizontally. They also had some other weird looking creatures I couldn't make out.

Students all dressed in their black uniforms predominated the passenger list today. Their hats were all different. Some looked like four-cornered graduation hats, with a beak on all of them; some were the usual captain's yacht hat. They all wore high white plastic collars. Some of their shoes were make of black rubber but had stitching and laces, sole and heel all molded in the rubber, and you had to look twice before you realized they were not real shoes.

The railroad wayside to Kyoto was like a parkway in a good many places, with grass, flowers and trees. We passed road junctions where I saw many bicyclists dressed in shorts riding racing bikes, waiting for the train to pass. They must have belonged to a club (all Japanese).

Every station stop had posters and ads apparently advertising Japanese movies. Also, on the trains, they had identical ads. I saw quite a few Japanese dressed in old odds and ends.

Getting off in Kyoto, I walked a couple of blocks just nosing around in the stores, then doubled back and caught a taxi at the train station for the Kyoto Army PX. What a place! Boy, there's nothing in the States like it. They have taken over this huge modern steel-cement office building right in the middle of Kyoto. MP's are everywhere and you've got to show them everything but your skivies in order to crack into the joint. They have a huge modern snack bar on the main floor where I ventured a snack--tenderloin steak, French fried spuds, peas, salad, *coffee, and chocolate sundae--$1.15. Then I went up on the third floor via elevator and the splendor that met me! The whole floor, 400' by 400', was covered with everything you could possibly desire in the orient: roll after roll of materials--tweeds and oriental silks. Dishes, vases, wood chests, kimonos, coats, oriental arts, books, toys, and household items were everywhere.*

I bought myself a beautiful Zenith trans-oceanic portable, DC & AC radio in black leatherette. I have it on the table next to me now and Bing Crosby is singing "Sin" on his canned stateside broadcast, being rebeamed by Armed Forces Radio in Kyoto. Humphrey Bogart and Lauren Bacall are now singing "Twinky Deedle Down, Twinky Deedle Dee, Old Fisherman," a song from Humphrey's latest picture. They are sure funny. Boy, I've heard some grand music and plays on my radio and I love it. It works beautifully.

Foster, Holland and I took a taxi to the station. We separated at Juso station. They went to Osaka and I came home to Itami and had dinner--chicken, which was very good. Then I retired to my lonely little BOQ room to write my girl and listen to my new radio.

Tell the boys I love them, and tell them they are going to get something from Daddy on about May 21st.

Love to you all, Daddy

CONVERSATION WITH THE F-86 SABREJET PILOTS

The R&R (Rest and Recuperation or, in the vernacular, Rack and Ruin) policy for the pilots of the 1st Marine Air Wing, similar to that of the USAF pilots, allowed temporary duty in Japan every six weeks. We were given anywhere from three to seven days to do as we darn well pleased. Some Air Force pilots maintained their families in Japan, but this policy wasn't condoned by the Marine Corps.

During these R&Rs I had the opportunity to meet any number of F-86 fighter pilots in an informal setting, most of them just fresh from intense air-to-air mortal combat in the skies over North Korea (MIG Alley), some that very day. They uniformly expressed very definite rules of combat in their own special lingo:

1. Their jet engines could suffer flameout during high-G turns above 20,000 feet, oftentimes not reigniting until they had glided to a more dense atmosphere, all the while being shot at by the wily MIG-15 pilots all the way down.

2. While in MIG Alley, they tried to conceal their presence by staying below 35,000 ft, thus avoiding the telltale contrails.

3. They had trouble "smoking" or "flaming" a MIG above 40,000 ft with their .50 caliber machine gun bullets due to the imbalance of the fuel-to-air ratio, whereas one single hit from a MIG's 37mm explosive shell could blow a Sabrejet out of the sky. Ironically, they all wished they had four 20mm cannons like my "obsolete" F4U-4B Corsair had.

4. "Punch your tanks!" meant "Jettison your drop tanks," which could be seen often fluttering down from a very high altitude.

5. They all stressed the absolute need for developing good relationships with every member of their team, since their lives depended on a cooperative effort.

6. They admitted that the UN radar team on the northernmost islands in the Yellow Sea gave them valued vectors that often resulted in their having a strategic advantage over the MIGs. They chose not to discuss this, however, in public. In fact, I didn't even know the team was there and never received any guidance from them. <u>We</u> had not been briefed on the existence of the radar control unit.

7. Radio silence was a rule unless engagement had already begun. However, we'd hear an awful lot of foolish chatter from these guys on the way home.

8. MIGs were often stacked at 4000 ft separations up to 40,000 ft.

9. The diligent use of dive brakes was as important as a burst of thrust from the engine. A good spray from the MIG pilot's substantial arsenal could spell the end of an overrunning Sabrejet.

10 These F-86 fighter pilots all turned tight if pursued, causing the MIG's fire to go wide of the mark.

11. The Sabrejet's "point of no return" came too fast because the high rate of fuel consumption often forced them to break off contact, or else swim home.

12. The Sabrejet pilots referred to the enemy flight leader as the "lead MIG driver." He was the one they loved to get first, causing considerable confusion for the rest of the flight.

13. "Tired A" was often heard over the VHF radio fighter frequency, which didn't mean their butts, but referred to the particular F-86 fighter model they'd been assigned that particular day--the F-86A was older and slower than the newer and faster F-86E, and they needed every advantage they could get over the 3000 lb lighter and faster MIG.

14. They complained about the short range of their .50 caliber tracer ammo, ie, early burnout.

15. They avoided pulling too many Gs, since that force would pull the bullets uselessly behind the target.

16. All pilots considered the political rule of disengagement at the demarcation point, the Yalu River (the border with China), incomprehensible. The Yalu River was referred to as the "Creek."

These guys were a rare and proud breed and our nation would owe them a heavy debt of gratitude. What would have been the consequences for the UN and the USA of having 841 MIG-15s wade into the obsolescent close-support aircraft such as I was flying?

This was the final number of MIG-15s shot down throughout the war, with another 52 kills in addition to that for all other types of Communist aircraft destroyed in the three years of fighting:

TEN OR MORE VICTORIES IN KOREA (39 TOTAL ACES)

Name	*Score*	
McConnell, Joseph Jr.	16.0	Killed in 1954 test flying.
Jabara, James	15.0	Killed in 1960 car crash. His daughter also was killed.
Fernandez, Manuel J.	14.5	
Davis, George A. Jr.	14.0	Shot down, killed Feb 1952. Won the MOH.
Baker, Royal N.	13.0	
Blesse, Frederick C.	10.0	
Fischer, Harold E.	10.0	
Garrison, Vermont	10.0	
Johnson, James K.	10.0	
Moore, Lonnie R.	10.0	Killed in 1956 test flying.
Parr, Ralph S. Jr.	10.0	

Upper Left: We visited the town of Kobe, Japan, which had been hit fairly hard by us during WWII; however, very little evidence was visible. We enjoyed shopping here.

Middle Left: View from our taxi. Kobe, a bustling town, had the best military PX in Japan, shown on the left through taxi window.

Middle Right: Capts Terrell and Johnson, my R & R traveling buddies in Kobe.

Lower Left: Kobe theater was showing "When the Worlds Collide."

Lower Right: Our avenue to everywhere, the electric train at the Juso Station, just outside Itami Air Base gate.

Upper Left and Right, and Middle Left: Scenes of the Japanese town of Osaka. The date 1 May 1952, May Day, and the Communists were making trouble.

Middle Right and Lower Right: Enjoying myself in the fabulous town of Kyoto and admiring the well landscaped grounds of the Miyako Hotel, where I stayed. I purchased a group of Japanese gods, all standing on a black stairstepped stand, which I still cherish today. The Miyako Hotel gift shop was the finest in all of Japan.

ACES IN TWO WARS
ACES OF WORLD WAR II AND KOREA

NOTE: All officers are assigned to U.S. Air Force except as indicated.

	WWII	Korea	Joint
Bolt, John F. (USMC)	6.00	6.00	12.00
Davis, George A. Jr.	7.00	14.00	21.00
Gabreski, Francis S.	28.00	6.50	34.50
Garrison, Vermont	7.33	10.00	17.33
Hagerstrom, James P.	6.00	8.5	14.50
Thyng, Harrison R.	5.00	5.00	10.00
Whisner, William T.	15.50	5.50	21.00

1 May 1952
Itami, Japan

Dearest Marion and boys,

I've missed you all very much today, little gang that I love. This morning I started out by taking Bill Higgins', Bob Foster's and Hugh Holland's greens, ties and shirts to the base cleaners because they had to leave at 0530 this morning for Tunp o ri, Korea.

I picked up the two rolls of pictures at the PX and they turned out swell, considering I was traveling at close to 200 mph and fairly near the ground when I took some of them. I think I'll send you only a couple at a time so that I'll have something each time to enclose in my letters to you. That way I'll keep your interest up. Ain't I the devil?

Capt Johnson, the officer on active duty at Los Alamitos at the Marine detachment, is overseas now and on his first R&R. He flies F9F Panther jets in Korea. He, Capt Terrell and I went out together. (Terrel and I took our physicals at Los Alamitos and went through VMT, the training squadron at El Toro. We got separated at El Toro and he came over on the 18th draft.) We all went into Kobe on the electric train, stopping on the way at the PX. I didn't need anything except a pencil flashlight and a couple of spare bulbs and batteries, and a few silk handerchiefs I wanted to enclose in my letters to you, just to add a personal touch. I forgot to tuck in the train tickets, but I'll do it tonight. We had a sandwich at the PX snack bar across the street from the main PX. They are closing the whole works May 5th.

We walked around town looking for a camera for Johnson and a set of china for Terrell, who finally ordered from the Nippon Kanko Shohin Co., the same place I bought yours. They had another beautiful set on display, 94 pieces for $69.00 (egg shell). Then we strolled up and down the little side streets and looked in all the shops. Took a few pictures here and there when I saw something unusual. We walked down to the harbor of Kobe and it's quite a place. Some of the dock buildings are still down and burned out from our bomber raids.

I heard on the radio tonight that there were 3,000,000 Communists holding 400 separate May Day meetings, and that Tokyo was out of bounds to all military personnel because the Communist demonstrators were burning and wrecking all American property, and even attacking American civilian and military personnel. Capt Van Dalsem came from Tokyo today and said he didn't see anything unusual. However, he pointed out that Tokyo is a huge place. It would be like the Communists having a riot in Pasadena and us living in Manhattan Beach, knowing nothing about it except by radio and newspaper reports. We saw nothing in Kobe today in the way of demonstrations, parades or speeches and gatherings. Maybe Kobe isn't one of their strongholds.

The Japanese government was quick to come out with the statement that it did not go along with the Communists' acts nor did it sympathize with them in any way. The Japanese Commies are trying to make it look like the Japanese people want the Americans to leave, but they certainly do not want anything of the kind.

We went into a huge Japanese department store in Kobe (5 floors) and shopped. I was especially interested in the Japanese furniture. Most of it was bamboo or wicker--glass topped wicker tables and a lot of very low, wide and long tables with legs only 10 inches high, beautifully finished woods, priced at around $15.00. They had some lovely lacquer ware; little jewel boxes with mirrors (2200 yen or about $6.50). They were the finest pieces of workmanship I have ever laid my eyes on. You'd love one and I've thought of getting one and sending it home to you. Maybe next R&R.

I took pictures of Japanese people in every walk of life today--at the stations, on the street, out of taxicab windows. I'll have this roll developed and will have the prints back before I have to leave again for Korea. The Japanese Red Cross is having its annual drive and I'll bet I was hounded by at least 500 little Japanese school girls today in Kobe until I finally gave one 10 yen and she gave me a feather with a red cross--find same enclosed.

We arrived back at Itami at around 1730. I cleaned up and had dinner, then met Bob Ferguson, who is here awaiting ship transportation home and discharge. We talked until 2000, then went and saw "Two Tickets to Broadway," a technicolor musical, with Tony Martin and Janet Leigh. It was fairly good, but not as good as "I'll See You in My Dreams."

Good news, dear. The Marine Corps has just put out a directive stating all volunteer reserves at the completion of their 17 months of active duty will be eligible for release from active duty and may resign their commissions! That's the best news I've heard in months. How about that, honey? Maybe if they get enough guys over here they will let us come home early too. Just think, darling, we'll be completely divorced from the Marine Corps. We can plan our lives without worrying about having to leave for any foreign shores again. I'm getting too old to fly or fight.

2 May 1952

Hello again, dearest,

I had to secure my letter last night because I was writing until 2330 and Lt. Nelson, my roommate, was in bed and I was afraid the light was bothering him. I just read my last night's letter through, and I guess I should have said we went to the show on the base. Also, I meant to tell you of the train's speed on our way into Kobe yesterday; we were doing about 65 MPH on a rickety, wobbly track that was highly elevated in many places and it felt as though the train were tipping over. The tracks are very close together, so whenever one train passes another they almost touch each other, and the breeze throws the trains apart because their closing speeds are around 130 MPH.

I really got a big charge out of going through the Japanese department store in Kobe yesterday. They had Japanese foods and goods on the first floor and the smell of fish was overwhelming. However, the whole store was really very clean. Just above the main floor, as in any stateside department store, they had the furniture level, toys, suits, dresses, radios, cameras etc.

This R&R has helped me get my mind off the war a little bit, but I can never forget it completely, knowing that in a few more days I'll be right back in the thick of things again. How I want to return home to my precious family! I miss you all so very, very much. The thought is constantly with me, gosh, I wish I had Marion and the kids here so they could be seeing what I'm seeing, but mainly to be with me because I need you all so very much. Better yet, I should be home with you because the thought is always with me that in spite of exceptions like that department store, the Japanese are somewhat careless about their general cleanliness in cities and small towns. I've washed my hands a dozen times because you feel as though everything you touch is filthy. I'd die if the kids were going around over here, or anywhere for that matter, touching things and putting their hands in their mouths.

I saw American children in Kobe and Kyoto PX with their mothers and fathers. They looked awfully good to me and I felt like going over and picking one of the little boys up and hugging and kissing him, and to feel his little soft face against mine. It's rough on a daddy to be away from his little family.

I love you, dearest Marion, and also the boys with all my heart.

Bye bye, Daddy

2 May 1952
Itami Air Base, Japan

Precious family,

Today was a nice, warm, sunshiny day. The birds were all out and singing. The grass is green and the trees are all getting their foliage. That's one thing I have really missed in Korea; there aren't any green trees or grass anywhere near our base.

I never left the base today. Got up late, ate in the snack bar and took a few pictures. Went over to the field operations building, checked out some navigation maps and drew you a sketch (free hand and not very accurate) of Korea and Japan. I tried to show you where I am, where I've been and a few of the highlights, such as the location of Atsugi from Tokyo and Mt. Fuji. Itami, as you can see, is inland and the dotted lines between Kyoto, Kobe and Osaka are the train routes. The other dotted lines indicate my general air travels. Miyasaki in Kyushu, if you recall, is the field I hit with the squadron in July 1945. Just offhand, without measuring it, I'd say the island of Honshu is about 400 miles long. There are a million little villages and hamlets, as well as large cities on every one of the islands.

My Zenith is playing some beautiful music, which sure helps a guy pass away the lonely hours. I'm listening to the Curt Massey and Martha Tilton show. They are the same two I used to listen to coming home from El Toro. Sounds just like home.

Just heard the stateside news about the steel and oil industry strikes. Isn't that a shame? Those people are sabotaging our war effort. Just heard also that about 30 percent of aviation gasoline was curtailed. Also heard of the atom bomb blast in Nevada. Boy, this is really wonderful, getting all the news right from the States via the Armed Forces Radio in Japan. I can get the 1900 news via short wave directly from Los Angeles. I heard Salt Lake residents were being evacuated because of rising waters. I can't picture the river there, can you, darling?

I have a newfound spirit and desire to go home and get to work at AiResearch, or maybe some other trade. Every time I return from a mission, taxi into the chocks and cut my engine, I breathe a sigh and say a little Thank You prayer. Each time, after listening to the roar of my engine for two or more hours, and feel the tenseness of combat, it seems as though I crawl out of my plane into a new, more wonderful world. It's very quiet, and seems almost like I am the only one on earth until finally we all gather into the ready room for a de-briefing and we relive the hop all over again. Then I try to forget the darn thing and get some happier thoughts in my heart.

Whenever I think of my beloved family waiting for me at home it gives me new courage, dearest. You and the boys are my strength. Maybe God is supposed to be, but through Him I have you, and you are His instruments to brighten my whole life.

I've had a very strong desire to get into youth activity when I return home. Maybe we could start a boys club or something, through Rick's Sunday school or grade school, one or the other. I want to get as close to my boys and my precious wife as I possibly can. We have a wonderful life ahead of us and we'll live every day with all our might.

Bye bye for tonight, my precious family.

Daddy

MY FIRST R&R IN JAPAN

3 May 1952
Itami, Japan
Sat., 1500

Hi there little family,

The daddy just returned from Osaka, where I went to a department store to buy Mama a little lacquer cabinet. A clerk in the store wanted to talk to me. He said he had been studying English for two years and wanted me to tell him how I thought he was doing. I told him fine. In fact, he was the best I've heard since arriving here. He expressed his regrets at the Communists' May Day Tokyo demonstrations and expressed his thanks that we were going to keep our troops here in Japan because, he said, "We are afraid of the Russian Bear." He was very nice and helped me along in his department. He wanted to know if I was married and what my trade was, etc. I showed him a picture of you and the boys, honey, and he said I had a fine family. I thanked him. He told me he had a very responsible position in the store and he drew 8000 yen a month ($24.00). I told him I made almost 8000 yen a day and he was amazed. But when I told him of the food and housing and general living costs in America he began to realize the true value of my money. His expenses are very nominal. He can buy enough rice for a week for 30 yen, and they live three families to a house, so his pay goes a long way.

We talked of the late Jap-American war in the Pacific and he said it was regrettable, "but through the occupation we have found true friendship with the American people we never had before." The truth of the matter is, they are enjoying a better economy than they had before the war, or during. They aren't having to support a terrific war machine as they were then. I enjoyed my talk with him because he was so interested in America, and expressed his desire to come over to see our department stores. I told him that in America we had mail order and delivery service which he said was a very good idea. He appeared to be astonished and impressed at my saying this, so I wouldn't be surprised if he becomes the Japanese Mr. Sears & Roebuck based on my suggestion. The train was crowded on my return and I stood up all the way back to Hotarikaike Itami station.

I've sure had my fill of walking since I came over here. I bet I've walked ten miles today! The other day, when we were in Kobe, we walked over ten miles, I know, because I checked the speedometer of the cab that picked us up to take us to the train station. I was all by myself today--me and around 100,000 Japanese. I snapped some pictures in Osaka. Just outside of the train station I caught a good one right on the main drag of a beat-up old horse pulling a huge load of lumber right in the middle of all the city traffic. Then I took a picture of one of the downtown trolley cars with a whole mess of advertising on the side of it, big signs hanging from the sides and top. Next came a two-wheeled cart with automobile size wheels and tires, being pulled by one tiny little old Jap, followed by a loudly honking new Cadillac with a Japanese business man inside and driven by a chauffeur. What a comparison!

The weather has been beautiful today, slightly on the warm side. I wore khaki shirt and pants. Tonight there is going to be a USO show here at the base and they are going to show a movie, so guess I'll try to get a seat and see them both.

In a way, I wish you were here. You'd enjoy the heck out of this strange but wonderful country. It's old and gives you the feeling that everything is filthy dirty, but outside of that it's interesting. If we'd sell all our assets and move over here we'd never have to work another day of our lives, providing we went on a rice diet. How about it, honey? Nope, you say? Well, me too. I'll take Manhattan Beach any time. It would be fun to set up a Japanese theme room, though.

Another day gone, which brings me just a little bit closer to my family. The Japanese children on the train were adorable. They took their shoes off and got up on the seats to look out the window. The sights you see in the backyards from the train would fill a good-sized book.

All for now.

Love,
Daddy

4 May 1952
Itami, Japan
Sunday morning, 1130

Hi little family,

One more day, then back to my Corsair in Korea in the morning. I've seen a lot of fellows I haven't seen since the war in the Pacific, and we've had long talks together. Itami is sort of a melting pot for the Marine Corps. Fellows going home to be discharged are here by the hundreds and you can see them parading back and forth in and out of the gate with packages they have purchased in town to be sent home. It's killing me, though, talking to some of these guys who are going home, to hear them tell how wonderful it will be to get back to their families and the grand times they will have again. Some of them are going to get married as soon as they hit the States to girls they have been writing to these many months overseas. Most of them will be home in a week. (Bob Ferguson is going to call you if he comes near Los Angeles. He'll be going home by ship, though, and won't be there until around the 25th of May.)

My roommate, 2nd Lt Nelson, is on his way home. His wife works in the El Toro PX and they have a home in Anaheim. He was a master sergeant and received his commission a short time ago in Korea. In 1941 and 1942 he was a sea-going Marine on the cruiser Chicago and we have been swapping stories about our Pacific experiences. The Chicago was with the Saratoga and Yorktown on many of our escapades when I was a white hat. Small world, isn't it? We returned to San Francisco about a month apart and he was to report to flight school like me, but he met his wife Kay in Frisco and married her in March 1943, and when the officer in charge found out they kicked him out of cadets. He's a regular.

Give my love to your mother and dad and Trooper and Peggy. They are often in my thoughts, and many times I have almost written to them but I figure that my letters to you get passed around, so it's sort of useless to write to everyone.

I'm listening to a Japanese program and they are singing American tunes in Japanese. It sure sounds funny. They have a strange sing-songy style to their singing, even though they are American songs. It's sort of pretty, though, just the same. Maybe I've been over here too long. A month ago I wouldn't have thought that.

I'm going to have quite a time carrying all my gear back on the plane--my little green handbag, radio, rug, bed lamp, greens, overcoat (raincoat) and dress oxfords. Bob Ferguson asked me to take a case of liquor back to his ex-mess cooks at Mag 12. He promised them a case and now doesn't know how to get it back. I told him I'd take it if he couldn't find anybody else.

Guess I'll secure this letter and let Nelson have a crack at the writing desk.

Bye bye little family, I miss you all very much.

Love,
Daddy

5 May 1952
Itami Air Base, Japan
Monday Noon

Hi darlings,

Didn't leave as planned because at the last minute they cancelled our seats on the transport and gave them to some new men going to Korea as replacements. I checked out of my BOQ room last night and was all packed and ready to go this morning at 0615 when we got bounced. We'll leave tomorrow morning for sure, though. It would be hard to explain to the Squadron if it weren't for the fact that Colonel Bryson is over here too and got bounced along with us.

Lt Nelson wanted to go outside the gate into the little shopping center that has sprung up since Itami Air Base has been occupied by U.S. forces. They have a lot of little souvenir shops, tailor shops, cleaning and laundry, and dives. Mostly beer joints. Nelson had some pictures developed at one of the little stores and wanted to pick them up. I went window *shopping with him because I'm down to my last $2.50 and I'll need that to pay my night's BOQ room charge of 25¢, my dinner and tomorrow's breakfast. The radio cleaned me out.*

After spending a month in Korea and returning here, everything took on a different appearance. Things seemed almost stateside as compared with anything we had in Korea. Flush toilets, urinals and lavatories, all Japanese make, at first appeared crude and funny, but look real modern and first class to me after the long metal handmade urinal and ten-hole crapper we have in Korea. I was just thinking how luxurious everything will seem to me when I return home.

Went to a movie last night with Nelson and saw, "The Man Within," an English technicolor of rum smugglers in the 18th century. It was the first time in any picture that I have seen the young man ask the woman in the picture for the privilege of sleeping with her and she said all right. It was the most sexy and uncensored deal I've ever seen. All the guys were whooping and whistling something crazy when they were in the bedroom scene. She was in a flimsy blue lace nightie that showed everything. They filmed a close-up of them just as they were kissing and she had her lips separated and looked like she was going to bite him. Boy, I can't stand many of that kind of picture. We're still talking about it and can't figure how even the British let that one get through. It's the first British technicolor I have seen. The photography and color were excellent. The story was pretty good too--ha, ha.

The radio is playing a Japanese version of an American barn dance, or square dance. The Jap is "calling" to the dancers in Japanese like a regular American caller.

Just heard the steelworkers are going to stay on the job during the talks on wages. The Korean peace talks didn't accomplish much today. They only met for 15 minutes. I wish something would come of those talks. I've had a feeling lately that they would come to a successful agreement, but then when you hear they have met and the meeting only lasted 15 minutes you begin to wonder.

I still have to pinch myself to make myself believe this is me over here. It's hard to believe, especially since being out of the Marine Corps and living as a civilian so long. I'm a civilian first, last, and always where my family is concerned, but a Marine where my country is concerned.

I'm going to secure this masterpiece, honey. Tell the boys how much Daddy misses them.

Love, Daddy

UNITED STATES, JAPANESE PEACE TREATY SIGNED

Japan and the U.S. finally got around to signing their peace treaty in May of 1952 which put a final touch to our occupation of their country since the end of WWII. The Korean War was pouring billions of dollars into their economy and we were their welcomed guests, as well as protectors. They were re-manufacturing thousands upon thousands of our military vehicles shipped back to them from South Korea and also providing ship repair facilities at numerous Japanese ship yards. We servicemen were buying their beautiful goods, bulging the pockets of their retail merchants throughout their land and boosting the whole nation's economy. In fact, the Korean War provided the economic stimulus which put Japan on the course of full recovery and ready to take their place among the industrial nations of the world.

GERM WARFARE PROPAGANDA

Two American airmen had been shot down over North Korea and the Chinese, after five weeks of intensive interrogation, finally forced a written statement from the two captured pilots, Enoch and Quinn, who had broken under the horrible ordeal. *Pravda* published their false statements on 6 May 52 which began a worldwide propaganda campaign claiming that we had begun operations and had dropped bacteriological bombs on North Korea. Of course there wasn't a shred of truth in it but, after that, a downed airman had virtually no chance of getting away from his wrecked plane or parachute; Chinese and Korean officers (who wanted the fliers for intelligence reasons) had to race farmers and villagers, with the latter usually winning--with their pitchforks.

On 8 Jul 52, Col Frank H. Schwable USMC, Chief of Staff of the 1st Marine Air Wing, was shot down on a reconnaissance flight. The Communists immediately recognized their prize and after hours of humiliating torture, they forced an untrue signed confession of germ warfare from the confused airman. True to form, if the Communists couldn't whip us on the battlefield or in the air, they would try it by lies, at which they were truly expert.

SUPPORT AND SERVICE

The prosecution of the war in Korea called for a tremendous administrative and logistical effort on the part of the Eighth Army. Decisions in Washington and Tokyo required that the army not only carry on its tactical mission but operate the supply lines within the peninsula, administer the rear areas, give relief to the disrupted civilian population, and run the prisoner of war camps--tasks normally carried out by the theater headquarters. In addition, the Eighth Army had to integrate the multinational forces fighting in Korea within its command structure. Multitudinous problems arose in carrying out these various responsibilities.

To integrate the ground contingents offered by member countries of the United Nations most efficiently, the U.N. commander's plan was to assign them, according to their size, to American units within the Eighth Army. Thus the Turkish Brigade came under control of an American division. The United Kingdom's two brigades and the one from Canada were placed under army control until July 1951, when the 1st British Commonwealth Division was formed and assumed control of all Commonwealth forces in Korea.

PRISONER OF WAR RIOT AND CHANGE OF COMMAND

The Communists had a trained cadre of agents spread among the 130,000 plus POWs in our Koje-do UN prison camp. Intelligence reports had it that the POWs planned to capture General Dodd, the commandant of the camp, and hold him hostage for further UN concessions. Nevertheless, on 7 May he agreed to meet with the POW leaders in Compound 76, known to hold the most militant prisoners. They rioted, rushed him and held him captive until 11 May, when they released him after forcing a statement from him promising prison reforms.

This event occurred on the very day that LtGen Mark W. Clark arrived in Japan to replace General Ridgway as the UN Commander in Chief. Gen James Van Fleet was the 8th Army Commander in Korea and Gen Dodd's immediate superior. Later, as a result of the riot, Dodd was relieved of command and broken to the rank of colonel, along with Gen Colson, who also had a position of responsibility at the POW camp, thus effectively ending both of their military careers. The riot did not accomplish anything for the POWs. Security was doubled and increased awareness of the cunning nature of the Communist prisoners taken into consideration by those guarding them.

PUTTING A FOUR-ENGINE R5D TRANSPORT INTO A STALL

6 May 1952
Tuesday morning
Pohang dong, K3, Korea

Dearest family,
I'm sitting here at G.W. Parker's writing desk knocking out a letter to my little crew while waiting for G.W. to return from a hop. He has been up ever since I arrived on the R5D this morning at 0830. The operations section (S3) I called told me he would return at around 1100, so I got in a truck with all my gear--my handbag, radio, greens with overcoat, and my reed

rug rolled up. The driver took us over to VMF-311 jet fighter squadron operations first, and I saw some fellows I hadn't seen in some time. I asked the driver to take me over here to MTACS-2 officers' quarters. I learned after I arrived that G.W. was airborne.

I woke up at 0430 this morning and thought I had overslept because it was as light as day out. The sun came up real bright at 0500 and it was a really warm, beautiful, clear morning as I walked down to the all-night mess hall and grabbed myself a bite of breakfast. Then I threw my gear on a truck outside the mess hall and went on down to the air freight office, where I learned I was on R5D four-engined transport No. 5 going to Pohang dong K3. We boarded the big old lady and were airborne at 0700, climbing out over the sleepy Japanese countryside and a very mountainous area north and west of Itami. There were about ten pilots aboard, and the rest of the load were enlisted replacements for the Wing, with their gear--rifles, back packs and the works. They looked like they were loaded for bear.

After about an hour out over the water at an altitude of 10,000', the crew chief came back and told us to strap in because the pilot was going to stall the plane to try and break something loose that was causing a drag on it. Needless to say, we were quite concerned as he pulled the huge nose high into the air and caused a large angle of attack. Finally the huge plane began to shudder and then the nose dropped and we picked up our flying speed. Then he put the flaps down and stalled it again. The enlisted men were more than somewhat concerned and I was too, although I had deliberately put my Corsair into a stall many times and was more or less used to them. Apparently, whatever he did must have corrected the problem, but it left us all in a quandary. We resumed normal flying attitude and landed at Pohang dong at 0835, just 1 1/2 hours out of Itami, Japan. I was mistaken in my map and earlier letters as to the location of Pohang dong (K3). It is located in the little hook on the southeastern end of Korea. I don't know how I became confused, but I'm glad it was only in my letters to you, and not in my navigation because I would have been lost for sure.

They are flying Banshee and Panther jets out of this field now. Up at K6 we now have two Corsair squadrons and one AD squadron which just moved up there from here.

I'm looking over G.W.'s pictures from home, while sitting here at his desk. His three little guys are sure cute. His oldest has lost a tooth. He's in about a dozen separate shots, and in every one he's grinning like a Cheshire cat to show what a big boy he is after having lost his first tooth (just like our Ricky). The older one looks a lot like G.W. and the two smaller ones look alike, but not like Marge or G.W.

Jets are taking off and the noise is terrific. I have all my gear with me here in G.W.'s hut because I don't trust that air freight office--that's the joint that burned down, at K3 where all the mail was lost. There are a lot of transient personnel down there too, and they'd snatch a radio or a pilot's handbag at a wink of an eye.

Our plane was taken from us to haul an emergency load of supplies somewhere and we were bounced. I have to check back at the air freight office at around 1215 to see if there will be another plane for K6 then. I'm sure I'll get to K6 by tonight anyway, because they have any number of flights going up there. I saw a load of Australian soldiers boarding an R5D Marine transport for a northern destination in full battle regalia; it's interesting to see the various UN forces in their native gear. The Aussies wear trooper hats, you know, with one side tacked up--very odd, to say the least. Korean ROK troops are at every field, not including Japan. There are more Marines at Itami than Air Force personnel, but they still say it's an Air Force field.

My radio is playing here alongside me as I sit on G.W.'s bunk. I've tried to get Osaka and Nagoya armed forces radio here at Pohang dong, but I can get only Kyushu armed forces radio; however, on short wave I picked up Tokyo armed forces radio. I imagine the reception at Tunp o ri will be only a slight bit weaker, because of the mountain ranges to our east and south. We'll see. If it is as good there as it is here I'll be happy.

This field sort of runs off over a high cliff, and, since I was here in April, they have filled in about 500 more feet of runway. They said they had lost a few planes off the runway, so the 500 feet would help some. Boy, those Banshee jets are beautiful taking off--low, fast and sleek.

I'll bet G.W. is anxious to get going home. I was surprized to find him still here. He has his desk calendar circled at 5 June; whether that has any significance or not I won't know until he returns. Gosh, it's 1115 now, so he ought to be returning soon. I borrowed some stationery *from him too, and I noticed on the cover he has spelled Marion three or four different ways. I'll bet it was when he wrote to you. He's almost as good a speller as I am!*

It's about 10° cooler here in Korea than in was in Itami. In fact, I have my leather jacket on, the heat is on in this hut, but my tootsies are still cold. The weather around this area is funny.

I can hardly wait to get back to Tunp o ri now that I'm in Korea, to get my hands on some mail from home.

Lots of love to my little family, Daddy

A WORD ABOUT G.W. PARKER

Since my letters were written to Marion and she had known G.W. dating back to our VMF-524, Congaree, South Carolina days of 1944, there was no need for me to tell her anything about my feelings for this guy. We had flown in combat together in VMF-223 in the Philippines and Okinawa and had kept in touch between wars.

G.W. (George) was a dedicated career Marine regular and as fine a F9F Panther jet pilot as had ever strapped himself onto one of those "stovepipes." Several of his VMF-311 pilot buddies had stopped by and we got to talking about him. He had lots of friends and admirers, it was plain to see. The Marine Corps had a lot of fine regular officers but I will always cast my vote as number one for my good buddy, G.W. (I'm sure that, after retiring from the Marine Corps, he made as fine a professor of Economics at the University of Mississippi as he did a pilot.) I will be forever grateful for our fine, warm friendship.

6 May 1952
Tunp o ri, Korea

My darlings,
I was in seventh heaven upon reaching here and finding I had letters from you from the 23rd to the 30th inclusive, even had a 31 March letter they'd salvaged from the fire. I am sending it on to you for your inspection. I enjoyed every word and you supplied me with a wonderful boost in spirit. You gave me a swell accounting of the little fellows' activities too.

George Parker (G.W.) finally showed up at 1200 and we dashed off to chow at his unit's separate mess. I phoned the air freight office and they advised that I had better get over to the flight line and stand by for the plane which was to be in by 1300 or before. Well, we tossed our chow down and G.W. helped me carry my gear over to Transportation, where we bummed a jeep and driver who took us down to the flight line by 1230. The plane did not leave until 1400 and G.W. stayed with me and talked all the time. It was awfully cold at K3, so we got behind the building to protect us from the wind and listened to some music on my Zenith portable; also listened to Moscow Mary. G.W. had never heard her before. She was putting out her usual propaganda in her flawless American accented English voice.

The R4D twin engine, beat-up old wreck of a transport plane they loaded us into, was filled up to the hilt and there was hardly room enough for any passengers after the cargo had all been tied down. She took off, and I swear to this day I felt as though we'd never make it alive to K6. Boy, my nerves are almost shot. After landing at K6 at 1530 I dragged my gear back to the hut, had a drink of water and washed my face. The squadron duty officer grabbed me and said, "Hey, Pete, get into your flight gear right away! We have a railcut up to Flak Alley, North Korea, for you."

I briefed at 1645 and was all set to take off when, at the last minute, they came in and said there were only five planes available out of the seven scheduled for the flight. Major Elliott, the Operations officer, struck Van Dalsem and me from the flight because our names were last on the list. I told Van Dalsem we'd just gotten another day's reprieve on our life and he said, "That's how I feel too." The flight returned at 2010 tonight, pitch black out, low

Above: G.W. in front of his quarters at Pohang dong, K3, Korea.

Above: Capt George W. (G.W.) Parker, my very dear friend. As a captain in Korea, G.W. was flying F9F Panther jets from the Marines' South Korean base at Pohang dong, K3. He flew with VMF-311.

Right: G.W. as a major, about to retire from the Corps in the early 1960's. He went on to get his doctorate in Economics and was a professor at the University of Mississippi until retirement in the mid 1980's. He served his country with honor and distinction.

Left: G.W. in his #10 F9F Panther jet headed for North Korea.

Above: G.W. Parker flying his F9F Panther jet in Korea.

Above, Right: G.W. Parker in the cockpit of his F9F, with VMF-311. Note bombs on wing rack. F9Fs were bombers as well as fighters in Korea, but they could never match the performance of the Air Force F-86 Sabrejet.

Above: Lt William "Billy" Bizzell, VMA-212

Middle Right: Capt Griffith, VMA-212

Right: Capt George W. Parker by his F9F, flying with VMF-311 out of K3 early 1952.

ceiling and everything. I would have hated a dark landing on this strip, as the lights are very poor.

The squadron has had a bit of poor luck lately, and every time I sit around and talk to the fellows who have had close calls, it only tends to get me all nerved up. Tomorrow morning I have an 0430 reveille, for I have the early, early strip alert, then breakfast at 0800, brief at 1000 for a railcut, and we're off again.

All the boys but four from our hut are gone on R&R and here we sit: Jack Ryan, Jim Feliton, Denny Clyde and I listening to Tex Beneke's music. They are really thrilled with my purchase of the Zenith. Jim lay in his sack and listened until he went to sleep. He'd had two real rough railcuts today, and besides, he's worried about his wife because she is supposed to have her baby now and he hasn't heard anything. He's nervous and worried and he's flying too hard. Jim's a very conscientious pilot--always eager to take somebody else's hop if they don't feel well etc.

All for now, precious family that I love,

Daddy

MY FRIEND, WILBUR PICKERING

The Marine Corps had again found a need for the expertise of many of my old buddies. Among those recalled to active duty was Wilbur Pickering, who hailed from Issaquah, WA, a few miles east of Seattle. A farm boy, Pick had gone through the CPT flight program before joining up with me at Livermore, CA, pre-flight school back in 1943.

Part of Class 5B-L in Barracks 7, B-Deck, we stayed together during our primary training in the N2S Stearman (Yellow Peril). Both of us well remember being in a group of 83 cadets who boarded three old WWI Great Western sleeper cars on the 14th of August 1943, and our smoky, dirty, bumpy ride through Winnemucca, Salt Lake City, Pueblo, Fort Worth and San Antonio to our destination, Corpus Christi, TX.

At Corpus we flew the SNV-1 Vultee Vibrator (the Air Force called theirs the BT-13) and the SNJ-5. Finally qualified as naval aviators, we were formally pinned with our Naval Wings of Gold as 2nd lieutenants in the United States Marine Corps Reserve on 21 Dec 1943.

From January to May of 1944 we flew SBD-5 Douglas divebombers together as part of Flight 121, VSB-5 Squadron at Masters Field, Opa Locka, FL. Our close-knit group consisted of 2ndLts Robert B. Robinson, Dub Woods, Joe Locker, Wilbur Pickering, Harry Taylor, B.W. Peterson (me) and Sankin, who perished when his SBD-5 crashed while doing field carrier landings at an outlying field. Our instructors were Navy Lts R.L. Gillum and J.S. Hannah, both regular guys.

Mid-May both Pick and I went to the Marine Corps Air Station at Cherry Point, NC, where we were assigned to different fighter squadrons, but not before we had each met our lifelong soul mates. Pick married PFC Donna Miller, the bugler, and I married Cpl Marion Gleason, of the Recruit Assignment office. Soon I was transferred to VMF-524 in Congaree, SC, to fly Corsairs, while Pick was sent to Vero Beach, FL, to transition into the most dangerous flying assignment going at that time--night fighters, flying F6F radar mounted fighters.

The last time I had seen Pick was in August of 1944 on his aircraft carrier *Block Island* CVE106. He'd been attached to VMF-511 in the 1st Marine Carrier Air Group. They had units of VMF(N)-544, the night fighter squadron, aboard also. When they pulled into Okinawa during the last days of WWII a few of us old buddies got together on the flight deck for our group picture; namely, Larry Berg, Les McFadden, R.B. (Robby) Robinson, Bill Hogue, Rex Ploen, Pick Pickering, Pete Peterson, Troyer, Jess Crone and J.T. Scanlon. At that time I was flying Corsairs with VMF-223 off an Okinawa airstrip called Awase.

Skipping ahead 49 years, Pick and I got together in March 1993 here at my home in Scottsdale, AZ. He brought me up to speed on what he'd been doing during those post war years. After he left the Marine Corps in

Top Row, L to R: Larry Berg, Les McFadden, R.B. (Robby) Robinson, Bill Hogue, (?), Rex Ploen. Front Row: Wilbur (Pick) Pickering, B.W. (Pete) Peterson, Troyer, Jesse Crone and J.T. Scanlon. The last time I had seen Pick was on his aircraft carrier **BLOCK ISLAND** (CVE-106). He was attached to VMF-511 in the 1st Marine Carrier Air Group. They had units of VMF(N)-544, the night fighter squadron, aboard also. When they pulled into Okinawa, during the last days of WWII, a few of us old buddies got together on the flight deck for our group picture. At that time I was flying Corsairs with VMF-223 off of an Okinawa airstrip called Awase.

Left: Pick in left hand seat of his R5D Douglas transport during the Korean War, with his co-pilot, Herb McDonald.

Left: Douglas multi-engined transport, the workhorse of the Korean War for all the services. Here a USAF transport picks up wounded to fly to hospitals in nearby Japan.

Right: My friend, Wilbur (Pick) Pickering, in Korea, ready to board his Douglas R5D transport. He flew with VMR-152.

Left: Pick, in his cockpit. We called him the farm boy from Issaquah, Washington.

Right: Pick, ready to fly another mission. We had been together as flying cadets in 1943, and during advanced training in 1944.

Right: Capt Wilbur (Pick) Pickering. Photo taken during his tour of duty in Korea. He stayed active in the Reserves, retiring as a LtCol, but still flew for Pan Am until he retired in 1983.

Above and Right: Pick, in his R5D Douglas transport planning his next flight, be it trans-Pacific, or evacuating a load of wounded, or just an R & R run to Itami, Japan.

Above: *Peterson just landed from a combat mission up north. We described it as defying gravity once again.*

Upper Right: *Marine Air Group 12, First Marine Air Wing headquarters, Col E. T. Dorsey commanding.*

Right: *Spud and his hardworking hut boy, Kim Jin Kil, at K6. Although we were told to pay them very little, he was earning more than ROK majors.*

Lower Left: *Peterson in cockpit of his Corsair.*

Lower Right: *A rare happening—the USO showed up.*

1945, he joined an active Marine Corps reserve squadron, VMF-141 in Oakland, while attending the University of California, then returned to Issaquah, WA, in 1948 and joined VMF-216 in Seattle. Trained in multi-engine aircraft while flying for Pan American, he was recalled during the Korean War to fly multi-engine R5D Marine transports with VMR-152, headquartered in Itami, Japan. They flew many hops across the Pacific and back, as well as to Korea.

Every one of us admired the transport pilots for their professionalism and for the service they were providing the war effort. Like Pick, many had been fighter pilots in WWII, and had left the Marines to fly commercial air lines. There wasn't much glory in being a transport pilot but the service they provided in transporting the wounded back to Japan (or even to the USA in many cases), hauling food and ammunition and providing air travel for all Marines in the war theater was truly a dedication to duty, even if the Distinguished Flying Crosses, Air Medals, Silver Stars and such weren't always there for them as they were for us.

Pickering stayed active in Marine aviation, retiring as a lieutenant colonel in the reserves, all the while flying for Pan American World Airways as second copilot, with navigation as his primary duty. His assignments with the airlines saw him stationed mostly in San Francisco and later in Berlin, Germany, as well as flying our troops into Viet Nam, under military contract, during that war. Pick retired completely in 1983 as a 747 captain and later moved back to the Seattle area. He enjoys playing golf and visiting his four kids and five grandchildren in various parts of the country.

OUR FLIGHT COVERS DOWNED AD-1 SKYRAIDER PILOT

7 May 1952
2110

Dear ones,
I am dog tired tonight but I am going to write to the precious family just the same. It all started like this--reveille went at 0415, which is an ungodly hour to meet the day. After breakfast we briefed at the Group Operations, then manned our planes at 0515 and taxied out to the end of the strip for a stand-by alert. We did not get scrambled, though, and at 0615 we brought them back to the line so our first squadron railcut could have our planes for their mission taking off at 0700. I had a cup of coffee and came back to the hut where I stayed until 0945, when I went over to the group headquarters and briefed on an 11-plane railcut.

On the way up to our target we heard an AD bomber pilot in distress and heard his wing man tell him to bail out. Capt Barbours was leading our 11-plane flight and called the 5th Air Force to ask if we could cover the pilot and direct rescue operations. 5th Air Force came up with an affirmative and we did just that. He had bailed out, but he was too low and did not make it. We flew down to Seoul and escorted the rescue helicopter to the spot, then stood by in case he was shot at. They informed us that the pilot was dead and asked if we would please stand by long enough for them to pick him up, and also if we would see that no guerrillas or enemy troops fired on the copter. We escorted him back to Seoul, then requested a secondary target because we were too late for our railcut interception and hook-up with the fighter escort.

We were given a target over on the west coast near Chinnamp'o, where we destroyed a huge railroad bridge and an auto bridge next to it. When we returned to K6 Tunp o ri I had logged three hours in the bent-winged monster and it was awfully hot up there circling at low altitude directing operations for about an hour. The sweat was pouring down my face and all my clothes were soaked.

After lunch, I found a huge box that rocket arming wires come in. I tore it apart for the wood and worked all afternoon on making myself a desk/shelf combination. It is now up against the end of the hut and is very comfortable for writing letters because the slant is just right. You can rest your arm while you are writing. I relieved the squadron duty officer tonight at 1900 after I put on clean clothes.

We had fried chicken and dressing, mashed potatoes, gravy, peas, cranberry sauce and pineapple, coffee for supper tonight. No mail. I went over to the squadron this evening to get the flight schedule and gave some instructions to the ordnance chief for tomorrow's hop. It's going to be what they call a maximum effort: the entire 5th Air Force is going to hit one area where troops and supplies are being assembled in great quantities. I am scheduled for two missions up there tomorrow. Somebody will stand by as duty officer for me while I fly there. Plane availability may keep me from getting one of the missions. Keep this in mind and when you read about the 5th Air Force maximum effort tomorrow you will know I have partaken in the fray.

I have to roll up my sack and sleep down at the squadron ready room tonight. I will arise at 0400 and wake up the 15 pilots on the first hop at 0430. Then I will get the hop out and will not have one myself until 1100. The second one will go at 1615 (4:15 PM) and I will return at 1815 (6:15 PM). It does not get dark here until 1945 (7:45 PM).

We have a gray rabbit that lives in and around our huts. I took two pictures of him this afternoon, fairly close up. They should turn out real good.

Signing off now.

With all my love, Daddy

CNIMAMPI (CHINNAMP'O) AND ANAK

I was a civilian and flew on weekends,
No sweat about flack and no sign of the bends.
But I am a reserve and older I grow,
And now fly a Corsair--it's old and is slow.
    CHORUS:
    Cnimampi and Anak, and P'yongyang and Sinmak,
    They'll drive you crazy, they'll drive you insane.
    Quad fifties and forties and 100 sorties,
    They'll drive you ape and they'll drive you insane.

We bombed and we strafed and we shot air-to-air,
Then off to Korea to the communist's lair.
We went to K-18 to fly with the group,
My hair is fast turning and my wings have a droop.
    CHORUS:

I flew my first mission and it was a snap;
Just followed the leader, never looked at a map.
But now I have 80 and lead a sad flight,
Go out on armed reccy and can't sleep at night.
    CHORUS:

We went to MIG Alley, S-2 said, "No sweat."
If I hadn't been lucky I'd be up there yet.
Six MIGs jumped our tails and our leader yelled, "Break!"
I jammed on the throttle; how my knees did shake.
    CHORUS:

Now I have a 100 and if they ask for more
I'll tell them to shove it, my butt is too sore.
They can ram it and jam it for all that I care.
Just give me a staff job, a desk and a chair.
    CHORUS:

8 May 1952
Tunp o ri, Korea

Dearest family,
Received two letters from you today mailed on the 28th of April. You sure do manage to keep busy, what with the garden, kids, washing, housework, cooking and shopping. You are wonderful, darling, going ahead with all your chores with a happy frame of mind.

I slept down at the squadron last night and we worked until 1230 getting the planes loaded and the bugs worked out of them so we would have at least 14 for the first hop. I got to sleep at around 0100 and my alarm rang at 0345. I woke up the first flight. It was really a scream going around from hut to hut hunting for the various pilots and waking them up. They all required a different wakening procedure. Some rise up in bed as though they had been shot, others mumble and roll over to sleep again, while some sit up slowly and say casually, "I'm awake." Strange, though, I never had to wake up anybody a second time.

I had breakfast at 0500 and went to briefing with the first flight. The second flight used the first 14 planes and I briefed with the flight with hopes of flying, but two planes were grounded and I was scratched from the flight.

The third missions briefed at 1515. I finally got a plane on a 13-plane interdiction to an area north of Kaesong about 60 or 70 miles at a red supply base called Suan. The entire 5th Air Force, including us, hit the area. Their supplies were piled high and there were lots of buildings, trucks, and hundreds of troops reported to be in the area. We clobbered them. The flak was meager and inaccurate 37 mm; none in any of our flights got it.

I made a screaming dive at a group of supply buildings and leveled the whole mess with (2) 1000 lb G.P. and (6) 100 lb G.P. bombs--quite an impressive blast. Carrying it low for accuracy, the blast felt like a mule kicked my tail on my pullout. I held it low to the mountains at better than 400 kts until clear of the heavy flak, then began climbing to rejoin the rest of the flight. Boy, my heart was in my throat from the very second we passed over the enemy line until we crossed back over it an hour later.

After landing at 1815 I enjoyed a ham dinner with boiled spuds, string beans, lettuce with dressing, chocolate ice cream, cookies and coffee. Returned to the line after dinner and took care of some squadron business. Then I had to find a pilot for a quick test hop before dark. Lt. Jacks took it and put on an air show over the field for 20 minutes prior to sundown.

Later, I went to the movie, "Sahara Hotel," a screwy picture if I ever saw one. Lt Olson relieved me from squadron duty and I was on my own at 2200 tonight.

I love and miss you all.

Daddy

THE DAILY BREEZE
Redondo Beach, California
Thursday, May 8, 1952

U.S. Hits Reds in Day-Long Air Attack

Big supply Base Target of War's Heaviest Attack

SEOUL, Korea (AP)--The U.S. Fifth Air Force said it made its biggest single attack of the Korean War today on the Red supply base at Suan.

A day-long attack left the prize target covered with "billowing flames and smoke," the Air Force said.

The assault on the town, 35 miles southeast of the Red capital, P'yongyang, began at dawn and lasted until nightfall. Both jets and propeller driven planes were hurled into the attack.

Two Red jets were reported shot down and a third damaged as they ventured far from their Manchurian bases, apparently in an effort to break up the raid.

Tops Sinuiju Record

The Fifth Air Force said more sorties were flown against Suan today than the 312 that hit Sinuiju on the Manchurian border a year ago this month in the war's previous biggest raid.

The Air Force reported Allied planes destroyed 97 supply buildings in the great supply complex, damaged 50 and knocked out 18 supply revetments and 16 vehicles.

Photo planes have been keeping an eye on the Red buildup at Suan, a feeder point to Chinese troops on the western front. Spokesmen said photos showed truck concentrations, great stacks of supplies and other equipment, well guarded by antiaircraft guns.

Shooting Stars opened the attack, hitting emplacements with demolition bombs.

The F-80 jets were followed by waves of Thunderjets, propeller driven Mustangs, more Shooting Stars and Marine Pantherjets, Sky Raiders and Corsairs.

"Tons of demolition and high explosives tore the Communist supplies to shreds," a Fifth Air Force communique said. "Thousands of gallons of fiery napalm (jellied gasoline) were spread over the target, turning piles of supplies into billowing flames and smoke."

TASK FORCE SMITH

Whenever we began to think we had it rough, we'd console ourselves by rehashing what it must have been like back when this terrible war first started. Back then, a handful of Army occupation troops had rushed to Korea in C-54 transports from Japan. Landing at Pusan in the southernmost part of the country, they'd been shuttled by truck and train northward to a blocking position on the main road between Suwon and Osan only a few miles south of the capital, Seoul.

These men of the 1/21st Infantry had been in Korea for only four days when, in the early hours of 5 Jul 1950, 403 of these bewildered, damp, disoriented Americans tried to stop 30 green-painted Soviet T-34 tanks rumbling south on the main highway. From a single battery of 105mm howitzers, this tiny troop of gallant soldiers fired numerous rounds at the attacking Soviet tanks, doing only minor damage to them. Several armor-piercing shells from their 105mm guns, however, did stop a Communist tank, setting it on fire. Unfortunately, they didn't have a sufficient supply of those shells. Their hand-held 2.36-inch bazookas proved totally ineffective in penetrating the thick armor plating of the T-34 tanks.

Why didn't they use the new 3.5-inch rocket launchers, which would have been effective? They hadn't been issued to MacArthur's Far East Army. One truly wonders who, if anybody, in the Pentagon was doing the planning out there.

As the remainder of the 30 T-34 Soviet tanks rolled past the 1/21st holding position, a Communist 85mm tank shell killed Lt Philip Day, making him the first American casualty of the Korean police action.

Most of Task Force Smith trickled to the south via foot, fishing boat or whatever means they could find during their pathetic and humiliating retreat in the face of the heavily armored Communist onslaught. They suffered 155 casualties in this first action at Osan; but five days later, exhausted and with terribly swollen feet, they joined up with friendly elements of another U.S. Army regiment.

Two years later the situation had changed considerably for the better. At least, by that time, we were well equipped and had ample air power to coordinate with the ground forces, so that sort of thing could not happen again.

HUGH HOLLAND AND I BRIEFED FOR SPECIAL MISSION

9 May 1952
Tunp o ri, Korea

Hi little gang,

My day started with a bang and ended the same way, but I am here to tell about it and that's all that matters. I was up at 0615, had breakfast and briefed at the group Operations.

Capt Hugh Holland and myself were selected to fly a special, important hop that was to require a great deal of skill and accuracy in order not to actually break off the truce talks due to another air violation of the conference area. With the list of special instructions of courses to be flown, times, headings, altitudes, release time and data, maps and armament, we took off for what we both felt was to be a hop of great importance and we were determined to do the best job we could.

We flew north over Seoul, then skirted Kaesong and Panmunjom to the northeast. We contacted our ground controller who handed us over to another ground controller located in very close proximity to the group of enemy artillery pieces that had been hammering our boys to the south unceasingly for days, with no fear of retaliation due to their closeness to the neutral area. Holland and I were at 14,500 feet flying level, our every move being controlled by radio instructions from our ground controller, directing us into the target, which we could not see. They, of course, were using radar to direct us.

The instructions came over similar to this: "Oxwood 25-1 from control, steer 270°, maintain angels 14.6 (14,600 ft.), close your formation up tight. Now turn left 275, now right 272, now maintain 272, you are 30 seconds from release point, steady on 272, turn right 273°, arm all switches, stand by--mark."

At "mark" we pickled off our load. We made five passes with three drops. The (16) 100 lb bombs dropped on a command post destroyed everything. The controller on the ground got jarred too, because his patrol had worked their way in very close in order to observe. Full of compliments, three different command levels handed us roses via radio. We had destroyed our objective and had come within dangerously close proximity of the conference without actually making an air violation. Had we failed, we would have been severely dealt with--but we'd succeeded.

They had kept us over their control point for a long time but we were so busy we hadn't realized we had been in the air for over two and a half hours. My warning light flashed on, reminding me that I had only 50 gallons of fuel remaining. Still, we hadn't made our kill as yet with our 1000 lb bombs. During the next ten minutes, we planted (4) 1000 lb bombs squarely on two heavy artillery batteries, finally hitting the jackpot, and they let us head for home. They gave us a steer of 190° to hit Seoul because the weather in the area was very foul and visibility was not conducive to good navigation.

On our return to home base we both decided we couldn't possibly make it back because of our low fuel state. We talked it over and agreed to make a landing at the F-86 Sabre jet base near Seoul. Now get this picture--Holland and I called for landing instructions at the jet field, and they came up with "Marine Oxwood 25-1 and 2, cleared no. 14." We broke over the field and wrapped her around in a tight left bank. Holland took the right side of the runway and I followed close behind him, but landed on the left side to avoid hitting his slipstream (which rocks your plane violently). Knowing we had an audience of dogfaces watching our two Corsairs coming into their jet field, I landed very smoothly.

After the weight of my plane cushioned on the oleos of the landing gear, I felt a violent chattering underneath that felt as though I had landed on our rough old Rowell Ave. at home. Saw horses and DO NOT USE, STAY OUT, KEEP CLEAR, RUNWAY UNDER CONSTRUCTION signs began flying past my wing and underneath me at over a hundred miles an hour. I had landed on the side of the runway they were tearing up for repair!!

By the time I realized what the score was, it was too late to pour the coal to her and take off again because I had to take off over another 5000 feet of the samie-same (Korean) stuff, so I popped my head out, first to the left, then to the right side and hit the brakes left and right as I needed to in order to avoid the deeper holes. It was like going down a hill doing a slalom on skis. Those tires and that old "U" bird (F4U) really got pounded to a frazzle, but I rode her out to a stop, taxied off the runway to the taxiway and back to the Operations area, where we cut our guns and crawled out, breathing a sigh of relief.

Upon inspection, outside of some big dents and bruises and a pair of very smoky brakes, the plane appeared OK. The tower had failed to notify me of the runway condition, figuring we were operating out of there on a day-in day-out basis and certainly knew the runway improvements program that was taking place. I got a little shook. We gassed up and, boy, our planes really drank up the gas. We couldn't have made it home.

We watched a stream of F-86s taking off and landing. They had just had a crack-up; an F-86 that had been shot up over MIG Alley had belly landed in the dirt to the right of the strip. We passed it, along with the crash equipment, as we landed. While fighting my plane to a safe stop, I saw the meat wagon pass beneath my right wing and the ugly thought flashed through my mind, "Hope I don't need you!"

After gassing up, we took off and 20 minutes later we landed at K6. They had begun to worry about us. Usually they don't send just two planes over the bomb line together because if one gets shot up the other can't do both the circling, strafing and protecting of the downed pilot and climb to altitude for emergency rescue equipment--copter etc. Anyhow, I was happy to be back here at K6. After my morning hop I figured anything would be a breeze, so I went to chow (lunch) confidently assured I was right in my assumption.

We briefed at 1515, were airborne at 1600 on a nine-plane railcut up to Sinanju, but as we reported in to our JOC (Joint Operations Command) controller on the way north, they advised us that our flight had been chosen for a diversion of targets because they had just uncovered an enemy buildup and found a strong point they wanted knocked out. We were vectored over to our airborne controller for briefing and control. The artillery lobbed a smoke shell onto the target and we immediately saw the area come alive with troops, AA, machine gun fire and "tocson" (lots of) small arms.

Called Sugar Loaf, the hill commanded a huge line of defense, as well as a large valley. The air controller was at 8000 feet, and we knew it must be "hot" down there because those guys come down lower than that lots of times to mark target, show direction of run, and to assess damage after the attack. He wouldn't come down, so we figured he knew the ground condition fairly well. We went into our attack from 8000 feet and made repeated attacks until all our ordnance had been expended. I got a direct hit with my 1000 pounder on an artillery piece dug deep into a cave, and my rockets went into trenches crawling with Commies lining the banks, every one of them firing at me.

On one run, which I remember especially, I happened to notice what appeared to be flaming basket balls coming over my cockpit. I was committed to my attack and had to bear it home, but I marked this guy's position in my mind, and, as I pulled through, I took it low to the ground and saw he had a bank of quad. 50s in a sandbag revetment. Next time around I put two five-inch rockets right on his nose. (Five-inch rockets have the same fire power as a blast from a gun of a destroyer.) I was so sore at him for shooting at me that I didn't even tell anybody else where he was because I wanted to score it up with him by myself. I did.

We had a very successful afternoon and, as my wheels touched the deck at good old K6, I really breathed a sigh. As I crawled out of the monster I looked at my watch and figured I had been strapped into the iron bird for over six hours today. It was 1800 and I had to go over to wash my hands and face before going to chow. Steak it was, an inch thick and done to a turn, just what I needed.

Good night now, dearest family.

All my love, Daddy

THE COMMIE'S LAMENT
(OH MY DARLING CLEMENTINE)

Once a flyer, do or dier, in his faithful Sabre true,
After bitchin', flew a mission to the town of Sinanju.
Still in flight, he saw some mighty Russian MIGs upon his tail.
With a quiver, and a shiver, he let out an awful wail,
    CHORUS:
    Sayonara, Sayonara, Sayonara a so des,
    If you find me, never mind me, I will be an awful mess.

Then a Mustang went in bustin', just to see what he could do,
But alas, he made a pass, and that was all, they got him too.
Thought an '80, I'm so great, he'll never get a shot at me.
Wasn't gone long when his swan song sounded just like this to me,
    CHORUS:

Then a Thunderjet, who hadn't blundered yet, thought he'd try it.
Like a blotter, hit the water, shook the hand of Davy Jones.
So the tally, in MIG Alley, isn't quite like all the claims,
But as a fair course to the Air Force, we won't mention any names.
    CHORUS:

Come a Corsair, for air warfare, built in 1941.
Ten years later was no greater than the day it was begun.
Then MIG drivers betting fivers on who'd get the F4U,
Instead of dying, would be flying if they'd known what Marines can do.
    CHORUS:

The wily Corsair, stopped in midair, went into a cloud to hide.
The MIGs went by him, couldn't find him, crashed into a mountainside.
If you spy us, go on by us or your flying days are done.
    CHORUS: (last line) - or you'll be an awful mess.

MPQ, RADAR BOMBING

The last mission Hugh and I had over the 1stMarDiv consisted of radar controlled bombing which allowed us to drop our bombs very close to our friendly troops on the front lines in darkness or in foul weather. It had been developed after WWII at Point Mugu, CA, under the direction of Marine Maj Marion C. Dalby and it was called MPQ-14. The Air Force had used it very effectively in Korea during the 1951 spring offensive. The Marine MPQ-14 equipment was smaller and could be housed in a one-ton van on the front lines.

Later, when I became a forward air controller with the 1stMarDiv, I planned for the use of this very valuable tool, especially during night battles and poor weather when we couldn't get our day fighters in on the target.

10 May 1952
Tunp o ri, Korea

Hello darlings,
    Just landed from a four-hour rescue CAP. We took off at 1615 and landed at 2030 on that dinky, narrow, little old runway we've got. My cockpit lights weren't working except on my instruments, and I had a heck of a time locating such things as landing gear lever, flap control lever, tab controls, light switches, radio selector, etc. It was pitch black and I was really

nervous because I hadn't made any dark landings since last December at El Toro. Everything came out OK, though.

We covered an F-84 jet pilot who bailed out east of Wonsan on the east coast. He was picked up by a mine sweeper and was OK except he was almost done in from the extremely cold water, they said. Boy, my bottom is sore and my back is tired! I haven't squared away from my six hours yesterday.

Tomorrow morning I have to get up early and fly way up in a heavy flak area to cut rails in North Korea. Then in the afternoon it's to be a JOC alert, which could be anything.

Hope all is well with my precious family.

All my love, Daddy

11 May 1952
Tunp o ri, Korea

Dearest little family,

I've had one mission this morning, which took nine of us about 175 miles up into North Korea in the center of the peninsula, where we cut railroads and enemy buildings with 1000 lb bombs, 100 lb bombs, 5" high velocity rockets and 20 mm. I was up at 0430 and had a cup of coffee, then went over to brief at the group at 0530, took off at 0645, and returned at 0900. After I landed I shaved and showered because I'd landed so late last night that I hadn't had a chance to catch the hot water. Hot water hours around here are very strange. Sometimes you can catch it and other times "hava no"--very inconvenient, to say the least.

Received your letter of May 2nd telling of my Ricky darling having the measles. How awful. The precious little guy shouldn't have to get anything like that. Kiss them both for me, dearest, and tell them how much their daddy adores them and misses them. I know you're taking the finest of care of the little guys. You're a precious wife and mother, darling. I'm so happy I married you, honey bun.

Tuck the angel boys into beddie bye and say a little prayer for them for me. I always say a little prayer for my whole family and I sneak the fact that I want to return home as soon as possible to my little family in my prayer also. I'll write a longer letter when I come down from my morning railcut tomorrow.

Love ya, Daddy

TEN THOUSAND DOLLARS GOING HOME TO THE FOLKS
(WRECK OF THE OLD '97)

*He was comin' on the downwind, goin' ninety knots an hour
When his Corsair went into a spin.
He was found in the wreck with his hand on the throttle,
And his body all covered with gin.*

*Now the Pratt and Whitney man said, "It can't be the engine,
'cause that engine never stops."
So upon examination, pulling plugs in every station,
They found it was the Hamilton prop.*

> *CHORUS: (Soft)
> Ten thousand dollars going home to the folks,
> Ten thousand dollars going home to the folks,
> Oh won't they be excited; Oh won't they be delighted;
> Just think of all the things they can buy.
> Ten thousand dollars going home to the folks.*

Sunday afternoon

Hi again,

The only thing I want is to return home to my precious family. I can't get interested in reading or hobbies or sports (even if I had time for them). When I'm flying I'm thinking of my wonderful little family at home that needs their daddy, and their daddy needs them too. I get so darn mad sometimes I can hardly contain myself.

Usually we can't see if we're killing any troops or not, but, instead, rely on Intelligence reports, which are made from an assessment patrol from our front lines. Whenever a hill is taken by the Commies, JOC calls on us and we dash over the first thing in the morning and clobber it. Needless to say, the Commies are content to stay dug in on their own side of the fence.

I know I will return to you, dear, but I always have to say to myself as I'm flying: I will return. I have to return to my precious family. Please, God, let the flak be light and don't let anybody get hit. Please end this killing.

Going to knock off until this evening when I return from my JOC alert, which will probably work into a close air support.

2130

I was right, it was a close air support hop, only about 2000 feet from our front line troops. They had been getting mortar fire from a reverse slope and they were unable to cope with the situation. Our troops had moved up to this Communist position just this morning and were pinned down this afternoon. We knocked the Commies completely out. A machine gunner was giving me the business, and the tracers were coming just over the cockpit. I caught him out of the corner of my eye. On my fourth run on the target I had him in my sights and let go with a blast of 5" rockets that did the trick. We got six direct hits with our 1000 lb bombs. The controllers, both airborne and on the ground, were really shook due to the intense fire they had been receiving, and they were amazed at what they called "the cool, calculated way" we went about eliminating the objective that had given them so much trouble. They were full of compliments, and said they were going to write it up and send it in to JOC for special mention. Made us feel good--Feliton, Maginnis and myself.

Feliton's wife finally had their fourth child last May 2nd. He just found out today by airmail, a 7 lb girl, Eileen or something like that. They have three daughters now and a son. He's a regular. She had the baby at Pendleton, no trouble at all.

We had to call for radar steers home tonight because the weather in the area was awfully foul and it was growing dark, which made it even worse. The haze moving down from the battle line made it almost like a heavy fog. Boy, there sure is a lot of activity going on, and I'm right in the middle of the powder keg. We were on the deck by 1900, not dark yet, thank God, and we dashed over and grabbed what was left of the chow: steak, mashed spuds, gravy, peas, peaches, coffee, salad--very good too. Then we washed, got out of our crummy, sweaty flight gear and into our shirts and pants, and went to a movie, "Lady Pays Off" with Linda Darnell; also a short subject that Ricky would have loved called "Under the Rails," showing model railroads and the men that built them. (Real 1" to the foot scale models that build up their own steam, miniature station, bridges, cars and everything.) Walt Disney had one on his estate and he was the engineer carrying about six of his nieces and nephews on behind, on a half mile track.

I was very much relieved to get your letter today mailed the 5th of May telling me Ricky boy was feeling better. I was pulling for him, you can be sure of that. I love you all and miss you with all my heart. So Randy sends his daddy kisses now, eh? That's cute. I saw his doodling on the letter.

Bye bye for now, dearest family.

Your very own, Daddy

THE CORSAIR PILOTS' PSALM

And so it came to pass, as the fourth hour before the dawn approacheth into the land of K-18 a messenger goeth forth to the tents of the birdman and he speaketh unto each verily, "Arise and don thy garments and go thou to the gathering place, for the master has decreed that it shall be thus."

The birdmen awakening, mutter into their beards and revile the messenger, saying his mother hath not morals, and that his father knoweth him not. And they arise and seek out their socks and go forth to break bread, and one breaketh his hand on the bread.

They are together into the sanctum of the sanctums called briefing, and their voices are hushed, for they are in the presence of the master, and disciples arise and speak unto them telling of routes, altitudes, and targets, for this is their manner of speaking. And at last the master ariseth and sayeth unto them, "Yea, verily, thou art indeed fortunate, for thine enemies are sorry put and will do naught to oppose thee, go ye forth, therefore, and gird thyself for battle and let him who would abort beware, for my wrath is great."

And the birdmen whisper one to another, "Yea, this will be a day of many tribulations, for the master returneth to his sack and goeth not amongst us." And they answer, "Yea, verily, it is so."

Then the birdmen go to their iron birds and prepare the rituals, and gird their loins for battle, and some are beset by trembling and redness of eye, for they have partaken too much of wine. And they go unto their friends and speak unto them saying, "Yea, many times thou hast been as a brother to me and I to you. Wilt thou therefore take my place in battle this day, for I am indeed overtaken by illness?" And their friends answereth, "Thou soundeth faint and I cannot hear thee. Go thou and disturb not my meditations." And they go.

And they go once more to the birds of iron, and there arises a great clamor as they make ready to go forth, and the great birds are risen into the air, all save one who aborteth for lack of fuel, and the master curseth him, saying, "Thou shalt know the full meaning of my wrath."

And the birdmen proceedeth unto the land of darkness, even to the doorway of the evil one called Joe.

Then the skies become darkened with mist and the birdmen stray from one another and miss their turning points and are lost, and they find not their targets, and great are their trepidations, and the birdmen cry unto one another, saying, "Oxwood-thirty-dash-one come thou unto me for I am set upon by bandits and my ammo runneth out." And Oxwood-thirty-dash-one replieth, "Verily, thou shouldst drop dead, for mine gas runneth low and flak hath found me."

And some falleth unto the land of darkness, while one and another scurrieth away like mice, and salvoeth their bombs into the sea and returneth home empty handed, there to tell of many deeds.

And the master gathereth them together and speaketh unto them of many practice missions, and of frozen promotions, and giveth them hell in general.

So be it--Amen.

CHAPTER 9

FLAK AND OUR MISSIONS

I have made mention of how devastating enemy ground fire could be to the airman, no matter how hot a fighter pilot he might be. Note the case of Lt Bob Hanson, the Marine Corps Ace with 25 kills, who was shot down and killed in WWII from a bullet fired by a Japanese rifleman during his strafing mission near Cape St. George on the island of New Ireland, northeast of Rabaul. We were all susceptible to ground fire. However, there were a number of considerations we could use to increase our chances of survival, one of which was to pay close attention to our flak officer during our pre-mission briefings.

SOME RULES THAT I FOLLOWED

Upon reaching our targets in North Korea, where we were flying at altitudes of between 15,000 and 20,000 feet, we'd then dive at approximately 35°-45° toward our target to the release point, which was approximately 2000 feet, before we'd start our pullout. As we came within range of the smaller caliber automatic weapons, hand-held or semi-stationary, the intensity of fire would be amazing. We'd experiment during our different missions, sometimes climbing out and gaining maximum altitude, and at other times flying the bird right down on the deck, as low as 100-200 feet off the ground. At 500 MPH this afforded the Communist gunners a very short time in which to level their sights on us. The latter method was the one I preferred and used on most of my missions. It was effective; I survived.

The Russians supplied the majority of weapons to the North Koreans and Chinese. Many of their weapons were of American manufacture, having been supplied to our Chinese allies during WWII, or captured in South Korea during their mad dash south in 1950.

The Russian 90mm antiaircraft weapon, Russian manned and radar controlled, was the one we most feared on our deep interdiction missions. We'd jinx our fighters every 10 or 20 seconds over North Korea and near known 90mm concentrations. Upon return from those two or three hour missions, we'd be wringing wet and exhausted from our workouts but mighty happy to be back home at our friendly airfield again, only to re-arm, fuel up and take off on still another mission up north.

Generally the antiaircraft fire was of the Continuous Pointed or Predicted type which moved along with your altitude and flight path. We, at least, gambled that it was, and often changed our altitude and

Above: Peterson in cockpit of his Corsair

Upper Right: Much of Korea was mountainous and helpful landmarks were few. This is our favorite one, the double bend in the Imjin River.

Right: Flooded rice paddies from the air. South Korea was Japan's rice basket for over 100 years.

Lower Right: Checking for rock bruises on the prop, which could make for a very rough engine vibration. I'm wearing my oxygen mask, binoculars, and carrying my map case.

Below: Peterson at the ready.

Upper Left: Marion, the love of my life.

Upper Right: Ricky and Randy, eyes fixed on the TV screen, no doubt watching their favorite program, "Beanie," with Cecil, the seasick sea serpent.

Middle Left: Ricky and Randy showing me the Korean won money I had sent them. Our home at Manhattan Beach, California, in background.

Middle Right: Ricky on Beulah, the donkey.

Left: The boys on their Easter egg hunt.

heading so as to fly through the black smoke from the previous burst, knowing that there would never be another round fired in exactly that position again. If we had miscalculated and they, in fact, changed to Barrage pattern, we'd have been just so much debris fluttering down to the ground.

12 May 1952
Tunp o ri, Korea

Hi there little family,

Well, let's see what we did today. Nine of us took off at 0830 on a railcut just a little below the Russian frontier. After we had been over the front lines about 20 minutes my plane began to run real rough and I could not get enough power out of it to stay with the formation, so I called up the flight leader, Captain Henley, and requested an escort to return with me to the base. He directed Captain Browning, of the old El Toro 232 squadron, who was on my wing, to escort me home. I nursed the plane back home again, but, before crossing back over the bomb line, Browning and I let go with all our ordnance and hit a large concentration of buildings from 12,500 feet in the air. We weren't taking any chances getting down low with my engine running like it was. On reaching the home base after one and a half hours in the air, I remained at 12,500 feet over the field and tried in vain to duplicate the trouble I had had earlier. I found the roughness again, but could not make it quit on me again. Browning and I landed and I reported my trouble to the Engineering Department. They believed it to have been supercharger regulator trouble with incipient detonation. I went along with them on their assumptions. I debriefed with the Intelligence section of Group 12 in "S2" and gave them the coordinates of the secondary target Browning and I unloaded on.

The days are rolling by, darling, and in only 13 more days I will have been gone two whole months. I can't say I'm enjoying these missions, but when one flies two a day the days just fly by, literally. I have to take off at 1710 for a 2.8 hour railcut up in the same target area they hit this morning. I probably will be making another dark landing tonight. Whoooie!! For some reason I have an aversion to taking off and landing at night. It probably stems from the fact that it's dark and you can't see a darn thing with these Corsairs at night because there are no landing lights on the plane and only very dim runway border lights to indicate where the edge of the runway is. I'll be OK, though, 'cause I had a night landing just the other day, and to have had one recently is a distinct advantage. One's judgement is poor at night, especially where the visibility from a Corsair is poor in the first place.

I've just been looking at all the pictures you have sent me and the cutest one of all is of the boys sitting on the divan watching their favorite television show--it's so typical. The ones of Beulah, the donkey, are cute too, and the one where they are standing by the fence on the west side of the patio in their bathrobes, with their Easter eggs and everything in hand at 0600--they have that excited look about them, and they both look exactly alike to me. The fellows in the hut here with me all say how much they look like me and each other.

Up in northern Korea today it was hazy and it looked like some weather might move down on us by tonight. Bob Barbours just called me and said, "We've got a hot one, Pete. Get down here to the line as fast as you can." I told him I'd be right down, but as I was getting my flight suit on he called again and said, "Skip it, Pete, we don't have enough planes for you." So that's how it goes. I will still have my afternoon railcut, though.

1830

I just **thought** *I would get a railcut. I briefed with the flight, then walked across the field to our squadron area and briefed again at the squadron, got into my flight gear over there and was all set to go when the line chief came in and said, "Sorry, Captain Peterson, your plane just developed engine trouble and it's down. You won't be on this mission because we don't have another spare plane." Well, I was a little put out after going through all the briefing and getting my gear on etc., but it was music to my ears to know I was not going to have to find that postage stamp in the dark tonight.*

I walked over to the mess hall and on the way over I passed the open air theater where there was a Korean USO type show going on. I went on into supper, which consisted of porkchops, peas, spuds, gravy, dressing, salad, ice cream and cherry pie, iced tea or coffee. They had light green plastic cloths on the tables, curtains on the windows, and all the mess furniture had been painted white. It was really looking nice. The food is sure swell for being prepared in a war zone, on battlefield stoves under very crude conditions. At K18 we used dishes, but here we are using Navy trays. I remember how crude and dirty everything appeared to me when I returned from my R&R, but now things seem OK again.

There is a big storm brewing out over the water just west of us and to the north there are towering cumulonimbus clouds with thunder and lightning. Gosh, I hope it doesn't get bad before our boys get home from their mission tonight. It's raining now, I hear the drops hitting the metal of our quonset roof. They will be home in another hour, I hope. Boy, those are the biggest raindrops I have ever seen. They were coming from a real black, stringy cloud that has already passed over. A front appears to be moving in from the east of us now, being pushed by heavy winds. The cloud formations here in Korea are entirely different from those back home, probably because of what I have told you before--the winds from off the icy waters blow in and pick up the warmer air from the land. There hasn't been any fog since I hit Korea. Weather is the airman's biggest threat, even greater than flak sometimes. I hope they don't make us fly any weather over here. They didn't at K18, but I don't know whether they figured to ease up on us because we were in the process of moving or what.

They landed and everyone got back OK! That's an awfully long haul up there and I was worried because if they had ever gotten jumped by MIGs up there they would have had it. The Air Force won't even bring the B-29s out in the daytime, yet they send us up there knocking on the Ruskie's door.

Remember that I love you all very much.

Night night, Daddy

BEATEN BEFORE YOU START
Author Unknown

If you think you're beaten, you are
   If you think you dare not, you don't
If you'd like to win but think you can't
   It's almost a cinch you won't.
If you think you'll lose, you're lost,
   For out in the world you find
Success begins with a fellow's faith,
   It's all in the state of mind.
Full many a race is lost
   Ere ever a step is run;
And many a coward fails
   Ere ever his work's begun.

Think big and your deeds will grow,
   Think small and you'll fall behind;
Believe you can, and you will
   It's all in the state of mind.
If you think you're outclassed, you are;
   You've got to think high to rise,
You've got to believe in yourself before
   You can ever win a prize.
Life's battles don't always go
   To the stronger or faster man,
But soon or late, the one who wins
   Is the one who thinks he can.

13 May 1952
Tunp o ri, Korea
0925

Dearest Marion and boys,

Reveille at 0300--I was too tired and sleepy eyed to eat at that time. We were airborne in the dark and over the target on the west coast of north Korea by 0620. We cut rails. There was flak in the area but we sneaked through OK; none got clobbered on our team. Back home on the deck at 0745, I was shoveling chow down by 0815. Nothing to do now except to brief before take off at 1300 for my JOC alert.

The duty officer just came in the hut and said that we (our sqd.) have been given two additional JOC alerts today because our availability was high and they have spotted some juicy targets for us.

Cameron, Kennedy, Jackson, Larson just came into the hut with all their gear, returning from R&R. They have just been told they have one of the JOC alerts today and they aren't happy. The comments are flying around thick and fast--"The poags can't even give us a half a day to get squared away after coming from a rough week in Japan; very inconsiderate," says Kennedy. Cameron is sitting on his cot reading his mail. He got a whole mess of it while he was away. His little girl, living in Costa Mesa, has the measles too. Feliton is still the proud papa. He was passing out cigars to the fellows he hadn't seen at the squadron meeting last night. Colonel Bryson brought over two cases of ice cold beer to the meeting and the boys promptly guzzled it up. I still haven't had a smoke or a drink and I don't intent do. Last time I was overseas I was nervous and required something to take the strain off. The same goes for this time, but I don't want to start in on either habit because under the strain and tension that exist now it could really become a habit that would be difficult to shake in future years. I haven't adopted an "all is lost" attitude, as many of the guys have apparently done. There's plenty of free liquor if a guy wants it. After every mission you are entitled to a shot at the debriefing office. The flight leaders are usually the only ones who have to debrief, and occasionally one of the others in the flight who had been particularly shook on the mission will drop in for a snort.

No mail yesterday. Maybe today, I hope.

1730

The hop went off as planned, except that after we got vectored over the target area our division leader's radio went out on him and he turned the lead of the division over to me. I was a little nervous about it until I located the control plane in our target area and established radio communications with him. He was at 10,000 feet and circling friendly lines, the "poag." So I figured it must have been a rough day over the battle line. (You can always tell by the altitude they are flying at when you contact them.) I gave him my call sign, number of planes, type of armament, how long we could stay on station, etc. He gave me the coordinates of the target in code, which I had to decipher, and then they called for "Willie Peter" (white phosphorous) to be laid on the target, which was promptly done.

It was seven artillery positions we were after and they were very well defended on either side by 3000-foot mountains. We had to dive down from 10,000 feet to below the mountain tops, while the Commies fired down on us on our pullouts. We got two artillery pieces destroyed and two damaged. We strafed and dropped 1000 lb bombs, and shot eight rockets into the four enemy gun positions. The controller was hilarious. He had done a good job of finding the guns and of spotting them for us. We did the rest.

Nobody picked up any holes, but a Master Sgt Edmunson in our division had engine trouble after his first high speed run and had to get back over friendly lines. He circled and waited until we had finished, then joined up with us. The controller never came lower than 10,000 feet all during the attack, except right at the very end he dove that old SNJ down and really gave the area a close look, then climbed back to altitude and gave me a damage assessment, which I passed on to two different air control units on return to K6.

I led the division home, did all the navigating and radio work, and they all said I did a first class job. We landed at 1415, which made it rather nice. I went over and debriefed at Group S2 Intelligence section and refused my slug of brandy.

Came over, showered and shaved and ate supper early so I could knock out a few well chosen words to you before having to brief at 1830 for the ready alert, standing by my plane at the end of the runway 'til dark.

2135

Back from the ready alert and went to a movie, but left early. The guys are all talking about the JOC alerts they went on today. Mine was fairly good, I thought, but to hear the rest of these snivelers talk, the war should all be over. I guess they really caught some good targets today. I just hollered at them to knock off the shop talk. I've had airplanes up to my ears ever since I got up this morning at 0300.

Love, Daddy

BE SURE IT'S TRUE
(Dedicated to Group Ops)

Be sure it's true when you say it's Haeju,
It's a sin to tell a lie.
Many a butt has been broken
Just because these words were spoken.
Kuneri, Namsidong and P'yongyang,
If you send me there I'll cry.
So be sure it's true when you say it's Haeju,
It's a sin to tell a lie.

14 May 1952
Tunp o ri, Korea

Hi dearest little family,

The whole hut was awakened at 0230 this morning by the duty officer, who advised us JOC had just called and wanted a railcut mission of eight aircraft from our squadron sent up to the Sinanju (MIG Alley) sector as soon as possible. We had eight planes loaded, but weren't expecting our first mission to go before 0600. The eight pilots were selected and, although I was awakened, I wasn't selected. What a sensation, being awakened at that hour for a mission! The way the duty officer talked, it was the crucial hop of the whole war. The boys were on target at 0515. I didn't have to brief until 1030, thank goodness.

We took off for our rescue combat air patrol up over Chodo Island, west of Chinnampo in Communist North Korea. As we circled the rescue helicopter, British and American cruisers, destroyers, British Sea Fury fighters, and F-86 Sabres made runs on us. We thought possibly the Sabres were MIGs, but weren't particularly shook because we had heard the Sabres call in a few minutes prior to their run on us and tell their controller they were inbound with negative contact, which indicated they had not engaged many MIGs during their patrol. The carrier based British planes were plainly marked and propeller driven.

The UN have a surprising number of naval vessels on the west coast of Korea, well above the 38th parallel, cruising back and forth. During the 3.4 hours we were in the air I had a very good chance to get acquainted with the west and north coast of Communist Korea. We scouted several road routes and towns, including Chinnampo and Haeju. The downed pilot had been picked up and covered by the patrol we relieved, so we didn't have any covering to do on our patrol. We strafed on our way back to K6 for a while, then landed too late for our railcut mission, so I was finished with flying for the day at 1445--not bad at all.

I received three letters from you today, postmarked May 6, 7, 8, and one from Mom acknowledging my Mother's Day card to her, a little early, but nevertheless I got it there.

Yes, I was right smack in the middle of the huge air attack on Suan. I'll send the clipping back so that you can keep it on record. Today I completed my 20th mission. They are mounting, slowly but surely. I'll be glad when they have reached 100 because then maybe they'll start tapering me off. They have a lot of jobs in the Group and with the Division and Wing that are filled with pilots. I'm not so certain I'd want some of the jobs because there is little or nothing to do in some of them and the time would drag, so it would seem forever and a day before I'd get home.

Today the Chance Vought representative attached to our Group gave us some baseball caps with the name Chance Vought and a picture of the new F7U-Cutlass on the bill. I boxed them up, along with a bunch of picture postcards for Ricky to take to school and give to some of his little friends.

Gosh, it will seem wonderful to get back to civilization again. Even the old Chevy will look new to me when I see it again. I'll need to have you give me a few driving lessons before I'll trust myself out on the road--ha, ha. Come to think of it, I haven't driven a car since I left. I haven't been off of this base either, through the gate, nor was I ever off the base at Kangnung, except of course to fly off.

Boy, I don't know what the score is, I swear. They have been flying every plane just as long as they possibly can. When they take off at 0430 they are going constantly until 2030 (8:30 in the evening). The enlisted men are working their tails off. Every man in the squadron is putting out. Those poor devils work from 0230 until midnight or 0100 the next day and turn right around and start over again. While we're flying they sometimes manage to catch a little shuteye but it's not the kind of rest that does a man any good. I wish the civilians could just peek in on our squadron during one average day's operation. They wouldn't believe what they saw. Even though they're worked long and hard, they always take time to play around and skylark. American boys are wonderful. There are a lot of young kids out here really putting out. They aren't getting shot at, but they are good fighting marines just the same.

Oh say, speaking of fine young marines, Ricky's teacher, who wants to meet a nice young jet pilot, has her opportunity in the shape of Nellie Sharpe. Nellie's name is Whitlock Nelson Sharpe, I believe. At any rate, I have spoken to him and I believe he is a little lonely and he said he would welcome a lovely pen pal. So now you get her to write him at VMF-323, Mag 12, 1st MAW, c/o FPO, or else give me her full name and address and I'll give it to Nellie. He's a fine fellow.

I miss my precious little family very, very much and I love each one of you with all my heart and soul.

Daddy

DAVE KENNEDY'S ROCKETS EXPLODE PREMATURELY UNDER MY PLANE

15 May 1952
Tunp o ri, Korea

Dearest baby girl and boys,
The daddy is one tired fighter pilot tonight. Reveille went at 0345 this morning and I had a cup of coffee, then briefed. It was still dark when we took off for our railcut up deep in North Korea. We hit them at about 0600 and boy, the rail junction was really jumping from our bombs and rockets, let go at low altitude in the heart of many Communist antiaircraft guns. They briefed us that we could expect heavy flak and they were correct. It was a long hop and I was keyed up the whole time because I couldn't get my plane's engine to run smoothly and expected trouble with it the entire hop, but nothing happened, thank God.

After we landed I had a full breakfast because I was really starved. I rested my tired back and took a short nap. Had lunch, then briefed again for a special interdiction mission they had just come across up in North Korea. A photo-recon plane had been over the area and through photo interpretation they had found one of the Communists' main truck overhaul and repair stations, and also a major truck and tank parts manufacturing point of North Korea.

Four of us--Col Bryson led the hop with me on his wing, Dave Kennedy flying section lead with McDonald on his wing--went on this hair-raiser. In order to give it the punch it needed they omitted our precious 150 gallons of reserve fuel we depend on so very much to give us the range the long railcut missions flown up into North Korea demand of us, and hung on an extra 1000 lb bomb apiece. Then they scrambled us up to N. Korea to about 60 miles north of the *capital city of P'yongyang, where, after much jockeying and evasive action (to avoid the antiaircraft fire) at 10,000' down to 8000', we located our target through a very thick haze caused by the many fires burning in North and South Korea. We dove on down, pressing our runs right down the throats of the Communist gunners defending their precious hideaway in the mountains. To say we clobbered them would be putting it mildly. Dave Kennedy, on my tail in the pushover from 10,000' down to treetop level, fired his rockets in pairs, and somehow or other one of them went off prematurely ahead of him and under me. The terrific blast lifted my tail, giving me a heck of a start. I thought for sure I'd had it, but managed to recover and climbed on up to altitude to take a look at my wings and fuselage. From what we could see, Dave also giving the bottom of my plane a going over, we decided I was a lucky boy. I had only received the concussion, but he had flown through the flak of it and had not been hit either, so he was pretty lucky himself.*

Concerning the premature explosion of Dave Kennedy's rocket, I'd figured the rocket itself had been struck by enemy fire just after he'd fired it. There didn't seem to be any other rational explanation, since rockets explode only upon impact. In any case, it was indeed a close shave for both of us.

Recovering to an altitude of about 8000', we began to worry if we'd make it home on our low fuel supply. We put our iron birds on automatic lean fuel mixture setting, decreased manifold pressure and engine revolution to a minimum, and pointed our noses home. A little over an hour later we began to see evidence of good old K6 and we were on the deck by 1600, after circling the field twice because of a plane dropping some hung bombs on the strip when it had landed. They cleared the strip and let us land. None of us had more than 50 gallons, some down to 20 gallons, which would hardly have been enough for an emergency wave-off on full power in a Corsair.

THE B-36
(Battle Hymn of the Republic)

The B-36, it flies at 40,000 feet,
The B-36, it flies at 40,000 feet, The B-36, it flies at 40,000 feet,
But it only drops a teensey, weensey bomb.
Tons and tons of ammunition,
Tons and tons of ammunition, Tons and tons of ammunition,
But it only drops a teensey, weensey bomb.

The PB4-Y, it flies at 30,000 feet,
The PB4-Y, it flies at 30,000 feet, The PB4-Y, it flies at 30,000 feet,
But it only drops a teensey, weensey depth charge.
Tons and tons of aviation gasoline,
Tons and tons of aviation gasoline, Tons and tons of aviation gasoline,
But it only drops a teensey, weensey depth charge.

Life certainly takes on a rosy hue after you've been shook a couple of times a day. Good old terra firma really looks good, I'll tell you. Too bad the folks on strike back home couldn't go along on a couple of rough railcuts, interdiction or close air support missions with us sometime-- they'd be so tickled to go back to the steel mills and the oil refineries AT ANY PRICE they'd be knocking each other over in the scramble. After every day's mission I always have a little thank-you prayer to offer, and believe you me, it's a a comfort to know I'm not doing the job all by myself.
I'll be content to return home and dig ditches for the rest of my life, if only I can be left alone to dig the ditches where and when I please, and to know somebody won't be along to take my shovel away from me and make me fight for the 3rd time for the right to dig my ditch when and where I please.

Just checked tomorrow's flight schedule and I have only one mission, a JOC alert, which will become a close air support or an interdiction. Yippee! I hardly know what to do. Guess I'll stay up late because I don't have to get up in the middle of the night to go flying. Our squadron's last mission tonight landed at 2100 (9:00 PM), and we are supposed to be day fighters/bombers.

I have some wonderful mellow music on my radio right now. I'd love to be holding you in my arms, precious girl, dancing around our living room, with the darling boys all tucked away in their beds. Kiss my wonderful little guys for me, dearest girl and tell them their daddy loves them and wants more than anything else in this world to get home and be with them. I'm always happy to hear that the little fellows ask for their daddy.

Night night little family,
Daddy

16 May 1952
Tunp o ri, Korea
Friday morn. 1030

Dearest Marion and my two precious little boys,

Daddy has been thinking of you all this morning. Since I don't have a mission until this afternoon, I wandered around the base taking pictures of planes, bombs, fellow officers, fox holes and stuff like that. There has been a C46 transport flying back and forth all morning over our field and living area, dusting or spraying DDT. It's in a liquid state and comes floating down on everything like a heavy fog. It's slightly irritating to one's nostrils, though, and I'll be glad when he's finished. He comes down real low, about 75 or 100 feet off the deck, and he really makes a noise.

Capt Budd just hit me for a donation for a going away present for Col Dorsey, our commanding officer of Group 12. It was a pleasure to give it because he's a fine CO. He flies missions with all the squadrons on the base and is a regular guy. Don't know who is going to relieve him.

The 21st draft should be showing up soon. When they do arrive it will give us fellows a little relief in flying because they took five of the pilots they gave us from the 20th draft and sent them to VMF-312. a Marine carrier-based squadron. We've got pilots on TAD (temporary attached duty), in the hospital, and on R&R, and golly, those of us who stay behind are really catching double duty. The AD squadron, VMA-121, now attached to our Group, has about ten planes available and they are only able to fly about every other day. VMF-323 has about 15 planes available and they only fly about every other day. We have 19 planes and about 30 available pilots, and we usually fly two hops every day.

They have taken the Koreans off the mess serving section and put on some enlisted men. The Korean laborers are being drafted into the Korean Army now and they are becoming conspicuous by their absence. The Korean labor office is hiring more and more papasans lately. Some of them are dressed real funny--their clothes are handmade, ragged and dirty, and they have those chin whiskers about four inches long.

One of the boys went into Seoul the other day and on the way in he saw Korean families living in bombed-out American and Russian tanks along the road. There must be thousands of homeless here in Korea. It's a shame everybody in this huge world can't have a small plot of ground to call their own. Thank God for our little plot. As small as it is, it's worth fighting for.

We enjoyed some beautiful music on my radio until 2300 last night. I knew about five fellows in the hut needed to get to sleep because they had the early early in the morning, but every time I turned it off they'd all yell, "Turn it on again, Pete!" The guys who should have been asleep early were the ones yelling to keep it on, so I did. It's sure a wonderful feeling to hear soft, sweet music in a godforsaken place like this. It takes you just a little closer to home and to more pleasant memories. This place could get a fellow down if he let it. I'm doing everything in my power not to let it. Your letters are sure a wonderful lift to me, honey. Hope there's some mail today.

2300

Hi again,

Just returned from the movie, "Streetcar Named Desire."

We briefed at 1500 at the Group but had to stand by until about 1530 when we got a rush call from JOC. We dashed off to our squadron, grabbed our flight gear, hopped into our four planes and dashed off up to a control area called Palomino, where we contacted the forward air controller with the ground forces and asked for the position coordinates of the artillery that was giving them trouble. He warned us of heavy flak and small arms fire, and he was right.

Never, I repeat, never have I seen so much flak in all my 23 missions. The stuff was sailing by my wings, canopy and engine. I jinxed all over the sky and made my runs from 9000', diving down on their position at as steep an angle as I could. I used full power and really picked up speed. A sickening feeling came over me every time I headed the nose of my plane down into their barrage. As I dove, I strafed with 20mm, which tends to keep their heads down in the immediate area. However, the jokers on every other ridge were popping away at me. (It's funny what you find yourself doing when they are shooting at you. I pull my shoulders in and keep my arms in as close to my body as possible.) The stuff they were throwing up at us today was 37mm, which bursts in a black ball about three or four feet in diameter at a predetermined altitude unless it strikes something; then it goes off on contact. I was wanting to get out of there after our first run on them, but we were forced to make a total of four runs each before retiring to friendly lines.

The controller gave us credit for 100% target coverage and 95% effective use of ordnance, which is nearly perfect. We were all right in there with our stuff. I was awfully glad to get back to good old K6 tonight.

Showered, shaved, had supper, which consisted of steak, French fries, string beans, salad, ice cream, chocolate cake, coffee. I went back for seconds on ice cream, and could have had another steak if I had wanted it. It was marvelous. You sure have to hand it to them-- they are really on the ball where the chow is concerned.

I don't know whether I'm getting it over to you, how I feel after returning from a mission. It's like a prisoner receiving a reprieve from the gas chamber, or something like that. You can't feel disheartened or discouraged; instead you feel as though you've been given a new birth and a new lease on life. It's almost like being born all over again. I always feel a terrific uplifting.

I'm happy to hear Ricky is getting to feel like his old self. The poor little guy has really had a session of it, hasn't he?

Give my love to Nanna and Grampa, Peg and Trooper.

Your very own, Daddy

THE RAT

*The pale moon shone on the barroom floor
And the place was closed for the night,
When out of his hole came a big gray rat
And sang in the pale moonlight.
He lapped up the whiskey from the barroom floor
And back on his haunches he sat,
And to that empty bar he yodled,
"Bring on your goddamn CAT! Hic - Cat, Hic - Cat."*

17 May 1952
Tunp o ri, Korea

Hi precious little family,
    The daddy was up at 0430 this morning and had breakfast, then got into my plane and taxied it out to the end of the line with Capts Sutherland, Browning and Cameron. We secured at 0700, came over for a second cup of coffee and got briefed at the Group. Then we briefed again for an interdiction mission which took off at 1130 and four of us flew up north of the bomb line to hit a heavy flak area and some very accurate antiaircraft guns that had been giving the UN aircraft a lot of trouble for some time.
    It was so "hot" with AA the air controller wouldn't come below 11,000', and yet, as he circled at that altitude, he was still getting 90mm bursts around him. He pointed the target out by voice description, and when we saw them firing at us we dove on down to nearly mountain top level (3500') and let go with rockets and 1000 lb bombs on their positions. Yes, we silenced them. My heart was up in my throat the whole time, though, and good old K6 looked awfully good to us--Capts Burnham, Sutherland, Jacks and self. We hit the deck at 1330 and had our lunch.
    I came back to the hut, stripped down to my shorts and took a 15 minute sun bath, but the sun was too hot so I secured that operation to an inside job of reading Dave Kennedy's recently purchased tourist guide book of Japan. It gave brief descriptions of the various resort towns, 13 national parks, religion, art, and history of Japan. Dave took a bunch of pictures the last time he was in Seoul and he gave me one that I liked a lot. It's of a cute little Korean boy he snapped in Korea's capital city. I thought you might like to send it to some paper or something because it is so cute. Poor little guys like him are just wandering around; most have been placed in orphanages, however, and I doubt if there are many who aren't cared for now.
    It's been almost as hot today as it was in El Centro in Sep '51. At about 1500, however, a gentle cool ocean breeze came in from the west and it's now very comfortable. It's becoming cloud covered now and I wouldn't be surprized if it didn't rain all over us tonight and tomorrow. I haven't been very accurate, however, on my weather predictions out here in this godforsaken country. Up near where we were today I did see a beautiful blue-green reservoir surrounded by thickly covered forests of pine, a beautiful setting. There are a few lovely white sand covered beaches that look as though they'd be nice recreation areas. There aren't any near K6 though. A huge, wide, fast-racing river runs from Seoul northeast to where we hit on our mission today. All along the river there were little towns, and occasionally there would appear a white sandbar of considerable size. They certainly have no water problem here in Korea.
    Due to the three or four foot water table here, wherever a 1000lb bomb has been dropped, the water then seeps into the bomb crater. Reflections from these pools can be seen from the air all over the country. That's one of the reasons we are going to have a bad mosquito problem here in a few weeks. I frankly haven't seen any yet. There are lots of flies, though, due to the proximity of the native farms to our airfield. They use their own droppings, which makes it rough.
    Tonight at the movie they are showing "Ten Tall Men." Guess I'll be there.
    Chow was very good tonight: roast beef, mashed spuds, gravy, corn, salad, coffee, apple pie (delicious crust too). Boy, those guys sure have the word. It couldn't hold a candle to yours, precious girl, but for over here, under field conditions, it's wonderful.
    I have a 1500 brief for a close air support mission tomorrow. Thank goodness I'll be able to catch up on my sleep tonight.
    Dave Kennedy just gave me two 100 wan notes to send home to my two "snivelers" (his favorite word, outside of "miserable slob"). A 100 wan note is worth about one and a half cent, so don't let the boys spend it all in one place.
    Dave K., Denny Clyde and Capt Lawler just left for some place outside the gate. They were pretty well charged up. Lawler "sniveled" the jeep from the Group transportation pool and off they went. I snapped their picture just prior to their shoving off, but I don't think it will come out because the sun had just gone down. I get a kick out of the fellows here in the hut. If I'm playing something on the radio and they don't like it they'll come over, and without saying doodley, start tuning it into something else. It'll stay there for about five minutes, then

somebody else will redial it. It goes on and on like that. It doesn't bother me any, and they just do it for laughs anyway. Nobody gets mad at anyone else in our squadron. I guess we all feel about the same. Life's too short to get mad about anything.

How's the garden coming along, honey girl? How about taking a picture of it for me?

Your very own,
Daddy

18 May 1952
Sunday - 1620
(Mission No. 25 today)

Dearest Marion and darling little boys,
    Just came down from a mission that took me up north and east of the Truce Talks. We worked with a forward air controller (FAC) on the ground and a tactical air controller airborne, who were assigned to the 1stMarDiv which is operating in that area.
    They gave us a round of "Willie Peter" on the target, which consisted of a group of caves, trenches and gun positions. "Toxon" (many) troops in those positions were engaged in a fire fight with our guys as we were being alerted. In fact, they'd hauled me out of the sack, for I hadn't expected to fly until 1500. Forty-five minutes after they woke me up from my nap I was dropping my 1000 lb bombs in a screaming dive on Communist troops. We did a very good job. The TACA & FAC were very happy about the outcome. They informed us of the fact that our attack had been observed by some very high rank, and that they'd sent a "well done" to us. It makes you feel wonderful to have a successful mission and to know you have done someone some good.
    Stretch Evans, a fellow who was with me on our mission, along with Bob Van Dalsem and Pittman, brought along his tiny Chihuahua dog, Scoshie on his mission. He had him sitting on his lap most of the time, except when he went into his runs, then he'd put the little fellow up on the dash panel in front of him. Scoshie made out OK, though, and was running around and barking excitedly after he landed. The men on the line got quite a kick out of it. I took a picture after we all got back to the hut area; that is, Denny took the picture of Stretch, Pittman and myself, and, of course, Scoshie.
    No mail today, darling, except for the AiReporter. Thanks for forwarding it.
    I miss you all more than I can possibly tell you, dear. Living in these darn huts with nine other men is lousy. Last night they had a drinking party and sang until 0200. I went to bed early and listened to the radio for a while, but there was another one going at the other end of the hut so I turned mine off, but I couldn't sleep until the party broke up. I was awfully sleepy this morning. The sleeping bag was too hot for me last night. It's beginning to rain right now.

Night night,
Daddy

AN EVENING AT THE SNIVELER'S BAR

19 May 1952
Midnight Sunday

Dearest girl,
    Just wanted to write this down before I forgot it. Tonight I saw "Lone Star," with Clark Gable and Ava Gardner. It was very good, I thought--didn't help my present condition, however.
    Col Bryson came through the hut at 2200 and announced that there was to be a meeting in hut 245, (the sniveler's bar), so I went down and had a wonderful time singing my fool head off with the boys. I had a Coke to quench my thirst from all my singing. John Snapper and I were standing close together in the circle and we harmonized real sharp together.

Above: A pile of mail ready to be delivered to the North Korean and Chinese Communists.

Upper Left: Capt John Snapper. John was my division leader during many a hairy mission. I respected his great flying ability and leadership qualities, and did my best to emulate him when I took over as division leader later.

Left: The geometrically perfect alignment of the Willie Sugar VMF-323 F4U-4B Corsairs at K6, our sister squadron.

Lower Left: The Group's Sikorsky HO-3S-1 helicopter. It later crashed, leaving us pilots without immediate rescue assistance.

Below: A slightly bent F4U-4B Corsair which crash-landed after being hit by heavy Communist antiaircraft fire.

Our very hungry and friendly rabbit mascot at K6.

A big day at K6--Korean laborers are relocating the outhouse, getting a little distance from our living quarters.

VMF-212 pilots moving from one quonset hut to another at K6.

Foxholes at K6 caused a number of injuries, especially at night to the unsuspecting.

That rabbit again.

Col Bryson played his harmonica. He can play anything on it. Then he played the uke and sang some Hawaiian songs, even a little hula along with it. The little dog, Scoshie, got drunk on beer and couldn't walk. His eyes were crossed, honestly. Gosh, it was funny! Bryson (Skipper) played the Irish Jig while Capt Lawler danced. Boy, what talent! We sang every dirty song that was ever written and also all the good clean ones any of us happened to think of. I never realized there were more dirty ones than there were clean ones. Live and learn. When you gather a bunch of grown men from every walk of life and toss them all together 8000 miles away from home and put them in a hole like this, it's no wonder they come up with the songs they do. Lots of them are about the UN and Harry Truman. The generals and the Marine Corps come in for their share too. I'll try to remember some of the funny ones. I didn't hear "I Ain't Got No Bean Bag" or "I've Got My A-Frame on Upside Down" tonight.

Wish I were home right now--gosh, I miss you.

Your very own, Daddy

P.S. *I went to church this morning and sang my fool head off there too.*

DOWN BY THE RUNWAY SIDE
(Down By the Riverside)

I'm gonna ground-loop my F4U
Down by the runway side;
Down by the runway side;
Down by the runway side,
I'm gonna ground-loop my F4U
I ain't gonna go to P'yongyang no more.
  CHORUS:
    I ain't gonna go to P'yongyang no more, no more,
    I ain't gonna escort a B-29.
    I ain't gonna go to P'yongyang no more.

I'm gonna tear off my wings and flaps
Down by the runway side;
Down by the runway side;
Down by the runway side,
I'm gonna tear off my wings and flaps
I ain't gonna go to P'yongyang no more.
  CHORUS:

I'm gonna turn off my IFF
Down by the runway side;
Down by the runway side;
Down by the runway side,
I'm gonna pull up my goddamn wheels
I ain't gonna go to P'yongyang no more.
  CHORUS:

19 May 1952
Monday evening

Hi little gang,

The weather north of the bomb line being marginal, I spent the day flying a test hop; then in the afternoon Denny Clyde and I went up for a GCA (ground control approach). We made numerous passes and the controllers certainly proved their proficiency. They brought us right down to the deck every time. I couldn't see very well either because it was raining quite hard at times and I relied entirely on their directions. We worked with them for about an hour and a half, then broke off and flew out over the ocean off the west coast and found an area that was clearing. Denny took pictures of me flying, and I took some of him. We landed at about 1630, came on over and took a nice hot shower.

I was in a lousy mood yesterday, honey, and I hope my letter didn't reflect it. At any rate, I'm in a much better mood today and that's all that matters. The boys have gotten the party business out of their systems now, I hope, and maybe we'll have a few days of peace and quiet. Two of the guys woke up this morning in the latrine! They had been moved bodily, cot and all, in there. One guy was put in the shower room, and this morning at about 0600 somebody went in and turned the cold water on him. What a rude awakening!

I only logged about six hours of rest last night at the most. Tonight, after the movie, "Texas Carnival," with Esther Williams and Red Skelton, I'm going to hit the basket because I have an 0500 takeoff for a railcut up in North Korea, then a 1000 takeoff for another railcut. It's going to be a busy day, weather permitting.

On my test hop this morning I wrang out an old tired goat and finally gave it a down check after it began hammering and running rough on me. After staying with it for a little over an hour, though, trying to put my finger on the trouble, I determined that it was probably an unbalanced propeller. They sent the plane over to the service squadron after I brought it down. Some of these old gals are really tired and should have been retired from the program many years ago. The fuselages are loose, they vibrate and shake like a dog coming out of the water when you put them into a dive.

Well, little family, it is almost movie time, so I'll knock off and give it a see.

2215

The picture was awfully funny, and I got a big bang out of laughing for a change. Usually the general run of pictures are real serious. It rained a little bit as we were watching the show, but hardly enough to matter when you're hungry for some entertainment.

Your description of the yard certainly sounds wonderful. You've really done a lot of work, dearest. You bet the time goes fast if you're busy. Some of my days really fly by. None can go fast enough for me, though, precious doll, until I'm home again and in your arms. Kiss my precious boys for their daddy that loves them.

Love, Daddy

CHOSIN RESERVOIR
(Ramblin' Wreck from Georgia Tech)

*Listen all you flyers, I'll tell you one and all
About an eager pilot with much less brains than gall.
He flew a weary Corsair in the North Korean war.
He made his fatal last mistake at the Chosin Reservoir.*

*He took off out of Wonsan, flew north to Sudong-Ni,
Then shot a loaded ox-cart on the road to Koto-Ri.
He charged his guns and looked around for something else to do.
He thought he'd find some targets on the plains of Hagaru.*

*Then a self-propelled gun in open view he saw
Along a slight embankment at the bottom of a draw.
With such an easy target he didn't stop to think
It might be just a flak-trap of the wily Commie chink.*

So eagerly he dove in, so deadly was his aim.
He knew he'd get his target and the Commies felt the same.
They got him with the first shot; he never felt the jar.
He now lies on the bottom of the Chosin Reservoir.

ATTACKED BY A MIG-15

20 May 1952
Tunp o ri
Tuesday afternoon

Hi there little family,
Received two letters from you today, which makes my day complete. One from your Mom today too. She told me all about some of Ricky's and Randy's antics. They were really amusing. I always love hearing about the two little guys.

I've had a very tiring day today and I'll be glad to hit the basket tonight. The hop went off about as I expected, although we attained remarkable accuracy, which JOC is going to doubt when they receive the damage assessment report tonight.

I got up early, had a cup of joe, briefed, took off (13 of us) at 0600 and flew to North Korea, below P'yongyang and above Sariwan, where we cut rails and marshalling yards. We got some AA out of them, but nobody got clipped and we were back home on the deck at 0815. After a big breakfast we briefed at 0900, took off again and flew up to the same target, only we worked it over a little south of our earlier mission. We got seven direct hits with (2) 1000lb bombs each and four damaging misses. There were twelve on our second mission, landing at 1215.

My bum and back were tired, so after lunch I lay down a while and then felt a lot better. I have 27 missions now.

The MIGs and Sabres were going at it while we were up there; one unidentified fighter plane made a run on us on our second mission--no doubt a MIG-15. We dove for the deck and firewalled our old U-birds, putting miles between us and North Korea, gradually climbed again to 10,000', rejoined our division and returned home. One of these days we're not going to be so lucky. I'm either going to have nerves of steel or else I'm going to be a nervous wreck. I'm in fairly good shape, so don't worry, dear; even though I get shook while I'm flying, I straighten out OK after I get back down on the deck.

I need your letters, darling, like I need oxygen, and I thank God I have you and the boys waiting for me at home. I sometimes feel as though I'm just a body, with my heart and soul removed, just going about my job as though I were a mechanical man. Sometimes it seems as though I've never done anything else in my life but fly railcuts and close air support, and when I think of you and the boys it's like thinking of my life hereafter--heaven, or someplace like that--someplace where all my dreams come to a focus and converge; not a rainbow, a pot of gold, a Cadillac, no, just my Marion and my Ricky and my Randy.

I enjoyed Ricky's drawing very much, and when I saw the little faces and doodles in and among the letters it reminded me of what I sometimes used to do.

I'm enclosing the poop on the pay raise--providing Harry S. Truman signs same--it will mean an additional $35.00 for us, or about $655.00 a month total.

The movie tonight is "Fixed Bayonets." I don't know why they send those war pictures to Korea. It's like sending coal to Newcastle.

1900

Just came from chow. It was very good--turkey, mashed spuds, giblet gravy, peas, carrots, cabbage salad, coffee, apple pie a la mode. Rough, isn't it? I guess they figure they better feed us over here, just to keep the morale up.

The sun is just setting, and if it were anyplace else in the world I'd say it was beautiful. I have my radio tuned into some lovely music being rebroadcast from the good old USA. I wonder if future immigrants will yearn for the shores of the "good old USA" as I'm yearning for *them now. Isn't it funny how things are rationed out? There are thousands of immigrants every year coming into America who are allowed to go their own ways and live their own lives in our country, while, on the other hand, there are thousands of our boys being sent half a world away from our shores in order to keep America free for all those who desire to live their lives unmolested there. Of course nobody ever figures things out in that light. I'm scared of the outcome, darling. Russia is bent on world domination and we're going to tangle with her sooner or later. It's in the cards.*

The radio is coming forth with "Baby, It's Cold Outside," in Japanese yet! Now it's "Somebody Loves Me" in English. Did I tell you my R&R date is 5 June? Just 16 more days. I'd like to go to Tokyo, only I don't know why I should travel so far when there are apparently plenty of recreational activities in and around Itami, Kobe, Osaka and Kyoto.

Smitty just walked in and handed me the two records you made and mailed 13 May. Gee, just imagine, only seven days old. I just went over and borrowed a record player from another squadron's officer's hut. They were good, honey. I sure enjoyed hearing all your voices.

Give my two darling boys a big hug for me. I'll be home in a few months and what a wonderful reunion it will be for all of us.

All my love, Daddy

BRITISH METEOR JETS MAKE THREATENING RUNS ON OUR FLIGHT

21 May 1952
Tunp o ri, Korea
Wednesday, 1715

Dearest girl,
I just had a nice refreshing shave and shower. It's been awfully hot today, and I shouldn't be using the past tense either because it's still bearing down hot and heavy, although there's a slight breeze coming up, but darned if it isn't bringing the smoke in with it from the shower room where the papasan is feeding the fire for our hot water. You just can't win, it seems.

I've had two rail bridge cuts today up in North Korea. If you'll look on your map at P'yongyang (the capitol of North Korea) you'll find a railroad coming in from the east crossing over a fairly wide river just east of the city. Well, if your map shows a railroad bridge crossing over the river it's obsolete, 'cause it ain't no more.

I jumped up at 0500, briefed and at 0715 I was over P'yongyang. The flak is extremely heavy directly over P'yongyang (we've learned from experience), so we skirted the city and made all our runs from west to east, recovering southeast. They threw a little AA at us which we neutralized right off the bat with VT (proximity fused) bombs set to go off 300-400' over the heads of the ground gunners. (When a thousand pounder goes off, with VT fusing, the earth quakes for a diameter of about 300' and you can see shock waves going out from around the bomb blast. It's terrific.) The rest of the flight let theirs go on instantaneous nose fusing with a secondary .025 second tail delay. The main railway bridge had been destroyed earlier in the war, but they had made a bypass just north of the main bridge about 100 yards. We'll keep them making bypasses until they're blue in the face.

South Korea sure is well preserved compared to North Korea. Hardly any of the railroads or bridges in S. Korea have been destroyed to the extent that the ones in N. Korea have. I'd say offhand it will take ten years to replace the bridges and road and rail system that the UN has destroyed in N. Korea. The dams and electro-power systems throughout both North and South Korea haven't been touched as yet. They sure have plenty of water reservoirs throughout their country, and nearly every one of them has a huge concrete dam with its hydroelectric facility combined.

The main north-south Korean rail system runs just east of Tunp o ri. Right next to it runs an overhead power system all down the nation.

GLOSTER METEOR MK 8

Gloster Meteor MK 8, of the Royal Australian Air Force, was the only British jet fighter to see action in Korea. Powered by two 3600 lb thrust Derwent-8, this fighter was used as a high altitude interceptor and as a bomber. It could carry two 1000 lb bombs or up to 16 rockets. Most versions carried four 20mm cannons. An early version, the Meteor MK 4, had set world speed records of 616 MPH in September 1946. The first Meteor to enter service was also the first Allied jet fighter to be used operationally in WWII. During the Korean campaign Australian pilots often made identification runs on our formation, scaring the living hell out of us.

Left: Hawker Sea Fury FB MK 11, used by British, Canadian and Australian Air Forces, carried two 1000 lb bombs or twelve 60 lb rockets, and four 20mm Hispano MK5 cannons. Sea Furies were used throughout the Korean War, and often tangled with the much faster Russian MIG-15 jets with some success. They operated almost exclusively off of British Commonwealth aircraft carriers. Recently, in the 1990s, re-engined with our latest and higher horsepower radial engines, they have proven to be a popular aircraft for air racing.

HAWKER SEA FURY FB MK 11

Right: Fairey Firefly MK5, a fighter reconnaissance aircraft flown off the British aircraft carriers HMS TRIUMPH and HMS OCEAN during the Korean War. Capable of carrying 2000 lbs of bombs or eight 60 lb rockets, it was armed with four 20mm cannons as well. A 1990 HP Griffon XII powered this radar carrying fighter which first saw active service in 1943 as an MKI and was rated as the best British specialized shipboard airplane produced.

FAIREY FIREFLY MK5

Above, L to R: My friends, Capts Jeff Crandall and Peter Thomas, on R & R in Japan.

Upper Left: Spud in his F4U-4B Corsair #16 LD (Love Dog), returning from a combat mission. Picture taken by Denny Clyde.

Left: Flight line view of VMF-323's F4U-4B Corsairs, armed and ready for next mission

A heavily damaged Corsair from a night landing pileup on the runway at K6.

Remains of an F4U-4B Corsair which crashed after being hit by enemy AA. We tried not to dwell too long on the prospects of this happening to us.

The first mission this morning I flew the survival plane on which, along with eight wing rockets and 20mm cannon, we carry a 150 gallon gas tank with a survival bomb that we drop to downed pilots. Fortunately, it was not necessary this time. We landed at 0830 and I went over to the mess hall for a bowl of Wheaties and a piece of bread and jam. The coffee was all gone. Anyhoo, I had to hoof it back to the briefing room at 0915 for a samie-same rail bridge east of P'yongyang. Took off at 1030. My plane was so hot I could hardly touch the metal as I climbed into it. It was sure warm this morning.

Flying up the west coast about 150 miles, we cut into North Korea east of Haeju. We hit the target, and as we were retiring we were attacked by two British Meteor jets coming down to investigate! They scared the hell out of us because of the way they came at us. We broke and went into a defensive weave, and when they saw we meant business, they broke it off. We were sure scared (shook is the word). Darn them! You'd think those bloody Englishmen would get the word sooner or later. Honestly, the next jet that makes even a feint at me is going to get sprayed with (4) 20mm cannons. I'm getting tired of being the goat in these deals.

We were on the deck by 1330 and had lunch. Boy, I was exhausted, it was so hot and I sweat my plane out the entire time we were over enemy territory. It wasn't running too well. During this morning's earlier mission my plane was pumping gasoline over the side due to a faulty fuel transfer pump. I stuck with it, though, and made the trip OK. I'm sure happy to get those two missions behind me, and now I can forget about any more flying until tomorrow.

I have 29 missions in now, darling. The 21st draft is coming in--yes siree, about 18 of them will have assignments to this squadron. At any rate, there are 103 pilots on the new draft. If we could only get the full allotment of pilots in this squadron we would only have to fly one mission a day. Golly, one is plenty.

Received your very sweet letter of the 15th of May, written just after you returned from the movie, "A Song in My Heart," with Peggy. It was sweet of you, dearest girl, to say you only desired to please me. I adore you, precious girl.

Tell Ricky that he shouldn't try to lift heavy things until Daddy returns home. I can teach him how to pick things up and maybe we can get some lifting weights like Mike bought Dale. I believe Ricky could get a lot out of weights even as young as he is. Both of the boys are going to have beautifully developed physiques if I have anything to say about it. I got a kick out of your telling me about the plastic goggles Nanga bought the boys. So they are really hot pilots now, eh?

Oh say, I wanted to tell you about all the radio communications that go on when we're on our missions. There are Greeks, ROKs, English, Canadians, Americans and South Africans, all talking and checking in and out with their various control units. It's very interesting. The British are really a scream, what with "15 bloody KIAs, (4) enemy bunkers destroyed and a bloody command post eliminated. Over."

The controller often comes up with a "Jolly well done, old boy. This is Shirley controller--out." The ROKs give their reports sometimes in broken English and other times in Korean. There are Korean interpreters at "Shirley." There are only about seven or eight P-51s assigned to the ROK air force and they are operating out of Kangnung on the east coast, where we were.

Guess I'll secure this for a while, baby girl that I love, and go over and have supper. Out.

1940

Hi darlin',
Just came from a delicious steak dinner.

Tomorrow our squadron is going to have 60 missions. I'm flying three myself, west of P'yongyang. Going to hit the basket early tonight if I can. Hope the boys go to bed early so that we can get the needed rest. Wish I could have a day off to rest my back, but it's an impossibility because we haven't enough pilots as it is. We're even borrowing pilots from the Group to help us out. Guess it's an all-out affair. I'll be flying nearly all day. Hope they run out of planes after my second mission. I'm not a sniveler, but my back and bum are.

Met one of my old buddies of 524 Congaree, Bill Brooks. I believe you knew him, darling. At any rate, he asked about you. He joined 232 just before I left it for over here. Hasn't got his squadron assignment as yet. He's a fine fellow. Golly, it's hard for me to believe I've got two months on him on my overseas tour. Time's a-slipping by, dearest. I'll knock off for the movie now with Groucho Marx and Marie Wilson.

Love, Daddy

A POOR AVIATOR LAY DYING
(MY BONNY LIES OVER THE OCEAN)

*A poor aviator lay dying
At the end of a cold winter day.
His comrades had gathered around him
To carry his fragments away.*

*The airplane was piled on his breastbone,
The Hamilton was wrapped 'round his head.
He wore a sparkplug on each elbow,
'Twas plain he would shortly be dead.*

*He spit out a valve and a gasket
And stirred in the sump where he lay.
To mechanics who found him came sighing
These brave parting words did he say.*

*Take the magneto out of my stomach
And the butterfly valve off my neck,
Extract from my liver the crankshaft,
There's lots of good parts in this wreck.*

*Take the manifold out of my larynx
And the cylinders out of my brain,
Take the piston rods out of my kidneys
And assemble the engine again.*

Some may wonder how we could concoct these grisly lyrics and then sing them with great gusto at our get-togethers. However, one must remember that we looked death straight in the eye on a daily basis, but didn't dwell on it. We had all made our peace with our Maker in our own individual ways. Most of us were fatalists, but also optimistic most of the time, feeling that we had a good chance of surviving if we didn't tempt fate too often.

*22 May 1952
Thursday afternoon*

Hi baby girl and boys,
Just came back from mission No. 31. It sure is good to get your feet back on good old terra firma. We hit a huge factory town area and supply build-up west of P'yongyang. I had two missions, one at 0730 and one at 1230, landing at 1430. We clobbered the factory for sure. The whole 5th Air Force made an all out effort on the same target area. When I went back on my second mission I hardly recognized the target, it was so completely clobbered.
Flying back over Seoul on our return to base, I saw a huge white hospital ship in Inchon Harbor. It sure gives you a good feeling to see that old baby down there. You know if anything happens they'll take care of you (if there's anything left to take care of).

Boy, it's been hot today, 87° and not a breath of air until just about an hour ago. We fly our missions at about 12,000' to and from the target and it's really comfy up there, but boy, when you land and hit that 87° heat it feels like 150°. All I wore today while I was flying was an undershirt under my flight suit, and I was still wringing wet when I landed. I'd welcome a little cool weather.

Some of the boys who have been with the squadron since last December just got transferred today to Group jobs, and they'll only have to fly once in a while now. They accumulated about 70 missions in that time. I have 31 missions and I haven't been here two months yet! They seem to think we guys who joined the squadron from the 19th draft will be with the squadron until July sometime. Then we're open for a Group job of some nature. When I get a Group job, dearest, you can begin breathing normally again. This squadron pace is purty rough on a guy.

The little jeep with a disinfectant gas tank on it just went cruising by the hut. They spray in the air and on the ground here at K6. It doesn't kill the flies, but it takes care of the other bugs, including the mosquitos. Those darn common flies are the hardest of all insects to kill, I think. There aren't as many bugs here in Korea as there were in the Philippines or Okinawa. Some of the bugs they had there would give ya the creeps. I used to dream about them.

I have to go to the Group briefing tonight at 1900 to get the word on a close air support with the Division tomorrow. We're giving it for the benefit of the top 5th Air Force brass, trying to impress them of the accuracy of the Marines' close air support effectiveness. We're hoping they'll give us close air support missions exclusively. To heck with these railcuts and interdiction.

2220

"Callaway Went Thataway" was the movie tonight and I really enjoyed it.

To beddie-bye now, darling. Say goodnight to the little boys for their daddy, honey, and tell them I want so much to be home with them.

Night dearest, Daddy

BOMB DROPS FROM MY PLANE UPON LANDING

23 May 1952
Tunp o ri, Korea
Friday, 1330

Hello dearest Marion and boys,

Mission No. 33 completed and am I ever glad of it. Got up this morning and had a couple of eggs and a cup of coffee at 0415. Boy, that's too darn early to eat breakfast. I'm so sleepy at that hour I can hardly get myself to swallow.

We took off around 0600 and hit a factory area west of P'yongyang. In my run, my strafing attack caused a huge secondary explosion that rocked my wings as I passed over the target. The entire 5th Air Force is working on this area today. It's a mile square, at least, full of all kinds of manufacturing. Our squadron was assigned this particular area that was supposed to be engaged in grenade and ammunition production. I believe, and so do the others in the flight who saw it, that I hit the powder storage area. You could see smoke and ruins for miles after we retired from the area.

I had a cup of coffee at 0900 when we landed and went directly to the Group briefing for my close air support mission. They gave us the word and showed us mosaic photographs of the area, warning us again and again of the proximity of Panmunjom to the target. When we got over the target area, we were almost as close to Panmunjom as the Manhattan Beach pier is to the water tank across the street from our house (about a mile). From an altitude of about 8000 feet, we could even see the balloons flying over the peace talk area. An airborne controller directed us onto the target and let us go at it.

I carried (2) 1000 pound napalm and eight rockets; the rest carried 1000lb and 100lb bombs. There were just four of us. We destroyed an artillery and mortar position and a CP (command post) up on top of a high hill. Our mission was observed from the ground by high rank of all nations in UN Command. We were giving them a demonstration of how it should be done. (If we had gotten off course and flown directly over Panmunjom we would have been court martialed. They told us that about ten times.) I was nervous before we took off, but after we got over the area and I began picking out familiar landmarks, all was OK. I'm going to send you the 1:50,000 map they gave us for this mission. I'll mark Panmunjom on it and our target we hit today.

In landing from my early morning mission, one of the 100lb bombs I carried on my wing fell off on the runway just as I landed. It came along with the plane quite a ways but finally slowed down and went end for end off the side of the runway. It gave me quite a start as I looked down and saw it flying wing on me. It didn't explode because of the safety nose fusing installed in it. Of course, though, there's always a first time on deals like that. The good Lord has his arms around me, darling, I am convinced of that. I know without a doubt, sweetheart, I'll be home safe and sound with my little family.

The following article appeared in the Manhattan Beach *Daily Breeze* 23 May 1952, covering my mission for that date:

ALLIED BOMBERS BLAST HUGE RED INDUSTRIAL AREA

SEOUL, KOREA (AP)--United Nations warplanes smashed a huge industrial complex southwest of P'yongyang today in the culmination of what the air force called the greatest saturation bombing attack of the Korean War.

The attack near the North Korean capital began yesterday morning and ended at 4 p.m. today. Nearly 800 fighter-bomber sorties were flown against the fat target.

Burned and blasted in the assault were a Communist *hand grenade arsenal*, the surface works of a coal mine, storehouses and nearly a half mile of machine shops and warehouses. They were along the north bank of the Taedong river between P'yongyang and its port city, Chinnampo.

Rain squalls sweeping down from Manchuria blotted out the target area late this afternoon.

Nearly 500 sorties were flown yesterday and 300 today.

The Fifth Air Force said it threw every type of plane it had into the strike.

The burden of the attack was carried by F-84 Thunderjets of the 49th and 136th Fighter-Bomber Wings. They splashed the area with bombs, rockets, napalm (jellied gasoline) and machinegun fire.

Supporting the Thunderjets were the Eighth Wing's F-80 Shooting Stars, the 18th Wing's Mustangs; *Corsairs* and Sky Raiders of the *12th Marine Air Group* and Australian Meteor jets.

During the night B-26s continued bombing the area.

The attacking planes were screened by F-86 Sabre jets.

On the ground the Reds threw a saturation artillery barrage at a small United Nations sector on the western front Thursday night.

CAPTAIN LARSON'S CLOSE SHAVE/
LOTS OF PROBLEMS WITH MY PLANE

24 May 1952
Tunp o ri, Korea
Saturday evening

Dearest wifey and my two little darlings,
How's everyone today? Fine, I hope. The weather has been very comfortable today after a cold front moved in on us last night.

Snapper came in and told me I had to take Captain Larson's hop at 0900 because he had just landed from a mission up in North Korea where they'd shot up his plane--knocked a big hole you could put a dishpan in right on top of his canopy. When he landed, a 100lb bomb dropped off of his plane, just like mine had done yesterday, but his blew up right on the runway. He had sufficient forward speed, however, and rolled ahead of it, escaping the blast, except for a few pieces of shrapnel in his plane's tail assembly. He was too shaken to fly his 0900 mission, so I had to fly it for him.

The bomb just about shook the tar out us here on K6. However, nobody was injured and only three AD dive bombers parked at the far end of the strip sustained any damage. Needless to say, the landing mat was a mass of twisted iron, as the steel marston matting was torn up. They set about fixing the strip as fast as possible, but when our flight took off we had to bear to the right of the hole as we got rolling down the runway.

My plane developed gas fumes in the cockpit, oil leakage from the top side of my engine covered my windshield, and finally the radio failed. I flew my mission anyway, however, to P'yongyang, central Korea, and hit artillery pieces in a pre-briefed target area, although we had a P-51 controlling us. I was happy to return because I was just a little shook from my plane's condition and the heavy flak in the area. Landed with a 20 kt 90° cross wind, a real cagy deal. Briefed immediately after landing for another hop just like the one I'd come down from. I finally landed at 1530 and called it a day.

Went over and had a haircut and shave--30¢ (2000 wan), nearly broke me. I can count the number of times I've been shaved. He has a vibrator machine that he works your back and scalp, arms and shoulders over with and boy, I could sit there in that chair all day.

The 41-year old barber told me he has been cutting hair for 25 years. He had a seven chair barber shop in P'yongyang in 1945. The Communists took all his equipment away and offered to let him stay and work in his own shop, which he did for three years, then moved to South Korea in 1948. He says the Communists took over everything--the markets, tailor shops--everything. He sure hates them, as you can well imagine. He says he has nothing today. Rice costs three times as much today as it did in 1950. He pays 20,000 wan for rent on a little room he stays in, but that's only 20 haircuts at 1000 wan (15¢) a go. His name is Park Joe San. I don't know what it means, though.

In the evening we all went over to the O'Club to give Colonel Dorsey a sendoff to the States. Colonel Bob Galer relieved him. He seems like a nice sort of Joe. If all goes as scheduled I'll have around seven hours in the iron bird tomorrow. My poor bum! I have 35 missions now. I got my R&R moved down to the 2nd of June.

No mail today, darling.

All my love, Daddy

26 May 1952
Tunp o ri, Korea
1130

Dearest baby girl and my two darling little guys I love so much,

Today was fairly easy for me as far as flying was concerned. I slept until around 0800 and then the traffic in the hut became worse than Hollywood and Vine, so I got up, showered, shaved, dressed and had breakfast.

Took off at 1000 and worked another close air support with the 1stMarDiv up within two and a half miles of the peace talks at Panmunjom. We destroyed troops, trenches, bunkers, command posts, artillery and mortars. During eight hours of the night and early morning preceding our strike, the Division had been clobbered with 2400 rounds and had received quite a few casualties from those pieces of artillery we destroyed, so of course the 1stMarDiv was especially well pleased with our success, and we felt we had accomplished a useful task.

We landed at around 1200, lunched and the four of us, Terrell, Kennedy, Cameron and myself, got a jeep from Group transportation and, for the first time in over two months, drove out the airbase gate to the town of Suwon, which is located about 20 miles north of us. We went to an Air Force field where they had F-84s, P-80s and F-86s. We wanted to buy some things we were running short of up here at K6. After we got there we found that the PX was closed on Mondays for inventory, but we looked the base over and saw how the Air Force did business.

Jets were taking off and landing constantly while we were there. Boy, there sure is a lot of activity going on here in Korea. I was glad I saw it for myself because I wouldn't have believed it.

After we left K6, we drove north through the most miserable, dirty, filthy towns and villages I have ever seen. The people, clad in rags, were, for the most part, barefoot. They were engaged in farming, of course, but, as we drove through the little villages, you could see little stores, opened in front, with only a handful of junk on a single table about four feet square in the middle of the room. The table was low to the ground, about 18 inches, and right up close to the street, and the dirt and dust from the huge string of military trucks, jeeps, tractors and road graders almost blocked the little establishments from our vision as we passed only six or eight feet from the storefront. They had some beat-up old dried fish, Japanese cigarettes, wooden sandals, Korean candy, all covered with dust. The people were covered with dust and everything in town, including ourselves, was covered with dust.

We saw babies, dressed in only a dirty little T-shirt, playing just a few feet from the active roadside, and mothers carrying their young in front slings if the baby was nursing, or in the back if the baby was just riding. The Korean women have huge breasts for their otherwise small size, and we saw many of them nursing in the open in many of the villages. Many of them appeared to be young, as best I could tell, and nearly every one of them displayed a toothless grin or a jagged brown set. Some had nice teeth, however, so it's not conclusive that their diet is responsible.

The old retired gentlemen of the villages had long chin whiskers and wore white smocks with a high black hat sitting on top of their heads with a strap under the chin. That was their mark of distinction. We saw lots of them dressed so. Usually they carried a cane or swagger stick and had a very important bearing to their walk.

In the town of Suwon we came upon a huge walled city, with a tunnel at the approach. I took a whole roll of pictures on the trip. Between Suwon and K6 I counted about 50 U.S. tanks along the roadside, having been destroyed during the advance on Seoul in 1950 and again in 1951. Artillery pieces, armored cars, trains and bridges all along the entire 20 miles destroyed by the hundreds. Caves and trenches can be seen everywhere. You'd have to see it to believe it, darling. We've lost our hat and ass over here in Korea. I can well imagine how this war has cost us five billions of dollars, and over a hundred thousand casualties. From what I've seen thus far, dear, since April first, and what I've gone through myself, it has been all as rough as the Pacific war and then some. I'm glad I went and saw things as I did, because now I have a better appreciation of what has been going on over here. Flying as we do, day in and day out, from the altitudes that we fly, we don't see these details on the ground. Nothing looks the same from the air as it does on the ground. I didn't recognize a single town, hill, mountain or road that I had flown over twice and sometimes three times a day for almost a month.

We went into an engineering Army unit near Suwon and bought some Ivory Snow soap, and a can of grape juice apiece, which we drank to wash some of the dust down our throats. On our return we dropped into the Air Force base again and went to the O'Club for an ice cold Coke. Boy, it sure hit the spot. We had left K6 at 1315 and rolled back in again at 1700, having eaten dust for nearly four hours and were we ever filthy.

PICKED TO LEAD A DIVISION

1945
27 May, 1952

Hi again precious girl,

Flew the 1400 MPQ, which I believe I have explained to you. At any rate, it's radar controlled bombing at 14,600'. It was near the peace talks and you have really got to be on the ball, or else--curtains. We had a good hop. Two of us. I led the thing, did all the radio work, and boy, there's plenty of it. We made five separate runs on the target. Flying horizontal all the time, we swung out to the east after releasing, so as not to fly over the peace talk restriction area. Mission #39 completed.

After supper we went over to Group briefing where they showed us some new survival equipment and radios which pilots can carry with them to use to aid in their rescue after they are on the ground. It's very small and has a mercury battery. Built in two parts, battery and radio set, it has only one frequency but it's the standard transmitter and receiver and is carried in a vest in two parts. They gave us all the details of the day concerning the missions flown and damage assessments. There were 93 MIGs reported being sighted last May 25, the day I got jumped. I guess I was even luckier than I thought.

I'm going to secure this, darling, and go to the movie, "Indian Uprising." Love you and miss you all very, very much.

Six of our squadron division leaders from the 18th draft are being transferred to Group jobs tomorrow. I have more missions than some of them. They are being transferred because of their length of time in the squadron. In other words, I am going to become a division leader. As such, I will have about ten times the responsibility as I do now. Leading missions consisting of as many as 13 planes, I will have to do all the navigating, radio work, briefing, and debriefing after all the missions. New pilots are coming in at a rapid rate; however, they have taken so many of the 18th draft men from our squadron we will still not be up to strength. It's possible that I may be taken off the 2nd June R&R schedule because they may need me as a division leader too badly. I'll keep you posted. I can hardly believe I'm ready to be leading. Thirty-nine missions are quite a few, though, just the same.

I saw Mac Kelly who was in 232 at El Toro with me. We're trying to work our R&R together. He's a golfer and a good one, I'm told, so maybe I can pick up a few pointers from him.

2225

The boys here in the hut with me are having a little beer party, celebrating their release from the squadron and flying missions. Can't say as I blame them. I have a few qualms about the leader responsibility I'm to assume in the very near future. Tomorrow at 1200 I brief for a JOC alert which could develop into anything.

Ricky's dream of my coming home while you were napping was cute. It's the first time I've heard him say he ever had a dream. The little guy is sure coming into his own, isn't he, darling? Where are all the enlargement pictures of you, honey? I'm still waiting.

I adore you, precious girl, Daddy

28 May 1952
Tunp o ri, Korea
Wednesday, 1745

Hi baby girl and boys,
 Received yours of the 19th and 20th along with the pictures. Gee, pictures sure are wonderful. It's just like taking a peek in on you all.
 Gosh, those little guys are really growing like weeds. I say again, honey, take a picture of the vegetable garden next time, won't you? I want to see the results of my other efforts (ha, ha).
 Most of the boys here are being transferred. Kennedy leaves for the Wing down at K3. Jackson is to become Group 12 Provost Marshall. Feliton is to become a Group briefing officer. Cameron and Snapper are to be retained a little longer in the squadron, although they are from the 18th draft. They are leaving fast and furious. Major Elliot went to the Wing. Smith is the new Special Services Officer. Golly, we 19th draft pilots are running the squadron. There are 63 new 21st draft pilots in the Group. Most of the fellows who filled up VMF-232 in December and January from the Seattle squadron are here. I saw MacFarland, who is a mutual friend of mine and Wilbur Pickering's. He says Pickering is going to be called in soon. Gus Dake will be put on the 22nd draft. I guess G.W. has left for home by now.
 Tomorrow I leave for the 1stMarDiv, for a two-day training session with the Marine Observation Squadron attached to the Division. They are the ones who control all our air strikes in close support. With enough gear to tide me over for a couple of days, I'll leave

tomorrow morning at 0800, flying to Seoul via TBM Navy Torpedo Bomber (as passenger), thence to VMO via a little lightweight reconnaissance plane. This is Wed., I'll return Sat., then maybe Sun. afternoon I'll get out of here for my R&R.

Today we took off at 1300 for a target up the east coast, slightly inland, and did close air support. Destroyed eight bunkers, damaged two mortar positions, cleaned out 50 feet of personnel trenches, resulting in 100 percent effective target coverage and 100 percent effective use of ordnance. "An excellent hop," so said the controller. Major Thorson led the mission, LtCol Axtell on his wing, Denny Clyde and myself. Our call sign was Oxwood 1255, and I carried the small UHF bail-out radio I have described to you, which is mounted in a nylon zipper vest; on top of that was my Mae West life jacket. The flight suit is warm anyway, because the fabric is very closely woven.

The movie tonight is "Retreat Hell," so I'm not going to go and see it. I've had all the war I need today.

Tell Ricky I heard about him crying because the ice cream man went by without stopping. Tell him the little boys and girls over here in Korea have never had any ice cream in their lives. And they eat fish heads and rice when they can get that. Many of them can't get any food at all. You tell him I don't like the way he cried. Tell them I love them, though, and tuck them into beddie-bye with my blessings. I love you, Marion, my precious wifey. You're doing such a wonderful job taking care of everything. I married the right girl for me. I love you, darling, and will for the rest of my life.

THE OCEANS AREN'T SAFE ANYMORE
(The Daring Young Men on the Flying Trapeze)

Oh they fly through the air with the greatest of ease,
Those daring young men in their B-29s.
They scatter their bomb loads all over the seas
And the oceans aren't safe anymore.

The bombardier peers thru his bombsight
And the bombs tumble down in a row,
And he says, "We're on target tonight, sir
For I'm sure that's the earth down below."

Repeat the first verse.

Above: Peterson back from a mission.

Upper Right: K6 foxhole--just in case!

Right: Capt Dave (the sniveler) Kennedy, examining an old Russian Communist T-34 tank, remains from the 1950 campaign near Suwon. We were on our inspection tour of the area during an off duty day.

Lower Right: 1000 pounders, ready for loading aboard our Corsairs at K6.

Below: Typical Korean papasan with his honey bucket on the A-frame, K6. They were as strong and tough as mules.

KOREAN PAPASAN WITH THEIR TYPICAL "A" FRAME. HONEY BUCKET. K6.

Above: Love Dog Corsair, involved in a three-plane pileup.

Upper Left: This is the standard 1000 lb napalm bomb. The Corsair could mount two of these on the belly bomb shackles. The hand grenade can be seen attached, which was the fusing detonator mechanism on the nose and tail. With the Chinese and N. Korean Communists increasingly digging in on the 38th parallel, it had become necessary to resort to this terrible weapon of destruction. 1000 lb bombs, if lucky enough to make a direct hit, would clear out a large pocket of the enemy; however, others only a few hundred yards from the point of impact would survive unharmed. Not so with napalm, a jelly-like gasoline substance which, upon dropping in a fairly low and dangerous approach, would spread over hundreds of yards and suck the air out of one's lungs. Later, when I was a forward air controller with the 1stMarDiv, I was on the ground and witnessed firsthand this phenomenal event.

Middle Left: A South Korean narrow gauge train bombed off its tracks during the mid 50's campaign near Suwon.

Lower Left: The ancient walled city gate of Suwon can be seen to the rear of Capts Dave Kennedy, Pete Peterson and Terrell.

CHAPTER 10

FAMILIARIZATION VISIT TO THE FRONT

29 May 1952
Up on the front lines
with the 1stMarDiv
Thursday, 1600

Dearest Marion and my two darling little guys,
    I sure have had an exciting day, which I enjoyed, except for certain parts of it. I arose at 0600 this morning, cleaned up and had breakfast, then went over to Group Headquarters and got my orders to VMO-6 Marine Observation Squadron Six, which has a very small landing strip right near the 1stMarDiv. Their job is very diversified inasmuch as they perform air taxi service, air evacuation of wounded--they go right up to the front lines with helicopters attached to this squadron. The whirlybirds take the wounded directly to the hospital ship lying at anchor in Inchon Harbor. They have ten OE-1 observation planes and eight HE-1 Bell helicopters like the one I flew in at Camp Pendleton. Located in a valley that used to be a rice paddy, the engineers came along and filled in a thousand feet of gravel, fifty feet wide, and called it a landing strip.
    A small Korean native village was only a few hundred feet from the strip and the children can be seen swinging on a gizmo that some enlisted members of this organization provided for them. The Korean children are awfully cute. I left K6 at 0830 with another pilot from VMF-323.

1910 (7:10 PM)

Hi, back with it again,
    Boy, what a day. As I was saying above, I left K6 this morning with another pilot from VMF-323 named Judge. We were flown to Seoul and from there we got into an OE-1 observation plane and flew to an outlying Army unit to pick up some mail and orders. From there we went to another field for the same thing, and finally here to VMO-6.
    They are surrounded by green covered mountains. Green everywhere. This little valley we're in is beautiful, if anything in Korea could be beautiful. After lunch I was assigned an observation plane (as observer) and the pilot, Capt Tinsley, and I went on a recon mission deep

into enemy territory, spotting troop bunkers and artillery positions. I had a pair of binoculars that were out of this world. I'm going to buy some in Japan next time, I believe. We flew over the front lines many times and actually called out artillery strikes against the Commies. The OE-1 is a two-place light weight observation plane, almost as small as a Piper Cub, only it has about three times the horsepower, 215 HP. It climbs like a homesick angel. Boy, I'd love to own one in civilian life. Would we have fun!

After we came down and made our reports I went over to Operations (VMO-6) where Lt White assigned me another mission with a Capt Keller, and we did almost the same thing again. He pointed out Panmunjom and we circled almost over the outer limits of the marker balloons. Within a mile of the truce tents, we were at 5000' and with my binoculars I could see people walking around down in a small clearing where the tents are that they use for the peace conference. Across the street from the site are about a dozen grass roofed houses which make up the village of Panmunjom. For a mile in either direction there isn't anything but checkerboard rice paddies.

I took two rolls of pictures today, honey, and even one of Panmunjom. We had a gray sky and no sun, so I'm afraid they won't come out too good. I took pictures of the area on the way up to Seoul, some of Seoul, and around the area here at VMO-6. I also took some over the battle line of trenches and artillery. I'll have a mess of pictures to send home to you after I get to Japan.

I took pictures of two jet airfields as we flew over them from our trip up north from K6 in the TBF Turkey this morning. The last time I flew in a TBF torpedo bomber was Jan '43 off the USS Saratoga during WWII. It really brought back memories. I'm finished for the day, thank goodness. I've been to five different airfields today, flown in four different airplanes, and can take credit for two extra combat missions, bringing my score up to 42. We put a piece of quarter-inch steel plate under our seat and wore the new flak vest that the combat ground troops are wearing to cut down chest, back and belly wounds. We received only small arms fire today. I actually saw Communist troops out in the open marching. If I'd been in my Corsair I'd have clobbered them. I had my .38 side weapon on me and felt like letting a few rounds go at them just for meanness.

You're wondering how we got so close to Panmunjom in the OE-1. Well, it's not a tactical aircraft, and they will allow them closer proximity than a tactical A/C. They have used the sanctuary provided in the truce talks to the fullest. My pilots today pointed out artillery that is right on the very edge of the restricted zone. We can't touch it without fear of violation. The Commies threw over 4000 rounds into this sector and other forward elements near here yesterday with many casualties. Everyone wears full combat dress up here in the Division, with their side arms.

Tomorrow is another big day for me up with the Division and flying more observation missions. I may even call a strike tomorrow. "Strike" out here means mission.

I'm sleeping in a tent with a wooden floor. I brought my little green Navy handbag and my bedroll and I'm using a cot that belongs to another officer who is away for a while. All day long I could hear the bombs and guns. Just heard some more thundering of guns--not very far off, either.

I took pictures of some little five or six year old Korean girls who were standing near the OE line this afternoon. They were very reluctant and ran away until a guy hollered to me, "Tell them 'presents,'" so I did and it worked--they came running back and I took their pictures. I'm going nuts with this camera but I see so darn much that I want to share with you and I think it's worth it. If you see any pictures that you think a newspaper would like, you can send it to them, as long as it doesn't show an airfield or installation, or as long as you don't tell them the location of the units I've mentioned to you. Don't actually say that the 1stMarDiv is up near the truce area. Actually there's more fighting going on here than in any other corps sector, and I know from first hand experience because I've flown missions over every corps area in Korea from west coast to east coast.

The mosquitoes are eating me up. Guess I'll try and find some repellant. The VMO-6 intelligence officer gave me a bunch of UN propaganda leaflets that the pilots of this unit drop periodically. I'll send you a bunch of each. You can let Ricky take them to school too if you wish. I can't make any of them out except that one that has 100 on it and looks like money. It says on it in English, "Safe conduct pass." The rest must be saying the same. There's a funny note to this propaganda drop. The messages in the past were printed on the cheap paper and the Commies were eager to gather them up to use as toilet paper, so we got smart and started printing the messages on smooth paper like the gay colored one enclosed. Dirty pool, ain't it? The other paper isn't used any more.

Guess I"ll secure this for tonight, darling. I love you, sweetheart and miss my little gang more than you know.

Daddy

30 May 1952
Up front with the Division
Friday morning, 1115

Hello dearest wifey and boys,

I just returned from a very interesting side trip up to the 1stMarDiv General Headquarters. Four of us jeeped up there from the VMO-6 strip south of their area about two miles, Capt Bolton VMO-6 G2 Officer (Intelligence), Capt LaVon G2 Assistant, Capt Judge and myself. We passed natives in their fields, plowing with ancient wooden handmade plows behind old beat-up oxen that looked to be a hundred years old. We crossed over rivers with water up to our hubcaps--no bridges up this close to the front; they've either been knocked out by artillery or bombs.

Arriving at 1stMarDiv G2 Section along with all the other brass (ha ha), we collected around a large map with various colored lines and square markings on it, which made very little sense to me at first but clarified as the briefing progressed. Each one would get up and brief on his various department. We heard from the C.I.C., (a branch of the Army Counter-Intelligence Corps with agents circulated throughout this corps sector.)

He read off the activities of yesterday alone and it was amazing the number of Communist spies they had caught--most of them Communist Korean prostitutes who infiltrate our lines and give themselves to our boys in the forward positions, gathering information all along the front. Then they captured some male Communists who were members of a six-man commando team whose express orders were to pounce upon jeep drivers in forward and rear areas and take the courier mail from them, kill all the passengers, destroy the jeep and retire back behind the lines. There are many such teams operating all over this area, and we hear of certain gruesome stories of whole units being killed as they slept. They kill the outer perimeter guards one-by-one, then have a field day from tent to tent. I'll be glad to get out of here tomorrow morning.

Last night the wind blew real hard and it rained. All night I could hear sounds and thought several times I heard Korean voices. I reached for my gun on two separate occasions. It turned out to be the wind only.

We heard from Capt Bolton who gave his spiel on the activities of VMO-6 for yesterday. They spotted hundreds of troops and gun positions all over the place. We were briefed (or de-briefed, I should say) in yesterday's activities along the entire battle front in general and along the Marine Corps Sector in very great detail. I have a greater appreciation of the critical nature of the entire ground problem facing us now.

I met the Division Air Officer, Colonel Gunther, who took us aside after the general briefing and gave us the picture, as far as Marine Air is concerned, of working along with the main ground forces. Gen Jerome talked the 5th Air Force into letting us send at least three close air support strikes a day up here to the Division. The 5th finally agreed. We, speaking as a fighter pilot from MAG-12, still have to maintain our commitments along the entire battle front, as well as deep penetration and railcuts.

While we were there I tried to get some free dungarees from the 1st Div supply, to no avail. It appears very seriously at this point, that I'm going to have to break down and buy some when I return to the Group. We'll probably attend some more briefings today here at VMO-6 and possibly another at the Division. We were hoping we'd get in a couple more missions and possibly get to control a close air strike on targets we recon'd yesterday, controlling *members of our own VMF-212. (I'd give them a bad time at first and on my damage assessment I'd cut it down to about 25 percent effective use of ordnance and 15 percent target area coverage. Then, after they hollered a while, I'd tell them their controller was "Pete" and give them a much higher damage assessment. Ha, Ha!)*

We presently have a ceiling of about 1000' and it's not clearing up very fast. The wind is blowing at about 15 to 20 knots in gusts. This little old tent is really shaking. Nearly all the VMO-6 squadron is on the deck, tied down, expecting higher velocity winds to come up.

I've met a lot of guys since leaving VMF-212 yesterday morning. On my return tomorrow to K6 I can honestly say I have gained considerable experience, especially from a ground picture. Ground means an all-over picture of the Division's problems. Likewise when the "crunchies" speak of air they refer to the entire 5th Air Force.

2000

Hello darling,

Well, just as I predicted earlier, the weather got worse, so the air strike was called off. I retired to the tent and read May 1952 Readers Digest for a couple of hours.

After supper tonight I played volleyball for two solid hours. Boy, did I have fun! It's the first time I've had any time to get into a game in ages. The officers played the enlisted men. After two hours it came out even. This side trip has been an interesting change for me. I'm glad I came. I'll be glad to get back tomorrow, though, because I want to get to my mail from the baby girl.

Kiss my little darlings goodnight for their daddy and tell them I love them very much. I adore you, my precious girl.

Bye bye, from the daddy that loves you

THE SPIRIT OF THE RED CROSS

31 May 1952
Tunp o ri, Korea
Saturday afternoon

Hi baby girl,

Well, I finally got back to K6 and the first thing they told me was that my R&R had been moved up to the 5th of June instead of the 2nd. I was planning to leave on Monday the 2nd, but I hadn't made any plans that can't be moved up to the 5th.

Last night at the front they showed some Mike Barnett television movies. Boy, were they horrible. I sat through one, but couldn't go the second. Later I listened to the thundering of the artillery not very far off. I got up once and could see the flashes of the guns in the night. Nobody crept up on us while we were sleeping, and now that I'm back here at K6 I can rest at ease. This morning they flew us into Seoul via OE-1 and from there we jeeped over to the Red Cross club on the air base. In the canteen they were serving donuts by the thousands and coffee by the gallons. Above the coffee bar was a sign that read:

> **The spirit of the Red Cross is like the spirit of Christmas. It dwells in the hearts of men everywhere. It knows no barrier of race, creed or color, and it helps satisfy the universal yearning for peace through brotherhood.**

I thought it was quite a nice creed, so I committed it to memory so I could send it on to you. Nevertheless, among the servers were a couple of pretty white women behind the coffee bar and, not having seen a female of my own race for such a long time, I must admit it was a pleasure to look upon them.

Seoul base is a transferring point for thousands upon thousands of all UN forces that are airlifted to their various units throughout Korea. They sometimes have to wait for days on end before their planes become available, so the Red Cross is a great meeting place for all UN troops. It's a beneficial service they are providing. You might pass it on to people you meet who wonder what the Red Cross is doing in Korea. This was the finest canteen I've seen, but that's as it should be; they have concentrated their energies at the point (Seoul) where they will serve the most men. It seemed as though I was entering a strange new land as I walked into the Red Cross Canteen and heard about sixteen different languages and racial groups assembled all around the room: Royal Helenic Air Force, British Air Force, Army Air Force, Navy Air, Marine Air, Marine Ground, Korean Marines, Korean Army, Dutch, African, Greek. They had blond beards, red beards and grey beards. I even saw some UN soldiers who looked older than Trooper. What an experience.

Kennedy was packing to leave for the Wing and his new non-flying job. I heckled him while he was packing, and someone said there was a troop show going on down at the base open-air movie. Kennedy and I went on down and saw the last 15 minutes of it. It turned out to be a group of GIs touring the Korean Theater with a six-piece band and about a dozen male singers and dancers. They put on the liveliest show I've seen out here. The M.C. was a scream. I laughed until my sides hurt. He imitated Winston Churchill, and at the close of his impersonation he said (still talking like Winston), "You know why they call England the mother country? It's because she's always expecting." He got a terrific hand. I'll bet he goes places in the States if he carries on his present performance, and adds to it while he's out here. The guys who danced were pretty sharp too. It's fun to see GIs knocking themselves out to entertain their buddies. Of course, they sang a couple of shady songs and their dances included the bumps, as when don't guys when they get together?

I just took my first shower since Wed., shampooed my hair, shaved and put on clean underwear and socks. Do I feel better! VMO-6 doesn't have any water except what they haul in by trailer. No showers, no hot water. Poor devils have to jeep about a mile. Guess I told you already.

On the flight over to Seoul from the Division we flew low over Korean cemeteries or shrines high up in the mountains. The areas were cleared right out of heavily wooded sections. Each area was about a half acre in size and on each plot they had a typical Oriental shrine with rock paths going up to terraced hills, where gravestones could be seen laid in grass that looked as green as a golf green. We zoomed down real low to get a a very good look. I'd have taken a picture, only I used them all up when I was at the Division. It looked like a heavenly retreat, "Shangri-la." Elevation was about 3000' and right on the side of this hill. At first I thought they were private mansions until we flew closer and could almost read the writing on the headstones--about 50' or lower. The little OE-1 would be a dream of a civilian plane to own. You'd love it, honey. We'll have to look into the possibilities of buying a plane. I want you to have some of the thrills that go along with flying. (Corsair combat missions are in a separate class.)

What a contrast as we flew along south toward Seoul. We could see huge hydroelectric dams as big as many I've seen in the U.S. Electric trains and steam locomotives chugging along, pulling hundreds of cars behind them. Railroad turntables and roundhouses, factory after factory building--many bombed out and the natives growing wheat in the floor, having torn out the cement floor for soil area. I saw the main street of Seoul from 150' or 200' overhead. Flew over the city hall and saw street cars, buses and taxis running every which way. At a huge stadium outside of town about five miles I saw tents and trucks by the hundreds parked inside the area, presumably Army.

As we proceeded to fly outside of the city limits and toward the farming area, we saw ox carts and ragged peons making their way along the roads, mothers carrying their young in slings on their backs and old men with their high funny black hats, canes and white rolls. Nearly every little patch of ground has its own open well, and they flip the water out of the well with the darndest types of contrivances. The man swings the paddle by the rope swing on the frame into the open well and flips it out into the trench. From the trench it goes on down to various other trenches and out onto his fields. There they have the usual oxen-turned water wheel and another flipper deal. They dip this box swung by ropes into the open well, then bring it up and flip it into the trench. I have to outline these crude methods to show you the comparison between the peons and the other terrific engineering accomplishments surrounding them, but seemingly not affecting them in any way. They are farming, living, eating, dressing as their ancestors did thousands of years ago. It's amazing. Someday I'll get up to Seoul and go into town on foot or jeep it because it looked fabulous.

In your letter, you told of Randy answering the telephone and talking to Nanna. Gosh, I can hardly believe the little tyke is old enough to do all the things you say he does. How about him telling Ricky, "I no seep, Icky." Ben tells me Ricky sure misses me. Bless Ricky's little heart, I love that little fellow, honey. I'd give anything to hold my two precious little guys in my arms and tell them how I love them and miss them. I guess this business of daddy being away works just the same on the little guys as it does on me. It's difficult for me to understand how I ever got into this mess. Seems like only yesterday I was reading the papers and feeling sorry for those poor devils over there in Korea having to be away from their families, and now I'm suddenly realizing that I'm one of those poor devils. How did it happen? It couldn't happen to a nicer guy--ha! ha!

You're right, "poag" means most anything. It's used about a thousand times a day around here. Also "sniveler." Ricky likes that word, does he? He would. Kennedy uses "slob" and "miserable slob" constantly. He's a scream. They all give me a bad time about being a reserve and I call them sniveling regulars. We go at it tooth and nail in a playful manner. We all hit it off fine. I'll miss Kennedy. I told him the kids thanked him for the wan notes so he says, "Here, tell them Uncle Dave sends two more home to them with his compliments."

Guess I'll wrap this up, honey doll. Tell the darlings I love them. I adore you, Marion, my precious girl. Bye bye until tomorrow.

Night night, Daddy

LOG FOR MAY 1952

Date	Aircraft Type	Aircraft Number	Flight Duration	Type of Mission
7	F4U-4B	63023	2.6	Railcut, Sinwon-Ni
8	F4U-4B	63012	1.6	Interdiction, Chinmor-tong
9	F4U-4B	97461	2.2	MPQ, Yudong-ni, Landed K14
9	F4U-4B	97461	0.5	K14 to K6
9	F4U-4B	63057	1.9	Railcut, P'yongyang
10	F4U-4B	63012	4.2	Res Cap
11	F4U-4B	62994	1.9	Railcut, Cheil-li
11	F4U-4B	63060	1.9	CAS, Oun-san
12	F4U-4B	97517	1.5	Roadcut, Poptong-ni
13	F4U-4B	97517	2.3	Railcut, Op'o-ri
13	F4U-4B	62927	1.6	CAS, Chombong-ni
14	F4U-4B	63005	3.3	Res Cap, Chodo
15	F4U-4B	62993	2.0	Railcut
15	F4U-4B	97470	2.2	Interdiction, Yonghong-ni
16	F4U-4B	62994	2.2	CAS, Sohui-ri
17	F4U-4B	97517	1.9	CAS, Sangch'ongsong
18	F4U-4B	62993	1.3	CAS, Sanmyong-ni
19	F4U-4B	62997	0.9	Test
19	F4U-4B	63005	1.5	GCA, 2 Approaches
20	F4U-4B	63057	1.8	Railcut, Tongsinch'on
20	F4U-4B	62919	1.8	Railcut, Tongsinch'on
21	F4U-4B	63057	1.7	Railcut, Imong-ni

21	F4U-4B	97489	2.2	Railcut, Imong-ni
22	F4U-4B	63005	2.0	Interdiction, Songho-ri
22	F4U-4B	63057	1.7	Interdiction, Songho-ri
23	F4U-4B	97489	1.8	Interdiction, Pobong-ni (P'yongyang)]
23	F4U-4B	63060	2.2	CAS, Sajang-dong
24	F4U-4B	97420	1.8	CAS, Chirung-dong
24	F4U-4B	62997	1.3	Interdiction, P'yongyang
25	F4U-4B	62997	2.8	Railcut, Taegwan-dong, Jumped by MIGs
25	F4U-4B	63057	1.6	Railcut, Tongsinchon
26	F4U-4B	63017	1.8	CAS
27	F4U-4B	97461	2.0	CAS & MPQ Waryongdae
28	F4U-4B	97461	2.0	CAS, Ounsan
29	OE-1	133789	1.3	Recon, Taedok-san
29	OE-1	133813	0.8	Recon, Yui-tong

1 Jun 1952
Tunp o ri, Korea
Sunday

Hi hon,

    Just returned from the evening group briefing and I don't like what I heard. We're cutting rails way up deep in North Korea. It's an all-out effort so I don't suppose they'll have the F-86 fighter cover up there in the amounts that we will need. The darn MIGs have been jumping fighter bombers, P-51s, for the past couple of days up north and the news has us guys down here plenty shook. There are other missions going out tomorrow too, JOC alerts, CAS and interdiction. I don't know what I've got yet; the schedule is late coming out tonight. If I've got a railcut I'll have to stay up tonight a while and plan my navigation and survival and rescue procedure for any downed members of my mission. A flight leader has lots of responsibility, and I'm required to dig out more information all the time. I've even been studying the tides because during low tides there are certain landing beaches available on islands along the coast that can be used in emergencies.

    You've done a wonderful job, dearest, and I'm so grateful to you for holding our little family together and keeping everyone, including me, in fairly high spirits. Your letters are my life preservers, dearest, and a crutch for me to lean on. I read them and re-read them over and over, time permitting.

    Let's see, what happened to me today of interest? 0400 reveille and 0500 brief. I led the mission--Peterson, Griffiths, Evans, Foltz. We went up to the 1stMarDiv Sector where the controller gave me my target and I led the flight in for a total of 18 separate runs. Napalm, 1000 lb bombs, rockets, 20mm strafing. We hit troops (50), mortars, artillery, OPs. They said it was a very good strike. We got a mess of 37mm flak thrown at us, but somehow or other nobody picked up any. Hugh Holland's flight of four, operating a short way from us, didn't fare as well as we did, however. He picked up small arms fire through his tail and something around the size of a 50cal knocked off his antennae. We returned, I debriefed the mission at Intelligence and then we retired to the mess hall for a cup of coffee and chatted about the mission.

    At 0930 I went to church which was conducted by a new young (29 yrs) Lutheran minister. I had met him at meals many times and he's a fine young fellow. He held Communion today and I participated. I felt odd sitting there in church after having just returned from a combat mission where I killed men. I suppose it's like the Crusaders, though, and I don't feel too bad about it. I can't help but think about the way I and other pilots, after having returned from a mission, go on with our business-as-usual attitude.

FAMILIARIZATION VISIT TO THE FRONT

Mission #43 completed, baby girl. If I get transferred to a group job or wing job at the end of this month I'll have only about 14 more days of flying after I return from my R&R on June 12th; that is, providing I leave on the 5th. Then the time will drag for me, but as long as it just drags and doesn't run out, I don't care. You can rest at ease after that, darling. I won't take any unnecessary chances, precious girl, if I can avoid them. I want to return to my little family so very much.

Give my darling boys a hug for me.

All my love, Daddy

MY SECOND SECTION, ATTACK COMMUNIST TANKS

2 Jun 1952
Tunp o ri, Korea
Monday, 2300

Hi dearest girl and my little guys,

The daddy is beat tonight. Last night when I checked the schedule I was thinking I was going to have an easy day, but little did I know. I only had a CAS scheduled, but at 0515 this morning, as I was pounding my ear in my nice warm basket, I was suddenly shaken by the duty officer who said, "Pete, I hate to do this to you, but you have to be over in the Group briefing room in five minutes. You're going to have to lead a TARCAP. This will be a support mission, working with our naval forces which are often British. Maginnis is sick and won't be able to do it."

I got up, dressed and was in the Group brief within five minutes, getting all the details of the mission. We took off, I gathered up my other three boys and headed out on course to a point 210 miles from K6. The weather was so stinking we had to climb on top of the stuff and I got radio navigational steers from some ground radar controllers to aid me. We flew at 8000' to the west coast, to a sector that the British Fleet units were patrolling west of Chinnampo. They had been shelling Commie gun positions all night and as we arrived they had them pretty well spotted for us. I had to fly down low on my reccy runs to find the gun positions under their very cleverly camouflaged screening. The daddy saw through it, though, and led his flight in and clobbered them. I also found some caves, with the British HMS Belfast shipborne controller's help, and we sealed them up. We were gone a total of 3.5 hours. I missed my breakfast but had a cup of coffee at 1000 to tide me over until 1130 lunch. We had to be radar controlled all the way home because of the solid overcast. Boy, this weather is for the birds.

This afternoon, on my second mission, we went up to the 1stMarDiv Sector and I led my flight into the target. We hit mortars and CPs, OPs and troops, caused some terrific secondary explosions, and just before dark they spotted enemy tanks, so I sent two of my boys in on them—because they were the only ones with any ordnance left. I brought myself and wingman on back to K6 and landed just before dark, while Feliton and his wingman landed in the dark in Seoul, gassed, and returned here to K6, landing at 2200. Jim Feliton just came into the hut. They got the tanks.

I had a nice steak dinner after debriefing, then caught the tailend of a British picture. Now for the sack. I'm leading two missions tomorrow.

I love you, sweetheart,

Your very own daddy

P.S. *Mission No. 45 completed.*

GIVE ME OPERATIONS

Don't give me a P-38, with props that counter-rotate.
She'll loop, roll and spin, but she'll soon auger in.
Don't give me a P-38.
    CHORUS:
    Just give me Operations, way out on a lonely atoll,
    For I am too young to die; I just want to go home.

Don't give me a P-39, with the Allison mounted behind.
She'll loop, roll and spin, but she'll soon auger in.
Don't give me a P-39.
    CHORUS:

Don't give me a Fox Thunder Jug, the ship that lands with a thud.
Etc.
Don't give me a Fox-51, with torque when you give her the gun.
Etc.
Don't give me a Fox 80C, those jets scare the hell out of me.
Etc.
Don't give me a Fox-84, into the target she'll bore.
Etc.

Just give me a Fox-86, the ship that's built just for kicks.
She'll loop, roll and spin, but she won't auger in.
Just give me a Fox-86.
    CHORUS:

3 Jun 1952
Tunp o ri, Korea
Tuesday afternoon

Dearest girl and little guys,
    For the first time in umpteen days I've stayed on the deck. It's been cloudy and windy and all our targets up north are obscured. Tough, isn't it? Well, I got up at 0715, had a nice quiet breakfast--three scrambled eggs, tomato juice, coffee and bacon--then came back here to the hut, took everything out of my foot locker and suitcase and repacked my suitcase for my R&R Thursday. I packed my greens away and broke out my tans. I doubt if I'll wear my tans, though, because I believe it will be too warm for them. My liberty uniform will probably be as before, khaki shirt and pants. I assume the Squadron Duty Officer Assignment tonight and we're expecting strong winds, so I'll have a busy night seeing to it that all AC are tied down, or at least sandbagged so they won't blow away.
    John Snapper gave me an assignment to do for him today in regard to an aircraft accident in our squadron. I've spent most of the afternoon in that regard and walking my legs off. Good exercise, though, and it's a pleasure not to have that "U" Bird strapped to me for a change.
    No mail today. Oh yes, this morning as I was packing, Evan's little Chihuahua dog was over here to see me. He comes over quite a bit. As I was sitting on my cot, bent over packing stuff in my bags, Scoshie crawled up my back and started chewing on my ears and biting and pulling my hair. His little teeth are like needles. I stopped packing and played with him for about ten minutes. Gosh, honey, he's a swell little dog. We ought to get ourselves a little short-haired dog. They are nice little guys to have in the house. Poor Lady's nose would surely be broken if we got another little dog and let it come into the house and not her. She gets mad at Gorgeous for being allowed in. Of course, Gorgeous rubs it in, flipping his tail in Lady's face as he walks in the back door.

FAMILIARIZATION VISIT TO THE FRONT

I got a haircut this morning. Can't stay away from that barber shop. Those 15¢ (1000 wan) haircuts are sure swell. Got a new barber shop now. Don't know where Parks went. The new barber couldn't tell me because he can't speak a word of English. He's very good but not as good as Parks. I paid Kim, our houseboy, his 14,000 weekly wan this morning (a little less than $2.50). He's glad to get it--a little over 30¢ a day, and he's a good worker. Whenever anybody wants anything done, he's Johnny on the spot. The houseboy next door has a brand new Japanese bicycle. He sure takes care of that bike. I think one of the VMF-323 pilots bought it for him on R&R. He hasn't even taken the paper off the frame and he's had it for over a month.

I was going to tell you that we are worried about guerrilla activities here at Tunp o ri and they are thinking of getting a company of ground Marines down from the Division to be a ready guard. We have our regular security police, but they are so thinly dispersed that their effectiveness in the event of an armed breakthrough of guerrilla forces is very dubious. I think we'll all sleep more securely too. Our planes, of course, would be their prime target. They could really clobber them if they set time-fused grenades on them, which is precisely what they would do. They've had guerrilla troubles way down in Pusan lately. Everybody is on guard. I was sure glad to leave that VMO-6 area. They haven't got security measure one.

Boy, the wind is really kicking it up outside, bringing with it the inevitable dust, and I do mean inevitable (I looked it up). I am affected by the wind and muggy, close weather to the point of indolence. It feels like it's going to rain any second.

I've been looking at all the pictures you've sent me, darling, and I guess I should send some home for the album, but I can't part with them. Isn't Randy a terror in some of those pictures Nanga took? It's just as well, though, because it shows just what he's really like and that's what snapshots are intended to convey.

Your choice of Texaco is wise. It's a better gas. Please send a copy of the Times *or* Examiner *used cars price list. I've just got to keep up on used car prices. Can't get behind on everything I'm used to doing.*

Just had a nice hot shower and shave. They have a water conservation program on now because they are having pump trouble. There's plenty of water in our well, but our pumps are petering out. They put a sign up in the shower today:

    (1) TURN WATER ON AND GET WET.
    (2) TURN WATER OFF AND SOAP UP.
    (3) TURN WATER ON AND RINSE.
    (4) TURN WATER OFF AND GET THE HELL OUT.
    Signed, Commanding Officer MABS-12 (Marine Air Base Sqd-12)

We're going to try and abide by it. Last night I went to the head after the movie to wash up and shave. I soaped up and got half my face shaved then the lights went out, but I carried on. Then the water went off so I came back to the hut and washed my face with our drinking water and finished up my shave with cold water. It's sure going to be a pleasure to get home to our wonderful modern conveniences, as well as many other items too numerous to mention.

Just heard the news that Ike is home and in his civilian clothes. I sure hope that man gets nominated. We need him. The Russians fear him and that's half the fight as far as the Russians go.

Gene Cameron said he'd stand by for me tomorrow afternoon if I wanted to snivel out on an afternoon R&R plane. Nice of him, eh? Cameron worked in the Broadway Hollywood department store prior to recall in July '52. We took our physicals together. There are quite a few guys here from that group who took their physicals with me at Los Alamitos--Terrell, Cameron, Whitmore. Whitmore is a 6th grade teacher. Terrell was a jalopy and stock car driver.

Until tomorrow, little family that I love, goodnight. I love you all very much.

Your very own daddy

4 Jun 52
Itami Air Base, on my R&R
Japan
2200

Hello darling Marion and boys,
    I had the squadron duty at Tunp o ri K6 this morning and had to get up at 0230. I awakened the pilots for the early flights and checked with JOC in Seoul on the weather situation. Found it was very bad up north so I secured one of the standby flights and kept one 4-plane division on hand. Finally got a bite to eat at 0530 and then around 1000 the hot phone rang and I dispatched a couple of 4-plane divisions post haste. We really started a busy day at that point. The weather cleared at the bomb line so everything went out.
    I was busier than a one-armed paper hanger with the hives when all of a sudden Tony Foltz called from Operations and asked if I'd leave at 1400 and fly a Corsair to Japan. There were two of us to go, Capt Edduns and myself. We gathered up all the necessary paper work, plane logs and files. I got a relief standing by on the duty for me (Gene Cameron), a good egg. Then we checked with Group Operations and Base Operations and they informed us that the weather over the channel was really stinko and we'd have to do a lot of instrument flying. We had our gear and everything all packed and down at the squadron. I was just going to load it into the belly of my plane when they told us the weather was bad. Edduns and I decided we wouldn't attempt it on our Corsairs because, for one thing, the planes were being sent to Itami for new engines. One of them didn't have any bird dog in it ("bird dog" is a radio direction finder) so we off-loaded, cancelled our flight plans and got our gear ready for loading on the R5D Douglas four-engine transport that was going to leave K6 for Itami at 1800. We grabbed supper (steak), hopped on the plane and were on our way by 1750. There were eight passengers aboard and two huge Corsair engines.
    We had an uneventful flight across the Sea of Japan, landing at night at Itami. Flying rather low over the cities of Osaka, Kobe and Kyoto, there didn't appear to be an area the size of a postage stamp without glimmering lights. It looked like a jewelled carpet. I've never seen anything so spectacular. The weather was beautiful and clear and the moon was glowing brilliantly above as we set down on Itami. I wondered where in the world the weather forecaster at K6 got his bum dope. I'd have really enjoyed flying my own plane over there. Oh well, maybe another time.
    Three brand new AU-1 Corsairs arrived at our squadron just as we were getting ready to leave. I looked at one briefly but what I saw I liked. The cockpit is completely new. The engine is a totally different type--more power, the plane's longer and will carry a much heavier bomb load. Most important of all, they are brand spanking new. They even smelled new. I'll be anxious to fly that rascal when I return.
    I'm going to hit the basket now, darling, because I'm beat. The pilot in command let me fly nearly the whole hop across, up front with the plane's navigator, radioman, pilot and copilot. I had the controls up to time to land. Those R5D Marine transports sure are well maintained. The cabin is as clean as a pin. The back end, where freight and passengers are carried, is crummy, but that's only to be expected. Passengers have a very low priority in Japan and Korea. We had 12,000 pounds of engines plus passengers on the plane. It handled like it was empty.
    I couldn't get a room in the main BOQ like I had last time, so they put us up in the TOQ dormitory, which has old army style narrow bunks of steel about three feet wide. I hang over the side. Thin little mattress, two sheets and one blanket, no pillow. I'll try to get a room at the BOQ sometime tomorrow.
    Good night little family.

                                            Love,
                                            Daddy

FAMILIARIZATION VISIT TO THE FRONT

5 Jun 52
Itami Air Base, Japan
Thursday

Hi again little family,

  Checked in at MWSS-1 office, turned in my R&R orders, went over and checked to see if my second sea bag had showed up yet. It hadn't, so I got after them to run an immediate search for it and to check with me in five days as to their findings. When the gift shop opens I'm going to turn in five rolls of exposed film for developing and buy some more. Then at about 1030 I'm going to head into Kyoto and start shopping around. I'll not mail this until tonight because I've missed the 0800 morning pickup anyway.
  Capt Ted Pittman saw me here last night and gave me $80.00 from our squadron officers' fund to buy Col Bryson, our departing CO, a Browning or Remington 12 gauge shotgun with a memento plate on the stock from his buddies of VMF-212. I'll buy it at Kyoto PX today maybe. Pittman just heard Bryson was being relieved yesterday and he was returning to K6 this morning and didn't have time to make the purchase himself.

6 Jun 52
0800

Hi again honey,

  I'm sorry to be stringing this out but I've been too late with my mailing to meet their early pickup schedule. Anyway, I'll give you the lowdown on my trip into Kyoto yesterday. I met Capt Woods and Jim Barber, the Chance Vought aircraft representative here, and they asked me if I'd care to go along with them to Kyoto. so we all went in together. It was about an hour's ride on the electric train, making one transfer at Juso. We took a cab into Kyoto Army PX and began purchasing our various items. I looked for a gun for Col Bryson, but all they had were Winchester 12 gauge shotguns so I didn't buy any.
  Woods, Barber and I ate lunch in the PX snack bar and then went over to the Damascene works where I bought some more earrings, charm sets and a necklace. The charm sets are for your brother who is a Mason and for Mike LaScala, who is going to become one. Then we went to the woodblock print shop and watched them at work. We bought some colored postcards and woodblock prints. I'll send them on to you right away. Every color on the prints has a separate wood plate for that color. They do it all by hand and they are really beautiful. Fifteen prints, 12"x14", all for my baby girl. Then we went to the silk mills and watched them making silk cloth. There were about a thousand looms all going like mad, making beautiful silk fabrics. They had it for sale by the yard, 36" wide. What a city!
  By that time it was getting late and we were hungry, so we went over to the Miyako Japanese civilian-run hotel, Kyoto's finest. Nestled among the trees on the side of a mountain, it overlooked the entire city of Kyoto. I took a lot of pictures, honey, so you'll get an idea of the layout. I was wishing so very much that you could have been there with me, dearest. You'd really have enjoyed the beautiful setting. We had supper in a huge, lovely dining room overlooking the city on one side and the open garden and patio on the other. Miyako is a continental hotel and there were both Japanese and American businessmen there, but hardly any other servicemen. I ordered the dinner special they had on the front of the menu: Spanish steak (Swiss steak), string beans and turnips with heavy gravy, julienne soup, after dinner coffee in little demitasse cups, and chocolate cream pie. We had to serve ourselves from the silver server held by the waitress. My check was 800 yen ($2.00). In the States for the corresponding setting, service and food, you'd pay triple. We looked the gardens over a second time and shoved off for the train station and Itami.

Got back here at about 2045, went over to the O'Club where I met about six VMF-212 boys in the process of being transferred home, to carriers, to Wing jobs, or just on R&R.

I'm thinking of you constantly, Marion dearest. I'm counting the days when I'll be home again with my little gang and our lives will begin all over again.

Give my little guys a kiss for daddy and tell them I love them and miss them very very much.

Love you all, Daddy

JAPAN'S NEW GOVERNMENT

Having aided in her almost total destruction during WWII, I took great delight in watching Japan's rapid rise from the ashes.

Seven years prior (1945) the Japanese people had been living under a national bureaucratic oligarchy. Today (1952) their government was one of democratic philosophies embodying features of both the United States and British systems of rule. As in the United States, the entire governing structure was laid on the foundation of a constitution which spelled out in clear and simple terms the nature and makeup of the state. It replaced the rule of men with the rule of law and established the principle of responsible government with sovereignty resting with the people.

While the new constitution had been promulgated 3 Nov 1946, the emperor had also been retained as a limited or constitutional monarch, serving as a symbol of the state and of the people's unity. He held that position only by the will of the public, retaining no powers of government, but carried out the purely formal, ceremonial functions of state on behalf of the people, and only with approval of the cabinet.

Since the formal signing of the peace treaty in May 1952, Japan had only been operating on her own as a representative democracy for less than a month, exemplifying one of the most complete and swift reversals of form in modern political history.

You could only wish her well.

6 June 1952
Friday evening
Itami, Japan

Dearest girl and my precious boys,
This morning I got a shine from a boy at the station (30 yen) and hopped a cab to the Kyoto Army PX in the big Daiken Bldg. in downtown Kyoto. It was noon when I arrived, so I had lunch at the snack bar (large thick tenderloin, $1.05, very good). Then I went up to the third floor, got my two packages I purchased yesterday, had another package boxed, took them all to the post office, sent two of them parcel post (20-25 day delivery) and mailed one first class which will go via air mail to San Francisco.

In the afternoon I took a cab to Nishimura's Lacquer Factory in Kyoto where I saw lacquerware the likes of which I never dreamed existed. Nishimura's company has been operating since 1657 and is being operated by the 8th generation. Am enclosing a folder explaining the terrifically painstaking process in more detail. The show room on the back is one of five I visited in the same factory. What workmanship! What patience! These articles defy any descriptive adjectives. Needless to say, I purchased a few well chosen pieces for our home.

Well, with all my packages in hand I departed Nishimura's for the Miyako Hotel again. I was a little early for the gift shop opening, also for dinner, so I sat and waited for about an hour and almost fell asleep in the yellow wicker chair it was so quiet and peaceful there. Finally six o'clock came and I went in and had dinner. They had "horse dovers" of salmon eggs, hard-boiled bird's eggs, caviar, two types of fish. They had the little strips of fish cut in the shape of fish and an olive in place for the eye--the olive was just a sliver. I ate everything except the olive because I thought it was a real eyeball for a while. Had roast veal, French fried spuds, peas, salad, potato soup that had curry and rice in it, Japanese style-- it was elegant, ice cream and a little coffee demitasse. (855 yen).

Every time I see a little Japanese boy I think of my two darlings waiting for their daddy to come home. I love you all.

Daddy

HOME GROWN JAPANESE COMMUNISTS GIVE US A SCARE

8 June 1952
Sunday morning
Itami, Japan

Dearest Marion and boys,

Yesterday Capt McDonald and I went into the town of Takarazuka and attended the opera. As we were departing on foot by way of the main gate here at Itami Air Base, we were informed that the Communists were having a demonstration in the little town just west, and another one east of the station, and it wouldn't be safe for military personnel on foot to be allowed off base. Mac and I caught a ride with two doctors we knew from K6, Korea, who were headed toward the train station in a jeep. We got off at the station and caught the train into Takarazuka, 30 yen each. It took us about 15 minutes. We didn't run into any Communists, fortunately. Takarazuka, located inland about 20 miles from the coastal town of Kobe, is surrounded by mountains covered with trees of every description. It's a vacation town with many tourist hotels, a zoo, a park, and the opera house.

After getting off the train, Mac and I walked down a tree-covered lane with grass and flowers growing along the side until we reached what appeared to be an amusement center. It cost us 60 yen apiece to gain entrance into the center which was surrounded by an eight-foot stone wall. Within the center there were small but very neat modern concession counters selling picture postcards, records, candy, cosmetics, soda pop, autographed photographs of the opera stars, train and boat tickets and guide service, hotel advertisements, bath house signs and many many colored posters of the Takarazuka Opera, "Les Chansons de Paris." The loud speakers were blaring forth with a voice of a Japanese girl, apparently telling of the various things that could be seen within the amusement center. There were no little car rides or swings, merry-go-rounds or anything of that nature. Of course, the main attraction within the center was the opera which began at 1300.

I had phoned for reserved seats at 1045 and they were awaiting our pickup at the box office. We had the best seats in the house, in the very center of the very first row, for 150 yen-- less than 50¢. For a comparable seat in a comparable opera in the U.S. it would cost $10.00 or more. The opera house, built of white stone, and ivy covered on the outside, was in fairly good condition as Japanese building go. With a huge main floor and two balconies, it seated about five thousand. They even had little seats in the aisle. As you can see by reading the program, there were 32 scenes. Not as elaborate as is used in the U.S., the scenery was nevertheless very artistic. In order to accommodate the more than 200 girls in the cast, the huge stage looped and came around the orchestra section.

They had about 25 or more gorgeous gown changes for the entire cast. The music was modern and very good. I haven't enjoyed seeing anything so much since I can't remember when. Scenes 20 and 22 were especially peppy and colorful. The girls were very beautiful and their dancing was to perfection. I was wishing with all my heart that you could have been enjoying this with me. I know you'd have loved it. After Part I which lasted about two hours, we had a forty-minute break, so we went to an outside garden with a fountain and pond and took pictures of little children who were there with their parents. I met about six other Marines I knew from K6 there in the garden and we gabbed until showtime again.

We found Part II every bit as enjoyable as part I, and the Finale the most fantastic musical presentation I've ever seen, the movies included. Everyone knew their parts perfectly.

There was no obscenity in the entire show. A couple of fellows I was talking to after the show stated that Scenes 20 and 22 were so far superior to the actual Follies Berge're and Can Can which they had seen while in Paris, that it couldn't be compared.

These Japanese are certainly developing an up and coming nation. Let's hope they don't digress under the tyrannical yoke of Communism. Communism is growing over here in leaps and bounds and I'm afraid it will grow even stronger as time passes. Within the Japanese Diet there are some 20 or more Communist members who stirred up the latest demonstrations in Tokyo and surrounding cities. I'd like to run into a Communist demonstrator--I'm afraid I'd kill the bastard. Pardon my French. Enough of that.

Back to Takarazuka again. After the opera Mac and I shopped at a little Japanese open-front toy shop and I made some purchases for my two precious little guys that I'm always thinking about and missing so very much. I took pictures of the little store. Wish it had been color because it was so very colorful.

I'd sure love to be in some of these guys' shoes that are going home. Wouldn't it be wonderful? I can dream, can't I? The mamasan did my wash for me--three shirts, 1 pr. khaki pants, 1 pr. socks, 2 undershirts, 2 drawers, 190 yen. The shirts are starched and ironed very nicely. There are four mamasans and one papasan working here in this BOQ. They get here at 0730 and the clacking of their wooden shoes gives us reveille. I wish they'd be more quiet this morning. An enlisted man woke me up at 0330 today saying, "It's time to get up, Capt Cox." I told him to go away, my name was Peterson. He said he was sorry, wrong room.

Kiss my angels for me. Honey, you can give them all the toys I bought. It's OK.

Bye bye, Daddy

The following article is taken from a late May 1952 edition of the *Pacific Stars & Stripes* and it confirms my explanation of the situation in the skies over North Korea at that time. While on my R&R I tried not to think about the fact that I would soon be returning to such a dismal state of affairs.

JET ACE SAYS MIGS BETTER; PILOTS SKILLED

TOKYO (Pac. S&S)--American Sabre jet pilots are now meeting top-notch Communist flyers in brand new MIG-15s--the most formidable opposition they have yet faced in North Korean skies--Fifth Air Force's sixteenth jet ace said in Tokyo Friday.

Col Harrison R. Thyng, commander of the 4th Fighter-Interceptor Wing from Pittsfield, N.H., said during the last few days, the Reds have put their best pilots and jets into the air in an effort to blast interdiction striking UN fighter-bombers.

The 34-year-old veteran fighter pilot who became an ace last Tuesday, said the enemy is also using strategy "which is a mark of a damn fine pilot."

He told reporters the Reds prepared for the springtime overcast weather by sending up "all weather" pilots who use "ground controlled interception" to strike fighter-bombers and F-86s in bad weather.

He said they fly directly into high overcasts and wait there--directed by ground radar--until Allied planes begin low level interdiction strikes beneath the ceiling. When the Reds' ground control guide informs them of the presence of the UN planes, he said the MIGs **dive out of the clouds and close with the Allied attackers at low levels.**

The system has been effective, he said, "against both fighter-bombers and Sabre jets."

"Not only are they good instrument pilots," he added, "but they are aggressive and want to fight."

He said they are a lot different from the MIG pilots of the past, who he believes were flying "training missions."

But the new pilots' increased aggressiveness and ability, he said, "makes us fight that much harder and we know we are getting the best of them."

"We have absolute air superiority to the Yalu," despite the effectiveness of the New Red flyers.

The stocky veteran of 105 missions over North Korea said there are indications some MIG pilots are not North Koreans. "When we find a good (Red) pilot we figure him to be Russian." He added others "might be doing it for pay." He speculated they could be Polish or German.

One of the indications that some of them may not be Korean, he said, is there seems to be a language barrier between the pilots.

"We shoot at one guy and there will be another right beside him who won't do anything about it."

Also, he said, Sabre jet pilots get close enough to see the Red flyers and have noted a difference in uniforms.

He said the MIG has steadily been improved but American jet improvements have kept up. "I wouldn't swap one F-86 for eight MIGs," he said.

He accredited the 8-1 superiority of the Sabre over the MIG to the quality of teamwork of the American pilots. He praised their training and spirit and said, "We are going to have a trained nucleus of combat pilots" if an all out war breaks.

Colonel Thyng got his fifth MIG--and thus became an ace--May 20 "without firing a shot." He told how the MIG made a sharp turn, too tight for the structural strength of the plane, and the tail section cracked. The plane went out of control and the pilot bailed out.

Although he is a wing commander, he already has five more than the required number of missions. He said, "I'm going to fly with the boys. . . no one tells me whether I've got to fly. My boss expects me to."

Colonel Thyng, who arrived in Korea last October, spoke at a press conference in Tokyo. He is spending several days in Japan before returning to Korea.

His wife and four children live in Pittsfield.

9 June 1952
Itami, Japan
Monday evening

Dearest girl and darling boys,

I've had a shopping good time today and I'll attempt to cut you in on the tour. First off, I slept late and missed my breakfast but caught a snack at the PX snack bar. I went over after 1000 (that's the hour the gift shop opens) and picked up my pictures. I bought four little china swans with roses on them. They are dished to form a little planter, like your big swan is. They're only about six inches long, only paid 60¢ apiece for them--nice little gifts. Then I had lunch and took the train into Osaka, where I caught a cab to the other side of town and went shopping in the newest department store in Osaka. About seven floors and every one of them stocked jam-packed with everything from soup to nuts.

I brought everything back to the base with me after fighting the evening crowd on the train. Had supper with John Snapper and Gene Cameron and we all went to "Fort Osage," a technicolor western with Rod Cameron.

I'm having a restful diversion over here anyway, dearest. The month of May in Korea was almost my undoing. I sure needed to get away from flying and the thought of the bastardly Communists just for a few days. I'll be back at them though, next Thursday, the 12th.

Snapper told me this evening that he's got his transfer orders when he returns from his R&R. He just arrived today from Korea. He's going to MACE-2 down in South Korea at the Wing level, Radar Tech. Officer--he's had the special schooling required for the job. He's a good man; I like Gene Cameron and John Snapper very much.

Tomorrow Higgins, Snapper, Cameron and I are going into the Takarazuka Opera again. It's wonderful. Gee, I wish you could see it, dearest, you'd love it--150 yen, I can't get over it.

I saw some real old fashioned Japanese sampans in a river in Osaka today. Whole families were living on the boats, kids running around, dogs, cats, old grandmas and papasans sitting around on them. What a picture.

Guess I'll close this deal out and hit the basket. The little narrow steel cots aren't quite wide enough for me. (This used to be a Japanese BOQ during WWII and the cots were probably adequate for them, being of smaller stature). The nice clean sheets are sure swell, though. I slept with two blankets on me last night and it was comfortable. It's been muggy over here with this overcast. The rain is rather refreshing. It's no wonder everything is so lush and green, with this rain.

Sayonara you.

All my love, Daddy

10 June 1952
Itami, Japan
Tuesday evening

Dearest girl,

The rest leave is gradually coming to a close. I've enjoyed my stay here this time because I truly have left most of the trials and tribulations normally associated with squadron life behind. The only thing I'm worried about is getting back into the grind after a week's layoff. Especially since, now that I'm a division leader, there are many extra things I have to spend more time on in preparing for my missions, in order to have the answer to any and every situation that might come up. I'd like to sit in on about three group briefings to bring me back up to date after a week's layoff. Flak areas and rescue facilities, as well as friendly and enemy troop positions, are my main concern in that regard. I'm not worried, of course, because I've done it many times before--really worried, that is--only concerned.

This morning Gene Cameron came in at 0730 and stirred me up into going to breakfast with him, so I did. I had been up early, however, because John Harkovnick left for the States this morning. What a happy cuss he was to be going over there this morning to climb on that 4-engined beauty that was to fly him to the good old United States of America. Golly, that sounds like it's an awful long way off. It seems as though it grows a little further away each day instead of closer.

Just talked to a captain from the First Marine Division who was on the lines the night I was telling you about, the night I was at VMO-6. He says that the night the Division received so much enemy artillery fire they hit a record of artillery received. Over 4000 rounds fell across our lines--no wonder I couldn't sleep, eh?

We went to the opera again today. It was just as exciting and colorful as it was the first time I saw it. The boys with me got a big bang out of it too.

I'm listening to Bob Hope's program. Rebroadcast, of course. My radio is working super. I can't pick up anything much over in Korea. There is a shortage of radio tubes of my Zenith's size over here, so the repairman had to substitute a tube he had in his shop with one more prong on the base than the one that went haywire in my set. It worked fine, though. The Japanese are very clever people.

I didn't realize how lucky I was, dearest, when I was home with my little gang all around me. I'll never let it slip through my fingers again. We Americans certainly have a lot to fight for, darling. The world situation has really got me confused--so confused I haven't even got an answer, either constructive or critical. I'm afraid I'm blinded by my desire to return home to you, dearest. I realize there's a need here for armed U.S. forces, but it cuts me because it came to close to suit me.

Bye bye, dearest doll,

Your very own Daddy

FAMILIARIZATION VISIT TO THE FRONT

11 June 1952
Itami, Japan
Wednesday afternoon

Dearest girl and little guys,

Howdee folks. I'm sitting here listening to the "Honshu Cowboy," and I'm getting all the latest cowboy songs. Just heard Roberta Lee sing "I Want to Play House with You." Now here comes Tex Ritter, the crying cowboy, singing "You'd Always Care." Boy, was it sorrowful. Oh no, it's called "This Lonely World." Hank Penny now singing "My Little Red Wagon." Takes me back home to the television shows I've seen him on.

Didn't leave the base today, although Cameron and Snapper tried to get me to go into Osaka and shop at the Sago Department Store with them. Today has been a warm, clear, beautiful day and I figured it would be even hotter in the Japanese trains, so I stayed here on the base. The movie tonight is the same as last night, "The First Time," so I guess I'll spend a quiet evening writing letters and listening to the radio, as I've done most of today. I've seen a lot of friends today, though, and have gabbed a lot. I'm all packed up and ready to go back to Korea in the early morning..

The food over here at Itami is very good. I don't think I've mentioned that before. The food is all prepared by Japanese cooks and served by Japanese girls. They knock themselves out giving you service. On the table they have jam, jelly, peanut butter, real country churned butter, sugar, salt, pepper, catsup, mustard, sweet bread and butter pickles, vinegar, soy sauce, meat sauce and toothpicks. This stuff is all lined up down the center of the table. Then they bring a carton of sweet milk and a carton of chocolate, and iced tea, coffee or lemonade. As you come in the door just after paying the sergeant your 50¢ per meal, they have a huge fresh salad bar with as many as five different types to select from, as well as several juices. It's very nice having all this fresh salad available. Often times they have a variety of cold cuts and cheeses on the salad bar. They always have soup for dinner, or supper. The waitresses hang over you and the very second the soup plate is empty they snatch it and in seconds your main course is staring you in the face. I get a kick out of them when they ask you if you want soup. They say, "You want zoup, sir?" They nod their head like mad indicating yes. If you say no, they actually seem disappointed. They have a heck of a time telling you what kind of soup or what kind of dessert they have. Sometimes they go get another waitress and bring her over and have you ask her. They speak hardly any English at all. This whole experience has been very interesting for me, honey, but I'd have gladly missed it if I could have. But I figure we might as well make the most of things since we've got no choice in the matter.

There's quite a bit of talk about the Koji Island prisoner deal. Boy, the Radio Moscowers are sure making the most of the situation. They sure are putting out a pack of filthy lies. Even though they are lies, I'm thoroughly convinced there are those in the United States who will pick it up, knowing full well it's a pack of lies, and pass it on--trying to drum it into the minds of the fools who will listen. Well, enough of that dribble. It's not even worth the trouble to write. I know how you feel about it too. You'd get a bang out of the Russian propaganda line. Too bad everyone can't hear it unabridged; then they could see it as it really is.

It's raining now and it's sure noisy bouncing off the tin rough. Japan seems to me to be a lot like the North American Pacific Northwest. Many, many trees, mountains and green valleys. The Japanese seem to be a happy people. On the train they joke and laugh and generally appear to be good natured. They are dressed in western garb and Japanese traditional, all mixed up. They sure are picking up American habits, traditions and dress. The Jap radio programs are almost completely taken up with American tunes, sung by famous Americans. Occasionally a Japanese will sing an American song in broken English.

Well, baby girl, guess I'll knock off now.

Tell my little fellows Daddy loves them and misses them very much. Tuck them into beddie bye real good, Mama.

Your very own,
Daddy

CRASH ON RUNWAY DELAYS LANDING

12 June 1952
Tunp o ri, Korea
Thursday evening

Dearest baby girl and my darling little boys,
      We climbed aboard the R5D Marine transport at Itami at 1330 and were airborne by 1345. After a lazy, uneventful trip over, we had to circle for about 15 minutes due to a crash on the runway. We finally landed at 1630, offloaded, and I came over here to the hut, unpacked my gear and went over to eat. Then I attended the general group briefing and got brought up to date on all the happenings of the past week.
      Oh, I almost forgot the most important part of the whole day--I went over and got my mail and boy, did I ever hit the jackpot! Got six letters from you, darling, one each from Ben and Mom, and one from Dr. Von der Nuell of AiResearch signed by about 30 of the top engineers and friends of mine in the lab and shop. I'll send it to you, darling, so you can keep it for me. I was sorry to hear about my Ricky boy and his tonsil troubles. Got all your letters from 31 May until 6 June. Your last one told of Ricky's apparently improving condition, which I pray will pull him through.
      Boy, do things look different. I've been gone seven days and during that period they built a new officers' mess hall and painted the inside battleship grey. They have cute black and white striped curtains hung at all the windows. Windows are only screened--no glass, don't need any over here. It's very attractive. Cement floor. Light green plastic tablecloths on each table with a white sheet underneath. All the chairs are painted a nice clean refreshing white. All the Korean mess men have white uniforms with white hats and MAG-12 over the lefthand pocket. In the head they have aluminum wash basins so we don't have to leave the water running while we're shaving.
      Hugh Holland just came in and said, "Go to bed right away, Pete, 'cause you've got to take off at 0355 for a close air support with the Division." (1stMarDiv), so I'll knock off writing soon and hit the basket.
      I was glad to hear you finally claimed victory over the gopher. I'm proud of you, darling. Determination always pays off. You and you alone have succeeded where others have failed miserably. You are indeed to be commended in this challenge that you so magnificently met. There must be some award for such determination. If I were there I'd kiss you, darling. Your Napoleon attack on the weeds to the south of our lot sounded to me like another matter that should receive some special mention. Well done, old girl. Boy, you sure mowed down the lawns too. You're a real fighter.
      In answer to your question, did I take any pictures of Nellie Sharpe, the answer is affirmative. Am enclosing same. Mom sent me a set of pictures, the same ones you sent to me, so I returned one set to you. Nellie is down at MAG-33 now at the wing. He's going to get into Panther Jets down there. Ann Driver can get him through his old VMF-323 address with MAG-12 1st MAW, c/o FPO San Francisco, and they'll transfer it on to him. Maybe we can start something there, honey. Nellie's a nice kid--very earnest, sincere and clean living.
      I was certainly surprised to hear from Dr. Von der Nuell, of all people. I had written to Eddie Butler and he posted the letter for everyone to read. I never thought I had made much of an impression with Dr. Von, but he apparently did know I existed after all because the letter was initiated by himself. Get the load of signatures on there. Even Homer Wood's. Can't understand why Cliff Garrett wasn't let in on the deal. I'm hurt--ha ha! If that's any indication of my worth at AiResearch, I guess maybe I'd better return. Maybe they'll give me a raise, who knows?
      Night, night darling. Will write again in the morning after I come back from my mission.

All my love,
Daddy

FAMILIARIZATION VISIT TO THE FRONT

13 June 1952
K6 Korea
1030

Hi dearest girl,

    Mission No. 46 completed. Browning, the SDO, woke me at 0230. It seemed as though I had just closed my eyes from the night before. Had an excited feeling in my stomach, like I always do when I've been out of flying for a while. We briefed at 0255, took off at 0355 and seven of us were over the 1stMarDiv area watching the fireworks display at 0430. What a sight, with all the machine gun tracers, artillery shells and huge bursts going on, one right after the other! I was carrying (8) 100 lb fragmentation bombs with a cluster of (8) smaller frag. bombs bundled together in each 100 lb cluster. It's for anti-personnel. Then on my belly I carried (2) 1000 lb instantaneous fused nose with a .025 sec. delay on the tail. Most of the others in the flight had a mixture of ordnance, including napalms. After we got over the area we were to orbit (turn in a circle), as a Major Frey had called up Holland, who was leading the seven-plane division, and requested that he be allowed to drop his ordnance immediately and return to the base (K6) because he was getting gasoline fumes in his cockpit. We were operating too close to the peaces talks to allow him to drop uncontrolled (our controller had not as yet reported on station), so Holland told him to return to K6 and directed me to escort him in. I was disappointed because, after going to all the trouble of getting up there that far, I wanted to go all the way. Besides, unless you cross the bomb line, it's no mission.

    After I escorted Frey back to Seoul, he called me up to say he was OK and for me to return to the Division, which I did. I got on the tail end of the flight just as they were going into their first run. We clobbered them on a reverse slope of a huge mountain, honeycombed with trenches, bunkers, caves, artillery pieces and mortars. In the early morning twilight we could see every tracer the Communists shot up at us. They would wait until we were climbing back out of a dive, and while we were still low, around 1500 feet, they would bore-sight us and their tracers were licking at our cockpit and wingtips, but somehow or other no one picked up any holes. It's amazing, how that can be with all that ground fire. When the bombs went off it kicked my plane just like I had dropped in on the deck from a height of about 20 feet. Boy, what a jolt! The whole area for about half a mile in diameter would light up from the white hot blast center and you could see the ground jump for a greater distance. The frag cluster did a very good job too. As we landed at 0610, I had precious little gas left. We received a 95% coverage score for this mission and the battle damage estimate will be sent up later, after the OE-1s confirm it later on this morning.

    Take care of my Ricky darling, sweetheart, and tell him his daddy is pulling for him. I love you so very, very much, my precious girl. You mean the world and all to me. The pictures are wonderful. Keep up the good work. I love you all very much.

                                    Bye bye, Daddy

13 June 1952
Tunp o ri, Korea

Dearest girl,

    I already wrote to you earlier today and mailed the letter, but your letter of 6 June arrived telling of Ricky's new case of measles. The poor little guy. Gee, I wish I could be there to help him. Did the nurse have any recommendations? You never said anything except that she said he had had the German, or three-day measles, the first time. Do you suppose you should take him to a doctor and have him look at him? Maybe his tonsils are still bad too and should be taken care of. How come all this is happening to Ricky? Isn't Randy getting **anything??!** In regard to Ricky's colds; do you take every precaution to see that he has a warm jacket on and that he's always in the house before the cold evening breezes come up? He always used to seem like a rugged little guy. Take care of him and tell him his daddy is pulling for him every minute of the day and night. He's been occupying my thoughts constantly every since you told me of it.

Got the boys' Father Day cards. Tell them I thought they were real sweet to think of me, darling. I'm proud of my two boys.

I love you, sweetheart.

Your Daddy

14 June 1952
Tunp o ri, Korea
Saturday evening

Dearest girl,

I just had a close call but the good Lord had his arm around me. Here's how it happened. All the missions that were pre-assigned yesterday and were coming off this afternoon were cancelled. We were told something big was coming off and every plane in our entire group was to be ready to go on a one-and-a-half-hour standby Finally the word came into the group and 35 pilots from all three squadrons were there and ready to go. We received a complete briefing, then went to our squadrons, got into our planes and lined up for takeoff.

The dust was flying as we all waited our turn to take off. I was number 32. As my turn came I headed my nose into the wind and pushed the throttle forward. My plane lunged out, my tail came up and I was really rolling when suddenly my propeller began changing pitch. I was slowing down and my engine was failing. I figured my propeller governor had gone out on me, so I jammed on my brakes, finally getting the old crate slowed down. As I turned off on a taxi way right in front of our squadron area the engine stopped cold. The men came rushing out to push my tail clear of the runway, to allow the rest of the planes behind me to take off. If it had happened 15 seconds later I would have been airborne and I'd never have been able to put it back down on the runway. I crawled out of the monster and said a thank-you prayer, and now I'm just beginning to realize what really did happen.

This propeller governor is the first one I've ever heard of going out on takeoff. It would have to happen to me!

1000

I was just outside having a little talk to you while looking up at a beautiful heaven full of stars. I miss you so very, very much, my darling, I can hardly stand this separation. It feels like I'm only half alive. I can't get interested in anything, don't often go to the O'Club and sing with the boys. Nearly everyone I knew very well has either been transferred or else is on R&R. This hut is practically a morgue.

Two helicopter pilots from up at the Division, friends of "Rainbow" Jackson, came down here to K6 to see him, so he brought them over here to our hut to stay. One of the guys said he'd teach me to pilot the big Sikorsky helicopter we have here in the Group for pilot pickup. That may be an interesting change. I'll keep you posted.

We have four brand spanking new AU-1 Corsairs in the squadron now. Tomorrow morning at 1000 I'm scheduled for a familiarization hop in it. I haven't even sat in the cockpit yet or read the pilot's handbook. They have one handbook which has to make the rounds of 40 pilots. The cockpit and engine are completely different and there's enough of a change to make it an entirely new airplane except for the outside appearance. It's a lot faster, and the most important thing is that they are NEW!

I'm checking the days off, slow but sure.

Night, night,
Daddy

FAMILIARIZATION VISIT TO THE FRONT

A VERY CLOSE CALL

While I was usually quite frank with Marion in my letters, the above incident regarding the propeller governor was watered down considerably to spare her the possible gory details.

Actually, my plane *was* airborne and climbing when the propeller governor and engine problem developed. I had already retracted my landing gear and was settling back down to the runway on my belly. Luckily, I hit my landing gear extension handle just in time, for the wheels dropped with a clunk in the locked position just a second before they touched the runway. I had missed settling on my belly, bombs, and belly fuel tank by seconds and, needless to say, had they exploded, they would have blown a fairly large crater right there in the runway. I had used up all of the runway and had to ground loop the old crate in the dirt. Fortunately, I didn't hurt the plane. This incident shook me up plenty.

15 June 1952
Tunp o ri, Korea
Sunday afternoon

Dearest Marion and boys that I love,

Finally I got ahold of a pilots' handbook on the AU-1 new type Corsair--about an hour before I took off in it. I read it through (over 100 pages) and realized I couldn't hope to remember everything I'd read, so crawled in and strapped up. After searching for the necessary gadgets that I had become accustomed to in the old Corsair, I finally got it going, taxied out and took off. After an hour in the air I had found nearly everything I needed to keep it in the air. I dove it from 11,000 feet to the deck at over 400 kts (around 500 mph) and it handled like a dream. More power than I knew what to do with--or almost, that is, because a few minutes after that, while cruising along at 10,000 feet, I spotted two F-84 jets flying along together below me at about 5000 feet.

I pushed my nose over at them and, feeling rather cocky with this sudden surge of heretofore unfelt power. I began a dogfight with them that lasted about ten minutes. We dove, climbed and turned in on each other, and finally I got the better of them both because as we lost altitude I gained more power, so I was on their tail and had them bore-sighted. They kept getting closer to K6 all the while we were fighting and the whole base was out watching us. I finally broke it off when they came out of a turn and took off on a course that took them home toward their base.

I landed soon after, feeling quite pleased with our new AU-1, and quite proud of my aerial accomplishments--so close to K6 too. Of course, I was greeted by the gang after I landed and they began firing questions at me a mile a minute.

"What power settings were you carrying? Did you have to use any flaps to out-turn them? What do you think of the AU-1?" etc.

I spoke to Col Galer, our new Group CO, at chow and he asked me a lot of questions about the fight they had witnessed. (He had served with VMF-224 at Guadalcanal, shooting down 13 Jap planes, and had won the Medal of Honor.)

Everyone feels a lot better about our chances now, in the event we get jumped by MIGs. We aren't using them yet on combat missions because we're still conducting familiarization syllabuses within the squadron. I'm very excited about the plane and its capabilities.

I'm standing by now for my 1800 takeoff for our close air support mission up to the Division. Our Group helicopter crashed today as I was up flying the AU-1 this morning. I had a look at it just as it crashed and saw three guys coming out of it. It's a mess and no chance for a repair job. They'll get a lot of salvage from it, though. I know all three guys and spoke to them after they were picked up and returned to the field. It was caused from hovering at low altitude near the ground at extremely high air temperatures. The air is thinner when it's a very warm day. They hit the ground from an altitude of about 15 feet. Glad nobody got hurt. They were on a training hop. It was the first time the pilot, McClure, had ever flown the SO3-1. Nobody in the thing had ever flown an SO3-1; they had flown others, but not the SO3. The Colonel (CO of the Group) is extremely mad at them. Don't know whether he'll do anything about it or not. Don't know whether it was pilot error or what. Probably poor technique. For now, that ends my chance to learn to fly a helicopter.

Maybe I'll get a letter this afternoon telling me my Ricky boy is better. I sure hope so.

*All my love,
Daddy*

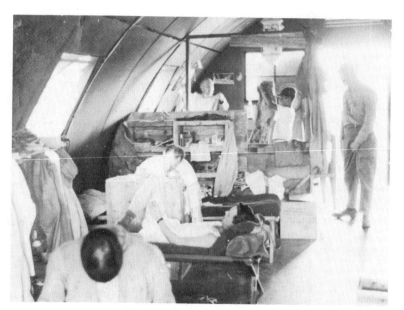

Upper Left: A typical afternoon between combat missions in the Quonset hut of Capt Robert Barnum and buddies of VMA-212. L to R: Capts Ivy and Holmes, Lt Welch, Maj Webster, Korean houseboy, and Capt Evans who received his majority after I left the squadron.

Left: VMA-212 Devil Cats Corsair flight line

Above: Capt Robert Barnum, in front of Japanese photo shop at Itami, Japan. Pictures on this page courtesy of Capt Barnum.

CHAPTER 11

BRAND NEW AU-1 CORSAIRS

Up until now we had been flying the older F4U-4B Corsairs. The Lord only knew and he wouldn't tell where they resurrected them, but they were all fugitives from some junker's melting pot, probably Litchfield Park, AZ. The airfield's rough condition, the harsh Korean weather, dust and constant hard use had taken their toll. I can't remember a single F4U-4B that I flew which didn't have something wrong with it--oil leaks from the rocker box covers that glazed the windshield, the odor of gas fumes, fluctuating fuel gauges, sluggish supercharger clutches, antiquated radios; mud, rocks and debris in the cockpit; foggy, unreadable instruments; nicked and marginally balanced propellers; noisy and ill-fitting cockpit enclosures; cockpit lights that didn't work; bald and fabric-showing tires; squeaky and grabby brakes and controls out of trim. None of these observed conditions would generally ground the planes.

We could hardly believe it when they announced that our squadron was to be refitted with the latest Corsair, fresh from the Vought factory. Vought had started the design work on its new F4U-6 back in 1950. The war in Korea had dictated a requirement for a strictly ground support type of aircraft. Upon the occasion of the maiden flight on 31 Jan 1952 it was redesignated the AU-1 ("A" for Attack and "U" for Vought). The major engine change consisted of eliminating the heavy, horsepower consuming, high altitude supercharger, and changing to a low altitude, single stage, two speed, manually controlled supercharger. The engine was designated the Double Wasp R-2800-83WA. Additional armor plating was added and the engine cowl supercharger air inlet ducts were eliminated. The basic armament remained about the same as the older F4U-4B with four 20mm M-3 automatic cannons. Vought made only 111 AU-1s, the last being delivered in Oct 1952. (The French Naval Air Arm ultimately wound up with 25 AUs from our sister squadron, VMF-211 of MAG-12, on 18 Apr 1954, for use in the Indo China War.) The cockpit had been completely redesigned and the pilot seat was comfort itself. Even the cockpit enclosure seal had been improved and the air leak was only a hushed whisper, for the first time actually allowing the pilot to hear everything clearly on his radio.

The removal of the high altitude supercharger had restored approximately 440 horsepower to the engine which improved its ordnance carrying capability and its general performance up to 15,000 feet. The AU-1 was no longer a fighter but had become a first class ground support machine. However, this is not quite so because I absolutely creamed two Air Force F-84s.

The F-84 Thunderstreaks that I tangled with in a friendly duel over our field in Korea were the notorious underpowered 5200 lb thrust J35-A-25, straight winged version. The Air Force had long since recognized its inferiority to the MIG-15 and was pushing hard for the new F-84F swept wing, powered by the 7200 lb thrust Armstrong Siddeley Sapphire, manufactured by Curtiss Wright as the J65. It did not reach production until Nov 1952, just as I was leaving Korea. But then, due to extensive problems, it never reached the Korean theater, so never tangled with a MIG-15.

My letter to Marion of 15 Jun 52 spoke of my first AU-1 familiarization hop. After landing, Col Bob Galer, our Group CO, questioned me in depth about my flight and requested my impression of the aircraft's performance. I gave it high marks.

On 16 June I led a strike to the North Korean town of Channampo. It was the first time the AU-1 had ever been flown in combat. I spoke of it in my June 17th letter to Marion.

COLONEL GALER MAKES IT BACK

Several months after being refitted with the new Corsairs, Col Galer, our new MAG-12 commander, was shot down after leading a flight of 31 Corsairs to their objectives, which were a supply area and tungsten mines in the mountainous northeastern part of North Korea, just below the 39th Parallel and 35 miles southwest of Wonsan on the east coast. After several hits had killed his AU-1 engine, the MAG-12 commander, preparing to parachute, climbed out over the side of his plane, but found that he had one foot stuck inside the cockpit, probably on the shoulder straps or the loop of the belt. He then pulled himself partially back towards the cockpit, freed his foot with a vigorous kick, cleared the plane, and headed in spreadeagle fashion towards the ground. Almost immediately the plane, falling in a nose dive, caught the descending pilot on the shoulder and pulled him into a spin. Col Galer recovered in time, however, to pull the ripcord and thus ease his impact onto enemy terrain. He landed within ten feet of his crashed AU.

"Immediately upon getting free of the chute, I ran as rapidly as possible, staying low, down through a corn field," he reported later. At the end of the field, he paused momentarily to survey the terrain for an escape route. Spotting a dry stream bed nearby, Col Galer dashed toward it and quickly but cautiously moved up it some 100 yards. Then he halted to put into operation a small survivor radio to report his position. The message was received by the rescue air patrol orbiting overhead which relayed the information to pickup aircraft. The patrol advised the downed pilot that the rescue helicopter had already departed for the crash area.

Before breaking radio contact, Col Galer told the air patrol his planned movements in order to facilitate pickup. He then quickly left the area which was located too near the crashed aircraft for a rescue attempt. Evading detection by enemy soldiers and curious teenagers moving towards the wreckage, the Marine worked his way to higher ground, keeping the air patrol advised of his changing position. By 1845 a search of the area was underway. Of the events that followed, Col Galer wrote:

> *At 1908 I heard the helicopter go down the next valley and saw it disappear. I called, told them to make a 180-degree turn since I was in the valley to the southwest and on the north slope. I did not get an answer but soon the helicopter came through a saddle in the ridge. . . . I immediately let the red smoke (day flare) go, and came out of the bushes. . . calling the helicopter on the radio also. They apparently saw me immediately and came over and hovered. The mechanic leaned out and swung the hoisting sling back and forth. . . . Finally, I grabbed it and got in. . . and the pilot took off. . . . The mechanic pulled me up and into the helicopter as we crossed the valley.*

The colonel was not yet out of the woods. The trip to a rescue ship at Wonsan was marked by intermittent bursts of enemy antiaircraft fire. On one occasion the chopper was hit hard enough to spin it completely around. As the rescue craft neared the coast, the patches of fog added to the hazards of night flying. About that time the warning light indicating low fuel supply came on but "the pilot gambled on making the sea at the risk of having to autorotate through the overcast into the mountains," Galer added. It was a correct decision. The fuel lasted until the helicopter landed on the rescue vessel. It was then 2100 and very dark. They were home safe.

I had covered downed pilots in a similar manner on several of my 60 combat missions flown in Korea, some being about as dramatic as Col Galer's. Knowing they would go all-out for you if you did go down in your plane over enemy territory gave us all the encouragement we needed.

Col Galer was a double Ace from WWII. That's one thing I liked about the Marine Corps. They exposed a lot of their ranking people to our air combat missions, instead of tucking them away behind some safe desk job.

MY PLANE IS HIT BY ENEMY GROUND FIRE

16 Jun 52
Monday 1030

Hello darling,

Yesterday will go down in my book as a red letter day. I sorta had to laugh too because it was Sunday (the Lord's day) and my day too (Father's Day).

We took off for our close air support hop at 1800 and were on station a half hour later. The airborne controller told me to orbit my flight and wait on station because they had something "hot" coming up. We did just that. We circled and circled and finally, at 1905, they gave us a call. It was growing rather dark now, as the sun was setting behind a huge storm cloud moving toward us from the west.

They gave me my target coordinates and I picked up my forward air controller who vectored us over to a hill position about 2000 yards in front of our friendlies (marines). We made two runs each on this position and we were getting 37mm, 20mm, 88mm and 90mm thrown at us by the hundreds. As it was growing dark, we could observe nearly every shot being fired at us, and it was coming thick and heavy. I wanted to get the heck out of there, but something inside me kept saying, "Go get 'em, Spud."

It was almost completely dark when we heard a frantic voice come up over the air wanting to know if we had any ordnance left. I came up with an affirmative and asked for the coordinates of the target. Due to very poor radio communications, I had difficulty reaching this controller, who was flying an OE-1. He was about ready to give me the coordinates when all of a sudden I saw a terrific blast come from an area about six miles north of Kaesong (right on the edge of the restricted area) and I knew what it was right away. It was Chinese heavy artillery 122 firing on our lines. After seeing the missile leave the piece and fall on our friendly lines, I headed west and north for their position. From an elevation of 8500 feet we were getting flak from hundreds of heavy automatic weapons firing at us constantly. It reminded me of the carrier days off Guadalcanal during the early days of WWII.

Due to poor visibility, I had almost lost their position, but then a hole in the overcast opened up and I felt I was in position for a run on them. The very second I dropped my nose over and began my diving attack at the (4) heavy artillery positions, the whole area, for what seemed miles around, lighted up from the many more hundreds of guns coming into my range as I came closer to the ground. I had only four rockets and about 600 rounds of 20mm left, but just before my release all four guns fired again and I could see the men all around them. I had them bore-sighted and let go with my 20s and four rockets. They landed right smack on the position. The rest of the fellows in the flight were quite a way off, except with their 20s. We stayed close to the deck, trying to avoid the heavies as much as possible until we got over friendlies, then started a high speed climb to altitude.

I hated the very thought of having to go back in there again, but darned if those heavies didn't let go with another barrage. Knowing we had to knock out those heavies at any cost, I led them back in again. With only 20s left, I dove down through that horrible sickening hail of fire that seemed to be licking my plane from every angle. I strafed, and the three others let go (2) 1000 lb 4 to 5 second delay bombs that landed extremely close, if not right on the heavies. I felt a thud in my rudder on my pull-out and knew I had been hit. However, I had full control, so it didn't bother me too much.

We got our damage assessment from the controller from the hill position--4 enemy bunkers destroyed, 2 mortar positions destroyed, and many KIAs (killed in action). The second controller wouldn't go in for a damage assessment run and I don't blame him. It was dark and he wouldn't have been able to make any assessment until daylight anyway.

As we retired from the area and headed home, we watched for some time and failed to see any heavy fire coming from the position we'd attacked, so we felt quite confident that we had knocked them out. We had another problem confronting us now, though, as I pointed my nose in the darkness toward K6 and a rain storm. During the excitement of battle none of us had realized our critically low fuel supply. In fact, we were very dangerously low. I leaned back my mixture and RPM and power settings, then just hoped for the best. We made it to K6, and as my wheels screeched on the metal matting when I touched down, a sense of complete relaxation came over me. It's quite a sensation to become suddenly scared, just momentarily, but when you stay that way for over an hour and the condition that scared you in the first place intensifies, it's another thing again.

As the four of us were sitting in the Group S2 Intelligence office giving the strike report, the other three boys had multiple shots of whiskey and water. We ate supper at 2145, then came on over to the hut and collapsed. My sleeping bag got too warm and I kept waking up with horrible jerks, while at the other end of the hut Jackson, McClune and Smith were playing with their radio, drinking and talking until 0200 this morning. I was restless. I'd go to sleep, then roll over, hear the music and chatter, and then stay awake for the longest time. Finally I yelled at them and they stopped the talking, but the music went on all night and was still playing this morning. I woke up at 0645, had a shave, showered, had breakfast and, although I feel like I never closed my eyes all night, I feel OK.

Early this morning I dashed over, crawled into the AU-1, took off at 0800 by myself and went up for 1.5 hours on another familiarization hop. I did a lot of practicing on radio and navigation, using my "bird dog" (they had one in this AU-1--didn't have one in the other one yesterday). Then I also used my "2B" navigation tower. Flying up to the bomb line and a little east of the center of Korea, I then operated my navigational radio aids to get me back to base. No dog fighting or acrobatics. Landed at 0930, then came on over here to Group Supply and finagled a nice wide mattress (30") with two mattress covers (both dirty). I have a blanket, so now I'll have Kim wash my covers, so I can slip one over me under the blanket. Kim and I shook the blanket and I've never seen so much dust and dirt come out of anything. Wish I could get it washed somewhere, but there's no chance. I know I'll sleep a lot better tonight. It's been very warm but not uncomfortable here lately, about 85° now but the door's open and there's a nice refreshing cool breeze coming in. I'm in my skivvy shorts and undershirt, with my boondockers on.

It's a shame a daddy has to be away from a family as precious as you. It's a crime. Tell my darlings I love them and miss them very much. Tell them to obey you, dear, because you only tell them what's good for them. They'll grow into fine men if they follow all our instructions, won't they, honey?

Bye bye, Daddy

TREADING ON THIN ICE

The peace negotiations hadn't been going too smoothly. Hardly anything was being accomplished. The night mission I led on the 15th of June was, in every sense of the word, treading on thin ice. The Communists had positioned their heavy 122 artillery pieces on the very perimeter of their neutral zone. I've mentioned earlier how Panmunjom had been designated as the center of a circular neutral zone with a 1000-yard radius and a three-mile radius around Munsan (the Allied camp) and Kaesong (the Communist camp). Also, a hundred meters on either side of the Kaesong-Munsan road had been neutralized as a further precaution to prevent any hostile act within the sanctuary. LtGen John W. O'Daniel, I Corps Commander, ordered an additional area forward of the formal neutral zone to be set aside. This zone could not be fired into, out of, or over. The Communists knew of this additional neutral safety zone and frequently used it as an assembly and artillery firing area. The guns we were attacking were in this zone and I was deliberately trying to knock them out. Their long range capability was permitting their huge projectiles to reach as far as our 1stMarDiv command post. Orders must have been circumvented for us in this case because we were ordered to "Go get 'em!"

Congratulatory messages from the 1stMarDiv CO immediately began pouring into our Group CO. Upon hearing this we were elated, since we now knew we had definitely silenced the heavies, and also that we weren't going to be court martialed for violating any neutral zone.

There was some talk of us receiving some meritorious award for that mission. We were just happy to have survived and not to have broken off the talks. My plane had been the only one hit that night. That's not too strange, however, since the division leader, being the first one to dive on the target, has a tendency to draw the bulk of the enemy fire.

17 Jun 52
Tunp o ri, Korea
Tuesday afternoon

Dearest girl,

Received your letter of the 11th of June telling of my darling Ricky's improvement. It was the best possible news I could have received. You work on him and just stuff the food down the little guy. Tell Ricky I'm so very happy he's feeling better. Please tell the boys that I think of them constantly and the time is passing right along--be it ever so slowly, it's passing.

Received the new address book, darling, and thanks a lot. So you've got gopher troubles again, have you? Boy, they can be almost as troublesome as Communists!

I got up at 0230 this morning, taxied out to the end of the runway with three other pilots and stayed there until 0545 when we came on back to the line, went over and had breakfast, then briefed again for a special interdiction mission into North Korea to hit some Commie supply dumps that were recently discovered by our photo reccy planes. Hugh Holland led the strike of eight planes but I led the second division of four. We clobbered the supplies and left the area in flames. They were dug in on a rugged mountainous area at 4000' altitude. Boy, they were hard to find, even with the special maps and photos and radar control to the target area.

Last night I led a strike to Chinnampo. It was the first time the new AU-1 type Corsair had ever been flown in combat. The daddy was chosen to lead. I had Watson, Eddens and Col Axtell (the Group tactical officer) on me. We made six runs each and we really got the feel of our new AU-1s. They are going to change the squadron designation soon to VMA-212. "A" for attack because of our new AU-1 planes which are made especially as an attack plane. My fighter spec. MOS has an addition now, 7331 VMA, Attack Pilot. I have 7302 already and maybe the engineer officer MOS 6410 will come through before 6 Dec 1952.

I have 49 missions now, darling. I've had quite a few familiarization hops and some others that don't count as missions. I signed my officer's fitness report today, made out by Col Bryson, who is being transferred. He wrote me up as excellent on 20 counts, and also in the remarks column he paid me some very favorable compliments.

COMBAT AIR SUPPORT FOR A BRITISH CRUISER

18 Jun 52
Tunp o ri, Korea
Wednesday, 2245

Dearest girl,

Honey, today will probably stand out in my life as a red letter day of all red letter days. I'm positive I'm only sitting here by the wonderful grace of God.

Briefed this morning at 0815 for an interdiction hop up into a Communist supply area in North Korea. The weather kept the whole 5th Air Force down except, you guessed it, your very own hubby that loves you. It all happened when a British cruiser, the Belfast, and two destroyers spotted some Communist gunfire on the North Korean west coast. They requested that fighter-bombers be called in to knock them out. My interdiction mission was cancelled and I was sent with my three boys up to hit them, almost 200 miles from our base. Because of horrible weather I felt very reluctant to take them out in the stuff. However, our Group operations department is so afraid JOC (the 5th Air Force) is thinking ill of the Marines that they almost insisted on us going. The final decision rested with me, however, regardless of MAG-12 Group or the 5th Air Force.

I took off, picked the boys up over the field and out on course. The weather west of the field was almost down to the deck. I began a climb out on full instruments with my three boys tucked up real close to me the whole way up. We hadn't broken through the stuff yet when Capt Strom's radio went clear out. Capt Watson called and told me because he was right up close to Strom. I instructed Watson to take Strom back to K6 and both of them to land. Then Capt Call and I continued our instrument climb out and, finally, after what seemed like hours, we broke through the stuff at about 5000 feet. As we did so, the sun almost blinded us because, due to a 2000-foot layer of fog on top, the reflection doubled the intensity. We got into contact with a radar controller who gave us radar steers (navigational control) all the way to our target area (Chodo Island). It was the darndest thing, all of Korea was completely socked in except our target.

I contacted a Limey controller called "Sitting Duck" who was on the cruiser HMS Belfast. Boy, it's fun listening to those rascals. We had quite a chat. He gave me the target coordinates and I was circling Chodo Island when all of a sudden my engine conked out! I had about decided to set it down on the sand at Chodo Island or alongside the cruiser when it began running again, and it kept running the whole time until I got home. We found the target they directed us to and Call and I clobbered it. I hit the gun position with a 1000 lb bomb, then clobbered a supply shelter that blew sky high and caused a large secondary explosion.

Note: While touring England in 1985, our River Thames tour boat brought us alongside the HMS *Belfast*, the very same cruiser that we worked with in Korea 33 years prior.

After checking out with "Sitting Duck," I climbed back up to 10,000 feet and got the radar controller again, who brought me home to Seoul at 10,000 feet and turned me over to the tower operator at K6. He gave us steers to the base which by this time was really socked in. The tops of the clouds reached 7000 feet and the bottoms hung at 1600 feet, with scattered rain storms in the area. They steered us to over K6 and then we made a tactical let down through a terrific storm.

Call was trying his darndest to stay on my wing, but the stuff got so thick it was impossible. I couldn't see out of the cockpit because of blinding rain beating on the windshield. Finally, after about ten minutes of terrible tension, I broke through, located the field and came in for a landing. Call was finally picked up by the controller and brought in OK too, but not until he went through a rough 15 minutes. You see, they can't bring you into the field on GCA until they get you down to controllable altitude, which is about 2000 feet here at K6. I broke through, however, at 1600 feet and a mountain peak went scooting just off my right wing. I was never so happy so see the ground in all my life.

Call and I contacted the tower operators, thanking them for a job well done, and this evening we each bought them a 5th of whiskey ($1.50) at the O'Club. They really appreciated it. The 5th Air Force called up and thanked them (Group 12 Operations) for sending their boys up in that stuff, and us for finding a target and destroying it, as well as giving them a complete weather report of nearly all Korea. (I had done it with me own two little hands.) Col Axtell, the Group Operations Officer, called me up and thanked me for going on through the stuff, and as a side he said, "It made the Marines look very good today, as we were the only ones in the 5th Air Force to get off the deck today."

Are you proud of the daddy, honey? I was shook for about an hour after I got down.

Went to the movies tonight and saw "The Tall Target," with Dick Powell and Adolph Manjou. It all took place on the train from New York to Washington, D.C., where Lincoln was to make his inaugural address. Dick Powell uncovered plot to assassinate the President and foiled it. He really got shook up in the process. I'd only grade it about 60%. Black and white.

Received yours of the 12th of June. Yes, dearest, I did enjoy my R&R very much. It took my mind off of flying long enough for me to realize there was something else in this world besides early-early reveilles and "U" Birds and Communists.

No. 50 mission completed. Guess I'll knock off and hit the pad for a while. Nothing cooking for me until 1300 tomorrow when I lead an eight-plane railcut with three majors in my division and two colonels. I'd better not make any slip-ups. I have to laugh at the situation: a lousy inactive reserve leading an eight-plane railcut mission with regular Marine colonels and majors under my command. There aren't many men in the squadron with 50 missions, or even in the Group with 50, who are flying any more. There are lots of pilots, however, who have racked up more than 50, but not in any shorter time than I have. I'd settle for 50 if they'd let me go tomorrow.

Cameron, who has been waiting for a Group operations job, was told today that any other Group jobs would be filled by VMA-121, VMF-312, VMF-323 pilots. However, there are other Group (MAG-33) and Wing jobs at other bases in Korea. I like to fly but can't stand to be shot at all the time.

I love you, my wonderful little family, and am waiting for that happy day when we'll all be together again. Tell Ricky I'm proud of the fine way he's acted during his bad period at home. I'm glad he's getting to be so grown up in so many of the nice little things he does. He's a fine boy, Mama, and I love him and Randy very much. Love to Nanna, Gramp, Peggy and Trooper.

*Night, night, precious,
Your very own Daddy*

19 Jun 52
Tunp o ri, Korea
Thursday

Dearest girl and my two precious little boys that I love,

I didn't fly today. Yes, you heard me right, darling. Last night I had a heck of a tight sinus condition and our squadron flight surgeon, Dr. Lindsey, gave me some nose drops that I've taken regularly to try and relieve the condition. Maybe it's caused from all this damn dust.

I was sure happy to hear Ricky has been sleeping all night long these days, and also that his appetite has picked up. Yes, I concur with you on the stomach shrinking deal. I have felt that way any number of times myself. I love that little guy so very much. I'm so happy he's growing into such a big fine boy and he has such a loving gentle way about him. I couldn't ask for a finer son. He makes me proud to be a daddy.

After the movie at 2230 the three of us went over to the mess hall and had a cup of coffee with a bowl of ice cream, of all things--first time it ever happened. Then at 2330 we went over to the Snivelers Club (a hut belonging to some VMA-212 pilots). They had a party going in honor of Col Bob Bryson's departure from the squadron.

Dick Francisco, an ex-boxer, and Lou Bass were putting on an act for the benefit of the gang. Francisco was supposedly buying beer from Lou, a liquor store operator, who was trying to wrap six cans of beer by stacking them on top of each other. They'd keep rolling off the table, naturally, and after three tries by Lou, with much to-do with his tongue, and help, help, ha, ha, from Fran, finally they all fell to the floor and Lou looked up into Fran's face (about six inches from his) and said, "We ain't got any beer."

The next act was Fran, the magician, and Lou, the straight man. Louie made the glorious introduction and Fran came out on the floor with a poncho over himself for a cape, and proceeded to tear Lou's shirt clear off of him. Lou just stood there and watched with a reassuring look on his face. Fran threw the poncho over Lou and said a bunch of mumbo jumbo, then pulled the poncho off of Lou and, of course, there stood Lou still with his ripped shirt (in absolute shreds) and Fran threw the poncho over himself and said, "And now I do a disappearing act," and made off of the stage with the gesture that Jackie Gleason does--"and away I go!" We almost died looking at Lou standing there like he lost his best friend. Boy, that Lou is a perfect straight man. Francisco is the perfect lead man. They're a heck of a lot funnier than Abbot and Costello.

I stayed about five minutes and paid my respects to Bryson, who had been presented the beautiful Remington shotgun and three shotgun shells with the name of each of his three daughters on them, "To get Patty married off," "To get Janie married off," etc. It was a cute idea. Bryson is really going to enjoy the gun. He's a great hunter. He's leaving for Miami soon to take over a new Marine Air Wing just forming down there. Lucky guy, he came out here on the 17th draft. Boy, would I love to be going home. I looked at him tonight and thought to myself, what a luck guy, going home to his loved ones.

I'm staying down again tomorrow, honey. We have a very light schedule because of the training going on in our squadron with the new AU-1, so the Doc said I'd better take advantage of it and give those sinus passages another day's break.

It's 20 minutes past midnight and I've got a musical program on. Nearly everyone has moved out of the hut except three of us, Cameron, Peterson, Snapper. We're all writing letters and listening to the music which really has a wonderful beat to it. Music sure helps a guy forget his troubles. Who's got troubles?

Tomorrow the hut is going to be invaded by Capts Codding, McMahon, Francisco, Thompson, McDonald, Budd, Hawkins--the biggest bunch of clowns and party boys in the whole squadron. I should move out and try and get a quiet hut, of which there isn't. At least Rainbow Jackson and his drinking buddies have left. Boy, there are sure some characters in this Marine Corps. Rainbow and his buddy, McClure (the guy that creamed the helicopter) went out on a raid of the houses of ill repute that have been springing up around the base. They arrested all the enlisted men they found there, then made them return to the base and turn themselves in to the guard house.

I love you, dearest girl, Daddy

20 Jun 52
Tunp o ri, Korea
Friday afternoon

Hi precious family,

Had another day on the ground, which I have enjoyed very much. I've read most of the March '52 Readers Digest, relaxed and listened to the radio. Tomorrow I'm going to start flying again. I think we'd all do a lot better if we only flew every other day. The tension sometimes catches up with a guy. My sinus is fine now.

This radio of mine has paid for itself a hundred times over. I helped some of the new men move into the hut today and the radio was going full blast. I'm getting the "Honshu Cowboy" loud and clear from Japan right now and he's playing all the latest cowboy songs.

We almost lost our swell little houseboy, Kim Jin Kil, to the group that moved out of here yesterday. Today the new boys moved in and brought their houseboy with them, so the houseboy papasan here on the base was going to take Kim Jin Kil but we talked him out of it, so now we have two boys. Kim is happy. He was with our squadron boys in Kangnung, K18, for a while and although his home is in Pusan he didn't want to go back there, so he came over here to K6. I saw him for the first time over here in late April when we moved. He's been a fine little houseboy and has been my good friend ever since we came over here. I think he likes me better than the group that moved out. (Feliton, Smith, McClune and Jackson stayed.) I brought Kim a fountain pen from Itami last time and he wanted to pay for it but I wouldn't let him. He has done a lot of extra things for me and he gets so little pay. He sends his money home to his mamasan in Pusan.

Six of our boys in the squadron all reported seeing a flying saucer over North Korea today. They all saw it very plainly and unmistakenly. Only last Wednesday the Group Operations officer told us to be on the lookout for such things and to report any strange or unusual sightings. Apparently other 5th Air Force pilots have made similar reportings in the past. Sounds very strange to me, but then, this is a very strange war.

Cameron slept in this morning and missed breakfast, so I grabbed a nice egg sandwich for him on my way out of the mess hall with Snapper; I can't see a guy go without his breakfast. Cameron was grateful and really enjoyed his breakfast in bed.

*Snapper is still with us but expects his orders to MACG-2 very shortly. He's had a lot of radar and electronic experience in the Marine Corps. It's kinda getting me wondering what sort of an assignment I'm going to land. I'll be happy if it's an engineering assignment with test hops, etc. There are a multitude of places I could go and many of them I'd prefer **NOT** to get, for example: front line FAC; OE-1 pilot at VMO-6; Marine Air Liaison Officer at the 1stMarDiv. Also they have control squadrons (radar) up near the front line that I'd not care about getting. This squadron duty isn't half bad compared to some of the remote outpost assignments they could put me in. Even though I get shot at when I'm flying, I can sleep at night without fear of anybody creeping up on me, or almost, anyway.*

It's nice having buddies to talk to and fly with, but boy, when you stack 12 men in a Quonset hut things really begin to happen: drinking, singing, radios, smoke, cards, etc. I can see I'm strictly a family man and this way of life isn't for me. Comradeship is a wonderful thing, though, and I'm always happy to meet new fellows and make friends. This has been quite an experience for me in that regard.

Francisco is directly across from me in the hut. Boy, we're going to be in for it now. I was talking to him today about what he was doing on the outside. He told me he was a coach and athletic director in or near Seattle. He coached a team of Marines from his reserve squadron and one of them has gone way up in his boxing profession. Francisco's nose is all busted and flattened out of shape. A guy sure does run into a bunch of characters. I guess I've said that a few times before, but it's sure worth saying again. Some of these fellows have been together ever since their Seattle Reserve Sqd got called up in October. They were lucky to get into 212 as they did. There must be about 15 or 20 of them, all from the same outfit.

Francisco just came over here and showed me pictures of his championship boxing team that he trained. The Hearst newspaper in Seattle paid all their expenses last summer to go to Boston by air. He took six of his boys in all the weights division, and they won second place back there. He also took his wife to take care of their diets. They boxed in Boston Gardens and stayed in the Magnus (or Magna) Hotel. Then he and his wife spent an extra week in New York, on Hearst, at the Waldorf Astoria. His team won trophies and they took the pictures he showed me. The bill he presented to the newspaper was for $12,000 and they never winced. They go every year (up to now, that is.) He has a little girl and a boy. Oh, I can see now I'll have a wealth of letter material. Hang onto your hat, honey.

Bye bye dearest,

Love, Daddy

21 Jun 52
Tunp o ri, Korea
Saturday

Darling girl,

Only two more days until Randy's third birthday, and only three more days until Mama's and Daddy's eighth wedding anniversary. I'll be thinking of the two occasions and wishing I were there to celebrate with you folks.

Today has really been a scorcher. I won't even try to guess how hot it was. Golly, when I came down from my mission this morning at 1100 my flight suit was wringing wet, and my underclothes could have had water wrung out of them. Got up at 0700, had breakfast and briefed at 0750. Took off on a close air support mission up to north of Kaesong with the control of the 1stMarDiv. We hit troop bunkers, trenches, mortars. Holland led the hop, I flew on his wing, and Maginnis and Budd were in the second section. We did a fine job of clobbering them. When I test fired my guns before my first attack, the nose cover on two of my rockets came off and blew back over the wing. It shook me for a second because I didn't know the method of arming the new type rockets. I fired them into the Communist positions about a minute later and got rid of them. I was glad to get them off of my plane.

When we take off from this field in the hot weather with no wind down the runway, and we're carrying 3000 pounds of external ordnance and a full load of gas, I sometimes wonder if the old gal is going to get off, and when she does it feels as though she were mushing back down into the ground instead of climbing, because of the heavy load. We landed without any mishaps. No. 51 completed. We could see the smoke and haze from our own destruction as well as that of others for many miles away. They've been having quite a fight north of Chorwon.

Our guys had a very bad day today. I won't go into it; however, just put this away and when I get home I can tell you all about it.

Kiss my little darlings and tell them I love them very, very much.

Bye bye, Daddy

22 Jun 52
Tunp o ri, Korea
Sunday noon

Dearest wifey Marion
and my darling Ricky and Randy,

I have to brief at 1430 for a CAS.

I've got some news, having just spoken with Paul Henley at chow. He's the Itami air base billeting officer and he just flew over a new AU-1 for our squadron. He says there are about 94 pilots at Itami right now from the 22nd draft. They will be arriving here (not all of them, of course) tomorrow. I'm almost positive there's a relief in the bunch for me, dearest. I'll let you know as soon as I find out. I was just counting the number of 19th draft fellows in our squadron: Southerland, Holland, Pittman, McGinnis, Barnum and I are to be relieved on the 19th draft. Snapper and Cameron are yet to be relieved on the 18th draft. A total of eight pilots. Snapper already knows he's going to MAC9-2 and Cameron knows he's going to the Group Operations Dept. None of us 19th guys know where we're going.

I had a nice breakfast, then went to church. It was a very good service and I was deeply touched. They passed the offering basket and collected quite a bit of money for the orphanage and other Christian missionary work around our base--outside of the base of course. I said prayers for my little family during the silent prayer period. I miss you all so very much. The only thing I want out of this life is to get home to my precious family.

I'll knock off until after my mission this afternoon.

BRAND NEW AU-1 CORSAIRS

Sunday evening

Hi baby girl,

Just came from the Group briefing. Something big is in the air. I can't tell you anything about it until it's all over with. Just keep this date and tomorrow's in mind and compare them with the news at a later date. There are sixteen of us going out tomorrow morning very, very early. This waiting kills me. Waiting, waiting, waiting--always suspense and not knowing what's next.

Completed No. 52 this afternoon up at the 1stMarDiv. We got credit for destroying nine bunkers and eight personnel shelters, destroyed mortars and troops also. **I led the division with our new CO, Col Benson, on my wing.** Stan Adams and Francisco were in the second section. We made a very rugged team. Nobody caught any hits from flak and all returned to base OK. I had to debrief, which is taking longer and longer because they keep adding more forms each time.

I was sweaty and tired but heard about the very important Group briefing that was coming off at 1900, so I ate supper in my flight gear. Had a wonderful steak with French fries, corn, peach pie and iced cocoa. Dashed over to shave and shower (thank gosh the water was on), then ran over and attended the Group briefing.

I found your wonderful letters of the 13th, 14th and 15th of June on my sack, so took them to the briefing with me. As important as the briefing was, I just had to read your letters. Gee, it's wonderful Ricky boy has been able to go outside and enjoy his trike and gym. The poor little darling has sure had a time of it, hasn't be? I'm so thankful he's out of trouble. Believe you me, honey, I sure sweated that little guy out.

I'm going to hit the pad early, lover, and try to get some shut-eye before this early-early big deal comes off in the morning. I love you, honey, with all my heart and soul. Give Ricky and Randy a kiss and hug from--

Daddy

LARGEST SINGLE AIR EFFORT OF THE KOREAN WAR

23 Jun 52
Tunp o ri, Korea
Monday, Randy boy's third birthday today

Dearest wifey and boys,

No mail today. Got up at 0500, had breakfast and briefed at 0530. We sat around until 0600--about 50 of us from all three squadrons. They said the weather had cancelled our mission, so we went on a standby basis waiting for the weather to clear up north. We finally briefed again at 1230, and for the first time they revealed the target to us. It was essentially the same type of target the 5th Air Force and four Navy carrier air groups were hitting today at 1600. There were over 20 major targets consisting of supply points and hydroelectric dams hit today by every plane in the 5th Air Force at exactly the same minute. Our target was a huge dam and hydroelectric point about 50 miles north of Wonsan and inland about 15 miles.

Fifty planes from our group took off at the same time and flew up to the target area some 250 miles from K6. We clobbered the dam. I flew an AU-1, carrying the heaviest load I have ever carried on any airplane. Can't reveal the load I carried, the AU-1 is still on the secret list. [It was an extremely heavy load of mixed ordnance, weighing over 4000 lbs, which was about 1000 lbs more than our old Corsairs could carry.] Some of the planes carried "Tiny Tims," the huge air-to-ground rocket which is eight feet long, and weighs over 1000 lbs. They whammed them into the dam and, along with the rest of the 50 planes' loads, we really gave them a blackout. Just imagine the punch the whole 5th Air Force could inflict upon 13 such dams.

It has been a standing order ever since the 5th Air Force has been in Korea to leave all dams and hydroelectric plants strictly alone. I guess they figured that now, since the peace talks are going so poorly, a blow of this nature would bring them to their senses. The knocking *out of dams will, in many places, cause floods and a complete lack of electricity throughout North Korea.*

Everybody in our Group came back OK. Two jet pilots had been downed, though, before we got there. Rescue plans were being carried out for them as we departed. We got loads of flak.

No. 52 completed. My head hurt, and aches so now that I believe I'm going to get grounded for a couple of days to get rid of this cold. We were at 15,000 feet before we started our dive, and the top of my head felt like it was coming off.

Today has been the largest single air effort of the whole Korean conflict. *I guess the reason they wanted us to hit it at 1600 was to indicate the combined single punch effectiveness of the Navy and 5th Air Force. I've been thinking of how this is going to shake the Communists. They never imagined we'd do anything as damaging as that. I'm dying to hear what they have to say at the peace tables tomorrow.*

Happy birthday to you, happy birthday to you, happy birthday, dear Randy, happy birthday to you. Gosh, what a big boy you're getting to be. Three years old! What I wouldn't give to be home with my family now. Birthdays don't ordinarily mean anything to me except now that my darling little boys are growing a year older every year, and before long they won't be babies any more. I'm sorry, Randy, that I wasn't on the ball with a birthday present for you, but there's one coming in a great big box. It will be there about 6 July. Mama will give it to you then, and sing happy birthday to you at that time.

You two precious little boys have enriched my life more than you'll ever know. You are very lucky boys, having such a wonderful precious, loving, devoted mother as you have. Your mommy and I will have been married eight years tomorrow. We love each other very, very much and being separated from each other is awfully hard on us. I want to ask your help, Ricky and Randy. While Daddy is away in Korea, you boys are the only men in our house. I'm asking you to look after Mama because she's a girl, and a girl always needs a man around to take care of her. You boys are getting big enough now to really help me while I'm away, by watching after Mama and helping her all you can around the house. I know Randy is still only a little boy, but you, Ricky, you're getting to be a big boy. You can really help me, honey. I want you to obey Mama by doing every single thing she asks you to do. Daddy has to take orders from his superiors all the time. I want you to kiss Mama and hug her a lot, and tell her how very much you love her. Mama needs a lot of love and kindness shown her while Daddy is away. You can straighten the garage out every night and put all your toys away inside and outside of the house. Don't go out of the yard unless Mama gives you permission. Pick up leaves and sticks and papers around the yard. Get the shovel and "play golf" with Lady's duties. You can water the edges of the lawn and put the sprinkler out. You can put the cans and garbage out the nights they are supposed to go out, and also bring them back in when they are emptied. I'm only telling you these things now because I think you've reached the age where you can take on more grown up responsibilities. When Randy gets your age he'll be able to help his big brother too. A big brother has a lot of responsibilities to his little brother too. You have to watch out for him constantly, Ricky. Don't let him go out of the yard, or even out front near the street. Tell him how fast the cars come by and how hard they can hit you if you get in their way.

The biggest thing you can do to help Mama is to keep your clothes clean and don't wear the knees out. Eat everything she feeds you and go to bed when Mama tells you to because you won't grow big and tall unless you get the right amount of food and sleep. Mama and Daddy know just exactly how much of each you need. Most important thing of all is to give Mama all your love, darling. I'm not there to love her and you boys are, so give her plenty. Tell her what a fine mama she is and what a grand job she's doing while I'm away at Korea. I don't think there has ever been a boy in the whole world that had a more important job than you do, Ricky boy. I'm so happy you're well again, honey boy. Take very good care of yourself. Always keep warm by wearing plenty of clothes and come in the house for a rest period or a nap so that you won't get too tired. The time you spend in the basket resting isn't wasted because even boxers and wrestlers and fighter pilots lie down and take a rest in the afternoon, and sometimes in the late mornings just before lunch. You're big enough, Ricky, so that you can start taking rests like big men sometimes do. It would be nice also because then the house would be quiet and Mama could have a little rest at that time too. Just think, Ricky, how busy Mama is every day for

Randy's and your comfort. You kids can afford to give Mom a little help now and then. The biggest help you can be, though, is to cooperate. Cooperation is obedience in action. You like action, don't you, Ricky?

I went to the movie tonight--"Iron Fist." I stayed exactly two minutes and shoved off. Boy, I'm sure getting particular lately. I can afford to, though, with a movie every night.

It's been miserably hot today. My flight suit is wringing wet from the three hours I spent in it today in the air. I've been in it most of the day, however. We landed at about 1530, ate supper and came over to take a shower and get out of our crummy, sweaty gear. No showers tonight, so poured a pan of water over myself, soaped up and rinsed off the same way. Shaved and put on clean underclothes, dressed and went to the Group brief at 1900. It's 2300, the door is wide open and the bugs are flying in like mad, but the air feels good. Every star in the heavens is out tonight. . .

Bill Crooks (of 524 Congaree, now of 323 here at K6) saw Gus Dake at Itami yesterday. He's out here finally, as part of the 22nd draft. I hope he gets MAG-12, I'd like to see him. Maybe he'll be my relief--ha, ha, could happen. I'll keep you posted.

My headache feels like it's going. Haven't seen the doc yet. Guess I'll wait until tomorrow.

Tell my precious boys that their daddy loves them and misses them very much.

I love you, precious girl,

Your very own Daddy

24 Jun 52
Tunp o ri, Korea
Tuesday

Hello little family,

This is Daddy talking to you from far off Korea. I sure do miss you all very, very much, but every day that passes brings me just that closer to the day that I'll be climbing on that big four-engined transport that will fly me home to my loved ones. We will surely make up for this separation in everything we'll be doing together when I come home. I'll be home for Christmas and it will be the most wonderful Christmas we've ever had. I've already written to Santa Claus and told him what I think you would like most to get for Christmas. I told him that Mama has told me that you boys have been pretty good so far this year, and if you continue to be good boys it would be OK to go ahead and give you the things you want the most.

Hello, Marion, my beloved wife. Today is our eighth wedding anniversary, and I thought it would be the best day to make a recording and send it home to you and let you know how very strongly I am thinking of you today, our day. First off, sweetheart, let me tell you how wonderful your letters are and how much they mean to me. Your loving thoughts and expressions are shared by me, dearest girl, you can rest assured of that. There isn't a day that goes by, Marion darling, that I don't thank God for His guidance in bringing you into my life. From the day I first met you, dear, my life has been fuller and richer than I ever dreamed life could be. Throughout our eight years we've been married we've been separated by two wars. Possibly when I return home this time we can look forward to no more separations and interruptions in our family's normal progress.

Today is a very warm clear day and if it were only southern California instead of South Korea everything would be perfect. How I'd love to take my little family for a ride up the coast, stopping at the beach along the way and having a picnic lunch. We've had such wonderful times together already in our rather brief but very full and happy life, and we've got a lot more happy times to look ahead to. Happy Anniversary, Marion dear, and may we have many, many more of them. I'm glad the gifts I sent to you arrived in plenty of time. I've enjoyed my R&Rs in Japan, but my heart is always so full for you and my boys that it's difficult to really enjoy myself.

Today the new draft is supposed to arrive from Japan, and I'm hoping there's a relief on the plane for me. I've completed 52 combat missions to date, honey, and I know how you feel *about my flying, so a transfer to a job that won't require me to fly quite as much will, I know, relieve your mind as well as mine. There are some very fine fellows in VMF-212 with me, and I have made a lot of new friends. That is one of the few things I can thank the Marine Corps for. All I can say to you, honey, is don't worry about me because I have everything I need here in Korea except you and my boys. The time is slipping by, sweetheart, and tomorrow we can cross three months off of the calendar.*

Give my love to Nanga, Ben, Nanna, Grampa, Peggy and Trooper, Lady and Felix, as well as all the neighbors that have asked about me. Kiss my two little darling boys for me and be sure to tell them their daddy loves them very much. Bye bye to you all.

Daddy

24 Jun 52
1645

Dearest girl,

I wrote this letter, then went over and cut some records this morning at the chaplain's office. The helper he had over there was a sergeant from VMF-323 who stopped working long enough at the squadron to come over and help me. The small ones are made out of aluminum and the machine had trouble cutting them, as you will be able to hear. The large one came out fair. It's made of plastic. I put them between cardboard and sent them airmail (80¢) this afternoon. I tried to cram too much on the records, and I'm afraid I didn't get what I truly felt over to you. We played them back and they didn't sound too sharp. Maybe it was the machine. I hope they sound better to you than they did to me.

Since I had a day off today, I got into three volley ball games. Boy, when we finished I was sunburned and sweating, so I took a bath out of a pan and felt better. Then I went down to the Group operation and stood by for a hot mission but they didn't need me. Francisco and I went over and met the R5D that came in from Itami. We were expecting the new boys (22nd draft) and I hoped to see Gus Dake. None of them have come over yet. Can't understand it--they've been in Itami since last Friday. Cameron is SDO today and he had the jeep, so Francisco and I went down to the squadron and checked on the mail with him. There wasn't any. Gosh, I'm spoiled. If I don't get a letter every day I'm sore. I just live for your letters, baby girl. I haven't the slightest idea what's to become of me. Hope it's an interesting job, at any rate.

Guess I'll knock off, baby doll, and post this little jewel. I adore you, honey girl, and can't wait until I have you in my arms again.

Love, Daddy

25 Jun 52
Tunp o ri, Korea
Wednesday afternoon

Dearest girl,

Boy, have things been happening around this place! Ever since we clobbered the Communists' hydroelectric plants we've been expecting some form of retaliation from them. The whole airfield went on alert last night when we got reports that a train had been attacked just a short way south of us by guerrillas. They'd killed ten Army men and 20 or 30 Koreans. We all carried our guns everywhere we went last night. They put on triple guards around the base and were just waiting for the guerrillas to hit us. The only thing that transpired, though, was some guerrillas were heard firing machine guns a long way off from the base. Then this morning we went on alert, every pilot on the base, to be ready to scramble every plane we had to some field south, out of Communist aircraft bombing range.

At 1200 I took off with three other fellows on a close air support mission with the 1stMarDiv. As we flew on the way north I could hear JOC (5th Air Force) giving vectors to the jets, "Steer 300° 50 miles at angels 5, unidentified aircraft approaching Inchon." We figured it was the incoming air raid and we were going to find ourselves right smack in the middle of it in *a matter of minutes. We proceeded north and switched radio channels to get our strike controller with the Division and lost out on what was happening in regard to the air strike. It may have been a dud, or else the friendly jets knocked them down. Will find out tonight on the news. Our strike went off very well--we knocked out two 76mm artillery positions and destroyed ten personnel bunkers. They were very pleased with the strike on the ground at the Division level. When we returned to the field at 1500 all the planes were lined up on the taxiways ready to be evacuated, but 15 minutes later they called down and cancelled the alert. I have a regularly scheduled strip alert tonight at 1855 until dark, then I'm secured. I have completed 53 missions now.*

Tonight we're going to get the same alert for the field on account of guerrillas. Boy, these alerts keep your stomach in a constant state of turmoil. No mail today. Re-read your letter of 16 June, dearest, and meant to mention how very pleased I am you're taking care of the Chevy on top of all your other work.

Despite the fact that sometimes flying keeps me busier than a one-armed paper hanger, I still think of you, darling. I need the feeling that I'm wanted and needed and loved. Here I feel like a very small cog in a very large wheel, just another fly-boy among many, just lost in this huge, messy shuffle, Korea. It's like we're sitting on a powder keg just waiting for somebody to light the fuse.

They have come up with some terrifying estimates of Communist strength just north of the bomb line. The radio has been full of news of our strikes up north on the hydroelectric plants, and last night a radio broadcast from Communist China (Peiping) told of our strike and hinted very strongly of retaliation raids.

The radio told of Communist uprisings in Osaka and Itami, Japan yesterday and today. They've cancelled all R&Rs for eight days on account of the Communist demonstrations in Japan, and also the need for every man at his station. Everybody is half shook around here at K6 for all the reported obits. Many men didn't get to sleep at all last night because they were pressed into special patrols around the base.

Later
1940

Hi baby girl and my darling boys,

The daddy is sitting out on the end of the runway writing this. There's a lovely orange sunset and a cool breeze blowing. Boy, this makes up for every bad thing that happened today. It would be heavenly if it were only like this all the time.

Hey, a great big four-engined Marine transport just came in and the huge wing passed only a few feet from my prop tip. Yes, you guessed it--the 22nd draft boys are on it. They are way down on the other end of the runway, but I heard the tower's unloading instructions to the transport pilot. I have Bing Crosby's stateside broadcast tuned in on my radio compass. Marilyn Maxwell is guest artist. They are putting the show on at Treasure Island Naval Station, San Francisco. None of the other guys could figure out how to pick up a commercial station on "bird dog" radio compass. I wouldn't tell them because it runs the batteries down too much. What's one little battery, though? Just think of the enjoyment it's bringing me as I stand my watch (sit my watch, that is). Bing's singing "I'm Nobody's Sweetheart Now." That's how I feel.

I'll have to go over to the transient quarters after I get off of this deal at 2030 and see if I can locate some of the new boys. Maybe Gus Dake will be there among them.

Kiss my precious little boys goodnight for me and tell them how much Daddy loves them and misses them.

Bye bye, angel girl,

Love, Daddy

THE HYDROELECTRIC STRIKES OF 23 JUNE 1952

Matthew B. Ridgway told members of the Senate Committee on Armed Services on 21 May 1952, the same month that 5th Air Force had begun to shift its air effort away from interdiction, "I think that the hostile forces opposing the Eighth Army . . . have a substantially greater offensive potential than at any time in the past . . ."

A number of factors contributed to the reduced emphasis on the interdiction strategy. The enemy, however, appears to have been most influenced with the inauguration of Operation PRESSURE, the name given the new policy of concentrating aerial attacks on major industrial targets considered of greatest value to the North Korean economy. Mounting 5th Air Force aircraft losses due to enemy flak (fire from ground-based antiaircraft weapons) and an insufficient number of replacements helped shape the new program. By April 1952 the 5th Air Force had received "only 131 replacement aircraft of the types engaged in rail interdiction against the 243 it had lost and the 290 major-damaged aircraft on interdiction sorties." These heavy losses had resulted from the increasing accuracy of Communist antiaircraft ground weapons, a capability Air Force planners had failed to consider sufficiently.

Although significant, this loss factor was not the final consideration in executing PRESSURE attacks against the power plants. More directly responsible were two other recent developments. These were the decision of the new UN commander, General Mark W. Clark, to take forceful action to bring the Communists around to an armistice agreement and a top-level Defense Department change of policy that had removed a major North Korean hydroelectric facility from the restricted bombing list. This was the Suiho plant, fourth largest in the world. Adjacent to the Yalu River, about 75 miles northeast of its mouth, Suiho supplied approximately 25 percent of the electrical power used in nearby northeast China.

Results of the PRESSURE strikes, carried on from 23-27 June, were highly successful. Marine, Navy, and Air Force planes flew 1650 attack and escort sorties in these raids. Of the 13 target plants attacked during this period, 11 were put out of commission and two others were presumably destroyed. North Korea was almost blacked out for two weeks. Chinese and Russian experts were rushed to North Korea to lend a hand in restoration. The hydroelectric strikes marked the first time that Marine, Navy, and Air Force pilots had flown a combined mission in Korea. The 23 June strike, moreover, was of particular significance to the 1st MAW since it was also the first time that MAGs-12 and -33 were assigned group strikes at specific adjacent targets at the same time.

Led by Col Robert E. Galer, the new MAG-12 commander since 25 May, Group pilots struck and leveled the single power complex, Chosin 3, in the 23-24 June runs. Col John P. Condon, who had taken over MAG-33 on 24 May, put 43 jets from VMFs-311 and -115 into the air during the two-day mission. The first time that its F9Fs had ever been massed for a strike of this type, the MAG-33 jets similarly destroyed the Chosin 4 plant, 11 miles northwest of Hamhung.

Although the jets carried a smaller payload than the Corsairs and ADs of MAG-12 (approximately 37 gross tons to more than 150 tons), the extremely precise bombing record made by the Grumman Panther jet pilots forever put to rest the doubts about jet accuracy that had been held by some in 1st MAW. As the Group commander later recalled, the capability of jet strike aircraft for extremely accurate bombing, an item of open discussion prior to this time, was never questioned in the 1st Marine Aircraft Wing after this mission. Another gratifying result was that flight personnel on all of the 150 Marine aircraft returned safely. In fact, of the total 1645 sorties, only two aircraft were downed; rescue aircraft successfully picked up these two pilots, both U.S. Navy officers.

26 Jun 52
Korea, Thursday

Hi honey
and Ricky and Randy boys,

  I have been looking over all the pictures I have of my little gang and three or four pictures make me wonder if Randy isn't straining himself, honey. I know I shouldn't worry about him, but I can't help it. Not having seen the little darlings for over three months is too much for me. You took the pictures of him pulling Ricky in the wagon with a load of weeds on the grass, also of him sitting on the bar of the teeter board. I know if and when I do any of those things, darling, I feel a strain on myself, and I know Randy will too. His condition is too delicate, dearest, to allow him to do everything a normal child his age could normally do; with those hernias he needs to be protected. I know what's going on in your head right now. You're saying, "The poor guy is over there with nothing to do but worry about his family." Well, you're right, but just the same, think about it a while, honey, and I believe you'll agree that certain types of strains of that sort aren't good for the little guy. Just tell me you'll not let him strain himself, honey. Talk to him, tell him what he can do and can't do. Tell Ricky about it too. If they hear it long enough and often enough they'll catch on. Don't get sore at me because I'm telling you this because I know you're probably too busy to watch him every minute of the day.

  Just came back from another all out effort that took our entire squadron of 13 planes, along with about 20 more from the other squadron, up to northern Korea where we hit the hydroelectric power plants again. Boy, it's a long way up. It takes three hours for a round trip, nine tenths of it over enemy held territory. The Air Force jets were clobbering another dam north of us when we got there. I flew an AU-1 again and carried a good size load.

  Mission No. 54 completed. Thirteen of the 22nd draft came into our squadron. Five of them are going to leave our squadron for VMF-312 aboard the carrier Bataan at the end of July. None of us 19th draft guys are being transferred this time. Tough luck. Oh well, maybe next month. Don't worry about me, dearest, I'll be OK. I'm going to go to work and try and get a Group engineering job of some kind. Maybe if I contact the right guy I'll be able to make them listen. If they turned me loose, I could fix most of these sick planes.

  Darn this mail situation. Received yours of the 13th, postmarked the 16th, the same day I received yours of the 15th, postmarked the 16th. Today I received yours of the 17th and 19th of June. You must have said something about Randy coming down with the measles in your letter of the 16th of June, which I haven't received, because in yours of the 17th you go right into your letter like I already know he had caught the measles. Darn this mail situation, I hate it. The poor little darling Randy boy has 'em now, does he? Doggone it, if it isn't one thing it's ten others. Take good care of the little guy, precious girl. Gee, honey, you're sure catching it from every angle. On top of all your other chores, you have to nurse two little guys back to health. I wish I were home to help out during these trying days.

  Glenn Smith received a letter today telling him his wife lost a $7 \frac{1}{2}$ month son, that is, it was dead at birth. It would have been their third boy. Smitty believes his wife lost it because of her worrying over him. He has a Group job now (special service officer). If only he had gotten out of flying two months ago, instead of one, maybe it would have been the difference. Every day I hear of awful things like that happening to my friends and it makes me realize that even though my little guys are down with the measles, they are OK and will get over it. You don't have to look around very much to find somebody else with a heap more troubles than you have, or I mean we have. Many of the fellows left their wives and children in strange towns in rented homes, with no friends or anything. It must be very lonely for a wife in a situation like that. I'm certainly thankful you're in the spot you are in, darling, even though you're working your tail off. It keeps you busy, and that's the most helpful single thing to keep from worrying.

  Cameron borrowed Snapper's camera a while ago and snapped a bunch of close-ups of the boys in our squadron. I'm sending them home for my scrap book that I'll get together someday, and probably give it to one of the boys at a much later date. I'm so happy Ricky is well again and running around engaging in his normal pursuit of happiness, as it were. Poor little Randy darling. I'm awfully happy to hear he's apparently got only a light case of it. I wish I could be there just the same. I feel so darn helpless over here.

I was sore at the Communists today, for a lot of reasons, and after I released my bombs I stayed on the deck and strafed a train, a bunch of box cars and some buildings, just to give them an extra dig. We were only supposed to make our bomb drop and get out because the flak was too hot in that area.

Tomorrow I have an interdiction mission up into North Korea. I'll sure be glad when my mission days are over. I work myself up into a sweat the night before, wondering what kind of a situation tomorrow's strike will get us into. This one today was an extra special deal the 5th Air Force dreamed up and only gave us thirty minutes notice. Everyone was shook when they learned the location of the strike, but everything came out OK. I'll sure be glad to return to a normal life like we were living, and be able to go to sleep at night and know that tomorrow doesn't hold anything in it that should shake you. I'll be able to sleep with all the security of a newborn babe all night long.

Tell Ricky and Randy that I enjoyed receiving the very nice drawings. They are doing real well.

Got a letter from Ben today. Told of getting a B+ in his exam. Good for him. He uses the durndest words. They aren't even in my dictionary.

I love you, precious wifey,

Daddy

27 Jun 52
Tunp o ri, Korea
Friday afternoon, 1800

Precious family,

The days are getting warmer and warmer, and longer and longer. It's daylight by 0445 and doesn't get dark until 2030.

My mission today took five of us (Pittman, Barnum, Col Axtell, Cameron and me) up to a red hot supply point 20 miles north of Kaesong. The weather was horrible and although it made finding the target very difficult, it made it equally hard for the Communist gunners to track us. We drew over 400 rounds of 37mm bursting type AA, and although there was lots of it all around us for the entire 20 minutes, we stayed over the target area seeking out supplies. Sighting them, we dropped out of the clouds from 8000 feet and clobbered them. Then we climbed back up, jinksing to avoid all the flak. They have hundred of guns of every caliber, and with a little more practice like we afforded them today they'll get real sharp. We missed our lunch completely and I doubt if I'd have eaten any anyway because the heat just plain old took everything out of me. It was 1500 when we got back and I was so tired and sweaty that I took a bath out of my pan, shaved and lay down for about an hour before going ahead with the other squadron chores.

Cameron got notified today he was to become the Marine liaison officer at Atsugi Air Base, near Tokyo in Japan. He'll be the only Marine there. His job will be to take care of all Marines coming and going through Atsugi. It's the spot of all spots. He'll have his own private jeep. Boy, did he fall into it that time. I'm tickled for him, though; he's a wonderful fellow. None of the rest of us have heard anything about our new assignments as yet.

Enjoyed receiving all the letters you enclosed. I received your letter of 20 June where you went for a walk around the block and had a cup of coffee with Mrs. Caruso and saw her babies. You said you were so lonely without me that you didn't know what to do with yourself. The same goes for me, honey girl.

I was so happy to hear Randy is free of all the measle rash. The precious little fellows have had their daddy pulling for them all along, dearest girl. You can bet your bottom dollar on that. Just knowing the darlings are well and that you are too, sweetheart, is all that I could possibly ask for. I love you, Marion, my dearest wifey, so very much. You're a real pal to me, darling, as well as companion and wife. We've got a whole world of happiness ahead of us, honey. We haven't begun to live, Marion dear. When I read Marge and G.W.'s letter saying the kids were glad to have their daddy home with them a choking feeling overtook me. I know how happy they must be to have their family all together again. No amount of money or any other kind of inducement will ever be able to tear me away from you again, precious family. I have always placed you at the very pinnacle of my admiration and enjoyment even before I had to leave you, and now it's driven the fact home to me a hundredfold over again.

2245

Returned from Group briefing and the movie, "Red Badge of Courage." It was fairly good--85%. Audie Murphy was in it. Civil War picture. He lost his nerve at first but regained it in the end to become a hero. Hurrah! Hurrah!]

Bill Crooks (of 524 Congaree) and I were having a chat about old times back in Columbia, SC. Boy, some of the tales Bill tells of Burns, Barnes, Greene, Foxworth, Chelson, Lease are fabulous. I never knew half of what actually went on. I guess the whole story can never be told.

Tomorrow I have a close air support mission with the 1stMarDiv at 1000. Budd, Barnum, Cameron, Peterson are the lineup. Budd is a rather new boy to the squadron and they are scheduling us older guys in second division to ride herd on the newer guys until they get more experienced.

They keep scheduling us guys every day. Can't understand it. We've got a mess of new guys that are ready to go, but still they fly us old guys every single day. I'll be glad when R&R comes again and I can say goodbye to the Corsairs and the Communists for a while.

Some of your letters are a scream, honey. You wait to write to me until too late at night and you're falling asleep half the time. Your writing shows it sometimes. You'll be writing along and all of a sudden you're off the page on a slant. Then you'll say, "Sorry, Daddy, I fell asleep." I love you and your letters and I don't care if you do fall asleep when you're writing to me, just as long as you keep on writing.

Kiss my little guys goodnight and keep a couple of kisses for yourself, angel girl. I miss you all so very, very much. This place can sure be lonely with all these guys around--funny, isn't it, honey?

*Your very own Daddy
that loves you*

P.S. Gus Dake is up at VMO-6 with the 1stMarDiv. I'll have to try to fly up and see him.

28 Jun 52
Tunp o ri, Korea
Saturday afternoon

Darlings,

Boy, has it every been hot and muggy today. Just like the weather we had when we were married in South Carolina.

We briefed for our mission at 0955 and were the first mission to get off of this field today because of the awful weather. Capt Budd led the hop, with Cameron on his wing, and I led the second section with McGinnis on my wing. The weather was so horrible when we got to our orbit point up near the Division that they wanted to divert us to a high altitude (over the overcast type of radar controlled drop). McGinnis and I had napalm, which doesn't drop like a bomb but tumbles through the air crazy-like, and would fall far short of the target if dropped from an altitude of 14,000 feet. They split our division up, sending Budd and Cameron, with the 1000-lb bombs, up to 14,000 feet and turned them over to another corps sector ten miles east. I had to work with a forward air controller who couldn't see me because of the poor visibility and I could only see the target through holes in the overcast. Nevertheless, we destroyed a village, making a total of nine runs. The whole village was burned out. It was located right near the bombline and enemy troops had long since run all the Korean civilians out. The Marine *forward air controller, whose call sign was Cassidy 14, said he had been posted on this one OP (observation post, forward) for a week and had been observing all the Communist Chinese activities. The Chinese figured we wouldn't clobber the Korean village because of the civilians, but hadn't taken into account the fact that we had spotters watching for a week to make sure before we did destroy it. Pat McGinnis and I really worked the area over and Cassidy 14 was so thrilled with our work he was screaming his head off every time we'd make a drop. He asked our names and unit and said he was going to write it up for special recognition. Cameron and Budd rejoined us an hour later and we all returned to the field.*

I took a shower, or a splash bath out of a pan, shaved and shampooed my hair. I have a clean change of scivvies on and I'm feeling pretty OK now. My flight suit and underclothes were wringing wet when I landed. The heat and the excitement were too much for me.

Received a letter from Ossippee, NH, written by your grandmother, Nanna Gleason, postmarked 21 June. Boy, that's really getting a letter out here fast, isn't it? No mail from anyone else.

Tonight they are having a welcoming party at the O'Club for the 22nd draft. Free drinks. There probably won't be much chance to get any sleep tonight. I may stop over to say hello to the new boys, then shove off early. Still haven't had a drink of any alcoholic beverage or a single puff of anything. The guys keep asking me if I'm going to become a chaplain or something. I tell them that what with all the spare time available, no place to go, nothing to do, if a guy got started he wouldn't be able to stop. They all agree, but do it anyway. Nobody overdoes it, though. It's very surprising, to say the least. Nearly everyone flying feels as though they need a clear head to fly these early morning deals they throw at us.

It's raining or sprinkling very lightly now. First time all day. My door is open and a refreshing breeze has just begun to blow. It sure is a relief from this heat we've been having. I'm going to chow now, darling. . . .

2000

Hi, I'm back again.

We had pork chops, boiled spuds, gravy, corn, peach pie, ice water. I couldn't drink enough ice water. I've sweat so much today I was almost dehydrated. They haven't broken out the salt tablets yet, but they probably will before long. Just checked the flight schedule for tomorrow and I have the early-early (ready alert, strip alert, what-have-you). Briefs at 0315, which means I'll be getting up at 0230. Then I have an interdiction mission later tomorrow; sounds like a rough schedule.

I'm listening to the Japanese Star Girl singing "Come On To My House" in Japanese. It's sure funny. Boy, those darn Japanese mock everything that comes out of America. I wrote Nanna Gleason in New Hampshire. I like to answer all my letters as soon as they arrive so they don't start piling up. Keep your spirits up, darling, and so will I. Every day that passes brings me just that much closer to you. Night night to the little guys.

29 Jun 52
Tunp o ri, Korea
Sunday afternoon

Dear ones,

How's my little family today? Received two letters from my precious girl today, postmarked the 21st and 22nd of June. Your mom had just returned from shopping in Inglewood for Randy's birthday gifts. You certainly did knock yourself out Sunday, baby doll. Boy, you're rugged, out there mowing that huge lawn. I've said it before, and I'll say it again, I'm not going to pick any fights with you when I get home, for fear of getting knocked on my butt by my (Mrs. Atlas) wifey. I was sure happy to hear my boys are doing so fine. . .

I'm listening to Amos and Andy. At 1900 tonight Jack Benny's coming on. I'll have to catch him at some other time, though, because I have to attend a Group briefing at 1900, in 15 minutes, in fact.

We had a rugged rain, wind and thunder storm last night. All day long today we had low ceilings and, although no rain, we were unable to get any missions off. I was supposed to have the early-early this morning, arising at 0230, but the duty officer didn't wake us up because it was raining, then we had about 50 kts of wind blowing. We briefed at 0845 for a 50-plane bridge cut at or near the Sinanju estuary. It didn't go, as I said before, on account of the weather.

2215

Back from the Group briefing and movie. Saw "At Swords Point" with Cornel Wilde, Maurine O'Hara. Very good--99%--lots of kissing, loving and excitement.

The Group briefing tonight was called especially because a Major Happy Harris of the Air Force, who flies F-86 Sabrejets, was down here to give us a few well chosen words about the Sabre and the MIGs, which he did for precisely 1 1/2 hours solid. It was very interesting and he answered many questions I had kicking around in my mind. He brought his gun camera movies along, showing a number of MIG kills.

I'm scheduled for the same thing tomorrow as I was today. 0230 reveille. 0315 brief for ready alert, then brief again at around 0845 for the big deal bridge cut up at Sinanju. More about it tomorrow, dearest girl.

I finally got my dungarees, caps, undershirts, shorts and jacket for free. I was confronted with paying for the whole mess because, for some vague reason, they said they weren't issuing any free clothing to any drafts except the 21st and 22nd. I thought it was a dumb decision and went directly to Col Bob Galer's office and told him so. He agreed and sent Col Gray with me to the supply officer and he immediately OK'd my slip. I paved the way for about 25 other officers that had been turned down. They sure arrive at some stupid decisions around here.

I'm going to hit the basket because it's 2225 and 0230 comes around awful early. Good night, darlings.

Love,

Daddy

30 Jun 52
Tunp o ri, Korea
Monday afternoon

Hello there little gang that I love,

Boy, what a place to be when the weather is hanging 300 feet off the deck, raining like mad. Arose at 0245 this morning, got into my plane and taxied out to the end of the runway, and the four of us parked ourselves there until 0540. It rained continuously the whole time. We got soaked to the skin getting in and out. If the Operations Dept had been on the ball like they were yesterday, they could have had the ready alert cancelled because of the minimum ceilings, visibility, and rain. Crawled back into the sack at 0615 after drying myself off and hanging my flight suit up to dry. Got a couple of hours sleep before the duty officer informed me they were having a division leader's meeting at Group Operations. I attended. It was boring. They talked of ordnance fusing and best type of delays to fuse bombs for railcut, bridge cut, etc. Nothing could bore me more completely. I was totally aware of everything they presented at that meeting.

For lunch we had weenies and sauerkraut and then I had a haircut. The barber has a vibrator he uses on your scalp, back and shoulders. It's wonderful and relaxing. I'm definitely going to get one in Japan next R&R. I can massage your back for you when I get home. You complain a lot of a tired back and this vibrator would really fix you up fine. Ricky would probably enjoy it too. I'd like to buy some binoculars; they cost around $18.00 for a 750X50 pair with case. They'd be nice to have for trips and sporting events. We'd enjoy them, I know.

My radio is playing some soft, lazy, dreamy music and it's befitting the way I feel today. It sure can get lonely in a place like this, so far away from everyone you love and everyone who loves you. The dreary, rainy days aren't for me, even at home, and at a place like this it's a hundred times worse. I guess it's not much different than being in jail. I'm not despondent, though, dear. I can feel your love coming out these many thousands of miles to me.

Sometimes I feel as though you were really very close by, but of course never close enough. It's very doubtful if we'll get a mail plane in today because of the flying weather. I haven't given up hope yet, though.

Signing off now with all my love,

Daddy

LOG FOR JUNE 1952

Date	Aircraft Type	Aircraft Number	Flight Duration	Type of Mission
1	F4U-4B	97470	1.3	CAS--Bunker and Trenches
2	F4U-4B	63057	3.1	TARCAP--Taeul-li - Trenches - Mortars
2	F4U-4B	62959	1.7	CAS--Chirung-dong
13	F4U-4B	97489	2.3	CAS (MD) Bunkers A/W Mor. Pos. Sokchuwon-ni
15	AU-1	129332	1.3	Fam.
15	F4U-4B	63057	2.2	CAS--Bunkers & Mortars Sajang-dong
16	AU-1	129335	1.4	Fam.
16	AU-1	129327	1.7	Railcut (Channampo) Yonan
17	F4U-4B	62993	1.5	Interdiction - Sangchongsong
18	F4U-4B	62997	3.0	TARCAP
21	F4U-4B	62993	1.6	CAS - Bunkers Mor. Pos. Nulmong-ni
22	F4U-4B	62993	1.6	CAS
23	AU-1	129340	3.1	Interdiction--Ryusui-ri Hydroplant
25	AU-1	129332	1.8	CAS
26	AU-1	129320	2.8	Interdiction--Ryusui-ri Hydroplant
27	AU-1	129320	1.5	Interdiction--Youdong-ni
28	F4U-4B	62933	2.1	CAS--Toksan-ni

1 Jul 52
Tunp o ri, Korea
Tuesday afternoon

Dearest girl,

I'm the SDO today and, although the weather is poor and most of the morning missions were cancelled, I've had quite a time contacting men for a special mission going out this afternoon. I have a truck to drive and the mud is terrific after the heavy rain storm we had, and you find yourself broadside half the time. Gosh, I haven't driven a truck in ages. It's been a pleasant change from flying a Corsair, I can tell you.

You sure had a time of it with all the chores, and the boys sick with the measles. I'm sorry things had to turn out as they did for you, honey girl. I'd love to have sat up with my little guys and rocked them all night long if need be. My schedule consists of every imaginable hour anyway. I'm getting used to going to work at 0230. At first I thought it was horrible, but you know there's something mysterious about the early morning calm. I can get along without it, however. . . . I think you've done really well with the pictures, dearest, and there's only one thing I could suggest, and that's to snap more action shots of the kids at play. Get your darling self into some of them too. I don't care if you're in your dungarees and are knocking yourself out. I want to see pictures of my loved ones. I wish I could go over the hill for a month. Oh well, honey, just think of the wonderful time we'll have when I do get home.

A smoke bomb just blew up down on the strip and the wind is blowing the smoke right over the area and into the hut. Everyone is coughing and it's really hard to see. The bomb is more correctly a smoke tank, carried on the belly of a plane which, when flown low over the battle lines, affords a smoke screen for our troops. Boy, it's really gagging me. Never a dull moment around K6!

I have 57 missions, dearest. I went over and counted them in my log book.

I had heard of the big ammo dump near Pusan going off, but it won't affect us. We've got more than we'll ever be able to deliver. As for your query about my becoming a forward air controller, I can't say, honey. I do know that it would be a dirty deal sending any of us 19th draft guys up there after we've literally busted our butts for them while we've been in the squadron. The practice has been to select men from the squadrons, regardless of the amount of time they have put in the squadron, so that may happen. They are quite sympathetic about us in the squadron, as far as squadron level is concerned. Group and Wing level is something else again. I'm making the fact very well known that I want an engineering job if one is to be had.

Lt Pierce just came in the hut, and his pants were half eaten away from the effects of the acid in the smoke bomb. He says the sun suddenly came out while the bomb was on a trailer out in the open, and the heat from the sun made the thing start smoking. Pierce asked the CO's permission to let him dump the remaining contents (which is an acid) and the CO consented. In dumping it, he spilled some acid on his pants and was fortunate in not getting any on his skin. As soon as the acid hits the air it turns to smoke.

The weather north of the bomb line is still very bad, but it's cleared up around here, so as squadron duty officer I've sent up some new boys on four hops in the AU-1. They are diving at the field and doing rolls, loops etc up above the field. The weather west of us looks sort of bad. I wouldn't be surprised to see another storm move in right behind this last one we've had. Got to get to work over at the squadron. Back to my truck and the mud.

Keep up your spirits. All my love,

Daddy

2 Jul 52
Tunp o ri, Korea

Hello little family,

Low clouds hanging overhead about 500 feet have kept us all on the ground today. Last night we attended a lecture which went clear past the movie, so consequently I didn't get to take in the movie. All day today has been spent listening to lectures and I participated in several of them, passing on some hints as to attack procedure and the characteristics of the AU-1 in combat, carrying a combat load. I rather enjoyed my end of it--guess I'm a born gabber.

As the situation appears at this writing, I stand to go on R&R the 7th of July.

Good news, honey girl. Capt Hugh Holland got his orders to the Group today. He leaves the squadron tomorrow for his new duty assignment. Hugh and I reported into the squadron on the same day from the 19th draft. I spoke to Maj Webster, our personnel officer in the squadron, this morning and told him how very much I desired an engineering job. He said he'd go to bat for me with the Group and see what could be done. I hope everything works out OK. I've knocked myself out in the squadron for them and now it's their turn to give me a break. Keep thinking right thoughts, precious wifey.

Three of the boys returned from R&R this morning and they were given two extra days to make up for the two days restriction they had placed on them at Itami, due to the Communist demonstrations in Osaka. The Stars and Stripes said there were 3000 demonstrators and they had a heck of a flight. I sure hope that's all over with by the 7th, when I go over there. If any of them get tough with me they'll get a knife between their ribs, and that's no fooling. A Communist is a Communist, whether he's in Korea, Japan or the U.S.

I received a swell letter from Mike LaScala--two full typewritten pages. He can sure write a fine letter. They are going to San Francisco on the 20th of July and when they return they are all going to the Great Lakes area. They are certainly a fine family, aren't they, honey? I just answered Mikes' letter last night. Like to get my answers off as soon as possible because that means another letter just that much sooner....

Brother, I'm still holding my breath. Maj Webster just came in the hut asking for volunteers for Forward Air Controller. He looked at me sitting here writing and asked where Capt Codding was. He asked if I knew anybody in this hut that wanted it. I told him that I didn't know of anybody. He said that if they don't hear from three volunteers tonight they are going to draw names out of a hat. Golly, I sure hope they somehow or other miss me. Maybe our little chat (Webster and I) this morning will keep me off of it. I'll keep you posted, darling.

I forgot to compliment Ricky and Randy on the very nice pictures they have been sending me lately. They sure are doing well with their art work. Ricky's tree was really sharp. I got a kick out of Randy's "eyes" in everything. Isn't it wonderful how the little guys develop? Each one of them has different talents, habits, likes and dislikes. They are most certainly individual. If we could afford it I'd like even more than three children, but I know, darling, how that would set with you. You've had so much of babies, boys and measles, colds etc all by yourself during the past three months I suppose your only thought on the subject is "To heck with it." I can sympathize with you, dearest, and I believe I know how you feel about more children at this time. Although you have consented to trying for a little girl when I come home, and that's exactly what we will do--any thought of a fourth will just have to wait for several years. I can hardly imagine life without a precious little Marion or a little Spud running around the house. It's certainly been a heartache being away from my little family. When I find myself getting too lonely, I break out my pictures and your letters and they help a heck of a lot to ease the pain, darling.

2000

Just came back from the Group briefing. They gave us the weekly intelligence summary; 39,000 enemy artillery rounds fell across our front line from 10-20 June, 18,000 rounds fell on the 1stMarDiv sector alone. Brother, that's a lot of rounds. The rounds vary in size from 75mm to 155mm. The lecture lasted one hour and we learned a heck of a lot of top secret info I won't be able to pass on to you at this time. We have Group meetings every Sunday, Monday, Wednesday and Friday evenings at 1900, and on Tuesday evenings at 1900 we have our squadron meeting, which lasted several hours last night and several more hours this morning. I've received so darn much information in the past year my head feels the size of a watermelon.

Due to the increasingly inclement weather we've been having, we are conducting an instrument training ground and air course, to be carried out during non-combat mission hours, aircraft availability permitting. At the meeting tonight Maj Webster asked for three volunteers for FAC. Two 2nd Lts have volunteered but they won't take them because they aren't experienced with the Korean close air support doctrine. Brother!!! They said two of the three will have to be either regular or reserves that have integrated. The other can be a reserve of any qualification. They also said they wouldn't select any of the pilots that just came into the squadron within the past month. That narrows it down considerably. Nobody else spoke up, so he said, "OK, we'll draw the names out of a hat in the morning and announce the winners tomorrow." I can really feel them breathing down my neck. If I can just sweat this out I'll be all set. I hope the good Lord is on my side again, as He apparently has been these past three months.

Going to knock off for a while and go see "An American in Paris" for the second time. See ya later, honey that I love. It's quite cool tonight. I'll need my jacket on at the movie, for the first time in a month.

2245

Boy, that was a long picture! Started at 2030 or thereabouts and just busted up. I enjoyed it just as much the second time as I did the first. The color and dancing, singing, and the love story were terrific. If you haven't seen it, sweetheart, do so at your very first opportunity.

Just saw the schedule. I've got quite a day, weather permitting tomorrow. I'm leading a four-plane interdiction into a supply center at 1010, then again at 1500 (3:00 PM). Cameron is leading a division of four and I the second four-plane division of new men up to the Haeju peninsula for a railcut and bridgecut. Should prove to be a very interesting day. Col Benson and Maj Webster are in my first strike. I'll have to give them a good lead, or else.

It's 2300, so guess I'll hit the basket. Tell my darling little guys that Daddy loves them and misses them very much.

Keep your spirits up, darling, our day is not too far off.

All my love, Daddy

Author in cockpit of his F4U-4B Corsair fighter, being assisted by one of our able VMA-212 plane captains. Our squadron was operating out of K6, P'yongt'aek, Tunp o ri, South Korea, June 1952.

Aerial view of pock-marked terrain in front of Boulder City as seen from HMR-161 helicopter. Photo credit: USMC

Top and middle of page: South Korean Won notes.

Below: F9F Panther jet fighter taxies down runway preparatory to takeoff.

CHAPTER 12

THE SHORT STRAW

4th of July 52
Tunp o ri, Korea
Friday afternoon

Hello dearest girl,
Well, it's official. I have been designated as a Forward Air Controller with the 1stMarDiv. They selected Cole, Pittman and myself from our squadron and three from each of the other two squadrons. We all leave for a week's R&R right away. I'm sitting here waiting for the plane to land any minute. Don't get shook, honey girl. This problem of selection fell upon our CO, Col Benson, who is a good egg, but, lacking volunteers, he was forced to choose three men from his squadron. Majors were omitted due to their rank, and 22nd draft men were not considered because they had not yet completed their missions. That left a total of 24 names from which to draw. The 1st Marine Aircraft Wing had placed the situation in the colonel's lap and he had no other choice. He pulled three numbers out of the hat: Cole, Peterson, Pittman, in that order.

Itami Japan

Hi honey,
Just landed at 1815, ate supper, and now I'm writing to my precious girl again. Let's see, where was I?
The best battle training ground in the world for training regulars or extended reserves in the art of forward air controlling is right here in Korea. These important coordinators are now being prepared for use in the new three-wing and three-division Marine Corps, which is soon to come into being. However, there are regulars out there with forward air controller MOS numbers from stateside training, but they are not being used up there at the Division--SNAFU!
I'm due back at K6 VMA-212 on 11 July, then 12 July K3 (Wing), then 20 July K6 again for my gear and checkout; then up to the Division to start a completely new phase of my short Marine Corps tour of duty.
There are many jobs as air controller that won't take me into the front lines, darling. Let me give you a breakdown of the situation. First we have the division (TACC)--Tactical Air Control Center.

```
                              TACC
              TADC                        TADC (Tactical Air Direction Center)
      TACP        TACP           TACP     TACP (Tactical Air Control Party)
   FAC   FAC FAC      FAC     FAC    FAC- FAC    FAC (Forward Air Controllers)
```

CAPTAIN BIBEE CRASHES ON TAKEOFF
I FLY MY LAST COMBAT MISSION IN A CORSAIR

They have FACs up with companies at the very front lines, TACP at the regiment levels, and TADC and TACC at the division level, as Dave Kennedy used to say, "In the rear with the gear." Hopefully I'll wind up in one of the latter.

Tomorrow evening about five of us are going into the Takarazuka Air Force R&R Hotel to attend a 5th of July, Saturday night party, steak dinner, floor show--for $1.00.

Last night I didn't write because I didn't land from my mission until almost dark. Then, after I ate and washed it was 2330 and I hit the sack. We had waited on a ready standby basis at the squadron for seven hours, from 1030 until 1730, before the weather cleared and our target information--coordinates and photographs--were flown down to us by the 5th Air Force courier plane. We studied the maps and photographs and I briefed my flight. We manned our planes, and mine developed a heck of a hydraulic leak at the wing-folding mechanism even before I taxied out. I cut my engine, crawled out and went over to one of the 21st draft men, who was in his plane turning up, and told him to give his plane to me. He got out and I got in, and just before we taxied out another division from our squadron was taking off.

Just as Capt Bibee got airborne while taking off about in the middle of the runway, he lost control of his plane. Off he went on one wing, cartwheeled, landed on his back and tore his whole tail off right in front of us. We just held our breath, waiting for his (2) 1000-lb bombs to go off any second, or for his plane to burst on fire, which would surely have leveled our whole line of planes (me too), but they didn't, fortunately. Capt Bibee only got his back wrenched. He was one lucky boy.

After the crash crew cleaned his wreck away I took my flight off, all of us still somewhat shaken from what we had just witnessed. The clouds were billowing, tall, cumulonimbus, and we encountered occasional rain squalls as we climbed out on course. The towering clouds reached all the way up to 12,000 feet and required considerable circumnavigating for the 125 miles to the target area. Our target, a group of bunkers containing supplies, was located north of the bomb line 12 miles, but required radar control prior to release. I radioed "Hothouse" radar controller and requested a bearing to my target, giving him the coordinates. He gave me my steer and I led the eight planes in on the target.

We were scoshe (low) on gas as we headed home because we had carried 3400 pounds of bombs each up there, with no external fuel tanks. That heavy load required considerably more power than normal. By following rivers and mountain roads, I made it home with my division and landed OK. No. 58 completed.

I was very upset over learning of my new assignment, but am gradually reconciling myself to it. It's mainly the fear of the unknown that's bothering me at this point. Keep your chin up, precious girl. We've got half of our tour over with and, if need be, we'll weather this new assignment.

Lots of love to you and the boys,

Daddy

Thinking back to that last combat mission, actually the last flight I would ever have in the F4U Corsair, I recall sensing a mixture of relief and sorrow all rolled up into one big emotional blur. As I cut the switches and heard that powerful Pratt and Whitney 2000-plus HP engine come to a crunching halt and, perhaps for the last time, read "Hamilton Standard" on the back of that big, wide paddle blade of the 13-foot diameter prop, a strange feeling possessed me.

I just sat there for a while, reflecting back to my first introduction to the F4U at Congaree Field, SC, with VMF-524, on that June day in 1944, eight years earlier. Then my recollection skipped forward to my last flight at Okinawa at war's end in 1945 after completing 80 missions in the bent wing bird with VMF-223. Upon leaving the service in November 1945, I had thought my flying days were probably over. At that time nothing could have been further from my mind than the consideration of voluntarily joining anything of a combative nature ever again. But how was I to know that the threat of world Communism would inevitably draw me closer to the one thing I dreaded most--killing my fellow man?

My fleeting thoughts carried me swiftly to the day I volunteered to fight once again for a free world, and I saw myself suddenly back in my old F4U Corsair at El Toro MCAS, CA, in July 1951. Here in Korea, a year later, after crawling out of my plane and debriefing my last mission, I felt as though I truly was saying goodbye to an old friend, who had always gotten me and most of my flying buddies home safely to terra firma.

This essentially ended all of my association with a squadron and all that it represented--the good and the bad, the ups and the downs, the joys and the agonies, carefree times and the tragedy of losing a buddy. And now I was embarking upon an entirely different tour of duty, completely foreign to me, and one fraught with uncertainty and fear of the unknown.

5 Jul 52
Itami, Japan

Dearest girl,

This evening Cozy Cole, Pittman, Moore and Peterson (all new FACs), along with Jack Rummel and Sutherland, boarded a station truck and rode into the Takarazuka Hotel where we had a very fine barbecued steak, cooked on an outside grill over charcoals. We took our plates inside to the dining room and ate, however. Had French fries, salad and coffee also. They had a dance band and about ten Air Force officers with their wives were dancing. They looked so very happy together it made me sick inside, missing you, my precious girl. There was a floor show, consisting of a magician and his cute little three-year-old son acting as his assistant. Six dancing girls in abbreviated costumes danced several numbers. It lasted about 15 minutes, after which Rummel, Moore and I walked to the train station, one and a half miles, and rode back here to Itami.

So now I'm an FAC. Oh well, at least I'm not getting shot at in my Corsair. Let's worry about it after I find out what it's like. Worrying never helped anybody anyway. I've had some rough assignments before and have always met them.

I drew my seabag (the brown one that was yours when you were in the Marine Corps) out of storage here this morning. It's got my steel helmet, web belt, canteen, mess kit, entrenching tool, two blankets and gas mask. I learned from Pearce that my other bag went over the side of the ship at Kobe last April. All my swell engineering books were in it, and most of my cold weather gear went too, but I can survey it. Can't retrieve my books, though, darn it.

Here's where the Marines differ from the Army Air Force and the Navy. When we left the States they issued us pilots this gear traditionally carried by marine foot soldiers, just as though they figured we'd be needing it somewhere along the line and, as Marines, we should be ready for anything and everything. Never dreaming that I'd ever use the stuff, now I'm eying it with the thought in mind that it could save my life up where I'm going. Hope I'm not out here long enough to have a need for the cold weather gear that went over the side. If I am, I'll draw some more.

Bought a few pieces of brass ware, bells and ash trays--$3.00--at the PX here, imported from India, crude art work but interesting just the same. I'm going to buy everything you've requested and box it up and send it all in one, just prior to returning to Korea. Am going into either Kyoto for your silk, or Osaka for the binoculars and brief case tomorrow.

All my love,
Daddy

MARINE ATTACK SQUADRON 212
MARINE AIRCRAFT GROUP 12
1st Marine Aircraft Wing, FMF
c/o FPO, San Francisco, California

FLIGHT SCHEDULE FOR 3 JULY 1952

PILOT	MISSION NO.	BRIEF	REMARKS
CAPT. COLE CAPT. SOREIDE CAPT. WATSON CAPT. KIME	1291	0315	READY ALERT
CAPT. COLE CAPT. SOREIDE CAPT. WATSON CAPT. WATERS	1251 4 AU 3-1000#GP NO NOSE 4-5 DELAY TAIL 4-100#GP NO NOSE 4-5 DELAY TAIL	0800	JOC ALERT
CAPT. PETERSON CAPT. HOLMES LTCOL BENSON MAJ. WEBSTER	1202 4 AU 3-1000#GP INST NOSE .025 TAIL 4-100GP INST NOSE .025 TAIL	1010	SUPPLY CENTER
CAPT. EDDENS CAPT. FOLTZ CAPT. STROM CAPT. MCCULLOUGH	1253 4-AU 3-1000#GP NO NOSE, 4-5 DELAY TAIL 4-100#GP INST NOSE, 4-5 DELAY TAIL	1300	JOC ALERT
CAPT. CAMERON CAPT. FOX CAPT. GIPPLE CAPT. MCARDLE CAPT. PETERSON CAPT. ALEXANDER CAPT. BIBEE 1stLT WELCH	1210 8-AU 2-1000#GP INST NOSE, .1 TAIL 8-100#GP INST NOSE, .1 TAIL	1500	RR BRIDGE (TRAINING)
CAPT. BARNUM CAPT. IVY MAJ. MICK CAPT. CALL	1243 2 A/C 3-1000#GP NO NOSE 4-5 DELAY TAIL; 6-100#GP 4-5 DELAY TAIL 2 A/C 3-NAPALM 6-100#GP 4-5 DELAY TAIL	1655	CAS (MAR DIV)

ALL PILOTS NOT SCHEDULED WILL STANDBY FOR INSTRUMENT AND FAM. HOPS.

O. D. O. - - - - CAPT MC MAHON

S. D. O. - - - - 1st LT. THOMPSON

H. R. FOLTZ
CAPT., USMC
ASST. FLIGHT OFFICER

ESTABLISHED IN 1657 - 8TH GENERATION

H. NISHIMURA'S LACQUER WARE FACTORY

MAKER OF ALL TYPES AND VARIETIES OF LACQUER WARE

Factory opened daily from 9.30 A.M. till 5.30 P.M.

OKAZAKI PARK (NIJO ST.) KYOTO

Tel. Yoshida ⑦ 3324.3310

三百年の傳統を誇る

象彥漆器店

陣列所には御実用向家具食器類御贈答品記念品等漆器なら
総て取揃へ陣列し何時でも御来店を御待ちして居ります

京都岡崎公園前　（二条通）　電話吉田⑦3324.3310

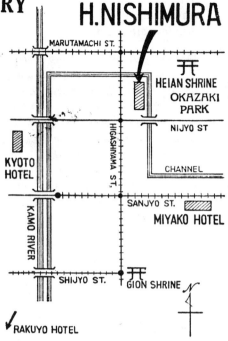

MANUFACTURERS AND EXPORTERS
OF
SILK FABRICS

Raw Silk Shantung,
KK Shantung, Satin,
Silk Gabardine & Brocade

MURASAKINO MIYANISHI-CHO'
(KURAMAGUCHI HORIKAWA HIGASHI)
NISHIJIN, KYOTO, JAPAN
TEL. NISHIJIN (4) 3162

KYOTO KIGYO GO., LTD.

京都機業株式會社
京都市上京區鞍馬口通堀川東入

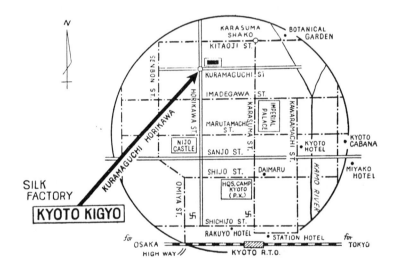

Your Favourite Souvenir Shop.

"OKUYAMA"

Silk Goods, Japanese Fine Arts.
Kimonos, Dressing Gowns, Shirt, Smoking Jacket, Jewel.
Table Cloth, China Ware, Camara, Binocular, and Fishing Set, E

No.26, 2-CHOME, SANNOMIYA-CHO
KOBE, JAPAN
TEL. FUKIAI ② 0966

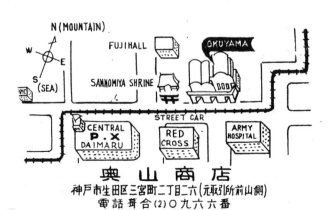

奥山商店
神戸市生田区三宮町二丁目二六（元取引所前山側）
電話葺合(2)〇九六六番

6 Jul 52
Itami, Japan
Sunday afternoon

Dearest girl and precious boys,
    I spent most of the day shopping in the big department store Damaru in Osaka. While making a purchase at the children's section I met an English speaking salesman who helped me the rest of the afternoon. He was just my age. He had been working at the store for 12 years, counting the interruption of the war years. He is a graduate of Tokyo University and held a rank of lieutenant in the Japanese army, based in Formosa. He never saw any action. His name is Yamamoto, a very likeable guy and he really put me at ease talking to him. He guided me all over the huge store which covers two blocks and rises seven stories. There was a special religious furniture room where he explained the different types of Buddha shrines and miniature furniture that they place in the shrines (in their homes) for worship. He is a Christian, however.
    I found some wonderful buys for the kids and bought my precious beloved wife five yards of silk cloth, four lacquer ware candy bowls and four lacquer ware trays, a leather brief case for myself, four toy cars for my darlings, three little fur covered toys (animals). If you squeeze the tummy of the little fur dog his mouth comes open. Had a heck of a time carrying all my packages to the train station and on the crowded train. Boy, was it hot too.
    Brought along your last six letters and all the pictures of my precious family, which I've looked at at least a half dozen times in the past day or two.
    The opera hasn't changed yet, so guess I won't go. May go swimming here on the base tomorrow. I've been so darn lonely for you and my darlings, honey, I just can't seem to concentrate on anything.
    All my love to you all,

                      Daddy

7 Jul 52
Itami, Japan
Monday evening

My darling Marion,
    There's a big beautiful orange moon shining outside, just made for you and me, dearest. I sure don't know what to do with myself, sweetheart. I'm a lost soul for sure. I might as well have stayed in Korea for all that I've been doing since coming over here this trip. It's doubly hard for me, seeing the Air Force dependents here. Every time I look at a little baby my heart cries out for my own precious little guys. When I see how happy some couples are over here it makes me bitter inside and resentful that I haven't got you beside me, darling. Don't worry about me; I'm not cracking up, just letting you know what's going on in this bonehead of mine half the time.
    Bought three more silk/rayon jackets just outside of the main gate at one of the new little gift shops that have sprung up. Got the large one for myself, one each for Joel and Mary. You decide between theirs. Bought you a birthday present, my darling, and I'll send it via 1st class mail tomorrow.
    Boy, those caliopsis and daisies have knocked themselves out, haven't they? Glad you weren't down long with your cold, sweety girl. Brother, I guess you're entitled to a cold or something, after what you've been through with the boys. Loss of sleep doesn't faze me anymore. In the past three months I have had so many nightly interruptions and early morning reveilles I have grown used to very little sleep.
    I got a charge out of Rick's and Butch's big conversation re the Missouri floods and Boulder Dam. I used to love to listen in on their conversations too. To me there's nothing sweeter in the whole world than watching and listening to one's little children at play.
    Went to a movie tonight and saw "Steel Town" with Ann Sheridan, in technicolor. It was only fair, about 75% is all that I can honestly rate it. Had a ham and egg and coffee breakfast at the PX, a malt for lunch, but ate a good supper tonight. Had pork chops, apple

sauce, mashed spuds with gravy, hot biscuits with butter and honey, milk and coffee, ice cream and peach cobbler, macaroni salad. Didn't eat a lot but had quite a variety of foods. I weigh 185 pounds dressed in my khakis and shoes, no more nor less than when I left in March. You say I look good and healthy in my pictures, honey. Well, I am well and healthy, but a little lonely, otherwise OK. You look your usual precious healthy self, dearest. The yard does provide you with a wonderful source of exercise, you must grudgingly admit, mustn't you, honey? I always hated it for its regularity but enjoyed it for its never ending source of invigorating exercise. (Who's fooling who!!?)

Hasn't Randy boy the sweetest little smile on in the picture with his birthday gifts? Boy, that Ricky guy is growing taller than a bean pole. You never said how you liked my part of the record meant for you, honey. Glad you played it for the darlings.

Kiss my precious little guys and tuck them into their beds with my blessings. Time's passing by, honey girl, even if only one day at a time. Love to all the family.

Daddy

8 Jul 52
Itami, Japan
Tuesday, 2200

Dearest girl and my precious boys that I love,

Today I dashed over to the post office and tried to get my huge box mailed but they haven't got the postal customs declaration cards in yet, so I left the box and went out on the strip, (shopping center outside the gate) and bought three Japanese copies of the famous American Ronsan cigarette lighters for a total of 700 yen. I'm going to give Eddie Butler, Ben and probably Mike LaScala the lighters. They are a real work of art for the money.

Decided I'd quit sitting around brooding and went into Takarazuka opera again this afternoon. They had the same opera and an additional one of a traditional Japanese legend. It was beautiful, as far as the gowns and robes were concerned. I'm sending a copy of the program. The Japanese legend part is on the back of the program.

Met a Dr. and Mrs. Drist (like in Christ). They are flying around the world via commercial airlines. They left San Francisco a short time ago and are on their way around. They had heard about the Takarazuka opera and made it a point to come all the way from Tokyo to see it. They were in their fifties. He's an eye, ear, nose and throat doc from Glendale, California. They asked about my family and where you were, and all about the flying in Korea. They'll be in Chicago in October and Glendale, California by November 1st. Boy, what a trip! I told them that was what you and I dreamed of doing sometime. We wished each other well and went our separate ways after the opera was over.

I walked around the corner and went into Abela's Italian restaurant where I had been last March. Had a nice platter of spaghetti and steak with garlic bread. It began raining as I was eating so I took my sweet time and finally, when the rain stopped, I made a dash to the train station, where I caught an Express by mistake. We never stopped until we got about ten miles past Itami. I got off and got on a local train that brought me back to Itami. The local had come from Kyoto and Osaka and it was filled to the brim with Japanese. I was squashed all the way to Itami. You sure get to know the Japanese people while riding on these darn trains. I was laughing to myself at how absolutely ridiculous it was. It kept getting worse too, as we went along. They'd stop and you'd swear another soul couldn't squeeze in and wham, here would come a dozen more charging in from the platform, the whistle would blow and bango, the sliding door would slam shut, and off we'd go. I was a full head taller than anybody else on the train and I was getting a bird's eye picture of the whole mess. Right under my armpit stood a little old grandma all squeezed up against a corner, and she didn't stand five feet tall. I saw a big toothless smile greeting me and I returned it (with teeth, ha, ha). Finally, after an eternity, Hatairagake station appeared and I squee-ee-ee-zed my way through, and what was that funny smell all of a sudden--fresh air?

I bought my houseboy at K6, Kim Jin Kil, a 170 yen (50¢) tee shirt, and myself a jersey short sleeved shirt for 350 yen, (less than a dollar). It's really swell. I'm sending it home for my darling to wear until I come home. Bought my binoculars on the strip on my way back to the base this evening. Haggled with the guy until he lowered the price almost 1000 yen and have me a genuine calfskin binocular case with leather belts to match, all for $18.00. They sell for $75.00 in the States. We'll be able to use them at races, on trips, up on Palos Verdes. They are made by the second biggest binocular company in Japan, Fuji. They make some of the finest cameras in Japan and also most of the Japanese film. The binoculars are called 7X50, which means they magnify seven times through a lens opening of 50mm, which is equal to about $2^{1/2}$ inches. They have a single finger adjustment which adjusts for both eyes simultaneously. Also it has an adjustable eye piece, in case your eyes are not the same strength. They have blue tinted and coated lenses for day or night work. I'm getting a big kick out of them. Maybe I'll take them with me to FAC because I suppose there will be a shortage of them up on the front lines.

    Time's passing, honey girl. Won't be long before I'm holding you close to me, my darling, telling you how very much I love you. Kiss my precious boys and tell them I love them and miss them very much too.

Daddy

9 Jul 52
Itami Air Base, Japan
Wednesday, 2100

Hello little family,
    Was just sitting here thinking about you all. I looked through all the pictures and talked with each one of you. I sure miss you guys, each and every one of you.

    I never left the base today, but stayed in my room most of the day reading the new July *Esquire* and *Popular Science* magazines.

    I forgot to tell you of a very interesting thing I saw on a little narrow street in Takarazuka yesterday in front of Abela's restaurant. An old Japanese man had a large box (portable deal) which had a tiny little stage and sliding cards with different scenes and characters and faces on each one. There were about ten kids gathered around real close, all wide-eyed, taking everything in with extreme passion and a hungry interest. He spoke in Japanese and made all kinds of weird and funny guttural sounds, according to the scene on the card he was showing the kids at the time. It was probably as close to television as they will ever see in their lives. The cobblestone and brick street was very rough and it was raining but, in spite of all this, the show went on. I'll never cease to be amazed at the sights I have seen here in Japan. Sometimes they seem so industrialized, educated and up and coming, and the next minute they seem 500 years behind the times.

    I saw a television for sale, however, several months ago in a Kobe department store. Maybe it's coming here too. With the electronic knowledge the Japanese have acquired, they certainly shouldn't have any trouble getting into the television business, if only they had the buying power that the American people have. They don't, that's for sure.

    I'm hearing from the Republican convention in Chicago. Herbert Hoover is speaking. Hope I can get this after I get back to Korea Friday. I guess he's trying to say we should only supply arms to the nations that desire to fight for their freedom, and more emphasis on air power. Enough of that....

I love you all dearly, Daddy

10 Jul 52
Itami Air Base, Japan
Thursday afternoon

Hello dearest girl and my two precious little guys,
    It began raining real early this morning and has continued to rain very hard all day long. I had thought of going into Takarazuka for a look at the zoo with my new binoculars, but the rain squelched my plans. I leave for Korea tomorrow, the exact time I will have to find out after 1900 this evening....

Above: Ordnance truck pulling empty bomb carts to depot for another load. K18 control tower can be seen off to the far right.
Van Dalsem photo collection.

Right: Napalm bomb being exploded in a test on our beach at K18, Kangnung.
Van Dalsem photo collection.

Left: Captain Robert Barnum on deck following a combat mission with VMA-212. Aircraft serial number shows it is one of our new AU-1 Corsairs.
Barnum photo collection

Right: Korean school children our air group helped to support near our air base at K6. On this day they had received some new baseball bats, balls etc.
Barnum photo collection.

Above: Our VMA-212 ordnance crew trying to put the guns on safe for this Air Force F-84 Thunderjet that made an emergency landing at K6.

Below: The flight line crew working out a wing folding problem on a Corsair of our sister squadron. VMA-212 Flight line is to the rear.

Photos on this page courtesy of Robert R. "Van" Van Dalsem, former Corsair pilot and squadron buddy in VMA-212.

Capt Barnum said this morning, after returning from Korea (K6) that Col Benson may not accept us as FAC because we are of the 19th draft and could possibly be returned to the States prior to a full four months tour as FAC. I'm not putting too much hope in this fact, however, and absolutely refuse to let myself get excited about it, so don't you, honey. We can hope, sort of on the side, though, can't we darling? It's raining so hard now I can't hear the radio. Brother, could we ever use this rain in California! No wonder Japan is so beautiful.

I was just thinking, you've probably received the boxes I sent home last June 8 and 9. I certainly hope you like everything, dearest, and will forgive me for being silly in some of my purchases. But my spending has come to a complete stop as of tonight, so it's all history now anyway.

Guess I'd better sign off for now, dear ones.

With all my love,
Daddy

11 Jul 52
K6, Korea
Friday afternoon

Hello darling,

Well, I'm back to the squadron, precious girl, and have been busy all day long. Had an 0430 reveille this morning, packed up my gear and took it out to the rear of the BOQ, but left it under cover because it was raining hard. The truck came by at 0500 and I got wet carrying my seabag, which I had gotten out of storage at Itami (containing my 782 gear), my little green bag (navy issue) and my portable radio. The truck parked in front of the passenger terminal and we all got wet again unloading.

I found out we had 30 minutes before we had to start loading into the R5D Marine transport, so we walked over to an all-night mess hall and had breakfast. We flagged a truck on the way back. We were wet to the skin, so it didn't make any difference to us after a while. My rain coat isn't any good at all. It gets wet and the clothes underneath act just like a blotter. Finally we got airborne in the middle of a terrific downpour, after hitting a huge puddle on takeoff in the middle of the runway which actually slowed that huge plane down. We climbed out on instruments for about 20 minutes until we got to 10,000 feet, when we broke out in the clear on top of the stuff. We flew on top all the way to K6, two hours and forty-five minutes to cross. I flew the whole crossing in the co-pilot seat and handled the ship for nearly an hour and a half. They didn't have enough seats in the rear of the plane, so four of us officers were asked to come up in front. The pilot asked me if I wanted to fly it, and of course I jumped at the chance. I had it on automatic pilot for most of the time, which simplified flying it to an absolute minimum. While it was on automatic it was only necessary to hit the rudder override switch to bring the nose around to correct compass heading one or two degrees, or to circumnavigate a towering cumulonimbus. What a comfortable seat they have! Top grain leather, arm rests, ash tray, the whole works. I got a big kick out of it. Hadn't had the controls of an R5D since September '45, on my way home from Okinawa, following the end of WWII, when I had over ten hours of it. I believe I could get completely checked out with only a few more hours of co-pilot.

After landing at K6, I got all my gear together and lugged it bodily back to my hut. The boys were happy to see me, and I them. They had missed my radio--ha, ha. I spent several hours this morning sorting through gear in my foot locker and seabag. Finally got all the gear I didn't need together with my sleeping bag and turned it in to the Group Supply and got my slip checked off. Went to the pay office and put in for my $1.00 a day while I was at Itami. Went over to the mess hall, had lunch, then to the squadron and had Mac take my picture in all my flight gear inside the AU-1 and standing by it--about eight shots. I figured I'd better do it now because I wouldn't have too much of a chance later on.

I'm going to get my orders tonight and leave at 0930 tomorrow for K3 for ten days, returning here to K6 and VMA-212 for a few days. They are sending us down there on TAD (temporary attached duty) orders. I can't figure out why they made them TAD, unless they *aren't sure of who they want to go to FAC, or maybe it's because they don't know when they want us up at the Division.*

Honey, when I returned here they told me I had been recommended for two air medals, one Distinguished Flying Cross, and get this, honey--the SILVER STAR. It made me very proud to even think I was being considered for one. There's a catch, however, and that will be when the recommendation goes to the Group awards committee for consideration. They may or may not pass on it. I had one exceptional mission that I led, and they are using it as a basis for the award. Keep your fingers crossed, darling, and don't say anything to anybody until I have it cinched. I'll be very proud to get the award. There haven't been but very few Silver Stars awarded to Marines in Korea. Even if I don't get it, it is nice to know I was well thought of in the squadron while I was attached, and the recommendation will become a permanent record of my fitness report anyway.

Got your wonderful letters of 1, 2, and 3 July, telling of the picnic at Nanga's. I love you, my darlings and miss you so very much.

Your loving hubby,
Spuddy

12 Jul 52
K3, South Korea
1730

Dearest girl and little guys,

Cameron and I got a truck, loaded our gear (he had most of it), and took it down to the parking area where the transports come in. The boys of MAG-12 were having a party because they had had quite a rugged day yesterday. The whole 5th Air Force was hitting P'yongyang, the North Korean capital. Our Group sent three multiple strikes during the day at the same target. The final strike they all carried napalm and incendiary bombs to burn it down. I, of course, didn't get in on it because my orders were already in my hand for transfer. At any rate, they all had free drinks at the club (I didn't even go over) and everyone who had been in the day's rugged flying was in the club getting stinko.

I went to the show and saw "The Harlem Globetrotters." Those rascals can sure play basketball. I didn't figure on being able to get to sleep early last night because when they get going on a Group party there's no stopping them. I was listening to the radio and reading when about 20 guys converged upon the quiet sanctuary of our home away from home. Music and song filled the night air, which was extremely volatile from the high percentage of alcohol being soaked up by the tables, chairs, cots, floor of our hut. They sang and drank, and drank and sang until 0200 this morning. Through the thunderous noise I somehow went off to sleep, awakening at 0545 to see the sun peeking in through the Quonset window this morning. The hut had about five extra cots in it, some lined up in the aisle, some squeezed up against each other. And the worst looking mass of humanity I have ever gazed upon was snoring a deep crescendo almost in perfect unison. Mouths were hung open, and arms and legs hung out over the cots. A couple of guys were under the table sleeping in the clothes they were wearing last night. Broken glasses, bottles and water littered the whole area.

I waded through the broken, twisted bodies, making my way to the Decontamination Center (as the sign over our latrine and head reads), where I shaved and refreshed myself, anointing my arms and face with Noxema to sooth the bites from the mosquitoes that had also entered our hut through the open doors last night, due to the forgetfulness of some of our drunken guests.

Lou Bass and Dick Francisco were really funny last night. They sang and danced and played tricks on each other. Example: pouring chipped ice down one another's shirt and over each other's heads. Bass had a mouthful of water or bourbon, or both, and Francisco dragged him up to an unsuspecting fellow in the corner of the hut who had just popped in to join the festivities. Francisco pumped Bass's arm violently for about ten pumps, the very engrossed stranger watching the entire proceedings. Finally, Bass gave out like a pump and squirted right in the stranger's face. Surprised expressions and laughter filled the night, only to be interrupted by an invitation to other partying pilots who came over to join the party in our hut.

Francisco and Bass would repeat the performance with another stranger, while the past victims and audience stood by with hushed expression until Bass poured forth--then everyone would knock themselves out with laughter, including myself. Those guys are the two most natural comedians I have ever seen. I hope I have painted a picture of the party in a manner to stimulate your imagination, because no matter what you could conjure up, I'm sure it was thought of last night.

After breakfast I came back and finished packing my gear. Then Cameron and I carried our gear down to the plane ramp and waited (listening to my radio) until the transport arrived at 1030. We boarded her and off we went to K3, making a GCA approach in some foul weather. The full-chicken colonel in charge of Wing G-1 was piloting and did a good job, I must say.

A truck met us and brought us and our gear to MACG-2 (George Parker's old outfit). It's officially known as Marine Air Control Group. We were greeted and turned in our orders, then had lunch and spent the remainder of the afternoon getting cots, mattresses, blankets, mosquito netting etc. Built a cabinet of boxes for my gear next to my cot. Brought my radio and voltage regulator, but not an extension cord, so will have to go without until I can pick up a cord. Battery only picks up a couple of local Korean stations.

Two Korean boys just came into the hut with large armloads of clothes for some of the officers. The shirts were nicely starched and ironed, and the white things looked good and clean. Guess maybe I'll have them do some washing for me.

Got a 3 July letter from my mom just prior to leaving K6 this morning telling of the picnic with you folks, and thanking me for the offer of the use of the trailer, but declining it because she said Scotty wants to work around the place. Mom sure loves you and our two precious little guys. Her every word just bubbles over whenever she talks about the boys; always reminds me of what a sweet wifey I married too. She's not telling me anything I didn't find out for myself, though, eight years ago. Golly, those eight years have been packed full of happiness, dearest.

Tomorrow we'll start our FAC instruction, I suppose, and get down to the business at hand. MACG-2 is a Marine Air Control Group, consisting of radar control units, plenty of radio equipment and guys with the know-how to pass it on to us, because we're going to be working with many different types of radio sets and devices used in aircraft control work. Parts of this training may prove interesting if I let it. My orders read to return to K6 and VMA-212 on 22 July to resume regular duties, which may mean we'll fly a few days more before we actually go to the front. Don't you worry, though, honey girl, I'm not flying any more than I can possibly get away with. I've had it in the air.

My first duty from now on is to you and my darlings. I'll return to you, precious girl, a daddy more in love a devoted to his precious family than I ever thought humanly possible before.

I love you all,
Daddy

P.S. It's cool here at K3; cloud cover makes it so. Ocean only a few thousand feet east. May get to go swimming yet.

NORTH KOREAN CAPITAL OF P'YONGYANG HIT

The reason my pals in my squadron were celebrating was as follows: General Clark explained the reason for dropping warning leaflets prior to the attack on P'yongyang, the capital of North Korea:

The objective was in part humanitarian and in part practical. We had to hit P'yongyang because the Communists had made it a major military headquarters and stockpile area. We wanted to warn the people away from danger areas. By warning them away we disrupted their daily lives and made it difficult for the Communists to maintain any kind of schedules in their work in the city.

Results indicated that both the destructive and the psychological aspects of the mission were successful. American, British and ROK planes completely destroyed three of the 30 military targets attacked. General Clark continued:

> *According to. . . reports, the North Korean Ministry of Industry's underground offices were destroyed and a direct hit on another shelter was said to have killed 400 to 500 Communist officials. Off the air for two days, Radio P'yongyang finally announced that the 'brutal' strikes had destroyed 1,500 buildings and had inflicted 7,000 casualties.*

Of the far-reaching effects of the leaflets, the UN commander later wrote:

> *The warning leaflets, coupled with the bombing, hurt North Korean civilian morale badly. The very audacity of the United Nations in warning the Communists where bombers would strike hurt morale because it emphasized to the North Koreans just how complete was UN mastery of the air. Contrarily, it made them see even more clearly that the Communists were ineffectual in their efforts to ward off our air blows. . . .*
>
> *As a result of the warnings, the bombings, the failure of the Communists to provide protection, and the refusal of the Communists to permit evacuation of the clearly defined target areas, civilian resentment was channeled away from the UNC bombers and toward the Communist rulers.*

The record set by the 1254 sorties flown in this 11 July operation was to last only seven weeks. On 29 August, 1403 sorties were employed in a new strike against the Capital. The massed raids against the military targets in P'yongyang, known as the "All United Nations Air Effort," turned out to be the largest one-day air assault during the entire three years of the Korean War. Attacking at four-hour intervals three times during daylight, Allied aircraft blasted a list of targets that read like a guide to public offices in P'yongyang, and included such points of interest as the Ministry of Rail Transportation, the Munitions Bureau, Radio P'yongyang, plus many factories, warehouses, and troop billets. Of the 45 military targets in the city, 31 received moderate-to-severe damage, according to post-strike photographs.

MY FIRST DAY AT FAC SCHOOL

13 Jul 52
K3, South Korea, with MACG-2
Pohang dong
Sunday evening

Hello little family,
 Well, school went along fairly well today and I picked up a few things that I had never heard of before. The radio gear we are to use is fantastic, with all sorts of portable equipment, as well as the radio jeep. I'm sending you a copy of our schedule so you will have an idea of what I'm getting. The lectures are, for the most part, being held in the movie building, where they have a stage and benches etc. We'll have field trips later on, after we get a little more ground work on the procedure and equipment. There's one heck of a lot a forward air controller has to know. It's going to be a very responsible position.
 The weather has been overcast and cool down south here all day. I didn't bring a jacket with me from K6 and I'm really regretting it now. No mail today, but we hope to have some tomorrow. We made arrangements to have it sent down here to us from K6. They get it in here at K3 originally, then distribute it all over to the various units by groups. The groups separate it by squadrons, and the squadrons by individual. That's why we can't go over here to K3 post office and ask for it. It has to go through the chain of command, like everything else.
 When we get a little time off tomorrow afternoon I'm going to go over the the Wing personnel officer and tell him about my discharge date of December 6 and the fact that I have to be returned to the States in November for release. They say that the 19th draft officers will

be going home around 1 November, except for 19th officers on FAC, who will have to complete their four months FAC tour. I'm going to get my two bits worth in anyway, and maybe they'll not forget me up there at the Division. We're out of touch almost completely with the Wing or Group, or anything, after we get up there.

2045

Just knocked off for about 45 minutes and went over to the MACG-2 club and played Bingo. They had 10 games and each game had a $4.00 pot. The last game had a $15.00 prize if you Bingoed in the 1st (7) numbers drawn, or $5.00 if you had to block out the whole card. Cole won $8.00 and Pittman $4.00. The daddy got nuttin. Cards cost $1.00 each, so I just blew a buck. Oh the sins of a gambler. The Bingo cards had little sliding black windows attached right on them, and as your number was called, all you'd have to do was to slide the little window closed.

I'm going to knock off now and go see the movie.

I had a nice shower and shave. Have a clean fresh, starched and ironed khaki shirt on, dungaree pants, dungaree hat, boondockers, clean socks and undershirt. Even got some Mum today. I'm as clean as a hound's tooth.

So long, little gang. Daddy loves and misses all of you very much.

Daddy

14 Jul 52
Pohang dong, K3 with MACG-2
Tuesday evening

Hi baby doll,

Had a nice creamed chicken on biscuit, mashed spuds, peas, chocolate ice cream and coffee for dinner tonight. They kept us so busy yesterday all day long that I didn't even have time to write.

Went over after school this afternoon and talked my fool head off until they gave me a pair of leather boots. They are ideal for hiking and rough terrain and are about 14 inches high. I'm going to look around and try to find somebody to put a zipper up the side, so that I can take them off easily. That lacing gets old. Bought two rolls of 620 black and white film and two rolls of 620 color; 35¢ for black and white and $1.55 for color, which includes the developing. Figured I'd better buy it because they tell me I won't be able to get any film up on the front line.

Picked up a lot of information on the FAC deal today. Talked about radar controlled CAS (close air support) and went into the radio business again. Toured the TACC here at K3. They control all the aircraft in the area. Very interesting. They said they had snakes up there, and also that you're required to wear leggings up with the Division. That's why I went to work so hard and got myself a pair of boots. These instructions have us guys shook, with all their stories about what we've got to expect up there, but I'm taking a lot of the tales with a grain of salt. From what these characters have been telling us, we've really got quite a tour to look forward to.

Saw Dave Kennedy (Sniveler Dave). He's been up on the east coast of Korea with a Marine GCI (ground control intercept) radar squadron for the past six weeks. He's been transferred down here to MACG-2 to be an instructor in FAC school, and also for instructor duty in Japan at an Air Force and Army school. He'll be going home in October. He gave me (2) 100 won notes to give to the boys. He said "Uncle Dave sends his love."

Went over to the Wing G1, saw a major, talked to him about my going home for discharge in November. He said he'd personally see to it that I wasn't forgotten up there. I don't like the thought of returning to the U.S. for a short time and then being returned to Korea to finish out the remainder of tour. They've done it to some guys. This FAC can't be as rugged as 58 missions over North Korea. Guess I can stand anything after that tour. Glad it's over.

Read some of your late letters over today. Looked at your pictures and had a chat with you. Sure miss my precious little gang that I love so very much. No mail as yet. Last letter I *received from you was dated 3 July. Called K6 today and checked on it. They haven't received any since we left there Saturday the 12th. Mail has been lousy lately. Can't figure it out.*

A helicopter pilot flew down from the Division and lectured to us today. Said the temperature there was 100°. Today here at K3 low clouds, 500-foot ceilings, some light sprinkles. The F9F Panther jets have been taking off all day long, nevertheless, on strikes up north. They are flying their tails off. Just as rough on them as they were on us up north. Dave Kennedy has been controlling B-29 traffic from Japan and Okinawa. He's a character. He's become somewhat of a legend, what with his radio chatter with returning B-29 night bombing raids. He gives them radar steers and controls them coming and going on their nightly missions. John Snapper and Shorty Thorson are up there with the same Group GCI. Dave said they are all alone and a very small outfit. They were constantly shook because of guerrilla activities. Boy, what a business this Korean War! Can't get out of this mess fast enough.

Try not to worry about me, honey. From all I've been through thus far, honey, I'm positive I'm a cinch to come home to you all. I miss you and love you very, very much. The light is very poor. No desks, I'm writing on my knee. Love ya all. Bye bye.

Daddy

16 Jul 52
Pohang dong, K3, with MACG-2
Wednesday

Baby doll and little guys,

I was a good boy at school today and got 100% on a field problem. They took us up in the mountains and gave us maps and compasses, then asked us to plot our position exactly to within 100 meters. I got my position by taking bearings on two mountain peaks, one three miles away and the other six miles away. I plotted my reciprocal bearings on my map and, after rotating my grid coordinates to correspond to true north instead of magnetic north, drew my bearing lines and arrived at my exact geographic plot. That's what we will be required to do up on the lines after we've advanced to a new position, which requires an air strike ahead of us. We'll plot our position so as not to call artillery or aircraft in on ourselves.

They will split us up after we get to the Division. There will be two FACs to a battalion. The Battalion spends 30 days on the battle line and 30 days in reserve. While on the battle line the two of us FACs will divide our time up being on the front line in our bunkers, so that we can advance to our outpost line of resistance with the maximum speed, with our radio teams of enlisted technicians carrying the radio gear. We will work with the forward observer of artillery, and the two of us and our teams will control all the artillery and air strikes in front of our Battalion sector. The two FACs will rotate--a week on the battle line in the bunker and a week on the battle line but back at Battalion CP (command post), to be on the staff of the Battalion commander. His staff will consist of three officers, one each from artillery, naval gunfire, and air. I will then become the air liaison officer of his staff.

Farther back down the line they have a similar staff at Regiment level, and further back than that from the battle line they have a similar staff at Division and Corps level. My job will be very important as I will be the air officer for a battalion of marines, which consists of about 1100 men. While on the staff at the CP I will be consulted as to whether the objective can best be attacked by aircraft or best be brought under fire by mortar or artillery. If I believe the target warrants air, I will make out a series of TAD (tactical air request forms) and radio it back down to my TADC (tactical air direction center), the Regiment, Division, Corps, will be monitoring my request and approve or disapprove it.

When the aircraft come on station my buddy FAC, who is doing his turn up on the front line, will take the aircraft under control through his radio and control the air strike, which will be **very** close to his position. Sometimes artillery can bring the target under fire better than aircraft, so aircraft are not requested and artillery is used and is controlled by the FO (forward observer for artillery). If the enemy position is on the reverse slope and mortars can't reach it, aircraft are used. Also, aircraft are used for heavily fortified bunker position because 1000-lb bombs are required to penetrate into the reinforced depths of some of these bunkers.

I can't tell you much about living conditions, honey, until I actually get up there and get with it.

Just saw Jack Ryan. He's in an F9F Panther jet squadron here at K3 (restricted information). He's had about 20 missions in them since leaving VMF-212 and loves them--says you can't miss with your bombs because in a dive you have no change on your rudders or controls and the engine doesn't change speed to cause you any correction. He says he can stay in the squadron several months, and will probably get a total of 100 missions. Their missions run two hours. Some guys get all the breaks.

No mail today. Sure do want to hear from my little family. Wish I could get home to my little gang. I love you all and miss you so very much. The time is going by, but not fast enough for me. I can hardly imagine what it will be like to get home. Home sure has a warm, friendly sound to me, darling. . . .

Bye bye, Daddy

17 Jul 52
Pohang dong, K3, with MACG-2
Thursday

Dearest baby girl,
Received my mail from K6 finally today. 5th, 6th, 7th and 8th of July from you, precious girl, one from Ben and one from Mike LaScala. It sure did give me a wonderful lift in my morale, which had reached a new all-time low here during the past few days, but now I'm on the road to recovery, thanks to you. . . I'm so happy you're keeping your spirits up, darling, and that you are taking trips to Laguna like you mentioned. Your descriptions of Ricky and Randy are very enjoyable to me and I always eat up every word about those two little guys. I'm sick about having to miss a single minute of their growing up. When I was home I used to love to watch and listen to their every action and word. It was always a high spot in my day when I kissed the darlings and felt their wonderful little arms around me. What an abundance of love and happiness comes built right into a tiny little helpless baby! Don't work on correcting Randy's or Ricky's speech too hard, honey, because I don't want to miss everything. Again, I want to reiterate, precious darling, how very wonderful your letters are, and how I hang on to every word, and never read them over fast because I want them to last as long as possible.

Tell your Mama and Dad and Peg and Trooper hello. I'm sure thankful you've got your folks right next door to you. Gosh, I'd worry myself sick if they weren't there. Tell your mom she's doing a very wonderful service to me and, if you will, indirectly to her country. As far as I'm concerned, her presence next door to my precious family is more of a service to me than all the Red Cross donuts, coffee, or canteens could ever possibly be. I appreciate having her there, darling, and please tell her I love her and think of her often.

As for me and what I did today, well, let's see. We loaded up a truck with all sorts of radio gear, field phones, wire and portable gear, and drove back into the hills. The instructor split us up into two groups. One group stayed at this first location, which would simulate the rear Battalion CP (or TADC) and the other group went on up into the hills about a quarter of a mile where they simulated the forward air controller and his radio team. We changed places to familiarize ourselves with both jobs. My head is absolutely bulging with all the information I have received in the past week, and today only heaped on the coals. We have radio gear 'til hell won't have it. Most of it is portable, in the sense that it can be carried on a man's back and either set down on the ground and operated, or else operated right off of a man's back in a standing position. There is the portable SCR/300 battery set with whip antennae, about the size of a GI water can, with which you're familiar, I'm sure. Then there's the MAW portable VHF 10-channel set with battery and antennae stand and phone jack box. Then we have the ANGRC/9, which we have nicknamed the "Angry 9." It has a 5-piece telescopic whip antennae 20 feet long, which has to be supported by three guide wires and it has a portable hand cranked generator and also a voltage regulator in the event you choose to lug a 6-, 12- or 24-volt battery along with you instead of using the generator, which weighs about 30 pounds. All this besides a reel of 110 wire one mile long, reeled and unreeled as required to two signal corps field phones at either end of our communication network. This is all topped off *with a radio jeep which is specially built and has a generator mounted between the two front seats that runs off of the transmission, and supplies current for a UHF (ultra high frequency) set, and a VHF (very high frequency) set with dynamotor and two 24-volt standby batteries, in case of motor failure of the jeep which wouldn't allow you to run the generator. The jeep is mainly a standby radio set and probably won't be used as often as the portable equipment, since we'll have to be very mobile, especially on forward outpost positions where roads we "hava no." This radio phase of it has been interesting inasmuch as we had to set up each piece of gear, tune each piece and operate each piece, carry each piece.*

We ran a simulated air strike with an "Oboe easy" (OE-1) which they brought down from the 1stMarDiv to work with us on this problem. Unfortunately the clouds precluded the chances of getting Corsairs in for a real honest-to-goodness CAS strike. The clouds are down to about 500 feet. When we get up to the Division in about four days they'll allow us to control a few strikes in conjunction with the experienced FAC who will be our partner. They have quite a schedule planned for us.

Heard on the radio today the Commies tried a push through in platoon strength (45 men) at the Marine sector near Panmunjom, but they were repulsed. Hope they don't try anything like that when I'm up there. I don't care if it's during daylight because I can run in an air strike on them if I can get the planes, but JOC (5th Air Force) allocates all A/C (aircraft) to all corps sectors along the front, a request has to be made through a long, tiresome channel prior to the approval, and it could be you wouldn't even be given the A/C you asked for in the end anyway. What a business!

Mike's letter was very interesting. It consisted of a four-page typewritten running account for my pleasure and edification (as he put it), of their visit to you and the boys, of the fireworks display at the Coliseum, and the Republican Nomination Convention, MacArthur's speech, which he didn't care for, his trip to a mountain resort with Terry and Dale. He left for Chicago on 12 July and is to stay at the Conrad Hilton Hotel. Boy, that guy is one swell fellow, honey. He sure thinks the world of you and the boys and is devoted to his family also. Terry would never have to worry about Mike running around with another girl. He's bubbling over with enthusiasm for her and Dale.

Played volley ball late this afternoon, seven games to be exact. Worked up a good sweat and won four out of seven. Got my hand, wrist and arm banged up from the ball, net, and other guys' heads and shoulders. They play rough here at MACG-2 and I played their rules. I had a good workout.

John Snapper and Shorty Thorson drove all the way (23 miles) down the coast to see us guys (Dave, Pittman, Cole, me) and we had a nice chat together for several hours prior to their returning to their camp. Dave goes to Japan tomorrow for schooling. Guess we'll have another field trip tomorrow.

Love you and miss you all so very much.

Daddy

18 Jul 52
Pohang dong, K3, with MACG-2
Friday 1600

Hello dearest wifey and my precious little guys,

Today at the crack of dawn they had us in the truck with all our radio gear and field equipment and away we went up into the foothills south of our living area. We all took our pistols with us and really looked like a reinforced rifle squad of fighting marines. There were 13 FAC students, two instructor officers and three enlisted radio technicians. Following some of the darndest roads and trails, finally we came to a river which blocked our way, so had to stop and set up our base of operation there. We went through Korean native villages and all the children were waving at us and crying for candy. Half of the little guys and gals didn't have any clothes on at all. Dirty, filthy, runny noses. What a sight! There were a few native villages around our position, and inside of five minutes there were 25 kids over to see us. We hooked up a microphone to our low frequency receiver and tuned in a Korean musical program for

Above: I made a wagon for these little Korean kids, from a metal ammo can. They loved it.

Upper Left: Our forward air controller (FAC) gang going out in the field for practical training at Pohang dong, K3, MACG-2, Marine Air Control Group

Left: Being trained in the use of all the radio equipment we would be using when we were with the 1st Marine Division up front. We'd have a more hostile audience then.

Lower Left and Right: Having fun with our radios and Korean youngsters. None had ever heard a radio before.

Above: Field trip for more training at FAC school, Pohang-dong, K3, MACG-2 Marine Air Control Group.

Upper Left: Spud at his fancy quarters at the Air and Naval Gunfire Liaison Company (ANGLICO), 1stMarDiv, 22 July 1952.

Left: Trying on the A-frame, while the patient Korean farmer looks on. In a few days we would be going up to the 1stMarDiv.

Lower Left: Spud with VMO-6 at the 1stMarDiv, up front where the real action is.

Below: My dear friend, Capt Melvin (Gus) Dake and writer on the stern of a hospital ship in Inchon Harbor. We had just flown a young wounded Marine out here in this Bell chopper.

them. They appeared to be so thrilled with it that I guess they had never heard a radio before.

We set up our radio equipment and the Oboe Easy (OE) acted as a fighter. We'd give it target location and information and he'd come down and simulate napalm or some other sort of attack. We all made out mission request forms and called in at least one strike apiece. The weather made it such that we couldn't get the Corsairs.

Due to the weather down here, we're leaving tomorrow morning at 0730 for K6. We'll spend the 19th, Saturday, at K6 and leave for the Division Sunday morning the 20th. We'll have a number of days of special training after we get up there prior to drawing our actual assignments. I'll have to leave my address the same until I'm positive what battalion and regiment I'll be assigned to. The squadron can forward my mail to me until my new address is known. Just keep on mailing to the same address, honey, until I notify you of my new address.

I snapped about six pictures today of our equipment and of the native children standing around. The country where we were positioned today was beautiful. Everything was so green and lush looking. They were growing rice and soy beans. Some squash was growing here and there, corn, and a rather large peach orchard and vineyard were doing very well. These people shouldn't have any food problems. Dave Kennedy said there are huge fishing fleets located along the east coast on the road up to where he had been stationed, and there were divers and fishing people located in every cove and inlet up the coast. They dive for sponges and abalone.

I got a credit slip for my cot, blankets, pillow, mosquito net, etc because we'll be leaving here before the supply opens up. We're all going to let Tommysan (ha, ha, it's a joke--really, he's supposed to be called boysan but we call him Tommysan and he answers, so that's all that matters)--anyhoo, we're going to let him turn in all our gear for us.

This school has been adequate, and I guess I've picked up enough info to get me along up there at the Divy. After I've controlled a couple I'll be fat.

Last night after Snapper and Thorson shoved off I went to the movie, but it was "Steel Town" in black and white. I had seen it at Itami in technicolor so shoved off. I sent a shirt, a pair of socks and underclothes to a local Korean laundry and it hasn't come back yet. I'm shoving off in the morning, so it looks like it will be without my laundry. The varmints told us we'd be here until around Monday. If I can't get word to him (laundryman) tonight I'll have Dave K. pick it up and mail it to me at the Divy. Boy, a guy sure can get sick and tired of moving around.

One of the student FACs here with us gave a Korean carpenter two cartons of cigarettes to make him a dandy footlocker to take up to the Divy with him. It will be nice to live out of while he's up there. I'm going to have to do something with mine when I get to K6 tomorrow. Haven't decided what, though, as yet. Itami is the best place but I'd have to catch somebody going over there and have him take it to storage. Don't like to burden anybody with it because they'll have enough of their own personal gear to fight while on the plane. Oh well, I'll come up with something. The chow has been horrible here at MACG-2. K6 chow is wonderful. Haven't heard any reports on the Divy chow. Hope it's good. No mail today.

Love you, dearest girl, and miss you so very much. Kiss the darlings for me and tell them that their daddy loves them too.

Your own Daddy

19 Jul 52
Tunp o ri, Korea
Saturday 2300

Dearest family,
Up at 0545, had a cup of coffee and a piece of coffee cake at the MACG-2 mess hall, packed up my gear, which consisted of my little green issued hand bag, radio, my old boondockers laced together and draped over my radio, my dungaree jacket, and roll of 1:25,000 maps of the Marine Division sector, similar to the ones I have sent to you of the area near Panmunjom. Thirteen of us climbed on the truck and went on down to air freight office where we sat and waited until three R5Ds came in. We watched the unloading until they finally called

out our flight number and we loaded. They had two huge prefabricated water tanks (all broken down and in crates), which took up nearly the whole deck of the plane except for just a tiny little bit of room on the right hand side where we were able to squeeze in.

I put on my parachute harness, strapped myself in, and away we went into a rain storm and low hanging clouds, climbing on instruments until we finally broke out on top of the storm and into a world of nothing but white fluffy clouds as far as the eye could see. After about 45 minutes we landed at a Marine night fighter strip and off-loaded the prefabricated water tanks. It was 1300 and we all went over to the snack bar. I can't mention the name of this field for security reasons. I can tell you that it was an Air Force field during the occupation and the dependents' bungalows are still in good condition and are being lived in by the officers. There must be about 25 of them. It was 111° there and brother, I almost died.

Had a Coke and a cheeseburger at the officers' snack bar for 35¢. Dropped 10¢ in a slot machine, admired the nude life size paintings of some gorgeous females they posted all around the club. Caught the truck and got the plane at 1400 and off we went to K6, Tunp o ri. K6 looked good as we circled prior to landing anticipating a reunion with my friends remaining there. After carrying my gear 1500 feet from the plane to my hut, I was sweating through every stitch of clothing I had on.

I went on down to the squadron and checked on my mail but they told me none had come in for about three days. Got yours on the 12th of July later on this evening. Also got a letter from the Coltons, Ben, and Nanna Gleason (in New Hampshire).

Unpacked my gear, showered and shaved, put on a clean undershirt, pants, socks, khaki shirt (my last, probably, because they only wear dungaree tops at the Division). Had supper, which consisted of French fries, hamburger steak, cucumbers, tomato, apple pie (lousy) and coffee. Attended the Group briefing, then went to the movie and saw "The River Queen" with Humphrey Bogart. I really and truly enjoyed it. The feeling they expressed as they survived the gun firings and the rapids and falls is similar to what I have felt on some occasions after a particularly rough mission. It sure feels good to be alive.

The humidity is very close tonight and a sheet will be uncomfortable on me. At K3 I required a blanket and a sheet. It was awfully warm here at K6 today too. Saw all the boys and was given a warm greeting by all my friends. K6 really seems like my home away from home to me now. I guess it's because I have watched for it to appear through the windshield of my plane so many times. Brother, I'm glad those 58 missions are BEHIND me!!

I'm going to secure this, dearest girl, because it's almost midnight and the light is disturbing my hut mates who have the early missions in the morning.

I leave for the Division on Tuesday, the 22nd of July at 0800 for good.

I adore you, dearest girl. Kiss my darlings for me.

Daddy

20 Jul 52
Tunp o ri, Korea
Sunday afternoon

Dearest family,

I've been packing and repacking my gear most of the day. I finally have all my gear turned in to Supply that I won't have any use for (I hope). My flight gear was all covered with dust because it had been sitting over in the pilots' ready room for two weeks, right near the floor in a little cubby hole. I cleaned it up a little bit and turned in my flight suit, head set, helmet, goggles, microphone, escape and survival gear, maps, and blood chit. My flight suit and helmet were sure crummy and smelly. Boy, a guy can get his flight gear in a sad state of affairs in a short time. I sweat a lot anyway, even on cool days. I don't get it; it must be nervous sweat.

George Codding offered to take my foot locker over to Itami, Japan, and store it for me when he goes on R&R August 1st. I packed my uniforms, khaki, oxfords, some letters and junk in

Upper Left: Howard Borman's mishap.

Middle Left: VMA-212 flight line at K6.

Above: Capt "Stretch" Evans posing beside 1000-lb bomb, with napalm bomb behind. VMA-212 flight line of Corsairs in distant background.

Lower Left: Flying Leatherneck Marine Captain Robert O. Barnum, 29, is strapped into his Corsair fighter-bomber by Staff Sergeant Calvin E. Kilpatrick, 29, North Quincy, MA, before taking off on a mission over North Korea. Both are members of the 1st Marine Aircraft Wing's "Devilcats" Squadron VMA-212, based at a forward air strip in Korea. Capt Barnum's wife, Bernita, and children, Roberta, 7, Howard, 5, and infant daughter, Shirley Ann, live in Jamestown, KS. He is the son of Mr. Robert L. Barnum, 443 West 7th, Concordia, KS. Sgt Kilpatrick's wife, Geraldine, and son, James, 5, live at 14 W. Squantum St., N. Quincy, MA.
Photo by Sgt Louis G. Oliver
Defense Dept photo (Marine Corps) A-133423.

Photos on this page from Barnum collection.

VOUGHT F4U CORSAIR

Typical of most radial aircraft engines, the propeller blades of the Corsair fighter are being "pulled through" before takeoff from the snow covered deck of the 27,000 ton carrier, USS PHILIPPINE SEA. The pulling through rids oil from the lower cylinders, thus avoiding hydraulic lock upon starting the engine.

it. I'm taking all of my socks, undershirts and pants, two sets of green dungaree fatigues, as well as my combat infantryman boots, two towels, two pillow cases, one blanket, two mattress covers, one air mattress, steel helmet, .38 pistol, mess kit complete, camera, knife, flashlight, pen, pencil, writing paper and toilet articles. Everything will fit into my seabag and green handbag.

I wrote letters to Ben, Mom, your Grandma Gleason, Mike LaScala, and now my baby girl. It rained today, sweetheart, and now it's muggier and closer than ever, but it was nice during the rain storm.

I'm sure getting excited about this FAC deal. I didn't get a real good chance to observe the control by an FAC while I was up with the Division because it rained so hard the day I was supposed to observe the strike from a forward observation post.

I made a wooden box today, packed the binoculars in it, jammed some of your old letters around the case to keep from scratching the leather case, and mailed it parcel post and special handling. The box may go air mail due to its size, so you may be getting it in a week or ten days. You'll enjoy the binoculars as much as I have. I'll have a government issue pair up at the Divy to play with.

I forgot to mention in my letter last night how wonderful Ricky's drawing and paintings are. His numbering is real good too. Gosh, the little darling is sure coming into his own. I'm so proud of my boys, dearest. I love you all with all my heart and soul, and with all my strength.

Major Dick Webster took a picture of me flying my last mission in tail number LD23. I'm returning to base from the supply strike I led. I had a hung 1000-lb bomb on my belly that I had a heck of a time getting rid of. I finally dropped it in the ocean west of K6. Webster is going to have an enlargement made and send it on to me.

2230

Saw Tyrone Power's new picture, "Buckskin." Takes place in a stage coach outpost. He's a mule team changer and inn keeper. Four bandits come to rob one of the stages--80%.

Give my little guys a hug and kiss from me.

All my love, Daddy

21 Jul 52
Tunp o ri, Korea, K6
Monday 2300

Dearest family,

Attended the Group briefing and they showed us camera gun shots taken by the F-86s during their fighter sweeps and dog fights with the MIGs over North Korea, and the Yalu could be seen very plainly below. They really clobbered the MIGs; you could see them fall apart right in front of your face. Boy, those fighter pilots sure must be having a field day. They knocked 13 MIGs down on the 4th of July. Those were the movies we saw.

Got my supply record sheet and checked out of the squadron and group. Every piece of equipment had to be accounted for. Also got my health records and pay records. Sure wish I could have kept my flight helmet, but everything had to be turned in.

Received your nice letter of 14 July. . .time marches on, dear, and our day is coming. Keep your chin up, honey, and I'll do the same. I certainly know what I want out of this life-- just you and the darling boys--nothing else matters. . . .

Our orders didn't come up from the Wing today, so I don't honestly know whether or not I'll be leaving in the morning. Some deal.

Kiss my boys for me, honey girl.

Daddy

22 Jul 52
Tunp o ri, Korea
Tuesday afternoon

Darling Marion and little guys,

I've been all packed up ready to go ever since 0700 this morning. There must be some foul up in the Group because they haven't notified any of us all day long. It's been miserably hot today. Everyone is dragging his body around like he's on his last leg. This heat can really take the ambition clear out of a guy. I like heat, but not when it's so darn humid.

The entire Marine Fighter Squadron VMF-312 came off the carrier and landed here last night. I've met a lot of fellows I've known from El Toro and some who were attached to this Group prior to going aboard the carrier. Just had a chat with Denny Clyde, who has been aboard the carrier for several months. He says they didn't get many hops in during that period because of bad weather, and the carriers were on two weeks rotation. They spent two weeks in Sasabo, Japan, then two weeks in Korean waters. Denny had heard aboard the carrier somehow that I got FAC. Word sure does get around. I joked that he'd better give me a good strike if he's working with me up on close support because I wouldn't give him a good write-up on my damage assessment report otherwise. He laughed. It will be a lot more interesting for me to work with the fellows I know flying the planes. We'll probably come up with some clever remarks over the radio that will really shake up the 5th Air Force. One of the boys who were going with us sniveled out today. His majority came through and they are sending him down to the Wing at K3 to be in G2.

G1 (Wing) Personnel
G2 Intelligence
G3 Operations
G4 Materiel (Supply)
G5 Executive Officer
G6 Commanding Officer

W=Wing, G=Group, and S=Squadron. Maj Charlie Greene is to be the W2 officer. The Marine Infantry, Army Infantry and Air Force all use the same system. Just thought you'd like to know 'cause I'm always mentioning it in my letters.

Major Kime told me today that all the medal awards were sent back to him for all of the officers, and the same for the other squadrons in the Group because the commanding general didn't like the forms they were using. He said he would let me know whether or not my awards were approved as soon as he found out. He'll write me a letter and then the awards will be forwarded to my Battalion CO and he'll present them to me. I hope it's approved because it will mean a heck of a lot more to me than the air medals and DFC. Not that they will do me any good, but the boys will cherish them, I know. Maybe my precious wifey will give me an extra yummy kiss for it when I get home.

I can hear the bulldozers and huge earth movers working like mad out near the strip. They're doing a lot of improving around here. The new officers mess hall is almost completed. Boy, they have really knocked themselves out on it. Real fieldstone fireplace, and it's on a knoll overlooking the whole airstrip. About two weeks ought to do it. I would be going now, darn it. The Korean laborers have done a lot of it with the Seabees' supervision. The Seabees have accomplished a lot since we first came here. They built work hangars for all the squadrons, rebuilt the chapel, tripled the mess hall and built the officers mess. They are building more Quonset huts here in our area also. They've trained a lot of Koreans and that has expanded their capabilities because they only have to put one or two experienced Seabees over a labor gang and the projects really begin to move. I'd like to have a dozen workers back home. I'd train them to build houses, pour cement, and really go into the business. Of course I realize it would be slave labor if I didn't pay them a good wage. It couldn't be done, anyway. I'm just talking to myself, don't mind me.

Some of the boys just came back from a rough hop. they got shot up pretty badly up in the 29th British Commonwealth sector of the line. The darn Commies keep moving in more and more antiaircraft guns all the time. I don't see how it could get any worse than when I was flying but the boys coming back swear it is, and by the looks of some of their planes I'm inclined to agree with them.

I have my doubts about leaving today, so I guess I'll get my cot and mattress from Supply and dig into my seabag for pillow, pillow cover, sheets and blanket. Haven't needed anything over me at night for the past two nights. It's really been hot.

Bye for now,

Daddy

23 Jul 52
With the 1stMarDiv in Korea

Dearest family,

Couldn't get a plane north to Seoul until 1230. Nine of us ate early chow and were ready a lot earlier than that. We loaded all our gear on the plane and boy, did we have the gear! The plane had brought the other three FACs up from MAG-33 at K3 to join us. I have never been hotter in my whole life. I haven't any idea of how hot it was but in that closed up DC3 twin engined monster it felt like it was 150°. The sweat was rolling off us like water running off a duck's back. You'd wipe your brow and two seconds later you had to wipe it again. Finally the pilot got his clearance and took off. He never got over a thousand feet all the way up to Seoul.

We were met at the plane by a major from Anglico (Air Naval Gunfire Liaison Company). We borrowed a truck, loaded our gear, and headed into the city of Seoul, crossing the Han River over repaired bridges. Nearly every building we saw had been bombed out and gutted, but the streets had been cleaned up and repair crews of Koreans were laying a new street car track in the middle of the street. A decrepit old trolly that looked like it came right out of the "Toonerville Trolley" comic strip was dong-donging its toilsome way down the street.

Seoul is really a huge city. While driving for miles and miles, we could see damaged buildings everywhere, some being large marble office buildings. Nothing at all like I had imagined. I'd seen it from the air, but had always been traveling too fast and too high to really get a first-hand look. Korean women were directing traffic at each large intersection. After an hour and a half drive north out of the city, we came to the 1stMarDiv. We off-loaded and had supper at the officers mess tent of Anglico. They gave us an empty tent and all 12 of us set up cots. I swiped a rubber mattress from MAG-12, so I'm fat.

Saw a movie (16mm) tonight about baseball. I think it's a tiny bit cooler here tonight than what we've been having at K6.

We got our assignments. You can use this new address:

Capt B.W. Peterson 033284 USMCR
3rd Bn 1st Reg 1st Marine Division
c/o FPO San Francisco, Calif

Under my name put Tactical Air Control Party.

I'm tired and dirty, honey. Gonna knock off and wash my face. I love you all. For the next few days we'll be touring the area. Saturday I join my unit. Will write tomorrow. Big early muster in the morning.

Daddy

24 Jul 52
1stMarDiv
Command Post
Anglico, Korea

Baby girl and boys that I love and adore,

Today has **really** been a day. They rolled us out of the basket at 0600. I shaved out of my helmet, and the cold water made it feel like I was pulling each and every whisker out by the roots. Put on my smelly dungarees and .38 side holster, hat and boots, and walked over to the chow hall for breakfast. Had two eggs "over easy," coffee and toast. Good food here at Anglico.

They split the 12 of us up into four groups of three and sent us to various units in the field for training. Our group hopped on a 6X6 truck and rode for about 15 miles up and down side roads, up and over mountains, eating dust from the other trucks, tanks and jeeps ahead of us all the way. Crossed over the Imjin River into our westernmost sector and went right up to the front lines and saw the troops in their positions, heard and saw our artillery firing, and watched two close air support hops run off while we were there. The noise of rockets, strafing, bombs and artillery going off is deafening. The troops looked tired, dirty and very haggard. I'm going to be right up there with them for **two** months on the line, starting Saturday, the 26th. Around the 1st of October we'll go in reserve, though, and I hope to talk my way out of going back up to the front again November 1st, on the theory that I have to be returned to the States for release by December 6th. I doubt if I can, but I'm going to work on it anyway.

We drove on back to the east side of the Imjin River again (the river is about 300 feet across, very deep and fairly fast moving). Upon crossing over, we went into the TADC (Tactical Air Direction Center), which will be the controlling agency for our air strike requests that we, as FACs, will be making, as directed by our battalion commanders. We were shown the intricate workings of their organizations. Located on high ground to assure the best radio reception and transmission possible, their call is "Devastate Baker." They also are the unit the aircraft check in with when reporting over station for a close air support mission with the Division.

Devastate Baker assigns the flight leader the target coordinate and gives him the direction and way to turn, upon recovering from his dive; also tells him distance and direction from nearest friendly troops, which would be me, the FAC. He gives him my call and channel number where he can contact me. The flight leader calls me and I direct him into the target area. I call for white phosphorous firing from my artillery commander and he marks the target. That's all there is to it. Of course, the goonies (as the crunchies lovingly refer to all Communists) are hiding in the toolies on every ridge line, lobbing mortar and machinegun fire onto our positions.

After leaving Dev Baker we came on back here to Anglico and I washed up. Boy, I was covered with dust and my clothes were wet from sweat. Had chow (goulash) and iced tea. Then our group went up to HMR-161, the helicopter transport squadron flying HRS-type helicopters, here in Korea with the 1stMarDiv on a trial basis. They have been transporting the UN truce team back and forth every day. After explaining the complicated operations of the organization to us, and showing us blueprints and photographs of the coming transport helicopters, as proposed by Sikorsky and Piaseuki companies (boy, they have some huge ones coming out of production soon), I crawled into the co-pilot side of the monster, and Capt Wek into the right hand pilot side. The rest of the boys got in the back. We took off straight up for about 20 feet, then the nose dropped over and we picked up speed to 65 kts. The engine is the identical one that's in the SNJ trainer.

We flew out over the truce negotiators' camp site and then over the train yard, where the news reporters are staying in pullman cars. They looked tired and dirty as we swished over them. Flew over a crashed AD-1 attack bomber. It was from our Group 12 from K6 and had crashed alongside the Imjin River two days ago. It had ripped in two, but the pilot got out OK. A crash crew was camped beside it in a tent and they were salvaging it. I took pictures of everything I've mentioned.

Flew over the new Freedom Gate Bridge crossing the Imjin. The truce negotiators use it sometimes, when they don't fly in the helicopter. The reporters drive over it every day. Saw the balloons circling over Panmunjom. The pilot took us over Hill No. 229, where I'll be doing all my controlling with the 3rd Bn, 1st Marines. Saw the troops in the trenches and our artillery positions, and lots of activity down there. We were low enough at times to read road signs the various units have placed out. The helicopter pilot stayed over existing roads as much as possible, though, because he said the area was heavily mined, and in the event of a power failure, he wanted to set it down on a road. Roads were crushed gravel and in horrible condition. To ride over them in a truck shakes your guts out. On the way back to the HMR-161 landing area Capt Wek let me handle the controls. I caught on OK. They are sort of crazy to handle.

We landed at about 1600, came back to Anglico and went over to clean up in a tent they have rigged for showers by pumping water up the bank from a dirty little stream next to our area. I walked over in my boots and pants, with a clean pair of socks and underclothes in my hand. When I got to the shower tent I was turned back by a guard who told me it was a Division order that you had to be fully clothed and carrying your side arm at all times. So I came on back to my tent (about a quarter of a mile), put on everything required and headed back. I washed my socks and underclothes, but not my dungarees because they were so bulky, shampooed my hair and washed real good in the cold river water shower. Felt good, though.

Now I'm writing to my precious girl and two darling little boys that I love. How I miss you, dear. Golly, I can hardly wait for the time to go by. I'd sell these next for months out awfully cheap if I could only find some fool that would buy them. Ha! Ha! Some joke.

These crunchies have gone mad with regulation, but I guess that's the way it has to be. My portable radio is sitting on somebody's foot locker at the foot of my bed. I have it on battery and I'm getting the AFRS in Korea very good.

Just returned to the tent from dinner chow. Had Swiss steak. Talked to a major of artillery over there at the mess hall tonight and he said the Commies have really been throwing the mortar and artillery over against our lines today. From what I saw today, both on the ground and in the air, I'd say the enemy could walk right through any time they had a mind to. The Korean Marine Corps had some very good defensive positions dug, however, but defensive positions don't stop hordes of Chinese such as what Intelligence has reported facing us (70,000). That's a lot of Commies, and life is awfully cheap to them.

This is an impossible situation over here, honey. The South Koreans haven't got a pot to pee in and never had a window to throw it out of. They, like any oriental laborer, only want a bowl of rice. The best we can hope for is a peace treaty that will fix the present battle line and give us time to train more Korean divisions to man the present battle line, and then it will be much the same as it is now, except the actual shooting will have ceased, and the endless, endless slaughter of our young Americans and our UN Allies will end, at least temporarily.

The Koreans have an air force of a sort, consisting of a few P-51 Mustangs. They fly out of Kangnung K18, and that's it. Of course, they represent a source of well trained instructors, but unless we supplied them and supervised them it wouldn't be any good. Everybody here in the Div is hoping and praying for a peace treaty. Not that it will do any good, except to stop the flood of incoming mortar and artillery fire that is really cutting us down, and to bring peace of mind to us that the 70,000 Commies won't be swarming across at us. The bridges available to us across the Imjin River, our necessary direction of retreat, are very few, and they represent an obstacle to us that is quite appalling. I'm glad I'm with a bunch of Marines, anyway, because they are all too gung ho to admit they are in a precarious position. They have a ten-mile or more front, with two regiments up: 3 battalions to a regiment, 3 companies to a battalion, 250 men to a company--up against 70,000--you figure it out. Even being Marines doesn't add that up to 70,000. The only consoling thing in this whole picture is that they haven't made a push for some months in any strength, so it can be hoped that maybe they won't. The battles have been for small outposts in front of our lines.

I forgot to tell you, honey, that yesterday we stopped at Seoul and visited the 5th Air Force and JOC, and saw the whole show. Boy, they really have a set-up. They have taken over a Korean college which somehow or other had escaped any battle damage whatsoever. Big new Air Force Blue Buicks were parked out front. Smartly dressed Air Force police lined up outside. Strict discipline and regulation everywhere. Very heartwarming. Someone is on the ball over here. Thank God for little favors.

I wish I were back flying Corsairs--honestly, I do.

Am flying with VMO-6 tomorrow.

Bye, bye, dearest girl. Sure do wish I'd get some incoming mail. I love you, sweety. Kiss my boys.

Daddy

P.S. MGen John T. Seldon is commanding the 1stMarDiv
BGen Clayton C. Jerome commanding the 1st Mar Air Wing
Artillery fire and flashes could be heard and seen all through the night.

25 Jul 52
Anglico, Korea
Friday

Dearest family,

I'm knocking this note out hurriedly because I was just notified that a jeep and driver would be here for me and my gear, to take me up to my battalion tonight instead of tomorrow.

This morning we were briefed by Col Cornell, the Division Air Officer, on the overall air picture here in Korea, and the 1st Div in particular. There are more darn restrictions we have to contend with than I ever heard of when I was flying.

I was wrong about the number of Commies facing us. Instead of 70,000 there are 85,000, which make up the Chinese 63rd and 65th armies. And we have 19 1/2 miles of front to defend, instead of 10,000 yards for a division of our size. The front line weaves in and out like a snake which is what makes it so long. Cornell talked to us for three solid hours on what we were expected to do, and what not to do, under all kinds of various conditions. Most of our air requests go through his office and he told us just about what we could expect to get through and what wouldn't get through.

After lunch I went to VMO-6, and although I couldn't get a hop in the Bell helicopter or the OE-1 or their new Sikorsky HO5S-1, I did take a few pictures and read the pilots handbooks on all of their equipment. I can fly any of it if I so desire; however, most of their aircraft was being used for emergency evacuation of wounded, from the Marine sector. The Commies have increased their incoming artillery to a fantastic number.

Just came back from chow and got a **happy** surprise. Here on my cot lay four precious, wonderful letters from my beloved wifey--10 and 11 July, which had been long lost, and 16 and 17 July. Apparently you mentioned receiving the silk pajamas in yours of the 17th, but I haven't got it as yet. You had tried them on, however, and said they fit you real well. Yes, I did receive Nanna's "I'm missing you" card. I just forgot to mention it. Whenever I hear of Ricky asking about me and saying things like, "Sometimes it seems like I haven't got any daddy," I get all choked up. Sometimes it seems to me that I've been gone for years and years too, honey. I was deeply touched by Nanna's beautiful card and wish for my quick and safe return to my beloved little family. Golly, with all the wonderful people I have pulling for me, how can I miss?

I guess that jeep isn't coming for me tonight. It's 1930 now and only one jeep has arrived, and that was for Capt Lane who is going to the 1st Bn, 1st Reg. (They refer to regiments as Marines; for instance, the 3rd Bn, 1st Marines.) Boy, am I getting salty. Maj French, the Anglico CO, gave me a farewell handshake, wished me well, and told me to say hello to Maj Christy, the 3rd Bn's executive. He also invited me down to eat in the officers mess here at Anglico any time I got into the reserve area. The boys in VMO-6 want me to come on down and control some air strikes from OE-1s at any time I want to. I would like to check out in the HRS-1 (the large helicopter transport that I flew yesterday). Darn it, there goes the mail truck! I'll have to walk this letter down to the Div CP tonight to get it mailed. I sure have done a heap of walking lately.

While at VMO-6 today, I took a cooooooold shower, and boy, was it invigorating! But I had to put back on my dirty clothes, which didn't make me feel too good. Honey, how I'm going *to appreciate your wonderful laundry service. You always took such wonderful care of me, dear (in every way!).*

I got a kick out of seeing Ricky's tooth. I can hardly believe he's big enough to be getting his second teeth. Is his first second tooth in yet? Ricky boy, Daddy misses you soooooo very much, honey boy. You bet you do have a daddy, and I'll make it up to you, darling boy. I love you, dear. Thank you, Ricky boy, for helping Mama water the lawn. Mike LaScala wrote and told me you told him that you did a lot of work around the house to help Mama while I'm away. I'm proud of you, dear.

Randy boy is pretty smart to be able to pick my picture out of a crowd. After all, he's only a little guy, and I've been gone a long time. Four months today, dearest. The time's agoing, but sometimes it seems ever so slowly.

My Bn and Reg are moving up to the front line tomorrow, and it's going to be rough taking up front line positions in a switchover proposition.

Happy you like the pajamas. I love you.

Daddy

26 Jul 52
Saturday evening

Darling girl,

First off, sweetheart, I'm dog tired. It's raining and I'm sitting here on the edge of my cot, wet through to the skin. Drove around in the rain for seven hours trying to locate my Bn on a 19 1/2 mile front. I found them on the line, but slightly in reserve, preparing to move up to front line positions tomorrow. Got here in time for chow, met about 15 officers of the Bn. My back is awfully sore and tired, and I'm going to lie down soon and rest it. I have really had an experience today. My driver and I went clear up to our forward outpost positions until we ran into roadblocks and then turned back. Hardly any of the many, many regiments and battalions are marked to help you find them, which makes it difficult, especially if you're a complete stranger to these parts. We heard artillery firing, but never had any rounds come near us. Boy, these battle lines are really spread out like mad.

My fellow FAC or TACP is named Bill Biehl, a new major. Bill has a regular Marine Corps commission.

We have a light in the tent, but the others are using it low to the table and I can't see by it, so I'm using my flashlight. This is a lonely and miserable existence. It's much harder for me to go through this ugly, soul wrenching war this time, darling, than before. . . .

Tomorrow, up to the front line positions, and a bunker. They broke off the peace talks for a week, I hear. Brother, there seems to be no hope at all, except in strength. Say a little prayer for the daddy, will you, hon, and I'll stroke my beads once or twice myself (figuratively speaking). Have Peggy say a couple of Hail Marys too, just to be on the safe side.

Night, night,

Your very own,
Daddy

Upper Left: Gus Dake and I were flying over Seoul, having dropped off a Marine casualty on the hospital ship in Inchon Harbor. There was scarcely a whole building left.

Upper Right: Of all the photos I took or came by, this little Korean orphan street urchin is my all time favorite. He personifies the entire reason for our being in Korea.

Middle Left: Countryside between Seoul and the 1stMarDiv.

Middle Right: One of the hundreds of bridges destroyed during the 1950-51 seesaw battles in South Korea. New bridge to the left now carries the heavy traffic, including tanks.

Lower Left: Two damaged Russian T-34 tanks sit harmlessly in a farmer's patch, leftover from the late 50's fighting.

Above: Crossing the Imjin River on a pontoon bridge. During flood conditions these bridges washed down stream by a 15 ft wall of water and were recovered at Inchon 20 miles south. This happened on three occasions while I was with the Division.

Upper Right: Marine engineer repairing a section of the pontoon bridge.

Middle Right: War damaged building in devastated downtown Seoul. I was attending an air controller's conference at 5th Air Force Headquarters at the time. The city was in total ruins.

Lower Left: Freedom Bridge, the permanent bridge across the Imjin River. This was the one our peace negotiators sometimes drove over going and coming to Panmunjom, unless of course they were transported by helicopter. After the war ended, our POWs crossed over it to freedom.

Lower Right: Another pontoon bridge crossing the Imjin.

CHAPTER 13

UP FRONT--BUNKER HILL

Across no-man's-land units of two Chinese divisions faced the men of the 1stMarDiv. From west to east, opposite the Marine regiment's frontline battalions, were elements of the 580th Reg (regiment), 194th Div (Division), 65th CCF (Chinese Communist Forces) Army and both the 352d and 354th Regs, 118th Div, 40th CCF Army. The 352d Reg held most of the area on which the battle would be fought. Enemy combat efficiency was rated as excellent and their forward units were well supplied.

Our battlefield construction was carried out by the infantry regiments to the limit of unit capabilities. The division engineers, one company per frontline regiment, augmented at times by shore party units, supplied the technical know-how and engineering materials and equipment. These combat troops processed the lumber for bunker construction and built fortifications for forward medical treatment and one bunker for observation of battle action by civilian and military dignitaries, irreverently called VIPs (Very Important Persons) who frequently visited the Division. Engineers also erected some of the barbed wire barriers in the forward areas and, when necessary, cleared firing lanes for weapons housed in bunkers. The bunker roofing material was 11-foot long, 12-inch wide, 4-inch thick timber. On top of this was placed a 2-foot layer of sandbags, tarpaper covering and a 4-foot high layer of earth that completed the structure and partially camouflaged it.

The processing of timbers for easier and faster bunker construction had begun on 28 July but this was hardly in time for the most difficult fighting the Division had faced thus far in western Korea. Given the name Bunker Hill, this battle would take place in the center sector of the Division line, manned since 27 July by Col Walter F. Layer's 1st Marines, who had taken over the command two days earlier from Col Fluornoy. On that date LtCol Gerald T. Armitage's battalion, 3/1, took over from the 3d Bn, 7th Marines on the left, while 2/1, commanded by LtCol Roy J. Batterton Jr., relieved the 2d Bn, 7th Marines on the right.

According to Col Armitage, Bunker Hill got its name from the heavy bunker building program going on at the time, in preparation for the important battle we were about to face. And this action was going to be supported by the greenest forward air controller ever sent up to the Div from the Air Wing--me. At the precise time that they were moving up to take over command of new and strange terrain, facing foul weather and an aggressive, persistent enemy, my joining the 1st Marine Regiment only added to the confusion. All I could do was try to do my best.

27 Jul 52
Sunday evening
Changdan, Korea
Up front with the 3rd Battalion, 1st Marines

Hello little family,
    I just had a bath out of my helmet and washed my filthy underclothes and socks. I still couldn't get myself to wash my still-damp-from-sweating dungarees cause they are so heavy, and I haven't any container large enough to hold them. The water has to be carted up in water cans from the water trailer, which is towed to a water point somewhere in the rear lines, so we're not loaded with water. I was so tired and dirty yesterday that I didn't care if school kept or not. My back felt much better this morning when I woke up at 0600, packed all my gear and struck the tent. I helped Bill Biehl pack his gear and boy, was he loaded. We had our enlisted team load our air team jeep, which they call the 4X4, and made about three trips up to our front line positions. I'm in the Battalion CP with Bill Biehl and Smith, the major in charge of the 3 Dept, and Capt Small who is the Battalions Weapons Co. commander.
    We had breakfast and lunch at our reserve area, then moved on up to our front line Battalion CP, where we off-loaded and brought our personal gear up the hill about 500 feet from the road to our tent. Our enlisted men have a tent next to the road. We split them up into two teams and sent one team up on top of a huge hill that sits between us and the commies. They have a bunker up there on the hill and have our portable radio equipment set up.
    Bill and I and Lts Stand and Olgren went up the Panmunjom corridor to a gate short of Panmunjom by about $3/4$ of a mile. We went up to the forwardmost outpost in "goonie land" and observed the area out in front of the hill mass that protects our Battalion CP. It gave me an odd feeling when we left our front line troops about a mile and a half behind us, and a relief when I saw friendlies dug in on this forwardmost observation post. We climbed up to the OP position and looked out over enemy territory and Panmunjom below us. We could actually see the tents and even a helicopter there, even though they didn't have any talks going on at the time because they had secured the talks for a week. I talked to the company commander, Capt Doug Ashton, who came out of his bunker long enough to tell us about a conversation he had had yesterday with General Harrison, a member of the truce team, and the general told him that the talks were going poorly and he had his doubts about a successful conclusion.
    We looked the area over real well and found the bunker we'll be using when we control air strikes. After spending about 30 minutes on the line at the OP we came back via a tank road, where the ruts, water and mud made it almost impassable. You can't imagine what those little jeeps will go through, though. We reported to the battalion commander, LtCol Armitage, and told him we were going to recon the rest of our lines and OPs in the morning.
    It rained harder last night than I have ever heard rain fall before. The flap on the side of the tent swished back and forth, so I didn't sleep very well, but seemed to rest anyway. It rained this morning too, and continuously until about 1530, when the sun broke through, and it felt real good. The bugs are flying around the lamp like mad, so I just sprayed the tent with an insecticide aerosol DDT and Allethrin bomb, but it doesn't seem to do any good for some of these bugs.
    Bill has a little plastic portable Motorola radio and boy, it sure plays well. I haven't used mine since I arrived. We're finally squared away in our tent and I have a mosquito net over my cot, so that will be some help. We'll get only two meals now that we're up on the line, or really at Bn CP. The meals will be hot while we're at CP but one will be a cold "C" ration and one hot when up in our bunkers. You should have seen the line of trucks and jeeps coming and going today. It sure takes a mess of equipment to move a battalion of infantry and supporting artillery. It was muddy and sloppy but we finally got the job done.
    I wish I were back in the squadron. Bill just got called up by a buddy back at Regiment TACP. He was told that his 17th draft was returning home the 1st of September. That means he can't go with them, though, because he has two months to do as FAC. I'm hoping and praying I'll get to leave in November, but from what I've heard happening to some of these other guys, I'm inclined to think otherwise.
    No mail today from my baby girl. Please note new address. I changed it slightly.

I miss you, darling girl, with all my heart and soul, and am praying for the day I'll return to you and the two darling little guys I adore. That's the only thing I want, precious girl. Going to hit the pad, honey girl. Night, night.

Your very own Daddy

OP2 (OUTPOST DUTY)

Perhaps one of the loneliest and most dangerous jobs was to man a remote outpost whose only defenses were sandbags, bunkers, trip wires and flares, and whose sole purpose was to give advance warning of the enemy, who took particular delight in attacking at night when our ability to sight his movements was at a minimum and when air support was grounded. The men on the outpost line were the first to hear the ungodly blowing of the Chinese bugles, and profanities screamed at them by the attacking hordes--sounds and oaths in English designed to chill your very blood. Even seasoned troops could never get used to this horrible sound in the night. Almost all ground action occurred at night and therefore you tried to get your rest during the daylight hours if you were on the ground and up front, as I was for the best part of four months. On many an occasion I would have been more than happy to have exchanged my foxhole for a Corsair. There was always a small amount of offensive action required, since patrols had to be maintained to fix the enemy's position.

I could not but admire the South Koreans who constructed our bunkers, dug our protective trenches, and carried the supplies on their backs on the primitive "A" frames their ancestors had been using for centuries. General VanFleet had set up this South Korean Service Corps of 60,000 laborers and porters. And in our sector, as in many similar sectors across the front, they worked feverishly--filling sandbags, carrying ammo and supplies to remote outposts and building bunkers--and died just as gallantly doing it as any soldier. They were unarmed porters and depended completely upon the protection of armed troops.

Capt Doug Ashton had to plan every conceivable way to provide protection of OP2, our outpost. Each evening the night patrol would assemble in our bunker and Doug would go over the night's prepared activity. The blackened-faced squads would carry radios and also string out telephone line, while Doug was in direct contact with them. They devised fiendish escape plans, including pre-planned artillery fire to be placed directly on friendly positions. They planned the use of the VT (variable time fuses), a type of proximity fuse, which depends upon an external source, such as an electronic signal, rather than the force of ground impact, to detonate the shell at a predetermined height over the target. This would be used only as a last resort, and after our guys had time to dig themselves a deep foxhole or bunker. I stayed up many a night to keep Doug company and listen to his squad leaders out on patrol.

I was beginning to experience a whole new world--that of the valiant ground Marines. While sharing this strange, sometimes horrendous and loathsome world, this humble fly-boy developed one hell of an appreciation for his infantry buddies--officer and enlisted alike.

28 Jul 52
Changdan, Korea
Up front with the
3rd Bn, 1st Marines

Dearest little family,

Up at 0700 and shaved. We have a battery of artillery attached to our battalion and they fired all night long. Didn't sleep at all and I felt it, too, today. Ate breakfast at 0930. We have only two meals, 0930 and 1630. Had a torrential rain last night. Our tent leaked and we were staggering our cots and gear to avoid the drips. The operations officer, Maj Smith and the artillery officer, Capt Small, came to bed at 0200 and I thought we were being ambushed by goonies (Communists)! The rain is terrible--mud, mud, mud. My team up on the hill in the bunker is digging out from the rain; pools of water are collecting in the bunker and a lot of trenches are caving in. The road to the top is inaccessible by our radio jeep, so we have to climb it now.

Brother! Here it is on a platter, honey. The commanding officer decided to send me up to our outpost position outside of the corridor to spend each and every night up there with the troops, and to return in the morning unless I have an air strike coming into our sector to control. My job up there, as explained to me by Col Armitage, is probably one of the most important jobs of the whole Korean War. OP2 was acquired by a rough fire fight only a short time ago. Since it lies outside of the no-fire corridor of the road to Panmunjom by only about 1000 meters, we have fortified it and have gone to very large extremes to assure ourselves that we won't lose it.

The goonies consider OP2 a thorn in their side, and it is anticipated they will try to recover it by any means possible. They could actually encircle us and wouldn't be in violation of the corridor because the corridor only extends to 500 meters on either side. If we should become encircled we would, by sheer necessity, be required to call in aircraft to aid in getting us out. And, if my request was granted, the aircraft would have to violate the air corridor and Panmunjom in order to get in close enough to give me close air support, and we would then be in violation of the peace talk arrangements--and Boom, WWIII!! So you see, honey, actually, and without exaggerating one little bit, I am really in an important command, under direct orders from the battalion commander. I'm frankly quite shook, especially after having studied the enemy situation map.

I went up to our OP position on the hill mass fronting our battalion, checked the bunker and studied the terrain with a 20-power fixed scope through a slit in the bunker. The men were digging trenches wider and deeper and trying to dry up the water pools that have collected from seeping down the sides. It's a useless task, however, because the rain continues to pour down.

The lights keep going out and I switch to my flashlight. There, they just came on again. The guard just came by and told us to put the sides of the tent down and door opening closed because the battalion is on a 100% blackout. We don't have a door, we have a flap. I have my little mat down on the deck on the dirt, so it's not too bad. However, I guess I'll be leaving my happy home for OP2 tomorrow.

Gus Dake came over here to my Bn CP and picked me up in his Bell helicopter at about 1400. He flew me around to about 10 of my emergency evacuation helicopter strips and set down on four of them. I plotted them on my map and finally he took me up to the OP on top of the hill mass in front of the battalion. The road was washed out and Major Bill Biehl and our sergeant had to walk it. I got up there a few minutes after they did and boy, did I give them the horse laugh as I stepped out of my private air taxi! Bill was sopping wet from rain and perspiration --some joke! Gus took a chance going where he did because he exposed himself to enemy mortar and artillery fire at the spot where he dropped me off, although luckily we didn't draw any fire. I bid Gus farewell and he said to come on down to VMO-6 and he'd check me out in the OE-1 so I could recon my battalion front firsthand. I said I'd try, but if I know me, and I think I do, I'll not be doing any such thing if I'm spending my nights on OP2.

No mail today, precious girl. I could go on and on, but I'm beat and I'm going to retire. I think of you, darling, every day so many, many times, and oh, how I need you, darling. Hope a letter comes tomorrow.

Kiss my precious boys for me and tell them their daddy is missing them so very much. Don't worry about the daddy, dear, 'cause you know me, hon, I've got a charmed life and a definite mission--and that's to return to you, darling, and make you happy and comfortable for the rest of our lives.

Bye bye, my darling

I love you, dear. Daddy

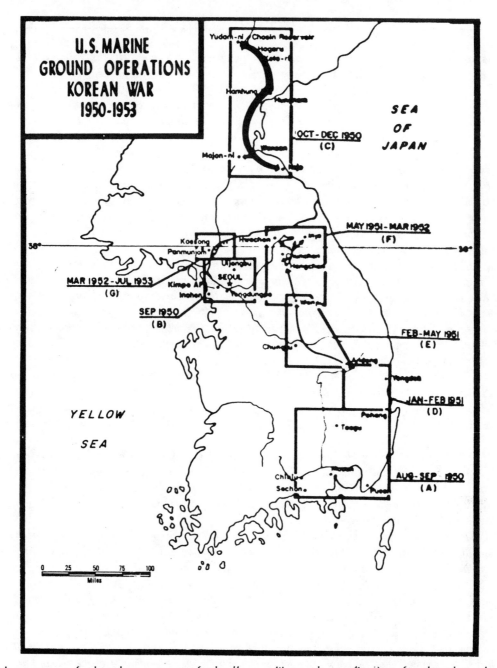

Over the course of the three years of the Korean War, the 1stMarDiv fought their battles over a wide sector of South and North Korea. The above map shows these various zones of action chronologically.

ZONE OF ACTION	DATES OF ACTION
A. PUSAN PERIMETER	AUG-SEP 1950
B. INCHON-SEOUL	SEP 1950
C. CHOSIN RESERVOIR	OCT-DEC 1950
D. POHANG OPERATIONS	JAN-FEB 1951
E. SPRING COUNTEROFFENSIVES	FEB-MAY 1951
F. EAST CENTRAL FRONT (PUNCH BOWL)	MAR 1951-MAR 1952
* G. WESTERN KOREAN FRONT	MAR 1952-JUL 1953

* The author's ground action (JUL 1952-NOV 1952)

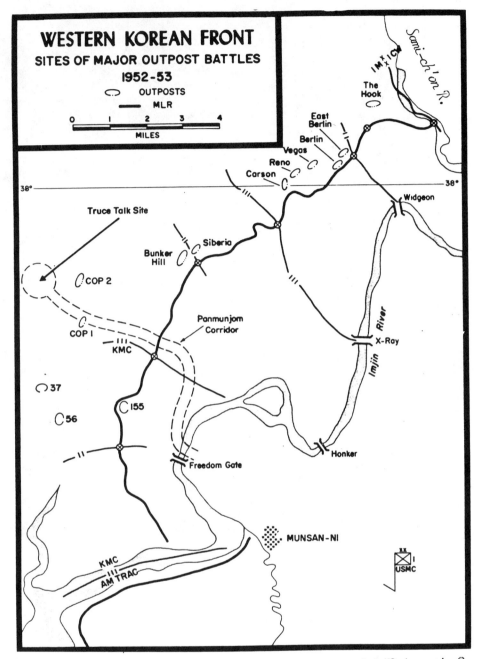

    The MLR (Main Line of Resistance) for the 1st Marine Division extended NE from the Panmunjom Corridor to the Sami-ch'on River, where it turned northward.

    The KMC (Korean Marine Corps) line extended south from the Corridor to the Imjin River; however, the 1stMarDiv had the training responsibility, and ultimately the total responsibility for this whole sector.

    As the FAC (Forward Air Controller) for the 3rd Battalion, 1st Regiment, of the 1stMarDiv, my principal activity, that of controlling our air strikes, took place on the MLR overlooking Bunker Hill, and actually within the confines of COP2, just a few hundred yards east of the Truce Talk site.

    Munsan-Ni was the campsite for our truce negotiating team and correspondents from around the world.

    Three pontoon bridges are shown—Widgeon, X-Ray and Honker—all of which washed out during the flood season, leaving only the Freedom Gate bridge the only means of crossing, except by helicopter. Whenever the bridges were washed out, the enemy intensified his unrelenting attacks upon us, knowing we were vulnerable.

1stLt Robert B. Robinson, Jr., standing in front of his F4U Corsair. Photo taken at El Toro MCAS, when Robby was flying with VMF-214, not long before the start of the Korean War. We had been together in 1943 as aviation cadets and later, in 1944, at Masters Field, Opa Locka, Florida, as members of Marine Dive Bombing Squadron Flight 121, VSB-5.

R. B. Robinson's Korean Service

* Forward Air Controller, 1st Bn, 1st Marines, 1stMarDiv
    o Inchon Landing, September 15, 1950
    o Wonsan Landing, October 26, 1950
    o Chosin Reservoir Area, Nov-Dec 1950

* Squadron duty following FAC tour
    o VMF(N) 513, K-9, Pusan, Korea F4U-5N
      15 Close Air Support Missions

BUNKER BUILDING. BATTLEFIELD CONSTRUCTION WAS CARRIED OUT TO THE LIMIT OF UNIT CAPABILITIES. 1STMARDIV PHOTO.

29 Jul 52
Changdan, Korea
With the 3rd/1st
Tuesday afternoon

Hello baby girl and boys that I love,
It hasn't stopped raining for three days. It's coming down hard right now and I'm just standing by until 1630 when I eat my second meal. After dinner and around 1700 I'm taking my team of two enlisted men and a set of radio gear in the jeep with a trailer, and we're going out the Panmunjom road to the road that cuts off to the right and goes out to our OP2. The captain who is in charge of the troops out there told Maj Bill Biehl (the other FAC) that our two men would have to pitch shelter halves, and possibly he could find a place in his bunker for me and a cot. Our radio gear would have to be kept in our jeep trailer under canvas until our bunker is completed.

I got up around 0800 this morning and felt quite rested, although I woke up nearly every hour--whenever our artillery or mortar opened up. Then over on our left flank the KMC (Korean Marine Corps) had one heck of a fire fight at around 2300, and it sounded like it was right next door. It lasted about two hours. They spotted three tanks and one truck in front of our battalion this morning at around 1000. Our artillery is hitting it now. Bill and I requested an air strike, but it's out of the question, what with this rain and 200- to 300-foot ceilings and zero visibility. None of the 5th Air Force has been doing anything for the past few days, due to the weather.

I had my team build me a board 24"X18" out of scrap wood. I got four 1:25,000 maps of our sector and put them all together. Then I placed it and a piece of transparent plastic that I'd brought with me from VMA-212 and plotted our MLR (main line of resistance), restricted corridor, our battalion and company positions, and all the emergency evacuation helicopter strips. It's very snazzy. Placed the positions that I plotted on reverse side of the plastic with black grease pencil, so it won't rub off. The situation of the MLR changes so often, I didn't want it on my map proper.

No mail from my honey yet. Keep your chin up, honey. There are happy times ahead for us, dearest girl that I love. Say a little prayer for Daddy. Kiss my darlings.

Love, Daddy

FORWARD AIR CONTROL AND CLOSE AIR SUPPORT

World War II produced many new opinions concerning how to support the ground troops with air power. In theory, this required the artillery forward observer on the ground to direct the aircraft overhead onto the target directly in front of the foot soldier or marine. But this proved unsatisfactory, due to misplaced bombs, rockets, or stray strafing attacks by friendly planes. This technique took a giant leap forward, however, when trained and qualified pilots were put on the ground with the foot soldiers on the front lines, bringing about a degree of air/ground coordination expertise, resulting in reduced accidental bombing of friendly forces. Later, when an airborne controller was added to the equation, things really began to improve. The Marines prided themselves for bringing this science to the maximum of their capability, although by 1952 most of the 8th Army along the 38th parallel in Korea had also improved their FAC training program, making close air support fairly safe and effective for the troops on the ground.

MY FRIEND, CAPTAIN ROBERT B. ROBINSON USMC

During the early stages of the Korean War, while the call up of the Marine Reserves dragged on, a variety of combat positions were being filled by regular Marine fighter pilots who had stayed in the Corps after WWII. As the campaign got under way, many of my old friends now found themselves out of their familiar role as pilots in the cockpit of a Marine fighter and, instead, learning strange new jobs. A good example of this was my friend, Robert B. Robinson, Jr. (Robby), who recently yielded to my urgent request to fill me in on his Korean experience, and on those many years that followed.

We had been very close throughout the cadet flying program in 1943 and, upon receiving our Navy Wings of Gold on 21 Dec 1943 at Corpus Christi, TX, I felt honored when asked that same wonderful day to become Robby's best man at the ceremony of his marriage to Lavonne, his longtime sweetheart. Both of them had come from Orange, CA, close to my own hometown of Huntington Park.

After commissioning, Robby and I received orders together to join Marine Dive Bomber Flight 121, VSB-5, at Masters Field, Opa Locka, Miami, FL. Wilbur (Pick) Pickering was also in that squadron. We flew Douglas SBD-5 dive bombers together for four months during early 1944 before going our separate ways. In 1945, during the closing days of WWII, Robby was flying night fighters, F6F-5N radar-mounted Grumman Hellcats, at Okinawa with VMF(N)-543, while I was flying F4U Corsair Fighters with VMF-223 at Okinawa. Briefly, we met aboard our mutual friend Pick's aircraft carrier *Block Island* (CVE-106) for our group picture. I would not see Robby or Pick again for 48 years.

Now let's get on with his fantastic story as an FAC (forward air controller) during the Inchon landing and later, during the taking of Seoul and on to the Chosin Reservoir. In my estimation, Robby's experience as an FAC in Korea was unparalleled in the history of the Marine Corps.

A BIRD'S EYE VIEW--FROM THE GROUND UP
By LtCol Robert B. Robinson USMC Ret.

Two facts were glaringly apparent as I swung my leg up and over. First, my foot wasn't encased in a size 10 flight deck shoe, and secondly, this wasn't the cockpit sill of my trusty "Bent Wing Bird." Actually, my foot was stuffed into a size 10 boondocker, topped by WWII leggings, into which my dungarees were neatly tucked, and my leg was going over the rail of an APA (U.S.S. Noble, APA-218) off the coast of Inchon, Korea. The date was September 15, 1950.

This whole scenario had its beginning back at MCAS El Toro when I received orders from VMF-(N)-542 to attend Forward Air Controller School at the Naval Amphibious Training Unit, Coronado, California. Upon completion of this training I was ordered to report to the Second Marine Division at Camp Lejeune, North Carolina.

During my trip from the West Coast to Camp Lejeune on June 25, 1950, North Korean forces crossed the line into South Korea. This action, of course, shed an entirely different light upon my initiation into the life of my "Walking Brethren."

I reported in to the Second Marine Division on July 11, 1950 and was assigned as Forward Air Controller, Air Naval Gunfire Liaison Company (ANGLICO FMF).

The next 18 days seemed to me to be an exercise in mass confusion. Supporting elements from many distant geographical locations rushed to Camp Lejeune, formed into an effective fighting unit, packed all equipment and personnel aboard truck convoys, trains, and transport planes and departed for Camp Pendleton, California on July 28, 1950 to report to the First Marine Division (Reinforced) where I was assigned as Forward Air Controller, 1stBn, First Marines.

Upon arrival at Camp Pendleton, around-the-clock ship loading operations commenced and the First Marine Division departed San Diego, California for Kobe, Japan, on August 13, 1950.

Upon arrival at Kobe, the ships were unloaded, reloaded for combat operations and sailed on September 8, 1950. Destination--Inchon, Korea.

The 36-foot tide in the Inchon harbor dictated a late afternoon amphibious landing in order for the LCVPs to approach the beach (in this case, the seawalls), disembark personnel and equipment and then retreat to deep water. At low tide, five miles of mud flats separated the shoreline from the seawalls.

The darkening sky was ablaze with a spectacular naval gunfire bombardment and scores of Marine and Navy close air support aircraft added to the fireworks as the enemy defensive positions were being neutralized prior to and during the actual ship-to-shore phase of the landing.

As my toe searched for the top rung of the cargo net draped over the side of the ship, I looked down 70 feet into what appeared to be a toy LCVP rapidly filling with an assortment of very heavily laden Marines. My journey down the net was an experience I will never forget! The only reasonably safe moment was when I was top man on the totem pole. From that point on down I was bombarded with various pieces of 782 gear that became separated from those above, my fingers were smashed by the boondockers of the too-eager Marines following me and the rolling of the ship only added to the general feeling of insecurity being experienced by those of us making our first trip down the net under any circumstance, let alone an actual combat amphibious landing.

With each descending step the LCVP seemed to grow magically to its proper dimensions, which, unfortunately, included a square foot or so for me and all my worldly possessions. When all of the space was completely filled, the order was given, "Shove off Coxswain, you're loaded." Depending upon the situation, this order can conjure up an enormous variety of wildly different feelings of anticipation. If you are departing ship for liberty ashore, anticipation is centered around life, love and the pursuit of excitement, bounded only by the hard cold cash in your wallet. If, on the other hand, you are departing ship for an amphibious landing on a hostile shore, anticipation is centered around life (basically, keeping the one you have) and fear of the unknown. The pursuit of excitement is unavoidable now and only time will tell if you are ready and able to meet the challenges ahead.

The trip ashore was uneventful and unexpectedly quiet. Each individual Marine was wrapped in a cocoon of his own thoughts and feelings. Talk was not necessary.

I was jarred out of my trance-like state as the LCVP banged against the seawall. The ramp lowered and the mass of humanity spilled out onto foreign soil and into a world that made men out of boys in a very short period of time.

My first order of business was to assemble my team and equipment and report to the Battalion Commander. Note: The composition of a Battalion Forward Air Controller team at the time of the Inchon landing was as follows:

1 - Naval Aviator
9 - Enlisted men
1 - Jeep, radio
1 - ANGRC-9, low frequency transceiver (back pack)
1 - MAW, 4-channel VHF transceiver (back pack)

As it turned out, this assembly process was not accomplished in a text book manner, mainly because all of my team did not come ashore in the same LCVP.

The late afternoon dusk rapidly turned into the darkest night on record. The flash of exploding shells and the ever present flares provided some light but seemed to be of little assistance in locating and identifying my team members. A constant din from a variety of sources rendered verbal communication impossible.

I was not alone in my frustration; the entire area seemed to be filled with people looking for other people--not just any people--only the people that fit correctly into their proper pigeon hole.

We have all observed ants streaming along a pathway in both directions. If you look closely you will note that individual ants almost never run into the back of the ant ahead, but almost always run nose-to-nose into every ant coming from the opposite direction. I don't understand why ants perform this oft repeated bumping ritual. Is it a form of communication to establish identity, is it to make sure they are on the right track, or is it because they can't see in the first place?

Those of you that have been involved in the act of joining up on your flight leader on a black night, overwater and under an overcast, understand the true value of two-way communications and proper identification. There isn't an aviator out there who can honestly say he has never tried to join up on some navigation buoy or has never joined up on the wrong tail light.

Let me tell you right now, finding and identifying nine Marines on a dark night, in a strange land, with no communications and no tail lights, is not a piece-of-cake either.

For whatever reasons ants go through their nose-bumping dance, they didn't have anything on me! I bumped into any number of unrecognized noses before I sorted out those that looked familiar and finally corralled my, as yet, untested fighting unit. That successful rendezvous solved only one of my immediate problems. Now I knew where we were, but didn't know where the Battalion CP was located.

Just about the time I thought I had a good handle on what my next move should be, word was passed that literally turned my world 180 degrees.

"GET BACK IN THE BOATS."
"WHATA YA MEAN--GET BACK IN THE BOATS?"
"GET BACK IN THE BOATS--WE'RE ON THE WRONG BEACH!!!"
"BUT SIR, I DON'T NEED THE PRACTICE."

The whole operation of getting back into the boats, proceeding to the correct landing site, and then disembarking again, remains quite hazy, although I did have the presence of mind to get my entire team into the same boat for the second landing of the evening.

From the very beginning, First Marine Airwing/First Marine Division Command, Control and Coordination worked in text book fashion. The First Marine Air Wing was used exclusively at this time to support the First Marine Division. When air support was requested, I could rest assured the aircraft assigned to my mission would be flown by personal friends, flying the "Bent Wing Bird" (F4U-4B Corsair).

Supreme confidence in the accuracy and discipline of Marine Close Air Support flights was rapidly established and I was given the green light to direct flights in as close as the tactical situation dictated, with little or no margin for error.

I considered that decision to be a tremendous feather in the cap of the FAC/Support Aircraft Team.

I served with the 1st Bn, 1st Marines, 1st MARDIV from Inchon landing to Seoul, the Wonsan landing, and to the Chosin Reservoir and return.

THIS WAS A PROUD TIME FOR THE UNITED STATE MARINE CORPS!
THIS WAS A VERY PROUD TIME FOR ME!

Robby elected to limit any additional disclosures concerning his memoirs of Korea, since his plans included producing his own book. (Refer to Appenidx Number 4 for additional background on Robby.)

In order to place the Chosin Reservoir operation in some perspective, as a follow-up I have included an account of the intensity of the action.

BGen Edwin H. Simmons USMC (Ret), the current director of the Marine Corps Historical Center in Washington D.C., was addressing some 54 members of Fox Company, 7th Marines on 12 Oct 91 during their reunion. Gen Simmons had been a major and commanding officer of Weapons Co, 3dBn, 1st Marines during the Chosin Reservoir operation. Fox Company had been to hell and back as they moved up onto Toktong Pass on 2 Nov 50. Its strength, with the usual reinforcements, according to official records, had been 240; when relieved, effective strength had dwindled to 122. This action may have been the most dramatic of the Korean War.

Among those present during the reunion was Gen Raymond G. Davis USMC (Ret), a former Assistant Commandant, but more important to Fox Company is that he, as a lieutenant colonel, had commanded the 1st Bn, 7th Marines, which came to their relief. For that action Gen Davis was awarded the Medal of Honor. The good general is now chairman of the KWVM (Korean War Veteran Memorial). On 28 Apr 93, site preparation began in Washington, D.C. The target date for dedication is 27 Jul 95.

Gen Simmons' concluding remarks concerning this redeployment sum up this operation admirably in his article appearing in the Fall 1991 *Fortitudine*:

The 1st Marine Division's commander, MGen Oliver P. Smith, thought that a winter line would be held around Hamhung-Hungnam, but MacArthur had given Almond orders to redeploy X Corps to the Pusan area of South Korea. More than a hundred thousand troops, thousands of vehicles, and mountains of supplies and equipment had to be gotten out. The 1st

Marine Division would embark immediately, while the corps' other two divisions, the Army's 7th and 3d Divisions, held the perimeter. We began embarking in the waiting transports on the 13th.

Since landing at Wonsan, we Marines had suffered 4,418 battle casualties and 7,313 non-battle casualties, mostly frost-bite and cold-induced respiratory problems. We had fought the 20th, 26th, 27th, and 42d Chinese Communist Armies, a total of at least 13 and probably 14 divisions. Chinese losses were estimated at 25,000 dead, 12,500 more wounded, but those are only guesses. Certainly the Chinese suffered more terribly from the cold and exposure than did we. The 26th Army reported: ". . . our soldiers frequently starve. . . some had only a few potatoes. . . . They were unable to maintain the physical strength for combat; the wounded personnel could not be evacuated."

The First Marine Division sailed from Hungnam on 15 December, a total of 22,215 men embarked in 21 Navy ships and seven merchantmen. I remember that a wishful rumor ran through the convoy: we were on our way to warm, tropical Indo-China to help the French. Instead we landed at Pusan and motor-marched to the "Bean Patch" at Masan where we recovered from frostbite and pneumonia, spent Christmas, got refitted and replacements, and with the New Year, moved out in an offensive to retake lost ground.

The Chosin Reservoir campaign was a dynamic one, very mobile in nature. By comparison, my Forward Air Control assignment turned out to be somewhat stationary, not unlike the trench and bunker type of warfare more characteristic of WWI, with the heavy emphasis on artillery and mortar barrages, and limited probing action on front line outposts day and night, rain or shine.

30 Jul 52
Wed. 1715
Changdan Village
3/1 CP

Dearest family,
Things went rather rough for me last night out on OP2, overlooking beautiful Panmunjom. It was raining when I got there and my two men and myself fashioned a level spot out, behind a rock, that would afford them some protection in the event of mortar or artillery. We got a shelter-half pitched and they had rubber mattresses that they laid down on the ground. We put our radio gear in their tent--what would fit--then cranked up the "Angry 9" with a hand cranked generator. The antennae was sticking through their shelter-half. The rain shorted out through our antennae and we couldn't transmit. Our receiver brought in our boys back here in the CP, however. It began raining so hard that I had them secure the gear and I bummed a spot in a leaky artillery bunker with three other men, on a two-hour watch rotation. They were in and out of the bunker all night. We had four inches of water on the deck in the morning. Shoes, "C" rations and boxes were floating around on the floor. What a mess! What a miserable existence!

My boys fared better than I did. They were dry and slept all night, except when two of our machine guns opened up on some suspected intruders at the base of the hill we were on. It started a fire fight that the Commies on an adjoining hill picked up and joined in. Our kids were very young and really shook. It rained all night and all day today.

Came on back here to the CP with a man who wanted to turn in to the battalion sick bay, and then I cleaned my filthy hair, shaved, and put on dry socks. My boots and pants were still wet, though. They have so many restrictions that I can't see how I'm going to be able to give them a good air strike, even if the weather does lift.

I took a Col Williamson of MAG-33 out to OP2 this afternoon on an inspection tour and brought him back. Then we had supper and now I'm writing to my darling. Oh, how I miss you, precious girl. I can hardly stand another day away from you. No mail as yet, honey.
Kiss my darlings and tell them I love them.

Night night, Daddy

Upper Left: Arrow denotes my position in photo. Korean laborers constructing our deeper, wider command bunker at 3/1 Battalion CP.

Upper and Midddle Right: Heavy timbers for vertical support of the massive overhead.

Lower Left, L to R: Lt Stapleton, Capt Peterson, Sgt Seaman, ?, but he's our Naval hospital corpsman, Capt Bill Whitbeck, CO of "G" Co. Thank God for our flak jackets. Picture taken beside our command bunker on OP 2.

Lower Right: Sgt Seaman at entrance to our OP 2 bunker.

Upper Left: Author controlling a support mission from his hilltop outpost overlooking Bunker Hill.

Upper Right: Ready for a chopper surveillance hop over my sector of control. Chopper strip at OP 181, Regt OP.

Middle Left: 3/1 Battalion CP, my home away from home if I didn't sleep in a bunker at the forward position.

Lower Left, Friends at 1st Regiment.
L to R: Maj Clyde W. Shealy, Maj Horace C. Reifel and Peterson.

Lower Right, L to R: Capt Douglas S. Ashton, of Portland, OR, and Peterson getting target practice with our 38 side arms. Doug was OP 2 CO, a Marine reservist whom I respected.

REPUBLIC F-84 THUNDERJET

F-84 Thunderjets, securely anchored aboard a carrier, en route to Japan for action over Korea.

Ridgway insisted that all weapons of every unit be employed to the maximum. The 75-mm recoilless rifle, whether mounted on the ground (as shown above) or on a jeep, proved to be useful in blasting out enemy bunkers.

Left: VMO-6 area. I took this photo from my OE-1 coming back from a spotting mission.

Middle Left: Spud at the controls of an HRS chopper belonging to the HMR-161 Marine Transport Squadron attached to the 1stMarDiv. LtCol John F. Carey commanded this fine unit which provided major support to all of us. A very comfortable ship to fly, the HRS was truly a valuable asset for the Division.

Middle Right: The boneyard for flak damaged OE-1s of VMO-6. We flew with a flak jacket on our upper bodies and put one on our seat to protect the "family jewels."

Lower Left: A hot volleyball game near the front lines.

Lower Right: About to take her up and recon the front lines.

31 Jul 52
Changdan Village
3rd/1st CP, Korea

Baby doll and precious boys,

It's only 1430 but I have a few spare minutes and I figured I'd better put them to the best possible use. After shoving off for my 25-minute jeep ride all alone up through the corridor on the way to Panmunjom and our outpost, I saw some suspicious looking characters on a haystack near the road. I thought they looked Chinese. I drove on but reported them to the company commander, Capt Doug Ashton, after I got to the outpost. He sent a rifle squad back, had them picked up and interrogated them. Sure enough, they were spies, so they turned them over to the Marine MP company.

Just after I got to the outpost I wondered why I didn't see anybody out of their bunkers or fox holes, and I no sooner cut the jeep's engine and began a 100-yard walk up to the Co CP bunker than I knew the reason for myself--we were under fire from a battery of 60mm mortars located on Hill 67, just a few hundred meters north of us. We received eight rounds and then they knocked it off. It was a new experience for me and one I can do without repeating. I had on my steel helmet and flak vest, and .38 strapped on my side. The Co CP bunker felt real secure, however. We received no casualties. I checked with my team and brought them up a new "Angry 9" radio, which we set up in the rain and tried to contact our CP back here at Battalion, but could not raise them. I had the boys secure and take cover in their shelter-half for the rest of the night. Then I talked with Capt Ashton (Doug) and his crew until midnight.

They made sandwiches out of "C" ration canned hamburgers, fresh raw onions and bread. Also had coffee. I only had the coffee. They are a nice lot. From a military standpoint they sure have an impossible situation to defend, but they're doing as good a job as they can. The telephone exchange for Doug's company is in the CP and they keep calling in, reporting activities from the various patrols the company has out, as they reach check points. It's interesting but I could do without it very nicely.

Skito, the top sergeant of Doug's company, is quite a character. He's had about 20 years in the Corps and really sounds like the old time rugged top kick one imagines would be running a company. Doug teases him a lot, but he is very well liked by all and they will miss him when he goes home in a few weeks.

The recon patrol leader came in to the bunker for a while to brief us on the patrol he was going to take out last night. It was so black out that I had quite a time finding my way to the artillery bunker at midnight, after I left the Co CP bunker. It had stopped raining and the whole skyline was visible in the far off distance. Seemed like we were an awful long way out in front of our MLR, and we were, too.

I flopped down on the air mattress, took my shoes and jacket off, and before long fell sound asleep. Woke up each time the watch was changed, though, which occurred every two hours. We tried contacting our rear CP early this morning and finally made a weak contact, but not sufficiently strong enough to work an air strike with them if we had to.

I came on back here to the CP (Battalion) and brought three "G" Company men along. After breakfast at 0900, I reported the night's activity to the colonel. Returning to the tent, I took a bath from my helmet and washed my underclothes. Now I feel a lot better.

Boy, this muggy weather really makes a guy sweat a lot. Nothing but rain off and on all the time lately. It's beginning to clear a little this afternoon and the sun is actually shining through in places. My clothes dried OK.

We have had a request in for an air strike for the past three days for Hill 123, in front of our sector, and I believe we may get it today. The controlling agency called us up and said we could count on a TOT (time over target) at 1700 today. If that's so, it means we will have to be up on the Hill 229 outpost at 1630 and we'll miss our supper. Oh well, such is life in the big city. Whenever anyone gripes about the upper command they use the term "city hall"; I guess it's appropriate.

Looked at all my pictures of my precious family today. I miss you all so very much. . . .

All my love, Daddy

LOG FOR JULY 1952

Date	Aircraft Type	Aircraft Number	Flight Duration	Type of Mission
3	AU-1	129336	2.0	Interdiction--Chugyop-san
24	HRS-1	127796	.7	1stMarDiv Front Line Recon.

1 Aug 52
Changdan, Korea

Hello baby girl and my two little darlings,

Last night as I arrived at OP2 they were having a mortar duel. The goonies lobbed ten 61mm mortars into our positions and Lt Fitzsimmons, the artillery forward observer caught a small piece of shrapnel in his hand and I don't see how they didn't get clobbered, except that they were really flat on their faces next to some sand bags. His OP is right up on top of OP2, overlooking Hill 67, which is held by the enemy, and they were the ones throwing the 61mm mortar at him. He was plenty sore, and by the time I got there (about five minutes after they had received the mortars) he was calling in our 81mm mortars and artillery from back at Bn CP. They put some good hits in there with 105s. He had them zeroed in and vowed he would hit them again last night around 2300 when they came out to repair the damage.

The weather turned clear and cool last night and the moon appeared about half full. Sitting up on the bunker looking out over goonie land, and south, back toward our lines, OP2 was a lonely spot to spend the night. It's bad enough during the day. I talked to you, dearest girl, and said almost out loud how much I love you and miss you.

Captain Ashton sent patrols out from OP2 up to the forward slopes of 67. I haven't heard whether they made contact or not. Some of our patrols did make contact over on our right flank of the MLR of our Battalion where we had one killed and five wounded. Maj Biehl, who was here in the Bn CP, called for an emergency helicopter evac and got one at 0230 this morning and another at 0430. He had quite a night.

We climbed our Hill 229 in front of Bn CP, (confidential) and at 1030 this morning we got our first air strike, four ADs from MAG-12, which hit Hill 123, 2000 meters in front of us. They got 90% cov. 75% effective, 2 mortars destroyed, 1 mortar damaged, 2 bunkers destroyed, 200 yards of trenches damaged, 2 KIAs and 3 WIAs. We spotted an enemy tank in the open, too, but the OEs couldn't find him under his camouflage and gave up. We were bushed after the strike, which lasted until 1200. I ran it myself, with the OE aiding. I called in WP ("Willie Peter", white phosphorus) to mark it.

Major Biehl and I climbed down the mountain. Then I got my maps and Sgt Walwood, our team sergeant, and we set out for three hours of searching and replatting our helicopter evac strips in our Battalion sector. We relocated several. We use colored cloth panels which we fashion into identifiable numbers from the air on each strip, plat its position, then call it into Regiment for recording. Tired, hot and beat on the way back to Bn CP, we spied a shower unit with truck etc along the side of the road. We stopped and inquired, "Is this for our use?" and they said roger. I took all my clothes off and swapped straight across for brand spanking new. Took an icy cold shower and dressed, and boy, do I feel a lot better.

We put in for an MPQ (night radar controlled air strike) on a supply and troop area 6000 meters northwest of our lines. They sent it back disapproved. We submitted another day strike this afternoon and have received some indication that we may run into trouble on it because it's only 500 meters from our front line troops, awfully close to control an air strike. If it comes through, we'll have to climb Item Company hill and control from there. Dug in on the north slope of Bunker Hill, the Chinese have brought in mortars which have given our right flank, Item Co, a bad time. In fact, we've taken some casualties from them. I'd like to be able to help them out with a good napalm air strike. Tonight at about 1830 I'll go out to OP2 again for the night.

My enlisted men finally got a bunker and got out of their shelter-half. Oh, I almost forgot to mention that a 61mm mortar missed our "Angry 9" radio by ten feet. It threw rocks etc on it. My men were going to man it in another five minutes. Lucky, eh? That was on OP2. We haven't got any incoming here at Bn CP as yet. The bridges crossing the Imjin are washed out and trucks are using the Freedom Gate bridge for all traffic.

Love ya all, Daddy

2 Aug 52
Changdan, Korea, Saturday

Dearest girl and precious boys,
  Boy, has the daddy had a time of it since I last wrote you, darling.
  Last night on OP2 was fairly uneventful, except that some private tossed a hand grenade at what he thought was a goonie creeping up on him. Then at about 0200 this morning we were awakened by drums and bugles in the distance and everybody figured this was it, but nothing materialized all night. Our patrols made a few small contacts.
  I got up at 0700 and drove on back alone the one and a half miles to the MLR and Bn CP, shaved and had breakfast, then got my crew and began a crusade to relocate some helicopter strips which we remarked with new panels, cleared weeds and shrubs from the area, working like beavers. Then at 1400 the general's helicopter landed in the Bn CP strip and I aided the 'copter in landing. Major Christy, the battalion exec, greeted the general and I stood off in the background because I didn't want to get roped into an escort deal for every VIP that comes up to the front lines. I have to meet the 'copter at 1500 on the same strip to pick up the general. After that I have to go out to the MLR and scout out another evac strip for our left flank company with the battalion doctor. Will eat at 1630, then work on my report of helicopter strips--their condition, location, and whether they can be used day or night.
  We submitted air strike requests for two more missions, one day and one night, in front of our battalion.
  Today the weather is low and not operational for VF aircraft. It's beginning to rain again right now. The general's 'copter just landed. Major Biehl caught it.
  We had two enemy tanks spotted in front of our sector and our artillery destroyed both of them and inflicted 135 troop casualties. How can they tell how many they have hit? By actual count through a 20 BC scope on our highest hilltop OP and by OE count. The goonies must be planning something, but I can't figure what it is.
  Mail came in yesterday, but the daddy hava no. Boy, what I wouldn't give for a nice fat juicy letter full of loving thoughts and a word from my precious wife about how she is and how my darlings are fairing!
  It's very close and muggy today and my clothes are sticking to me as never before. What weather! The countryside is green, with beautiful rolling hills and meadows, but not very many trees. It's quite lush right here where we have our CP.
  There are happier days ahead and oh, how I'm going to live every day to its fullest!

All my love, darling, Daddy

Here's Ricky's tooth. I want you to hang on to it, honey.

FROM THE FRYING PAN INTO THE FIRE

3 Aug 52
Changdan, Sunday Noon

Precious family of mine,
  The daddy spent a "clutched up" night on OP2. They sent out five separate assault teams from our position and several of them made contact. One team assaulted Brown Hill, fronting our outpost, and killed eight goonies in hand-to-hand combat. I talked to the recon leader, Lt Watson, before and after the assault, in the "G" Co CP bunker. During the entire

period from 2000 until 0100 I stayed in the CP with Capt Ashton, and kept abreast of all the patrol activities with Ashton's situation map. The patrols would call in via ground line which they'd strung out as they left the OP. They were all tied in on the same net and Capt Ashton gave them on-the-spot directions via phone. They had fire plans evolved around the activities of all the patrols. For instance, they sent up colored flares if the ground line went out, which several did during the course of the evening; two red flares indicated "Give me plan Victor mortar barrage around my patrol position," etc. There is a heck of a lot to this ground fighting.

They had expected heavier casualties from this encounter. However, we received only two slightly wounded by burp gun, skin cuts by near misses. They all wear flak vests and steel helmets, as do all of us on Hill OP2. We expected a platoon-size assault on our OP last night because we'd intercepted an enemy communication to that effect. It came, however, on the Commonwealth sector to the right of the Marine sector.

I certainly have picked up a lot in regard to ground fighting. I prefer the air, however, and am actually hurting a little bit to get back into my old pal, the bent-winged monster. My bum is sore from bouncing along in my jeep this past week. I had a tiny little roll of fat starting on my side, but all the mountain climbing I've done this week and the terrific amount of sweating has slimmed me down and I'm wearing a pair of 32" dungarees, with room to spare. I'm in wonderful physical shape, darling, and have never felt better in my life. These two meals a day have cut my weight a little also.

I miss my precious family so very much, though, darling, that it's really tough on me. I try to push you out of my thoughts sometimes so I can concentrate on the situation at hand, but you all just keep worming yourselves right back in there, so I don't fight it any more.

1800

I just came back down from OP 229, where I spent the best part of five hours waiting for aircraft that never showed up. Two other battalions got some, but I didn't make out. Boy, that little jeep of mine is really a mountain climber. It's about a 15% grade and it really labors going up there. It would be fun to have a jeep and blaze our own trails through the desert and mountains. I'll bet it would be good for pulling a trailer too. I pulled a loaded trailer up to OP2 the other night over the roughest sort of road and it just pulled it along as nicely as could be. Capt Doug Ashton was running low on ammo and chow, so I resupplied him.

It's 1900 now and I have to get ready to go up to OP2 in a few minutes for my nightly surveillance. I sent Corporal Boone back today to this Bn CP and borrowed another man from the 1st/1st to replace him. Now Evans is our only man from the 3rd/1st and he's going to be relieved in a few days. My men on OP 229 asked today if they could come on down to get a change of clothes and a shower. Of course I said yes. I have one negro boy named Stamps, along with a white boy named Skinner, up on 229. My three boys here at the CP are named Walwood, O'Gara and Bowman (a carrot redhead). Not one of them is over 20 years.

Last night on OP2 Boone and Evans kept asking me all about flying and radio navigation, and I talked to them for several hours. Then I talked to the doctor for another hour while looking out over goonie land. It was cool but the mosquitoes kept giving us a bad time. The Army signal unit had their search light on right at the Panmunjom site, shining straight up and staying in one spot. Over on the KMC sector another search light played out over no-man's-land searching for goonies. All during the night I heard mortar, machine guns and heavy artillery pounding away.

Enough of that! No mail! Has me disturbed somewhat and I'll feel a lot better when some comes in.

I love you, precious family.

Love, Daddy

4 Aug 52
Changdan
Monday 1320

Dearest family,
I'm standing by to move out to Item Co OP which is on our right flank. I'm supposed to get air around 1700 this afternoon for a coordinated air strike and battalion battery of 105mm and 81mm. We used to be able to count on about 12 A/C from MAG-12 daily, weather permitting, but now there's a new regime and we cannot look forward to our 12 aircraft daily. Our requests for aircraft have to go through Devastate Baker, our TADC, then monitored through the 1st Reg TACP and on to Division Air FCSS, on to 5th Air Force and JOC. We have no idea when we can count on our strike A/C, and, consequently, either Bill or I will probably have to man 229 or Item Co OP all day every day, weather permitting.

We monitor our Angry 9 all day and maybe we'll be able to beat them on station by driving like mad to either one of our OPs. We're moving out to Item OP at 1400 and we're taking our AN/URC 4X4 radio jeep and MAW along for remote control. We've alerted our artillery to stand by for my order for "Willy Peter" to mark the target because 500 meters is very close to have to control A/C, but I think with a closely coordinated effort we'll make out OK. Item Co has been receiving incoming mortar and artillery all morning from the Commies on the north side of Bunker Hill, the target we're going to put our air on.

5 Aug 52
Tuesday, 0830

Hi darling,
We stayed in a slit trench on Item Co front lines waiting patiently for our A/C to arrive. Finally, at around 1905, Devastate Baker called and told me he had four F-84 Air Force Jets.

We had received machine gun and sniper fire, and also many, many rounds of 76mm artillery very near our position, throwing rocks and sand on us it came so close. Then we heard the zing from the machine gun bullets about every two minutes regularly. I had no OE to assist, but I directed the F-84s in with WP and gave them a good mark. They had 1000-lb GP and 5-inch rockets really working Bunker Hill over. The terrific blast effect shook us up considerably because we were so close. As we were securing our gear, Devastate Baker called me again and gave me three P-80s which I brought back on a target near the others and used them until dark.

After sharing a can of beans with some troops in Item Co I came on back to CP and saw Col Armitage. He congratulated Bill and me on running an excellent air strike. I drove on out to OP2 at 2300 and arrived about five minutes before a mortar barrage began hitting us. I was inside the Co CP bunker, though, and safe as could be.

During a lull in the attack, I went up on top of the hill and hit the pad in the artillery bunker. Another barrage opened up at midnight, lasting about a half hour. It was uncomfortably hot last night but, after tossing and turning and batting mosquitoes for an hour or so, I went off to sleep. I don't have a mosquito net up on OP2, so I'm taking one up tonight. The kids in the bunker I sleep in are really shook up on account of the mortars. They haven't taken many casualties, though, thank God.

I came on back here to the Bn CP at 0800, shaved and had breakfast. Capt Butler told me I had a court martial at 1030, so this will prove a new experience.

I have finally received seven letters, honey girl. The lunkheads at VMF-212 mail room put the wrong forwarding address on my mail, but it has been corrected.

Looking back to 26 July, I believe I forgot to wish you a happy birthday, honey girl. At least I got your gift off in time.

Ricky is sweet telling you he dreams about me almost every night. The precious little guys, I'd give anything to get home.

Love from your very own Daddy

5 Aug 52
Changdan, Korea
Tuesday 1715

Dearest Family,
    I wrote to you this morning on the bottom of yesterday's letter, but I felt like having a scooshie little chat with all of you anyway.
    Today I had the court martial. It was for a young 19-year-old PFC who had accidentally discharged his carbine through another fellow's neck while standing in the chow line. The fellow he shot is on the hospital ship at Inchon and will be OK. We tried him on a special court martial. I was only one of the four-member team. We met from 1030 until 1600 this afternoon solid. We gave him as light a sentence as we could, and then recommended clemency, 30 days at hard labor and two thirds of one month's pay. They have held him over here in Korea from going home on 1 July, awaiting trial. I believe the CO of the 1stMarDiv will knock off the 30 days hard labor because of it. He'll only have to pay $60.00 and he's leaving for the U.S. almost immediately. I felt sorry for the kid (Julian Torres).
    After the trial I hurried on over here to the tent to take a helmet bath, and put on a clean change of underclothes and socks.
    Bill dashed up on the 229 OP today when they called to inform him he had an air strike. After he got up there the darn radios wouldn't work. He had to turn them over to the KMC to the south of our sector. We sure were sore. An FAC isn't any better than his radio gear. The 2nd Bn 1st FAC to the right of us ran an air strike on Bunker Hill this morning, so we did get a little benefit out of our air today. Bill was going to use them on Yoke Hill, fronting our sector. Oh well, we will get another chance tomorrow.
    Ricky's drawing and writing was very interesting and I think he'd doing fine, don't you, darling? I miss the precious little guys so very much. My wants out of this world are very simple, darling--just my precious little family would complete the most wonderful picture I could ever paint in my wildest ambitions.
    I'm listening to Jack Smith's radio program with Ginny Sims. They are good together. Bill's little radio really puts out. I'm going to peddle mine to the highest bidder, I think. It's nice, but I don't use it anymore. I don't have any radio at all, of course, at night out on OP2.
    I'm glad you gave the maroon hanky box to Nanna. No mail today.

                                      Love, Daddy

6 Aug 52
On top of old 229
Changdan, Korea
Wednesday

Dearest girl and my two darlings,
    Happy day--got two wonderful letters from you today, 23 and 31 July. The 31 July letter was the first one I've received with my new address. I got hot finally and mailed the dumb jerk of a mail clerk at VMA-212 my address the second time. He keeps putting on 3rd Pl.
    The kid show sounded swell down at Hermosa. You were sweet to take Ricky and the girls. I'd love to watch the expressions on Ricky's face. He's very expressive in the face, isn't he? Randy too, for that matter.
    Last night after the battalion meeting (officers from all companies and all departments) at 1800, we (Maj Bill Biehl and myself and a Lt Malone) went over to the 1st Regiment CP and had a meeting, where we tried to work out an artillery flak suppression on some of the heavy anti-aircraft concentrations fronting us. We are also working out a deal with the "Four Deuces" (4.2" mortar group) to mark our targets for us on our command. The entire plan requires infinite patience and coordination because we have patrols out all over the place and we have to exercise extreme care not to clobber any of our own men.
    I arrived on OP2 at 2130 last night and boy, it sure is a long, scary ride alone in a jeep at night, without any lights, on that lonely stretch of no-man's-land on the way to OP2. I stopped briefly in the "Bloody George" G Co CP bunker and passed the time for a while with Capt Doug

Ashton. Told him of a goonie or two I noticed on the way out to OP2. He thanked me and sent out an eight-man squad to try and make contact. I brought my mosquito net and poles along and set them up in the bunker, so I had a much better sleep last night.

  Came back down to Bn CP for breakfast, then got a three-man work party together and cleared an area not too far from the Bn CP for a helicopter strip, large enough to accommodate three large 'copters all at once. I numbered it in colored panels "42" and laid out the border in part panels and part 2" white cloth marker. Cleared an area down from the plateau (strip) and laid sandbags in for steps.

  We are supposed to get toksan (many, many) VIPs tomorrow to observe our air strike. They will 'copter to Bn CP strip "42" and jeep to the top of 229. I am up here on 229 now sitting on a sandbag in a slit trench with all my radio gear before me. I have checked it all and am just waiting for Dev. Baker to call me on my "Angry 9" down at my radio jeep, and then I'll come up on my VHF remote set or my VHF (MAW) portable and contact my aircraft and hit Yoke or 123. My mortar man is to my right and my artillery (105mm) to my left. I have 3 (EE8) field phones to aid me. I'm the senior officer and it's my show. Where are my planes now? My 4.2" mortar and 105mm guns themselves are, of course, to the rear of our position near Bn CP; just the observers and field phones are up here on the front lines with me. I have called in my own artillery and mortars, and have adjusted fire. Lt Monroe is going to check me out on the sighting adjusting, firing of the 105mm and the 155mm as soon as we get some time. Lt Lawry, the 4.2" CO, is going to cut me in on the operation and etc of the "Four Deuces". OP2 has "Bloody George" G Company on it. Hill 229 has "Hairy How" H Company on it. Right flank has "Fight'em with Item" I Company.

1615

  Just knocked off the letter long enough to control two air strikes. I got (8) F9F Panther jets and ran them all in on the targets inside of 20 minutes. Had a little radio trouble during the strike, but everything came out OK at the end. Dev. Baker gave the jets to me because they were low on gas and had to return to base in a very few minutes. I ran them in and gave them adjustments as I saw them. They destroyed several bunkers and OP positions and lots of trench lines. One of the planes had hung napalm and tossed it about 1500 meters and burned off a whole hill. I wouldn't be surprised but what they knocked off a few goonies, just the same.

  Bill came dashing up in his jeep after we got the call from Dev. Baker. I can see four aircraft circling our other battalion (the 2nd/1st); they have some good targets over there. They receive a lot of 76mm from the back side of most of the goonie hills fronting their line. Those are Corsairs from MAG-12 working over there. Boy, it's good to see those old Corsairs. The rocket and bomb noise takes about ten seconds to reach our ears. It's funny, seeing the rockets leaving, then ten seconds later hearing their sound. I guess it's all over with. Our mortars are still adjusting their fire for our targets tomorrow.

  It sure is hot today. I'm only wearing my boots, pants, flak vest and hat, but I'm still wringing wet.

  Sure hoping I get some more mail tonight. I love your wonderful letters, dearest girl, and my every thought is of my wonderful family that means the world and all to me.

  I got a kick out of the newspaper clipping about me. Boy, I'll be glad when I'm home reading about somebody else for a change. I'm sick and tired of war.

  Kiss my boys and tell them their daddy loves them. Randy sounds like he's doing fine on his trike. I'd love to see him go.

Love to my little gang, Daddy

7 Aug 52
Thursday noon

Dearest girl and my two precious boys.

  Last night as I approached OP2 I sensed that all was not serene, and my feelings were not unfounded, for it wasn't two minutes after I stepped out of the Co CP bunker and on my way to the top of the hill that all hell *broke* loose with a terrific barrage of 60mm and 80mm goonie mortars. About (12) 60s exploded near me, the closest one landing about ten feet away. The blast knocked me down and I stayed for about 20 seconds, thinking I'd been hit because the blast tossed rocks, gravel and dirt against me and the rocks stung like shrapnel. When they kept coming in at the rate of one or two every five seconds, I jumped up and made a run for my bunker 200 feet away, up near the top of the hill mass. Others landed as close as the first, showering me with rocks and debris. Somehow I made it to the bunker and hit the deck with two other guys already there.

After it was all over I examined myself and counted several rock or shrapnel bruises on my arms and legs and one on my cheek--no blood. I was OK, completely unscathed but shook. Thirty minutes later we got a similar 60mm barrage, and it came at different intervals all through the night. Again at 0800 this morning, just prior to my leaving the bunker, we got another blast. I made a dash for it down the hill to my jeep, cranked it over, and away I went back the Panmunjom road to the Bn CP. Ate breakfast at 0900 and wrote up two more air strike requests.

Attended an hour briefing for our big coordinated artillery flak suppression/mortar spotting air strike. We are going up to the 229 OP at 1300 to prepare our radio equipment for the big deal. A lot of planning has gone into this and generals from all branches of the services will be there.

It was 106° in the shade here yesterday and every bit as hot today. I slept in my clothes because they anticipated a goonie attack to back up their heavy mortar barrage. It was hairy all night and our patrols out in front of OP2 ran into some goonies but they managed to turn them back. I got about two hours sleep between mortar barrages and the men changing watch from our bunker.

I found the nose and tail of the mortar that knocked me down. I'll send it home soon. No post office here at Bn CP.

Bye bye, dearest girl. I love you. Kiss my darlings and tell them to be good boys. Don't worry about me, honey. The bunkers are **well built**.

Love, Daddy

P.S. Remind me to write a book when I get home.

AN OVERVIEW OF THE GENERAL SITUATION AT THE FRONT

To fill in the central part of the EUSAK front where the change of IX Corps boundary had created a gap in the line, the UN commander inserted the ROK II Corps with three divisions (ROK 6th, ROK Capital, and ROK 3d) forward. Immediately to the right of this new ROK Corps sector, the X Corps continued in approximately its same position on the east-central front. Its ROK 7th and U.S. 25th Division remained on line, while the ROK 8th had advanced to the former sector of the Marine division in the wild Punchbowl country. At the far right of the UN line, the ROK I front was held by the ROK 11th Division at the X Corps boundary and the ROK 5th along the Sea of Japan. By 1 May 52, nine Republic of Korea divisions had been emplaced on the UNC main defense line, three more than had been there in mid-March.

Throughout Korea in March and April there had been a general stagnation of offensive action of both sides because of fog, rain and mud. In May, however, the Chinese launched no less than 30 probing attacks against the ROK 1st Division in the I Corps sector without gaining any significant advantage. To the right, the enemy and the U.S. 45th Division traded blows in several patrol actions. In June major EUSAK combat action was still centered in the 45th sector but the following month was marked by sharp battlefront clashes in nearly all Eighth Army division areas. For a two-week period in July and August heavy seasonal rains limited both ground and air action. With the return of normal weather, heavy fighting again broke out, concentrated in the I Corps sector. That action did not abate until late August, when the onset of the heaviest rains of the season again drastically reduced military operations.

Communist ground activities in the spring of 1952 were marked by increased artillery support which resulted in telling damage to UN infantry and artillery positions. Thus, during May, the enemy expended approximately 102,000 artillery and mortar rounds against the Allied front, roughly 12 times the number fired the previous July just prior to the period of stabilized battlelines in Korea. The artillery buildup was accompanied by a sharp decrease in hostile air support activities. While the Chinese had flown 3,700 jet sorties during the first month of 1952, by June the monthly total had dropped to 308.

8 Aug 52
Changdan, Korea
Friday, 1115

Dearest family,

Yesterday, amidst a multitude of very high Army, Navy, Air Force and Marine brass who had chosen Hill 229 to observe Bill's and my eight-plane AD Skyraider strike on targets Yoke and Hill 123, we had a dynamotor burn out in our radio jeep one hour prior to the time the planes were to arrive on station. I sent Sgt Walwood back with it to the Division Anglico which is about ten miles behind our front lines and he exchanged radio jeeps but didn't get back until 2300. Meanwhile, I got the 1st Regiment TACP team's radio jeep up on the hill and, between three portable MAW VHF radio sets and running a remote line down to the radio jeep, we managed to have good communications.

It was about 110°F yesterday and Bill and I were drenched when the strike was finally over and our men secured our gear. At 1900 we came on down from the hill and had dinner. (Harry, our officers mess sergeant, kept some chow for us.) We attended the colonel's nightly briefing and he complimented us (Bill and me) on the beautiful way the air strike went off. The colonel said the generals were really pleased at the coordination between mortars marking the target and 105mm and 155mm VT (proximity fused, air bursting artillery) flak suppression. They complimented the colonel, and he in turn us, for a beautiful job well planned and executed. We were tired and beat but well satisfied with ourselves that we had run off the air strike like one should be run.

*Later, after briefing, I took a bath from a helmet and put on clean underclothes. Then Capt Ashton, the "G" Co commander, and I drove up to OP2 for the night. I stopped in at their Co CP bunker for an hour, then at 2200 I started up to the top to my bunker and the goonies tossed in some 60s, so I dropped back to the Co CP for 15 minutes and tried again. Got all the way up OK. Had a relatively quiet night except for an occasional 60mm or 82mm coming in every hour or so during the night. At 0615 this morning they tossed some 82s at us and one landed squarely on top of **our** bunker. The terrific noise and explosion really rocked us. It tossed rock and sand all over the place. Another dropped just outside our door but the sandbags protected us from it.*

On examining the 82 that hit our roof, I found that it dug a hole measuring about three feet across and fourteen inches deep. I picked mortar fragments up that were lodged in sandbags which I'll be sending home soon. I dashed down the hill this morning, hopped into my jeep and headed for the Bn CP.

Bill had to roll out of the basket at 0700 to run an air strike we hadn't known we were getting. He rushed up to the hilltop, only to find that our new radio jeep wouldn't work, so he used one of our portables (MAW) and just barely made out. He had (4) F-84 Air Force jets.

I have been planning another air strike on Bunker Hill for this afternoon or tomorrow morning and selecting the coordinates. I want mortars (4.2") to mark WP and flak suppression points for our 105s and 155s. The company commander's personal supporting weapon is 81mm mortar. He can employ it any time anywhere without coordinating with the Battalion or Regiment FDC (fire direction center). He employs it in close support of his platoon patrols etc.

I'm listening to the Jack Kirkwood show and boy, it's hard to concentrate on writing a letter. No mail today. None yesterday.

I just sent Sgt Walwood back to Div Anglico to get another radio jeep. Hope he gets it back in time for our afternoon air strike. The MAW VHF has a wet cell battery that doesn't allow much of a power output to transmit. We receive OK, however.

This water situation here at Bn is critical. All water is hauled in by water trailer and transferred to five gallon cans. We started out here with five cans; now we're down to two. The four of us use it up faster that we can keep supplied.

Bill took several pictures of me with my camera while I was crouched in my slit trench up on 229 controlling the air strike yesterday. It completed another roll that I'll have to have developed whenever I get a chance.

Kiss my darling little guys and take a few for your precious self. I love you, honey.

Love, Daddy

OPERATION RIPPLE

Just as things began to quiet down on the front, the Marines would quietly move their multiple rocket launchers up behind my hill. Marine Helicopter Squadron HMR-161 would transport the 4.5-inch rocket battery and its personnel to the various firing positions in this newly introduced tactical innovation known as Operation Ripple. A characteristic of a 4.5-inch rocket launcher is the discharge of 24 rounds in quick succession called a ripple. A battery of six launchers can fire 144 rounds on a target in less than a minute. They would let go with a salvo that absolutely scared the living hell out of us and it seemed like we could feel the heat and the disturbed air as the rockets went screaming over our head. The Marine rocket launching crew would then get the hell out of there by helicopter as fast as they could, for within minutes the Chinese would return an artillery barrage on the rocket position (no longer there, of course), with numerous rounds falling on my position. I always failed to see any advantage in this practice. I suppose the generals back at the Division got their kicks, but I sure didn't appreciate it. On cloudy days when we had a very low ceiling, I'd get sprinkled with shrapnel from my own friendly artillery batteries whenever their VT fused rounds exploded prematurely over my position due to the affect of the low cloud ceiling.

This was actually a well thought out plan by the Division artillery planners. One provision required a battery in each battalion to select counter-counterbattery positions and occupy them for 24 consecutive hours each week. Another provision of the program was the selection by each battalion of ten roving gun positions, which were to be occupied by a single weapon, rotated to each place at least once weekly. By these tactics, the artillery regiment hoped not only to mislead the Chinese in their estimate of the strength and location of Marine artillery but also to dilute enemy counterbattery intelligence by causing him to fire into areas just vacated by friendly guns. The effectiveness of the program was demonstrated on numerous occasions when the enemy fired counterbattery into unoccupied positions. An added advantage was that of providing deeper supporting fires on target areas.

THE BATTLE FOR BUNKER HILL BEGINS IN EARNEST

As the western anchor of the Eighth Army front in Korea during the summer of 1952, the 1st Marine Division guarded the critical corridor leading to the South Korean capital of Seoul. The 35-mile Marine front was aptly compared to the trench warfare of World War I, as the front lines, or Main Line of Resistance (MLR) consisted of trenches and bunkers running along the ridgelines of hills. Across a precarious no man's land, the Chinese began extending their own trench system during the spring of 1952 towards Marine lines.

Early on the morning of 9 August, Chinese forces assaulted 1st Marines positions at Outpost Siberia, on Hill 58A, and the Battle for Bunker Hill began in earnest. The ensuing 9-16 August struggle for the heights which commanded parts of the Marine MLR developed into some of the fiercest fighting of the Korean War. Intense Chinese small arms fire, along with mortars and artillery, was answered in full by Marine coordinated support fires--tanks, rockets, artillery and mortars. Though successful in repelling the Chinese assaults on the division center during Bunker Hill, Marine casualties stood at 48 killed, 313 seriously wounded and several hundred treated and returned to duty. Increasing use of bullet resistant vests along with timely helicopter evacuation of the wounded saved the lives of many Marines. In the final analysis, it was the determination and courage of the individual Leatherneck in defending Bunker Hill which resulted in the first major Marine victory in west Korea. **CREDIT: Robert V. Aquilina, Ass't. Head Reference Section, USMC Historical Center, Washington, D.C.**

9 Aug 52
Changdan, Korea
Saturday 1400

Darling family,
Happy day--got two letters from my darlings yesterday, Aug 1 and Aug 2. Gee, it's wonderful hearing from you. My whole day is shot unless I get a letter from my honey. You sure had an experience at the Boston store fighting the old bags for the bathing suits. I'd love to see you in your new swim suit. I'm glad you had Nanna take a picture of you in it.

I thought that was sweet of Ricky boy buying the American flag when he had a selection of all those toys. He's shaping up into a fine little specimen.

Let's see now, what have I been doing? Well, yesterday afternoon five congressmen and several generals came up to observe our air strike and also a United Nations war correspondent from NBC with a tape recorder. His name was Carlson. He recorded my every word to the strike aircraft and really got himself an exciting bit of conversation. I had (4) AD Skyraiders on target and one of them got clipped in the left wing with a goonie 20mm and had to jettison his load on the target and head for home. His voice came over the air in a frantic pitch and I responded by directing him back over friendly lines. The other three returned to the target and gave them a good show. Carlson said he would return to Tokyo Monday and shortwave my tape to New York for use on or about Wednesday's program. I don't know who the congressmen were. As usual, I returned to OP2 where they'd received (30) 82mm mortars on their position five minutes before I got there. I heard the noise on my way out. None fell during the night, so we got some sleep.

In the morning I drove back to Bn CP, had breakfast and shaved. Then Bill and I prepared a briefing for five VIPs that we met at the colonel's tent. They were all big wheels from Douglas Aircraft, El Segundo, except one, Navy Cmdr Brown of the Bu Aer (Bureau of Aeronautics). Maj Bill Biehl and I escorted them in a three-jeep caravan up to OP 229, broke out our radios and monitored an air strike in the 2nd Battalion's sector where the Communists have broken through and are threatening our right flank. We have suffered 75 percent casualties to (2) full size platoons trying to regain the outpost. They hit us at 0355 this morning, along with a push off toward the KMCs on our left flank last night at 2230. They fought all night long. Tracers could be seen and cannon roar heard until morning. Machine gun chatter sounded so close that we felt as though it was being directed at us. They left OP2 alone last night, however. The VIPs were all project engineers and heads of their various engineering groups: Cox, Devan, Quick, Nichols--all from Douglas Aircraft Co.

I struck up quite an acquaintance with Mr. Quick who is chief project engineer on the new AD Skyraider. He said he'd either look you up or call you in ten days and give you a first-hand report on me, so stand by. Doesn't hurt to make a few acquaintances. His wife is very friendly with Mrs. Garrett. Who knows what may come of it? I, of course, told him all about my AiResearch connections. He invited me over to Douglas on my return.

Mr. Quick's party had been on the Boxer *when it had experienced its trouble. He said he didn't want to go through that again soon. The story goes, an ordnance man fired a gun and the bullet went into a gas tank of a plane ahead of it. It burst on fire and the fire exploded a 500-pound bomb, all down on the hangar deck. Fire broke out and seven or eight F9F Panther jets were destroyed, seven men killed, 30 or more jumped overboard and many others were hurt. Some ordeal for a civilian!*

After we pointed out Panmunjom to them through our 20 BC scope and gave them a word and visual picture of our panorama of goonie land that spreads out before us in front of 229, we took them all back down the hill and six or seven miles down to 1st Regiment, where we had lunch--my first noon meal since 26 July. We left them at that point after I took some pictures of the group. They continued on their tour of our radar control party and are going back to Seoul and 5th Air Force and JOC. Back home by 18 August. A 30-day deal for them.

Some trip, eh what? Maj Jack Shoden, from TACP 1st Reg, briefed Bill and me on the goonie breakthrough in front of the 2nd Bn. Capts Daniels and Hayden have been up all night. Jack's been up all night also and really shows it. We sent two MAW radios up to the 2nd as standby for them, and just a few minutes ago Jack called from regiment and asked either Major Biehl or me to come up on the 2nd Bn's front line where they're catching so much hell and control the aircraft for them. Apparently, Hayden and Daniels are worn out. They have controlled about six air strikes already since early this morning. . . .Bill went because I have OP2 tonight.

A call came in from the doctor at Bn aid station requesting helicopter evacuation for two casualties. I called Wind-Wonderful Forward and got the helicopter up there in five minutes. I lifted them on the stretcher carrier of the 'copter, strapped them in, and the 'copter was on its way in 60 seconds back to Able Med, back by Division CP. Some service. The two boys got hit a few minutes ago over at the 2nd Bn area and were brought over here by mistake. They should have been evacuated from 2nd Bn aid point. Boy, they've had about a hundred casualties already today. The Communists have an unlimited supply of mortar, machine gun and artillery ammo. Those darn Russians are the cause of this whole rotten mess.

Bye bye for now, honey. I loves ya and adores ya. You're my everything back there, darlings. Take care of yourselves and keep happy--I'll try and do the same.

Wish your folks and Peg and Troop happy vacation!!

Bye bye Darlings, Daddy

STRAYED FRIENDLY BOMB ALMOST HITS US

10 Aug 52
Changdan, Korea
Sunday 1330

Hello little family that I love,

Finally got all your letters, honey, from 19-24 July, all those that I had been missing. Got them last night, five of them from you, sweetie, and one from Ben thanking me for the leather brief case and telling of your trip to the beach. Your letters arrived at about 2000 and had it not been for the fact that Bill hadn't returned from helping control air strikes in front of the 2nd/1st and I had no jeep to run me out to OP2, I would have missed them. Read them under candle light until 2100 when Bill finally returned, tired, beat and hungry. One of our boys had snatched some fried chicken from the galley tent earlier and put it away for Sgt Walwood and Bill Boy. They tore into it like a couple of mad, hungry wolves--hadn't had anything since 0900 yesterday (32 hours). I hopped into the jeep and in total darkness (blackout is mandatory up here on the front) I started my six-mile journey alone to OP2.

The road out is bumpy and dusty now and bordered by hedges and trees that are slowly but steadily narrowing the road down to almost one lane in places. While creeping along in no-man's-land, a huge truck suddenly loomed up in front of me going about 40 mph--no lights, the blackest of nights and on a curve. I swerved to my right and drove into the hedges as the truck went screaming by, just barely scraping my two left fenders. He never did see me and must have been scared to death, driving like a mad man coming back out of no-man's-land. I backed out of the hedges and proceeded on my creepy way to OP2. It seemed like I would never get there last night and for the first time since I've been going out there I was shook, mainly from the truck episode.

Upon arriving, Capt Ashton told me to move my jeep to another location because they had been pounding my parking place up on the hill all day long and he promised if I left it there the goonie on the tube at the other end would clobber it, so I backed it up against a ledge and sandbagged it. I stayed in the Co CP bunker until 2300 reading over your past five letters and talking over the very shaky tactical situation with Ashton. He has frankly warned me that in the event anything happened to him during an attack I would become "G" Co commander and would be calling all the shots.

I studied all the code names, patrol numbers, squad numbers and ambushes he has set up and am learning all about supporting arms (30 cal machine guns, 4.2" and 81mm mortar, grenades) and what to do in case we should be cut off and overrun during the night. If we are ever cut off, I'll call in VT air bursting artillery **on our own** position and we'll take shelter in our bunkers, hoping to clobber the attacking goonies in the open. It's a nasty thought but a tactical solution.

It was hot and muggy last night and the mosquitoes made me very happy that I had my net up there on the hill. I was very tired and slept straight through until 0700 when I got up and returned to Bn CP and aided the doctor in loading two casualties on a helicopter. They had 13 air evacs from our CP strip alone and Bill handled it all night. I just happened by at 0720 to assist the last one.

The 2nd Bn/1st Reg, flanking us to the north (right), has been receiving many casualties from over 3000 rounds of mortar and artillery logged in the past 24 hours. They made a platoon-size push on a Commie OP in front of their position and were driven off. A second platoon attempted it and were also driven off by the enemy. Then this morning after running (17) 4-plane air strikes on that hill, our forces made a company (300 men) push on it and received many, many more casualties. I get weak and sick whenever I look upon those pitiful youths--17, 18, 19 years old--lying there on those stretchers biting their lips to hold back their great pain. I have seen the hill they have been fighting for and I'm at a loss to find in my heart the need and worth of their great suffering. From a fighter pilot's viewpoint, I knew how I could have covered it with napalm and made it impossible for a human being to survive there. However, with our own troops so close, it would have been very difficult to put an air strike so near them.

I went to church this morning and sat there and prayed with all the rest to bring a cease-fire to end this bloody mess. As we sat in the makeshift church under canvas, the bomb blasts from the unending air attacks would puff out our tent and interrupt the chaplain's every other word. I couldn't help but feel very deeply moved and I felt very close to God as I searched my heart for a justification of this horrible killing. Pray, dearest, for peace, for we need it. God, how we need it!

Maj Biehl and Maj Smith have been out on the front line examining our positions. Biehl will take on great responsibilities if our battalion is struck hard, over and above the tactical limits, and I will be very hard pressed running air alone. However, we are only playing it safe and--

A plane just dropped two 250-pound bombs near our area by mistake. One went off and the other didn't. No one got hurt. What an explosion! Bob Small, our battalion weapons officer, just got the phone call and we're going out to find the darn thing and detonate it with a black powder charge so no one will get clobbered later on. Brother, the TACP sure inherits a headache with a battalion at the front.

Enough for now, darling--have to go chase those bombs with Captain Small.

Tell Ricky and Randy I liked their paintings and drawings very much. They are really improving. I love the darlings and miss them so very much.

Much later, we found the unexploded 250-pound bomb, set our charges and exploded it. Some blast!

Love ya, Daddy

11 Aug 52
Monday evening
on beautiful OP2
overlooking Panmunjom

Dearest family,

On my return from OP2 this morning I found three letters on my cot, two from my precious family and one from George Codding, of VMA-212. He sent me back a roll of pictures he had developed for me while he was over at Itami. They are mostly of Koreans we ran into while we *were on maneuvers during training in the field as FAC down at K3 and MACG-2. I'll enclose them in the morning in this letter when I reach Bn CP.*

I've truly had a day, darling. Probably not one like it in my entire life. I was confronted with neutralizing, by air, all enemy mortar, machine gun positions, goonies themselves and OPs fronting our Item Co on our right flank. Major Bill and I worked through our 2 Section and Artillery Section and learned all we could from them. At 1000 this morning we moved up to our right flank on Item Co line (in front of them, in fact) and began running air strikes on our plotted goonie position. During an eight-hour period we poured on six 4-plane divisions of aircraft and we feel we have really done a complete job of clobbering them.

The reason we worked so hard and long in the planning and execution of this attack today was because a company-size push is leaving Item Co line to try and retake Bunker Hill tonight at 2100. You'll hear all about it in the papers and radio. Just look back to 8 August when we began getting clobbered here on the western front, especially today or tonight, because our battalion is more closely connected with this operation than the other. However, we did receive toxan casualties and that was sufficient to make us feel we were part of it.

I spent eight hours on the radio controlling air today, switching with Bill. We helped each other with the mortar marking the artillery HE (high explosive) marks by which our aircraft spot our targets. Bill and I adjusted fire with the artillery FO (forward observer) but we didn't like the way he was doing it, so we took over and did it ourselves, finally getting what we wanted.

The front line OPs are very sparsely manned, and by green men. The men trust and respect our expertise, while we depend on their obedience, strength and ability to help get the job done. Major Bill isn't as aggressive as I am, so occasionally I have to take the bull by the horns and even tell him what should be done. Some of the time he tells me, however. This all takes place under the heat of battle and it's only in the line of duty. We get along fine. The Colonel and Exec are beginning to like us a little bit more; as much as a ground cruncher can like an airdale. I've been plugging at my job with all my heart and soul and have been getting a tremendous sense of satisfaction out of helping those kids, especially today.

Sgt Walwood and I left the line early and came on back to Bn CP. I attended the meeting at the COs, then reported my air activity and the Colonel was very appreciative. I secured and got some cold chow because it was late--two hours after chow secured. I'm tired, dirty and sweaty, sitting here in the OP2 "G" Co CP writing my precious family by very scoshy candlelight.

I'm listening to all the incoming phone calls from along our battalion front--all the forward listening posts calling in reporting enemy patrols in this sector and machine guns firing at us from such-and-such an azimuth. An ambush team from "G" Company is reporting in from their very advanced position forward of our outpost line of resistance. The bunker is very warm because it stores up all the heat from the day and brother, it's warm in here. It's cool outside but the mosquitoes are horrible. Incoming mortar on OP2 was heavy 30 minutes before I arrived tonight but they haven't received any in the two hours I've been here.

An interesting sidelight: as I've been writing here, a pile of white sawdust has been piling up on my left knee. I asked what it was and the corpsmen answered, "It's the droppings from the termites or worms that are eating up our bunker's overhead beams." I didn't believe it, so they scooped out a worm an inch long, a grayish brown. Boy, what they haven't got in Korea isn't worth mentioning. I wondered why all the goonie bunkers up here were falling down--now I know. The fellows here say they are frankly worried about the worms causing a weakened condition of our own bunkers.

I've been so darn busy lately I haven't had time to feel sorry for myself. You're always on my mind, darling, and your wonderful words of encouragement truly help me along. I'm just living for the day when I can hold you in my arms, dearest girl, and cash in on some of that loving I've missed out on. I left the CP tonight before the mail came in and now I'm wondering if I haven't got a letter waiting there for me from my darling. Tell my dear boys how much I love them and how sweet Ricky boy is to pray for his daddy's safety. Tell him I too am waiting for that day of days when we can go out to the garage together and build some little boats and cars out of wood. I have so much I want to pass on to my little guys. You've given me so much, dearest, in presenting me with my two little guys. I'm as proud as punch of my whole family and never pass up an opportunity to show you off to my friends.

Night, night, darlings. The daddy is going to hit the basket and prepare to arise early in the morning to take up position on Item Co's front line to direct more air for our boys.

Love, Daddy

PS. It's 2200 (10:00 PM) now and the battle is really under way. The booming is terrific. Shakes our bunker.

On August 12th we were interviewed by an Associated Press war correspondent up in my frontline trench and Marion cut the following piece out of the local paper, the Manhattan Beach Breeze.

MARINES DIG IN TO DRIVE REDS OFF 'BUNKER HILL'

By Sam Summerlin
Western Front, Korea, Aug. 12
(AP)--American Marines stealthily moved up Bunker Hill today, casting wary eyes at a tiny pocket of Chinese soldiers dug in on the dust-caked summit.

From an outpost overlooking the hill, I watched the hunters stalk their prey.

The Chinese were in deep trenches. A few scattered boulders gave them added protection.

The marines, dripping sweat in the fierce sun, zigzagged on the slopes 300 feet from the enemy. They took cover behind scrawny shrubs and in small crevices on the slopes.

Lt. William H. Thousand of Mt. Horeb, Wis., pinpointed the Red position and called in artillery and white phosphorous shells, used to guide air strikes.

An Allied gun boomed on a hill behind us. Everybody suddenly ducked. The Marines in the outpost realized it was defective. The shell made a weird flip sound as it went over head and exploded on the bottom of Bunker Hill, far short of the target.

"Phew!" muttered Sgt. Jim E. Howard of Burlington, Ia. "That thing went end over end. They sure give you the willies."

Howard, wiping sweat from his suntanned, unshaven face, said he had not slept in four days except for short naps.

"Nobody much likes it here," Howard said. "But it's a job that has to be done."

Howard pointed over our trench to a majestic ridgeline towering behind Bunker Hill. The ridge is enemy territory.

"That's Taedok-San," he said. "Every time you open your mouth, they can put a bullet in it."

Rifle shots crackled. Ping, ping. "They're ours," Howard said with a broad grin. Each time the Chinese on Bunker Hill poked their heads up, a Marine sniper just below our trench opened fire.

"That keeps their heads down so our boys can move around easier," Howard explained.

In recent days, the mercury has hit 106 and 108 degrees on the Western Front hills. But the Marines still prefer to keep on their plastic vests. Every Marine seems to have a story of some buddy who escaped certain death when his vest stopped bullets or shell fragments.

Suddenly, there was a loud "whoomp" in front of the outpost hill. A Chinese mortar shell exploded on the trail the Marines used to move up Bunker Hill. Everyone ducked again. "Whoomp, whoomp, whoomp."

"Guess our planes didn't knock out that mortar crew after all," remarked Capt. Bernard W. Peterson of Manhattan Beach, Calif. He and Maj. William Biehl of Richmond Hill, Long Island, are forward air controllers. They direct the warplanes in strikes on Communist ground targets.

U.N. artillery soon boomed behind us again. Shells zoomed overhead and crashed into the hill beyond. The Red mortars became silent.

Over the hills to our left, silver balloons hovered high in the blue sky over Panmunjom. The blimps warn away airplanes from the tiny truce site, a neutral zone in the midst of warring armies.

Climbing down the hill, I ran into a weary sergeant who had just walked off Bunker Hill.

"Those boys are pretty tired--but they're in good spirits," reported Sgt. Robert C. Coleman of San Diego. The sweltering heat bothers the Marines on the shadeless slopes.

"I never felt like this in Alabama," Coleman remarked with a wry smile. "But then, back home I never ran up and down hills all day. And I worked in an air-conditioned hardware store in Birmingham."

The husky sergeant said the Marines are swiftly digging in on Bunker Hill. They are building sturdy bunkers as cover against enemy shelling.

"Once the boys get dug in," he said confidently, "those Chinese never will get us out."

12 Aug 52
Changdan, Korea
Tuesday 2130

Dearest family,
    The daddy and our whole TACP just returned from the front lines again. We have had one heck of a day up there covering our boys that have pushed off on Bunker Hill. We're tired and dirty--unshaven for three days and no prospect of shaving again for a day or two. Nevertheless, with as much incoming and shrapnel, flying rocks and timber, and hail of machine gun fire as we took today up there in our slit trench, I still feel fortunate because out there on Bunker Hill tonight, at this very moment, those kids are receiving a murderous hail of 60 and 82mm mortar and machine gun fire.
    The large Mt. Laedocsan overlooking our whole position is infested with goonie mortar and artillery spotters, and the reverse slope is loaded with mortars and artillery. The high ground of Bunker Hill (the nose, we call it) still has a few goonies on it spotting mortar on the reverse slope of Bunker clobbering our boys. They really located our position today and the incoming was continuous all day long. It got so bad while I was controlling one of our twelve air strikes today that I had to call off the planes, duck down in my trench and just hang on for dear life. Each air strike consisted of from 4 to 6 planes. Some of our fellow Marines in our trench said they had been with the 1stMarDiv for about a year which included the east central front (Punch Bowl) and had never seen so many aircraft or such ferocious fighting or enemy mortar or heavy shelling. Every minute or two we'd get another one and it would really rock us. The FO standing in front of me got hit with some shrapnel from an 82 that landed behind me. Figure that one out! I never got scratched today, in spite of all the incoming. We've taken a huge number of casualties and tonight will even be worse than before because we are gradually securing a little more of Bunker Hill all the time.
    I watched the faces of those kids as they passed through our trench line on their way out to Bunker. Oh, honey, this is a horrible war--worse than anything I have ever imagined possible. Everyone is shook. Major Bill and I controlled the 4.2-inch and 60 and some 82mm mortar as well as all the air today because nobody was up there to take over the control when the battalion control switched from the 2nd to the 3rd. Bill controlled the whole show for a while, then I took over. We really saved the day for a bunch of those kids but couldn't help a lot of the poor devils. Haven't eaten but one meal today, at 1300. Nothing tonight. Am going to leave for OP2 in a few minutes, dearest.
    Pray for us out here, honey. I love you and adore you, my sweet. Kiss my darlings and tell them their daddy loves them. I've got a guardian angel, precious girl, so don't worry about me.
    Got interviewed during a little lull by Sam Something-or-other of the AP. Gave him the dope on the whole situation and the heavy incoming sent him scurrying off.

                                  Love ya, Daddy

P.S. Rec'd yours of 30 July and 6 Aug. and Eddie Butler's of Aug. 1. Sent him a cig. lighter--he likes it.

PURPLE HEART TIME FOR YOURS TRULY

13 Aug 52
Changdan, Korea
Wednesday 1700

Dearest family,
Another day has almost come and gone and I'm sitting here back at the Bn CP, clean body, shave, clothes, and my tummy is full of ham steak. One hour and a half ago I was filthy dirty, crummier than I had ever been before in my life. My beard was about a quarter of an inch long, my skin black from the dirt and dust of three days.

After writing to you last night I drove on out to OP2, arriving there about midnight. I briefed the new "G" Company commander on the activities out at Bunker Hill. We practically ran the show, since we know this front line like nobody else at this point in time.

The battle progressed; deafening artillery and mortar fire thundered and machine guns chattered unceasingly all night long. Artillery forward observers changed watch every two hours. It was hot and muggy and I lay there, sweating up a storm, listening to the battle. Hearing the rumble of tanks--our tanks and machine gun chatter, I didn't sleep a wink because I was never completely sure but what OP2 was being assaulted. It wasn't, so at about 0600 I got up and put on my filthy, slimy, dirty clothes and flak vest, steel helmet, .38 and side holster and came back down here to Bn CP.

I picked up today's shackle code, went out to our right flank overlooking Bunker Hill and relieved Bill who had been up there directing air strikes since 0400. On the way, I met a steady stream of beat, torn, worn kids, having tasted battle at its grimmest, coming down the road from atop our frontline outpost. Stretcher cases were strewn all along the road in the weeds, behind rocks to protect them somewhat from the steady hail of incoming mortars. They were awaiting jeep evacuation to the Bn aid station. From there they are carried to a helicopter strip where Bill and I have placed two of our men to direct and aid operations.

I took over for the next nine hours, (from 0700 until 1600). I planned and directed 11 air strikes on known goonie mortar, artillery, machine gun positions and the air boys really put out.

Bill stayed and let me secure to get cleaned up and to have a meal here at Bn CP. He'll get another seven or eight strikes before 2000. The incoming mortar and artillery fire on our position where we were directing was the heaviest I have seen yet. During the more severe barrages we'd lie flat down in the trench and pray. Then we'd get up, pop our heads out and continue the air direction. I got hit with a little piece of shrapnel across the bridge of my nose and it bled. Larger hunks were falling in our trench, missing us by inches. One piece fell on my toe--no damage, however, because it was well spent after striking a sandbag over my head.

The third company of troops are now on Bunker Hill. Baker Co and Item Co, suffering very heavy casualties, were pulled off last night and this morning and replaced by fresh troops. Bill and I are beat. So are our men who have been right in there all the time plugging.

I prayed today, honey--you may be sure of that. You said you and Randy and Ricky prayed for me, honey, but right now I'm not praying for anybody but my boys that are going out on Bunker Hill tonight. If there's any justice in this world the peace talks will surely be concluded to our satisfaction.

No mail tonight, honey. I love you, sweetheart. You're on my mind constantly, dearest girl.

Love to all,
Your very own daddy

Left: Surveillance of the Enemy—Men of the Reconnaissance Company, 1st MarDiv, scan CCF positions across the Imjin River.

Right: HMR-161 choppers airlift 1st 4.5-inch rocket battery into position during August 1952 maneuver. They had the nasty habit of landing unannounced, firing their rockets, and minutes later flying off to another position. The enemy would immediately counter fire on the empty position. The friendly fired rockets would zing right over our heads, scaring the living hell out of us up on Hill 229 CP outpost.

Left: Marines of the 1st Armored Amphibian Battalion empty 75mm shell cases from armored amphibian after a shoot-out on Independence Day, 1952.

Photo credit USMC.

Right: My forward air control partner, Maj Bill Biehl, and author at our bunker on top of Hill 229. We are awaiting our close support flight of aircraft to come on station.

Middle Left: These enlisted Marines are my constant support group. All are radio operators and wiremen, and darn good ones.

Middle Right: Our TACP, Tactical Control Party for 3/1/1. These men are all enlisted radio operators.
L to R: Cpl A. Skinner, Sgt C.J. Walwood, Cpl D. Evans, Cpl M. Stamps, Cpl R.M. Boone and PFC E.J. Bauman.
Kneeling: Maj Biehl and Capt Peterson.

Above: Author and Gus Dake, back from our R&R pheasant hunt in the OE-1. Our 3rd Battalion was in reserve for a few days of rest.

Above: The OE-1, one of 11 planes of VMO-6 at the 1stMarDiv. A real workhorse.

CHAPTER 14

HELLFIRE

The FAF (5th Air Force) was losing altogether too many aircraft, both in deep interdiction missions over North Korea and during close air support. Various measures attempted to reduce mounting losses of personnel and aircraft. In all Marine air units, evasion and escape tactics were stressed. In addition to the de-emphasis on interdiction of communication routes due to heavy aircraft losses, the FAF decreed that beginning 3 June, with the exception of the AD and F4U aircraft (1st MAW types) only one run would be made for each type of external ordnance carried and no strafing runs would be made. FAF also ordered that in all attack runs, aircraft would pull out by the 3000-foot altitude level. The Marines, combining their air and ground efforts, came up with a positive program of their own, the first known instance of Marine ground forces supporting Marine air.

Although the originator of the idea cannot be positively identified, the time that artillery flak suppression firing was first employed can be traced back to late 1951, when the division was still in East Korea. It was not until June 1952, however, that a published procedure for conducting flak suppression firing appeared in Marine division records. That same month another type of flak suppression, this by an aircraft, was utilized by the 1st Marines, commanded at the time by Col Walter N. Flournoy. The procedure called for the FAC to relay gun positions to friendly strike planes, which then temporarily diverted their attack in order to silence the located gun. Although the method worked with good results, it was not destined to become the system adopted by the Marines.

On 30 June 1952, the 11th Marines published a new SOP (standard operating procedure). Since the objective was to prevent enemy fire from interfering with friendly strike planes, the key to the entire procedure was the precise coordination of artillery fire with the delivery of aircraft ordnance. When the infantry regiment received word of an air strike, the air liaison officer plotted on the map the target of the strike, the orbit point, the direction of approach, the altitude, and direction of pullout. Then the artillery liaison officer, by looking at the map, could determine which of the Chinese positions could bring effective fire on the strike aircraft. The artillery battalion had prearranged code names and numbers for every antiaircraft position. All the artillery liaison officer had to do was pick up the phone and tell the FDC (fire direction center), "Flack suppression," and read off which targets he wanted covered.

These fires were then delivered upon the request of an FO (forward observer) who was with the FAC. When an FAC was up in the front lines controlling the strike, we would put an FO with him. Then the planes were ready to go, the FO got the word, "Batteries laid and loaded," and the FO would tell them to fire. The minute the FO got the word, "On the way," the FAC would tell the planes to start their run. As a result, we had cases where the planes were in their bombing run within 30 seconds after the flak suppression was fired, which meant that they were in on the target while the positions were still neutralized. The question of control and split-second timing was of exceeding importance because the aircraft were going 300 to 400 miles per hour.

Early in the program the MAG-12 commander reported that, although the flak suppression procedure was not flawless, it was proving very capable and workable. Shortly after it was put into operation the success of the 1stMarDiv's pioneering efforts in flak suppression was made obvious by a steady stream of influential visitors to the Marine CP to find out how we were doing it and to get copies of our SOP. Other Eighth Army units eventually adopted this system.

Marine air losses from hostile ground fire during CAS strikes immediately began to drop from the June peak and never again reached that level. In 124 close support sorties flown by 1st MAW on 13 August, not one plane was shot down and only four received even minor damage. Bill and I controlled the majority of these sorties in support of the Bunker Hill battle. It was very gratifying to know we finally had come a little bit closer to perfecting a system to reduce the losses our fellow pilots had been sustaining.

MARINES CUT REDS DOWN
750 Chinese Wiped Out
(Associated Press)

SEOUL, Korea (Thursday), Aug. 14.--United States marines and artillery cut to ribbons 750 Chinese Communists assaulting leathernecks entrenched in prefabricated bunkers atop Bunker Hill on the Korea western front.

The battalion-size attack--second major bid of the Chinese to recapture the height--was broken at dawn today. Chinese losses were described as very heavy.

The marine commander, Major Gen. John T. Selden, said the strategic ridge overlooking the Panmunjom truce site "is marine territory now. We certainly are going to hang on to it."

Marine foot soldiers, supported by flame-throwing tanks, captured the strongly fortified height and nearby Siberia Hill early yesterday. The Reds counter-attacked at dusk yesterday, but were thrown back with heavy losses.

There was no indication the Chinese had given up hopes of retaking the position. In mid-afternoon a marine spokesman reported that Communist artillery and mortar fire was falling on Bunker Hill.

The navy said its carrier planes yesterday struck a heavy blow against major Red supply and troop concentrations south of Wonsan, heavily battered east coast port city. The navy said 40 buildings, including barracks, were flattened with heavy casualties to Red troops.

HILL 122 (BUNKER HILL)

The primary objective of the Chinese over the past couple of days, Hill 122 (Bunker Hill) lay only a short distance to the west of us and we were assaulted along with it. Following the battle, the 1st Marine CO, Colonel Layer, reported to General Selden that the Bunker Hill action during 12-13 August had resulted in 24 Marines killed and 214 wounded. On our right flank, in the 2d Battalion sector, an additional 40 Marines were listed as casualties, including 7 killed in the Stromboli defense. Chinese known dead numbered 210, plus an estimated 470 killed and 625 wounded. Artillery FOs, along with aerial observers such as Bill and me, reported that between the hours of 1500 on the 12th and 0600 the following morning an estimated 5,000 to 10,000 rounds of enemy fire had fallen on 1st Marines positions, the heaviest incoming fire the Division had ever received since coming to this sector. Just as though it was raining hot steel, it filled the air. I caught a chunk on the bridge of my nose, and my flak jacket was cut to ribbons but it had saved my life.

Bill and I assisted in calling in helicopters, loading the many wounded onto the litters and strapping them in. Most of the wounded seemed like teenage kids to us--especially heart breaking to me, a father of two sons back home.

14 Aug 52
Changdan, Korea
at Bn CP, Thursday

Dearest family,
It is now 1600 and Bill and I are preparing to go up to 229 OP and spend the night controlling MPQ radar drop bombing and flare plane direction. Last night, after I wrote to you, Col Armitage informed me that I was to go up to 229 outpost and remain up on the radio all night, to stand ready to drop aerial flares for illumination of Bunker Hill, in the event the goonies assault our boys. The night was very black and as I was preparing to leave for 229 with my two men and radio jeep I heard a helicopter circling our CP, so I dashed out and lit up the area with flash lights. A few minutes later an ambulance arrived and we loaded the kid on the plane, strapped him in, and away the copter went.
Maj Biehl (Bill) came back down at 2045 from Item Co where he had controlled about six more air strikes after I'd left yesterday afternoon to come on back here to make out strike requests and consult with the colonel on tactical plans regarding air for today. Maj Biehl turned in about 2300 and got up this morning to resume control from Item Co trench overlooking Bunker Hill.
I went up to 229, set up my equipment in the dark overlooking the goonies and got my next door neighbor in the 2nd Bn (1st) to control the R5C, which was carrying 125 flares on parachutes that burn approximately three minutes, giving off one million candlepower of light. The battle raged up to a fever pitch and I observed the whole affair from 229.
Our tanks, 13 of them, climbed up to the summit, turned on their powerful searchlights and opened up with their 76mm cannon and 50 cal machine gun fire. I could see the tracers in the night hitting the target and bouncing, or ricocheting, and I'd watch them burn out. I waited all night long up there. Didn't close my eyes. The colonel called at about 0200 and asked me to arrange to have an OE over Bunker Hill at first light to search out the reverse slopes of the hill surrounding Bunker to the north and south.
I was still up when he checked in at 0500. Then I cancelled the flare dropper plane, or rather, sent him home after seven hours in the air because we didn't need him, thank God. The enemy made their assault on our boys at 2000, then broke it off at 2200. Our boys really killed a lot of goonies. Lt Kelly went out and searched their bodies today, gathering a lot of intelligence dope. He got burp guns, ammo clips, potato mashers (hand grenades) and some papers off of some of them. I was looking over all the stuff he retrieved. The burp gun is quite heavy.
I fell asleep up there after I secured the net and slept until 0800 on an air mattress out on the ground. The mosquitoes ate me up. Returned here to Bn CP, shaved and had breakfast. Prepared strikes for today with Col Armitage's and Maj Smith's requests for targets that are affecting the successful securing of Bunker Hill, also known as Hill No. 122. Our boys fought off the night's onslaught very well. Their bunkers are being completed and that will give them a much better chance to weather the terrific hail of mortar fire that has hit them so steadily.
I escorted a Col Bolman, new executive officer of MAG-12, up to 229 and OP2 today. We got incoming mortars at OP2 and that really shook him up. Our whole team went up to 229 OP tonight and controlled a flight of ADs carrying one- to six-hour delayed fused 1000# bombs, which I laid in the expected corridor of their assault route for tonight. We killed 32 goonies and got four active mortars at 1945 tonight; also Bill ran three from Item this morning. The incoming had dropped off to a very scoosh degree up there, but business picked up considerably this afternoon and, as I'm writing now, I can hear the thunder of a huge eight-inch gun (secret, don't mention this) moving along our front behind us, firing from behind each battalion on the front, giving the goonies the impression that we have many of them behind us--eight-inch guns, that is. They just let another round go and, boy, it really is LOUD. It sounds exactly like a freight train is passing by.

Just got two nice letters from you, precious girl, dated 7 and 8 Aug. You mentioned in your latest letter, darling, about Randy turning Trooper's hot water faucet off. It's an awful thing for him to have done but I couldn't help laughing to myself. Ricky-boy sure comes out with some cute and sentimental little sayings--he's a darling.

I'm not going to OP2 tonight because I have to be up by 0500 to possibly control the OE on the search and attack mission that I have planned for first light tomorrow. Bill is getting up there too. We're both very tired and I don't have my air mattress here. It's on OP2, so I'll borrow Bill's mosquito netting and sleep on my cot with no pad. It's rough in the field. Ate three meals today because I was at OP2 this noon with Col Bolman and that's the time they have a hot meal.

Miss you all so very much. Don't worry about the daddy, precious girl. I'm in very good health. The cut on my nose has healed already. Bill says he's going to recommend me for a Purple Heart. Ha, ha! (Got beat out of two of them in WWII during the carrier battles.)

15 Aug 52
Changdan, Korea

Page 1 and 2 lost

. . . of the beating we took there for three solid days. It was brutal, honey. I've never experienced anything like it, dearest girl, and I hope I never have to again, but I'd do it if it meant getting up there close to our boys to control any aircraft strike that will help them in any way. Bill and I have the radios and authority to call in the medics and helicopters to rescue these many wounded boys. Our adjoining Bn FACs will control air to the right flank, we'll control air to the left flank, and I hope we can stay out of the middle (Item Co MLR)

After a company is relieved from Bunker Hill they either return back to their reserve CP or come over here to ours at Changdan, and they haven't any tents or anything else for them, so they put up cots in a long line and they crap out there. Nine-tenths of them have been wounded but if it's not bad enough to be evacuated they keep them on duty with the company. They have really fished down into the bottom of the division barrel for reliefs and they are committing such men as special service personnel--barbers, truck drivers and cooks--it's been a rough go for everybody.

It's not over by a long shot. A captain who had just brought his company off of Bunker was here in our tent giving Maj Smith, our operations officer, the gory word. It made me sick to hear it, but he told it with a calm and grace that made him stand out in my mind as a real man. I've seen boys made into men these past four days and men turned into fodder. I hate everything Communism has done--with a purple passion. I wish they'd take the honey-coated cover off the whole dirty word "Communism" and call it by its true name, "Slaughter."

I find myself saying little prayers to our beloved Creator off and on throughout the day and night, to please spare those kids out there on Bunker and all other places like it in Korea. I hope the people are getting a true picture of what's going on over here. This is not a business-as-usual war; it's war in its every gruesome color. I can't honestly see why we need Bunker Hill except that it had been taken over by the goonies and gave them a closer OP. With our boys on one side and the enemy on the other, it was really hard to order the air drops or supporting ground fire to aid them. If they weren't there I could level it with napalm.

2230

Something happened this afternoon and I lost page 1 and 2 of this letter. Col A. called me over to his tent and asked that I show Doctor Lamb the enemy positions etc fronting us. I got word almost immediately that we had three missions for this afternoon early, and three this evening or late afternoon. Dr. Lamb is a scientist hired by the Navy and loaned to the Marine Corps to make a study of CAS and air support in general, to suggest ways of improving the effectiveness and to cut down on pilots and planes lost. He went with me up to 229 and it began to rain. The water was flooding our bunker, so we had to secure the radio gear. Finally, after two hours in the bunker, we decided we'd better make a run for it down our hill to our jeep and call it a day, not thinking for a minute we'd get any airplanes with the storm that was over us.

We got soaked coming down the hill--what a hill! I'll take some pictures of it one of these days. The rain was washing the road out fast too. I have to drive up and down it in 4-wheel compound low. Then, at that, you feel like you'll never make the grade. Anyhoo, we had chow and while we were at the mess tent Lt Wilson came over and told us the colonel wanted us to get up to 229 again as fast as we could because the weather would clear and we would have air.

We (Maj Biehl, Doc Lamb and I, our radio jeep and boys) dashed back up while it was still raining--all the time asking ourselves, "Air, in this rain?" Oh, I forgot to add that Gen Seldon was the one who told the colonel to get us up there. On the way up the weather actually cleared up, so we got on the horn (radio), called Dev Baker and asked for a TOT. They didn't even have a mission request in for us. Regiment had failed to relay them in for us, so we never got any air. We waited until dark, then left Doc Lamb at the artillery forward observer's bunker for the night--he wanted to observe the artillery fight tonight.

After we came down the hill I made up six more mission requests, including a request for a continuous air drop of flares. They refused to give us the flare plane over our station all night but told us that in case of emergency we could request one and they would get one over us in an hour. Not much good in an hour--when you want flares you want them now. The goonies have hit our boys on Bunker Hill every night and we have needed flares, artillery or other types, every night. They've almost exhausted their supply of artillery flares and they really need the air drop. Can't understand why we couldn't get it, unless it was because we didn't use them the other night. The goonies hit between 2100 and 2200 and they illuminated by artillery. Plane came on station at 2200 or thereabouts.

Don't have to go to OP2 tonight. Have to stand by here at CP and be ready to call in flare plane if a big emergency comes up. Then I have to go up to OP 229 and control it in conjunction with "Dev Charlie" radar. If we don't need it I'll have to get up at 0500 anyway and come up on the radio for control of the OE over our sector.

A whole mess of rockets just went off behind our CP. Boy, it really makes you jump through your skin. The eight-incher does too. What a bang! Never any warning either. They call it (the rockets, that is) the Rocket Ripple. I bet it really shakes the goonies up, providing they have them spotted properly.

Heard on the radio tonight that ten congressmen were coming to Korea to learn firsthand about the conditions in Korea. Bet I'll have something to do with them. Maj Bill Biehl had two colonels today that he briefed up on 229. We sure get the colonels, generals, newsmen etc. up here.

The fighting on Bunker remains grim. We never directed any air today. Weather was reason, mainly. Request foul-up helped too.

No mail from my darling, but got one from Skee Codding of VMA-212. Said he got my foot locker into Itami OK and sent me a claim check for it. Says they have really been flying their tails off supporting us up there. I know they have. They've been working my tail off controlling them.

Looked all over the place for page 1 and 2, but can't locate them, so I guess you'll just have to go wanting to know what I said--me too. I love you, precious girl, with all my heart and soul. The time is slipping by slow but sure--tomorrow is the 16th--half of another month gone. Keep happy, dearest, and I'll try and do the same. Don't worry about me, dear. Kiss my darlings and tell them how much Daddy loves them and misses them, and give them big hugs and kisses for me.

Your very own, Daddy

CHANGING THE GUARD

Confusion Reigned Supreme would be a better sub-title. While still a squadron member, I had attended briefings as to the nature of the Chinese forces opposing the 1stMarDiv. These numbers were in serious variance from later numbers I was given in briefings after I reached the Div as an FAC. The magnitude of the main line of resistance (MLR) for which we were responsible was given as 10,000 yards, then 19.5 miles, and finally 35 miles. The makeup of the enemy varied all over the place. What appear to be the actual numbers filtered out after the war was over, from information derived from the 1stMarDiv, Comd D, Jul 52:

> *A shift in units occurred on 26 July when the 7th and 1st Marines traded places and missions. At that time the MLR, from west to east, was manned by the KPR, 1st AmTrac Bn, KMC, 1st Marines, and 5th Marines.*
>
> *Opposing them in mid-July were an estimated 27 infantry battalions, whose primary missions were to defend the sectors assigned. The division credited these units with the capability of launching limited objective attacks at any time or of taking part in a major attack with a force of up to 57 infantry and 16 artillery battalions, augmented by 40 tanks or self-propelled guns. It was estimated also that the enemy could cross the Han in battalion strength in the vicinity of the northern shore of Kimpo Peninsula at any time and that Communist aircraft could attack anywhere in the division sector. Enemy forces identified at the end of July, from west to east, were the 193d, 195th, and 194th Divisions of the 65th CCF Army; the 189th Division of the 63d CCF Army; and the 118th Division, 40th CCF Army, which had recently moved from a position opposite the Commonwealth and U.S. 3d Infantry Division. Infantry strength of the Communists was established at 28,328.*
>
> *Chinese infantry units were not only solidly entrenched across their front line opposite the Marine division but were also in depth. Their successive defensive lines, protected by minefields, wire, and other obstacles, were supported by artillery and had been, as a result of activities in recent months, supplied sufficiently to conduct continuous preparations. Not only were enemy ground units well-supplied, but their CCF soldiers were well disciplined and well led. Their morale was officially evaluated as ranging from good to excellent. In all, the CCF was a determined adversary of considerable ability, with their greatest strength being in plentiful combat manpower.*

Sunday
16 Aug 52
Changdan, Korea

Precious family,
    Bunker Hill remained rather quiet last night and it looks as though maybe the worst is over, at least I hope so. I slept all night, although not as comfortably as I might have, had I had my rubber mattress down here from my bunker on OP2. Gosh, my friends out at OP2 will probably feel as though I've given them up. Bill stayed on 229 all night waiting for the word to call in a flare plane, which didn't show up but could have been scrambled from Seoul on a minute's notice.
    They illuminated with artillery flares for a short period last night but knocked it off after 2200.
    Maj Stone, who is in our tent here at Bn CP, is the "Operations Snatch" commanding officer. He has the job every day the truce talks meet to stand by in a tank with troops on OP2, and to dash out and snatch the truce delegates if the goonies knock it off and grab them. He's been acting as assistant SAC (supporting arms center) officer and assistant S3 during our Bunker Hill deal. You have probably deduced that Bunker Hill is the main responsibility of <u>our</u> Battalion, the 3rd/1st. Due to our large front, however, we drew companies from the 1st/1st and 3rd/7th to support Bunker Hill operations. We have only three companies in our Battalion, "G", "H" and "I". "G" is on OP2 and "H" is on 229. "I" (Fight'em with Item) was already committed to Bunker and did a fine job under the direction of Capt Slim Connolly on that tiny little hill. Maybe the indication of the goonies moving out was a good one, perhaps to lick their wounds, of which they have plenty.
    At 1500 today Bill and I are going to charge up 229 and run three air strikes until dark. Then I guess I'll stay on 229 tonight, in case they need aircraft night illumination. It's only 102° today. The sweat is running off of me by the gallons and dropping on my letter, as you can see. Maybe it will be a little cooler up on the hill.

The story is going around here that two MIGs over the 1stMarDiv sector were the cause for the Red alert sent out by the 5th Air Force air defense net. It is said they made a pass on a division of F9Fs, then turned and headed for home. It caused a lot of excitement around here.

Dearest girl, I went to church at 1030 this morning and really enjoyed the service. There weren't but about 20 people there. We sang our heads off. I took communion after, as I have done for the past month.

Your letters are certainly a blessing to me, my darling. You'll never know what an uplifting they give me. Your patient description of everything my darlings do is most interesting to their daddy. I'd love to have been there when the box was opened and watched their faces light up. Those little cars are the best ones I've seen. I'll bet they are the talk of the block with their monthly overseas special toy shipments coming in as regular as the mail, aren't they? I'm sure glad they liked the clothes I sent and I'm looking forward to seeing them in them.

Just came down from 229 a little while ago. It's 2100. Our radio jeep's engine froze up tighter than a drum going up to 229 this afternoon at 1415. We called motor pool and they hauled it down. We just traded our other one off yesterday because the radios weren't any good. We ran an air strike on the southern slope of Taedoksan, the main goonie mountain stronghold that most of the artillery hides behind in caves. They waited today until all aircraft were out of the area, then they opened up with a heck of an artillery barrage on our boys on Bunker and Item Co. I called in an OE to try and spot the fire but he got over Taedoksan a few minutes too late to spot many of them. However, he gave me some very good dope on a few 76mm artillery positions and we ran an air strike on the bastards at 1900 this evening, then came on down the hill and had supper. I was starved--not having any lunch is hard on you when you're active. It's too hot to eat, anyway, at noon. Guess we're just as well off without it.

The goonies are firing like mad right now and our counter-battery just opened up from behind us a few hundred yards. Boy, what a noise! Well, the artillery this afternoon hit the targets I phoned into them after the OE gave them to me. It's a roundabout way to get any artillery on target but I didn't have any air on station, so I figured we'd better clobber them with what we had available. There's more than one way of skinning a cat--and killing a goonie. The artillery is VT fused to cover the max area by exploding a few feet in the air, then throwing shrapnel down on the goonies. The news says we've clobbered 3700 goonies in the last few weeks in our sector and I'm not one to disagree. That's a lot of goonies in anyone's language. We lost some too, darling, and for my money, it wasn't worth a single casualty. Boy, what a stupid war! But I won't go into that.

Well, precious girl, the weather man says there's a typhoon coming in at us, moving NE from the Yellow Sea. Part of it is over us now and there's thunder and lightning but no rain as yet. Very muggy and close. I took a pan bath--poured the water over me, soaped, then rinsed, so tonight I feel cleaner and cooler. Got clean underclothes too. Keep cheery, darling girl, and keep busy is my motto, and the time has a way of slipping by. Our day is coming, baby girl, and it will be a day of days when I hold you in my arms once more, never again to let you slip away from me, darling, and I do mean <u>never</u> this time. I love my wonderful family so very much, darling. You have certainly given me eight wonderful years, dearest girl. I wouldn't change them a tiny speck if I could turn back time. The next fifty years will be lived to their fullest, you can bet your life on that. We're going to have so much fun--our little family.

Night, Daddy

No mail today.

Oh, honey, I forgot to tell you not to get shook or excited if you receive a notice through Marine Corps channels that your hubby has been wounded in action because I already told you about it. I got hit on the bridge of my schnoz and it bled a few minutes, then it stopped. I didn't even report it, but Maj Biehl did, and the doctor looked at me today and wrote it up. He had to look twice, too, because it's all healed now, since it's been four days. I caught a few pieces in my back, but my flak jacket stopped them from hurting me.

Bill and I are going to receive some award for our part in Bunker Hill, but I don't know what it will be at this time. I would imagine it to be a Bronze Star; however, don't spread the word until it happens. The wound I got will get me the Purple Heart finally, and I don't feel funny about accepting it because of all the wounds I received during those carrier battles in WWII without turning in a report.

THE MAKEUP OF THE UNITED NATIONS COMMAND

Basically, the situation boiled down to a United States operation supplying most of the money, troops and aircraft. However, token troops and aircraft plus carriers were eventually supplied by 18 other Western nations. Of these, 14 contributed combat forces and four sent only small noncombatant medical contingents.

Although the air and naval forces of the contributing nations were important, the burden of the war in Korea, like all wars in history, was borne by the infantry. The ROK Army started with eight infantry divisions and added more as the war progressed. The United States provided seven divisions, six Army and one Marine. The British Commonwealth (United Kingdom, Canada, Australia, New Zealand) contributed one division. Turkey sent one brigade. France, the Netherlands, Greece, Belgium, the Philippines, Thailand, and Colombia each provided one battalion.

While flying my combat missions with VMA-212 Devil Cats, I supported all of the infantry clear across the 38th parallel, which included a mix of those allies mentioned above. The KMC (Korean Marine Corps), on our left flank, came under the 1stMarDiv control for training and supply. The 1st British Commonwealth extended on our right flank, so we exchanged intelligence information, sent them our overflow close support aircraft and, in a reserve status, met them socially upon occasion. What a grand bunch they were.

Since our Hill 229 claimed the highest ground overlooking Panmunjom and, as such, drew a lot of UN visitors, Bill and I found ourselves as tour guides on many an occasion. Although most seemed to arrive just when we were trying to catch up on our lost sleep, or do our filthy wash, or write a letter home, for the most part it resulted in an enjoyable and rewarding experience because it included many of the UN contributing countries' journalists, politicians, diplomats, generals, admirals and many members of the peace negotiating team.

17 Aug 52
On top of old Paekhak Hill
(OP 229)

Dearest family,
Here I sit in my favorite foxhole or slit trench, as you wish, and am looking over the beautiful panorama of goonie land before me 229 meters below, a sight to behold with its valleys and rivers, trees, rice paddies and sage. It's 1830 and the sun is at a rather low angle, casting odd shadows from off each ridge line, throwing them into every unworked and deserted rice paddy to the east. The paddies come down the draws in even terraces of perfect half concentric rings, probably improved year after year by generations of farmers.

Just got a call from somebody saying troops were reported in a certain area and wanted me to come up on my radio, call in an OE to reccy and report, which I did and which the OE did. He said that, sure enough, the goonies were moving out, using the trench lines, and he could even see packs and radios on their backs. I reported same back to S3 and Maj Smith ordered Hellfire (VT fused artillery) poured in on them. They lobbed some over and I guess they clobbered some.

This morning, or I should go back to last night and bring you up to day, which I will. After working over our air requests, I hit the pad at around midnight. At 0245 I was awakened and told to get up to 229 as fast as possible, which I did in my jeep post haste in the dark of night. Boy, it's rough going in the daytime but at night, with no lights, it's really rough going. I made it with no hitches. Skinner and Stamps (the negro boy on our team, who is a hard worker and credit to his race) were up on all the radio gear and waiting for me. We set up and contacted Dev Charlie at 0300, and at that time the black of night was interrupted every 15 to

20 seconds with an illumination from our own mortar and artillery flares. At 0315 I coordinated with two radio control centers, Dev Charlie and Gary Cooper 14, to run two R5Cs throughout the night or early morning, as it was. A thick fog, cold and with a 20 kt wind behind it, came up at about 0430. The flare plane circled and dropped five at a time; they'd last until he circled and dropped again. He dropped them from 12,000 feet and they illuminated at 2500 feet on down to the deck. When the fog rolled in I was really afraid the goonies would get the kids on Bunker Hill, but they didn't, thank goodness.

The enemy hit them three times during the night, supported with toxan mortar and artillery fire, which they use very effectively. Our boys called for a "Box me in," and clobbered them, although they have only a small corner secured. They use the fire support all the time during heavy probes. If they come over the top they ask for it "on the ridge" and get it there. Accuracy is very good at the close range that they employ it.

At daybreak I had three air strikes on station and used them throughout a three-hour period, working them between my control and the OE. The OE would identify an active enemy mortar position and in would go the A/C and clobber it. They had a very lucrative day. And at noon Major Bill came on up the hill with two generals. He briefed them on the targets fronting us and introduced me to them, but I was so busy controlling I didn't even remember their names. They shoved off 15 minutes later.

Bill stayed on the hill and controlled, then came on back to Bn CP at noon, talked Harry, my cook, into scrambling three eggs for me, and came back up with steak and eggs, coffee and canned plums. It was delicious. Harry's a good kid. Normally, he's our good radio man, but had to help out in the mess tent for awhile, since some of the cooks were injured in battle recently up on the line. He wouldn't have done it for anyone except me. I'm his boss, you know. He doesn't need any bossing, though.

The colonel gave me orders for air and I submitted same, then had supper at 1630 and went up on 229 to spell Bill so he could come on down and eat. When he returned I had the 1930 mission all set up--eight aircraft we worked on goonie approaches to Bunker Hill with six hour delayed fused 500# and 250#s. I secured at 2030 and came down. Bill remains all night and controls illumination until 0500. I sleep, maybe.

So far there hasn't been any out-and-out fighting this evening and it's 2300 already. I hope it holds off all night. Maybe our six-hour-delayed fused bombs will help hold them off.

A helicopter crashed tonight. I picked the pilots up with my jeep and sent one of my men and jeep back to VMO-6 with them. More darn excitement!

I adore you. Glad Ricky snapped out of his fever and dizziness OK. Night, precious doll--another day closer to heaven, my heaven on earth--1410 6th St.

Love, Daddy

18 Aug 52
Changdan, Korea

Dearest family,
It's noon straight up and raining up a storm, the tail end or edge of a typhoon moving up the Yellow Sea from the China Coast. I saw this day start at 0500 up on OP 229, having stayed up there to work with the OE on this first-light morning recon of Bunker Hill and enemy approaches. The weather became unoperational at 0515 and I was up there with no OE to work for me, so I stayed on 229 until 0630, then came down here to Bn CP, lay down again and listened to the rain beating on our tent top, which by this time is stretched as tight as a drum and each drop bangs a tune of its own, saying, "It's going to stay a while, Pete, don't get excited about your aircraft and air strikes today because it looks like you'll hava no for a couple of days at least." I don't mind one bit. It's a break for us because it will take a little pressure off our team. But at the same time, I'd gladly go without sleep for a week if it would save just one of those kids' lives up there on the hill.

Bill and I have been searching in our hearts and minds this past week for the true reason or purpose behind this huge pressure we have placed on the Communists these past ten days. We have run hundreds of aircraft in this front and thousands upon thousands of rounds of artillery, mortar and machine gun fire, in preparation for the assault on Bunker Hill. I have reached the conclusion that this request for pressure to be placed on the Communists came directly from Washington, in order to shake the goonies at the peace conference, at any cost. The true cost will never be estimated. I have never seen such mass slaughter in my life, and if I hadn't seen it I wouldn't have believed it humanly possible. The guts, courage and fortitude displayed by our kids out there on Bunker and on Item Co MLR was probably as heroic a stand in the face of the overwhelming hordes of enemy assaulting us than any battle I have read about, heard about or participated in.

I have been praying for today to come, because 18 August was the date the peace delegates had set aside as the day they would resume peace talks. At breakfast, Maj Stone told us he just got a call from the delegate camp that his Operation Snatch wouldn't be required today because they are postponing it another day. I've placed my faith in God to bring this bloody, senseless thing to an end, and at the same time have been holding onto a very slim ray of hope that those peace talks would end in the affirmative.

The Communists did not start this pressure on Bunker, as such. They have been taking all our outpost lines of resistance, listening posts, and forward observer posts that we previously held, up to a few months ago. The M.C. at that time felt as though it was not a particular threat but it seemed to be developing into an envelopment. The goonies thought, I believe, due to the terrific pressure we placed on them, that we were on our way through. Therefore, they countered with everything they had and it really was a hassle. I'm so sick and tired of the thought of it I think I'll stop talking about it, except that I have to keep constantly abreast of developments for those kids out there on the hill.

After what Bill and I went through on Item Co Hill the 11th, 12th and 13th of August, I've felt so darn good to be alive and kicking I could hardly contain myself. I have lost about ten pounds but it looks good on me and I've never felt better in my life. Bill said yesterday, "Pete, you're getting as skinny as I am, and I'm skinny." I've completely lost those two little rolls of fat on my side, and my pants (size 32) are loose. My bum is slimming down too.

The rain has continued all morning and afternoon. I've been writing a little and working a little; it's 1410 now and I haven't finished this yet. I hardly ever finish a letter to you in one sitting. The field telephone of mine is humming most of the day and night, and between it and the artillery in our area we have to sandwich what shut-eye we can.

I mentioned the word "sandwich" and I got to thinking I was hungry, so I opened up a "C" Charlie ration and had a small can of boned chicken on crackers. Very tasty. That should carry me over until 1630, two hours from now. How I'd love to be sitting down to one of your deliciously prepared meals, precious girl. I never knew when I had it so good. You did so much for me to add to my personal comfort and well being, and I took so much of it for granted. I'll always appreciate your cleanliness and alertness to small things--really never did say anything about it in a complimentary way. I'm sorry for it now and I'll rectify that shortcoming of mine when I get home. I'll rectify a lot of shortcomings when I get home.

Oh, how wonderful it will be to resume the position I held as daddy and husband and master of my home! And the three most precious people in this whole crazy world. Needless to say, precious girl, I love you and need you close to me forever and ever. I regret every second I've missed being with you and the boys, but maybe in some way those days we've been apart may have been insurance for the days we'll have together again, and soon, honey. Time is passing by, angel girl.

Time to secure now and do my paper work. I have to make out a complete report of all the air strikes we've run in support of Bunker Hill--a monumental task, but tut tut, here goes nothing. Bye bye.

Your very own Daddy

P.S. *Don't let the boys break their daddy's "binopulars," will you, dear.*

19 Aug 52
Changdan, Korea

Dearest family,

The battle for Bunker Hill continues and the boys have had some time to dig in a little deeper and improve their bunkers, which has cut down on the casualties considerably. The goonies have fairly well knocked off assaulting the Hill and have concentrated on an artillery and mortar barrage of our boys. Bill and I have an OE over the area now spotting their fire and as soon as this weather lifts we'll throw some air on them. We were expecting high winds from the typhoon last night but it didn't materialize. The main blow was south of us. Between midnight and 0230 we had to arrange helicopter evac for two marines, one killed and one wounded. It was so black and the ceiling so low that they wouldn't come until almost daybreak's first light. I haven't heard about our casualties on Bunker last night.

Read the 13th, 14th and 15th August Stars and Stripes and the account of Bunker. It varies somewhat with the actual fight but I guess it will be some time before the full story can actually be told. It gives you a squeamish feeling being so near the fighting, and the reports of thousands of goonies assaulting our territory only a few hundred yards away. You never know what they are backed up with or how far they are coming.

Col Armitage is leaving the 3d Battalion and is to be rotated home. His relief is a big burly, hairy ape of a guy named LtCol Sidney J. Altman. He was previously 1stMarDiv provost marshall and CO of the Military Police Co.

I learned last night that Bill and I are being recommended for the Silver Star for our part in Bunker Hill operations from the 11th through the 14th, and then I'll get the Purple Heart. We're both getting recommended for the Bronze Star for our part in the development, execution, and sale to the 8th Army and 5th Air Force of our flak suppression plan, and it will cover the entire period that we will be in the Battalion. Still no word, however, on my Silver Star from the Wing. I don't much care one way or the other on any of them except for the boys-- they'll be proud to have them. (Ricky and Randy meaning boys in this case. I'm always using the term boys to mean Rick and Randy and also my air team, and also those wonderful kids on Bunker Hill.)

Since the weather is marginal today and air hava no so far, I'm still down here at Bn CP. However, three LtCols from 1st MarWing are coming up here for a look-see at 229 around 1500, when Bill and I have to escort and brief them on the goonie land out in front of us. We are working hard preparing our air report and Cpl Boone of our air team is really knocking himself out. Cpl Boone is the kid Bill and I are trying to get into officer candidate school. He has three years of college and a heck of a high GCT--135. As well as being a good worker, he showed great courage when we were under mortar and artillery fire for those three days. Everyone did a superb job and I was proud to have been there doing what I could to help those kids. No company is there more than 48 hours. They are returned to reserve and replaced afresh. The kids crack up out there on the hill if they are left longer than that. They called one outfit the "Clutched Platoon" because they were so scared. Can't blame them though; who wouldn't be, under the circumstances? Those who say they aren't scared are just damn liars, that's all.

Kiss my darlings and tell them their daddy loves them and misses them very much. Chin up, honey, our day approaches.

Love, Daddy

CREEPING TACTICS BY SHOVEL

Under interrogation, the Chinese prisoners had stated they were part of a force of one thousand men who were infiltrating to form a guerrilla force somewhere in South Korea. Six days later, after a brief fire fight between a small group of Chinese and a Marine outpost in the center of the division sector, the defenders discovered that two of the three enemy dead wore under their own clothing various articles of Marine uniforms. Neither of the Chinese had identification or any papers whatsoever. According to the surviving prisoners, both were enemy agents and the attack on the outpost was only a diversion "for the express purpose of detracting attention from infiltrators."

The enemy's tactics and attempts to penetrate Marine positions demonstrated a good deal of soldierly skills, and his conduct of defensive operations proved nothing short of masterful. This was especially true of Chinese construction of underground earthworks. It appeared that the Chinese had no single pattern for this type of field fortification. Like the Japanese in World War II, the Chinese Communists were experts in organizing the ground thoroughly and in utilizing a seemingly inexhaustible supply of manpower to hollow out tunnels, air-raid shelters, living quarters, storage spaces and mess halls. Americans described the Chinese as industrious diggers, who excavated quickly and deeply for protection against UN bombardments. From numerous reports of ground clashes in the 1st Marine Division sector and from observations made by Marine pilots, it became known that the enemy was quick to seek cover whenever he was exposed to sustained artillery bombardment or air attack.

What was not known, however, was the extent of those subterranean shelters. One Chinese account, allegedly written by a reconnaissance staff officer named Li Yo-Yang, described the protection of a CCF shelter to a recently captured UN prisoner as they were under Allied artillery bombardment. While shells exploded all around the position the enemy boasted, "There's no danger of being killed on a position fortified by the Chinese People's Volunteers."

The Chinese attack by "shovel" proved effective and difficult to combat. They burrowed forward almost continuously, even under direct observation. Every foot of advance provided added opportunity to attack Marine COPs with greater impunity. While this activity possibly provided Marines with target practice in both small arms and mortars, these CCF working parties in a narrow trench 7 to 10 feet deep probably took very few casualties.

We fully recognized the excellent protection which those defensive positions afforded the enemy and we took that fact into consideration when ordering our strike aircraft munitions loading. They could be destroyed with napalm and .3-second delayed fusing on a 1000 pound bomb which went deep in their penetration.

20 Aug 52
Changdan, Korea
1600

Dearest baby girl,
Two wonderful letters from you, precious girl, 11th and 12th, mentioning the Bunker Hill deal. I don't suppose there ever were two aviators in the history of the Marine Corps that ever found themselves in quite the situation as did Bill and myself. We were committed to a battalion that happened to catch the brunt of Bunker Hill.
Today I have had no less than a dozen handshakes from various company commanders, colonels, and even Col Walter F. Layer. They thanked me and Bill for sticking to our guns (meaning our position in the trenches) when they needed us the most. I only heard as hearsay night before last that we were being considered for the Silver Star for our performance on Bunker. Today no less than six people have said, "Congratulations, Pete, on your Silver Star." It certainly makes a fellow feel good hearing the word from his buddies. There is also a definite Bronze Star and Purple Heart for me too. Still no word from the 1st Marine Air Wing on my other "star." Let's see, the only other Silver Stars were given to the battalion operations officer, Major Smith, and the company commanders who had companies on Bunker. The battalion commander was recommended for the Silver Star by the 1st Regiment, but all of us signed a petition trying to up it to the Navy Cross, although we have our doubts about them honoring our request. He's left the battalion now and Col Altman has taken over command as of today.
Pat Magginis of VMA-212 dropped in on Bill and me today and said, "Hi, Pete, I'm Devastate Baker." You could have knocked me over with a feather. He's been there about a

week, all during our heavy air attacks, and I talked to him a dozen times and didn't know it. Bill and I took him and a Lt Muller up on the hill (229) and gave them the tour with all the trimmings.   He got a lot out of it and appreciated what we had to contend with.

I took Maj McClair out to OP2 and, sure enough, in came the mortars while we were there. I got my sheet, pillow and air mattress and brought them back with me here to the Bn CP.

There was a woman reporter out on OP1 and Col Armitage asked me to stop on the way out and see if Miss Scott had a guide. When I got there I spotted Lt Wilson's jeep at the base of the hill and saw him showing her the sights, so I didn't go up to meet her but drove on out to OP2 and called back to tell the colonel that Miss Scott was in good hands.

No air for us today because the pressure is still on the 5th Marines on our right flank. The goonies are distributing the pressure along the line, feeling us out all along the front. Can't figure the goonies and I'm not even going to try. Bill Whitbeck, Co commander of "G" Co on OP2, almost caught three goonies on an ambush last night. They got away from him because he had received orders to make no contact with the enemy last night, so he let them go without disclosing his patrol's position.

I've got two rolls of film all exposed and seven snaps taken on my 3rd roll. Pictures of bunkers and fellows I've worked with, me on the battle line and on my horn (radio) controlling air over our sector. I may mail the film home to you for developing after I expose the 3rd. I'm sure in the mood for some snaps from you, honey. It's been ages since you put that roll of color in there. While I'm over here I'd just as soon get black and white once a month than color once every two months. We'll take color after I get home, baby girl. I sure have been feeling fine, honey girl. In fact, as the time over here dwindles away and the time for the daddy to come home approaches, I'm getting so darn excited I can hardly contain myself. Oh, won't we have fun, baby girl? Life has taken on a brand new picture to me, dearest. I came so close to getting it that it wasn't funny, and more than once.

I've been meaning to tell you about the follows who were killed while I was in the squadron with them. Now that I'm not flying and you can relax, I think I can tell you. Tulk was the first one, then one week later Porter got it. Yes, he was the same 232 El Toro radio announcer Porter. Next my very good buddy, Johnnie Johnson got it, followed by Harry Soladay, a good friend too. Duke Williams was shot down and seen to be taken prisoner, so he may be alive. All the rest are dead, though, because they were seen to go in. Then Bobby Foster, the big happy-go-lucky kid from Tennessee (you have his picture taken a few days before he died). Then Fred Sell got it, followed by Soreide, and I just heard today from Pat that Major Phillips was killed yesterday. He joined the squadron just as I left it. All the rest I mentioned were killed while I was in VMA-212. Almost as tough as the Philippines and Okinawa. We had eight killed, one prisoner of war and about 10 guys shot down but recovered, out of an average squadron complement of 30. At one time we went down to 22 pilots and then up again to as high as 42.

Many a night I couldn't sleep, honey girl, after looking at the schedule and knowing where I was going in the morning's mission. I was sick at heart and so afraid something might happen that would prevent me from ever seeing my precious family again, but nothing did and nothing will, I'm positive, dearest. I've got it made, sweetheart, and don't you ever worry about me again while I'm over here. I play it safe, sweety girl, and have the incoming fairly well timed wherever I go along our front. Tonight I signed my fitness report and every mark was either "excellent" or "outstanding," and in the remarks column it read like a Medal of Honor. Col Armitage was certainly more liberal with me. Sorry to see him leave us.

Heard tonight I was going to the Regiment to take over Maj Jack Shoden's job as Regimental TACP officer, or 1st Marines air officer with no assistant, a very responsible position and one that I'd like to try and handle if given the opportunity. Jack Shoden and Bill Biehl were both here at 3/1 until I came along and Jack went to the regiment. Now Jack and Bill are both on the 17th draft and their draft left today for home, but because they are FACs they have to stay another 30 or 40 days. Jack hasn't had an opportunity to control any air strikes and wants to be a Battalion TACP. Originally Jack and Bill made an agreement to take the regimental TACP for one month and then change with one another. A month is almost up for Bill as Bn TACP. I think Bill and Jack both want to be Bn TACPs and hence are giving me the boost in responsibility. I don't know whether I want it or not but, at any rate, by the 25th or

26th of Sept, two brand new FACs will be coming into the battalion and, unless I can pull some strings, I'll have to go to the regiment at that time. Maj Christie asked me tonight to try and stay with the battalion if I could because they needed me, wanted me and liked me. Then, after I read over my fitness report from Col Armitage, I had a tiny little tear in my eye. Golly, I'm proud to have been a member of **this** battalion. I wouldn't have passed up this experience, darling, for anything. I know now what those kids are made of. Gads, but they were marvelous in the face of death. What an uplift it gives a man to see such a performance by another man—or boy, as it was in most cases up there on that hill.

Lt Wilson just popped in and I interrogated him on his little deal with Miss Scott. He said every time he tried to show her the bunker she would say, "I've seen the inside of a bunker and would rather see Panmunjom this time." Wilson said she was 23 years old, very good looking and couldn't be touched--at least by him. She's a correspondent for a Japanese newspaper for English speaking people living in Japan. Wilson is the talk of the battalion. Boy, even an ugly beast of a white female could make out over here. I went on up to OP2 and just mentioned that a woman was stopping back at OP1 and Lt Fitzsimmons said, "I'll see you later, Pete, I'm on my way back to OP1." Ha, ha!

Something more important than Korea, or anything else in this world is now in order--I love you, darling, and need you so very much. No letters, sweety, but I know they are on their way. I already mentioned receiving 11 and 12 Aug. mail yesterday but nothing tonight. Maybe it'll come in though. Had a haircut by a Korean today--only fair.

Kiss my darlings and tell them I adore them. Have Ricky kiss my girl for me.

Your own, Daddy

21 Aug 52
Changdan, Korea
Thursday, 1300

Dearest Baby Girl and my two darling little fellows that the daddy loves,

Bunker Hill was fairly quiet today and last night. I was up on our OP 229 early this morning working with the OE who was giving me targets, which I called down to artillery and they sent out a few rounds of VT on them. We worked about eight targets that way until Bill showed up and relieved me for breakfast. He's doing the same thing now himself. We have air requests in for four air strikes but we aren't sure whether we'll get them or not. The air picture has been rather slow over the Division the past couple of days. They seem to be sending most of the air north for supply and deep interdiction. I guess it's the most profitable target at this time anyway. Our artillery can do a very good job if given the proper information and direction. They have an AO (air observer) spotting targets and adjusting fire for them while we (the TACP team) have our TAO (tactical air observer) working roughly the same area, but spotting air targets; also giving us any kind of a target that we can call artillery on if it's available, in case we don't have any air to put on it, which we haven't had for a few days now.

It's interesting controlling artillery fire for a change. We got some incoming mortar fire on a line 600 meters north of our OP this morning. It's the nearest mortar fire I have observed on OP 229. Today 229 has been relatively quiet since we came up to the line. "G" Co, Item Co and Bunker Hill are the hot spots. Guess the goonies figure they are going to spread the stuff around to keep everybody on their toes. It's really very beautiful up there on 229 looking out over goonie land or back toward Seoul. I'll soon put my roll of color film in and take some color of the area.

The new colonel is touring the area with Maj Stone. Stone is weapons company commander as well as "Operation Snatch" CO. He acts as Maj Smith's assistant operations officer also.

It's warm today and rather quiet on the front here. The quiet is broken once or twice every 15 or 20 minutes by a volley of artillery and an occasional burst of machine gun fire.

Reread your letters of 11, 12, 13 and meant to mention I enjoyed the verses you sent, darling. With you pulling for me, honey girl, how could anything go wrong? Gosh, how I love you, darling girl, and miss you so very much. Tell my darlings how Daddy misses them and how much fun we'll all have when I get home. I got a kick out of one of your letters where you were saying when I get home all I'll have to do is to clap my hands and say, "Woman, mow the lawn," or, "Woman, wash the car." Yeah, and turtles can fly too!

With all my love, Daddy

22 Aug 52
Friday
Changdan, Korea

Dearest family,

Last night the boys on Bunker Hill repulsed a goonie probe estimated to be of squad or as heavy as platoon size. We took two KIA and several WIA, and so far I haven't heard any estimate on goonies killed. I woke up this morning to the vibration and rat-a-tat tat of machine guns firing on the MLR of the 5th Marines on our right flank.

Received your letter of 14 August, honey girl, stating how sorry you were to have missed me on the NBC national hookup. I knew I wouldn't have time to notify you early enough, but wrote as soon as I could and hoped you'd, by some quirk of fate, have the TV off and the radio on just at precisely the right moment. We were having so many visitors at that time that I wasn't too carried away with any of them. Different fellows have received articles from their hometown newspapers mentioning my name etc. I hope you have been watching the AP and UP and others because right during some of my busier moments of an air strike some nosy reporter would ask me my name and hometown and outfit. Too bad Ricky boy didn't hear his daddy on the radio. He'd surely have gotten a thrill out of it, as you would have also, honey girl.

I've thought more and more of putting some of my experiences down in short story form and have you type, edit and rewrite it. I believe one of the most interesting items might be the fact that although I was not a "Sunday morning warrior" like so many of the reserves were, I went into combat flying, then up to the Thundering Third (3rd Battalion) as Forward Air Controller in the Battle of Bunker Hill and controlled as many, or possibly more air strikes than any other FAC in any outfit, save only Captain McDaniels of the 2nd/1st on our right flank. During many FAC's entire four-months tour on the line they had only about a dozen or, at the most, two dozen air strikes to control in their area.

The fellows were kidding me last night about all the medals and ribbons I'm entitled to wear. Majors Smith, Biehl and Stone (all regulars) have been after me to integrate into the regular MC. Biehl said that I'd be a cinch for major by June of next year and said my colonel commission would be cinched also when I came up for it, what with my Korean record. They make it sound good but I'm still not completely sold. I love to fly and I like the MC--that is, certain parts of it, but as long as there's a MC they'll fight every war and anybody's war just because they are Marines and Marines can do anything. I want to remain with **you**, dearest girl, for as long as I can and I'm never going to let anything get into my life that will ever again say, "You **must** leave your precious, beloved wife and children and champion another cause 10,000 miles from nowhere." The thing that is bothering me now, darling, is the thought of our Ricky boy possibly having to face a war in eleven years. I'd rather fight another one myself with any odds than to think Ricky or Randy ever had to go through this hell.

Ben's letter of 15 August arrived telling of how Randy and he had a tilt with the lawn mower and trike. Randy must be awfully cute, honey. I'm longing to see all of you wonderful people again. I wonder if everyone there at home, neighbors and public in general, fully realize how very fortunate they are. They have nothing in this world to fear but death and taxes. If only I could show them how very much they have to be thankful for and how we should share what we have with the underprivileged peoples of the world. I'll never curse the taxes again *as long as our wonderful country remains strong and free. Some people think of the Communists as barbarous natives with nothing but clubs, rocks, bugles, drums and makeshift weapons. How wrong they are, honey. We are facing a well organized, well equipped, trained and supplied foe of high morale and vicious cunning, with the will, know-how, and ways to force us into near submission if he chose to throw his weight at us. Even his airplane is on a par with ours, and recent intelligence reports revealed he outnumbers us in jets available to him just across the Yalu. They have more planes than we do of every kind, and especially more jet fighters.*

If the truce talks ever broke down we'd really be in for it. (Confidential) Maj Stone's sole purpose for maintaining his "Operation Snatch" team is based on the possibility of complete breakdown and a mass breakthrough up the Panmunjom Corridor. Naturally, it would place us in a very tough predicament, being as we are spread so thin across the front and especially along the corridor. "G" Co would be cut off unless they fell back with our tank squad. The bridge situation across the Imjin is very critical, the only dependable one being the Freedom Gate. This is all confidential, honey. Don't pass it around because the "Operation Snatch", bridge situation, number of regiments and battalions up are all top secret. I hope you don't let any of the friends or family read it because it would not be healthy to have it get out. They mention battalions by number in newspapers and over the radio but not any indication as to how many or how few.

Last night at 1900, as I was coming down from OP 229, I saw seven large helicopters land at our battalion CP, all carrying rocket launchers. Men jumped out of the copters and the cranes lowered the launchers to the deck. Copters hovered over to one side and landed. The rockets were aimed at Taedok san and a 144 rocket ripple went off; the copters hovered over the launchers again, hooked onto them, and away they all went to another location along the front, all in six minutes from the time they landed at our battalion. It was the fastest moving operation I had witnessed in a long time. (This information is confidential also.) We are trying to make the enemy think we have many, many rocket launchers strung out all along our front. The copters fly at about 100 feet or so and are never seen by the enemy because our MLR ridges are about 200 meters average or 500' to 600' high. The Marines are trying to use their helicopters in as many ways as they can to warrant their continued requests for more and more helicopters.

There were two admirals here at 0800 this morning and it caused quite a furor. Maj Biehl got up at 0500 while I slept until 0800, shaved, had breakfast, then came on up to relieve him. He'll come up at around 1700 and I'll go down for dinner and stay, unless we get some aircraft.

The day is very warm but I'm inside our bunker where it's about 75°; outside over a hundred. My boys up here are brewing me a cup of Joe. They have "C" rations and make out fine. They like it up here better than down at the battalion CP.

*Last night around midnight Doc Craighead called me for a copter evac and I got one in ten minutes. Went down and got three of my boys with flashlights, and we brought the copter in and loaded up two young marines who'd been hit out on Bunker. I feel so deeply for those kids. I want to help them all I can but **air** hava no these past few days. We're not hurting real bad because we do have our artillery available in emergencies. We're down to fighting Trooper's kind of war now--snipering and mortar and artillery like he did in France during WWI. I can go outside, look down across our MLR and see incoming nibbling at our bunkers and mortar positions at the rate of one or two a minute. They just toss it in as H & I (heckling and interdiction, as the school books call it). Not **barrage** and **concentration** or **search** and **reach** type firing, as they were doing to us 10, 11, 12, 13 and 14 August at Bunker Hill when we were on Item Co line. Bunker and Item are receiving the bulk of all of the incoming, shared by "G" on OP2.*

*Majors Shoden and Biehl told me again last night that I would replace Shoden at Regiment on or about 25 Sept. Regiment is about 1500 meters to our rear, and we call Shoden a rear area poag or tell him he's "in the rear with the gear." I guess I'll become the rear area poag after 24 Sept. My job will be to coordinate between my three battalion air teams and instruct them in air control, helicopter evac and strips. I'll have an eight-man team with responsibility to supply any emergency radio needs to any of the three battalion teams and, of course, to see that they get helicopter rescue support **when** they need it. We will probably go* *into regimental reserve around 1 Oct and return to the battle line 1 Nov. That's when I'm hoping Maj Cole down at Wing Personnel will come to my rescue and relieve me. Keep your fingers crossed, baby doll. My big job at Regiment will be to advise the regimental commander on all policies re **air**--some job. How do I fall into these darn jobs? I'm a civilian at heart and I find myself almost running a war--certain aspects of it anyway. Life sure can be strange if you let it.*

My boys up here on 229 were complaining about the size of the rats. They said they woke up last night thinking that they heard goonies creeping up on them. Hurriedly turning their flashlights on the floor, there were two huge rats lugging off their only "C" ration carton.

Looking around the bunker, I can see flak vests hanging up, steel helmets, a box of candles, carbines and M1 rifles, extra batteries for our MAW VHF radio, a five-gallon can of water and two cots. No mosquito nets. The bunkers are the answer to this incoming and heat, but not to the problem of mosquitoes and rats. Mosquitoes have bitten us all terribly and they make you swell up like when a bee stings you. Everyone scratches his bites, causing scabs, and we all look like we've got the crud on our hands and arms. It's too hot to wear your dungaree jacket and vest, so we just wear our flak vests and let the mosquitoes eat. They got some rat poison yesterday but didn't have any luck last night. The mosquito repellant is too greasy and we'd all rather have the bites.

My boys camouflaged our trench with pine boughs and other greenery. Maybe the goonies won't be able to see our movements now (I hope).

There goes another blast. It was our own dynamite team blasting another bunker position up near us. Makes you wonder about incoming, however.

*All for this time, honey girl. I'm going to check on my **air** from Devastate Baker. Love and miss you, precious family.*

Your very own, Daddy

"OPERATION SNATCH"

When they took over the peace corridor sector, the 7th Marines also assumed the responsibility for emergency rescue of the Allied truce delegates at Panmunjom. The regiment advanced a mile nearer the objective when it moved the pick-up force's assembly area to within 400 yards of the line of departure. The 7th Marines also replaced the tanks in the force with the M-39 personnel carrier, a U.S. Army developed tracked vehicle similar in appearance to the Marine amphibian tractor. Another vehicle the 7th Marines retained in its task force was the M-46 medium tank equipped with additional radios. This armored communication and control vehicle was used as a radio relay station on the MLR. It was dubbed the "Porcupine," due to the number of antennae sticking out. This force with its mission at various times was known as "Task Force Jig" or "Operation Snatch." The Porcupine became my radio control center, and I was the air control officer in charge when our peace negotiators met at Panmunjom when the 1st Regiment relieved the 7th. It was our mission to "snatch" them, in case the Communists made an attempt to capture them.

Taking advantage of the peace corridor in the western end of the center sector, a Forward Covering Force would speed tank-riding infantry to the high ground one-half mile beyond the objective, Panmunjon. Following would be the Pick-Up Force, from the 1st Tank Battalion Headquarters Platoon, which would retrieve the principal UN delegates and take them quickly to the assembly area two miles to the rear of the MLR. A Rear Covering Force, composed of a tank-infantry element, would follow the Pick-Up force both on its way towards the objective and on the return trip. Withdrawal of both covering forces was regulated by a series of phase lines.

The full company of Marines on OP2 were there also as part of our rescue plan, as well as to provide the eyes and ears to the division.

23 Aug 52
Saturday 1600
Changdan, Korea

Hi honeys,
It's raining and has been all night. Good sleeping, though, and after my session on Hill 229 yesterday I fell asleep last night at 2030 and slept until about 0600 when the field phone rang and woke me up. Bunker Hill had a few light probes but nothing as earth shaking as last week's. Artillery and mortars did their usual H & I last night in counter battery on the goonies' fire.

Had a nice breakfast, then prepared to receive eight aircraft company VIPs from Douglas, Grumman and BuAer. Bill and I rustled up eight helmets, eight flak vests and two jeeps, then took them up to 229 and gave them our 75¢ tour. The weather was too foul to see Panmunjom and the top of Bunker but they enjoyed themselves very much just the same. I, of course, told them I was an old AiResearcher and we really touched ground. They personally had worked with many of our AiResearch products and we were all talking on very familiar subjects. They all took my picture and several said they'd personally stop into AiResearch and give Eddie Butler, John Brammer and Paul Reed my best regards.

Colonel Cram, USMC pilot and CO of MACG-2 down at the Wing, was with them and he asked me how I liked duty here. I told him fine since the hellish incoming had stopped at Bunker Hill.

Boy oh boy, is it ever raining hard now! The water is splashing through the hole in the top of our tent, darn it, and my letter is getting splashed. Darned if I can see why I'm not sick at heart and despondent, honey, but I'm not. I have absolutely nothing over here but a job to do, only a cot to sleep on and rain, mud and incoming mortar and artillery as well as creeping goonies in the night, but as each day is checked off of that calendar I grow stronger and happier all the time. I have noticed a terrific difference in my mental outlook here of late, honey. I can't explain it, but I have really undergone a change in my complete mental outlook. I've told you that now nothing gets me down anymore and how good I feel all the time. Haven't felt this good for years--no pain in my side even hiking up the highest hills. I've lost weight in the right places and can't for the life of me figure out why I'm feeling so darn good. Have you ever felt that you, and you alone, had a very special mission to perform, the stage was being set and plans were being made ready, and everyone was working along the same lines, but you couldn't put your finger on the thing you were readying for? That's me, honey. Guess it's 6 December and my homecoming. That's all I can figure it to be.

Your very own, Daddy

JACK CRAM, MARINE HERO IN WWII

Maj Jack Cram, personal pilot and aide to Gen Geiger during the Battle of Guadalcanal in WWII, was the hero of the PBY Torpedo attack on two of five Jap transports unloading their cargo eight miles from Guadalcanal's Henderson Field. Alone in the cockpit of Gen Geiger's borrowed personal PBY, with two torpedoes hung on the wings (with which he had had no experience), he attacked the transports, which were under the screening protection of eight Japanese destroyers. Disregarding their murderous antiaircraft fire, he hugged the water and let go his two torpedoes at 500 yards, striking pay dirt with both--getting solid hits that blew up a transport, causing it to sink in a few minutes. Rog Haberman, a Marine pilot flying a Wildcat, shot down one of five Zeros chasing Cram back over Henderson Field, and it disintegrated in a blinding flash just off the runway where Cram had set his bullet-riddled PBY down safely. Cram was awarded the Navy Cross for his fearless suicidal mission. [Roger A. Haberman shot down a total of seven enemy planes during WWII.]

This wasn't the last of Cram's heroics. Summoned to rescue Marine Capt Joe Foss, who had ditched alongside the small island of Malaita, Cram landed in a bayou close to the Catholic mission where Joe was staying. Taken by native canoe to Cram's idling PBY, Joe was soon lofted back to Henderson Field, where he resumed his relentless pursuit of becoming the Marine Corps' top ace.

Much later, as the CO of VMB-612, flying stripped-down PBJ (B-25) twin-engine medium bombers, Jack Cram and his pilots conducted daring raids on Japan. Their PBJs, flying missions some 1500 miles in length at night and in foul weather., were the first Marine land-based aircraft to strike the Japanese main islands. Flying from the newly acquired island of Iwo Jima, his squadron completed 74 low altitude missions, sinking or damaging numerous Japanese ships. Conceived in the cunning mind of Jack Cram, these missions took place during April, May and June of 1945. Maj Cram, in my estimation, equalled the daring of Jimmy Doolittle in his B-25 raids three years previously, flying off the carrier *Hornet*.

What a wonderful privilege to be spending a little time with my hero of WWII, Jack Cram! He and I became good friends as I showed him the front line situation during my tour in 1952 as FAC at Bunker Hill in Korea. A warm and caring person, Maj Cram in no way reflected the hard-charging PBY pilot associated with the above exploits.

L to R: At the MLR near Bunker Hill, Capt Bernard W. Peterson USMCR, Forward Air Controller with the 3d Bn, 1st Reg, 1st MarDiv, and Col Jack Cram USMC, CO of MACG-2 at Wing HQ.

24 Aug 52
Sunday afternoon
Changdan, Korea

Hello little family,

Got your letter last night, honey girl, telling of how you went down to the radio station and listened to me, and how you and Peg gripped each other with emotion when I came on the air. You're a precious girl, honey, and I love you so. Little things you say like the above make me realize more and more how much you do love me and how very much I love you, my darling... How did little Ricky feel about hearing Daddy, finally, after he thought he had missed me? I'd give anything to have seen their precious little faces when they heard my voice.

It rained and the wind blew last night something terrific, and for a while we thought that we would lose our tent and everything in it. The worst that happened, however, was that we got wet from all the holes in the tent.

The goonies hit Bunker Hill last night at around 2130 and right in the middle of a heck of a rain storm. Our boys repulsed them OK, however, but not without quite a bit of excitement back here at Battalion CP because the word always gets garbled by the time it gets back here as to the size of the probe.

Maj Smith's ground line, or field phone, rang all night off and on. All in all, we had quite a night of it. This morning it continued to rain just as hard and now, at 1400 it's still pouring and the wind continues to blow.

We went to church this morning at 1030 but, due to the rain, the attendance was very light. About 12 men were there but we sang and had a very nice service just the same, followed by holy communion, which I took. We had a new chaplain from Regiment today, hadn't heard him before.

Not much activity on the front today because of the rain. The swollen rivers have all run over their banks and washed a lot of our temporary bridges away for the third time in a month. We are in a very poor situation over here on this side of the Imjin River, with the bridge situation such as it is.

The junior officers asked Bill and me down for bacon, tomato, onion sandwiches at noon today and we jumped at the chance. I ate two huge sandwiches and a mess of extra bacon because I took over the frying end after I ate. Lt Monroe was cutting onions, tomatoes and bread and making the sandwiches. I was frying the bacon in a mess kit over a little tiny GI one-burner gasoline stove. Biehl mixed martinis and Kelly put the green olives in the "glasses" (beer cans with the lids removed). Monroe (artillery officer), Lt Milen (communications officer), Wynn (transportation officer), Kelly (intelligence officer), Wilson (assistant operations officer), Stone (Weapons Co commander), Biehl and I. Three loaves of bread, a dozen huge onions and 24 tomatoes, three 3-lb cans of sliced bacon--we did it all in. The junior officers finagled this chow from some rear outfit and, boy, it was really a treat. We had a fine session. A grand bunch of fellows.

Lt Valentine, officer in charge of a recon squad that is going out to try and take prisoners on Bunker Hill tonight, stopped in. Kelly and Wilson gave him a briefing and a big fat sandwich before sending him on his way.

No air today, of course, so I'm catching up on my letter writing. Wrote Coltons c/o PM, Palos Verdes Estates; also Mom and Aunt Edna. Wrote Ben just a few days ago so I'm pretty well caught up now.

Boy, is it ever coming down now, honey girl. I guess the monsoon season is really here now. It's the sort of day I'd like to be cuddled up to my honey beside a nice big fire and stealing little kisses now and then. Won't we have a time this Christmas, baby doll? Golly, I get excited just thinking about my homecoming. It sure will be grand, dearest girl, and we'll really begin living again, honey. How are my darling boys today? Fine, I hope. Be sure and tell them that their daddy loves them and misses them very much.

Keep your powder dry, baby doll, and remember the daddy loves you. You'll probably be all decked out with a new permanent wave and tint and dress when I get home. You'd look good to me if you just crawled out of the drink soaking wet, hair and all. I loves ya, baby doll.

So long until tomorrow, dearest.

Love ya, Daddy

25 Aug 52
Monday, 1340
Changdan, Korea

Dearest family,

Received your letters of 16 and 17, Sat. and Sun., in the same envelope, saying the nicest things about the daddy. I'm human, I guess, 'cause I always react to praise. You're sweet, honey girl, taking my record around to everyone and playing it for them. I can see you're proud of me, honey, and I can say the same about you too, dearest, because you're the most precious mate a daddy ever had. Randy was cute playing games, the hide game with Grampa and then calling him stupid. He sure must be getting to be a cute **and** fresh little rascal. I'm dying to see both of them so very much. Randy kissing the radio and saying, "That's my daddy" was cute, wasn't it, dear? So Ricky boy is going to be an archaeologist or geologist, is he? He does things that remind me of myself. I used to do things like that, I can very well remember.

Bunker Hill had another probe last night but our boys successfully repulsed it. Lt Valentine, who has the recon platoon, came off of Bunker Hill this morning early and was giving his report of his activities to Maj Smith in our tent. His face was still covered with black burned cork and his body covered with mud from head to foot. He had been to within twenty feet of a trench full of goonies and almost got himself a prisoner, but the rain was coming down so hard and there was so much mud that his weapon wouldn't fire. He didn't want to give his position away, so they returned to our side of Bunker and came off the hill to make his report. They'll attempt it again Wednesday night. I took his picture because he was such a mess--told him I'd give him a copy. Up all night crawling around in the mud and rain in goonie land isn't my idea of longevity.

Bill and I handled wounded evacs last night and today we had a few more. Those kids are still getting hit up there. Bill and I help every department we can when the weather is bad and there's no chance of getting any air. The weather has been terrible, raining and blowing almost steadily for three days. Just this afternoon it let up slightly and there's a little blue hole up there now, which may indicate clearing weather. I hope so because we could sure use some air over our battalion. The air is very muggy and humid, my clothes are all wet, and the mold or mildew on my green navy issue handbag grows thicker every day.

Our battalion bunker here at CP is flooded, so we had to have two men with buckets bail for two days. We just got a pump installed. The not-too-distant thunder of artillery can still be heard and remains a constant reminder to us that those kids up there are depending on us back here for all the support we can give them. They sent clean dry clothes and extra socks out to them today. Water is two feet deep in their fox holes and no sleep for anyone while they are in the bunker. They effect complete company size relief nearly every 48 hours because the men begin cracking up if they are there any longer than that and start shooting at shadows and weeds etc. The company commander who just came off the line was in our tent reporting to Maj Smith that they had 67 casualties, five KIAs and 13 wounded evac, the rest walking casualties. Mostly mortar and artillery injuries.

Well, well, here comes our water can (5 gals). It disappeared several days ago and water hava no. Now I can shave and clean up this carcass of mine. Smitty is taking a shower, or pan bath now and splashed my first page of this letter, so I got after him.

Chow goes in ten minutes and I'm starved, I can tell you. Hardly any exercise today because of the weather. Gets old staying in this darn tent, but then, I'm dry and mortars aren't dropping around me at the present time, and I haven't a leaky bunker or fox hole. The story could change any day, however, and we could be up there giving them air if they need close air *support again. We'll be able to give them nearly all the air protection they'll need from 229, however, so don't worry about the daddy, will you, dearest.*

Kiss the darlings and tell them how very much their daddy loves them and misses them. I love you, precious girl, and need you so very much the rest of my life.

Night night, dearest, love Daddy

26 Aug 52
Tuesday afternoon
Changdan, Korea

Dearest doll,
Another all night session and our kids took a shellacking out there on Bunker Hill. All day yesterday it was fairly quiet and we felt as though the goonies would lay off for a while because of the three days of rain. We knew our own particular problems arising from the rains-- bridges out, fox holes and bunkers flooded, resupply of food and ammunition very limited. We believed the goonies to have had their spirits dampened but, oh boy, how wrong we were! At 2030 last night it hit the fan and lasted all night.

The weather was foul but the colonel ordered me up to 229 and up I went at around midnight. It was pitch black out and the jeep got stuck a third of the way up to 229, so Cpl Stamps and I had to hike it the rest of the way. The road had washed out in about ten places and we slipped in the mud and had a heck of a time. I felt every one of my 29 years when we finally reached the top, so tired that I couldn't talk for about five minutes. Then no flare plane. At 0100 this morning they notified me the flare plane couldn't make it because of the weather, so I waited up there in the bunker (229) until 0430 when Maj Biehl called to tell me the colonel had ordered our team to Item Co MLR immediately, to arrange for close air support at first light this morning--weather permitting. We brought all our radio gear down from 229 on our backs and finally got to the jeep and a 6X6 truck Bill had sent up to meet us. Fifteen minutes at our battalion CP, then we climbed in a truck (6X6) and proceeded to the rear medical aid station with all our radio equipment and three men--Evans, Boone, Stamps, Biehl and I. The road to Item Co MLR was out completely except by tank, or APC (armored personnel carrier) which was making regular runs back up to the front and to the aid station carrying supplies up and casualties back. We boarded it and off we went.

I was amazed at the smooth ride we had. The road up to Item is terrific but the APC made it. We saw some horrible sights at the rear aid station and the forward aid station point where they let us off. I had to turn my head. The South Korean stretcher bearers were so exhausted they were falling down. They had been assaulted by a full battalion last night and this morning, and we took eight KIA and around 60 WIA.

Purposely, I spared Marion the terrible sight we came upon at the aid station. The wounded, the dying, the exhausted, the dead lay on the ground or on stretchers covered with their Marine blankets or ponchos. Hospital corpsmen and doctors slept nearby. Most of the wounded had been given morphine shots or plasma, and were resting or fast asleep. All were waiting for the APC (an all-terrain tank-like vehicle sometimes used for transporting the wounded) to pick them up and carry them off to the next level of aid, which would be the Battalion aid station or the hospital ship in Inchon Harbor. Med evac helicopters were shuttling the wounded off as fast as they could manage.

I asked a corpsman where I could find my friend, Dr. Craighead. "He's over there asleep on the first cot in that row, sir," he said. The cots were actually short legged canvas stretchers, standing six inches off the ground. Since all the bodies were completely covered with a blanket, I kicked the boot of the man on the first stretcher. Thud--it didn't move. He was dead. The same for the second and third, but the fourth one moved, uncovered his head and spoke to me. "Hi, Pete, it's been a hell of a night. Got any chow?"

My friend, Lt Valentine, had been hit pretty bad. No word on him as yet but I'm checking.

Set our radio gear up by 0530 and worked an OE but couldn't get air. At 1030 we left Item line and returned to our CP by APC with a full load of wounded. It's still raining and we're expecting another battalion assault tonight. Lay down an hour at noon but got up to help square our operations away for tonight. Nobody had any sleep. If the rain doesn't let up soon the situation will get worse. I'm safe, baby girl, so don't worry about me, but pray for those kids, darling.

I love you, honey. Kiss my darlings. Received your lovely letter of 18 August.

Love ya, Daddy

27 Aug 52
2030
Changdan, Korea

Dearest family,

I went to bed last night at around 2230, fully expecting to go up on 229 at any minute to direct a flare plane all night if the kids on Bunker Hill got hit with any force and needed me. They only got probed lightly, thank God, and the casualties were mostly from mortar and artillery.

We did get up at 0500 this morning and I brewed a cup of instant coffee over our little Coleman stove in my canteen cup and shared it with Bill. We were really cold last night and this morning, and it looks like another cold one tonight.

Bill and I and three members of our team jeeped on the good portion of the road to the battalion forward aid station and waited 15 minutes for the tank to carry us up to Item Co line. As per usual, we observed the pitiful sight we are so used to seeing collected there at the aid station. I'll not dwell on that, though. We boarded the tank and up we went to Item through a lot of incoming artillery and mortar. The roads are still a mess of mud and muck and it will be days before a jeep or a truck will be able to use it. The tank is a godsend, worth every nickle the tax payers paid for it. No telling what the death rate would be if it were not for the tank's ability to travel these hills and ruts and swollen rivers. At night, when we have rain or fog as we have been having, helicopters hava no. I can't impress it upon you how smooth the tanks ride. It's just like riding in a Cadillac.

The South Korean labor battalion is working on the roads but the tanks have torn them up so badly they have an endless job. We passed a tired, beleaguered company (250 boys):--wet, bearded, dirty and completely exhausted--walking through the mud back out to a reserve area. They had spent 72 hours of hell on Bunker Hill, and the horrible story could be read on the face of every man and boy of them.

The tank let us off at the company aid station and the same old story held true there-- dead and wounded Marines all over the place. We walked the last quarter mile to Item Co trench overlooking Bunker and had set up control by 0630. We had observation of all goonie land lying west, north and south of our kids on Bunker and, although the valleys were fogbound until 1000, when we got our first strike A/C, we did manage to call in 4.2 inch and 81 mortar on some goonie positions we'd spotted. They were brazen this morning, with the fog, and felt safe to expose themselves. I had about 20 of them in my 20 power BC scope and called in the 81s on them. When the smoke cleared goonies hava no. They didn't know what hit 'em.

You know, you can't hear a mortar fired. There's only a dull thud and a woosh, and off it goes. Our mortar battery was directly behind us and, after our fire mission was laid, the goonies counter batteried us and our mortar team really got sprayed, but they are ever ready from past experience and hit their bunkers seconds after they fired, to avoid the inevitable counter battery. We heard them whistling over our heads, both our 81 outgoing and the goonies' counter battery incoming. Gives you an eerie feeling, believe me. We get all the goonie counter battery shorts--really shakes you, ("clutched" is the new word, "shook" is very popular too).

Cartoonist in 1stMarDiv paper showed two front line radio operators talking to each other, "Hello, Shook, this is Clutched, how do you read me?" Very appropriate, believe me.

No mail tonight, dearest.

Maj Stone took his rescue team out and set up his station for "Operation Snatch" because the truce team met again for the first time in a week, only to adjourn again for a week. What a dismal failure those people are. Bill and I were too busy to make it to our Snatch job this time.

This Bunker Hill deal is the most senseless mass slaughter I have ever seen. It's not high ground--Item is higher. We could keep it neutralized by napalm, bombs, mortar and artillery without putting those kids out there. I'm sore, and so is Bill. We have observed this deal closer and longer than any other officers. Every time a company comes off Bunker it pulls its forward observers with them. The FOs usually take up their stations on Item Co line with us. We see new faces there every time we go up. Maj Biehl and I have briefed the colonel and the operations officers, as well as the intelligence officer--a situation that should be reversed. We are a little sore about that too.

We ran three strikes in the valleys and ridges west of Bunker, where the goonies have been observed in great numbers moving through trenches, carrying supplies, mortar and recoilless rifles on their backs. We napalmed and bombed a large area and laid nine 1000-pound one-to-six hour delayed bombs tonight at 1930 across their known avenues of approach. When they go off it'll shake them, believe me. The colonel was pleased with our day's work.

We bugged out from Item Co MLR at 1400, and it took two and a half hours for us to get back out to the main road and our jeep. A weasel was broken down and the tanks were being used elsewhere. We directed operations on the repair of the weasel (jeep with tracks--amphibious also). We got another one, at long last, and had the driver go up to Item Co MLT to pick up a load of weapons, then out we came, a 15 minute rugged ride. Weasels are not here to stay; the roads are too rough and steep for them. Tanks are the only answer.

We got back to CP and ate. Then I bathed from my helmet and put on a clean change of clothes. After that I controlled the one-to-six delay drop through an OE and radio relay from our jeep at CP. Finally, after working up four air strikes for tomorrow and submitting them over our TAR net to Dev Baker, I settled down to my letter to my precious family that I love and adore and miss so very much.

I feel fine, dearest. The Bunker problem upsets me, though. Guess I worry too much.

Love ya, Daddy

P.S. *Still no word on Lt Valentine's condition. Will keep you posted.*

Upper Left: Peterson taking a short break prior to moving up to front lines. Old house is at Changdan, near the Command Post (CP) of the 3rd Battalion. The date is 5 Sep 52. We had to order the Korean families out of houses too close to the fighting, for fear of them taking a good dose of mortar and artillery fire. They were mostly farmers, eager to get on with their lives. This house we had obviously let slip through the cracks, because the Korean family was still living in it. Note the wash hanging from the clothes line. Life goes on.

Upper Right, L to R: Peterson, unknown, Gus Dake. Hunting was great this day. The Chinese ringneck pheasant tasted a lot like gamey chicken. They were delicious.

Middle Left: Good hunting.

Lower Left: This was once a helicopter.

Left: KANSAS Line. 1stMarDiv recently completed secondary line occupied by 1/7 while in reserve in late 1952. It's plain to see that reserve duty did not imply R & R.

Right: Marines of the 1st Tank Battalion raise radio antennae on their Sherman Medium Tank. This type of tank would be my air control vehicle for "Operation Snatch."

Left: Tactical problems are reviewed (from left) by MajGen Edwin A. Pollock, CG, 1st MarDiv; LtGen Paul A. Kendall, I Corps Commander; and Col Russell E. Honsowetz, AC/S, G-3, 1st MarDiv.

Photo credit USMC

CHAPTER 15

THE DEATH OF A TRUE HERO

28 Aug 52
Thursday, 1510
Changdan, Korea

Dearest family,
 The boys on Bunker had a relatively quiet night, thank God. I had a fine night's sleep and was prepared to get up at 0600 but at about 0545 I woke up and heard rain falling on my tent, so I reached over and turned off Bill's little (Big Ben) clock and proceeded to snatch a couple hours more sleep. At 0800 I got up and put on a pan of water and shaved, then kept putting on more water for everyone else in the tent and as their water got hot they'd get out of the basket, shave and dress. When all were shaved and dressed we went to breakfast together. I had four scrambled eggs with coffee, toast and strawberry preserves.
 As the weather was still bad, I prepared a summary of all air strikes flown in support of our battalion front since we arrived and also submitted three more air strike requests--one for 1 to 6 hour delayed 1000# bombs to be laid in the goonie approach corridor, and two strikes for MPQ night bombing radar control in known active goonie artillery positions.
 After putting all the men to work doing general cleanup and equipment repair, I got powerful "hongray" at 1430, so put on a small can of beans and ate with gusto. They hit the spot. Now I think I'll survive until 1630 when chow goes. The sun is coming out, so it's entirely possible we may get air this afternoon. I sure hope so. I've got some good targets an OE gave me last night.
 The large Corps 8" gun is firing in back of us here at Bn CP and every time it goes off we jump, the tent puffs out and everything on the little makeshift table of ours hops into the air about a quarter inch. I wish they'd shove off. The rocket ripple is the one that shakes you. Boy, when they go off it sounds like about 100 jet fighters all buzzing you at about 25' altitude.
 No mail last night or today, as yet. Failed to mention I received yours of 19 August, honey girl.
 I guess we'll be on the line for at least another 20 days, then battalion reserve for 20 days or thereabouts, then regimental reserve. I'll sure be ready for reserve, I'll tell you, darling.
 Got some sad news today. 2nd Lt Earl Lester Valentine Jr. died on the hospital ship from head wounds received on Bunker Hill. I took a picture of him the day before, which I'll

send home and have you get it developed, enlarged and framed. I'll get their addresses so you can send it to his sweetheart and family.

All for this writing, darling. I love you and miss you all so very much. Your trip to the Redondo Fish Aquarium sounded interesting. I'd love to have been with you, dear. Grace's new addition sounds interesting (restaurant on the pier). You've got a date, honey. Kiss my darlings and tell them to be good boys. Tell them their daddy loves them and misses them very, very much.

Your very own, Daddy

THE DIVISION SPECIAL RECONNAISSANCE COMPANY

The Chinese order of battle (OOB) information was fed into the division intelligence network by higher commands, I Corps and EUSAK, and adjacent units but a large part of the data about Communist forces was produced by the division itself. Frontline units, in contact with the enemy by observation of his activities, supplied the bulk of intelligence about enemy defense tactics, employment of weapons and combat characteristics. Supporting Marine division units, particularly artillery and armor, fed more facts into the system, mostly through identification of the caliber of enemy shells fired at the Marines. As a result of its missions forward of the line and actions in defense of it, the division reconnaissance company also contributed to the intelligence network. Individual Marines performing as tactical air observers, artillery air observers, forward air controllers, as well as the VMO and HMR pilots, were other important sources readily available to the 1st Marine Division.

G-2 directed the division intelligence effort, including processing of raw material and supplying of updated reports to 1st Division units. The G-2 section also maintained OOB and target identification data on Chinese units and their commanders. Members of the G-2 staff also assisted in interrogation of prisoners of war (POWs), screened the civilians apprehended in unauthorized areas, debriefed Marines exposed to enemy intelligence and conducted inspections of division internal security. In areas where the 1st Marine Division had only limited intelligence capability, it turned to EUSAK for assistance.

Eighth Army teams augmented the division counterintelligence efforts and provided most of the translation service. In addition, three radio intercept units furnished information to the Marines. The importance of this service had been proven during several combat patrols in May when critical information had been instantly radioed to a friendly unit under fire.

Other intelligence activities proved less beneficial to the Marines. These operations were conducted by Tactical Liaison Officers (TLOs), friendly Koreans trained by U.S. intelligence teams and members of a Higher Intelligence Detachment (HID), a Korean unit assigned from EUSAK. Both the TLO and HID proved of limited value to the division, due to the generally poor educational background of the agents and their inadequate training.

Communist forward positions were gradually encroaching upon us. Since April 1952 the division had noted every month that the enemy was continuing to extend his trenches in the direction of the Marine MLR. The Chinese technique was to occupy key high terrain at night, prepare the ground during darkness by digging trenches and constructing bunkers, then vacate the area before daybreak. After nightly repetitions of this process had produced a tenable position, the enemy moved in and occupied it. By means of these creeping tactics, the Chinese hoped to acquire the dominating terrain. The ultimate goal of the Communist forces was believed to be Paekhak Hill, my Hill 229, because this represented the Marine high ground position just over a mile east of the road leading to Panmunjom and Kaesong, and a straight shot into Seoul.

At night my forward bunker high up on my 750-foot vantage point had become the gathering point for an elite group of individuals from the division reconnaissance company. I had grown to know and admire Lt Earl Valentine, who showed up at my bunker more often than any of the other recon people. Since he was attached to our Co H, 3d Bn, 1st Marines, he would ask me for a briefing of the day's activity in my sector and any bits of advice I could throw his way. My two bits' worth was simply the last of several he had received before each of his hazardous missions. He'd blacken his face, check the grenades and smoke flares hung over his flak vest and give his CO one last call before jumping off into goonie land to ply his trade. At it all night, he'd creep directly up to Chinese Communist positions and gather intelligence information. A knife served as his only protection, since any other weapon would reveal his presence and he'd be a gonner. The incredible stories he related to me about his risky business made me realize just what caliber of man Earl Valentine had to be--a very special person who liked what he was doing, had volunteered for it, and died doing it.

When word reached us that Lt Valentine had died from wounds received on his last mission it broke my heart. I had lost a friend and a true hero in my book. It was a small thing that the division did in his memory, naming our parade ground in his honor, but to his many friends and buddies, his name would live on in his deeds. **THIS WAS A MAN'S MAN!**

THE OFFICIAL CITATION

VALENTINE, EARL L., JR., Second Lieutenant, USMC
H-3-1, August 25-26, 1952, KIA

Assigned the mission of restoring the company defensive perimeter when an overwhelming enemy force overran a key ridge line on the right flank, Second Lieutenant Valentine bravely led his platoon through intense enemy artillery and mortar barrages to the line of departure in preparation for a counterattack. Undeterred by persistent hostile fire, he boldly reconnoitered the terrain in the darkness, called in a mortar fire plan to the company command post to support his attack and, although wounded, moved his unit forward in the assault. At the height of the battle, he assumed a position forward of the platoon and spearheaded the attack in the face of a heavy barrage of enemy fire until he was mortally wounded.

Second Lieutenant Valentine was posthumously awarded the NAVY CROSS.

— — — — —

30 Aug 52
Changdan, Korea
Saturday, 1930

Dearest baby girl,
I had a happy surprise this afternoon. Maj MacMahon and Capt Strom from VMA-212 dropped up to OP229 to see me just as I was in the middle of controlling an air strike on the southern slopes of Taedok san, the main Communist stronghold fronting our battalion, where 72mm artillery and 61 and 82mm mortars, troops, bunkers and supplies are located. We hit them some pretty hard licks and the OE gave a good damage assessment. Strom and Mac got a kick out of it, and I called in arty (VT fused) on the troops that were still running around after my planes had expended all their ammo. We used flak suppression and they were very much impressed with our plan. We were expecting the new general of the 1st Marine Division, MGen Pollock, to inspect the OP but he only came as far as the company CP, then went on back.

My friends and I secured to the battalion CP. I called for a helicopter, then we had chow. They took pictures of me and I of them, and the three of us together, taken by Maj Biehl. I showed them the new colored pictures of my precious family that I'm so very proud of, and they got a kick out of it because they both had colored film in their cameras and had never seen colored prints before. They had seen slides etc., but not prints.

Aided by some able FOs (artillery forward observers), I prepared air missions and arty supplements for each enemy position and submitted them for tomorrow, then stayed in the 2/3 bunker until dark.

Your very own, Daddy

31 Aug 52
Sunday morning
Changdan, Korea

Dearest family,
Another rainy day looms its ugly head over our little village of Changdan by the Imjin, and air hava no today. The wind blew so hard last night that we all were certain our flimsy little old tent would surely take off, but luck was with us and we didn't lose it. The tent flaps banged against my cot all night and I didn't get much sleep but I can nap today, I think, because of the rain.

Just wrote Ben. Wrote Mom yesterday.

OP2 was hit by a goonie probe and they killed two of our boys and wounded three. Hit the bunker next to the one I stayed in for 25 nights. How do I ever escape those deals? Scares me, honey. The Chinese walked up to it at 0200 this morning as the boys were changing watch, tossed in three grenades and opened up with burp guns. The enemy all got away. Their lines are so close to ours it's pitiful. Glad I'm off of OP2. Bunker Hill is what drew me back here to the battalion CP and MLR.

Keep up those prayers, honey girl. Went to church this morning--the little squad tent (enlisted mess hall) served as usual for our gathering place and we sang our fool heads off trying to drown out the rain beating on the tent and the sound of the wind. About 12 were there. I took communion afterwards. The sermon was about St. Paul and the 276 shipwrecked people who landed on the Isle of Malta 1900 years ago, and he was the only one who had vision enough to gather up the wood for the fire. The chaplain drew a parable for us in our Battalion of Bunker Hill (or Butcher Block Hill, as the men call it now).

Bunker was quiet last night except for over 500 rounds of mortar and arty--no probes. Only probe was on OP2 George Co. They frisked the bodies of eight goonies killed on Bunker the night before last and I examined the loot that Lt. Kelly, our intelligence officer, had and was going to turn into the regiment for study--one low white tennis shoe, a small brass spoon, a couple of dirty old bandage compresses and a couple of documents in Chinese.

I was just asked to brief the company commander of Easy Co. They are going out to Bunker Hill to relieve the company that's been there for three days. The company CO brought with him his three platoon leaders, snipers, FO and mortar men. I briefed them on the whole Bunker situation and the effectiveness and limitations of their supporting arms; the tactical situation now and what it has been in the past three weeks; what to do in case of an assault or probe in regard to calling in supporting arms. Also briefed them on the Yobo (our So. Korean civilian support people) supply system, routes, best trails and hours of travel. Communications, observation posts and goonie resupply and approach corridors were discussed. Boy, those kids sure have to be briefed on a mess of various things: whose machine guns and mortars are to be used, whose radios, situation maps, and mortar and arty overlays are to be used--on and on, too numerous to put down on paper.

I certainly have found myself in some peculiar situations of late. The last month I have directed mortar and arty fire, called in air, briefed company commanders, taken charge of wounded helicopter evac., directed Yobo supply teams, ridden in a tank and a weasel up to our front line positions to direct air, worked as SAC officer and VIP guide service on the Changdan-by-the-Imjin "resort" town, directed aircraft night flare drops, inspected and supervised the cleanliness and general appearance of my enlisted team, set up radio repair and maintenance on our equipment, kept regimental officer briefed on all our battalion air activities and any other matters relative to battalion and regiment liaison. I grade my men, father them and correct their many mistakes without blowing my top in the process.

Darling, I have enough material for a dozen books if we just sit down and apply ourselves. I've gone on and on and I'm tired of hearing myself. Your letters were sweet, dearest girl. I love you so much and my boys too. Our day is coming, honey girl. Keep a stiff upper lip, like Cecil. Love you heaps and heaps.

Your very own Daddy

A RECORD MONTH FOR CLOSE AIR SUPPORT

August was to become the record month for 1st MAW attack and fighter pilots during 1952, with a total of 5,869 sorties flown.

While the air people in August were maintaining a good weather pace against the enemy following the July downpours, the Communist ground troops apparently found the going too difficult to mount any sustained attack, other than Bunker Hill. The enemy merely continued his active defense with an average of two contacts daily, while busily engaged in advancing his OPLR by creeping tactics. Even the usually assiduous Chinese artillery was strangely quiet. With respect to the enemy's excellent artillery capability, the 1stMarDiv in July learned that the Chinese had introduced a 132mm Russian rocket in their combat operations. The presence of this truck-mounted launcher, the Katusha, which could fire 16 rockets simultaneously, was indicated by a POW who had been informed by his platoon leader that there were two Katusha regiments in the CCF. In addition to this new enemy weapon, the Marine division reported the same month that positive sightings had been made of self-propelled guns emplaced well forward, and that there was an "indication that these guns were being used to fire direct fire missions from frontline revetments."

This wasn't the first time these big self-propelled guns had been brought to bear on the division. When I was flying close air support for the 1stMarDiv we were fortunate to be over the division at dusk when these big guns opened up. I was leading the division at the time and we were successful in silencing them. My plane was hit during this mission.

August was the record month for the number of close air support missions flown in support of the 1stMarDiv, with nearly 1000 aircraft, predominantly Marine, dropping their ordnance on the Chinese. The Marines still felt that they were the champions of close air support and they *were* excellent, but of course, I controlled all types of aircraft and some other types from other services were also good. I had good and bad missions flown for me by all services.

At any rate, Major Bill Biehl and I would like to lay claim for having controlled more aircraft in a single month than anyone else in that war, or perhaps any war. Lord, were we busy!

1 Sep 52
Monday, a brand new month

Dearest family,
OP2 was hit with another Chinese probe last night, or rather at 0300 this morning. We had 1 KIA. Maj Biehl and I took care of the helicopter evacuation after they brought the dead and wounded here to Bn CP aid station at 0400. It was foggy and cold and the copter was delayed because of it. Bunker Hill wasn't probed last night. OP2 and Bunker Hill are both untenable ground and worthless to us. I don't go along with the strategic concept of their tactical solution in the slightest. Major Jack Shoden, the regimental air officer that I am relieving, called this morning and said that Col Layer (the Reg CO) had told him he wanted me as his regimental air officer when Shoden left at the end of this month with Biehl. So I guess I have made it, honey. Shoden sprained his ankle last night and has to go to Div Aid for Xrays. Bill or I may have to assist at Regiment if he's delayed more than two or three days.
The weather is clearing, darling, so maybe we'll get a little air this afternoon. I hope so--I have some good targets I'm itching to clobber.
If the picture I took of Lt Valentine turns out well, I'll send one to his mother and father who are separated but living in Lexington, Virginia. I'll try to locate his girl friend and send one to her also.
No mail yesterday. Love you so and miss my darlings.

Your daddy

1 Sep 52
Monday afternoon
Changdan, Korea

Dearest family,
I mailed four rolls of film home to you airmail, honey, and enclosed it, but just the same, I felt like writing to you to tell you what happened this afternoon.

The weather cleared up around 1030, so Bill and I went up to 229 hoping we'd get to control some air strikes. The aircraft arrived but they gave them to the KMCs on our left flank. Then the VIPs started to arrive. First Col Altman came up with Gen Baird USMC, the assistant Division commander who was with a Mr. McKay, the president of the Navy League. We gave them a briefing and they all took our picture, so I took one of them, or I should say Col. A. took it of us and I was in the group, then shoved off. A couple of hours later three others arrived and it proved to be very interesting. One was a Pathe News camera man (with his movie camera) named Pierce, another a Major from the 1stMarDiv P.I.O. office and a Methodist missionary named Elmer MacQuarie. The latter was most interesting--a man of approximately my age, born in Japan and has lived in the orient for over 21 years. What he didn't know about Japan, Formosa, China, Korea wasn't worth saying. His wife and child are living in Formosa and he knows Chang very well. He'll be home in a week or two. He says Chang's army is shaping up and that if the United Nations' forces don't hit China soon they won't be able to utilize all the young Nationalists that are still alive. The Communists have purged by killing over 30 million of them this year and are increasing it all the time. His parents were missionaries. He was in Korea 8 years ago. He skied in the mountains northwest of Wonsan. According to him, missionary life is the best kind of life to live. Pierce provides him with movie equipment and film for his orphanages and missions. He likes Koreans best of all the orientals because they make the best Christians. They had a Willys station wagon which they parked down at the Bn CP and took a jeep up to Hill 229.

While we were on our way up the hill this morning our jeep boiled, so we stopped at a stream, filled up our helmet and poured it into the radiator. For several days after it rains there's a regular little stream coming down from 229. OP2 had some probes last night again and Bunker was quiet--guess the goonies are playing it cool over at Bunker.

Had a nice dinner tonight--steak, string beans, baked beans, macaroni and cheese, cookies, lemonade, sliced pineapple. I opened a little can of spaghetti out of an assault ration at noon today, heated it and used the little plastic spoon provided.

Pierce took movies of our panoramic view from 229, as well as of us. Don't know whether we'll make the movies on it or not. Seems as though he wanted it for his personal collection. Said he wanted to film an airstrike and he was sick he couldn't have been with us on Bunker from the 10-14 of August. It would have made exciting movies. He may come up there to 229 some night and film the night fighting.

I loaded my camera with color film and have taken three already today. The view from 229, green and beautiful, belies what's taking place out there. Watched through my 20 BC scope the goings-on at Panmunjom, which placed it as near to me as "Colton's Fort" is from the top of our hill at home. I could see them building a frame house at the truce site, the dimensions of which were approx. 30'X30'. The roofline looked like our garage and in the front it has a little stoop. It's only framed, so far. It's a mutual thing, you know; the goonies are supplying the lumber and the UN the plumbing, lights and fixtures. Winter's coming on, so I guess they decided to converse in comfort. One helicopter flew in and out of there at about 1500 carrying junior delegates, according to Maj Stone who gets all this hot dope because he's the Operations Snatch CO for the top delegates. Mortars have been registering in all day on the northern slope of hill G7 which, of course, is goonie-occupied. Hill G7 contains the mortars that have hit OP2 so hard of late.

Talked to Capt Melansen, commander of How Company, which just came off Bunker Hill at 0200 this morning. Said he played it cool and stayed loose. That's the standard saying of nearly everyone here--"Play it cool. Stay loose. Don't get shook. Don't get clutched."

Maj Smitty got some new brown leather high boots yesterday and we teased him so badly he took them off. We called them Seoul R&R boots and he's a rough, tough ex-company commander, always having to give that impression to his company commanders because he's the operations officer and gives all the orders. He put his old beat-up black leather mud-covered boots back on. We sure got a kick out of him.

No mail tonight, honey girl. I love you, dearest girl and am just living for that wonderful day when I'll be heading home. They sent one man from each company today to cold weather lectures back at the regiment. Looks like it's not too far off. Brrrr!

How are my darlings? Fine, I hope. Tell them I love them.

Your very own Daddy

2 Sep 52
Tuesday afternoon

Hi dearest family,
    Received yours of 25 and 26 August today and was very happy to read the sweet words you always have to say about me, and the very descriptive manner in which you so capably describe the activities of my darlings. Randy must be a cute little guy, carrying his blue teddy bear wherever he goes. I'd love to hear him chatter. The only thing I ever heard him say was "Icky." There will be so much for me to see and do when I first get home, I won't know where to begin.
    I visited Lt Kelly's recently completed bunker adjoining our Bn CP. It's a first rate piece of workmanship, dug practically out of solid rock (the red decomposed granite type of rock), 6"X12" overheading, 12"X12" uprights. It's as cool as can be inside. I'm sold--I'm going to have a cellar in our next house, honey. They are grand.
    Not much activity for me today--sky is overcast. Had a colonel and a major up on 229 this morning. VIP tour. Put my boys to work making a map 5'X4' on a 1:10,000 scale for the VIP bunker on 229. Two reporters from United Press came by today. I didn't talk to them--crummy looking individuals.

    Bye bye, love ya,
    Your very own Daddy

3 Sep 52
Wednesday afternoon
Changdan, Korea

Dearest doll and boys,
    Today is strictly not a day for an aviator. Typhoon Mary is upon us with buckets of water, wind of about 20 knots in gusts. We've got our tent flaps secured as best we can but the water still comes in. We are standing by for winds up to 50 mph by 1800 this afternoon. The war practically comes to a standstill with weather like this, which is OK for my money, except that it drives me nutty to be cooped up in a dark, dreary, old leaky tent.
    Stone, Smith, Biehl and I--oh yes, Monroe also--worked up a SAC watch officers duty list and responsibility schedule. It will aid the battalion relieving us (about 15 or 20 Sep) a lot more than it will us. We've progressed fairly smoothly with our old system but it needed a lot more improvement. Roughly, the system is this: we wired into the Reg FDC (Fire Direction Center) and lines to all our 4.2", 60mm, 81mm, 105mm mortar and artillery. We built a 20' long bench in the bunker, placed large maps on the bulkheads and platted all the individual ranges of the various supporting arms on it, as well as the existing fire support plans that the company commanders on OP2 and Bunker Hill would need in case the goonies hit again in force. The maps have clear plastic over them and we use grease pencil to plot all the fire missions as they are called in. In a few days, when the system is completed, I'll stand active watches at night, acting as SAC officer for the battalion during my watch and make decisions as to which supporting arm should be employed in support of our troops. During good weather and daylight hours I'll be up on the hill awaiting aircraft. They never mentioned this type of duty in the FAC school!

Bill just came in with Col Hutchinson, an aviator touring the Div. He's to be CO of VMF(N)513 night fighter squadron located at K8 down south of K6. The old CO was shot down (Col Lambert). This colonel is his replacement. We won't be able to show him around, though, because of the rain and restricted visibility. We can't even see the top of 229. Those kids in VMF(N)513 have really had a rough time. Night flying is tough going with the weather and navigational aid such as they are.

Reread your last two letters, dearest, and enjoyed them all over again. Love you, darling, so very much. Miss you all like everything. Not much news on my end today.

Bye bye, Daddy

4 Sep 52
Changdan, Korea

Dearest family,
Happy day, I received two letters today from you, darling, and one each from Mom and Ben. Sure does give the old man a terrific uplift to hear from home.

Mom said she and Ben got a big kick out of Randy saying, "All boys out" whenever he gets out of the car, just like I used to say. Imagine that little tyke remembering! How I'd love to be home watching all this firsthand. Mom also said she got a big thrill out of hearing me over the radio on the news program.

This medal awards thing runs hot and cold. They hit a snag at the Wing at K3 and it had to be rewritten and resubmitted. At the Division a lot of the Silver Stars have been downgraded to Bronze Stars, and Bronze Stars to Legion of Merit. Bill and I don't know where we stand now and probably won't for several weeks to come. Oh well, such is life. The only thing I care about is coming out alive and, so far, I've been able to keep just a few steps ahead.

What really counts with us is that those wonderful youngsters who have fought so valiantly during the bitter fighting through August and September are properly rewarded. It's interesting to note that four of the seven Medals of Honor were posthumously awarded to 1stMarDiv Marines for gallantry in action during this time period. This alone shows the awful intensity of the battle to hold these hills, and I fear that many more months and resultant casualties will be required to bring this terrible war to an end.

Today Bill and I greeted a brand new sunshiny day after that monster we had upon us last night. Outside of a few good husky blows and lots and lots of rain, Typhoon Mary petered out. We manned OP229 after breakfast and got an airstrike at noon. Had two separate VIP tours up with us during the day, including three LtCol air Marines. After learning of my FAC experience and 58 missions, they tried to talk me into shipping over after 6 Dec 52. I told them it would all be a bed of roses if it weren't for being separated from my family. Said I couldn't stand any more separations. They agreed it was tough, especially so for them, having just left the States. I was far worse off during late March and early April myself than I am now. I've steeled myself to the situation after five months and feel as though each day I cross off the calendar is another day closer to my family, especially now since I'm over the hump, as it were. Five months down, three to go. It's downhill all the way now, darling. About 10 more days and into battalion reserve we go, then a few more weeks and I go into regimental reserve and can breathe again free and easy. What a relief it will be to get off of the line! The tension is always with us, no matter what the situation is at any one time. Always ready and waiting for another attack, never knowing when the field phone will ring, saying this is it.

Just called in for a helicopter to go to strip No. 54 for an emergency evac over at Item Co line. It's now 2145 and they have been receiving incoming all day. The goonies have somehow managed to get observation on some bunkers and are really clobbering them during the daylight hours. Killed three lieutenants up there today and wounded several others.

Every time I hear of casualties I curse the stupid peace delegates. They met today again for the first time in a week. I was up on OP229 and watched the UN delegates arrive by helicopter at 1030 sharp, through my 20-power BC scope; then at 1045 I fixed the scope on Kaesong and soon I could just make out a caravan of cars moving south and east along the

Panmunjom road to their meeting place. OP2 lay just below the Panmunjom site in the scope and, even as they drew nearer that site, mortars could be seen hitting our positions on OP2. They finally arrived at 1055, being led by a new light colored sedan of unknown vintage, behind which followed four jeeps of apparent Russian manufacture--quite different from our American made jeep in every way, larger and wider especially, and black in color.

Just as the delegates parked at the truce site, my airplanes came on station and we must have shook them up considerably because we directed them onto a target that was closer to Panmunjom than to our control position, and we felt the bomb blasts very decidedly. I was wondering why we happened to get aircraft and nobody else did for several hours, either before or after--at exactly 1100, when the delegates met; and especially significant also is the fact that we are the air control agency closest to Panmunjom. I'm positive 5th Air Force JOC and I Corps, 8th Army and the 1st Marine Division engineered the timing on our air mission today. We never have any idea whatsoever when our aircraft will be on station. The goonies were pounding our OP2 for effect and we were adding to the thunder with our aircraft.

Bill and I labored about six hours today and this evening, writing out an FAC SOP to pass onto Dave "Sniveler" Kennedy who is up here at Div to pick up some finer points on FAC'ing to pass on to his new class of FACs soon to arrive at K3's MACG-2 FAC school. We knocked off ten full pages of suggestions and ideas that we thought would materially aid a new FAC coming up here to Div. Bill and I both felt as though the 10 days we had put in at MACG-2 turned out to be practically useless to us as FACs. We learned later on by ourselves, the hard way.

Dave gave me 1000 wan for each of the kids and said, "Tell the little darlings Uncle Dave sends his love." He's quite the guy. You'd get a kick out of some of these characters I've picked up as buddies. Nearly every one of them is a hard-charging, drinking, loud-mouthed regular officer, and nearly all have just made major, including Dave. I absolutely love these guys. They all have helped me get through this lousy mess.

So Troop thinks I make a good soldier, does he? All I can say to that is that I make a good soldier when I'm soldiering, but I'd like to try and make a better civilian. Don't care to be making a move every time I turn around. Want to remain in the same place and enjoy it while I can. This pursuit of life, liberty and happiness deal sounds great, but you've got to take time out to analyze the situation in every one of its sinister meanings. Namely, you can get creamed flying, whether in Korea or El Toro. I couldn't remain in the Corps and not fly. BU AER appeals to me very much but it would peter out in six or eight months, then I'd find myself on some other overseas draft and away I'd go to England, Italy or some carrier in the Mediterranean or Caribbean for a year. Nothing doing. If I have to dig ditches to remain with my family, dig ditches I will. Security is a wonderful thing and a military retirement would be grand but you've got to outwit a Corsair or a jet or a dark landing and instrument let-downs in foul weather in order to collect. I think I'll gamble the other way--on security that is achieved by a savings program, with sound investments and wise expenditures of all our funds. I think we've got it made already, darling. Don't you?

Enough of that. Now to tell you how very much I love and adore you, sweetheart. Keep that side of the beddie-bye warm because before long I'll be home! Kiss my darlings. I love you all--you're all on my mind and the days are slipping by.

Your very own Daddy

Clear skies tonight. Full moon
I can read a newspaper outside.

2030, 5 Sep 52
Changdan, Korea

Dearest girl,
Was up all night and all day today. Our kids on Bunker fought off an estimated enemy battalion. We took 12 KIAs and 50 WIAs. Enemy losses haven't been estimated. I called in helicopters and lighted strips, worked in the SAC bunker until daylight, then went up on OP229 and controlled airstrikes by myself all day because Bill was busy here at the Bn CP. I

ran in 24 aircraft today. Received the last 16 after 1830 and clobbered an enemy assembly area where they were reported to have gathered for the push last night.

In the heat of the day, between air strikes, I knocked off long enough to take a bath in a cold mountain stream. I almost froze but, gosh, it relaxed me. Arrived back here at Bn CP, had a good supper and began working up our air targets for tomorrow. Got four good ones I hope work out for us tomorrow.

Am tired, honey, so will close for tonight, may write in morning. Love you, sweetheart. Kiss my darlings.

            Love, Daddy

6 Sep 52
Changdan, Korea
Saturday morn.

Hi honey,

Boy, am I ever thankful for last night's sleep. I slept all night and we never had any enemy assaults nor any casualties, so I wasn't disturbed for helicopter evacs. I'm sitting on my edge of my cot looking outside at the sun shining through the flap. A bright beautiful new day in the making. Am going to cut this short, dearest, and shave, eat breakfast and charge up on the hill to stand by for my strike A/C. What a difference it makes in me to get a night's sleep! We can't figure the goonies out--fully expected another heavy assault last night. Glad it didn't materialize. I prayed awfully hard for it.

Kiss my darlings for me. Tell them I love them and that I'll be home before very long. I love you all and miss you terribly. Will write again tonight. Love ya.

           Your very own, Daddy

6 Sep 52
2225
Changdan, Korea

Hi darlings,

Here's the daddy up on Hill 229 with Dave Kennedy. Just as I started this letter the goonies began a terrific artillery barrage on the KMCs on our left flank and also on the 5th Marines on our right flank. I had never seen such continuous pounding as that, not even on Bunker Hill. As I write, I can still hear the guns pounding on our right flank. Can even hear machine gun firing not far off. KMC sector has quieted down. Our battalion is fairly quiet tonight except for an occasional fire fight out in front of 229 where Dave and I were parked. We tuned into the VHF frequency tonight and monitored an MPQ drop. A lone F4U-5 Corsair was up there and dropped his load during several runs.

The air today was purty scoosh, only had one mission which Bill and I let Dave control. He got a kick out of it. They were VMA-212 Corsairs. Dave went back to regiment tonight to stay with Jack Shoden because they have a cot for him. He's going to return to K3 and his school tomorrow morning. He's had a good chance to pick up a lot of good poop to pass on to his new class of FACs starting on the 12th of Sept. He's getting 13, plus two for standbys.

The staff is down in the S2 and S3 bunker, all shook over the probes and heavy artillery attacks we are receiving to our left and right. Guess they figure the goonies will be coming over the big hill any time, meaning of course 229. The standing joke around here lately is, "Keep your air mattresses inflated at all times 'cause we may be using them to move east across the Imjin River."

No mail today, honey girl.

Oh say, big day today--Bill Biehl manned strip 32 and I manned strip 42, waiting for Gen Van Fleet and four other generals to arrive at our Bn CP. We waited in the sun for two and a half hours before they arrived, landing on strip 32. Bill and I dashed up to OP229, expecting them to arrive there, but instead they went to the Co CP on the hill just next to ours. I saw Van, tho', but didn't meet him.

Took a pan bath and put clean clothes on tonight, so I'm clean from the skin out again. You're on my mind constantly, dearest girl. I love you and miss you all so very much. Kiss my darlings and tell them to be good little boys.

Your very own
Daddy that loves you

From The Redondo Beach Daily Breeze (Redondo Beach, California):

Saturday, September 6, 1952

BUNKER HILL
HAND-TO-HAND FIGHTING ERUPTS ON KOREA FRONT
ALLIES WITHDRAW FROM OUTPOSTS; BOMBERS BLAST RED HEADQUARTERS

SEOUL, Korea (AP)--Chinese troops charged three outposts on embattled Bunker Hill tonight under cover of a thunderous artillery and mortar barrage and may have forced Allied troops to withdraw.

However, Allied troops on top of that Western Front ridge held firm in their bunkers.

The fighting slackened off before midnight but a front line officer said the wary Allied troops wouldn't sleep the rest of the night.

The officer said Red artillery pounded the hill outposts with 2,500 rounds, "a very heavy shelling." A reinforced company of at least 200 Chinese attacked two outposts on the south slope and other Chinese hit an east slope position.

Savage hand-to-hand fighting erupted. The officer said reports that Allied troops withdrew from at least two of the outposts could not be confirmed immediately because of the darkness.

U.S. Fifth Air Force fighter-bombers pounded a big Red Army headquarters Saturday in Northeast Korea.

On Sandbag Hill, Too

At the eastern end of the battle front, U.S. 25th Division infantrymen hammered back a Communist attack with fists and bayonets on Sandbag Hill, an allied outpost.

U.S. Air Force, Marine and Australian planes hurled high explosives, rockets and machine gun bullets at the North Korean Fifth Corps headquarters near Kowon, the Air Force said. Pilots said they set 10 large fires, demolished 56 structures and damaged 20.

"The buildings just seemed to collapse like they were made of playing cards," said Capt. Felix Fowler, Cleveland, 0.

Other fighter bombers and B-26 light bombers blasted a tungsten mine southwest of the Northeastern Korean port of Wonsan. Fighter bombers also pounded west coast and other battlefront targets.

U.S. Sabre jet pilots reported they probably shot down one Russian-built MIG and damaged another in air battles involving 39 allied fighters and more than 50 Red jets.

New Unofficial Record

In Tokyo the air force said that Sabre pilots last Thursday rolled up a new unofficial record for a single day when they downed 14 MIGs--13 shot down and one which crashed without being hit. The latter isn't listed officially as a kill.

The revised score resulted from a study of gun camera films which confirmed that Capt. Norman L. Box shot down a MIG. He bagged another Friday.

The Air Force reported the first Sabres lost in aerial combat since Aug. 1. Two F-86s were shot down by Communist warplanes during the week ended Friday. Five other U.N. planes--including two Sabres--were lost to other causes. The 21 MIGs shot down during the period made a victory ratio of better than 10 to 1.

7 Sep 52
Changdan, Korea
Sunday 1730

Dearest family,
My tummy is full of fried chicken and french fries, plus lettuce and celery salad, donuts, chocolate ice cream. The rear area poags felt as tho' we deserved a little something extra, so they made a special effort, and, boy, I ate until it was coming out my ears.

This morning early, Boone came in and said, "Captain Peterson, we have a flight of jets on station, do you want them?" I said sure, dressed like mad and dashed up on the hill. Evans had already called for a mark (smoke round). When I got there the target was marked and we were ready to go but Dev Baker said they had given the air to another battalion. I was really sore about it.

I opened up a can of "C" rations, took out powdered chocolate, heated a canteen cup of water and mixed it up. It tasted good, since it was rather cool up there on the hill this morning. Had a small can of pears too, so I made out OK for breakfast. Stayed up there until noon before I got air. Ran them on the western side of Taedok San, hitting observations posts, bunkers and troops. Gave them a damage assessment of 95% coverage, 95% effective use of ordnance, 3 bunkers destroyed, 10 KIAs. They were AUs from VMA-212, my old squadron. Didn't ask pilot's name.

Came down to Bn CP and went to church services at 1330, staying for communion. At 1400 five lieutenants from Anglico and Dev Baker showed up and wanted the tour. I took them on up to 229 and gave them the works. Arrived back down here to Bn CP in time for supper, ate, and here I am writing to the most precious girl in the whole wide world. I'm counting the days now that stand between us, darling. Rec'd yours of 30 Aug. Looked at all my pictures of you and my darlings again today. My, but I have a fine, wonderful family to come home to. I love you all so very much.

Let's hope the boys in the 5th Marines on our right have it easier tonight. They received a heavy probe along with the over 7000 rounds of artillery and mortar fire. KMC on our left were hit hard also. Hasn't rained for 2 days.

Love ya, Your own Daddy

NORTH KOREAN MP SURRENDERS AT PANMUNJOM

8 Sep 52
Monday, 1100
Changdan, Korea

Dearest family,
I meant to mention more about what Dave Kennedy and I observed from atop OP229 on the night of 6 September. The Chinese had about 20 batteries of 76mm artillery placed within their no-fire sector near Kaesong and were blasting away at the KMC hill on our left flank prior to making an assault. I watched the whole show, including their colored flares shot into the night to call off their artillery when they had reached position to assault the KMC hill they had under fire. They lifted the artillery barrage several hundred meters (yds) to another KMC hill and assaulted the first one. Then followed a terrific fire fight and the KMC were still holding their hill, but with heavy casualties. The Chinese have really mastered the art of artillery and mortar support of their attacking forces. They are every bit as good as our forces in that regard. More and more, the fact is driven home to my mind that we are fighting a highly trained, well equipped, vicious foe. It's kill or be killed. I see no immediate peace in the offing.

The Panmunjom permanent building is shaping up. Forget whether or not I mentioned the fact that one of the Chinese MPs at Panmunjom surrendered to our OP2 outpost guard on 6 Sept. They brought him into our Bn CP where our intelligence officer and our Chinese interpreter got a heck of a lot of wonderful information from him. The Chinese MP prisoner is a master sergeant who had been a lieutenant but was broken down. Well educated, clean, close shaven and armed with a Russian pistol, he was neatly dressed in an ironed shirt, creased pants and shining leather boots. Made us look crummy.

*The prisoners captured the other night on Bunker gave out with a lot of good dope too. The pressure had been on our battalion for six weeks to take prisoners because we needed info concerning the goonies' assembly area for Bunker Hill, so we could lay down a concentration of mortar and artillery on them. Also, we wanted to know the size of the unit facing us. Found out it's an **army**!*

During the height of the battle 5 Sept, 0100-0200, a call came into the Bn CP , "This is Moody [the company commander on Bunker Hill at the time]. We've got a live one but the mortar and artillery barrage is so heavy we're afraid we'll lose him and also some of my men getting him back to Battalion aid." Col Altman told him to risk it, put a helmet and flak vest on him and bring him out. They did and he lived. I saw him here at Battalion aid on a stretcher, all bandaged up, smoking a cigarette, being interrogated by our Chinese interpreter. Seems as how they only wear tennis shoes, pants, no shirts, beanie hats atop. Black straight hair about three inches long. Could have had his picture but was hurrying up to OP229 to control aircraft on station at the time.

Battalion Doctor Brodrick requested I try and procure a plane to spray Bunker Hill to get rid of the stench of dead bodies and to prevent the further spread of disease. I passed the request on to Jack Shoden at Regiment and he in turn to Division air officer, but he felt as though it would cause an international incident. Probably would claim gas warfare. It'll be interesting to see what develops.

The Jack Kirkwood show is on Bill's little portable radio. Very good show. Haven't heard it for ages. Jack's always good for a couple of laughs.

McDaniels is coming up this afternoon for a tour of our Battalion front, helicopter strip, air control points, other points of interest and edification.

Going to knock it off for now, precious girl. Love you. Kiss my darlings and tell them I miss them something awful.

Daddy

OUR BRAVE YOUNG MARINES ARE STILL DYING
THREE AIRMEN SHOT DOWN--FATE UNKNOWN

9 Sep 52
Changdan, Korea
Tuesday, 1945

Dearest family,
The daddy has had an active day looking over maps, reading intelligence reports, planning and running air strikes. Had a nice breakfast at 0900, then trooped up to 229, controlled a mission of three AUs from VMA-212 led by Major Thompson. A large party of visitors were up there observing, including the I Corps communication CO, Col Kelley. I briefed him a half hour before the mission and had him out in my slit trench amongst all my telephone wires, sound power lines, radio portables and remote lines, my two plotting boards and binoculars. Very impressive display. The Corsairs laid their napalms right on the button at about 150' altitude. I've never seen such beautiful drops of napalm.

After the hop Thompson came up on the radio and asked if that was Peterson controlling. I replied, "Affirmative. I believe I'm talking to Thompson of 212, am I, Charlie?"

"Charlie, Pete. I'll see you in two weeks. I'm coming up to be an FAC. How did we do today?" he inquired.

"You came within about 3000 yards of the target!" I joked.

"Pete, you dog!" Thompson yelled.

All this time the CO of communications for the entire I Corps area was listening to the conversation over three loud speakers I had rigged up for the occasion. He was a good sport about it, though, and congratulated me on running a very nice air strike. I had arranged for a regimental fire mission to fire seven batteries of VT-fused flak suppression on the target areas, known A/W (automatic weapons) and AA (flak points).

When Col Kelley returned to the command post he put in a very nice compliment for me to Col Altman, who mentioned it at supper tonight. Had lamb chops, french fried onion rings, string beans, corn and limas mixed, sliced peaches on vanilla ice cream and iced lemonade. It was a very delicious meal, best we've had since we came up here on the front lines.

Major Bill went back to the Battalion reserve area and inspected the locale that we will be moving back to in a few days. I'm sure looking forward to it. There's been just too darn much pressure on us all up here ever since 26 July--every single day something.

Had to call in a helicopter this morning at 0200 for a lifesaving mission. One of our patrols had run into a land mine called a Bouncing Betty. While on a deep patrol forward of our MLR, they accidentally hit the darn thing and tripped the wire, causing it to spring up and explode at waist level, killing one of the kids and wounding three critically. The evacuation proved to be extremely hazardous because the goonies, of course, had them spotted by the mine explosion. It took about three hours to get the kids back to friendly lines and to the helicopters.

My heart was breaking as I observed the dead and wounded, so young they had barely started their adult life. We had to handle the living very gingerly to get them on the helicopter stretcher side mount, strap them in safely and see them on their way.

I love you, precious darling, and oh how I miss you! I re-read your letters over and over and each time I get enjoyment out of it, honey. Kiss my darling boys and tell them they'll have a real live daddy that walks, talks, reads funny books, has nickles and dimes in his pocket, can show boys how to make little boats, trucks and cars, and a daddy that will stop every half hour and tell them how happy he is to be home, and hug them a thousand times a day.

Bye bye little gang that I love, Daddy

A SALUTE TO THE NAVY CORPSMEN

General Alfred M. Gray, Commandant of the Marine Corps, in the Summer of 1989 issue of the Marine Corps League magazine had this to say about the Corpsmen:

"Whenever you find the Marine Corps or the Navy, you will find Navy Corpsmen. In times of peace, they provide quality health care to our Marines and their families. In times of war, Corpsmen are employed in amphibious operations, on the beaches, and on the battlefield with our Marines. In fact, 21 Navy Corpsmen have received the Medal of Honor, 18 of them while serving in the Fleet Marine Force. Whenever medical service is required, the hospital Corpsman is there, willing and prepared to serve our Marines and our country. I salute our Corpsmen for their courage, valor, and willingness to serve above and beyond the call of duty."

LT GEN JAMES VAN FLEET VISITS MY BUNKER

10 Sep 52, Wednesday
Changdan, Korea

Dearest family,
The VIP air show went off with no hitches. Congressmen and generals, including LtGen James Alward Van Fleet, Commander of the entire 8th Army in Korea, was present.

I ate breakfast here first, then dashed up the hill at 0830 and set up the gear. Had the Regiment's radio jeep up there too, as a standby. The VIP bunker was wired for sound with a speaker box and all my phones and sound power hook-ups were in place and functioning. I controlled (4) ADs and (4) AU Corsairs, putting them on a company of Chinese dug in behind a little hill in front of our positions about 1500 yards, and creamed them. The VIPs, delighted with the fine demonstration, went on their way after Van had given us a "Well done."

At the end of the strike, however, while the OE was making his damage assessment, my VHF radio went dead. (We had a remote line run up the hill to a transfer box that had a short in it, which caused all the trouble.) I ran down the hill to where I had the standby radio jeep and used our other radio.

After eating two hard boiled eggs with my boys on the hill, I came down and worked in the SAC bunker planning a couple of airstrikes for the PM, prior to the helicopter arrival of Capt Barnum of old VMA-212, who came up on the lines to see how the Intelligence end of Air functions on Battalion level. He's the new S2 at MACG-2 working with Dave Kennedy instructing FACs. I took him up on the hill and gave him the 50¢ tour. Came down, had chow, attended Bn briefing, then secured to the tent where we gabbed about the good old days (ha, ha) in VMA-212. My boys found a sack for him tonight in their tent. He'll leave in the morning when the helicopter, bringing two more colonels and one general up here for a tour, arrives. He'll return to the Division CP.

My work is cut out again for me tomorrow. In reserve by the 14th PM. If the ordnance we dropped today were turned into Cadillacs, they would amount to about five brand new 1952 Coupe de Villes at $4500 a crack.

No mail tonight, honey. Love you all. Miss you terribly.

Your very own, Daddy

CORSAIR PILOT DOWNS MIG-15

I had flown my 60 missions and was doing my time as a forward air controller with the 1stMarDiv when, on 10 Sep 1952, word reached us that a Marine Corsair pilot, Capt Jesse G. Folmar, had shot down a MIG-15. His squadron, VMA-312, was flying off the aircraft carrier *USS Sicily* at the time.

Folmar and his wingman, Lt William Daniels, while looking for targets of opportunity near the North Korean town of Chinnampo, were jumped by eight MIG-15s. Tracers from one of them were coming very close when it pulled up and ahead of Folmar, who opened up his four 20mm cannons and smoked the MIG. Shortly thereafter another MIG damaged Folmar's Corsair so badly that he had to bail out but, fortunately, he was rescued. He became the first American to shoot down a Russian-built MIG-15 with a propeller driven fighter.

Marine fighters shot down a grand total of 35 enemy aircraft, including 26 MIG-15s. As mentioned before, Marine Maj John H. Glenn of VMF-311, in July 1953, while on exchange duty with the USAF, shot down three MIG-15s.

I was fortunate in having met John Glenn briefly at El Toro, and years later at Kitty Hawk, North Carolina, when my son Eric and I went there for a youth seminar on aviation and they dedicated the museum and the replica of the Kitty Hawk. I took a lot of 8mm movies of John crawling aboard the Kitty Hawk and manipulating controls. If John had scored only two more MIGs he'd have been a jet ace. Of course that was the same John Glenn who became an astronaut, and later a U.S. Senator from Ohio.

11 Sep 52
Thursday, 1240
Changdan, Korea

Dear family,
As the companies were relieving each other, the incoming artillery and mortar fire cut our boys to ribbons at 0200 this morning. Bill and I called helicopter evacuations in until 0800. It was a long and bloody night. I won't dwell on it any longer because I'm trying to push it out of my thoughts. But let us not forget that those kids still need a lot of prayers because it seems everyone is powerless to prevent this horrible slaughter that seems to go on and on with no apparent letup. This could all come to an end if only the powers that be at the truce talks could

agree to the prisoner exchange issue. Our side still believes that the prisoners we hold should have a choice of returning to North Korea or not.

It rained last night and this morning, so we had about a 100' ceiling and a half mile visibility, but the 'copter pilot came on in and did a wonderful job. Doc Broderick was grateful for our assistance because he had his hands full. One kid had lost his right leg and was so far gone that the doc couldn't even find a vein in his arm to administer plasma. We put him in the 'copter along with another youngster in critical condition.

The medics, who had arrived a few minutes after we did, nudged the feet of the Marine casualties lying on the row of stretchers, all covered completely with blankets. The feet of those that were dead felt like you had nudged a brick, since rigor mortis had set in. If there was any movement the medics assumed that there was still a shred of life there and set upon their task of loading those stretchers cases onto the T-34 medium tank's special litter racks for a muddy, bumpy dash back to the med center.

Sometimes, when the thought of resigning my commission in December occurs to me, I feel sort of cowardly for leaving a sinking ship. I suppose, though, there are many qualified men waiting to take their turn up here in this senseless mess. My feelings are all mixed up as to what I should do. Patriotic duty would be to stay; obligation to myself, you and the boys would be to leave, get associated in defense industry and concentrate on being a daddy. The latter, of course, is the most appealing and compelling force upon me at this time. I pacify myself by the thought that if I'd been knocked off, which is something that could have happened any number of times, I'd have required a replacement. My morale is still high, dearest girl, in fact, never higher. It's odd how disastrous casualties surrounding a person can instill in him a stronger than ever desire to live. I feel very lucky and that's the big reason I'm in high spirits. Also I'm so darn glad you and the boys are healthy and happy and aren't in need of anything, except maybe a daddy.

Jack Shoden just called up and told us about (6) F9Fs that are missing on a training flight in South Korea. No word about them since early yesterday when they took off from K3. We can't figure out what could have happened to them. Probably all hit a mountain someplace. Golly, that's a terrible loss.

The sky is still overcast but looks like it may be breaking up a little. Maybe we'll have some air late this afternoon. We are going into Battalion reserve during the daylight hours of 14 Sept, Sunday. Our Companies Item, How, George will remain either on Bunker Hill or along some point of our MLR, and rotate with each other and companies of the 2nd Bn/1st Reg and 1st Bn/1st Reg. Actually, just the Battalion staff are going into reserve, but not completely in reserve either because Bill and I will be the air officers on "Operation Snatch" until around the 23rd of Sept, when Bill goes home and I take over as Regimental air officer. Then I'll have to worry about all the Battalion TACP teams along the Regimental front and "Snatch" and reserve. Some job, huh? We'll work it out. Still looks like around 15 Oct for Reg reserve. Barnum told me he's leaving for home on the 21st of Oct with the first planeload of 19th draft returnees. The bum. Can't see how I can get home before mid Nov, honey. So what, we'll make out OK, won't we, darling? I'll be there for Xmas, though, and that's the real important date.

Here are some propaganda leaflets. Read the intelligence release on this Panmunjom security guard that surrendered the other day. He was a North Korean. Had been in the NK Army since 1942. Some story to it--I'll tell you at another time.

Love, Daddy

P.S. Chinese soldiers carry a little brass spoon with them to eat their rice. It's called an "itywa" spoon, so now the trend is to call the Chinks "itywas", as well as goonies, yobos, bastards etc.

There was precious little humor on the main line of resistance, but every once in awhile some would creep in. Whoever wrote the following Laws of Combat certainly must have been in our 3rd Battalion, for it fits the situation to a tee.

LAWS OF COMBAT
(Murphy's Law)

1. You are not a superman
2. If it's stupid but works, it isn't stupid.
3. Don't look conspicuous--it draws fire.
4. When in doubt, empty your magazine.
5. Never share a foxhole with anyone braver than you are.
6. Never forget that your weapon was made by the lowest bidder.
7. If your attack is going really well, it's an ambush.
8. No plan survives the first contact intact.
9. All five-second grenade fuses will burn down in three seconds.
10. Try to look unimportant because the bad guys may be low on ammo.
11. If you are forward of your position, the artillery will fall short.
12. The enemy diversion you are ignoring is the main attack.
13. The important things are always simple.
14. The simple things are always hard.
15. The easy way is always mined.
16. If you are short of everything except enemy, then you are in combat.
17. If you have secured an area, don't forget to tell the enemy.
18. Incoming fire has the right of way.
19. Friendly fire--isn't
20. If the enemy is in range, "SO ARE YOU!!!"
21. No combat ready unit has ever passed inspection.
22. Beer math is: two beers times 37 men = 49 cases.
23. Body count math is: two guerillas plus one portable plus two pigs=37 enemy killed in action.
24. Things that must be together to work usually can't be shipped together.
25. Radios will fail as soon as you need fire support desperately.
26. Anything you do can get you shot--including nothing.
27. Tracers work both ways.
28. The only thing more accurate than incoming enemy fire is incoming friendly fire.
29. Make it tough for the enemy to get in and you can't get out.
30. If you take more than your fair share of objectives, you will have more than your fair share of objectives to take.
31. When both sides are convinced that they are about to lose, they are both right.
32. Professional soldiers are predictable, but the world is full of amateurs.
33. Murphy was a grunt.

Happy birthday, Ricky
Happy birthday!

12 Sep 52
Changdan, Korea
Friday 1930

*Happy birthday
Ricky boy,
happy birthday
to you*

Dearest family,

My tummy is so full of strawberry ice cream I can hardly move. They got it sent up from the rear area and boy, we sure went for it. You know me and ice cream, anyway. They had a very nice meal for us tonight: mashed spuds with gravy, dressing and string beans, corn, salad, iced tea, cookies and coffee. One of the best meals we've had since we've been up on the line. My thanks to those rear area poags.

This morning at 0600 and last night around 2000 I had to call in three helicopters for wounded. One fellow was unconscious and as stiff as a board from hemorrhagic fever, a Korean disease, usually fatal. Golly, they have the doggonedest sicknesses over here. They've got a name for it, though, but not always the cure. There's a special hospital set up just to handle hemorrhagic fever victims alone. [Author's note: refer to Appendix Number 2 for further discussion about hemorrhagic fever]

(Happy birthday, Ricky boy that I love. This should arrive on the 17th, the day you become 6 years old.)

Three lieutenant colonels and two majors from MAG 12 came up to visit us today. Bill and I didn't get any air but we gave them the $1.00 tour and they appreciated it. Col Robinson is up at our bunker on OP 229 for the night. I sent Bowman and Boone up in the jeep with him, and a cot, blankets, mosquito net to set up for him. He wanted to watch the battle front at night, so we obliged him. I've seen it and wasn't impressed. I don't get a kick out of watching our lines get pounded because I know somebody is going to get clobbered, and usually does. We are in a better position here at Bn CP to call in the helicopters and aid the wounded during the night.

(Happy birthday, Ricky boy, happy birthday, Ricky boy. Happy birthday.)

Bill's calling the Division air officer now to see how many generals are coming in tomorrow morning via helicopter because we have to direct them to land at strip #32 in only one 'copter, or #42 if more than one.

Brother, there goes a 144 round of rocket ripple on the goonies--that ought to shake them up. It shook me up when they started firing. They sneak up behind us and set up shop, and you never know they are there until all of a sudden they let out with a tremendous thundering roar and, swoosh, they go sailing over your head at a terrific pace.

We're getting all squared away to move to our reserve area. We've been checking our equipment, tents etc. and taking stock of all our gear. The kids will be glad to get off the hill, out of that darn bunker and into a nice clean dirt-floored tent--ha, ha. Three meals a day and a movie every night will make it seem better anyway. The big thing will be the fact that the responsibility will have shifted to another Battalion staff and we can at last breathe easier.

No mail today, darling. Oh, I meant to mention that I ran into Lt Jacks and Lt Olsen. They left their jeep at the bottom of the hill and walked up because they didn't have any brakes. My jeep hasn't any either but I use it all the time. (Lt Jacks is the guy who checked me out in the T-33 jet trainer at El Toro last year. He and Olsen had left VMA-212 to fly F9Fs for several months and I had controlled them on Bunker Hill on their last mission in jets. They'd run a swell strike and I'd given them a huge assessment. Then they came to VMO-6 as OE pilots.)

More leaflets enclosed. Got another goonie prisoner. He drove his Russian truck through the UN checkpoint at Panmunjom and surrendered to our forces yesterday.

Happy birthday, Ricky pants.

Love,

Daddy

13 Sep 52
Changdan, Korea
Saturday afternoon

Dearest family,
I've had guests, two majors and a colonel from MAG 12. I got them on a 'copter at about ten o'clock and am done with them. A British general showed up at the same time as their 'copter arrived, and **his** had to circle our strip twice before landing, which shook Col Altman and Maj Christie up somewhat.

The weather has been low hanging alto cumulus and not operational--no air. Burrr, it was cold last night. Had on two blankets but three would have felt good. Boy, honey, will I be glad to get into that basket with you. These darn cots weren't made for comfortable sleeping.

Bunker Hill got a mortar and artillery pounding last night but not probed. The sky lit up about once every minute for several hours stretch, around 2200 to 2400. Of course, they took the usual casualties.

Jack Shoden has been up here talking to me about the Regimental air officer's job. Says Col Layer is a grand guy. I've met him four or five times but don't know him very well. He's heavy set and greying, about 43 years old; a reserve called back in '51 but is integrating this time.

Wrote Mom and Ben today. Very little activity today to report on, honey. We're moving out to reserve area tomorrow, as per schedule. Shoden says I've got the 1st Reg Air Officer job as of 24 Sep. Continue with this address, though, honey, until I tell you differently. The 3rd/1st will only be a short way from the 1st Regiment CP and I'll drop over and pick it up. When I'm definitely established at 1st Reg I'll tell you to change.

Yours of 6 Sep rec'd last night, honey. Wonderful service, isn't it? Wish I could crawl into one of these letters to you, honey girl, and mail myself home. Wouldn't you get a terrific surprise when you opened me up? Ha, ha.

Bill and I are going to try and get down to K6 when we get into reserve. I want to see the boys of VMA-212 again before they all go their various ways.

I'm going to knock off and find a cracker or something. I'm starved, my stomach thinks my throat's been cut. I love you all and miss you all so very much. Our day is coming, honey girl.

Your very own, Daddy

Above: Due to our proximity to Panmunjom and Bunker Hill, Maj Bill Biehl and I were asked to brief VIP's of Congress, aircraft companies, UN and foreign representatives. Here we are giving a pre-briefing at 3/1 Bn to Maj Jack Shoden, Col Revetta, and Douglas Aircraft Co. representatives Quick, Nichols and Cox, before taking them up to the front.

Upper Right: My partner, Maj Bill Biehl, controlling an air strike near Bunker Hill.

Middle Right: 29 Aug 1952 at 1st Regiment. MajGen Edwin A. Pollock addressing the troops as the new commander of the 1stMarDiv. He had an admirable reputation as a 30 year Marine with grit and stature.

Lower Left: Our TACP team of enlisted wiremen/radiomen at 3/1 Bn.

Lower Right: Peterson on right and two companions with "Operation Snatch." My radio command post, Sherman Medium Tank, is in the background.

Left: Spud and Gus Dake have shot their supper. Wild Chinese ringneck pheasant were abundant in our sector. Standing beside the famous OE-1 Marine observation plane which I would see plenty of in the next five months.

Middle Left: OE-1s that didn't fare too well. Flying over enemy positions to spot for air controllers or artillery batteries drew thousands of rounds of flak. All were attached to the VMO-6 squadron at the 1stMarDiv.

Lower Left: Peterson and Gus Dake buzz a Seoul railroad marshalling yard in our Bell chopper.

Lower Right: This little chopper was easy on the controls. Spud just landed from a familiarization flight and reconnaissance around the Division.

The CO of the Marine Observation Squadron VMO-6, when I was using their equipment, was at first Maj Wallace J. Slappey, Jr., then LtCol Elkin S. Dew took over from him. These professionals were fine, cooperative individuals. VMO-6 deployed 11 single-engine OE-1 observation planes, which averaged over 500 flights in any given month, including forward air control, observation, photo recon, weather, liaison and checkout work for rusty pilots.

Upper Left, L to R: The General's aide and Gen Lemuel C. Shepherd, Jr., Commandant of the Marine Corps, during a battlefront tour of the division in September '52. Coordinated assaults during this period were repulsed by the division in bitter close-in fighting. I was privileged to be in the general's tour party as the air officer.

Upper Right: Valentine Field, named for my friend, 2nd Lt Earl Lester Valentine, Jr. of HOW Company, 3rd Bn, 1st Marines. Killed in action 26 August 1952.

Left: The North American SNJ-5 advanced trainer was used extensively for aerial spotting along with the OE-1. Air Force called them the T-6.

Above: Dave (the sniveler) Kennedy and Peterson. Dave traveled 200 miles to visit me.

Above: Col Walter F. Layer, CO of the 1stMarReg. I would become his air officer.

Upper Left: Peterson controlling an air strike, mike in hand. Radios at my left and right, near Hill 229 outpost. Map board for target coordinates in front. Beyond the hill in background is Panmunjom, site of peace negotiations.

Upper Right, L to R: Capt Peterson, visitor, Maj Biehl, visitor.

Middle Left: Friends at 3rd Battalion.

Middle Right: USO show at 1st Regiment.

Lower Left: We made a model of our control area in front of the main battle line. It proved a valuable tool for us and visitors to our bunker on Hill 229.

CHAPTER 16

GUS AND THE WHIRLY-BIRD

Not very many fighter pilots had the mixed blessing of drawing a Forward Air Controller assignment. I did not relish the task but, since I had no choice, I decided to do the best damn job I could. While at this position in Korea, my old friend, Capt Merlin "Gus" Dake, showed up at VMO-6, the helicopter support squadron attached to the First Marine Division. We had served together as cadets and later in VMF-524 squadron during WWII. He and his lovely wife, Gladys, had kept in touch with Marion and me between wars and we had watched each other's family grow up. I felt very close to Gus, respected him tremendously, and sensed that he felt the same way about me. A regular officer, he was, in my estimation, the finest helicopter pilot in the Marine Corps.

I called for Gus to come up to my front line positions and help me rebuild and re-mark the many helicopter landing pads carved out of the mountains and ridge lines. Later, as we were under fire and taking casualties, night or day, rain or shine, Gus would risk his neck getting in there to help me and my buddies fly out the wounded to the aid stations or hospital ships in Inchon Harbor.

Whenever I could spare the time I went flying with Gus. These helicopter check rides were a source of great pleasure to me. Although I felt like I had two left feet and ten thumbs when it came to handling those strange controls of that odd little Bell HTL-4 with its bubble canopy, Gus was a fabulous teacher, albeit the kind of guy who would tell you once and expect you to listen. Typically, while I was flying, the tail would drift around and it would be 90° from the ground track we were making. Pressing on the pedals, similar to rudders, would change the pitch on the tail rotor and control the direction the chopper was going. I had a hard time remembering to make pedal adjustment to compensate for engine torque whenever I changed power. Understanding the main control stick was the least of my problems because it reacted almost like an airplane's control. Moving it caused the craft to fly in the same direction as the stick was moved, whether forward, sideways or backwards. They called it the "cyclic" because it changed the pitch of each rotor blade once cyclically per revolution. It felt almost airplane-like in the hovering mode.

The strange little horizontal stick between us with the motorcycle twist grip throttle was just that, the throttle. Because this handbrake-looking lever controlled the pitch of all the rotor blades at once, it was naturally called "the collective stick." If you pulled the collective stick up, the pitch of the rotor blades would increase and the chopper would climb. If you lowered it, you would descend. If you added more collective pitch, you had to remember to add throttle immediately. Trial and error plus practice soon had me fairly well coordinated. These were merely beginning basics and the real test would come later when Gus cut the power and demonstrated autorotation. He used such terms as, "dead man's curve," which he interpreted as, "the height-velocity diagram." Basically, your kinetic energy is stored in the rotors in the form of speed or altitude, which you ration out gingerly. You actually glide and don't drop out of the sky.

Gus demonstrated the "flare" which dissipates your forward speed and puts a few Gs on your ole bod. The rotor blades felt to me like they were going to snap off under this violent maneuver but they returned to normal as we slowed our air speed. It's mighty strange hanging under a whirling rotor blade, and you never quite answer the nagging question, "Where are the damn wings?"

Gus had me practice climb-outs from an initial ground hover of about four feet position. I had to rev her up to 3100 RPM, then pull the collective back, which felt for all the world like I was pulling myself up by my own bootstraps. This, after about 15 minutes of hovering practice a few feet off the ground. I had to control the position over the ground with the cyclic, the altitude with the collective, the RPM with the twist grip throttle and the nose position with the pedals. For me, the whole affair seemed uncoordinated and I felt like I was pumping the controls. Gus hollered at me, "Pete, ease off, just use light finger pressures!" and, what do you know, everything calmed down.

Cruising along at about 80 mph felt airplane-like, except that the vibration could be felt clear down to my liver. If you goofed off and let the nose rise, the airspeed would drop off markedly but, strangely, you didn't get that old familiar stall warning and spin, as in a fixed-wing, even when you reached 10-15 mph. I think I might have been better off with zero fixed-wing experience and just gone into it cold. Gus disagreed and before long, with his patient instruction, I began to get the fever. They are just plain fun to fly. But having fun wasn't the name of the game there in Korea and we had to get back to the serious business at hand, that of saving lives.

WE MOVE TO BATTALION RESERVE

14 Sep 52
Camp Joseph J. Meyers, Korea
by the Imjin River
Sunday, Battalion reserve area

Dearest family,
At last we made the move to our reserve area. Old hill 229 is within our sight, however, and only about a mile away. This area is heavily covered with green foliage, trees and vines on rolling hills. The chow is served in a squad tent with a dirt deck but, at least, we got three squares today. It took our boys about four trips with our cargo jeep and trailer to accomplish the move. I stayed over there until the last load, while Bill had come on over here to direct the unloading of the gear. We had to strike the enlisted men's tent. When we got here, however, there was a swell newer tent standing near the enlisted men's site, so we talked to the special service officer and he agreed to take our old one and give the standing one to our team. Bill and I and Smitty put up this tent we're in now. Dug rain ditches around it and had electric lines run into it, as well as a telephone system. We laid a wood deck in our tent today also, from packing boxes--better than dirt.

At 1700 this evening Bill and I set up a bar outside our tent and served cocktails to about 25 officers. Smitty broke out cheese, crackers, olives, shrimp and fish his wife had sent him. They enjoyed it and it really was the first of its kind we had ever had since going up to the line. Ate supper at 1730, very nice fried chicken.

At 1930 we went over to a little 16mm movie site laid out on the side of a steep hill and, due to a faulty sound tube, we didn't get to see "The Halfbreed." Saw Bugs Bunny, though, without sound. Sat there for two hours waiting for the repair that didn't materialize. Tomorrow night "Pat and Mike." Am going to Division tomorrow morning to accept an air medal at Anglico. Jack Shoden and Bill are going along for the same purpose.

Love you all so very much. Our day is coming, honey girl.

Love, Daddy

16 Sep 52
Camp Joseph J. Meyers, Korea
0900

Dearest family,
    The daddy had a big day yesterday and got back to the tent at around 2300. Didn't want to keep the light on and disturb the others, so I'm writing to my darling now. After Bill and I had breakfast Pvt Red Bowman, of our team, came up with our jeep and away we went to the Division and Anglico via the Freedom Gate Bridge. It took us about an hour, with all the detours etc., to get to Anglico, where the whole formation was lined up waiting for Bill and me. A lieutenant briefed six of us on what we were to do in regard to marching out from behind the formation up to the front. As our citations were read, we stepped forward and came to a halt in front of Col Glick (the CO of Anglico) who pinned on the medals, or handed us stars in lieu of the medals, such as in my case. I received my star in lieu of my 9th air medal. When he said 9th in the citation the crunchies in the formation were heard to mumble a little bit, They (200) marched in review before us.

    We knocked off and had a cup of joe with the colonel and Maj French (his executive officer) and another major. We asked for a trip pass to get us into Seoul, the capital of S. Korea. He had orders not to pass any of his Anglico jeeps into "Seoul Area" but bent over backwards in Bill's and my case and passed us. We went to the Division HQ to see whether or not the letters of commendation we had written for four of our men had been approved. They had. While there they told Bill and me that, by the way, our Silver Stars had been downgraded to Bronze Stars by Col Layer, the CO of 1st Regiment. Col Armitage tried to get them through as Silvers, but hit the bottleneck at Reg, they informed us.

    Two hours and several rain storms; about thirty Korean villages with hundreds of kids; thousands of bumps and field after field of rice all ready to be cut--later, we arrived in Seoul. We went directly to 5th Airforce HQ and looked up Maj Bob Barbour who was on liaison duty there. He didn't know I was the FAC up here at Bunker Hill that was getting all those airplanes he was sending up. We had a nice chat, then Bill and I ate lunch, hit the PX and I bought a new shaving brush and some Rinso washing powder, 2 rolls black and white 620, Listerine. Went on to Seoul's main U.N. PX and found it to be in a four-story well-constructed department store building that somehow had escaped any damage from the ravages of war. They had items in there that were representative of Korean art--very crude, and a bunch of Japanese imports. Didn't see a thing that did anything for me. We took turns sitting in our jeep parked outside in an alleyway, where about 20 filthy raggamuffins, ages four to 15, were trying to polish my boots--reached inside the jeep and smeared black polish on them as they were resting on the clutch and brake pedals. One little guy who was tugging at my pants and sleeve (five years old) was so ragged and dirty I couldn't even see any of the brown Korean skin on him. He had a little pail with a wire handle on it, and kept giving out with a moaning sound while rubbing his stomach and pulling on my arm. I bought a watch band from one kid, 7000 wan ($1.00) to get rid of him, which only aggravated the situation and brought about 10 more kids over to the jeep selling rings, scarfs, paintings etc. I was about ready to start the jeep and drive around the block to get away from them when Bill and Red came out. As we drove off the little beggar kid spit at us and hit me on the arm. I only felt sorry for them and the uninhibited environment they are growing up in, and couldn't help but compare their condition to that of Randy and Ricky.

    It's hard to believe one half of the world can be living in luxury and the other half starving, ragged and filthy. There are a number of orphanages, missions and relief centers in Korea, the Seoul area in particular, but they can't hope to cope with the huge masses. Half of Seoul's streets are asphalt paved, 25% cement, and 25% cobblestoned. An occasional taxi of 1932 or '34 Chevy or Ford vintage can be seen, also a bus or two here and there on every block. We looked down many little side streets where they were selling their wares and produce. Even some old street cars were running, but had not been painted in 20 years, I bet. No glass in the windows--reminded me of the San Francisco cable cars. Kids and papasans and mamasans hanging all over them. What a place!

Seoul seems completely out of place, as compared with all the other Korean villages, which are nothing more than grass covered frames. On the way out of town I saw a couple of women grinding something (grains of some sort) on an old rock grinder. They were working like mad, and right around them sat about five middle-aged papasans smoking and talking over the activities of the day. They don't sit on anything; they sit on their haunches in a circle. There were a number of Korean houses under construction along the way. For the most part, they look like this: the floor is some two feet above the ground, and there's no siding below the floor level. Sliding doors on the front are left open most of the time. The outside wall is woven bamboo with mud plaster placed on it about two inches thick. The roof is either slate or tile, or mud with grass placed over it. People in the country are doing much better than the city people appeared to be doing. The mothers all nurse their babies right on the front steps of the main street, and most women only have a little half-vest affair that doesn't tuck in and their breasts are 9/10 out. They look and live like animals for the most part. [Refer to Appendix Number 5 for more on refugees.]

We got back to our Bn CP reserve area here at Camp J. E. Meyers (named after PFC Meyers, killed in action). No permanent buildings here at all--only tents. Got out of my dusty, dirty dungarees and cleaned up at the shower unit truck about 300' from our tent. Clean clothes and a nice supper. Saw "The Halfbreed" and "Pat and Mike." Sure was nice seeing a movie, for a change. This reserve area allows you to relax and almost forget there's a war, except that artillery is located just a few hundred yards behind us and it blares out every now and then. You can hear the incoming at Bunker Hill and see the sky light up from the flashes. The company that came off of Bunker Hill the night before last was there and they were cutting up and clowning, as kids do. It's marvelous how high their spirits are, in spite of the casualties.

A Korean from the KSC dropped dead in front of us as we were leaving the movie. Had some sort of a virus, the corpsman said. I"ll be glad to get out of Korea, if for nothing else but to get away from all these bugs. [This was later diagnosed as a virus in the family of hantavirus. Refer to the appendix for additional background].

Received your letter of 8 Sept. and am now up on all the finances. Sure miss my little gang. I love you all so very much. You're constantly on my mind, sweetheart.

Your very own, Daddy

17 Sep 52
Camp Meyers, Korea
My big boy's 6th birthday

Dearest family,
I flew the OE today on a checkout familiarization hop and general recon. of the front lines. Bill and I drove down to the Division HQ to see Col Armitage at the Div G3. He's a big wheel at the Div now and introduced Bill and me as the two FACs that saved the day for his battalion at Bunker Hill. Met a half dozen colonels, and Col A. had his arm around Bill or me the whole time we were there, a fine fellow. Said he was sore as a wet hen about the downgrading of our Silver Stars to Bronze Stars, but said he would always feel as though it were silver.

Went over to Div Air office, saw Whiskey John (Major John Cox) and chewed him out for the lousy cooperation we had received from his department. Drove on down to VMO-6, crossing two rivers that were flooded--jeep almost flooded out--ate lunch there and then checked out the OE. They have lost three in the past week and are down to seven, which is really purty scoosh to carry on all the tactical commitments they are obligated to perform. Bill talked them into letting us take one by saying we would fly an hour recon and make it a checkout at the same time. Bill took off and we reconnoitered the front lines clear up to the Commonwealth sector and then returned to a small air strip located alongside the Pullman cars where the UN reporters stay at Munsan-ni. Then I climbed in the front seat and took off, flew it 30 minutes and shot a few landings at Munsan-ni, then returned to VMO-6. What a narrow and short runway they have there--about 1300'. I have always been used to landing on a runway about 7000'-8000' long. Got her down OK and Bill said I was officially checked out. We cleared with Operations and they gave me a call sign to use, "Codfish 91," whenever I come down to fly for them. VMO-6 is "Codfish Base."

Drove home at 1400, arrived 1530. They were having a meeting at the colonel's tent in regard to the purchasing of dishes in Japan for our officers mess. The colonel wants dishes but nobody else seems to want them. I personally prefer navy mess trays such as we are using. They collected $5.00 per head (officers' heads) for the purchase of whiskey for the cocktail hour they want to set up between 1630 and 1715 PM daily now that we are in reserve. Bill and I built a bar and Cpl Boone painted same. In fact, on the front of it he painted the Third Battalion 1st Regiment Bull, which looks something like this:

Boone painted it about 3'x4' and it really looks fine. Boone volunteered to act as bar tender and he did a wonderful job. The morale has been quite low because of all the casualties from Bunker Hill and you'd have really been pleased, as Bill and I were, when those company commanders and lieutenant platoon leaders arrived yesterday afternoon and saw their Battalion Bull painted on a little old packing crate for a bar. My admiration for these men is beyond my ability to express. They have been through hell and back. Bill and I know all of them since we had briefed them as they had passed through our trench line on their way out to their various hills.

We managed to get a hold of some ice and cokes, soda water, crackers, cheese, sardines, olives, crème de cacao and crème de menthe, gin, whiskey, vodka and fruit juices. Bill and I had purchased 24 blue tinted glasses in Seoul when we were there last time and we have set up a nice little bar for them. It's surprising how little it takes to make so many guys happy. When we left here last night at 1715 they were a different bunch completely. Yes, they all had had about three cocktails and had relaxed a little bit, but they have been under such tension. And the companies are still on call at Bunker Hill, even though they are temporarily in reserve area, resting.

The show tonight was "The Return of the Texan." It was wonderful--gripping and dynamic. Walter Brennan was the Grandpa. He was great. Try and see it. A strong emotional plot. Love, of course.

18 Sep 52

Hi dearest girl and Ricky and Randy,

Burrr, it was cold last night. I had two blankets on, a shelter half over that and my new winter field jacket tucked over my feet, and I was still cold. It went down to about 30°. Papasan (our Korean house boy--age 35) came around at 0630 and rolled up the tent flaps. Boy, it was really cold then. We got up and had a glass of tomato juice (ice cold from sitting out all night) and then sent down for some coffee. We didn't go to breakfast.

The Commandant, Gen Shepherd, is coming here this morning to give us an inspection. He's due to arrive at 1100 and is to land at our helicopter strip #38. We all are supposed to be up there to greet him (officers, that is). We ran around here and policed up our area like mad this morning, then knocked off to await his arrival. Lt Morgan has four Korean laborers working out front now putting a canvas tarp over our bar, blocking the view from our tent.

Darling, the goonies pounded our lines all last night with heavy artillery and mortar fire, and I couldn't sleep on account of it. I worry so darn much about those kids up there that I just can't seem to get to sleep. Then, of course, our counter battery artillery just about raises me out of the sack every time it goes off. We didn't get any rounds here in our reserve CP. It's not out of the range of their guns, however, but it's out of mortar range.

Enough about me and the goings-on, except to mention the fact that we have a green olive tree with olives over our bar. It'll show in the picture I took. Also, we have a chestnut tree over our tent. Papasan picked some yesterday and roasted them for us over our little gasoline burner. They were wonderful. We'll have to get some for the kids sometime, honey girl.

Happy birthday, Ricky boy. Gosh, isn't it wonderful to be SIX years old? You're going to be a man before your mother at the rate you're going, Ricky. It's hard for me to believe I have a son in the 1st grade. I remember how grown up I felt when I was in 1st grade.

Love, Daddy

I could not understand why our Bn reserve area couldn't have been located a mile or so away from the Artillery Bn which was situated just behind us a very short distance. Every time they'd fire, the Chinese counter-battery would lob a few rounds back at us. We, in fact, were marking our own positions for them, to say nothing of the lost sleep.

Another disturbing thing was the grave registration area. Located at the 1st Reg CP, right near us, it remained a constant reminder of death and the loss of our buddies. Surely that could have been placed in a rear area, out of sight of people who had just come off the battle line and were supposedly being given a little R&R to regain their composure before returning to fight again.

A VISIT FROM THE COMMANDANT OF THE MARINE CORPS

18 Sep 52
Camp Meyers
3rd Battalion Reserve
1815

Dearest family,
   Even though the sun just went down it's beginning to get real chilly. I'll bet it drops to below 32° tonight. I drew another blanket from supply today and now I have three blankets over me, one folded double with a shelter half over that.
   A volley ball game is in progress a few feet in front of me. I was at supper when it formed, so I'll have to wait for a relief team to form--50% enlisted and 50% officers. Boone and I set up the happy hour this afternoon. I got a gallon of processed cheese from Harry (the officers mess man) and several boxes of soda crackers. Bill and I had purchased sardines and kippered snack in Seoul and the fellows loved them. We served about 20 officers from 1630-1715. Boone and I cleaned up when they finished. Boone worked on the painting again to day at his leisure. He enjoys puttering around like that. I helped rig a canvas over the bar earlier today.
   At 1115 General (4 Star) Shepherd, the Commandant of the Marine Corps, arrived as per schedule on our strip #38. We were up there to greet him, Col Layer (1st Mar Reg CO) and Gen Pollock (1st Mar Div CO). The 'copter sprayed us with dust, so we were filthy when the general stepped out and Maj Christie introduced him to each and everyone of us. He's 57 years old and quite grey. A fine fellow, though, with a warm friendly smile and a wonderful strong handshake. He looked right in my eye and said, "Peterson, the forward air controller?"
   Christie answered, "Yes, and a damn good one too." The same personal remarks were in store for each of us. We had five jeeps awaiting the party but Shepherd said, "Let's troop it." He inspected the area and especially took notice of the Item Co flag (famous for its presence on Bunker Hill) and also the colorful Battalion flag. I snapped colored pictures of the general by both flags. He was with us 20 minutes and I'll bet in that period of time he endeared himself to about 300 of our hearts. The nicest guy you'd ever want to meet.
   Bill went to the Canadian sector today and procured some Scotch for the happy hour. Haven't seen anyone drunk here yet--a fine bunch of fellows.

My 8th Air Medal is floating around down at the Wing somewhere. Don't know how they gave me my 9th before my 8th.

"Operation Snatch" tomorrow morning. It will be the first tactical job I've done since coming off the line last Sunday.

No mail from my darling today. Burrr, it's getting awfully cold at night. Love you, dearest girl, with all my heart and soul. Kiss my darlings and tell them Daddy loves them.

Your very own Daddy

19 Sep 52
Camp Meyers, Korea
Friday, 2115

Dearest family,

Went to the movie but couldn't stand more than 10 minutes of the "Rose of Cimarron." Bill and I drove over to see Bill Ranson, FAC, at the 1st Bn 1st Reg, also his partner, Lane. Ranson had our railroaders hats for us and took about six pictures to send back to the president of the Southern Railroad System in Washington D.C., who had sent Ranson the hats for the Korean railcutters. Of course, you know that when we were cutting the rails in North Korea we became members in good standing. Ranson's father is the commissioner of the Brotherhood of Locomotive Engineers in Washington, D.C.

Bill and I had lunch, then drove over some rugged back roads to the 1st Reg, where we talked with Maj McCloud about "Operation Snatch" for tomorrow. We had originally planned on today but found we were one day early. Jack Shoden wasn't there but I looked the 1st Reg over quite well and have a much better idea what I will be getting into when I take over there in a few days. We drove on back around 1400, the same rugged back road. Boy, some of this country is really deserted. The rice paddies are all mined and the villages deserted. They seem like ghost towns and are sort of creepy up here near the front lines.

When we returned to the 3rd Bn CP we picked up Doug Ashton and went out to the pistol range. I got a big kick out of those two. Bill had been on a pistol team at Cherry Pt. for years and Doug Ashton had been CO of George Co. They talked about all the shooting they had done in the past and I kept mum, figuring I didn't have a prayer. When the count was made after firing 50 shots each, I had 371 points, Bill 352, Doug 275. Expert requires 320 points. I surprised myself.

Returned to CP, showered in icy cold water, changed underclothes. Tended bar with Boone for 45 minutes, had supper, then played volley ball until dark, working up a heck of a sweat. Went to a movie, secured early.

Kiss my darlings and tell them I love them. I adore you, my precious girl.

Daddy

20 Sep 52
Camp Meyers, Korea

Dearest family,

"Operation Snatch" went off with no hitches. The delegates flew over us in their helicopters on the way to Panmunjom. Bill went out to OP2 and I stayed at the tank assembly area. I checked out all the radio equipment at my disposal, both in the special porcupine tank and in my radio jeep. After Bill and I monitored our various radios with each other, we checked in with Devastate Baker. At exactly 1200 the delegates came fluttering over us again on their way back to their base camp at Munsan-ni. We stood by until 1300, however, because some of the sub-delegates hadn't returned.

Major Adams is the commander of the team, with Bill Biehl next in rank and then myself. After briefing on the whole problem before us, we now have it fairly well formulated in our minds. We had 12 Sherman tanks and one radio tank on our team, besides a full company of troops and two helicopters. Stew Monroe, artillery support officer on the team, was also *standing by with his radio jeep. I took a lot of pictures while we were standing by for the possibility of the goonies snatching our delegates and busting up the peace talks. Although it's a very remote possibility, we nevertheless are prepared to recover the delegates at any cost if the goonies ever do attempt anything.*

Sure have missed you something fierce lately, doll girl. Oh, how I'm counting the days until I'll be home with you, my very own precious wife. I'm so lonely for you and the boys. It will be the happiest day of my life when I finally arrive home and once again get you in my arms, never to let you get loose again.

Your very own Daddy

21 Sep 52
Camp Meyers, Korea

Dearest family,

Happy day! Received your letter of 12 Sept.; also one from Nanna and Ben. The Daddy had a big day and an enjoyable one. Bill made arrangements yesterday to be picked up here at our helicopter strip at 0900 this morning. I figured it would be a good chance for me to get an OE down at VMO-6 and recon the front lines. I also found out that Frances Langford would be appearing at the Division today at 1430. Figured I might as well combine business with pleasure so I picked up Cpls Boone and Evans in my jeep at 0905 and off we went to "A" med (meaning 1st Medical Company), which is located some 10 miles behind the main lines, back by Division. We drove for an hour before reaching our destination. Dropped in at "A" Med and watched while Cpl Boone got his eyes examined and arranged for glasses. I asked the doc to examine Cpl Evans' eyes also because I was planning on recommending Evans for flight school but if his eyes were not good enough (the most important part of the physical examination) I wouldn't bother with the rest of the paper work. The doctor examined his eyes and said they were very good, so now I'm going to go ahead and prepare the necessary paper work for Evans.

We drove over to Div PX, then to Anglico, then to VMO-6. I requested permission to fly a recon in one of their precious few (7) OEs. They were a little leery but figured as long as I was the new 1st Regiment air officer it would be OK. Evans and Boone climbed into the rear seat as I hopped into the front and off we went for 1.3 hours. I picked up a lot of valuable information concerning the Bunker Hill area as well as the other zones of the 1st Reg's responsibility. Meanwhile, Boone and Evans were thrilled beyond belief.

Back on the ground at the Div Lt Jacks and Lt Olsen, now of VMO-6, joined us at the Frances Langford show. There must have been 2000 Marines there watching.

We ate dust all the way back to our Battalion (10 miles of it), arriving just 15 minutes late for our evening responsibility, the happy hour. Boone, Evans and I turned to, however, and had it all set up in a few minutes, with the drinks flying across the bar just like stateside. We had the company commander and four platoon leaders who had just come off of Bunker Hill (7 days up there) up tonight and, boy, did they appreciate the cocktail hour! Even Boone said how much he enjoys setting the thing up every night for the fellows.

Maj Smith just returned (2200) from Div. He saw Frances Langford's 1900 show and ate dinner with her and her group. Smitty said she was old enough to be his mother; in fact, he said his mother is a heck of a lot better looking than her. Just the same, she deserves a lot of credit for coming over here to a hole like this. She could earn herself a better living in the States, I'll bet.

The movie tonight didn't have a name. Anyway, that part of it didn't appear. It started out without any introduction because the first part of the film had been clipped off. Pat O'Brien was a big time lawyer in it. Very good (new picture, too).

Got my sleeping bag tonight. Hot dog, I'll be warm now. Brand new one, too--either brand new or newly processed--it's a dandy.

Love you, sweety, so very much. Kiss my darlings. I got a big kick out of Ricky crossing up his new girlfriend, Helen. I'll bet you 10 to 1 Suzy saw the locket and asked him for it. The poor little guy, getting all tangled up with women at his age. Wish I were there to straighten him out.

Lt Jacks hit mission No. 100 *(flown in F4Us, F9Fs, OEs)*.

I flew mission No. 61 today. We got shot at a couple of times, only light or small arms however.

Love you all,
Your very own Daddy

22 Sep 52
Camp Meyers, Korea
Monday

Dearest girl and my two darling little guys,

Bill returned from K3 with a couple of cases of whiskey for the bar. He couldn't get a ride to K6 so he went to K3 from Seoul. He jeeped from Seoul up to here and he was covered with dust; even his eyelids were covered. He arrived just about ten minutes after the happy hour started. We got a big laugh out of him.

Boone puttered around painting some more stuff on the bar front. I did paper work most of the day flaked out in the sun, enjoying myself completely. The sun was warm and it felt wonderful. I never left the CP today. Did some research in regard to air support tactics.

Bill talked to the commandant last night down at K3 for about 30 minutes and, of course, under the influence of several martinis, gave him a few well-chosen words on how *he* thought Shepherd should run his Marine Corps. I'd given a month's pay to have heard him. He told everybody down there how we were pinned down with mortar fire and how I was wounded directing a/c on Bunker Hill. He played it up big and had a large audience around him, including the commandant. If the CMC believes everything he told him last night, Bill and I will probably get the Medal of Honor. This, of course, is according to Bill and he probably played it up to us here tonight as much or more than he did last night down at K3.

Kiss my darlings. I love you, dearest girl, with all my heart.

Your very own Daddy

24 Sep 52
Camp Meyers, Korea

Dearest family,

Missed writing to you last night, sweetheart, because it was so darn late and so cold by the time I got back to the tent that I just crawled into my sleeping bag. Then I couldn't sleep at all because our own artillery, located a few hundred yards behind us, kept firing nearly all night long. When they fire, the blast really rocks you, the shell whines over your head at a low angle and you ask yourself each time, "Will the next one be an air blast," (premature explosion), "and spray the whole area with hot steel?" None did last night, but this morning I've got bags under the bags under my eyes from no sleep. The dopes that located this camp under the barrels of our own artillery ought to have their heads examined.

Yesterday Bill and I went over to Regiment where Maj Jack Shoden briefed me on my duties, introduced me to my seven enlisted members and at noon chow I met all the officers. They all gathered at around 1200 and those officers that are members of the colonel's staff stand until the colonel arrives, then are seated when he sits down. Tableclothes, stateside silver and dishes complete the formal scene. Some change from the field conditions I have been under since 26 July.

Upon return to our Bn CP we carried out an assignment Col Altman and Maj Christie had requested of us the day before, that of setting up a barbecue and party for the "H" Company and "I" Company officers coming into reserve yesterday. "Item" had been with us several days but "How" just came off of the battle line and Bill and I were only too eager to comply. Capt Ashton had a set of grills made which Boone and Evans mounted on a stand. Harry, the officers' messman, brought two tables and two field stoves, steaks, barbecue sauce, sliced spuds for french fries, salad, and a huge 24"x19"x2" chocolate cake with USMC across it.

We started the fire for coals at 1500 and by 1700 we had a wonderful hot bed. Harry barbecued about 25 steaks on the coals but had to switch over to the field stove grill for the last 25 because the coals weren't hot enough. We made another fire, though, and put the steaks on the barbecue grill after they came off the field grill, for the smoke flavor. Everyone ate their fill and we sang every song I've ever heard (dirty and otherwise) until dark, then went to the movie and saw Micky Rooney in "Sound Off." Everyone had a wonderful time and I almost forgot I was in Korea, until after I got in the rack and our friendly artillery began its night long barrage.

No mail yesterday; however, the night before I got three letters from my precious darling and the pictures were wonderful. Those I sent were lousy and the one of Lt Valentine isn't worth bothering with--too bad, too. Those you had taken were super, honey. You look awfully good to the daddy in your new pajamas. Ricky's girlfriends are cute. The one of Randy with the butterfly is priceless. Ricky is certainly growing into a fine tall boy.

I'm planning on going up to the 1st Bn/1st Reg CP to pick up Ranson, so we can drive up to his OP to observe his front line air targets, if any. I'm not going to stick my neck out any further than I have to, though. I've had my fill of dodging hot steel for this tour.

Peggy wrote me a nice letter and expressed herself very warmly. I'll send the letter. It's a cold overcast day today. My spirits are very high, though, honey girl. I'm feeling wonderful, and as I cross each day off of the calender I feel just a little bit happier. Hope all's well with you and the darlings. You are on my mind constantly, dearest girl.

Love, Daddy

P.S. Yes, Paekhak san is 229.

FIRST REGIMENT GETS NEW AIR OFFICER

25 Sep 52
1st Marine Regiment CP
Thursday 2130

Dearest family,

The daddy has finally made the big move to Regiment. Things are getting plusher all the time. Before long we'll be in Regimental reserve area (approx. 10-15 Oct.) and we'll have stoves to keep us warm. Brother, it's been cold. Last night it dipped down to the 30s and didn't get over 55° all day today. Started raining yesterday at 1700 and has been coming down continuously ever since. It's strange because it seems too cold to be raining. I usually associate rain with a warm frontal system but there's a cold system upon us now and that's for sure.

Let's see now, what happened that's interesting? Oh, yeah, I wanted to tell you about last night's movie that I didn't see. Well, on account of the rain, the skipper said we'd have the movie for the officers in his tent at 2100, after it was first shown to the men at their mess tent. The projector broke down about 15 minutes before the last reel was shown and they never got to see the last part.

All the officers began gathering at the colonel's tent at 2100 as planned, not knowing they had had a breakdown with the projector earlier. When the colonel saw us all arriving and sitting on the floor (sand) of his tent with the expectant look, he made up his mind he wouldn't disappoint us. He ordered Lt Morgan, the special service officer, to bring the equipment up to his tent, regardless of whether it worked or not and we'd try and fix it. We worked on it, found a small bulb burned out, put in a replacement bulb and away we went. Maj Christie called the man at the generator for more juice and they revved it up as fast as it would go, but there were too many electric light bulbs coming off of the main line and the projector wasn't receiving all the juice it required. Maj Christie called in the bugler and told him to sound taps, which he did. The lights went out which gave us a little more current but still not enough for the sound amplifier. We didn't see a movie. We knocked around there until 2215, then secured in a blinding rain storm.

Bill and I, upon reaching our tent, found everything soaking wet. We had about five big leaks and many little ones coming at us through more little holes in the canvas than we could count. My sack was located fairly well out of the drips, but Bill's was right under them. He managed to maneuver it out of the way.

I checked out of the Bn today at 1300. Bowman drove me, with all my gear, back to the 1st Reg, where Maj Jack Shoden gave me some more dope on the Regimental air officer's job--mainly being the colonel's advisor.

My driver and I then returned to the 3rd Bn in my new regimental jeep, loaded with sardines, canned shrimp and cigars and I gave them to Lt Morgan for the fellows. Had dinner with them and we said our goodbyes. When they saw my new jeep and driver, they all kidded me about being a rear area poag.

Got back here to Reg in time for the 1830 briefing. The weather being as it is, Shoden had a negative air report, of course. The other officers then very seriously presented him with a copy of *fake* orders from Gen Jerome, CO of 1st Marine Air Wing, stating that Maj Jack Shoden would remain with the Reg until 10 Oct. Jack's mouth fell about two inches as it was being read; it all looked and sounded so official! When everyone stood around chuckling, he finally wised up. I had been cut in on it earlier. Jack lives in Santa Ana, is married to a 21-year-old and has a little girl. I gave him your address.

After a 30-minute brief we saw "Diplomatic Courier," a pretty good show. Tyrone sure had to fight off that she-wolf, didn't he? Everybody was jeering at him to grab her, but he never put his hands on her.

It is now 2200 and beginning to get mighty chilly. Think I'll knock off, baby girl, and hit my pad. I'm in a tent up on a hill, all by myself. It's lonely up here and I keep hearing strange noises. In a day or two, after Shoden leaves, I'll move down and be with Maj Honeycutt, the Reg artillery officer and Maj McLeod, the Reg operations officer. I'm the Reg air officer.

Eight more weeks, baby girl, and I'll be home with you. Imagine, six months completed today. Hot dog! Ricky is fortunate getting his cowboy boots. I always wanted a pair and to this day haven't ever had any. Maybe I'll get some someday too.

All for now. Love you more and more with each passing day.

Your very own
Daddy

26 Sept 52
1st Reg CP, Korea

Dearest family,

So far so good as the Reg air officer. Both of my front line battalions have received a/c thus far today. This made Col Layer very happy. I arranged a helicopter pickup for him at 0830 tomorrow morning. He wants to fly out to the hospital ship. I also arranged a copter pickup for him here at the Reg CP at 1500 and an OE ride over the front lines. He's striking for an air medal, I believe. The guy is on the go constantly.

The sun broke out this morning and it's been a lovely warm sunny day--makes such a difference in my attitude, whether the day be bright and sunny or cloudy and gloomy--I reflect the weather somehow. It's been around 78° today as compared to yesterday's 55°. Last night was a cold one, but I slept snug and warm in my sleeping roll. They are certainly marvelous. The food here at Reg is very good and so is the service. Today for breakfast (0715) I had two scrambled eggs and three sausages, coffee, hot biscuits and jam.

At noon the new FACs, Capts Norlin and Brunsworth, arrived, and Jack and I took them to chow with us. I gave them a lot of scoop about the 3rd Bn and called Bill Biehl to come over with his jeep to pick them up. As we sent them off to the Bn with Bill, he was beaming all over. Shoden and Biehl can hardly contain themselves for the excitement of going home. I guess I know how they feel.

Golly, honey, just think, eight more weeks and you're mine once again. I have to pinch myself to believe we've got in six months already. Time has flown some months and dragged others. Oh, how I've missed you, my beloved wife. It's been awfully hard on the daddy to be *away from all my loved ones. You've been blessed with the darlings, but at the same time have had the full responsibility, which should normally be shared by a daddy. I keep thinking about coming home, darling. Will all the neighbors, relatives, kids be there? I'm dying to set eyes on my little darlings and to hold them, hug them and kiss them. Golly, how I've missed my little gang. If ever there was a daddy that loved his wife and kids, it's me. I'm nothing without you all and I know it.*

Love you, Daddy

27 Sep 52
1st Marines, Korea
Reg CP

Dearest family,
Jack Shoden and Bill Biehl moved out at 0730 this morning. I heard them singing, "I'm on my way, I won't be back; Yes, we're on our way, we won't be back." I got up at 0650, had breakfast with them and helped load the jeep trailer. Now I'm completely on my own. I spent several hours in the command bunker studying situation maps, enemy positions etc. We had the 65th and 40th CCF fronting us with the 63rd CCF Army in reserve. A total of some 90,000 Chinese Communist troops. The total has increased somewhat since I last checked some two weeks ago. I procured three target coordinates of some (122) heavy artillery pieces, then called Capt Daniels at the 2nd Bn and asked him to submit them today for MPQ14 night radar controlled targets. We had a big air day yesterday and the colonel was very happy over the results. His recon. hop yesterday provided him with some more target info which I plotted and sent in for air strikes.

Received three letters from you last night, honey. You asked me where Old Baldy was, dear. Well, it's about 15 miles east of us. Kelly Hill is two miles east of us in the 1stMarDiv sector and under control of the 7th Reg. Capital Hill is the ROK's main struggle on the east coast of Korea and Finger Ridge is part of Capital Hill. The fighting south of Panmunjom is being done by the KMC (Korean Marine Corps). They cover the area north up to the Panmunjom corridor and we take over north of the corridor clear over and around to the large river running north and south coming into the Imjin River. The Commonwealth Div takes over from there and runs across to Old Baldy, which is US Army controlled. Hill 229 doesn't have any other name other than Paekhak Hill. I'm about two miles SE of 229 now. This is confidential, of course, honey. Glad you spotted Taedoksan. That's loaded with goonies and mortar and artillery. Taedoksan is their MLR 2nd line of defense. Their primary line is forward of that about 2000 meters SE up to Bunker Hill.

My new job as Reg air officer will keep me busy for some time and the weeks are flying by. Keep happy, darling.

Love, Daddy

28 Sep 52
1st Marines CP
Sunday evening

Dearest family,
I just now finished writing a complete report of the air activity in front of the 1stMarReg from the period of 28 Aug to 28 Sep--12 pages and it had to be written in the standard Marine format, narrative and chronological summations of all the air strikes of all the battalions. It's some report.

This morning Dave Kennedy flew off in the helicopter I arranged for him last night. He's returning to K3 and then will go to Johnson Air Force Base in Japan for his weekly lectures to the doggies regarding air control. He had his relief with him, a Capt Tony Caparilla, a ground officer, inactive reserve returned to active duty. Tony had been an FAC on Iwo Jima, Peleliu and Okinawa during WWII, very experienced boy. He's going to take over the FAC school about 15 Oct and Dave will come home. (Dave left 10¢ in MPC script for Ricky and Randy.) His next duty station will be C.C. schools, Quantico for a two-year period, he thinks. His home is in Mass. and so is his wife's. Said he'd try and get me a spot there if I wanted it, instructing at aircraft engineering maintenance school--ha, ha, don't get excited about it, honey. That makes two guys that have got the duty station of their choice.

Last night Maj Christie brought me my fitness report that Col Altman had made out on me because of my transfer from the 3rd Bn. Besides an almost perfect score in the grade columns, he wrote the following under Remarks: "Capt Peterson has the capacity for handling the assignment of air liaison officer at Battalion or Regimental level. He actively sought to improve himself professionally; was cool and efficient in the performance of his duty as an FAC under heavy enemy fire; participated in combat operations against the enemy during the period covered. Qualified for promotion to Major." Signed LtCol Sidney Altman. How's about that, darling girl?

I had to go over to the 3rd Bn and brief the two new FACs on "Operation Snatch," then joined them on the operation. Thought we had peace for a minute when, at noon, we got a call saying the delegates had recessed until 1400 today. We ate lunch and Brunsworth and Norlin returned to the Snatch operation at 1500 today. They adjourned until 8 Oct.

I was called over to the 3rd Bn to take over as defense counsel on a negro Marine I befriended during Bunker Hill operation. He's charged with stabbing a fellow Marine at Seoul on 26 July. I'll tell you more later. He asked me to defend him during his court martial trial. I don't believe he did it.

Had air today. Cold tonight. No mail today. Have been awfully busy. Watched an artillery duel at my old OP229 for 30 minutes today. Copter pilot Maj Joe Frieta joined me on my rounds of the front lines today. Played four games of volley ball this afternoon--won three. Even Col Long was out playing ball.

Love you darling,
Daddy

29 Sep 52
1st Marines CP, Korea
Monday evening

Dearest girl,

This morning I prepared the final page of my report, turned it over to the sergeant major and asked him to type it for me. I called all the battalions and talked to all the FACs in regard to their enlisted members making application for flight training. Out of all the teams, and there are four with eight men each, only three men were qualified in having a recommendation from their FAC officers, and having any college or a high enough GTC. I fooled around doing all my paper work and also planned a training course for the air teams when we go into reserve.

Got a call from the Div air officer, Capt Lape, telling me of Col Cram's arrival at Strip #32 at Changdan by the Imjin, along with two other air colonels he had brought up from the Wing. I picked up Capt Gilman, another copter pilot, who had asked me to take him along the next time I went up on the front lines. Col Layer asked me and Gilman to accompany him over to the 2nd Bn CP and Strip #32 to meet, greet and escort Col Cram and his two colonel friends. Col Cram landed the big Sikorsky copter himself at Strip #42 and we waited for about 10 minutes as they loaded into a jeep and finally drove over to Strip #32. Three jeeps of us drove up to OP 229 which, incidentally, had received some artillery fire on the far right (north) side. (My quiet little home isn't quiet any more.) Gave them the 50¢ tour and lucked into two air strikes. After jeeping down the hill to the 2nd CP Col Layer bummed a ride for me, Gilman and himself in Cram's Sikorsky helicopter. He gave us a recon. just to the rear of the front lines, dropped us off here at the 1st Marine CP and turned the copter over to his copilot who flew it back to HMR-161 CP at Div. Col Cram is staying all night.

I played volley ball for 30 minutes and secured. Took a pan bath, ate chow and at 1800 went down to the bunker, where I got all the air strike information across the Corps front, and then prepared my air report which I presented at the usual nightly briefing at 1830.

Attended the movie (colored film) "Has Anybody Seen My Gal?" (75%), in a squad tent. Made corrections on the rough copy of my air report they'd typed. Awfully cold tonight, brrr, my feet were cold last night.

Love you and need you always, precious family.

Your daddy

30 Sep 52
1st Marines CP
Tuesday 1300

Hi honey,

Finally have a few minutes to myself after working on helicopter strips and air diaries for the past months, as well as activities training schedules for all the enlisted members on TACP's teams under my control in the 1st Marines. Arranged air priorities with the Div and Bn air officers. Did liaison between operations and artillery officers. Worked on system of signals for the peace delegate and sub-delegate members.

Yesterday the Communists snatched two jeep drivers and took them to Kaesong. This morning one of the Army majors, a member of the subordinate team, came into our tent to talk over this "Operation Snatch" rescue mission with Maj McLeod and myself. We suggested he go to see the general because it was a higher echelon policy problem. This afternoon, along with full chicken Col Cram and Maj Honeycutt, I am going up to the front to check things out.

1700

Just as I was writing this letter, Col Cram and Maj Honeycutt came to pick me up and we shoved off for the 1st Bn 1st Marines sector, which is way over on the right flank. Thirty minutes later, a thousand bumps and a couple of terrifically steep hills saw us on top of OP8 where we spied down on the goonies crawling around in trenches and moving supplies. A fire mission was called in on them and, in retaliation, the Commies began lobbing artillery very near our position. We shoved off and drove all the way across the division front to OP229 in hopes of watching an air strike that was scheduled to come off at 1530. Arriving there 10 minutes early, we waited until 1545 and no A/C, so I called back to Div Air and learned that they had been on station over us but JOC 5th A.F. had diverted them to the 3rd Army Div which was being hit very hard at 1530. After finding out the reason for diversion, Col Layer felt OK about it, but until I found out, he was furious.

Got back in time for two fast volley ball games--love that game--keeps a guy fit. It's so darn cool I don't take any showers because they are ice cold. Heated some water and took a sponge bath and am now writing to the most precious family anybody ever had. Fifteen minutes before dinner and I'm starved. Can hear the artillery firing now. Drove near a battery of 155mm artillery just as they were firing and our jeep jumped a couple of inches off the road, shaking us clear to our boots. Wow! What a noise when you're not expecting it.

Received three wonderful letters today from you and Ben. It's so wonderful hearing from you, dearest. My whole day seems so bright and cheery whenever I hear from you. Ben's letter was full of the Sunday ride and steak dinner and all about Randy. Told me nearly everything Randy said to him Sunday. I really never realized Randy spoke so many words. You told me he was talking up a storm but I never realized he was putting any words together like, "I want to be as tall as where my hand is now." I'm amazed. Honey girl, I wish you'd tell me more of the sentences Randy is speaking. Ben said Ricky called Peg and Troop to dinner with "Come and get it, the flies are already on the meat!" I thought that was awfully funny. That's my boy.

2200

Back from the movie, "Waves Ahoy!" Esther Williams.

Went to the bunker and plotted some coordinates for Col Layer. I gave them to Maj Honeycutt, the artillery officer, and they are going to put a regimental TOT (Time On Target:) on the enemy. We didn't get any air today and the goonies are creeping up to our outpost on 124 near Bunker Hill. We have a patrol out near there, though, so we must coordinate the TOT with the patrol's return, for their protection. Three of our tanks are dozing a road out on a ridge leading to 124. After they get out on the point of 124 they can put the goonies on the west side of 122 (Bunker Hill) under direct fire. One of the tanks threw a tread and two tank retrievers went out to recover it about an hour ago. Then one of them got stalled, but fortunately, the one good retriever was able to bring the other two out. Just after they got back to the MLR, the enemy opened up on them, showering them with mortar and artillery fire but the tanks got back to the rear of the MLR safely.

The bunker here at Regiment is a huge affair--artillery charts, intelligence section, phone watch and operations section. It could take 122mm direct fire, no strain. Down the road from us a few hundred yards the goonies must have taken azimuth flashes from our artillery and they zeroed in on it. Joe Frieta, the copter pilot, was driving by the artillery battery at the time three 122mm (real big gear) came sailing in, and one round landed near the road about 40' from Joe's jeep. It landed in swampy ground where the mud and water absorbed most of the blast, but covered them with mud. Two other rounds hit the friendly artillery positions directly. Didn't hear how many casualties were taken because Joe Frieta bugged out. We, of course, heard the explosions over here at 1st Reg. Enough about this darn war.

Glad Ricky is all married off happily to the little girl down the street; now we've only got one more son to marry off and we're all alone again, honey. Boy, they sure grow up fast. Bye bye, dearest girl. The daddy adores you. Only a few more weeks and I"ll have my honey in my arms again.

Your very own,
Daddy

2 Oct 52
1st Marines CP
Korea

Dearest family,

I didn't write last night because I was swamped with telephone calls until 0200 this morning. Maj Gen Pollock, CO of the 1stMarDiv, called Col Layer last night and told him to be prepared to execute Plan VIP at 0630 this morning. I had the whole thing tossed into my lap, which really amounts to a king-sized headache. Had to coordinate the flak suppression fire mission with the artillery and set up a sound (radio) system up on OP229 through my 2nd Bn air controller. Had to call them and explain the entire fire mission plan, air plan, and also the fact that the VIPs would land at Strip #42 at 2nd Bn CP and would have to be given the tour at the Bn bunker and taken to OP229. Throughout the night we had to call in regard to whether or not the weather would be operational and whether or not we could count on the aircraft arriving if it was operational. I was awakened at 0230, 0330, 0430, 0530 and finally got up and stayed at 0600. Anglico is constantly calling me to relay information to the three Bn teams.

I recommended Boone for meritorious promotion to sergeant. Hope the kid gets it; he deserves it. Yesterday was an extremely busy day for me too. I could hardly get all my paper work and phone calls in.

At 1145 Col Layer, after returning from a recon. of Bunker Hill in an OE, demanded an air strike be put on there immediately, adding that if we didn't, we'd lose the hill at any hour. It was a very risky thing to attempt because we had friendly troops only a few yards from the enemy positions that were to be attacked. Nevertheless, I said I'd get him air if it was the last thing I did. Somehow I managed to get air and the planes were on station at 1300, which didn't provide us with enough time to execute "operation catch'um" because of the necessary *withdrawal of troops from their forwardmost positions to some prepared bunkers about 100 yards from their forwardmost bunkers. I called in a helicopter that picked up Capt Walt Daniels, the FAC of the 2nd Bn/1st now occupying our old MLR position, and flew him down to VMO-6 where he took an OE up and controlled the strike himself from the OE, while his assistant, Lt Buechler, was in OP6, overlooking Bunker Hill where I used to control air (the old Item Co position). They called in artillery flak suppression which practically nullified the goonies' automatic weapons fire. They knocked out three mortars, four bunkers, 75 yards of trench line, killed five and estimated five WIA. Then our troops moved back to retake their old positions, the goonies opened up with mortar and sniper fire, hitting only one of our men. Then, last night at 2300, we sent a mop-up team up there but they got hit with machine gun fire, hand grenades and mortar, and were driven back with two KIA and eight WIA. I can't understand how the goonies could have had anyone alive on 122 (Bunker Hill) after the air pounding they'd received, but they sure did. I'm trying to get some more air for them today, but the KMCs on our left cried wolf so they got some just a few minutes ago.*

We just had a flash storm with lightning, thunder and wind. Got a call from a MLR Company saying two of the big silver Panmunjom balloons had been blown over to a point near our MLR. Gotta try and recover them.

Last night after the movie I took a walk under a beautiful full moon and spoke to you, dearest girl that I love.

*Your very own,
Daddy*

TWO FRIENDS SHOT DOWN FLYING IN AN OE OBSERVATION PLANE
CORSAIR EXPLODES AND CRASHES NEAR OUR POSITION ON THE LINE

4 Oct 52
1st Reg CP, Korea
0830

Dearest girl,
Yesterday I worked like a little beaver on air requests, assigning targets and priorities. We had priority air over the Div all day because on Thursday night and Friday morning the KMCs and 7th Marines had been clobbered by around 15,000 rounds of mortar and artillery, followed by a heavy probe of enemy troops. Yesterday morning we had air, and I do mean air. Eighty-eight planes worked with us during the day, unloading around 440,000 pounds of bombs on the goonies. Last night enemy action was practically nil as a result of yesterday's heavy air activity. Boy, they are sure having one heck of a scrap up here. The KMCs got clobbered the heaviest from Communist artillery. The helicopters were going all night on their evacuation hops, and they fly right over our tent at about 100'. Needless to say, nobody got any sleep.

Last night I briefed the colonel on the air activity and stayed for the movie, "Singing in the Rain." Gene Kelly--100%. Story all about moving pictures, from silent days up to the first sound movie. They never got past about 1926 or '27, and all the women, of course, wore the clothes of the times. "Wait for me, Nellie" also took place at roughly around those dates; both were color films and very enjoyable. The Nellie picture, however, started during the Spanish-American War period and went clear through the Roaring '20s and up to 1952. I certainly enjoy movies. Guess I'm a ham or something deep down inside.

Yesterday afternoon, late, an enlisted man, while installing a stove for our tent, climbed up the tent on the outside and was replacing the cloth top with a metal top, which has a hole for our stove pipe. The old, worn canvas tore loose and he came tumbling down, tent and all. Of course we had to move lock, stock and barrel, next door to a VIP tent and it was a little while before we got squared away with our gear and lights connected, so I didn't get around to writing to my darling. It was so cold we kept the fire burning but we only had a five-gallon can of diesel oil and sometime during the night it went out so the water we had on top heating for our shaving water was cold this morning. When we get up at 0645 every morning, we all race each other for the little stove and heat our water in a small pan for shaving.

The full moon shone so brightly last night that we feared another goonie push but, thank God, it never materialized. Had our usual afternoon volleyball game and lost four games in a row. The fellows just wouldn't set them up for me to kill. Volley ball relieves the tension of the day. Doc Mitchell (dentist), Doc Murdock and Doc Craighead, (surgeons), Maj McLeod and Col Long, along with about six 2ndLts usually comprise our teams. It's hard to believe that Murdock and Craighead could muster enough energy to play, after some of the rugged days and nights they put in working on the casualties that filter in here to our regimental aid station. Even so, they come out every day to enter into our game, to laugh and generally forget for a spell the urgency of the situation confronting every one of us. However, despite our distance of better than a mile from their target, the air strikes and our nets shaking from the bomb blasts wouldn't let us completely remove our consciousness from the ongoing battle.

1730

Hi again,

Tony Foltz of VMF-212 and Capt Woodberry came over to see me today. Col Layer asked me to take them up to the front lines and give them the tour, which I did for about four hours. We went up to an outpost and observed a fierce tank (friendly), mortar and artillery fire fight in the KMC sector to our left. I saw Chinese troops by the hundreds crossing a river (knee deep) over to the KMC's side and manning positions on Hill 37 they had taken the other night in a fierce fire fight. We had 12 air strikes in close support of the KMCs and, through my 20-power glasses, I observed the goonies carrying off their wounded, and others moving across open fields. The tanks were firing at positions now occupied by Chinese that previously had been held by KMCs. I have never seen so many Chinese in the open. There must have been thousands. We, of course, were also under fire and bugged out after watching a Corsair crash and explode while doing close support for the KMCs.

A friend of mine, Capt Moran, who came to the Div in July with me and who was the regimental air officer for the 7th Marines, was shot down and crashed in an OE along with his passenger, the intelligence officer of the 7th Marines, a Major Owens. Both were seen to be dragged from the crash which landed some 1800 yards inside goonie land. Artillery later demolished the OE. Both appeared to be dead, according to our front line observers. A copter crashed today also. Good old 229 is getting incoming now and big gear 122mm artillery. Action has increased all along our division front.

Your letter today smelled wonderful, honey. You're on my mind constantly, precious doll. Our day is coming--yes, you can tell everyone I'll be home next month or at least will have left Korea by late Nov. Clear and cool today. Our stove feels good tonight but my feet are cold. I'm certainly going to enjoy my homecoming like I never enjoyed one before. It's been such a long, long time. Keep happy, honey--know the daddy is OK. I'll not take any more chances than necessary, honey. I'll stay off the front lines and away from OEs as much as possible, I promise.

Your own Daddy

6 Oct 52
1st Marines, Korea

Dearest girl,

This morning I jeeped to all three battalions and talked to all six of my FACs. I had a lot of business to talk over with them and didn't want to use the land line phone because it's low security. The goonies have some of our lines tapped and we don't like to use them for top secret info. If we do use the telephone we talk in broad terms and use gizmo and thing-a-ma-jig and the code which we change every day. The KMCs and 7th Marines caught hell last night. Both our own and the enemy artillery were at it all night long. It was difficult to relax and get any sleep, what with our phone ringing off the hook. Maj McLeod, the regimental operations officer, has calls coming in from all three battalions' operations officers.

It was cold last night and the basket felt really good. I crawled out, turned on the heater and put a bucket of water on to heat at about 0600. Brother it was cold--brrrrr!

The goonies are showing strength all along the Div front. Air has been on station all day working for two of my battalions and also the KMCs and 7th Marines. When we get an emergency situation here we get plenty of air. We tried to take the hill known as Seattle fronting the 7th Marines. The Marines were repulsed, with quite a few casualties. Of course the goonies suffer a huge number of casualties too, but to us one Marine's life is worth a battalion of goonies.

2200

Hi again,

Just returned from the Reg bunker where everyone assembles when "it hits the fan," as they say. The goonies hit us hard on Bunker Hill and another outpost nearby. At the same time, they attacked all along the 7th Marines sector and we are taking heavy casualties right now. We suffered about 15 or more near Bunker.

The incoming being very heavy, Daniels called me to see if I could get him an MPQ immediately on some 122mm guns they had plotted. I called Anaconda Baker, the radar control agency, posthaste and found out they had planes on station. I got them diverted and they hit the 122s and stopped a lot of the firing. An hour later Col Cornell called and really tore into me about going over his head. He didn't bother me much, though, (the rear area poag). Next time I will go through Div air but that means just another call. Daniels got up to his OP and, through a hail of incoming, managed to observe some excellent hits from the radar drops. He called and thanked me for my cooperation. Div air wouldn't have done it for him. Everyone is up and I guess we'll all stay up the rest of the night on account of Bunker Hill and the 7th. It's a clear moonlit night and I don't think they will need any illumination for support.

7 Oct 52

0800

Dearest girl,

I didn't have to stay up all night, only until about 0100 this morning. The goonies relaxed their pressure on us at about 2200 so we gradually left the bunker, came to our tent and handled the multitude of telephone calls until 0100. We had about two KIA, 29 wounded evac. and quite a few wounded non-evac. They captured one very badly wounded prisoner, a PFC, and he couldn't supply them with much info. before his evacuation by helicopter. We're planning a helicopter rotation of the 2nd Bn 1st Marines. McLeod and I are going to select the pickup points and letdown points for the rotation sometime this morning. We're waiting for the copter now. It went over to the 2nd Bn first and will swish around here and pick McLeod and me up in a few minutes.

Col Layer and I met this morning for a conference regarding the best air targets and general close air support. I sure hate to see the nights roll around because it means the goonies will resume their activity, and what proportions their attacks will amount to, nobody knows.

The artillery officer from the 5th Marines, who will be relieving us, is up here this morning. Maj Honeycutt is taking him on a tour of our regimental front and all the OPs. It's my job to give the air officer a tour if he ever gets around to coming up here to see me. I had a full tour yesterday. These roads really knock our jeeps to pieces, to say nothing of the passengers.

We passed within 200 feet of some heavy artillery that was firing a mission and, brother, it really gets noisy. It's cool and I wouldn't be surprised if it snowed instead of rained.

I figure I'll be relieved on 26 Nov. In other words, from today I have only 50 days of Korea to do. If we're in reserve for five weeks, that will mean I'll have only 10 more days up on the lines when we come up again in Nov.

Received your wonderful letter of 29 Sep last night. It's swell hearing from my precious girl so often. I love you, darling. You're my everything, sweetheart. Kiss my darlings and tell them their daddy adores them and is looking forward to coming home to them.

Daddy

7 Oct 52
Korea
2135

Dearest doll,

Everyone is very concerned about the enemy making an all out push tonight in our sector, and also on a large scale across the entire Korean front. The peace talks are scheduled for tomorrow morning and they must have a show of strength. They hit with some estimated 12,000 troops along the whole front, but very heavily in the 7th Marines sector and also at Bunker Hill and the KMC sector. Our division sector received around 8000 rounds in 24 hours. The three-quarter moon is slowly cutting into the black sky, emitting more light as it rises. I'm holding my breath and have said my prayers several times today. I pray nothing happens tonight. It was such a hectic scene last night, and the reserve battalions are all committed, plus there's no reserve in sight for the battalions of our regiment--only our CP group. (This is all very confidential, honey, and don't repeat it because it could bring dire consequences if it filtered into some wrong person's hands. I'm writing it only to record for any future use we may make of this info.)

Something funny happens almost every evening at briefings. The young lieutenant of engineers and his crew, who are doing all the road work and construction for our regiment, are presently building a tank road in plain view of the enemy and it disturbs the Chinks no end. The lieutenant is constantly bringing in handfulls of artillery and mortar fragments fired at him during the day. We've all grown to expect his nightly display.

We have a pet rabbit by the name of Bugs, naturally. He's very friendly, comes into our tent, lies down and goes to sleep. I petted him to sleep today. He's gray and white. I'll take a picture tomorrow.

The movie tonight was "They Weren't Married"--Marilyn Monroe, of course, knocked everyone for a loop. She's the rage here in Korea. Sza Sza Gabor, Ginger Rogers, Fred Allen--75%.

My relief, the air officer of the 5th Regiment, Capt MacAgorski, came up here at 1000 this morning and I gave him a briefing as well as a tour of 229 and all three battalion CPs. We drove approximately 20 miles in the tour and didn't return to the CP until 1600, dusty and dirty. He had to shove off right away, so I got into a volley ball game. After washing up and eating dinner, I drove up to the bunker, gathered all the info on today's activities air-wise and presented it at the briefing, which lasted until the movie started inside the same squad tent where we hold our briefings. There are two space (tent) heaters now in there, making it super comfortable. The same type we had at Fallon, Nev., they burn diesel oil.

Got a letter from the Commandant of the Marine Corps, Gen Lemuel C. Shepherd, today, thanking me and all the reserves for our part and asked me to extend. Nice of the old codger, wasn't it? No mail from the most precious wifey in this whole wide world.

It's 2230 and still quiet, except that the goonies are hitting Hill #39 over near the KMC sector right now. It's 1500 meters closer to the KMC lines than their last hill the Commies took from them--getting closer all the time.

Kiss my darlings that I love. Love you, honey.

Daddy

8 Oct 52
Korea
1800

Dearest girl,

Last night produced its bit of excitement. OP2, where I spent so many nights, was hit by a mess of goonies and our kids took quite a few casualties. At about 0200 this morning we got the first word about it and the first report said they were even out in our neutral corridor, which would, of course, mean the truce talks had been chucked and this was the beginning of the end. I found out later it simply wasn't the case. However, some 10,000 goonies did attack all along the front, hitting the Army the hardest. After a while things simmered down and I finally managed to get about two hours sleep. Tonight we've been alerted again for heavy enemy activity in our sector.

Col Cornell, the Div air officer, flew into our CP today by helicopter with a bunch of top secret plans concerning the hitting of targets that lie within the six-mile no-air circle around Kaesong. Enemy artillery positions. The OK and original plan came from the top in Japan, routed through the Wing, up here to the Div and now to me--I have yet to brief my FACs on it.

Collected the usual air info for my brief, then briefed the colonel. About 20 people gather there each evening, making quite an impressive show. Spread on the table are about six 4'X6' maps of Korea covered with clear plastic and marked with all sorts of secret info of troops, artillery positions, mortar positions, roads, tanks, troops, anti-tank preparations, and air no-fly circle. Every phase of our command has his own map. I have mine--plot all my air strikes in grease pencil etc. Worked for about an hour on approach headings and pullouts, put a mess of info in code and sent it over the land line to Walt Daniels who will set up control on OP2 tomorrow at 1000. The planes will hit all seven targets that lie just within the no-fly circle, which have never been hit. The Commies placed their guns inside the circle knowing they wouldn't be hit by us. Now they'll get it. Four AD Skyraiders will hit each of the seven targets.

At the present time everyone is fairly relaxed, for some reason. It's dark out now, but the moon will be high by midnight and that's when things begin happening. We had five killed, I found out at briefing tonight, poor kids. They all seem so young and innocent. The graves registration tent is about 150' from my tent. All KIAs come in there--a sickening sight every morning.

I want to tell you about Casey, the young Irishman I have on my team. He came to the USA over two years ago to live with an uncle, took out his 1st citizenship papers and joined the Marine Corps. His parents don't know he's in Korea. His FPO San Francisco, Calif. address has them thinking he's enjoying himself in sunny California. He doesn't want to worry them. Says he wants to stay in the M.C. long enough to get a military transport (air) ride back to Ireland and visit his family, then return to good old Uncle Sugar. Casey says homes cost about the same in Ireland and carpenters and plumbers receive only a slight bit under what they receive in America. Says food is very plentiful and English come over to Ireland to buy food. Food is cheap. Clothes are funny; 24-inch bell bottom pants are the style for men. Says he had a hard time changing over to American styles. Last year he and his two American cousins made a tour to Colorado. He's homesick for Ireland, I can tell. Still has his brogue. Nice kid. Always smiling. Good radioman.

Kiss my precious little guys. Tell them daddy loves and misses his little guys. Don't worry about me, honey girl. I'm getting plenty of good chow and sack time. Love ya.

Daddy

9 Oct 52
Korea
Thursday 1700

Hello honey girl
and my two precious little boys that I love,
 I broke out all of my pictures of my wonderful family and had a nice visit with all of you. I think I'll keep you all, can't find a single thing I'd want to add except a little Marion Jr. and myself. What a wonderful family combination that would make.
 I wanted to go up to the front lines and monitor all the air strikes today but I had so darn many things to do here at CP that I didn't have a chance to get away. Forty-three a/c flew interdiction missions very close to Kaesong today and really clobbered the Communist artillery batteries. The Army and ROK forces have been having an awful time over on our right.
 We're moving to a blocking position on the night of the 12th, then will spend the night and return to Div reserve on the 13th. Probably will be a miserable night in the blocking position but it's necessary as a rehearsal; in case we have to move up there some night during a Communist break-through, we'll all be familiar with the terrain. I have to make <u>all</u> arrangements for a helicopter lift of an entire battalion on the morning of the 13th, so you see, honey, I have considerable to do. Have to draw up plans to map scale, locations of pickup and drop area, time schedules by companies etc.

       Love ya, daddy

10 Oct 52
1st Marines CP, Korea
Friday afternoon

Dearest girl, Ricky and Randy-boy,
 Another day has almost slipped by and, as far as I'm concerned, the 49 or more days remaining can slip by as uneventful as today. Tomorrow my boys are moving to the other side of the Imjin into the Div reserve area, leaving two of my boys here, one radio jeep operator and one kid for my bunker watch. I'm sending the bulk of my gear with them because Sunday morning I'll be moving to the blocking position to set up an advanced command post (CP) remaining Sunday night and then finally moving to Div reserve Monday. We, of course, are on 24-hour around-the-clock call to back up the units on the line. I'm going to go down to K6 if it's the last thing I do, though. I want to see those kids down there before I go home because they are all wonderful fellows and we've had a lot of experiences together.
 Major McLeod, my tent mate here, had the opportunity today to volunteer for duty in the Philippines at NAS Sangley Point, near Manila. Brand new Naval Air Station. He of course accepted and is leaving for his new assignment in December directly from here. His wife and family (one boy five years, I should say) will meet him there. Quarters (new) are available and Filipino house girls. He's going to become the Commanding Officer of the Marine detachment. His wife doesn't know about it yet. She was with him in China, though, and says she likes foreign duty. He's been over here in Korea since April.
 Played volley ball for an hour as usual this afternoon. We have a super fast game, lots of setups and hard drives from the net. We play "no net;" that is, you can't even touch the net a tiny little bit, and, brother, do we get into arguments with each other--all friendly though. We have a swell bunch of kids. The dentist, Doc Mitchell, is a character; so is Doc Murdock, both about my age. The mail truck came in this afternoon chuck full. Hasn't been delivered yet and I'm chomping at the bit until it is delivered.
 It was quiet in our sector last night. They woke us up at midnight, as we had to make some command decisions. Seems as though the commander out on OP2 reported he heard tracked vehicles moving around within the Panmunjom circle and then a few minutes later McLeod got a call from the base camp, where the peace delegates stay on the other side of the Imjin, saying their troops out in Panmunjom reported enemy tanks. Three truckloads of Army

troops (U.S.) came charging out from Panmunjom because the M.P. at the checkpoint had told them to "bug out--the Communist tanks are coming!" The general got word of it, ordered them back and they returned. Don't know whether there were any tanks or not. Somebody was all fouled up.

2015

It's raining now and our little tent is warm and comfy. My sack is better now because I've learned to deflate some of the air from my pneumatic mattress which makes it more comfortable. I'm having to use two blankets over my winter sleeping bag. Boy, when we turn our heater off it really gets cold in a hurry. Bugs, our little rabbit, hasn't been around here for a couple of days. We had roasted pheasant again. Is it ever delicious!

The special services officer announced at briefing tonight that he received $26,000 worth of PX items which will go on sale when we move to reserve. The regiment starts moving tomorrow at noon, but as I've mentioned, we won't move until the morning of the 12th to our blocking CP and 13th to Div Reserve CP. Maj Charlie Reifel asked me today if I'd like to sell my radio. I told him when the time comes I'd let him know. It's been banged up quite a bit and is dusty and rain spotted from the 3rd Bn tent Bill and I shared, so it's no beauty any more. Brother, did that thing leak!

Ricky is doing real well in his reading, isn't he? I'm proud of both of my little guys, I can tell you. Tell them their daddy is looking forward to those scuffles and games we'll play together and the little boats and cars we'll build together when I get home. We'll have to keep Rick out of school for a few days when I first get home. All for now, precious girl.

Your very own Daddy

Eternal Father
    grant we pray,
To all Marines
    both night and day,

The courage, honor,
    strength and skill
Their land to serve,
    the law fulfill,

Be thou the shield
    forever more
From every peril
    to the Corps.

Marine Corps verse of the Navy Hymn

Upper Left: Standing beside my radio jeep, with the Sherman Medium Tank in the rear. If required, I would man the tank for the rescue of our peace negotiators. The WWII Willys Jeep quarter-ton 4x4 was loaded with radio equipment.

Upper Right & Middle Left: In position to control air support activities, should these be required during any rescue operation. My tank was especially equipped with an assortment of radios for my job as air officer.

Middle Right: Maj Stone and Peterson. Bill was our 3/1 Bn Weapons CO and had primary responsibility for "Operation Snatch." We were tent mates as well.

Lower Right: Crossing over a bridge Marine Engineering Company constructed to cross the Imgin River, which often flooded, washing everything out. The enemy would take advantage of our precarious situation then and increase his hostile activity against our forward positions.

Upper Left: On Guard at Critical Site—Korean Marines (KMC) clean their 3.5-inch bazooka at blocking position near Hill 155, just on the left of the Panmunjom Road corridor.

Upper Right: Gen Lemuel C. Shepherd, Jr., CMC (Commandant of the USMC) observes fire placed on CCF position during frontline visit to 1st MarDiv. The good general visited my Hill 229 on one occasion and we had a long chat about my work, where I was from, whether I was a regular or reserve. A very pleasant individual.

Right: Aerial shot of 1st MarDiv CP at Yong-ri, as viewed from mess hall, looking north. In the over four months that I was an FAC, I had not managed to visit this rear area but on two or three occasions. My flying buddy, Capt Dave "The Sniveler" Kennedy, referred to anyone this far behind the lines as a "rear area poag."

Left: Marine OP reports on Chinese dispositions during August 1952 battle. Photo could have been of our TACP team at Hill 229 and my ANGRC/9 radio, with author at left of photo controlling an air strike.

Photo credit USMC

Right and Middle Right: I covered this crash of an AD-1, #14 from VMA-121. It had been struck by ground fire while supplying close air support for the 1stMarDiv. My partner, Bill Biehl, and I would later perfect a system of artillery fire support and flak suppression to help reduce the number of planes shot up over our sector during close air support. We called it HELLFIRE.

Middle Left: View of Seoul from our Bell chopper on return from a medical evac to the hospital ship.

Lower Left: The Bell chopper had two side litters; however, summer temperatures, which affected the lift, prohibited more than one. Designation Bell HTL-4.

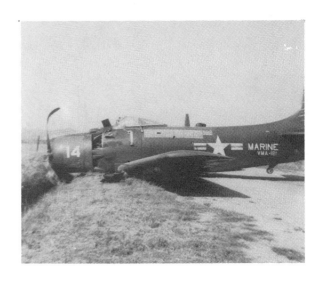

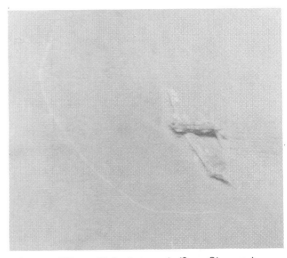

Above: This flak damaged AD-1 Skyraider crash-landed in a mine field near our division. They cleared a path to get the pilot and placed a white ribbon around the cleared safe area. Very dangerous duty.

Above: My partner, Maj Bill Biehl, striking his hard-charger stance in jest. We were in position for controlling an air strike near Hill 229.

Upper Right: Peterson showing where we are on his map. The Willys jeep is the standard WWII ¼ ton 4x4. This is one of two issued to our TACP.

Middle Right: View from the 1st Regiment Command Center.

Lower Left: Another successful Chinese ringneck pheasant hunt while our Bn was in reserve.
L to R: Cpl Evans, PFC Bauman, Peterson.

Lower Right, L to R: Maj Bill Biehl, Capt Peterson, 2nd Lt Morgan (ass't Operations officer), and 2nd Lt Kelly (ass't Intelligence officer).
The black berets were gifts presented to us by our British friends of the 1st Battalion, a famous regiment of the Black Watch.

Right, L to R: LtCol Glenn Long (Exec of 1st Reg), Col Walter Layer (CO of 1st Reg), MGen Edwin Pollock (CO of 1stMarDiv) at an inspection tour of the front lines.

Above: 3rd Bn Command Post personnel for a group photo. Peterson on right.

Left, L to R: LtCol Glenn Long, MGen Edwin Pollock, Col Walter Layer, Capt Peterson, and ?, aide to MGen Pollock, during a tour of the front lines.

Middle Right: Peterson at 1st Reg CP bunker, at my right. Regiment's rear position rarely received incoming, but it was nice to have when needed. Capt Dave (the sniveler) was now referring to me as a "rear echelon poag"—not quite an apt description because I spent 50% of my time on the MLR advising my three Battalion TACP teams. The incoming was still coming in there hot and heavy.

Lower Left: Peterson and Biehl in a borrowed armored Willys ¼ ton 4x4 Jeep. This war had, for the most part, deteriorated into an artillery duel, and the daily incoming Communist shells fairly rained on all of our positions.

Upper Left: A team of VIP's from the Navy and the Douglas Aircraft Co. I am about to jeep them up to my Hill 229, to the north of the 3rd Bn CP and show them gooney land. The purpose of their visit was to learn divebombing tactics for future aircraft design.

Middle Left: Gus Dake and the writer on the way to the hospital ship in Inchon harbor, carrying a wounded Marine in the helicopter's side litter.

Middle Right: USO show at 1st Regiment, in reserve.

Lower Left: Getting autographs from the USO group following their performance. Just getting a quick close-up look at a white woman was a treat.

Upper Right: Our pet rabbit.

CHAPTER 17

1ST MARINE REGIMENT IS RELIEVED ON THE MAIN LINE OF RESISTANCE
(IN THE REAR WITH THE GEAR)

11 Oct 52
1st night here at Reg CP
brrr, it's cold, Korea

Darlings,

    The regiments made the big switch today. All chairs, benches, tables, telephones, maps, a lot of the communications and all the cook stoves have been switched. Trucks coming and going like mad. My team moved--lock, stock and barrel--except two of them that I kept behind to drive the jeeps and run the radios. Most of the day has been spent arranging details of the move and briefing the 5th Regiment air team.
    It's been cold today. At 39° late this afternoon, winter must be nearly upon us. I'm up as near as I can get to our stove without getting burned and it feels good. I finally broke out my leather flight jacket, and right now have my woolen sweater on over my cotton undershirt, plus my dungaree jacket over that. I think I'd be cold even with all these clothes on if I moved away from this heater, so I'm sticking pretty close. The mess halls or tents switched personnel and stuff like I mentioned, resulting in a loused-up chow this evening--no coffee, just water. I'm dying for a cup of Joe. Don't even have any instant coffee. I used to keep some on hand over at the Third. The kids up on the lines don't have any heaters yet and I'll bet they are miserable. It's been very quiet the past few nights in our sector and I pray it continues. I'll be glad when we finally relinquish command to the 5th and then go into reserve.
    Looking through McLeod's Sears and Roebuck catalog today, it brought me back home, almost. All the beautiful clothes, furniture, tools, etc. We'll have fun, honey doll, shopping and eating at nice little restaurants of our choosing. Your wonderful cooking is what I'm looking forward to, honey. Golly, I've missed so many of the little things you did for me and that I took for granted. I'm never going to allow myself to drift into this business-as-usual routine again. We're going to enjoy life to its absolute maximum. Our day is just around the corner, honey. I love you.

Daddy

13 Oct 52

Dearest family,

  After 79 days on the line, yesterday morning the 5th Marines finally relieved us. Brother, was I ever happy to pull back. Everyone was getting shaky from being under constant pressure day and night since 26 July. The infantry companies had caught hell and our regiment as a whole had suffered over 50% casualties. I haven't an accurate figure on the number of boys killed, but Major McLeod said over 1900 casualties had been reported through his office during that period from 26 July. Of course the daddy counted as (1) and many amounted to only light cases but, for the most part, they were heavy and critical. Bunker Hill, Hill 124 and OP2 were the heaviest points of contact for us while we were up.

  Well, anyway, after the 5th relieved us yesterday, we formed a convoy of jeeps and trucks, drove several miles up to the front lines, set up a blocking position, and staged a defensive maneuver, just as though the goonies had broken through our MLR. Communications and tents, stoves, cots, maps, phones etc. were checked out and we ran the regiment all night. The battalions had been relieved from the MLR and moved back several thousand meters to fighting holes and trenches along a five-mile line to the rear of the MLR positions they had held. We were fairly comfy in our squad tent, but it was crowded with so many men in only three squad tents for the whole command group. I had radio contact with my three battalion teams all night. In spite of getting only about two hours sleep during the early morning hours, by first light this morning all equipment had been packed up, tents torn down and we were ready to deploy to our reserve area.

  The large Sikorsky copter air lifted the 2nd Bn across the Imjin in two and a half hours. Col Layer's copter arrived at our advanced CP at 1030. After he left, the remainder of us moved back to reserve, arriving here at 1130. Big tie-up crossing the pontoon bridge--trucks, jeeps all lined up in both directions awaiting their turn. Got the team squared away here at the reserve area. Made out my reports on the move. Found all my gear and tossed it in my tent shared with Majors Charlie Reifel, McLeod and Honeycutt.

  After I got my phone hooked up a lot of work had to be done. Major French, CO of ANGLICO, called and asked me to select an FAC and send him down to the Korean regiment for a month. I hated to do it to any of my battalion FACs, especially since they had just come off the line. However, I made my selection, a Lt Buechler of the 2nd Bn 1st Marines, who is Walt Daniels' partner. When I notified Buechler, it didn't go over very well and I can't say that I blame him. This business of handing out decisions isn't to my liking. It places Daniels in the poor position of not being free to leave his battalion while he's in reserve because the Bn CO wants at least one FAC at the Bn all the time. However, Buechler is the best man and can help the KMCs because he's familiar with that sector.

  The news from our neighbors on our left flank isn't good. The ROKs are taking heavy casualties but, at the same time, are inflicting heavy casualties on the goonies. The fighting is the heaviest near White Horse Mountain. I doubt that our position is in any particular danger, even in a breakthrough. Things could get terribly confusing here for a while if they did, however. They are fighting on the main northern approach route to Seoul. We're back far enough here that I don't think we'll be hearing any artillery firing except our own 155s. It's been rather quiet here in the Marine sector, since the goonies' major effort is on White Horse. The hills the goonies took from the KMCs are still in Communist hands, but the situation doesn't pose very much of a threat to the KMCs because the enemy has to resupply over open terrain in plain view of KMC artillery. The KMCs are assaulting the captured outposts daily to no avail. Bunker Hill is being probed by goonies every night but our kids seem to have the situation fairly well in hand. I guess we'll be having lectures, field trips and map reading exercises on our new sector that we'll be moving up to around 15-20 Nov. Of course I'll be leaving on 27 Nov. so I'll have my relief here from one of the battalions around the 15th to learn my job and to meet all the officers here in 1st Regiment, a fine lot of fellows, every one. There's a big "Hearts" card game going on in our tent right now--first cards I've seen since joining the Div. The fellows are beginning to relax. I can't go cards. Now volley ball is another matter.

1ST MARINE REGIMENT IS RELIEVED ON THE MAIN LINE OF RESISTANCE

Had a wonderful hot shower tonight inside a heated tent over at the 11th Marines CP. Drove three and a half miles for it with Charlie Reifel, but it was worth it. Although crowded, I managed to squeeze in, had a nice shampoo and shower. Felt fine after a clean change of clothes--I'll have to wash clothes tomorrow.

All for now, dear. Give my boys a hug for me.

Daddy

A CONFIRMATION FROM A SURRENDERED NORTH KOREAN SECURITY OFFICER
I SAW HIM THE NIGHT HE GAVE UP

When I was still flying with VMA-212, our flight got jumped by MIG-15s up near the Yalu. I was able to catch several fleeting glances at my attackers, and I swore they were Russian pilots flying them. The following newspaper clip helps confirm this feeling.

SURRENDERING—To Allied forces, Lt. Lee Dong Yup, ex-North Korean security officer, confirms reports Russians have been piloting some of MIG planes in combat. (International)

14 Oct 52
In Reserve CP
1st Reg, Korea

Dearest family,

It was cold when I crawled out of the rack this morning, but about 30 minutes after lighting the heater my shaving water was hot and the tent fairly comfortable. After breakfast I went up and checked over the men's tent radio equipment, then jeeped into the Div CP, VMO-6 and ANGLICO. Met Denny Clyde, ex-VMA-212 pilot, now with Anaconda Baker the TADC. We gabbed about old times and set up plans for an OE hop to K6 together tomorrow morning. Ran into Tom Catarino, Dave Kennedy's assistant in the FAC school. Tom is up this way to gather a few facts for the new FACs who will begin training on 10 Nov and will be up here at Div ready to take over on or about 22 Nov, which means a few days cut from the original schedule. I, of course, can leave this peninsula of panic that much sooner.

Dropped in at ANGLICO and made out some long overdue forms for the good Major French. Did a few errands at Div Headquarters, stopping in and saying hello to my good friend Capt Lape at Div Air Office. He informed me that our mutual friend, Capt Morin, who had been shot down and killed over enemy territory while flying the OE several weeks ago, left a wife and three children. I was sick when I heard it.

Gus Dake had a terrible thing happen to him yesterday. He flew a Col Thomas over to the KMC sector and they set down in his helicopter (H05-S). Col Thomas, a Marine liaison officer to the KMCs, got out and spoke to some officers. When he finished talking he turned and walked square into Gus's tail rotor, which killed him instantly. He leaves a wife and four children, so Major Honeycutt told me tonight. I tried to contact Gus today at VMO-6, but he's up at Wonderful Forward on the front lines. I swear I'll be glad to get away from all this death and sorrow and return to more pleasant surroundings and happenings.

Dave Kennedy sent Ricky and Randy some British occupation money. Find same enclosed. It's about a ten-mile drive back to Div CP from our reserve CP, through valleys and over hills. The Koreans are cutting their rice now. Everywhere you drive the women are flailing it on the ground to knock the kernels loose. Then they put it in a framework with a screen and sift it back and forth--very crude. For miles around, you see yellow fields of rice waving with the wind. Food for the soul, the beauty of the colorful autumn foliage all around us contradicts the widespread human misery.

Farmers were all out plowing today with their crude plows and oxen. While one plowed, another followed with a basket of B.S. Then one cast seeds and the other covered the seeds with about six or eight inches of top soil. Couldn't figure out what they were planting so deep. Old papasans, with their long grey beards, were standing by the sidelines supervising in their white robes, high silk black hats and long pipes. What a sight! Kids, thousands of them, dirty, playing in the roads, all begging candy ("hava yes candy, hava yes candy") and when you drove past without an offering you'd hear yourself cursed in Korean all the way from age two to six.

No mail today. Love you and miss you all so very much. Kiss my darlings.

Love,
Daddy

15 Oct 52
1st Marines CP, Reserve area, Korea
2130

Precious family,

Hello Ricky, Randy, Mama, that I love and miss so very, very much. It rained very hard last night, and up until noon today the clouds were hanging very low (500') which loused up plans I had made yesterday of getting an OE and flying down to K6 to see the boys that are about ready to be rotated back to Uncle Sugar, or Conus, as we refer to the good old United States of America. Conus of course means Continental Limits United States. Col Long told me again today I could go tomorrow. It's about a hundred miles from here and will take me a little over an hour flying time from VMO-6 in the OE. May take one of the team boys along for the ride. Hope the weather stays clear. I believe it will because it's clear tonight and very cold.

The boys got their class-six rations in from Japan. They sent a lieutenant back to Japan last week on a whisky run and R&R. He returned with the rations and everyone is having a party. Charlie Reifel, my tent mate, is enjoying a tot of rum right now.

All regulars and a swell bunch of Joes, they haven't had any drinking parties here in Reg since I joined around 16 Sept, until now. They treat me fine. In fact, they have been trying to talk me into extending my overseas tour, and even to integrate into the regulars. I can't see it, though. I believe I prefer to devote myself to my precious family than to the USMC.

Earlier this evening a bunch of machine guns opened up behind us and we were 15 minutes tracing them down. They were a tank outfit firing, and hadn't notified us. Brother, we figured the goonies were coming over the hill. We have one heavy arty outfit close by but, outside of them, this is a quiet sector. The goonies are hitting the 9th ROKs fairly hard. Reports come into us all day long concerning the activity. Bunker Hill has been quiet except for a light probe nightly.

Had my teeth checked yesterday by my good friend, Doc Mitchell. He proclaims I have a perfect set and found nothing wrong whatsoever but did give them a light cleaning. I'm getting my weight back fast, back to my old 185+. Can't push myself away from that table. I'll be nice and cuddly, dearest.

Worked on a helicopter evac indoctrination and a mess of paper work today. Bet I had over 100 phone calls. I need a secretary. Want the job? Kiss the darlings.

Love,
Daddy

1ST MARINE REGIMENT IS RELIEVED ON THE MAIN LINE OF RESISTANCE

THE FESTIVAL OF THE HONEYBUCKETS

16 Oct 52
1st Marines, in Reserve, Korea

Dearest little family,

I received yours of 7th and 8th Oct this evening and was sure happy to hear from you, precious girl. Golly, when I go for two or three days without hearing from my baby girl it's awful.

Called Denny Clyde up this morning and he came over here. We took my jeep into Division and on to VMO-6, several miles south of Div and waited about an hour for an OE to become available. Denny flew it down to K6, Tunp ori, and I flew it back. We took off at 1130 and 45 minutes later landed at K6. Met about 50 guys that I recognized from my old squadron VMF-212 and we ate lunch together in their new mess hall. Brother, you should see the bar and club room next to it. The Seabees worked on it for three months before they moved in. Almost, but not quite as good as stateside. Of course a large blown-up portrait of Marilyn Monroe graces the club over the bar. Also, over Dick Francisco's bunk in his hut, he has a 3'x4' photograph of Monroe lying in bed with only a sheet over her and that sultry look in her eye--signed, "to Dickie, with fond memories of our night together, Love, Sweetie Pie." Dick claims he stopped in Hollywood last month when he flew home on emergency (his father died, I believe). Anyway, he swears Monroe gave him the picture.

Last month Bass and Francisco put on a gigantic "Festival of the Honeybuckets," with a barbecue, parades, races, games etc. They said it really went over big.

Still there, Kim, my old houseboy at K6, greeted me with a big grin and a "Hi, Captain Peterson." He was ironing a shirt for one of the fellows. He's a good kid. My old desk and shelf arrangement are still in place and being used. Most of the faces have changed, though, in the squadron and hut. Pilots come and go. It felt strange calling up K6 Tower requesting takeoff, and even stranger becoming airborne in that little OE after using only a few hundred feet of that long runway, whereas the fully-loaded Corsair chewed up runway like crazy. They are building a huge all-concrete runway 10,000' long and 300' wide between Seoul and K6. Flew over it to give it the once over. They must be planning to use it for jets, or possibly B-29s. The B-29s are coming from Okinawa at the present time--a long haul. Kennedy used to direct them. Seoul, a huge city, has been totally devastated but it's being rebuilt. Flew out over Inchon Harbor and close by the two hospital ships, Repose and Consolation. On that clear, cold, sharp day, with ideal flying conditions, the erratic wind made that little OE really hop around in the air--it's fun to fly. Flew over 200 miles today, about like L.A. to San Diego and return. Landed at VMO-6 at 1430, drove back to Anaconda Baker and left Denny off. Came back to Reg CP, got my soap and bucket and a clean change of clothes, then drove down to the service battalion shower unit to wash my clothes and clean myself up. Feels so good to be clean from the skin out.

Doc Craighead is leaving for home on Tuesday the 21st. I'm going to fly him down to Ascom City, where he can pick up his suitcase at the Marine storage warehouse near Seoul, and then I'll fly him over to K16 and get him on the transport plane for the States. Doc Mitchell, the dentist, is leaving around 1 Dec. He wants to fly home westward through Asia, Europe, England, etc. I'm going to investigate the possibilities for him through my "agents" at Atsugi (Cameron), Hanada (Evans), Itami (Larson), and K3 (Kennedy). I might even do it myself if it's feasible. Is this me talking about going home? Can it be true, the daddy that loves his precious girl and his two little guys is really going home? Happy day!

We saw "The Scarlet Angel" tonight. Technicolor picture--95%. You'd enjoy it, I believe. Our heater was fouled up tonight. Charlie and I worked on it for 30 minutes and almost froze to death in the process. Brrrr. It sure gets cold after the sun goes down. I wonder how on earth the Koreans keep warm in their little grass and mud huts. Glad my little gang is comfy cozy. Don't worry about your old man getting cold, honey, I've got it made.

I love you,
Daddy

Friday, 17 Oct 52
With the 1st in the rear
with the gear, Korea

Dearest doll girl,
    Col Jack Cram of MACG-2 forwarded a picture of us taken by Harry Hjorth, the assistant to the vice president in charge of military sales of the Douglas Aircraft Co. of Santa Monica, California. I wrote Harry this morning and thanked him. I'll send it on to you, darling. It's a 4"x7" enlargement of his snap. I believe it turned out fine, don't you? Wait until you see it and I'm sure you'll agree. I sure have made a lot of contacts in my capacity as air officer. They may do me some good either in the Corps or in civilian life, who knows?
    The whole camp was covered with a thick white frost this morning and, boy, was it cold! We had heater troubles again this morning for a while but finally got it squared away.
    I'm going to buy the very first Christmas tree that's sold in Los Angeles and decorate it, and those kiddies of ours are going to have the finest Christmas any two kids ever had anywhere. I believe Ricky is ready for a bike this time. I'll build the boys another car and give the old truck I made to Beck Satzky for her kids. Ricky could use some nice woodworking tools, and I'll devote a lot of time instructing him in the use and care of tools because a man really needs that knowledge all through his life.
    I think some of the pent-up feelings inside me have been replaced by a more calm, relaxed approach to many things, including having more patience than I used to have. I think you'll be very pleasantly impressed by the new daddy, possessing all the best traits of the old daddy and some late improvements. Just drive it and you'll buy it--ha, ha, sounds like an ad for a new car, doesn't it? I'm in rare form today--wish I were home right now.
    Today I have to do some work on my air report for the month and also Major McLeod has asked me to prepare an Air Annex to his Amphibious Operations Plan for the regiment. Some title, eh? I can do it, though. Better get to it.
                               Love you all,
                                      Daddy

18 Oct 52
1st Marines in Reserve, Korea

Dearest family,
    I spent a very interesting and unusual day today. I drove into the Division CP and ANGLICO where my radio jeep was undergoing a checkup. We left the cargo jeep, picked up the radio jeep and went over to the special service section of ANGLICO, where I checked in the two shotguns I had checked out on the 14th. I'd let my men use them the whole time. They have been bagging on the average of three birds a day, with this morning as no exception. They cleaned the pheasants and will give them to me tomorrow. I'll have our cook fry them for us officers at noon. My boys are getting a little tired of pheasant.
    Scrounging for a new windshield and top for our jeep, we finally located the survey dump for trucks and jeeps and found a perfect windshield with two wiper motors, lines and blades, and switched the whole works. Even found an old top which we took to use as a "changie change", as the Koreans say. If you've got something to turn in for something else, you can usually make an exchange. They are in the process of winterizing everything, which includes side curtains, water heaters for the jeeps, anti-freeze and light weight oil in the engine and gear boxes.
    When we arrived at VMO-6 it was almost lunch time, so I went in and sat down to eat. There I ran into Gus Dake who had just come to the rear (VMO-6) a few minutes before to carry out a special errand for his CO. Seems Gus had met an Army colonel down in Seoul, or Japan--I forget. Anyway, this colonel is in charge of all railroads in South Korea. There is plenty of lumber available in Pusan, where nearly all the shipping is unloaded, but very little space available on the freight trains for such items as lumber. Gus invited me to go along while he delivered two beautiful, fat pheasants he had shot this morning to the colonel in Seoul. We took off at 1400 and twenty minutes later (I flew it, honey! What a thrill to fly a copter HTL-4

1ST MARINE REGIMENT IS RELIEVED ON THE MAIN LINE OF RESISTANCE

Bell!) Gus landed it in a parking lot with a bunch of Army trucks, leaving the engine running with me at the controls, while he contacted his friend and gave him the birds.

As I waited, about 50 Koreans, who were working for the Army in this truck compound, came and sat about 50' from the copter, laughing, pointing, and jumping all around like crazy. Apparently they had never seen a copter before, especially not one so close. It wasn't a copter landing site we set down on, just a parking lot. Fifteen minutes later off we took, zooming low over the housetops and looking down into the private yards of the Korean dwellings, over school yards and old bombed-out factories, busy streets, and finally into the outskirts and never-ending fields of yellow rice waving in the breeze. Koreans everywhere were cutting their rice and beating it beside every road and in every village, house and yard along the way.

I certainly got a thrill out of our flight today. Gus let me handle the controls all the way from VMO-6 to Seoul, a distance of about 20 miles, I'd guess. I flew in and out of valleys, up rivers and over roads and had a whopping good time. The low altitude of 300' allowed me to see a heck of a lot more than I could from an OE. We are required to fly a minimum of 1000' near Seoul in the OE. No limit on copters. I took two rolls of pictures today, some on the ground and some in the air from the copter. One especially interesting picture is of about 3000 Korean children, all in white, parading on their school yard.

I took care of Col Layer's Air Medal also at VMO-6, and found out he had flown about 28 red missions since July, easily qualifying him for an Air Medal, which is issued on the basis of twenty missions. Additionally, his missions have nearly all been in OEs on dangerous recon flights over the front lines. About five OEs have been shot down and 10 Marines lost due to enemy ground fire since I've been here. I won't be taking any more front line recons, so don't you worry about me, honey girl.

Major French of ANGLICO told me today I could go to Japan on a special mission for him and stay five days if I wanted to. I didn't care to go, so I selected Capt Layne of the 1st Bn/1st and he was tickled pink. He leaves tomorrow morning. I asked him to buy a set of wood block prints and send them to Harold and Mary Colwell, which he said he'd be glad to do for me. By the way, dear, please tell me what you'd like me to buy on my way through Japan on my way home. I can't remember a thing you've asked except "binopulars" as Ricky calls them, for your dad. Don't mention too many things or I'll be delayed in Japan too long.

After my talk with Tony Catarino the other day, I believe the new FACs will arrive here about the 20th of Nov, so I'll be shoving off any time after that, honey girl. Golly, that's only 33 more days. When this letter reaches you, I'll only have 26 more days to do and when I receive your letter in answer to this one, I'll only have 19 days left. I can go through 19 days with my eyes closed.

I ran into Capt Watson of the 1st Bn/1st today while at VMO-6 and he expressed a desire to relieve me as Reg Air Officer. I had asked him first, though, and also had talked to Col Layer about him. Watson could relieve me earlier if I could swing it, but I'm not counting on it because it's a matter of waiting orders from the Wing down at K3.

Rec'd yours of 10 Oct today, darling. Love you, precious girl. Kiss my two little guys and tell them their daddy loves them very much.

Your very own Daddy

19 Oct 52
With the 1st Marines in Korea

Dear Marion,
I've got to get busy on my report tomorrow and also the Air Annex to the Amphibious problem. Everyone keeps telling me how lucky I am, only having to do one more month on this rock.

Here come four aircraft on station overhead to work with the Div. First a/c we've had for some time. Thank God things have been fairly quiet up there for the past couple of weeks. I hope and pray it stays that way. I attended church services at 1030 this morning in the mess hall. The chaplain tried to show us that God is not responsible for all this killing. I know God isn't, but it's hard to figure things out sometimes.

I heard Radio Moscow today, broadcast in English, claiming that America says there isn't enough food for all the peoples on the earth and that Americans have come up with a plan for killing millions of people in certain parts of the world to alleviate this problem. He says the Russians have a better plan, Communism, which will put food in the mouths of all peoples. What a bunch of trash they are putting out! I can't stand to listen to more than a minute or two of his jabber because every time I hear it I feel like busting up the radio. They are sure planting the seeds of WWIII, honey girl, just as sure as you were born. If it comes, I hope it happens before our little guys are of military age. I've often hoped my participation in these two wars might somehow keep my little guys from it. Perhaps it's too much to hope for. Maybe we'll prevent it if we get strong enough.

We had our briefing this evening and the engineers announced that a new bridge crossing the Imjin would be completed by the 23rd of Oct. I'm glad to hear this because those kids on the other side of the river would be in rough shape if the goonies chose to put the pressure on them. They'll do anything for you short of the impossible.

All for now, dear. Give my boys a hug and keep one for yourself.

Love, Daddy

20 Oct 52
1st Marines, Korea
Monday 1630

Dearest girl,

Just finished a razzle-dazzle volley ball game. Our side lost but I was in there pitching all the way. We won the first game, then they won the second and we were up to 13-13 on the third game and they snatched the last two winning points, drat it. It was the best game we've had here in the reserves. We had a lot of swell games when we were up on the line at Reg CP. No games at Battalion, however.

Let's see, what happened today that would be of interest? Oh yes, honey, my Silver Star from the 1st Marine Air Wing is confirmed. They called me up from ANGLICO and told me this afternoon. I'm so thrilled. Nothing could mean more to me, next to the Congressional Medal of Honor, and my precious family, of course. Silver Stars are hard come by, honey, in this man's war, especially aviators. They told me the ceremonies would be at Division Headquarters on the morning of 10 Nov, with parade, pomp, band and the works. Happy day, oh happy day! Wish you were here, honey, and we'd celebrate. Oh well, darling, we'll have all kinds of time when the daddy gets home to do everything under the sun.

My training program came off very well today, thanks to Gus Dake. You remember I had told you about it some time ago about having the new HO5-S Sikorsky helicopter fly around to my three battalions, land and give practical instruction to all the hospital corpsmen and air team enlisted men. The copter arrived here at 0830, when Gus picked up Doctor Murdock (the regimental surgeon) and flew to all three battalions, giving an hour's lecture at each spot. Doc Murdock said Gus gave them a lot of very helpful advice. Some of the fellows were new draft men who would be handling casualties, lighting strips, making copter strips, bringing copters in at night and so forth. They all profited from the lecture and demonstrations; perhaps it will mean the saving of lives because of their added knowledge now. I sure hope so. Gus and I have made a date to meet at VMO-6 on 1 Nov to have dinner and a chat. Otherwise, I won't get to see him because he's across the river now at Wonderful Forward Echelon. I could drive over and see him but it's a long, dusty, bumpy trip by jeep and, if he's had a hard night of flying evacs, he'll probably not welcome any visitors.

Wrote Ben and Uncle Art and Aunt Julia, enclosing the picture you sent of Randy sitting on our driveway wearing his new Japanese clothes and holding his car and elephant. I think his expression there is very much like Uncle Art's. Perhaps they can see it too. I'm anxious to find out if they do think so because Randy is their little dream boy anyway. I haven't heard from them for months, have you?

My radio has been full of static lately, so much so I can hardly make anything out. Climatic conditions, no doubt. Bugs Bunny just came up through a hole in our floor. It gave me a

1ST MARINE REGIMENT IS RELIEVED ON THE MAIN LINE OF RESISTANCE

little start there for a second. His nose came out, then his ears popped out, and then the rest of his body. He knows his name and will come to anyone who calls him Bugs. Charlie Reifel is feeding him soda crackers now. I'd love to have Bugs at home for the boys. They'd love him.

It's been very warm today, the warmest we've had for several weeks. The dentist, Doc Mitchell, is always pulling wise cracks on the volley ball court. Today he said, "You've got a lovely set of teeth, but your gums have to come out." Then he asked Stan Craymac if he didn't think his hair was getting too thin and Stan came back with, "So who wants fat hair?" We have our little gags now and then. There are a bunch of swell guys here in the regiment and I'd like to hang on to them, even if only through letters. I'll drop them a line or two every now and then after I get home.

Col Cornell called today and asked me to appoint one of my FACs to go to the Air Force ground support school in Japan for a week. I selected one of the two that replaced Biehl and me at the 3rd Bn. I told them to draw straws. Oh yes, the letters of commendations Biehl and I wrote for our four enlisted men came through; I believe they'll be presented to them at ANGLICO on 10 Nov also. I called and told them and they were happy to hear of it. They are PFC Bowman (Little Red), Cpl Boone, Cpl Evans and Sgt Walwood.

I finally got Col Layer a hop in an HTL-4 helicopter to recon our sector that we will occupy when the 1st Reg moves up to the front again. Had a heck of a time obtaining one for him, parts and availability being so low. At present VMO-6 has about (12) HRS Sikorskys, (8) HO5-Ss and (8) HTL-4 Bells. As for OE scout planes, of the four VMO-6 got from the Army a few weeks ago, there is only one left but, together with the six they had previously, they now have a total of seven. Most of those lost have been disabled by enemy groundfire. At this rate, I'd say we'll soon be in dire straights as far as recon aircraft are concerned.

Don't know what's for dinner yet. Am about ready to depart for the mess hall, however, and find out. No mail. Love you and adore you, precious girl.

Daddy

HELICOPTER QUALIFIED AT LAST

Tues. 21 Oct 52, 2000
1st Marines, Korea

Darling Marion and precious boys
Ricky and Randy,

Happy day--received three letters from the baby girl--13, 14, 15 Oct and one from Mom and Aunt Edna. Felt great getting some mail. Randy is a rascal, going out of the yard without permission, telling fibs, being mean to his little playmate, spilling water in the garage and all kinds of naughty things. Tell him Christmas isn't very far off and, if he expects Daddy or Santa Clause to bring him any toys, he'd better snap out of it.

You're killing me, telling me of all the luscious pies and cookies you're baking. You'll have to do plenty when I get home, sweetheart, because I've got a powerful hankering for your home cooking and baking.

So Ricky is kissing his sweetheart already, eh? He's making out better than I ever did. Guess he must be his mother's in that respect. He doesn't take after me. I don't think I got the nerve until I was around 12 or so, then in a game of post office at a party. This younger generation, I don't know what they're coming to. Ha, ha! Brother, I hope I never find myself saying that in earnest about those kids. From what I've seen lately, I can only say let them live and get as much out of life as they can because life can be very, very short for some of those kids.

As I'm writing, the tent is shaking from a windstorm of upwards of 30 mph. It's raining very hard and the cold wind is whipping up through the cracks in our floor. This morning, as promised, I took Doc Tom Craighead down to VMO-6 and got him a hop in an OE to Ascom city, then to K16 Seoul where he could catch another plane and, if he made proper connections, he would be in Japan by 1500 and be able to catch the evening plane for Uncle Sugar. I didn't fly him myself because another pilot was already scheduled. I did get in a flight, however, in an HTL-4 Bell copter with Maj Joe Frietas. I was sitting in the ready room reading some late air *publications when an emergency call came in for plasma. Joe asked if I'd like to go along, so I did. We took off for "A" Med. and I flew it and landed it, then took off after we loaded on the plasma. I flew it on up the Imjin River to avoid the heavily mined area (in case of power failure) and about 15 minutes later came to "E" Med., where I landed it and we transferred the plasma to an ambulance that sped off a few seconds later.*

Our mission completed, Joe let me fly it around, heading generally back toward VMO-6 across valleys, along roads, over Koreans working in their fields harvesting rice. Hedge-hopping in a copter is just about as much fun as in a plane. We were perking along at 80 mph carrying 22" manifold pressure, 3000 rpm on the engine. What a thrill! Of course it can't be compared to flying in a jet, but it's a thrill in a different way. I'll try to explain it to you honey: The pilot and copilot each have a set of controls complete. Each has a collective stick with throttle and a set of tail control pedals (sometimes called torque control pedals), and a cyclic stick. After the engine is started, it is revved up to 3000 rpm and remains at that rpm throughout takeoff, climbing, cruising, letdown and landing. The collective stick is full down when you're sitting on the ground; as the hand throttle is turned counter clockwise and 3000 rpm is registered on the engine, you know that you then have the necessary rpm on your main rotor blades which turn only 300 rpm, or 1/10th the speed of the engine. As you read 300 rpm you raise up the cyclic stick, hold hard left rudder to compensate for the heavy torque of the main rotor and you're off in a cloud of dust--literally. What a wind machine a copter is!

Now, after you pick up forward speed of approximately 70 mph, the main rotor begins to receive the effect of the forward motion of the plane and you can gradually come back down on the collective stick to about 22" of HG (manifold pressure) which is nothing more than an instrument that measures engine power but is handy to watch in order not to over stress your engine. Cruise setting is 22", where you clamp down on your throttle and collective, and you needn't bother about using them again during your flight until you want to land the little monster. The direction of flight is controlled mainly by the cyclic stick, the rudders having little more to do than to keep the tail end in back of you where it belongs. (It's possible to fly along with your tail off to either side of the flight path without appreciably affecting your flight path). To climb at any great speed it is necessary to come up on the collective a few inches of HG, which is in effect increasing the blade angle of the main rotor only enough to increase your lift needed for the climb desired. It is possible, however, to climb at a slower rate by the sole use of the cyclic stick pulled aft slightly, or to lose altitude by a forward pressure. Left or right can be accomplished by pressure on the cyclic stock in the desired direction of bank or turn as you wish.

Next, the landing is really the thing that fouls up a conventional fixed-wing pilot. Actually, it's the exact opposite of the copter's takeoff. First, it's necessary to lose your altitude and approach your landing site at about 100' altitude. You ease down on the collective to 15" HG and the copter begins to settle toward the ground--you still have forward speed, however, and you can lose that very quickly by coming back on the cyclic which raises your nose slightly, slowing the plane down. <u>Now</u> is where it gets rough. Remember, I told you when we took off, our forward speed allowed us to come off on the collective, but now we've lost forward speed and we'd plop to the ground if we didn't come up again on the collective, increasing our angle of attack of the main rotor blades, which fairly suspends us in the air--all forward motion being stopped. It's a small matter to let yourself back down to the ground by gradually easing down on the collective and, finally on the ground, pushing the collective full down and turning the hand throttle to the right, cutting down the engine rpm to around 2200 for on-the-ground idle. That's all there is to it. Simple--yeah, all except coordinating the darn things.

I heard a good joke today. Seems as how the commander of a stateside regiment returned to the base camp with his troops after 30 days in the field. He thought it his duty to give fair warning to the WAC commander of the necessity of keeping her girls in the barracks for a few days until his boys cooled off. The WAC commander in reply and tapping a finger at her head (indicating brains) said, "Oh, you don't have to worry about my girls, Colonel, they have it up here."

The colonel came back with, "I don't care <u>where</u> they've got it, my boys can find it." Ha, ha!

1ST MARINE REGIMENT IS RELIEVED ON THE MAIN LINE OF RESISTANCE

Let's see now, I've given you an account of my day's doings except the trip back in the jeep without a top in the pouring rain. I was soaked to the skin and the four streams we had forded previously without any strain were running swift and deep. In places I thought the darn jeep was going to flood out, but luck was with us and we made it home safely. After I dried off and ate a good dinner, all was right with the world, at least for a little while.

At 1830 I gave the colonel's briefing up on top of his hill, and going to and from his briefing tent got wet again. Boy, is that rain cold! The little old heater ran out of oil tonight and, in the rain, I went out and changed cans with Maj McLeod's help. Can hear the artillery booming away tonight; even in the rain and cold the hammering goes on.

Out of the entire reg't TACPs I selected two men to go on R&R in Japan, leaving on the 25th. Capt Lyon of the 1st/1st hasn't left yet on his R&R but will tomorrow; likewise Capt Norlin of the 3rd/1st. I don't care for an R&R. All I want to do is come home to the most precious girl in the world and to pick up where we left off, honey. I hope I can forget world affairs for a while and just concentrate on my little family for a change.

I will try for some more helicopter flying whenever I have the chance. I'm well checked out now, according to Captain Gus Dake and Major Joe Frietas of VMO-6. In fact, they are telling me I'm fully qualified.

Daddy

22 Oct 52
1st Marines, Korea
Wednesday, 1900

Dearest family,

This morning Maj Charlie Reifel and I jeeped into VMO-6 where we waited several hours for our HTL-4 Bell copter. Charlie took the first one at 1130 while I stayed at VMO-6 and had chow, then took off at 1300 in another Bell piloted by Maj Mitciff. We dropped a sergeant off at Ascom City, then proceeded over to the hospital ship Consolation, landing on the stern of the ship in a 30-mph wind. I dashed on down to pick up Maj Reifel. He was visiting Maj Bud Honeycutt who had been operated on Monday, the 20th, for hemorrhoids. He was lying on his side still suffering from his operation, and he'll be another three weeks on the ship. Saw one nurse who directed me to Bud's room. Homely but smelling of perfume, it was a treat just to see a white woman after so many weeks. When she spoke, it was a surprise to hear a high-pitched voice after hearing nothing but men's voices for so long.

I found Charlie talking to Bud and I chatted with him for a few minutes, then Charlie and I shoved off for our copter that was turning up on the fantail.

Maj Mitciff took off and we buzzed down close to the water to pick up speed, then banked her over toward the docks where the Korean boats--thousands of them--were lined up along the shore, high and dry because of low tide. Coal was being unloaded from them. They will shove off when high tide comes in again this afternoon, according to Maj Mitciff who flies over there on hospital runs quite a bit. Inchon Harbor only had a few ships in there and amphibious trucks were cruising back and forth from ship to shore. There are a lot of little islands with just one hut on them and every inch of land under cultivation. Lots of bombed-out factories and docks. Must have been a thriving harbor prior to the war.

We were airborne exactly one hour and the wind really buffeted that little Bell around. Things pass by fast when you're cruising along at 70-80 mph at 100' off the deck. Every piece of land flat enough to be flooded with water has been planted to rice this year and the harvest is booming. Everywhere you look there are acres upon acres of yellow waving rice and the Koreans of every age are out harvesting it. They cut it off at the base which is the water line, tie it in bundles 8" in diameter, stack it and dry it. Then a few days later they beat it over a log and the rice kernels fall off. They use the straw for roofing and siding on the houses and for a ground cover.

Arrived back at VMO-6 at 1400 and jeeped back to our CP by 1500, had five volleyball games--won four. Received a package and letter from Joe Marshall of AiResearch signed by 37 of the boys. Joe sent a tooth brush, tooth powder, shampoo, pepperoni sausage roll, olives, canned chicken soup, pills, 1/2-pint Welch's sweet wine, canned clams, can of mushrooms, chapstick and hard candy. Charlie and Mac and I made short work of the sausage, and they have their eye on the clams and chicken already--the dogs. I'll write Joe and thank him. It had been packed and mailed by AiResearch shipping department. Boy, they really had it wrapped up but good!

Received the AiReporter today too, honey, postmarked 14 Oct on the regular 1st class postage. They must send everything air mail.

Let's see, what's new with me tonight. I'm still tasting the sausage--brother, is it highly spiced! I shouldn't have eaten it so fast. Don't you send me anything, dear. I don't need a thing.

Bugs is cute. He pushes the door open to come in, jumps up on your cot, licks your hand. What a rabbit--spends a lot of time in our tent. My legs are a little tired from all the volley ball this afternoon. Beat Charlie four games straight running in Ping-Pong at VMO-6 while waiting for our Bell rides. My El Toro skill hasn't been lost. Love that game!

Love you, dearest girl--am counting the days remaining--29 to go. Can it possibly be me going home to my darlings in only 29 days? Yippee! I'll love taking up where I left off. Kiss the little guys for me.

It's been quiet in the Marine sector, for which I am very grateful. Keep up the prayers, dear.

Love, Daddy

23 Oct 52
1st Marines in Reserve, Korea
Thursday 1900

Dearest family,

The friendly artillery is very active tonight. The tent is billowing from the shock waves even though we are several miles away. It's been a continuous pounding for over an hour. Hope a push doesn't develop. We don't get the complete picture here in reserves like we used to up on the lines. We get it all in the morning, however. The Div, of course, is up on everything and in case of a breakthrough or a big enemy push where our assistance would be required, we would be notified posthaste.

The biggest part of the day I spent writing my air report for the month and I believe it will be a "masterpiece" by the time it's typed once in the rough, corrected and then final typed. I've edited it twice with my dictionary for misspelled words and found quite a few. I wrote 2000 well chosen words on all the special activities conducted within the Regiment from 28 Sep until today, including the air strikes inside the six-mile circle; also our experimenting with tank searchlights marking targets at night for close air support; also the move from the MLR to our blocking positions and the whole story about the helicopter lift of the 2nd Battalion during the move. Wrote hundreds of words about our training program and suggestions for equipment changes and team organizations, both at Reg and Bn level. I didn't hold any punches and, since it's all going into ANGLICO diary to become a permanent part of the 1stMarDiv Command diary, I suppose Col Glick and Maj French at ANGLICO will ask me to take it easy in the future. The darn equipment is shot and it's really a pity what they hand the air teams and still expect them to do the job.

The air has been scoosh over the Division front since we pulled off the lines 12 Oct. Today was the heaviest day for air over the Divy since then. We had three air strikes all coming on station after 1700 this afternoon. I got a call from Col Glick of ANGLICO asking me if I would let Capt Layne of 1/1 replace Capt MacAdersky, the air officer of the 5th Reg. I talked to Col Long today and he doesn't want him to go. Seems like Mac of the 5th has rubbed his colonel the wrong way. His colonel is probably down on him for not getting much air for his regiment. Actually, there is little a regimental air officer can do for his battalions besides going through normal TAR channels, which is what Mac has been doing. None of these other regiments are as on-the-ball as the First. All the battalions within the 1st have a heck of a high spirit and pride in their respective units. The 5th and 7th seem sloppy somehow.

1ST MARINE REGIMENT IS RELIEVED ON THE MAIN LINE OF RESISTANCE

My boys drove to Div today to pick up some 10-gauge shotgun shells, to do some pheasant shooting for me on special request of Col Layer because the general will be here for lunch tomorrow and he wants to treat him with a feed of fried wild pheasant. What a delicious meat it is, honey. Have you ever eaten any? They keep five 10-gauge shotguns here in Reg CP special services tent for the men to use for hunting purposes, but the guards (security) have been using them to shoot yobos (South Koreans) they catch stealing from our area at night; then they don't turn them back in to special services for the men to use in the early morning hours to go hunting. I talked to the special services officer and asked him to reserve two guns last night for my men this morning, but the jerk didn't do it and my kids got up at 0500 in the freezing cold for nothing. He told me they would be available this evening for the boys again but my sergeant just called me and said all the guns were gone again. He's sore and I don't blame him--especially after driving over 20 miles to get the shots for it and not getting back until after dark. He stopped in to see me when he returned and his nose, ears and cheeks were cherry red from the cold night air. Our jeep hasn't any top, either, so it's extra cold riding in it. I'm going on a campaign tomorrow to procure a jeep top somewhere, someplace, somehow. My boys spent three days digging out by hand, using small entrenching shovels, a tent area and radio jeep parking area and road up in the new sector where we will be moving when the Regiment moves up in middle Nov, only to find out today that we are moving into a new area. Just little tidbits like that are what shakes a guy up. The Div makes these changes without regard to the Regiment's feelings.

We saw a movie the other night and one of the funny men in it kept saying, "Let's live a little," so it has taken hold here in the Regiment, especially among the young 2nd lieutenants, and you hear it said about 50 times a day . . . .

Love ya,
Daddy

COMMUNIST FORCES OVERRUN THE CANADIANS ON OUR RIGHT FLANK

24 Oct 52
1st Marines in Reserve, Korea
Friday 1815

Dearest family,
   Never left the CP today, just hung around here and tended to a few loose ends that have come up from time to time. Handled an investigation in regard to a jeep accident and also piddled around with a report or two, gandered at the Sept issue of <u>Life</u> and almost started Two Years before the Mast, *but never quite got into it.*
   Played seven games of volleyball this afternoon and we won five. Charlie Reifel and Col Long really set them up for me to spike. We have a wonderful time playing. Everyone argues profusely about whether or not the ball landed on a line or whether someone was in the net. We go around and around and have lots of laughs. Golly, it's absolutely the only form of recreation we have here in Korea except hiking, which is hazardous because of land mines unless you stick to the roads and then the dust from the traffic is terrible, so it narrows down to volleyball anyway you figure it, but we all enjoy it so we've got no gripe.
   We had a little excitement around here. Seems a patrol around the area here found a body of a Marine, supposedly, that had been dead around a year to the best of the grave registration man's ability to guess. He had on last year's winter issue Marine type clothing, and wore a Marine type issue wrist watch too, but he had on spike shoes of the Australian or Canadian variety. They are searching records now to determine who it could be and will probably resort to dental examination.
   The Canadians, our neighbors, got hit very hard last night by an estimated reinforced battalion (1200 men). They overran the Canadians' main line of resistance, a very serous loss, but by 0300 this morning they had regained their lost positions and were consolidated. It must have been a rugged attack supported by thousands of rounds of artillery because we could hear the fight all night. You never know when you're lying in the basket what's going to develop

from their pushes. They aren't very far from us. We could be deployed in their support at any time because we are in their same Corps area. I don't think it will happen, however.

This is top secret--no mention of what I'm going to say. The enemy is always interested in our maneuvers. The Canadians are shifting their lines left towards ours a bit and the shift will necessitate a move of our Regimental CP. The 7th CP will not be utilized. In other words, when our regiment moves up we will move into a new sector. I'm not sure whether we will have time to construct a new Reg CP, troop the area and learn the terrain prior to 30 Oct which is the date we have been informed will be the move date. I hope to be out of here by then though. Capt Watson, my relief, will be up here a few days before we move and will learn my job and meet all the officers here in the 1st Reg CP.

Had hamburger patties, mashed spuds and gravy, string beans and chopped ham, coffee, spice cake. I was starved, especially after all that volleyball. I showed all my pictures to the boys as they gathered here in our tent. They have never seen that type of colored print before. They are going to try it themselves as soon as they can get some of the colored film.

My radio is knocking itself out on shortwave from Australia. They have a swell request program they present every night for the Australian and British forces in the Australia area, Korea and Japan. Most of the tunes played are American, however. The announcer's name is Leslie. May send in a request song some time.

Finally got a copter approved for the 1/1 CO and the 2/1's-XO tomorrow morning. Took a lot of doing but finally got their blessing up at Div Air Office.

Movie tonight is "Drums in the Deep South." Seems as though I've seen it but I'm not sure. Guess I'll go and find out. My time is so valuable I hate to waste it in any duplication. Ha, Ha.

One of the Captains going home on 15 Nov said that returning reservists are being processed to inactive duty directly out of the San Francisco office in a matter of some 72 hours. Isn't it fun just talking about it? Golly, coming home. Can it be true? I've thought about it, hoped and prayed for it, and now it's almost here and I can hardly believe that in only 27 days I'll be leaving for good old Uncle Sugar and the most precious family any daddy ever had. I'm sure crazy about you, honey doll. I always have been head over heals in love with you right from the start. You knocked me for a loop with that first kiss and I've been in a tailspin ever since. Love that spin I'm in!

Bye bye, Daddy

PLAYING TIPPY TOE WITH LAND MINES

25 Oct 52
Saturday evening

Dearest family,

My tummy is full of wild pheasant deep fried in oleo by my enlisted men. They invited me up to their tent where they had a pan of flour, pheasant all cut into nice sizes, a can of oleo and a nice hot fire going in the space heater. I had my choice of coke, beer or coffee. I took the coffee and pheasant. It was wonderful. I have never tasted anything so delicious in my whole life, honey.

Charlie and I drove over to the new Regimental CP area this morning and cased the joint. Only a KSC (Korean Service Corps) outfit is over there at the present time. It's a very nice area, completely untouched by tractor, jeep or truck. The KSC is near the road, as they were afraid to venture too far back up the draw because of land mines. Charlie and I went hunting up in the draw and thrashed around for three and a half hours without touching off any mines. We scared up about 10 pheasants. Charlie had the only shotgun and he got two roosters but we could only find one, try as we might. The grass was deeper than our armpits and it was very difficult going.

General Baird and Col Layer came up at 1100 to inspect the proposed new CP site and there Charlie and I were shooting pheasant. The general complimented Charlie on his kill

1ST MARINE REGIMENT IS RELIEVED ON THE MAIN LINE OF RESISTANCE

and wished us success in finding the one in the tall grass. No luck. We sent down to the KSC camp and had about 10 yobos come up in the draw to help us look for it but they were scared to death. They kept shouting, "Mines! Mines! Mines!" pointing to themselves and adding, "Hava no!" throwing their hands in the air, apparently trying to indicate what would happen to them if they hit a mine. Charlie and I figured it out, though, and it just wasn't good mining area. It wasn't a through draw and didn't afford a good approach corridor for either tanks or troops in an assault. So, being a good infantry officer, I plowed right along behind Charlie-- about 15 feet (ha, ha, just in case he tripped one, I'd be far enough in back of him to avoid getting clobbered). I seriously doubt if there are any mines in there and it's my opinion the KSC said there were because they didn't want to break up their camp.

No mail today, darling--maybe tomorrow. It's getting colder and colder over here. I'm sitting on my cot some eight feet from the space heater with my dungarees on, woolen socks, boots and a woolen sweater, cotton undershirt, leather jacket, and I'm still a little chilly. Bet it will dip way below freezing tonight. It's had an early start.

Finished my reports all up. No more until next month; then I think I'll have my relief do it. Twenty-six days until the 20th of Nov, honey girl. I'm so darn excited about coming home I can't think about anything besides it any more. I love you all so very much. Kiss my little guys for me, honey.

Your very own Daddy

MEMORIAL SERVICES FOR OUR FALLEN COMRADES

26 Oct 52
Sunday evening

Dearest girl,
Today was rather unusual in that I met MGen Vernon E. Megee, who is on tour out here in Korea. He is presently commanding general of Air Fleet Marine Force Pacific, of which First Marine Air Wing is a part. Col Layer called me at about 0800 this morning and told me of the general's arrival by helicopter here at our CP at 1040. He asked that I contact all of the battalion FACs and have them here when he arrived. Only Daniels of the 2nd, Watson of the 1st, Brunnworth of the 3rd and myself were on hand. Col Layer and I were at the strip to meet the general and his aide, a captain. Col Cornell was also with him. We walked over to Col Layer's quarters, perched on a hill above the rest of our camp, where we joined the other FACs. We talked of air support for 25 minutes, with Layer giving Daniels and me a verbal pat on the back with his praises every now and then. Daniels requested of the general an extension to remain out here in Korea, but to rejoin his F9F Panther jet squadron, VMF-311 at K3 for several more months. The general said he would see to it that it was carried out.

Gen Megee is a small man, standing only 5'6" tall and weighing about 135 pounds. I'd estimate his age at 55 years. He's quite gray and wrinkled but a nice little guy, very informal, put us captains at ease right away. He shoved off at 1105 for a visit with the 5th and 7th Marines before leaving again for the Wing and possibly the States, although there was some talk of him relieving General Jerome of the 1st MAW.

We four FACs ate lunch together while discussing problems pertaining to our various units. They read my report and made some constructive comments regarding some omissions. We planned a course of instruction with regard to the TACP teams while in reserve. I have to go into ANGLICO tomorrow morning to check on availability of training films that will aid our boys, especially in regard to radio procedure, maintenance and security. If they have the proper film, I'm going to grab it and show it here at Reg, splitting the TACP teams into two separate groups so they will always have one half of their team available in case of an emergency.

At 1400 this afternoon I went down to Randall Field, a newly constructed OE field around the bend from our CP here, and attended the memorial services for the kids killed in the 1st Reg while we were on the line. The majority of the 170 killed, 1709 wounded and 28 missing in action were under the 3rd Bn's control during Bunker Hill. The other battalions turned their *companies over to our control because our battalion was on the line in the Bunker Hill sector. The 2nd Bn relieved us on about 14 Sep or thereabouts, but the fighting had tapered off and the majority of the casualties had occurred with our battalion prior to the battalion change date. Our battalion shows the least killed, but that's because our companies, attached originally to the 3rd Bn, had outposts and MLR positions and the other battalions fed their companies through our MLR. Our 3rd Bn companies were later relieved on the MLR. The figure of 170 sounds rather light to me in view of the number of terribly battered bodies, though apparently still alive, that I either saw at collecting points or aided in the helicopter evacuations during those terrible middle and late days of last August and part of September.*

There were about 3000 infantrymen there at the memorial services and I had my picture taken with Col Layer and Gen Pollock (CO of the 1stMarDiv) on my camera. That film is completed now and it contains about six pictures of the services today.

Right now the 7th Marines are being hit and Maj McLeod's telephone is ringing like mad, giving the blow-by-blow account of the fighting. The artillery is hammering out hundreds of rounds of shells in support of our 7th Marines now being overrun. Brother, won't there ever be a let up in this horrible killing? Don't worry about the daddy, honey, because we're the reserve regiment and things would really have to come to a sorry pass to get the 1st Marine Regimental Staff up there in the fight. They will commit the battalions of our 1st Regiment, however, if need be. I shouldn't have mentioned it to you, darling, because the Marines can handle the situation, I'm confident. I'll add a few lines in the morning, honey, to let you know how things turn out.

The 1stMarDiv band was there today at the memorial services and they played beautifully. The national anthem and then marching songs, or tunes, I should say. When the service ended, the troops certainly looked sharp and marched well to the band music as they left the area. There wasn't a parade nor did they march in review. [Also see Appenidx Number 7.]

I'll enclose a copy of the memorial service, honey, in my letter. I have a second copy I may send to Eddie Butler and the boys at AiResearch, just to let them know too that there are kids fighting and dying out here in far off Korea for a principle. If we let Communism run rampant, everything we hold dear to us in our wonderful United States of America will be swallowed up. It seems hard to believe that we are fighting for our very lives and the lives and freedom of our loved ones, but a guy only has to stick his head up out of his trench on the MLR at the wrong time and he'll get all the convincing he needs. Turn on the radio to Radio Moscow and listen to the poison they put out. Read Vishinsky's address to the latest UN congregation in N.Y. if you need any more convincing, and if then one can't judge the situation in its true light, there's no use going any further because he's probably a Communist and wouldn't believe you if you spoke the truth. A Commy in the U.S. had better keep out of my way, honey, or else there will be dire consequences. They are spreading the same poison as was spread in China and North Korea and we are paying the horrible price. Or better I should say, our kids have paid and are still paying with their precious lives. All for tonight on this subject.

It was only 28° this morning but it felt like zero. We might as well be sleeping outside for all the protection our tent affords us in the way of warmth. Darned if I can keep warm in my sleeping bag. Tonight I put on my long underwear for the first time. I've had my upper on a couple of times during the day but haven't worn either part to bed as yet. I have been wearing my woolen sweater and socks every night for some time however. The cracks in the floor are a quarter inch wide in places and the old wind just comes a-racing in here. The only way we can keep warm evenings is to huddle around the stove, which the three of us are now doing.

We had our usual volleyball this afternoon and it really pooped the old man, I can tell you. My legs felt like Jello when we finished but they feel fine now. Chow tonight was pretty good--ham, sweet potatoes and peas; donuts and coffee for dessert. Bugs was cute today, eating apple and graham crackers out of our hands. Then he'd lie down beside the fire like a cat or dog. I've never in my life seen a rabbit so tame. Once in a while he'll hear a noise and jump up and dart for his special hole in the floor. He has his own special water can and he had part of McLeod's beer again this afternoon. Loves beer! I realize this is all probably very hard for you to believe, but wait until you get my pictures developed; they will back up at least part of my

1ST MARINE REGIMENT IS RELIEVED ON THE MAIN LINE OF RESISTANCE

story. I hear a fellow talking to Bugs right now. He's up the hill in back of our tent about 25 yards. Everyone chats with him just as though he understood every word they were saying.

Precious girl that I love, our day is slowly but very definitely and methodically approaching. My little guys will probably knock me for a row of tenpins but I'll love it. The whole lot of you have been on my mind almost constantly since I left home, darling. I'm lost without you and I'll never leave you again if I have anything to say about it, sweetheart. We'll have so much fun together, all four of us, when I get home. Won't it be a wonderful Christmas? We'll celebrate the New Year too, darling, and begin to live every minute and every second of our lives together. Only 25 days to go now, honey, until 20 Nov. I'll hardly be able to stand it when it gets down to two, then one day and finally I start the long air voyage home. First I'll check out of the 1st Reg, then DivAir, then ANGLICO; then fly to K6 Seoul, catch a plane down to K3, the 1stMarAir Wing HQ, and pick up my orders there; then fly over to Itami, Japan, to MWSS-1 and get an endorsement and arrange air transportation to the States via Atsugi, Japan; then Wake, Midway, Hawaii and San Francisco. May take Mars again from Honolulu to Frisco as before, but it's hard to say what accommodations they'll give me. It shouldn't take over five days to get home once I get signed out of the Wing. They may horse around at Wing and not get my orders right out however. Bill Biehl and Jack Shoden breezed right through Wing, no strain, on their way through. Left here on 27 Sep, arrived Honolulu 1 Oct, delayed one day, then off to Frisco.

Good night, dearest

Monday morning
27 Oct 0730

Hello honey,
All's OK. The 7th held last night but we had to commit one of our battalions in the fight (the Thundering 3rd went up at midnight to reinforce them). Haven't any details yet, dear. Don't worry about a thing; we've got everything under control.

Love you, darling

THE BATTLE TO REGAIN THE OUTPOST CALLED THE HOOK

27 Oct 52
1st Marines, Korea

Dearest baby girl,
I made a footnote on my letter to you this morning saying everything was under control and the MLR had been taken back. The goonies really hit the 7th Marines last night and made considerable headway. It was the heaviest action across the Korean front. I won't go into details because they aren't pleasant, but I will say that we had 140 aircraft today clobbering the goonies on the new positions they occupied (took from us) and it's my conviction they were hurt plenty hard, with over 300 enemy killed. Our regiment is concerned because we sent our Third Battalion up to reinforce the 7th Marines; in fact, good old Item Company went up and regained the MLR positions from the goonies. The two outposts that were overrun lost all the boys out there and tonight we are planning a counter-attack to regain those lost outposts. One is called The Hook.

Two AD Skyraiders were shot down over us today. One crashed and the pilot was killed, the other landed wheels-up at the Munsan-ni Strip and the pilot got out OK, thank God. Last night's ground action and today's air action was the heaviest the division has encountered since occupying this sector last March. They originally occupied the East coast sector.

Spent most of the morning at ANGLICO and got a lot of unfinished business straightened out with Maj French, the CO. When I made recommendations, he listened and *said he was glad that I took the time to come in and visit him. He acknowledged the fact that I had taken keen interest in this air support program, and was happy to go along with a lot of my suggestions because he realized that I had had the experience to back it up, which he lacked because he was always back at ANGLICO when all the fighting was going on.*

Maj French said my relief wouldn't be here until 26 Nov (the dog). I'm still hoping for 20 Nov. We'll see.

Am going to secure this because I still have a little air work to do. It's been fairly quiet thus far tonight. Let's hope they don't hit again. The radio is playing "My Heart Cries for You." Mine sure cries for you, darling!

Night, dearest,
Daddy

West of the Sami-ch'on River lay an outpost named The Hook. The 7th Marine Regiment had repelled a heavy attack by the Chinese on 26-27 Oct 52. On 3 Nov the 1st Battalion of the Black Watch, a famous British regiment, relieved the 1st Battalion of the 7th Marines on The Hook.

On 18-19 Nov 52 the Black Watch fought a furious defensive battle, taking many casualties, but once again proved their fighting ability and heroism under fire. Whenever Bill and I had more aircraft overhead than we could handle comfortably, we dispatched them over to the British Commonwealth on our right flank, an act for which they would forever be grateful, the reason being that the 1stMarDiv had the air priority and they didn't.

We had the pleasure of meeting a number of members of the Black Watch while we were in reserve. They announced that they had put Bill and me in for a special medal, but we haven't received it after a more than 50-year wait. Their gift at that time of our black berets and some booze more than filled the bill however. They were all a fine bunch of lads and their countrymen could be proud of them.

The following citation exemplifies the fierce fighting that took place on The Hook.

O'BRIEN, GEORGE H., JR., Second Lieutenant, USMCR
H-3-7, October 27, 1952, Jamestown Line, The Hook

With his platoon subjected to an intense mortar and artillery bombardment while preparing to assault a vitally important hill position on the main line of resistance which had been overrun by a numerically superior enemy force on the preceding night, Second Lieutenant O'Brien leaped from his trench when the attack signal was given and, shouting for his men to follow, raced across an exposed saddle and up the enemy-held hill through a virtual hail of deadly small-arms, artillery, and mortar fire. Although shot through the arm and thrown to the ground by hostile automatic weapons fire as he neared the well-entrenched enemy position, he bravely regained his feet, waved his men onward, and continued to spearhead the assault, pausing only long enough to go to the aid of a wounded Marine. Encountering the enemy at close range, he proceeded to hurl hand grenades into bunkers and, utilizing his carbine to best advantage in savage hand-to-hand combat, succeeded in killing at least three of the enemy. Struck down by the concussion of grenades on three occasions during the subsequent action, he steadfastly refused to be evacuated for medical treatment and continued to lead his platoon in the assault for a period of nearly four hours, repeatedly encouraging his men and maintaining superb direction of the unit. With the attack halted, he set up a defense with his remaining forces to prepare for a counterattack, personally checking each position, attending to the wounded and expediting their evacuation. When a relief of the position was effected by another unit, he remained to cover the withdrawal and to assure that no wounded were left behind.

Second Lieutenant O'Brien was awarded the Medal of Honor. He currently lives in Austin, TX, and is a close friend of Beaumont Cooley, my squadron VMF-223 buddy of WWII.

1ST MARINE REGIMENT IS RELIEVED ON THE MAIN LINE OF RESISTANCE

28 Oct 52
1st Marines, Korea
1715, Wednesday

Hello darlings,

No mail yet today. Just finished three fast games of volleyball. Major Clyde Shealy, our SI, took some pictures with my camera of us playing.

PX supplies came in today and I bought two cans of tuna, two boxes of Ritz crackers, three rolls of 620 black and white film, two boxes of assorted cookies, two cans potato chips, jar of Borden cheese spread, two boxes of stationery. That ought to keep me in snacks until I leave. Oh, I forgot, I bought a case (24 cans) of chocolate Toddy. Those are the first goodies I've bought since I left home. I'm really living now.

Funny how you get used to things and take them for granted until you do without them for a long period of time, and then everything seems very special to you all over again. I know that's how my whole homecoming will be, darling. You have always seemed special to me, dearest, but you'll be even more lovely and precious when I see you again. The same can be said about many things in one's life. You go along day in and day out taking everything and everybody, and even your freedom for granted, until one day everything you hold dear is threatened and you have to go out and fight for it. In the process of fighting, you see others die and you become even more convinced that life itself is precious, and everything you have waiting at home for you is sort of a wonderful bonus thrown in, besides having your life and limbs spared.

The big question that I asked myself in WWII and have asked myself a thousand times over here in Korea is: How come I keep coming out smelling like a rose all the time? I can't hope to ever be able to answer that question, but I will always try to make my friends realize they have a precious heritage that is worth fighting for and working for, regardless of how low they may feel and how fruitless their own personal fight seems at times.

I can never feel low again, honey, not if I allow myself to picture those kids going into the battle on Bunker Hill and other places along the line. What an inspiration they were to us poags standing in our trenches 350 yards from them. Even though we were drawing incoming too, we did have our trenches to protect us somewhat. As far as I'm concerned, Americans have never had it so good but, from what I can judge after reading week-old newspapers, they are griping about everything under the sun. Lots of those that gripe the most aren't necessarily to blame, however, because they haven't had the opportunity to see how the other half lives and to make the on-the-spot comparison, or to rough it a while and do without, for a change.

Although heart wrenching, I am actually grateful for certain phases of my Korean tour- -those experiences that have shown me how my fellow man gives his life that others might live, such as when I see Korean farmers working unmolested in their fields and returning at night to their crude grass covered houses, but to their own family circle, while almost within shouting distance truck loads of young American Marines are riding or marching to the front to what fate, what sacrifice?! And all for that Korean whom they passed on the road, and for that Korean's family. Some of those same kids that fall dead on the battlefield will never have a woman, children, a home of their own, or return to any of the fruits of that cherished freedom they gave their all fighting for. Yet how many Americans are totally unaware of the privileges they have had thrown in their laps without having lifted a finger to defend them. And, if asked what contributions they have made toward our great struggle of WWI, WWII, and Korea, they will produce a stack of war bonds large enough to choke a horse and state, "This is my contribution," and feel as though they have every right to be proud of that contribution. But at the same time they are completely unaware of their real heritage or the staggering debt that was paid for that heritage--not in money, but in human lives.

It's a futile fight, as far as I'm concerned, because there isn't an end in sight. I don't imagine either side could call themselves the victor in this conflict. Nevertheless, the old question keeps cropping up: Is this war necessary? No wars are necessary, but where communism is concerned, I say "Yes, hit them every chance we get, every time they show their ugly strength anywhere in the world." I believe we'll eventually knock them down to their original size, but it's going to take a long, long time.

My radio isn't working worth a darn. I can't get rid of the static. Wrote Ben and Mom today. Just received yours of 23 October, honey. You said I had the cleanest family in town—you had just had baths and shampoos.

Love ya,
Daddy

29 Oct 52
1st Marines, Korea

Dearest family,

How I love to write 29 Oct! I've looked forward to writing it for seven months and now I've finally written it. I can say the same for 26 Nov also. But when I get home I hope time stands still because I want my happiness with my precious family to last and last, and if only the kiddies could stay young wouldn't it be a blessing? But of course it wouldn't be fair to them because there's a driving force in all kids to reach that next birthday, for some unknown reason. My absence has surely created an interest for Daddy on the part of the kids, I must say. When I was home so much I was just another adult around the house to keep them from doing what they wanted to do. I only hope that we can all feel this strong love for one another clear up through their manhood. I'd love to be looked up to and respected by my wife and children. There wouldn't be any higher honor that could be bestowed upon me.

You and I have been the best of pals, dearest girl, for these eight years and I hope we can always hold the same interest for one another. The boys will have to be taken on hikes and camping trips and be taught how to build fires, cook things for themselves and clean up the gear after they are finished with it. Even though I've been camping out, as it were, for these past seven months, I'm still anxious to do it some more with my little guys and you, precious doll. We've got some wonderful times ahead of us, darling. We're a perfect little family. I don't know of a happier, more contented little family troop anywhere. It's a great pleasure for me to know my family wants for nothing (except their daddy maybe).

This morning Sgt Koch, my team chief, and I went down to Div ANGLICO, and 1st Signal Battalion, then over to Munsan-ni where we examined an AD Skyraider that had belly landed the other day (Monday, 27 Oct) during the heavy air support missions flown for the 7th Marines. I took pictures of it. Arranged for eight movies (training films) to be brought up from an Army unit film library in Seoul, for training of my air teams.

I'm listening to Radio Australia and they are comparing American tunes with theirs. It's very interesting. Frank Sinatra just sang "All of Me."

Had the usual volleyball games this afternoon, also took a nice hot shower down at the 11th Marines CP shower. Shampooed my hair and now it's a mass of ringlets--the colonel was kidding me tonight at briefing.

I have to call Div Air office and get all the important activities concerning air last night (MPQ radar drops in support of the Div) and also CAS flown during the day. Last night they dropped within 1000 meters of our front line troops. Very close for night radar drops. Guess those night drops shake up the goonies considerably.

Fortunately, we had a fairly quiet night on the Div front. Thank God for it too because those companies had sure taken a beating. I can hear the artillery pounding out right now. I believe it's our outgoing, but one can't be sure because the goonies' incoming 122mm is just about as noisy.

Oh, something funny happened this morning. I awoke early this morning to a sound that I thought was a rat chewing on a package. It was dark and I reached for my flashlight. Who should I find there but Bugs--he had chewed the whole corner off one of my assorted cookie boxes, reached clear into the cookies and taken two of them. I shooed him away and put the cookies up high were he can't reach them. I had seen little bits of paper on the floor several mornings in a row and couldn't figure out what it was, except maybe rats, but it was my little old buddy, Bugs.

1ST MARINE REGIMENT IS RELIEVED ON THE MAIN LINE OF RESISTANCE

Talked to Col Long today and he thinks Capt Watson will be the best one to replace me. I saw Watson at Div today and told him. He was very pleased. I told him I wanted him up here, bag and baggage, around the 20th to snap in on the duties of Regimental Air Officer. We may be on the line again by that time, but won't be there long before I'll be shoving off.

All my love to my little family,
Daddy

30 Oct 52
Korea

Dearest family,
Today the daddy went over to the other side of the Imjin and selected a helicopter landing site for our new CP. Maj Christie (former exec of Thundering Third) is now in charge of building our new Regimental CP. Can't say when we'll move over there. Attended a ribbon cutting ceremony at 1000 today at the opening of a newly constructed bridge across the Imjin. Generals Hart and Pollock attended. They had a band and the engineers that had constructed it were congratulated in speeches by Gen Pollock, 1stMarDiv CO. After they cut the ribbon, about four jeeps drove across, turned around and came back; then the MPs opened the bridge to the first traffic. My boys and I drove across and over about two miles of newly constructed road, hit the main supply route, then drove on up to the 7th's area and to our new CP site. Completed my business there in about 30 minutes and came back by way of Xray Bridge. Had lunch, then lay down for a while and tried to shake a headache. Finally got rid of it and took care of a few items of air interest and then had the usual volleyball, pan bath, supper, briefing, and now my letter writing time.
Denny Clyde stopped by to tell me about the big party he lucked into at K6. The Seattle boys were celebrating their one-year birthday since being called to active duty. They had lobster (Korean), shrimp, crabs, oysters, steaks, beer and drinks. The Seattle pilots tossed in $5.00 apiece for the deal and Denny says it was fabulous. He told me of three more deaths of some friends of mine in VMF-212.
Bugs is in visiting us and having some Ritz crackers--loves those crackers--wouldn't eat his carrot yesterday.
Strung an antenna for my radio by hooking up a wire from my radio to my field phone. The field phone has several miles of wire and really increases the radio reception.
Div Intelligence has made some intercepts indicating that the enemy is planning a major assault. Even though we are in reserve, we are standing by to render any assistance that they might need up on the MLR. All's well so far.

Love you all dearly,
Daddy

Just a few miles south of the 1stMarDiv Korean farmers actively harvested their bountiful wheat crop. This area had been cleared of Communist mine fields so that they could resume their farming. Other farmers, eager to return to their homes and farms, were blown up along with their water buffalo while plowing in uncleared mined areas. I witnessed this one day through my telescope from Hill 229.

These photos of Korean children were taken at various times near the VMO-6 Marine observation squadron, within the 1stMarDiv sector. The village was out of harm's way and in near proximity to the squadron. This gave us ample opportunity to enjoy their friendly and beautiful little faces. The older girls packed the younger ones around on their backs and had the primary care for them, rather than their mothers.

These scenes depict the plight of the Korean peasants—washing their clothes in the river and on the march to the Lord knows where. Millions of Koreans, whose lives had been a struggle for a meager existence before the war, had to leave for the southern part of their country by foot and oxcart, embarking on a three-year odyssey, barely subsisting on American milk powder and herbs picked along the way until after the war ended. Scarcely a family in that unhappy land had been spared.

Upper Left, L to R: Col Walter F. Layer, CO of the 1st Regiment, and his exec, LtCol Glenn R. Long. When Maj Jack Shoden left for the States, he nominated me to take his job as Air Officer of the 1st Reg, serving Layer and Long. This was an unusual privilege for a Reserve captain, since the job had always been filled by no less than a major. I was honored to take this position, and especially to serve these two fine officers. My duties as a full Regimental Air Officer took a huge jump and I had a lot to learn, but my earlier time served as a forward air controller at Company level at the forward outposts would prove to be a big help in my new job. Maj Bill Biehl would return to the States with Shoden, so I was without a sidekick in my new job.

Upper Right: Two of our hardworking TACP team, L, Cpl A. Skinner and R, Cpl D. Evans. We traveled for miles throughout the Bn sector, always on call for another air control mission. We always packed our mounted map along with us. This map board was eventually set up in our Hill 229 bunker, to use in briefing visiting VIP's.

Lower Right: Peterson, in position for controlling his aircraft for another close support mission. Bunker Hill in distant background, scene of some of the bitterest hand-to-hand fighting the 1stMarDiv experienced during the Korean War. The 1stMarDiv, a component of the Eighth Army, faced a large portion of the formidable enemy forces spread across the 38th parallel at this time. Seven Chinese armies and two North Korean corps, totaling about 270,000 troops, manned their front lines, while eleven more Chinese armies and North Korean corps estimated at 531,000 waited in reserve. Together with their service and security forces, the total amounted to more than a million men. One could not expose himself for long before drawing heavy enemy fire.

Upper Left: Maj Horace C. Reifel taking a shot at a flying pheasant. We were out scouting a new location for the 3rd Bn command post. This area had not as yet been cleared of mines.

Upper Right: Resting at roadside between 1stMarDiv and Inchon. Trusty Willys jeep ¼ ton 4x4 by my side. Wheat growing in background.

Middle Left, R to L: LtCol Sidney J. Altman (new 3/1 Bn CO), LtCol Carlo A. Rovetta, and ?

Middle Right: Biehl and Peterson controlling an air strike at HOW Company position on the MLR, 38 pistol in side holster, radio gear by my knee. Standard uniform of the day, flak jacket and hard hat for me.

Lower Left: Peterson serving volleyball at 3/1 CP headquarters, my back to camera. Great for relaxation between battles.

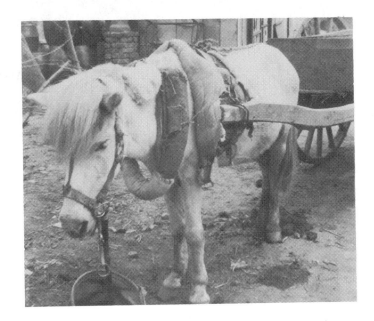

Upper Left: Korean farmer plowing with his water buffalo, a few miles south of the 1stMarDiv.

Upper Right: These little Korean ponies pulled their weight in many diverse ways for their owners.

Middle Left, L to R: Capts Browning, Anderson and Peterson at K6.

Lower Left: Typical scene of a Korean mother packing her baby while carrying a big load on her head. Tents in background belong to VMO-6 squadron.

Lower Right: Korean children playing jump-board near VMO-6, Marine Observation Squadron at 1stMarDiv. They could bounce six feet in the air with ease.

CHAPTER 18

INN OF THE OPEN DOOR

DAILY BREEZE, REDONDO BEACH, CALIFORNIA

Thursday, October 30, 1952

ONE-WORD DESCRIPTION OF TRIP TO PANMUNJOM: IMPROBABILITY
By Rembert James

MUNSAN, Korea--This is the jumping-off place for Panmunjom, the improbable little place where truce talks with the enemy have been going on for 15 months.

The last time they had a talk I went to Panmunjom, riding in the back of a two-ton army truck in a caravan that included 49 other correspondents.

From this town of Munsan, inside the Allies' lines, you travel 13.9 miles over twisting, dusty roads. Once you cross the Imjin River, four miles above Munsan, you are in Communist territory, except that under the agreement there is a "no firing" zone for 200 meters each side of the road, and in the 2000-yard perimeter at Panmunjom itself.

LIKE L.A. COUNTRYSIDE

Panmunjom is supposed to mean "Inn of the Open Door," and there actually are four small Korean buildings there, in addition to three tents and a matting-covered meeting building put up for the truce talks by the Communists.

The countryside itself, on a bright Indian summer day, looks pleasant enough--a valley with low hills rising around about, like you can see in the Southland back country. You might believe you were back on a back road to Escondido except for the unfamiliar sight of rice paddies with their yellowing harvest.

And of course there is something else you don't see in Los Angeles County. This is the spectacle of a war still going on, with Allied forces' planes dropping bombs on hills in easy view.

SHELLS LOBBED

Artillery from both sides lob shells onto each other's positions too, and you see the smoke and dust rise, and then feel the blast.

There are security guards at Panmunjom, 20 Allied soldiers commanded by a former New York policeman, Capt. Joseph Foley.

The routine of a truce talk is simple. Today's meeting was set for 11 a.m. The Allies' caravan pulled into the area at 10:55. There were a dozen jeeps, two truckloads of correspondents, and one truck loaded with rations.

At about the same moment the caravan stopped, two U.S. helicopters landed. From one of them stepped the top Allied forces delegate, LtGen William Harrison Jr., and he was followed by the other delegates and top staff members.

ENEMY ARRIVES

Down the road from Kaesong, on the north, came a caravan of Russian-made jeeps, then a gray 1949 Ford sedan with the right side battered in, followed by a 1947 Chrysler seven-passenger sedan with white sidewall tires.

Out of the Chrysler came the Communists' top delegate, Gen Nam Il (pronounced "Nah-meel"), a medium-sized man wearing a Russian-type uniform. Without delay, the delegations entered the meeting hall from opposite ends. Correspondents lounging outside, kept 20 yards away by military police of both sides, could see through the screens that the delegates were seated.

A couple of Air Force planes dropped bombs on a Communist-held hill to the south, and the earth trembled a little but nobody paid any apparent attention. Artillery boomed on both sides of Panmunjom, but you couldn't see where the shells were landing.

There were four Communist correspondents, three of them Chinese or North Korean, and one Englishman, Alan Winnington, correspondent for the London Daily Worker. The three Oriental Communist correspondents sat rather primly on the porch of a Korean building across the road from the truce meeting hall. Winnington circulated among the Allied forces correspondents.

DUCK PRAISED

He is a slender man, around 40, with a thin face and a restless glance. He wore a light-colored uniform with a high collar. His role seemed to be considerably more than that of a correspondent. He produced a copy of Nam Il's answer to the Allies' war prisoner repatriation proposal, showing it around to the correspondents while Nam Il was reading it at the meeting.

How are things in China? Wonderful, Winnington said. You should visit Peiping sometime. The Chinese are wonderful cooks, and Peking duck, a world-famous dish for epicures, is never better than in Peiping.

"You don't have the right kind of ducks," Winnington said. "Now in Peiping, the ducks are raised in a basket, and never move a muscle and so when they are prepared for eating, they're perfect."

No one asked Winnington how many of China's 400 million eat Peking duck.

One of the American correspondents, the representative of the National Catholic News Service, Father Patrick O'Connor, listened patiently to the speech about the ducks, then in a quiet moment he held out a little white booklet to Winnington.

"Oh, thank you!" Winnington said.

"You'll not only be amused," added Father O'Conner, "You'll be interested."

Winnington glanced at the cover. It read: "From Communism to Catholicism," by Douglas Hyde, former editor of the London Daily Worker.

The two men parted and Winnington went back to eating with chopsticks out of a can of Chinese jade fish.

The meeting in the truce hall ended, and it was a failure, and after briefings the Allied correspondents ate baked ham and peas and canned peaches in a tent operated by the American security guard.

The road back from Panmunjom seemed longer and dustier than it had been on the trip north. There were the same sights and sounds of war on the surrounding hills. There was a group of Korean kids alongside the camp--caves in a hillside-- and there were the rice paddies and the maize fields with a few Korean farmers working in them.

It seemed strange, and a little improbable, most of it. You could wonder if it wasn't unreal, but not for long. If you got too far away in imagination the truck would hit a chuckhole. When you bounced on the wooden seat, you were back in reality.

THIRTY THOUSAND ROUNDS OF COMMUNIST ARTILLERY IN ONE DAY

1 Nov 52
1st Marines, Korea

*Dearest girl and precious boys
that I love,*

The KMCs and 7th Marines got hit hard last night again. We were alerted at an early hour this morning but our assistance wasn't needed. The KMCs clobbered literally hundreds of goonies when they caught them assembling in the open for an assault. Artillery landed right in the middle of their assembly area. Today they had eight CAS missions in support of them, and the 5th and 7th had one apiece.

Received your letter of 25, 26 Oct telling about the heavy attack the 7th had at the Hook. Yes, dear, that was a terrible battle and poor old Item Co of the Thundering Third took 100 casualties, 17 dead on the last count. Poor kids got pulled into it from reserve too. It's not so about pulling off of Bunker Hill. The news got fouled up that night and the word even came over the radio here about us giving up Bunker Hill. It just ain't so. I talked to our Regimental Operation Officer (the guy that would definitely know) and Mac says we are still on Bunker and have never left it. The papers get hold of a lot of bum dope. The Hook really caught it, though, and some estimates I have heard place the number of incoming rounds of mortar and artillery at around 30,000 for one 24-hour period. Horrific! You also wrote that our neighbor, Lynn, got choked up when Randy said he didn't have any daddy. I hope Lynn knows how lucky he is. Some guys will never be able to look back on hectic war days of intense battle and recount the things that scared the tar out of them. Those recollections make a man truly appreciate what he has and realize how fortunate he is to just plain old be alive. Out here in Korea, where life is cheap, you have plenty of time to evaluate things in their true proportions.

You know something funny happened to me a while ago. As I was reading your letter, Bugs was licking my hand. When I came to the part in your letter where you said, "Imagine that crazy rabbit licking your hand," I almost flipped. What a coincidence--especially because I don't believe Bugs had licked my hand since I wrote you about it a couple of weeks ago.

Just came from the colonel's briefing. For the first time in five weeks we met at 1930 instead of 1830, and also he announced there wouldn't be a briefing tomorrow night. Just full of exciting announcements. Ha, ha! The exec officer, Col Long, is driving the staff officers out of their minds with his old maid ideas. He's really rough on them, insisting on absolute adherence to the letter of every order ever published by the Div. McLeod does about 9/10ths of his paper work over about five times. He's fit to be tied; also Maj Charlie Reifel, the communications officer, because of this new CP on the other side of the Imjin. We're building bunkers etc and rewiring the whole thing for lights and telephones to all the battalions, companies and divisions. Supply remains a never-ending problem over here. Lumber is especially scarce and these tents are icy cold unless you have a wooden deck underneath them. They scrounge most of the lumber from mortar boxes etc. The darn stuff is available down in Seoul from the Army, but the Marines are too proud to beg it. Yet, as we are part of the 8th Army just as the Marine Air Wing is under operational control of the 5th Airforce, we have every right to draw from their supply. We are getting 12"x12" heavy bunker material, which is an absolute must in order to withstand the withering enemy fire. You can't imagine the is an absolute must in order to withstand the withering enemy fire. You can't imagine the amount of incoming they throw at us. I don't understand where the Communist supply comes from. I must admit to a certain extent that "Operation Strangle" has been a failure inasmuch as those darn goonies are getting the stuff to wage war, and _how_!! Air interdiction can only do so much.

This is all the news for now. Hugs and kisses to all from your ever loving--

Daddy

2000, Sunday eve
2 Nov 52
1st Marines, Korea

Dearest family,
Just now returned to the tent after seeing "Lone Star," with Clark Gable and Ava Gardner. I had seen it once before but was hard put for amusement so I stuck it out. Some mighty potent love scenes in it that made my old ticker skip a couple of beats. Clark has still got "it" as far as I'm concerned. That guy is ageless. Ava's got all the fixtures too, for that matter. Who said I wasn't ready to come home? Look out, come early Dec, girl!

This morning I saddled up old Betsy and headed south for the VMO-6 ranch. The cold morning air made me wish I had lingered a spell longer by the warmth of my fireplace back at my diggings. It was fairly early when I pulled into VMO-6 and, even at that early hour, I missed Gus who was out with nature's fowl life, shooting ducks and geese. I tarried a while in Joe Frieta's corral jawing about his two-month extension imposed upon all helicopter flying machine pilots by one Gen Megee. Joe was hurt at the extension and his vocabulary was most interesting, expressing adjectives unheard by other ears prior to this morning. I venture to estimate if the sun had been a little higher over the yardarm he'd have wet his words with alcoholic beverages. However, he was on the hook which is the expression used by us pilots meaning to be "on call" for a hop.

Gus's voice was soon heard mingling with others as they approached Frieta's tent and, in less time that it takes to tell it, Gus and I were shaking each other's hand in a gesture of friendship because Gus was my friend and I am Gus's friend and we are each other's friend. Mighty friendly cuss, Gus. I lingered most of the day, swapping yarns and telling lies. Gus had one evac at noon, outside of that, no other flights.

I read a couple of magazines and the new _Stars and Stripes_ which, of all things, had an article in there about your ever loving daddy winning the Silver Star. No mail today, darling. I've got about six copies of the paper which I'll send. The article is at the bottom right hand corner of page 6.

Your very own
Daddy

A TRUCKLOAD OF UNEXPLODED ENEMY SHELLS GIVES US A SCARE

3 Nov 52
Monday, 1720
Korea

Dearest family,
Spent the best part of the day over at our new CP site working out details with Maj Christie. We selected a nice spot up on a hill, where we'll be able to put our radio jeep, thereby getting maximum range. We have to be able to reach our battalions, Anaconda Baker (the primary air control agency for the Division) and strike aircraft. Bulldozers were churning up the dirt, making roads and shelves for our tents and other things.

The new area has quite a few Korean civilian graves in it. Dozers are uncovering a lot of them today. On the way over there, via the Xray bridge, we saw a mine demolition team clearing a field for some communication wire teams. Wouldn't relish their job!

They are also digging out huge holes in the sides of mountains in our area, for bunkers. The KSC (Korean Service Crops) is digging and preparing each hole, so they can install the prefabricated sections of 12"x12" timber. Brother, will it be rugged! The whole thing will be covered over with tar paper, then dirt about 10 feet deep. Today there were about 50 KSCs digging on the large bunker hole. Their Honshu (boss man) was sitting on a pile of dirt and whenever one of them stopped working he'd throw dirt clods at him. Then they sure would turn to. The Honshus are just Koreans with a little education, but they act like a commanding general over those yobos. They wear Marine dungarees, leggings and a nice green jacket (Marine issue). The one today was carrying a swagger stick. Some pumpkins. I'm going to take some pictures, maybe tomorrow--too busy up there today.

Today, here at our CP, a near tragic thing happened. A truck, loaded with duds (mortars and artillery shells) they had recovered in our area, pulled up next to Maj Clyde W. Shealy's tent, which is near the parking space, and not far from mine. He looked out of his tent and found himself staring at a sign, "BEWARE, KEEP WITHIN 100 YARDS OF THIS TRUCK AT ALL TIMES. CARRYING EXPLOSIVE DUDS!" Shealy jumped out of his chair and ordered the young driver out of the CP poste haste. Off he went down the road which is rough as a cob, duds banging around, knocking against each other in the steel bed of the truck. None went off, thank God. How stupid can a guy be, bringing an explosives truck into and area like this? Then again, I was thinking, maybe he had not been well enough informed by his superiors about the potential harm his deadly truckload could cause.

The guys threw a cocktail party as a going-away present for Capt Xanders--yes, that's the way he spells it. He was supposed to leave tomorrow morning, but tonight at briefing they notified him that it wouldn't be until Friday, 7 Nov. His face dropped a mile, poor fellow. It's rough on a guy, these last few days especially.

Col Layer just started on me tonight, in a kidding way. You remember how I wrote you about the bad time he gave Maj Jack Shoden, the fellow I relieved, right up to the hour he shoved off. Well, as he was leaving the briefing tent he said, "Pete will be giving the next party because he's leaving <u>next</u> month." He knows perfectly well I leave 25 or 26 Nov., but he's starting on me already. He forgets I'm wise to his kidding. I'll go along with it though and play like I'm all shook up.

They are playing "Sweet Leilani" on the radio. Golly, it's nice. Makes me think of my precious girl that I love and miss so very much.

Oh, a funny thing happened last night, or was it in the wee hours of this morning? Anyhoo, it was cold and dark when I heard some stuff juggling around on the box I have next to my cot. Then I heard some chewing noise and I figured it was Bugs at my cookies again. I flashed my light at the box and there, sitting on top of my radio so he could reach my cookie box, was a great big rat. My light blinded him for a few seconds and he just stood there with his teeth hanging out and his eyes popping out. He was one surprized rat. I was too tired and cold to get up and cover up the hole he came in through or to put the cookies in a place he couldn't reach, so I just zipped up in my bag again and went off to sleep after about 30 minutes of listening to him chew.

This morning, after arising, shaving and eating chow, I did some work on my air reports and administrative work, then drove to the other side of the Imjin. Boy, I really covered the ground today around our new site. Bet my crew and I hiked three miles over hills and valleys. Fortunately, we didn't hit any mines.

Tomorrow is Election Day back in the states. We'll hear the results on Wednesday the 5th, so the radio tells us.

Love you,

Daddy

4 Nov 52
1st Marines, Korea

Dearest family,

Today the H&S Company SgtMaj had three PFCs up here to our tent throwing the dirt up around the bottom of it to keep the cold air from coming in. They had done it before about a week ago but Bugs had dug it out in five or six places and it required fixing again. The three men had worked the whole thing over and were just finishing up on one corner when Bugs arrived and began digging in again. The men came over and watched him, then filled it in with rocks and covered it again. Bugs just sat and watched and when they finished he went over on the other side and dug in another hole. The fellows were really baffled as to what to do about it. They filled it in again just before they left, but I just noticed there's a new tunnel freshly dug, and when I came in the tent from chow, there lay Bugs by the stove stretched out on the floor. He comes up through the floor in a special hole we left for him. I guess you could say he's won this round.

My team and I are making a sand table model of the sector we are moving up to. The boys are using Korean mud and water and are really having a time. They will cover it with plaster of Paris and paint it for the finish coat. It's on a 6'x6' board which covers an area of 2000x2000 meters on the map. Mostly goonie land. I went over to 1st Regiment CP today and talked over plans for some air strikes on a few Communist hot spots in our new sector. Saw Capt Layne who had just returned from Japan.

I'm wondering how the election is going to turn out. Don't hear <u>any</u> talk of it around here. My absentee ballot never arrived from California, even though I wrote for it on the regular absentee form back in June, from K6. But hava no.

Been quite a bit of <u>cannonading</u>, as the Canadians call shooting artillery, tonight. Haven't heard any word, however, as to what's going on.

Love you, precious girl,
21 more days!!!!!
Daddy

5 Nov 52
1st Marines, Korea

Dearest girl,

No mail from you today, honey, but I didn't luck out completely because I did get a letter from Winchell Atwater, the laboratory machine shop foreman at AiResearch. He wrote about how much everyone enjoyed my letters and wondered how I could keep up my good spirits over here where the fighting is so heavy. (I figure a letter should be both informative but not too personal, and to stay on the light side wherever possible). Said he didn't want to have me take the time to write him a special letter but to keep them coming to the gang. I reread your last three letters, dearest girl, and it was <u>almost</u> as good as getting one new letter from my darling.

This afternoon I went over to the 7th Marines CP up on the line and discussed plans for relieving Capt Woodbury on or around 15 Nov. I gave him details of an operation that is to transpire at a date I cannot divulge, except to say <u>I have planned</u> the <u>air</u> for it. When it takes place, baby doll, you will read about it in the newspapers and you will then recall that I forewarned you about its coming.

Later this afternoon I went over to our new CP up on the line, surveyed the layout, made recommendation for my area, looked over the helicopter strip, 65'x100', and took pictures of the new bunker diggings and of the lumber used in the construction. The yobos posed with me in one. Maj Christie took one of me in the bunker hole the yobos were digging.

The bulldozers were really knocking themselves out cutting shelves and roads for us today. Maj Christie has been doing an excellent job over there. I have advised him on several items regarding helicopter landing pads and he has carried out my suggestions to a tee. The copter strip is way up on high ground and required about 50 tons of fill to be carried up and *unloaded on the spur   It's imperative that the copter site be located on the highest possible ground in the CP because it has to be higher than any of the communication wires or lighting poles, especially for night operations. It's the finest strip in the Division sector, bar none. My boys are going to rock the border and lay out the strip number in six-foot high numbers painted white. Christie is going to have the dozer cut me a shelf for my enlisted men's squad tent, and also for the radio jeep so it will be on high ground but protected from enemy observation.   VHF radios require line-of-sight in order to function properly. Mountains etc in between radios will block the transmissions; hence the requirement of getting the radio jeep onto high ground.*

Got back to our CP here at 1600. The volleyball game was in full swing and I joined them. Charlie Reifel began accusing me of getting in the net. I wasn't in the net and stood my ground. He blew his top, and after the game when we got back here in the tent he got after me for arguing with him. He's a major, you know. I told him off in even stronger words. He was flabbergasted and kept saying, "Remember, Captain, I'm a major." I told him what he could do with those major leaves. I also told him that when he steps on the volleyball court he should leave his rank back in his tent. He was sore enough to go to the colonel but didn't do it. We're talking again and everything is copacetic(spelling?). If there's anything I can't stand, it's someone pulling their rank on me. I never use my rank for anything, not even to gain a place in the PX line, and I'll be darned if I'm going to let a sniveling major (a regular) pull his on me. Reifel is a funny cuss and is forever getting into riffs with other officers in our CP group here. Maybe my standing up to him today will take some of the wind out of his sails.

How did your election bill passing go, honey? Guess I'll be getting a report on it in your next letter. Guess you can take some of the credit for Ike's being elected, eh honey? Haven't decided about this college deal completely. Maybe full-time days at AiResearch and part-time nights at college will suffice. We'll see when I get home. Of course, I won't qualify for the GI Bill, though, if I'm earning a full wage, darn it.

Twenty days to go. Yippee!!! Love ya, honey. Kiss the darlings and tell them I love them. Won't be long now!

Daddy

6 Nov 52
1st Marines, Korea

Hi little family,
Seems the sister of Cpl O'Gara, who was on my 3rd Battalion TACP team, wrote her congressman from Illinois, one Melvin Price, inquiring as to when her brother would be returned to Uncle Sugar. Congressman Price wrote BGen R.H. Ridgely Jr., Hdqs. MC, Wash., who advised Price that O'Gara would be eligible for rotation soon. I am going to write Price tonight and tell him O'Gara has already departed our Asian shores for good old Uncle Sugar. I'm also going to write his sister, Miss Shirley O'Gara, and tell her what an outstanding job O'Gara did while a member of my team during the heavy fighting at Bunker Hill. He didn't qualify, in my estimation, for a Letter of Commendation, as did four of my other men. Major Biehl and I were limited to four citations to be awarded to the four most deserving in our team. O'Gara hadn't been along with us up to Bunker Hill as many times as the others nor had he experienced the number of rounds of incoming mortar and artillery fire as the rest of the team, but he deserves a pat on the back which I intend to give him, also making it part of his service record book.

So you and Randy-boy passed out circulars together, eh? He's probably the youngest member now in the Young Republicans Club. The Halloween deal sounds like fun. I always enjoy myself completely on Halloween watching the kids. It's such a <u>serious</u> business with them and they all are so cute.

Spent half a day at VMO-6 today. Gus was in Japan on R&R, the dog. They gave me a wind sock for our new CP helicopter strips. Spent quite a bit of time at Div Air Hdqs. arguing with Col Cornell. He's so used to having everyone agree with him that he's dumbfounded when somebody doesn't. I don't and I told him so, and he listened. He talks so darn fast you can't get a word in edgewise, so I let him run down, then tore his theories about close air support all to pieces. When I finished after about ten minutes, he was standing there nodding his head at everything I said. I hope I may have knocked some sense into his head that will make it a *little bit easier for the new FACs coming up here to the Div. I'd rather fight the goonies bare handed than to try and squeeze a request out of Col Cornell.*

Took a picture of a papasan in his white robe and high black hat. Took snaps of some Korean farmers knocking the rice from the stalk. They push a pedal like an old fashioned sewing machine, which is connected to and turns a rough surfaced drum that flicks off the rice onto the pile. It was doing a good job of it too.

I am listening to Radio Australia. They sing a lot of the popular American tunes, but every now and then they toss in some Australian tunes and they sound sort of corny, like most English songs do.

My pen isn't what it used to be since I dropped it last night. Guess you can't treat these pens like darts and expect any service out of them. The <u>Christian Science Monitor</u> predicts Ike will be over here in Korea about 10 days after the election. How about that? The only living thing he can do over here that hasn't already been done is increase the number of ROKs in training, but then, they have been doing it right along at as rapid a pace as equipment and training would permit. It's a darn shame a single boy of any other nation should have to sacrifice his life over here. The Koreans make good soldiers, provided they are backed up to the hilt with mortar, artillery and aircraft. They are rough on equipment though. Their trucks, jeeps and tents are all falling apart. Guess they haven't been trained properly in maintenance. This is surely a costly war. New recruit replacements are coming in tomorrow (400). They are worried about tentage and chow for them. Seems they held up the last draft that was supposed to go home, in order to build up a backlog of troops during these heavy fighting days. Now they haven't tents to accommodate them. They will go to the various battalions, though, in a short time to make up for their battle casualties and there they will have plenty of tentage, except when we move up to the line and bunker shortage looms up again.

All for tonight, dearest girl. Our day is coming, baby girl. I adore you, honey doll. Bye, bye.

Love, Daddy

7 Nov 52

Dearest family,

Guess what! We had our first snow this morning. I heard it begin at about 0430 this morning and it was strange too because it sounded like a slow rain with great big drops falling on the tent. It got a heck of a lot warmer all of a sudden, then the snow. Guess it has to be just right before it will snow. About a quarter of an inch fell and we had a white blanket over all the tents, jeeps and trucks, and all the hills were white. Very exciting for me because I haven't seen it snow but about half a dozen times in all my born days, being from sunny California. The hills were still snow covered when I arrived in Korea on 1 Apr but it hasn't snowed since. Just rain and not a heck of a lot of that, when you get right down to it. July and August were the two rainy months. We were especially concerned, however, in case the Imjin River should swell, overflow its banks and knock out our bridges, which are our only means of escape in case the goonies start an all-out deal, as they appeared to be doing on Bunker Hill. We're fat with bridges now and I see no immediate danger to our forces over there on the other side. They have several foot bridges crossing it now too, which would be a great help in the event of a retirement. I have taken pictures of nearly all the bridges in the sector with two exceptions, the Widgeon and Teel bridges, which are up in the Canadian sector.

Oh say, there's a bunch of Scottish "Black Watch" troops with the Canadians. (Scotty Neish, Mom's second husband, was at one time a member back in Scotland.) They call their area up there the Commonwealth Sector. There are British, Australian, Irish, Scotch and Canadian troops among them. I see them down here in our sector occasionally, with their screwy looking hats and leggings, and some strange looking tracked vehicles. Guess they have a good reputation, though, of being fearless fighters. They have anywhere from 10 to 20 patrol contacts in their sector nightly, ranging anywhere from a squad to a company of Communists. They go out every night just the same. The forward patrols act as an early warning to the rest of the MLR troops. Our sector is quiet, or relatively quiet, that is. Today we've had an overcast *that looked and felt like more snow all day--no aircraft flying in support today. It may still have time to clear before sunset and we'll have some air if it does. I hear copters buzzing overhead already.*

A little deal came up this afternoon. I received the new operations order for when we take over in the right sector. Had about 10 pages of enemy capabilities, defensive fire plans, expected weather outlook, enemy mortar and artillery positions.

The enemy is in very good shape. He's already been issued his winter clothing and his bunkers have been winterized, according to our intelligence people. Prisoner information, etc.

This afternoon we played volleyball for one and a half hours. I'm bushed but feel good anyhoo. Brother, I've really been getting the practice lately. I swear my spelling gets worse every day. Some days I can spell like mad without ever consulting my dictionary, and then other days I can hardly spell my name. I wonder why that is. I don't believe Maj Reifel has written a letter since I've been in the Regiment. Can't figure the guy out. Guess he's not on speaking terms with his wife and child. He doesn't ever get any mail either. Poor guy, I feel sorry for him. McLeod is just as faithful as I am; in fact he's the first guy I've run into that writes every day, besides myself. I get a lot of pleasure out of sitting down and having a pen chat with you, honey. It's a way to get a lot of things off my mind. I know it will reach you in only five or six days and, as long as there's one on its way every day, the chain is never broken and you hardly realize that the letters are a week old. Won't it be wonderful, honey, when we can thumb our noses at writing these nightly letters, when we can grab one another and tell each other what we feel and want and be able to receive an immediate response? Every time either one of us asks a question it takes two weeks to get an answer; yet, I have asked you things and it's seemed like I had only written of it two or three days before, and what do you know, here's my answer. At times like that, you realize the time is flying by.

I answered the letter Congressman Melvin Price of Illinois put to me re Cpl O'Gara. Also added a line or two giving O'Gara a pat on the back. Maj French was up here to see me today and had a traffic citation against my Sgt Koch. I asked him to take it easy on him, but he said Col Glick of Signal Bn was rugged on tickets. Poor Koch, I tried to help him but doubt if I can. They may bust him, and he doesn't deserve it. My hands are tied though.

French said he was going to cut my orders to read Nov 28 or when directed. The varmint, he keeps adding a day or two every time he comes up here. Doctor Mitchell and I want to go home together. Mitch doesn't know anything about Japan and wants me to accompany him on a shopping tour to the Nishimura lacquerware factory and to the silk fabric factory. If I'm very close to 1 Dec in getting out of Korea, I may as well hang around until that date and get another $200.00 income tax deduction, but if I can get out of here on 28 or 29 <u>I'm gone</u>. I got gypped out of my $200.00 March deduction by only one day, you know, landing in Korea on 1 Apr. I don't know why I have to arrive and depart on the days so near but yet so far from the allowable deduction dates.

Let's see, no mail today so I have no questions to answer for you. Might tell you of a raid a friendly platoon pulled off last night on a goonie outpost, and they really creamed the goonies. It happened over in the 7th Marines sector, right in the area we're moving into on 15 Nov. Hope it didn't agitate the goonies too much. When you jab those chinks it's like knocking over an ant's nest. We took about 20 casualties on the deal but they consider the raid successful because they killed 40 Chinese. It's one of the first raids <u>any</u> friendlies have pulled off anywhere in Korea for about a year. Usually the goonies have been the aggressors and our troops the defenders.

Nearly all the staff officers are sore at Col Long and Col Layer because they don't take anybody's suggestions. The new CP has been the crowning blow. They want to stick <u>all</u> the Regimental officers into three squad tents, except themselves. It won't work because we won't all have space in the bunker, so we'll need working space as well as living space in our tents. It will be a crowded mess. We're all going along with the deal because nobody wants to argue with the old man. Everyone is really sore. He runs the whole show and he doesn't really need any staff as long as he persists in running the whole show himself. As far as I'm concerned, Col Layer treats me fine, takes all of my suggestions and never bothers me. By 1 Jan this whole Regimental staff will be relieved, going home and reassignments etc. Too bad too because the

Regiment will be on the line and it goes without saying, it's not healthy to change staff in the middle of the stream.

Just read in the operation order under Intelligence heading that the Imjin wouldn't freeze over in our area because it's mixed with too much salt water backing up into it. Up near the Commonwealth sector, however, it will freeze over to a depth of nine inches by 9 Dec. So you see it's going to get rather cool here, honey. This is all supposition, though, based on last year.

How nice it will be to be back home in the center of my wonderful little family that I love and adore. It will be such a pleasure to get away from this constant pressure we're all operating under.

Love,
Daddy

8 Nov 52
1st Marines, Korea

Baby girl,

Brother, is it ever getting cold over in this country! This morning we didn't have any snow but did have a heavy white frost that looked just like snow. It lasted until around 0930.

Bugs came in early this morning to get his cracker, then shoved off again. A big white Alaskan husky dog is dogging poor Bugs's footsteps these days and, as a result, we don't see very much of the little guy.

Capt Watson, my relief, came up for lunch this noon and we chatted a while afterwards. I filled him in on some dope regarding my job and also gave him a chance to meet some of the officers here in Reg. Watson is a nice guy, easy to talk to, and I believe will make a good Regimental Air Officer. He will have 10 days on the line with me after we move up a week from today, so he'll be quite familiar with the front enemy situation, pertaining to his area at any rate, and with a little more recon he'll be pretty well up on our whole Regimental front. He was originally a transport pilot, which he said kept him away from his family quite a bit of the time. They stuck him in Corsairs, though, when he arrived at El Toro for a fighter refresher prior to his Korean assignment. He's a Marine regular.

No mail as yet from my precious girl, but it's early and there's still a chance some will come in.

I went over to our new CP across the Imjin this afternoon to make a check on our new positions. Maj Christie has the situation fairly well completed. From all indications, we'll start moving over there by 13 Nov and be completely moved and operating by 15 Nov. I still have quite a bit of liaison to do with the 7th Marines Reg Air Office and have to tramp the lines in order to get the picture of the new sector well in my mind. The washboard roads really shake you up if you do much driving. It's a wonder the equipment lasts as long as it does under these conditions. We still haven't any side curtains or heaters on either one of our jeeps as some of them do.

I estimate the temperature this afternoon at around 40° at the most, and from the way it's dropping this afternoon, I'll bet it's going to be mighty chilly tonight. I still haven't gone to my long underwear, but come tomorrow I think I'll switch. Somehow or other I just don't care for cold weather--a common complaint from all of us California boys. It must be because I'm not used to it and it's unnatural for me. Our little old heater just can't cut the mustard on keeping our tent warm. You have to cuddle up right around it in order to keep comfortable. Our generator has been on the blink and we've been without lights for several days. They bummed another one from Div Engr's and they just hooked it up, so we've got lights again.

Bye bye,
Your very own daddy

9 Nov 52
1st Marines, Korea

Babydoll,

    No air strikes today. But tomorrow, being the 177th birthday of the USMC, we are going to run a 100-plane close air support for the Div. It should be one grand show. Hope that we have used good planning in our selection of targets, to be sure and get the full benefit of such a gigantic effort.

    Sgt Koch and I drove into Div area this morning and took care of his traffic violation. We both signed statements and talked to the reviewing officer. We won't hear of the outcome until next week. This guy has really put out for me under fire and I want to help him if I can.

    Talked to Maj French for about 30 minutes. He's a nice guy and we have a lot in common. Drove over to VMO-6 for lunch and watched Capt Layne feed raisin pie to about 20 little Korean kids. Honey, it was the cutest thing, but due to an overcast day, I couldn't take a picture and most tactical flying was grounded. They were all lined up, while the captain was sitting in a swing, and one by one they came to him with their little filthy hands out and the sweetest expectant look on their faces. Capt Layne would ask each one what they should say. Some said, "Me one, me one," others, "Sank u, sank u." The little tykes gobbled it up with gusto. Golly, they are cute.

    After lunch Koch and I drove off to the forward air strip, got an OE-1 and I took him flying for an hour. Of course he was thrilled to death. We flew up to the Canadians' sector and up and down our new MLR over our new CP at 100' at 150 MPH, and of course buzzed this CP. Returned and made my best landing to date in one of those crates. Stopped at ANGLICO, signed our statements they had typed from our roughs, picked up our radio jeep that had been there for repair and proceeded home, arriving in time for our usual volleyball game, between the Rinkydinks and the Hijinks. The Rinkys skunked us three out of five games, but we didn't go down without a fight. Tonight at supper, there sat the volleyball with a note on it, "RINKYS 3, HIJINKS 2." Ha, ha!! Doc Winchell's doings, the rascal was rubbing it in.

    Saw an amazing movie last night. They showed us "Happy Time," with Charles Boyer. It was hilariously funny. Took place in Canada. They were a family of three brothers and a gadabout grandfather; and Charles Boyer and his wife and their 13-year-old son who had discovered all about the birds and the bees too soon. I laughed and laughed. One of the brothers was a wino; drank it out of a water cooler. One was a traveling salesman--young, dashing devil-may-care type who fell madly in love with Charles Boyer's maid. Everyone was in love; even Grandpa, who was going on 65, was on the make. It was wonderful. Charles Boyer sat down and actually explained things right in the movie to his son, in a way that a father could do in real life. I got such a kick out of it because I put myself in his place seven years from now. At the very end of the picture Pe Pe's (the son's) voice changed, showing he had reached puberty, and all the men of the family were thrilled to death. <u>Go see it</u>, honey.

    Like I said, tomorrow being the MC birthday, they are dedicating the football field they pushed out near our CP for a combination helicopter strip and football field, naming it in honor of Lt Valentine.

    At 0900 I'm going down to ANGLICO and be present when my men--Boone, Evans and little Red, along with a number of others--receive their Letter of Commendation medals for their part in Bunker Hill. At 1300 our volleyball team will play the NCOs in a no-holds-barred game. At 1730 Col Layer will cut our Marine Corps birthday cake, and then they will hand out menus for us to send home to our families. We will have ham, turkey and trimmings. Probably a party in the evening too. When I announced at the briefing tonight about the 100-plane strike tomorrow, I colored it up quite a bit with flowery language--how us airdales are going all out for you crunchies etc. They got a big kick out of it.

    Lucille Ball is in the movie tonight, "Dream Boat." Bet it will be good. Our movie projector was broken for quite a while, but it's working fine now.

    About 17 days, lover.

                                        Your very own
                                            Daddy

Left:
Captured Enemy Weapons Various types of mortar and artillery shells, machine guns, rifles, and a 60mm mortar are displayed at 1st Marine Division CP. At least these would never be fired at us again.

Right: Main Logistic Link to the Front--View of the Freedom Gate Bridge from shore of Imjin. This bridge was the only one left standing after August 1952 floods. Our position was across the bridge, on the northern side of the Imjin River.

Left: Truce Talks Resumed. Marine helicopter approaches truce site at Panmunjom as negotiations reopen in October 1952. With my high powered telescope I could nearly make out as clear a picture as shown, when I manned my Hill 229 bunker.

Photo credit USMC

Upper Left: Doc Mitchell, 3/1/1 dentist. He was more than a dentist, assisting our surgeons, Doc Brodrick and Doc John Kennedy, all of them performing wonders administering to the many casualties as the battles for the outposts raged on, particularly during July through Sept 1952. This picture was taken when I flew Doc Mitchell in an OE-1, borrowed from VMO-6, from the Division to Seoul, ASCOM City, to catch his plane home. Building in background is the USMC air freight and passenger terminal in Seoul. Praises to Doc Craighead also.

Upper Right: 3/1/1 Executive Officer, Maj Wesley R. Christie and Peterson

Middle Left: The helicopter carrying our peace negotiators to Panmunjom. I was on standby alert to man my tank if anything went wrong.

Middle Right: This is my personal bunker at OP 2. It was showered with enemy incoming many times; in fact I was hit by mortar shrapnel at the entrance once. It did a number on my flak jacket.

Lower Right: Our friendly rabbit at OP 2.

CHAPTER 19

177TH BIRTHDAY OF THE UNITED STATES MARINES

Seventy-eight days and nights on the firing line had taken its toll on my fellow Marines who had been under intense strain from the constant shelling and hand-to-hand combat with the enemy. Having witnessed many of our friends and companions killed or wounded, most of us had fallen into a deep depression, not knowing when it might befall ourselves.

While on the MLR during all that period, I personally had not seen anyone drinking, perhaps mainly due to the fact that no liquor was available, but also because we had been on 24-hour duty always at the ready, expecting that we would be called upon to repel the next enemy offensive.

We all longed for the day when we could relax and let our hair down a bit and, now that we had finally made it to a reserve status, the Marine birthday celebration was presenting just that occasion.

10 Nov 52
1st Marines, Korea
Monday 1630
177th birthday of USMC

Precious family,
The boys can be heard singing in the tent next to mine. They have been drinking martinis for the past couple of hours and their singing sounds like it. It's been declared a holiday routine here in the Regiment and the boys are cooperating, and how! All they were waiting for was an excuse like this.
We fell out for the dedication of the parade/football field in honor of Lt Valentine this morning at 0830. I prepared a large map of the new sector we are going into, and laid out all the Div, Reg't, Bn, Co boundaries, as well as the locations of the 4.2" mortars (used by the FACs for marking air targets with smoke mortar for air strikes); have to know the max range and radios. Laid out all the helicopter strips, MSR, MLR and outposts. I secured the four maps together, then attached them in a piece of cardboard for easy folding and carrying.
At lunch today Col Layer cut our birthday cake for us because he will be up at the Div this evening. After lunch I prepared my maps a little more, then at 1330 I went out and played volleyball. There were three teams: one NCO, the Rinkydinks and the Hyjinks. We Hyjinks beat the NCOs in our 1st game, Rinkys beat NCOs, then Rinkys beat us. They were far more sober than about three of the players on our team. McLeod, Joshlin and Kramer had been

drinking since before lunch and were sure loose. They had a big time and we had lots of laughs, but they lost the game for us, that's for sure. We played until 1500, then knocked off and went up to our outside movie arena on the side of a hill and watched a USO show--six men and three women--the usual singing, acrobatics, singing cowboys, hillbillies, a puppet act, banjo player and lady magician. Now I'm writing to my precious baby doll that I miss so very much. Gosh, darling, I love you so much. Waiting for those 16 days to pass is going to be pure torture. I can hardly believe I'm going home, honey. I have been over here in Korea so darn long. It seemed as though I would never reach my rotation date, but now it's going to arrive just as sure as you're born.

The boys next door are singing "From the Halls of Montezuma" again for the 50th time today. Gets flatter all the time.

I'm hungry tonight, sweetheart, from all the exercise I've had today. Boy, we're having baked ham and turkey, yummy. They have certainly done wonders in feeding us guys over here in Korea. Nobody ever complains. Certainly nothing like the last war (in many ways).

I am enclosing a menu.

1st MARINE REGIMENT
*Commemorating the 177th Anniversary
of the U.S. Marine Corps   1775-1952]
In the Field   Korea*

Colonel Walter F. LAYER	*Commanding Officer*
Lieutenant Colonel Glenn R. LONG	*Executive Officer*
Major Clyde W. SHEALY	*S-1 Officer*
Major John N. RENTZ	*S-2 Officer*
Major Stanley N. MC LEOD	*S-3 Officer*
Captain Stanley E. KRAMEK	*S-4 Officer*
Captain Bernard W. PETERSON	*Air Officer*
Second Lieutenant Elroy SUDEK	*Commanding Officer H&S Co*
First Lieutenant Jerome MC LAUGHLIN	*Mess Officer*
Master Sergeant Clinton O. SKEEN	*Mess Management Chief*
Technical Sergeant James H. NELSON	*Mess Management Chief*

MENU

APPETIZER - Shrimp Cocktail

DINNER -   Roast Turkey, Virginia Baked Ham, Giblet Gravy, Sage Dressing, Cranberry Sauce, Snowflake Potatoes, Candied Carrots, Buttered Corn, Hot Rolls, Butter - Jam, Pickles, Celery Sticks.

DESSERT - Birthday Cake, Ice Cream, Fresh Fruit, Chocolate Milk, Coffee.

It was every bit as good as the menu pictures it. After dinner we had a lot of laughs. Doc Murto stood up and tried to make a speech. He's in the Navy, of course, and was half tight, as were nearly all the Marine officers. Nobody was drunk but all had had a few drinks and were really in the spirit of the evening. Doc would say, "I want to pay a tribute on this auspicious occasion to the glorious United States Marine Corps on its 177th birthday." Every time he said the word Marine everyone yelled and whistled, and every time he said Navy they booed. We had quite a time, I must say. Those doctors sure had a big time this afternoon. They are all a swell bunch of guys, all about my age. Seems odd that I can be as old as a doctor or lawyer or dentist, but time rolls on. Everyone treats me swell and makes me feel as though it takes a certain special kind of person to be a pilot and also makes me feel good about being one.

They all ask me questions pertaining to flying, navigation, engines and radio etc. I, of course, have all that stuff cold and snap back with an easy explanation that leaves them half way up in the air and halfway squared. Seems funny sometimes, being asked something about flying, or airplanes, from a high-ranking ground officer. I have always been around air officers that knew as much or more than I did on the subject and hence we often talked of other subjects.

Tomorrow afternoon at 1400 I am supposed to deliver a lecture to the new officers on the incoming draft. I have to work up a little program, so as to present to them as complete a picture as possible in as short a period as possible, of all the important facts on air that they will need to know. They are arriving tonight at 2100, travelling from Seoul on the slow old Korean train. I'll bet they will have a warped idea of what they are coming up here to, especially riding in a rickety old train in the black of night, transferring to truck for the last 12 miles up to the assembly area where they will be mustered and billeted. There's something strange and mysterious about arriving in a new place at night. I've watched the arrival of many new men, all wide-eyed and with that lost look about them. Maj Shealy says there are roughly 400 officers and men and, in addition to his regular duties as Regimental SI, he has had to arrange orders, chow, billeting, lectures, training etc. for them.

New men coming over is certainly a welcome sight. It means replacement and rotation for these other kids that are fed up to the necktie with war--and nearly 90 percent of them have one or more Purple Hearts to show for their tour in Korea.

All for now, angel girl. I love you, precious. Tell my little guys that their daddy loves and adores them, and is counting the days until I'll be home eating waffles and reading funny books again with them. Honey, we can look forward to a wonderful life together. No mail today, darn it. Maybe I'll get one tomorrow.

Your very own daddy

11 Nov 52
World War I Armistice Day
1st Marines, Korea

Dearest family that I love,
What a miserable day this is. Rained all night and it's still raining. The mud is terrible too. Can't figure out for the life of me why it didn't snow. It sure missed a good chance, that's all I can say. It's been cold too, but your old man has been doing some administrative chores that didn't require his setting foot outside more than half a dozen times today.

This afternoon we gave the incoming draft officers a one-and-a-half-hour briefing which they apparently enjoyed. We covered a heck of a lot of territory. They also enjoyed my two bits' worth on air. Arriving at the Div this morning at 0330 in a blinding rain, they really saw Korea at its worst. I'm sure glad I'm going home instead of just coming out here. Some of them stand to be here a year. They had already been given their assignments to Bn and Company. Several drew assignments to the outposts in our new sector that are being hit almost every night by the goonies. They looked like a bunch of worried boys. After General Pollock talked to the officers, Col Layer introduced each one of them to him. And then the general left and we commenced our briefing. Col Layer returned at the completion of the briefing and gave a nice talk to the new men.

A guy doesn't have much to his credit out here in Korea except the fact that after you've put in your time you have that on your side, and you treasure that time like a bag of precious jewels. I guess life is like that. I've waited a long time to be first on that waiting list and now that I'm on top I'm feeling awfully good, but sort of sorry for the kids that are just coming out.

I'm arranging a schedule now for the (3) Bns because we just picked up (6) films for the training of the TACP enlisted men. I suppose I'll attend myself, for my enjoyment, education and edification.

Talked to Walt Daniels of the 2nd Bn. He went down to K3, bummed an F9F Panther jet, came up here the other day and gave his Bn and Anaconda Baker a real buzz job. He said he came over on his fastest run (I saw him) at 640 MPH, out of a dive, of course. Brother, that's *moving, I hope to tell you. The day I buzzed you in the T-33 jet (P80) over our house at Manhattan Beach, we were travelling 550 MPH; that's moving too! Walt said it was like a real tonic for him after being cooped up here at Div for four months. That's a heck of a long time away from jets to just jump in one and fly 250 miles, then put on a show like he did. He's requested extension out here in Korea for F9Fs again. What a guy! He's single and a hot jet pilot--I think I understand.*

I'm happy I have my little family all squared away and waiting for me when I get home. I remember the thoughts that were going through my mind a little over seven years ago, when I was about ready to return home from Okinawa to my precious wife, and I thought of where we would live and what we would do. Could I make a good living on the outside? Would I be sorry for chucking the Corps? Would Marion still think I was the top brick of the chimney when she saw me in civilian clothes? What would our first baby be?--and over and over again, how very much I loved you and missed you, precious girl.

Just returned from supper chow. Col Layer told me he was going to be transferred to Pusan to be the senior advisor to the Korean Marine Corps Academy, on or about 20 Nov. A wonderful break for him. He'll be a good man for the job. He'll really snap those Korean officer candidates in proper, like he did with our gang. He's a fine man and a dedicated Marine. Glad he's decided to integrate and become a regular.

Winds of 50 kts expected tonight. Also freezing rain and snow for in the morning, and 20° temp. expected on the morning of 13 Nov. Brother, the roads are six inches to eight inches deep in mud; now if it freezes it will be worse than a washboard. Some of the units are moving tomorrow up to the new CP and set up in the mud. No wooden deck as yet for them, but I'm trying my darndest to procure some wood for them. A good bunch of kids.

Happy day! I received three letters, all dated Nov 5th, from Mom, Ben and you, dearest girl. Golly, it's wonderful getting letters from you all. Wasn't Randy-boy cute, telling the little kids his daddy is flying an airplane in "Kera." Golly, he must be awfully cute now, honey. I know I'm in for a real surprise. Oh honey, I want you to tell the kids that Daddy won't be carrying any presents with him when he comes home because of the space problem. I will buy them presents, though, and ship them parcel post and they will receive them prior to Xmas. I don't want them to be disappointed if I return empty handed, but you know how hard it is traveling with a bunch of extra gear. I got a big bang out of Ricky's test papers; he's doing a fine job in school.

Mom says Scotty is proud of me and talks me up to all their friends. Can hardly imagine him giving me lip service. Maybe the old bird isn't as hard hearted as he tries to make you believe.

Ben was his usual well-expressed self in his letter. If he needs another hundred or so, let him have it, sweetheart. He's getting a lot of contracts lately. Hope they all materialize for him. He is certainly to be congratulated on his aggressiveness and, if there's anything I admire in a person, it's that trait. I think our Ricky boy has it too, for which I am very happy.

You occupied my thoughts, precious girl, most of the day. Can't get you off my mind. You mentioned in your letter that you'd be a new woman--can't say as I go for that; I loved the old one too much for any changes. Happy day, honey bun. Won't be long now--15 or so more days before I shove off for heaven and my precious family.

Love,
Daddy

12 Nov 52
1st Marines, Korea

Dearest family,
  Early this morning, at the crack of dawn, Maj John Rentz and I, his staff NCO and mine, all went for a recon of the left sector we will occupy. The road up to the OP had been washed out from the rain, and the mud made it slippery going for us. They have just completed this bunker which is on commanding ground, affording one a wonderful view of our left regimental sector, including all outposts and MLR. Maj Rentz wanted me to check a helicopter strip up on a

nose just to south of his OP a few hundred feet. He wanted it there because he feels during the coming winter months he'll need it for evac and resupply.

I've been getting a lot of calls lately from any one of a dozen various units attached to our regiment that are moving up with us. We will assume operational control of the sector at noon on the 16th.

Dropped in at the new forward Reg't CP also this morning and found it wasn't ready for us yet. The bulldozers have been working over the shelf where our enlisted squad tent will be situated, and also the artillery liaison squad. Our radio jeep will have a good location as far as communications are concerned.

Last night the wind blew up a storm and it was really cold. Then a cloud cover moved in but it didn't rain. The clouds raised the temperature but it still stayed in the high 30s during the day. Should be powerful cold in the morning. Our little oil burner stove burns between 7 and 10 gallons of oil per day. Just imagine how many stoves like it there are in Korea and you have some idea of how much oil is burned each day.

The problem of Supply (logistics) boggles the mind. The quartermasters certainly do a wonderful job of supplying us, though. Think of all the tentage, food, clothes, ammunition, transportation and personnel problems. I have my share, being in Reg't, of personnel problems. Five men are returning home from the 1st Reg't TACP. I am getting five replacements in the morning and will send them off to the various Bns. There they will receive firsthand front-line experience from the old timers and be given additional training as their Bns drop back in reserve. The boys of the 15th draft are the ones returning home. Stephans, a corporal on my Reg't team, is leaving. He came out here last Nov. Some tour for them. Fourteen days from today the new FACs will arrive at the Reg't and Battalions. Twelve days from now Capt Watson will move over here to learn my duties.

Time is scooting right along, isn't it, honey? I can hardly wait. Not much news from the daddy today. I love that little picture you sent me of Rick taken in school.

Love ya,
Daddy

1st REGIMENT TAKES UP FORWARD POSITION AGAIN

13 Nov 52
1st Marines
Up on the battle lines again, Korea

Dearest girl,

We moved, lock, stock and barrel, today from the reserve CP up here to our new CP near the battle line. We're far enough back, however, to be classed as rear area poags by the battalions. It was a lovely day today, fortunately, and the sun dried up some of the mud from the roads, which was a big help. Most of the tents in our new CP here had been put up by the H&S Co and they were ready for use. But since our team is detached from ANGLICO and has separate tentage, we had to set up the enlisted men's squad tent and also put up a small blackout tent for our radio jeep. With the staff officer's tent already up, it remained a simple matter for me to get squared away. There are eight officers in my tent. We have electric lights, two space heaters and a wooden deck, also wood side board up two feet. It's very comfortable.

At noon today I went over to the 3rd Bn/11th Marines and had lunch with Capt Bob Zugler, our artillery liaison officer. Had a fine lunch--meat balls cooked in deep tomato sauce with tomatoes, sliced onions, celery and sliced carrots in sauce, creamed spuds and peas with a tomato gravy, pears, coffee. It was delicious, honey. Then I drove over to the 11th Marines CP clear back on the other side of the Imjin in the reserve, where I attended a briefing of air officers and artillery officers, mostly colonels. Those present included the CO of the 11th Marines and the CO of VMO-6. Several were from the 5th Marines.

On 10 Nov they flew 98 sorties in support of the Marine Div. We talked about flak suppression and the other various activities. Two-hour meeting. People had flown all the way up from K3, in the southernmost part of Korea, to attend. Big deal. I added my two bits' worth every now and then.

Tomorrow morning I have to go over to the 2nd Bn where MGen Edwin A. Pollock will award me my Silver Star.

No mail today. Love you, darling. I'm back in Air business again. Kiss my darlings and tell them I love them. Keep a couple of kisses for yourself, honey. I have to knock off to set up my cot and break out my sleeping gear now.

    Love ya,
        Your very own Daddy

14 Nov 52
1st Marines
On the line, Korea

Family o'mine,

The day dawned damp and dismal and the daddy departed for the distant side of the darn Imjin. My departure was delayed due to the fact that there was a big traffic jam in the CP area, bogged down from mud. I got out of the basket at 0630, shaved and put on all clean clothes. Had breakfast and by 0800 was on the way back to the 2/1 reserve CP. After 30 minutes of riding in the open jeep, raining all the time, colder than an Eskimo's nose, we arrived. A formation of troops standing in the cold drizzle showed evidence of their long vigil. I reported to Major McClure, the 2/1's executive officer, who directed me to the center of the formation, where I joined two enlisted men, the three of us to be presented with the Silver Star Medal.

After some 10 minutes of standing at attention, the general's helicopter arrived and the formation (250 men) stiffened a little more. The commanding officers of each of the S.S. Medal recipients was also present. We three marched forward and, as the citations were read, MGen Edwin A. Pollock, Commanding General of the First Marine Division in the Field in Korea, FMF, pinned on our medals, shook our hands and said to me, "Captain Peterson, it's to aviators like yourself that we ground troopers give thanks, for you save countless lives of your brother Marines by your tireless efforts in air support. Thank you." The photographer snapped two pictures of me, and every one of the top brass shook our hands. After the P.I.O. Marine correspondents asked us for the names of our wives and mothers for hometown release purposes, we shoved off for our CP back up on the lines. I was proud to have received my Star from Gen Pollock, a fine man. I guess I'll hold on to my medal and citation and carry them home personally so nothing happens to them.

A Cpl Howard, whom I worked with a great deal when up on Bunker Hill, was one of the S.S. Medal recipients. He had been hit a good many times in his OP up on 6A in that darn trench from where I used to direct my air strikes. Very proudly, he told me his wife had given birth to twin girls on 28 Sept. Howard should be an officer and I wouldn't be a bit surprised but what he's been recommended for same.

Bob Zugler, the artillery liaison officer, and I drove over to the 3rd Bn (Thundering Third Reserve CP) this afternoon and had a shower. The shower unit was outside of a squad tent, with the shower pipes and heads inside the tent and wooden grates to stand on; an adjoining tent served as a dressing area. No lights in either tent, clothes piled all over everywhere, hot water in the shower room causing steam, and the rest of the bodies all groping around in the dark and steam-filled tent, it made quite a picture, I must say. I couldn't help but laugh to myself at the total confusion unfolding before me, and I right in the middle of it. What a luxury our shower will be when I, at long, long last, stand my body beneath its wonderful hot water, in the privacy of our very own (and Union Federal Savings and Loan) shower and bath combination.

Oh! Oh! I hear incoming rounds hitting the MLR in our sector. It's 2100 and awfully dark and cold out. Heck of a night for a push and I hope and pray things remain on the quiet side, at least for the next 12 or 13 days.

Speaking of short time and the thought of coming home etc, Doc Mitchell, the dentist, received a letter from a doctor friend of his that just returned home and is presently in Frisco, *stating all the info Mitchell might need on his return trip to Uncle Sugar. The most important item of the text was the fact that the good doctor snagged onto one of 39 available seats on a Pan American commercial line leased by our government to fly the Pacific. Seems he made it home from Frisco in 33 1/2 hours--10 hours from Tokyo to Wake, 12 hours to Honolulu, 11 1/2 to Frisco. Some time, eh? I imagine the Marine transports will be nearly as fast, but if I can manage it I'll try to work the commercial end. Boy, those guns are really pounding tonight!*

Miss you so, my precious wife and partner. Can hardly wait for the 12 or 13 days to roll by. They'll move along, as all the others have, but darn it, they seem to be dragging something awful, in spite of the fact that I try to avoid dwelling on days remaining. I have been awfully busy today checking with the Reg't air officer of the 7th Marines (Woodbury) as well as all of my Bn air control officers. Checking helicopter strip numbers, evac pickup points, code names, our radios and other equipment. I'll be so happy to leave this outfit and forget all these darn problems of air. I've written two reports also today, besides preparing my briefing material for tonight's brief. Gave a lecture on flak suppression tonight during briefing.

Love you darling,
Your very own Daddy

15 Nov 52
1st Marines, Korea
On the line, 1630

Hi Honey Girl, Ricky and Randy,

The Daddy just returned after being gone all day. Doc Mitchell has been asking me for ages to please fly him down to Ascom City near Seoul and pick up his suitcase, so he'll be all set to leave for home when he gets his orders on 1 Dec. My team chief, S/Sgt Koch, was going into ANGLICO this morning to pick up some gear and have the jeep looked at, so Mitchell and I went along.

We arrived at VMO-6 at around 0930 and, on a hunch that he wouldn't be allowed to pick up his gear without going-home orders, we called down to Ascom City and found out he absolutely couldn't get his gear without orders. We called the Div Dental office and asked if we could get a set of orders for the doc so he could pick up his stuff and they said they would knock him out a set. We drove all the way back to Div, picked up his orders and I dropped into the awards board and checked on Col Layer's Air Medal. They didn't even have any record of receiving a request for one, so I'll have to start it through the proper channels all over again.

Doc and I ate lunch after we got back to VMO-6, then hopped in an OE and off we went. I climbed to 5000' and flew over K14, the big Air Force jet base, and Doc took a lot of colored pictures. Sure hope they turn out good. As we landed at Ascom City (an old Japanese munitions factory), the telephone poles and chimney stacks made it really rough trying to judge my approach to the tiny postage-stamp airstrip. No tower, no radio, no wind sock, but I came in and, after making three passes to be darn sure I had it measured right, I set her down. It was quite muddy, so we stopped rolling in a hurry.

We hiked over to the huge warehouse which had previously stored ammo made by the Japanese and used against us in WWII. Fortunately, the Marines were on the ball and, for once, I ran into an outfit that had a system. Doc hadn't seen his suitcase since he had turned it over to a Marine supply sergeant in Japan last March. They had his card filed and in two minutes, out of the thousands of suitcases, seabags and footlockers stored there, to Doc's amazement, out he came with his bag.

We hoofed it back to the plane but, because it didn't sound just right to me on my engine check, I cut it and got three mechs from HMR-161 hangar and they found I had a loose muffler. We were on our way a short time later and I took the Doc over our DIV MLR at 4000'. Seeing it for the first time, he was taking pictures like mad all the while.

We landed at 1430, loaded his gear into our waiting jeep and began the long, bumpy, cold ride back to our CP--took 1 hour and 15 minutes. Boy, what horrible roads! Arriving at the CP at 1545, I took care of a bunch of phone calls that had accumulated during my absence. Then Sgt Koch and I tried hooking up my radio to the storage batteries but I can't get a strong signal. Problems!

Maj Shealy stopped us from using the little road they had cut for us up to the hill where the enlisted men's tent is. Looks like we have to park it in Reg't Motor Transport area now, a quarter of a mile away. Two 55-gallon drums for our diesel oil burners have been rigged up just outside our tent which will help us out a lot. We won't have to worry about running out of fuel one of these cold nights. Bulldozers and graders are knocking themselves out pushing a flat area out just in front of our tent. We are on a shelf about 60 feet above the road level and have quite a steep hill to climb to get up here. High rank all over the place. They are all assembling for their beer and cocktails prior to supper.

Passed Signal Battalion communicators all the way back from Div; they were in the process of laying an entirely new phone system, consisting of about 50 wires all wrapped together and hung on poles 20' off the deck. Very good job. In the past many of the lines were lying on the ground and oftentimes the moisture rendered the entire system inoperative. Many improvements are being made. VMO-6 strip is really in fine shape. Ascom City was a mud hole as compared to VMO-6.

Had bread at noon out of wax paper, pre-sliced, just like stateside. Understand new bakery at service Bn is operating now--very good. Everyone is getting wooden decks and are building doors for their tents. People will be in fair shape for the coming winter months. The roads will be a problem, however.

No mail up to this writing today. Everyone is running around getting squared away for the big changie-changie tomorrow at noon, when we assume operational control of this sector. The troops have been moving all day. Many hundreds of trucks could be seen on the roads today. Will knock off for supper and resume same after eating, honey. Love you, dearest girl. Can hardly wait until I'm holding you in my arms, precious girl.

Back from chow and briefing. Had fried chicken dehydrated spuds and gravy, peas, coffee, apple sauce--very satisfying. Had a scoosh piece of chicken--could have eaten more but none available. Left full, however.

Talked of a new fire plan for artillery, utilizing batteries that can best parallel a terrain feature while deflated (behind a hill). My FACs will occupy their front-line bunkers tomorrow and be set up to direct air strikes. I have to alert them about submitting more requests for air. They ran five air strikes today: 1 each for KMC, KPR (Kimpo Provisional Regiment), 7th Marines and two for the 7th Marines. The colonel wants six missions on request at all times. MPQ radar strikes are still not forthcoming, due to Anaconda Charlie's gear, which is still not operating.

Maj Charlie Reifel just drew his pay he had let accumulate since coming over here last June--$3000.00. His wife has been living with his folks, saving her dough. He has only a $150.00 a month allotment going home to her per month. Maj Christie's wife is living in Compton--649-B Santa Fe Apts., South Santa Fe St., Compton.. They have a five-and-a-half-year-old boy. Chris wanted me to stop in and see her, or phone on my return. I thought maybe you could look her up prior to my return and establish liaison. Mrs. W.R. Christie. Maj Christie, you remember, was the Bn executive officer under Col Armatage, then under Col Altman. He always treated me OK. He's a quiet sort of a guy, wants to live in Georgia or some other southern state but his wife wants to live in Compton, where her parents are living. She's from Compton, went to school there, hates earthquakes and may accept Georgia on account of them, according to Chris. Chris, you remember, had the responsibility of building this new CP and now is relieving LtCol Rentz as the (S2), Intelligence of the 1st Regiment. Maj Bud Honeycutt has returned from the hospital ship and he's looking fine. Came to the briefing tonight, along with his CO, Col Rogers, CO of 3rd Bn 11th Marines, Artillery Officer.

The boys are talking over the Battle of Bunker Hill. Said the newspapers did more for the Marines than any other battle they have participated in for some time. McLeod said after the newspapers built it up they couldn't move off.

True, the Marine Corps, as well as the other services, had been shaved to the bone by budget cutbacks during the years preceding Korea. However, due to the dismal situation Korea presented, Congress mandated the size of the Marine Corps and wrote in the 1952 House/Senate Conference Report that the Marine Corps "must be the most ready when the Nation generally is least ready." That decree assured the Marine Corps that it would always remain as "a balanced force-in-readiness--ready to suppress or contain international disturbances short of large-scale war." Living up to the expectations of that conference report put the Marine Corps ever on its toes to fulfill that mandate, and it was made very obvious there to all of us that we must always perform as expected.

Capt Melanson is now Maj McLeod's 3A assistant operations officer. He was "H" Company commander and had his hitch in <u>hell</u> on Bunker Hill. Spent as much time on the hill as any company commander. You remember the Commonwealth took over a small sector to our right. The 1stMarDiv had occupied outposts Ransom and Warsaw. However, when we turned it over to the Brits, they said, "To hell with occupying the bloody things, we'll go out every other night and let the goonies have it the other nights." That's the way it's been going on ever since. Col Rogers just said that they are the darnedest lot. If there are two limey officers, they'll start an officers club and, come hell or high water, come 1600 the war stops for a spot of tea. "I say, old boy, have you plenty of bullets to support us in cannonading?"

"Righto, old bean."

Enough blabber for tonight, sweetheart. Talked to Maj White of VMR-151, Marine Transport Squadron, today at VMO-6 mess. He said that ComNavFed has jurisdiction over the 39 seats of PanAm commercial airlines under government contract and that Marine transports can only guarantee through passage as far as Honolulu and delays of up to five days in Honolulu, whereas PanAm is straight through to Frisco, 33-and-a-half hours. I'm going to try my darnedest, honey girl. I adore you, precious girl, and am crossing the days off my calender with great gusto and vim. Still no mail tonight. Perhaps tomorrow.

Kiss my boys, honey, and save a few for yourself, dearest. Love my little family so very much.

Love,
Daddy

16 Nov 52
1st Marines, Korea
2300

Dearest girl,
    My team Sgt handed me two letters today and boy, was I happy. Yours of 10 Nov arrived and also one from Ben. He's overdoing it. Sure is good hearing from both of you so often.
    I've been trying to set up a helicopter evacuation of a hemorrhagic fever victim*. He's not long for this world and Doc John Kennedy called me during the movie tonight, ("Affair in Trinidad," with Rita Hayworth--very good, I thought). It's raining and there isn't a bit of a horizon, pitch black out, so I talked him out of it tonight but called DivAir and set up a copter evac for first light in the morning.
    Had a busy day today. Spent some time in the bunker but it's such a darn overcrowded deal and confusion reigns supreme, so I bugged out and set up shop for the rest of the day in my enlisted team's area where I could monitor my radio jeep. The 5th Reg got two air strikes today but none for us. This morning a white frost covered everything and the ground was frozen harder than a brick. We literally slid down our hill. Had to get a bunch of extra batteries and chargers to my front line battalions this morning. So far our sector hasn't been hit since we took over. Our artillery is firing their normal H&I missions now and they sound as if they were right in our back yard.
    Am going to make this a short one, honey, because I'm tired and want to hit the basket before midnight, since I'll have to get up for the evac in the early morning.

Night, darling,
Daddy

* *See Appendix #2*

17 Nov 52
1st Marines, Korea

Dearest family,
    Received the two most wonderful pictures of the two most precious boys in the whole world. Golly, honey, I hadn't realized how much they had changed. You probably hadn't noticed but the closeness of the pictures certainly brought out those changes. The everyday snapshot doesn't tell what's taking place in the face. They are adorable, and I love them so very much. I'm proud to be their daddy, I'll tell the whole world. I've shown the pictures around to my fellow officers and they think they are two very handsome boys. They don't all agree that they look like me, however. My enlisted team could hardly believe I was old enough or had been married long enough to have two boys as grown up as they are.
    I just happened to think about what you had mentioned in your last letter about Ricky putting the cartoon I had drawn in his treasure box. It brought me back many, many years to when I had a treasure box and put the darnedest things away in it for posterity but, for the life of me, I can't remember where it is now or what I ever did with the junk that was in it. At the time, it was my most cherished possession.
    Had one air strike today for Evil-Eye-14, which is the call sign of my 1st Bn. The weather wasn't conducive to close air support in our sector today, due to a 4000-foot layer of clouds. They made one run and decided against continuing because it was too close to friendly lines. Bill Watson, my relief, was controlling it and the OE (aerial observer) came up on the radio and said he would not assume responsibility for their control, with the possibility of their hitting friendly positions only some 1000-yards away. The Marine F9Fs were finally directed to fly north of the bomb line and hit targets of opportunity. Watson is coming up tonight to snap in at our Regimental briefing and will attend them for the rest of the time. Sure seems nice having one's relief so close at hand. I feel like packing up and shoving off, but of course that's not possible.
    Got up at 0630 (brrr it was cold) and checked the weather. It was too foggy for the copter, so we couldn't evac our hemorrhagic fever victim until 1045.
    Time is growing short, dearest girl, and before long I"ll be holding you in my arms once again. I love you, precious girl. Our day is coming. Only nine or ten more days, dearest.

                                            Your very own,
                                               Daddy

18 Nov 52
1st Marines, Korea
2030

Dearest little family,
    Brother, will I be glad to get out of here. From 1700 this afternoon until 1800 the artillery outfits across the river from our CP got lambasted by Chinese heavy artillery, 152mm, which is <u>big gear</u>, and the count ran up and over 300 rounds. The friendly artillery positions are only about 1500 meters to our east and the shells were sailing right over our CP. We could hear them whistling and, of course, hitting their target. They caused two secondary explosions of powder ammo storage and small arms ammo that continued to go off after the artillery let up. We expected a few short rounds to land here in our CP at any second, but the good Lord was on our side and they all kept sailing over our heads on their deadly way. They were so close to us they sounded like a freight train going by.
    The radio outfit with our Regiment intercepted a Chinese communication that I read in the bunker tonight after the briefing. I make it a point each night to check the bunker and follow very carefully all of the action on our front. Lt Ewing, the young British liaison officer, was calling his unit, giving them the info on the radio intercept because it is in his sector that they anticipate the enemy raid tonight. They usually hit the Hook, which the British now

control. We gave them the Hook a couple of weeks ago when we shifted left. As I'm writing right now, it's quiet; let's hope it stays that way.

This morning it was cold, 22°, and it never got over 35° all day. I worked with the engineers building another helicopter strip today. Sure feels good tonight sitting here by the heater. My wash was frozen solid this morning--first time I've ever seen clothes frozen, being a southern California boy.

Watson came up tonight for the briefing. Have to attend a flak suppression meeting at the 3rd Bn, 11th CP tomorrow at 1000. Trying to perfect our flak suppression program to aid the pilots when they are up here working with us on close air support.

Col Layer is being relieved by Col Adams on the 21st. Big ceremony is being planned here at our CP and Gen Pollock is going to officiate. Got Layer and Adams both a copter recon this afternoon. Copter pilots hate to fly Layer because he makes them go forward of the MLR most of the time and our losses from this type activity have been high.

All for tonight, honey. I love and adore you, honey girl.

Your very own,
Daddy

P.S. *I may have a little surprise for you.*

FOLLOW-UP TO LOST KOREAN LETTERS

The happy day finally arrived when my orders were received rotating me home. The First Regiment and several battalion FACs held a going-away bash for me, and it was a good feeling to realize the rapport and goodwill that had been developed over the past five months between the air and ground forces in our little area. I found out that the gravel-pounders love us airedales because we save their bacon so often.

Leaving Seoul, I caught a transport down to 1stMarAir Wing Headquarters at K3, Pohang, then flew to Itami, Japan, to pick up the balance of my gear. Japanese Air Lines was on the base recruiting Marine pilots headed for home. Their offer seemed very attractive but I was too anxious to return home to my little family to consider it seriously. Among other things, it would have involved flying Convair 240/340 type transports in the foul weather conditions that prevailed a great deal of time in the Orient. A number of my fellow Marine airmen did accept and, after a 60-day home leave, returned to Japan Air Lines for a long successful airline pilot career.

Continuing my long trail homeward, I caught a plane to Tokyo and checked into a military transient hotel to await further transportation orders. While there I checked out all of the major sites and sampled some of the delicious foods and wines. The next day I boarded a Northwest Air Lines DC-6 airliner, under charter to the military, and flew to Shimya, an Aleutian island, landing in a dense fog on instruments. Upon landing, the stuff was so thick we had to taxi behind a follow-me jeep to the headquarters building. This was a fuel and chow stop.

The big mess hall was crowded with Canadian soldiers on their way to Korea. They finished and boarded their transport after exchanging a few words with us. Following our meal, we reboarded our plane and were soon winging our way toward Elmindorf Air Force Base in Anchorage, Alaska. About an hour's flying time from our last stop, word was received that the transport carrying the Canadians had crashed into the sea, with no survivors. What a shock!

In our final approach to landing at Elmindorf the night lights of the city confused us with the runway lights of the airfield for a moment. But then we were safely on the ground, soon fed, refueled and on our way to McChord Air Force Base, near Seattle, Washington. Upon arrival, we learned that a troop transport had just crashed on landing, with numerous deaths and injuries. The base was running wild with emergency vehicles. Something told me that this business, with its sudden death and everyday turmoil, was no longer for me and I'd be glad to relegate it to the past.

I managed to get to a phone and called Marion. How wonderful to hear her voice after all those uncertain months of separation! A military bus took me to the Marine Barracks in Seattle, where I was to report in for further orders. Upon checking into the office I couldn't believe my eyes. Sitting there, smoking a big black cigar, was the very same Marine master sergeant I had checked in with when I returned from WWII seven years before! He endorsed my orders and, with a puzzled expression, queried, "Don't I know you, Captain Peterson, from some place before?"

I replied that I had stopped off here in 1945 when returning from the South Pacific. He remembered me as the guy that had given him an especially hard time while cooling my heels awaiting my orders to Treasure Island, San Francisco, for processing out of the Corps. It had taken weeks! He reassured me that I would not have to wait this time and could proceed to Treasure Island immediately.

Leaving the boys with her parents, Marion had caught the train in Los Angeles and was all settled in at the Marine Hotel in San Francisco by the time I arrived. What a joy to hold her in my arms once again! I was soon given orders to inactive duty, free to return home. We had three wonderful days together seeing the sights of that fair city, a place forever enshrined in our hearts. I couldn't take my eyes off Marion or the Golden Gate Bridge--both symbols of what I had been hoping and praying for over those lonely months. We caught the train back to Los Angeles, and I was engulfed by greetings from the family. Son Eric, six now, came running to me, leaped into my arms, wrapping his legs about my body and his arms around my neck, but it wasn't until we got into the house and I had lifted three-year-old Randy up and banged his head on the living room ceiling beam that he warmed up and admitted, "Yup, you my Daddy."

A few days later Eric led me to the French door between the living room and the porch saying, "Daddy, the house is going to fall down. I can hear something down there. Are they termites?" Then he was down on his knees with his ear against the door jamb. Reaching down, I scraped the paint away and, sure enough, the termites had left the paint and riddled the wood beneath. Yes, you could actually hear something going on there. So, instead of relaxing and taking a short trip with the family, I proceeded to sledge out our concrete porch, treat the termites, and repair the damage for the next 30 days. Even so, I was thrilled to be home again, and I definitely felt I was needed.

The local Manhattan Beach press arrived for pictures and a short interview, seeming figuratively to put a period at the end of the long sentence I had just completed. The Santa Monica Marine Corps Reserve held an awards ceremony in my honor, inviting my friends and family, and that was my last official act involving the United States Marine Corps.

The local American Legion asked me to come down and give them a talk. A number of AiResearch friends showed up at the meeting and wondered when I was going to return to my old gas turbine experimental development technician job in the test lab. I was uncertain as to whether I should return to AiResearch or go back to engineering college on the G.I. Bill, while living off our savings until they were exhausted. While still contemplating what my next course of action would be, I received a telephone call from our chief engineer at AiResearch, Homer Wood, asking me to come in and have lunch with him. I had a good visit with Homer the following day at his office, covering my activities since leaving the company. Homer then popped the question: would I like to come back to work for him as a development engineer, working under Hal Greenwald in the Gas Turbine Auxiliary Power Group? I immediately accepted, for that was the main reason I was planning to return to college, to complete my formal engineering degree and then apply for the job Homer had just offered me. It was understood, however, that I would continue my formal education in my free time. Homer Wood had reviewed my past education in the military, aeronautical engineering school, correspondence courses with the Marine Corps Institute, and past experience. He had concluded that I could handle the job. Thrilled with his offer and the confidence he had expressed in me, I was determined not to let him down. I knew I also had a number of other engineers to thank, whom I had worked with since 1946, such as John Harkenrider, Carl Paul, Charlie Stone and Hal Greenwald.

It was around January, 1953, that I reported to work. The first week on the job was a total washout as far as getting down to any productive work was concerned, since everyone I ran into at work wanted to know all about my Korean experience. I had been corresponding with Eddie Butler, my former boss, on a regular basis. He always posted my letters on the bulletin board and everyone read them faithfully. Korea, unlike WWII, did not have a massive call-up, and mostly reserves answered the call. Many of my friends at work had served in WWII, but hardly any of them were called for Korea. We all shared a common bond, however. They never failed to compliment me and to show me in many ways that they appreciated my contribution in our nation's attempt to save the world from the threat of global communism.

PEACE TALKS AND PRISONERS

The peace talks had been in permanent recess since 8 Oct 52. On 3 Mar 53 Josef Stalin, leader of the Soviet Union, died. Having no successor, it flung the Soviets and their eastern satellites into a turmoil. President Eisenhower, newly elected, was eager to press forward on any and every peace initiative put forward by the Communists. On 30 Mar, Chou En-lai, then foreign minister of Red China, said that China and North Korea might accept the proposed neutral screening of POWs. Russia, eager to be done with foreign aggression for the time being, while it put its own house in order, applied the necessary arm twisting that pushed the two parties together once again at Panmunjom, which finally resulted in the full armistice and cease fire on 27 Jul 53 and the exchange of prisoners, with the sick and wounded prisoners being released first. It was only then that our country became aware that 58 percent of our POWs held by the Communists had perished due to starvation, sickness, and just plain neglect. This proved what everyone already suspected, that the Communists were barbarians, demanding that their prisoners in our POW compounds be inspected by the Red Cross and their general welfare be observed, while doing absolutely nothing for our people under their control and refusing to permit inspections.

When the Korean War finally wound down, fewer than 90,000 Communist POWs of the 132,000 captured chose to return to North Korea or China. The 13,000 Chinese went to Taiwan and the 29,000 Koreans just stayed in South Korea.

FOLLOWING THE CESSATION OF HOSTILITIES

In Korea the American soldier, with his Korean and United Nations allies, fought with bravery and skill against his communist foe and met the test in accordance with the best traditions of the service. His valor and determination defeated the communist aggression and stabilized the battle along the present demilitarized zone. The location of this line largely above the 38th parallel is historic evidence that in Korea aggression did not pay.

> MAXWELL D. TAYLOR
> General, United States Army
> Chief of Staff

The conflict in Korea had lasted three years, one month, and two days. It had destroyed Korean homes, fields, and factories, wrecked the nation's economy, and threatened the populace with famine and disease. It had consumed the lives of hundreds of thousands of civilians and soldiers from nations all over the face of the globe. Many had died who a short time before had known Korea only as an exotic place name on a map. The signing of the armistice brought an end to the shooting; it did not bring an end to the ideological war. "We have won an armistice on a single battleground," said President Eisenhower as the Panmunjom negotiators reached agreement, "not peace in the world. We may not now relax our guard nor cease our quest."

Despite the failure to settle the issue in Korea, the United States and its partners in the fight against aggression had gained some insight into the manner of foe that opposed them. They learned that the communist adversary would use every means at his command to gain an advantage, both political and military; that he was willing, as in his use of human-sea tactics, to expend his soldiers' lives prodigally in order to offset superior fire power. And, most important, they learned that the enemy, though powerful, was not invulnerable.

The countries that fought under the flag of the United Nations to prevent the conquest of South Korea had demonstrated their ability to put aside differences and act in concert against a common enemy. That nations of highly diverse cultural, religious, and racial background were willing to place their forces under a single command, in this case the United States, was evidence that free men could rise above national pride in their never-ending fight to remain free.

> CREDIT: Department of the Army and
> President Dwight David Eisenhower

Left: Scene of See-Saw Fighting. View of enemy-held outpost Yoke as seen from Marine trenches.

Right: VMO-6 helicopter returning from front lines, landing at Field #19. My buddy, Capt Merlin "Gus" Dake, may have been pilot this day. I flew with Gus many times.

Bottom Left: Support for Battle of the Hook. Marines heading for embattled Hook carry machine gun ammunition. Note bandoliers around their necks.

Bottom Right: Captured CCF equipment taken in October 1952 battle included prima cord, cartridges, Soviet hand grenades.

Photo credit USMC

Upper Left: The A-frame, earliest mode of carrying heavy loads on the back, always amazed us when we saw these small people backpacking huge loads.

Middle Left: Typical scene on nearly every road in South Korea, the peasants on the move.

Middle Right and Lower Left: Having completed my tour of duty, I was flown down to Seoul City Air Base to catch my plane to Itami, Japan, the first long leg of my return home to my beloved family. This is one happy day, Nov 1952.

Lower Right: A Korean papasan, the most privileged person in Korea. Tanks and trucks, everything stops for him, the aged Korean, honored by all.

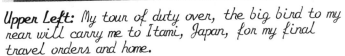

Upper Left: My tour of duty over, the big bird to my rear will carry me to Itami, Japan, for my final travel orders and home.

Upper Right: My last look at the Korean countryside as our big transport plane heads for Japan. My mind is racing a mile a minute as I ponder the next few days.

Middle, Left and Right: At the Itami, Japan, air base awaiting my plane to Tokyo and home. Here, at this time, a representative of the Japanese Airlines (JAL) interviewed me. I could have signed up as a commercial pilot, flying the Convair twin-engine transports of JAL. Good pay, my family with me, annual leave home, family allowance etc. Many of my buddies did just that. I would consult with Marion upon returning home, and the answer would be No way, José.

Right: A low approach to Itami Air Base, Japan.

Upper Left: I'm standing in front of the Central Billeting Office in Tokyo, looking for a room for the night before flying home to good old Uncle Sugar.

Above and Middle Left, L to R: Capt Jeff Crandall and Peterson, looking Tokyo over.

Lower Left: In front of the Ernie Pyle Bldg. in Tokyo. Pyle, a famous newspaper reporter, was killed at Okinawa by the Japanese in a firefight during WWII.

Lower Right: By the Air France Airways office in Tokyo. Actually, I landed a flight home on a United Air Lines DC-6, via Shimya Island in the Aleutians, then on to Anchorage, Alaska, and Seattle, Washington. The United Air Lines plane was chartered by the military.

Left: The author and his nephew, Joel Gleason, of Marblehead, MA, shortly after Joel wrung us out in his Citabria aerobatic plane. Marblehead, MA, early 1970s.

Below: Captain Bernard Peterson receiving the Silver Star, Bronze Star with Combat V, Navy Medal and Purple Heart in Korea, October 1952. Commanding General E.A. Pollock USMC, of the 1stMarDiv is making the award. Peterson left the Marine Corps at the end of WWII and put all flying behind him until the advent of the Korean War. After six years out of the cockpit, he volunteered for active duty and was retrained as a fighter pilot. He flew 60 combat missions in Corsairs while a member of VMF-212 Devil Cats before moving up to the 1st Marine Division as a forward air controller for the final five months of his Korean tour of duty. Peterson also had a 37-year civilian career as a gas turbine engineer with AiResearch Manufacturing Company (later renamed Garrett Turbine Engine Company), a division of Allied Signal.

Captain Bernard Peterson, just back home from Korea, November 1952. Shown with his wife, Marion (former Corporal USMCWR) and son Randall (3 yrs) and son Eric (6 yrs).

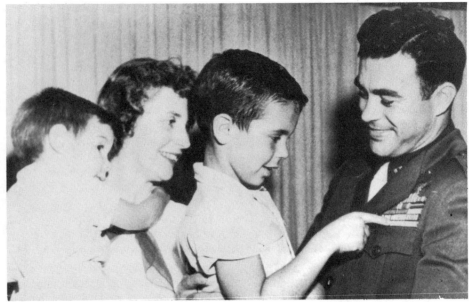

Below: Captain Peterson in the trenches with "G" Company of the 3rd Battalion, 1st Regiment, 1st Marine Division, near Bunker Hill, Korea. 1952 Peterson served for five months as a Forward Air Controller, following his 60 combat missions in his Corsair with VMF-212 "Devil Cats." L to R: Lt Stapleton, Capt Peterson, Sgt Seaman, (next person's name not available but he's our Navy hospital corpsman), Capt Bill Whitbeck, Commanding Officer of "G" Company. Author was wounded by enemy mortar fire. Everyone is wearing their flak jackets.

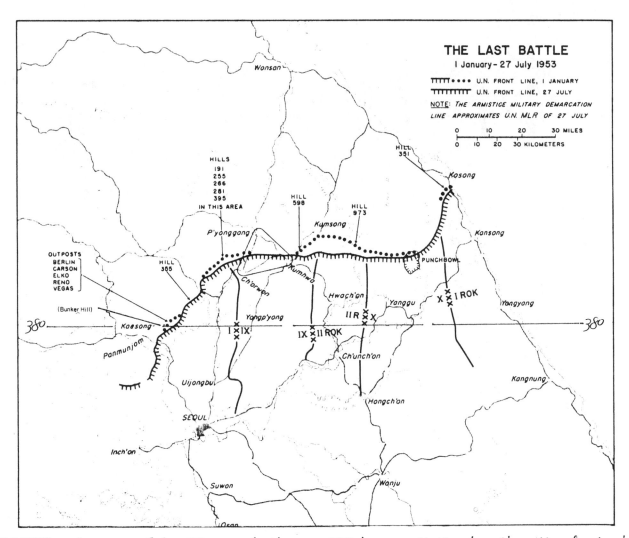

THE LAST BATTLE, 1 January–27 July 1953 . . . As the year 1953 began, activity along the entire front subsided. Patrolling and small-scale harassing attacks characterized the fighting during the winter months of the new year. Then, as spring began, the enemy renewed his assaults upon the Eighth Army's outpost line, attempting to seize terrain that overlooked the army's main line of resistance. These attacks increased in frequency and intensity until, in July, they approached the scale of the enemy's heavy attacks of May 1951. . . .

To oppose the Eighth Army's twenty divisions the enemy disposed a formidable array of strength along his front. Seven Chinese armies and two North Korean corps, totaling about 270,000 troops, manned the enemy defense line. Another eleven Chinese armies and North Korean corps with an estimated strength of 531,000 remained in reserve. With service and security forces, the total enemy strength in Korea amounted to more than a million men. . . .

Enemy losses in July were tremendous. The army estimated that the Chinese lost over 72,000 men, more than 25,000 of them killed. Out of the five Chinese armies that had been identified in the attacks upon the II and IX Corps, the enemy had lost the equivalent of seven divisions.

While the fighting raged on the central front the negotiators at Panmunjom rapidly approached an agreement on armistice terms. On 19 July agreement was reached on all points by both sides. The next day liaison and staff officers began the task of drawing up the boundaries of the demilitarized zone. All details of the armistice agreement and its implementation were completed in a week. At 1000 hours on 27 July Lt. Gen. William K. Harrison, Jr., the senior United Nations delegate to the armistice negotiations, signed the armistice papers. At the same time the senior enemy delegate, General Nam Il, placed his signature on the documents. The signing took place at that time to permit the armistice to go into effect at 2200 hours of the same day, as required by the agreement. Later General Clark, for the United Nations, General Kim Il Sung, for North Korea, and General Peng Teh-Huai, for the Chinese forces on the peninsula, affixed their signatures.

The conflict in Korea had lasted three years, one month and two days. It had destroyed Korean homes, fields and factories, wrecked the nation's economy, and threatened the populace with famine and disease. It had consumed the lives of hundreds of thousands of civilians and soldiers from nations all over the face of the globe. . . .

CREDIT: Condensed from Department of the Army, *KOREA 1951–1953*.

Defense of Boulder City—Men of 1st and 7th Marines receive supplies during CCF assaults in July 1953 against Boulder City. Photo credit: USMC

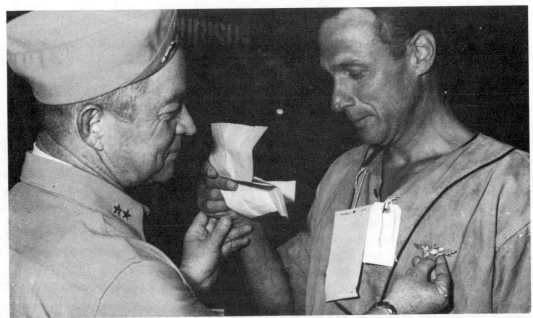

LtCol William G. Thrash USMC receives naval aviation wings upon his release as a POW, at Freedom Village, from MajGen Vernon E. Megee, Commanding General 1st MAW.
Of the 221 Marines captured during the three-year conflict:

- 49 were officers and 172 enlisted;
- 190 were ground and 31 aviators;
- of the 190 ground troops, 19 were officers and 171 enlisted;
- of the 31 aviators, 30 were officer pilots and 1 was enlisted. Photo credit: USMC

APPENDIX 1
MESSAGES FROM THE MEMORIAL

Adjacent to the Lincoln Memorial, the Korean War Veterans Memorial in the Nation's Capital will complete the west end of the Mall. The site, Ash Woods in West Potomac Park, is located across the Reflecting Pool from the Vietnam Veterans Memorial. The Korean War Veterans Memorial was authorized by the US Congress on October 28, 1986, by Public Law 99-572.

The Korean War Veterans Memorial reflects the spirit of the time--a time when America's sons and daughters were asked to go to a country they did not know, to defend a people they had never met. They did so without question, never doubting the rightness of their actions.

Appropriately, the Memorial pays tribute to this response to the call of duty and expresses the Nation's gratitude to all who served. As a salute to the bravery of the men and women who saw combat or supported those in combat, the Memorial honors all who served in the Armed Forces of the United States.

The sculptures of 19 ground troops are clad in foul weather ponchos and fully equipped for battle. They emerge from the protection of woods, suddenly exposed to the potential of enemy fire. They are tense, alert and ever courageous as they advance up a gently sloped triangular field, moving resolutely toward their objective, symbolized by the American flag.

The 19 statues are made of textured stainless steel, stand 7'0"-7'3" tall, each weighs nearly 1,000 pounds. There are fourteen Army, three Marine, one Navy medic, and one Air Force Ground Observer representing the service personnel who fought the war on foot.

The diversity of the U.S. Armed Forces are honored as well: Caucasian, African American, Hispanic, Asian, and Native American. As it was in Korea, some are seasoned soldiers, while others are young and new to combat.

A 164' long, 100 ton, highly polished black granite mural wall forms the backdrop of the Memorial. More than 2400 photographic, archival images of both men and women representing, land, sea, and air personnel units, symbolically join those whom they supported. From a distance, the faces are not always distinguishable--rather appearing to be silhouettes of the mountains of Korea.

The American flag stands at the threshold of the "Pool of Remembrance", surrounded by a grove of clipped trees. An extension of the granite wall slices into the smooth and reflective pool dramatically paying tribute to the sacrifice of those killed in Korea, taken prisoner, or missing in action--a poignant reminder that FREEDOM IS NOT FREE!

Recognition is also given to the Republic of Korea and the 20 other countries who sent men and women to counter communist aggression. A raised, granite curb along the left side of the entrance walk into the Memorial lists each of the nations that formed the United Nations' first multinational military mission.

An extension of this UN curb stone, projecting into the pool with USA and UN casualties, testifies to the magnitude of the "Police Action" that was in fact a major war. . . a war that changed the world. There will be a computerized data-base of all known KIAs, MIAs and POWs which will be accessible at the kiosk near the Memorial. Information including the name, rank, serial number, and home of record can be viewed as well as a picture of the deceased, if available. Printouts will be available to visitors.

American veterans have donated the majority of the $18 million for design, construction, and maintenance of the Memorial. Approximately $6 million was raised through the sale of a special Korean War commemorative silver dollar that was produced by the US Mint.

DESIGNERS OF THE MEMORIAL	
Architects of Record:	Cooper-Lecky Architects, PC of Washington, DC
Muralist:	Louis Nelson Associates of New York, NY
Sculptor:	Frank C. Gaylord, II of Barre, VT
Dedicated:	July 27, 1995

Below: Betty Perrin (lower right in photo) during recent visit to the Korean War Memorial. LtCol John Perrin USMC Ret and Betty live in La Conner, WA. John flew with VMF-214 during the Korean War.

APPENDIX 1 cont'd

A STATISTICAL SKETCH

KOREAN WAR:
June 25, 1950 to July 27, 1953

NUMBER OF US PARTICIPANTS:
Actual Service in Korea during war: 1,500,000

STATIONED IN FAR EAST COMMAND
(Korea, Japan, Okinawa, Sea of Japan):
1,789,000

ON ACTIVE DUTY DURING THE KOREAN WAR: 5,764,143

US PRISONERS OF WAR: 7,140
RETURNED: 4,418
DIED IN CAPTIVITY: 2,701
REFUSED REPATRIATION: 21

US CONGRESSIONAL MEDAL OF HONOR RECIPIENTS: 131

UNITED NATION ALLIES WAR DEATHS

COUNTRY	DEAD	MISSING	CAPTURED	WOUNDED
Australia	339	39	29	1240
Belgium	95	5	1	350
Canada	291	21	12	1072
Colombia	140	65	29	452
Denmark	0	0	0	0
Ethiopia	120	0	0	0
France	288	18	11	818
Greece	169	2	1	536
India	0	0	0	0
Italy	0	0	0	0
Luxembourg	2	0	0	0
Netherlands	111	4	0	389
New Zealand	33	0	1	79
Norway	0	0	0	0
Philippines	92	57	40	299
Republic of Korea	570,947	460,428	84,715	950,073
South Africa	20	16	6	0
Sweden	0	0	0	0
Thailand	114	5	0	794
Turkey	717	167	219	2246
United Kingdom	1109	1263	766	2278
United States	54,246	8177	7140	103,284
TOTAL	628,833	470,267	92,970	1,064,453

CREDIT:

The American Battle Monuments Commission and
Korean War Veterans Memorial Advisory Board, 1995

APPENDIX 2
HEMORRHAGIC FEVER -- A FATAL VIRUS

As a forward air controller in Korea in 1952 I had assisted numerous victims of this awful virus while calling in airevac helicopters for their transport to a special hospital set up in the 1stMarDiv sector in Korea. I had always wondered about the history of hemorrhagic fever all these years. The following article helped answer some of this mystery.

LIVES OF A VIRUS:
The Mysterious Navajo Epidemic is New Only for America
by Robin Marantz Henig

The mysterious epidemic plaguing the Navajo territories in the Southwest should come as no surprise. We have seen such epidemics erupt, seemingly out of nowhere, many times in the past, and are likely to see them again.

The difference is that this time they're erupting on American soil.

Many details of the current outbreak--which has been attributed to an Asian arena virus (one carried in rodents) in the family hantavirus--are essentially the same as details seen in other situations in which the environment changes sufficiently to bring viruses into new proximity with human beings.

In western Argentina in the late 1940s, for instance, the pampas grasses were cleared to make way for new farms. When the tall grasses disappeared, so did predators of the calomys, a mouse-like rodent that carried the junin virus. Beginning late every summer (which is February in Argentina) and ending early in winter, the calomys population increased.

The human population also increased in these months as transient farmers moved in for the harvest. The result: an annual outbreak of Argentinian hemorrhagic fever, a new and terrible infection caused by the junin virus, which killed up to 20 percent of its victims.

A similar change in Bolivia in the late 1950s, also involving a species of calomys, led to the emergence of what came to be known as Bolivian hemorrhagic fever. Cowboys living on the dry plains of the Beni department, in eastern Bolivia, had long depended on a Brazilian-owned company to export their beef cattle in exchange for rice, maize, beans and fruit. But after the 1952 revolution, the new government reclaimed the land and the Beni cowboys were left to fend for themselves.

They moved to more arable land at higher altitudes and set up farms there--in the very backyard, as it turned out, of the little calomys. By 1960, the rodent population had skyrocketed; they thrived near homes and gardens. And the first cases of Bolivian hemorrhagic fever began to appear.

Another viral emergence happened in Brazil in the late 1970s, when people in the north were falling ill with a new disease called oropouche fever. Scientists suspected that the oropouche virus, which could be isolated from human patients, was an arbovirus--a virus carried by a mosquito or other arthropod--but they didn't know precisely how it was transmitted. None of the mosquitos in the immediate region of the outbreak tested positive for oropouche.

So scientists began testing other arthropods that carry viruses, such as ticks and mites, finally finding oropouche in a biting midge, or sandfly. They ultimately traced the origins of the epidemic to chocolate. As cacao, whose seeds are used to make chocolate, became an important cash crop in the impoverished regions of northern Brazil, more and more land was turned over to cacao trees. When the cacao hulls were discarded, they piled up into huge mountains, each hull containing a mini-pool of collected rainwater--the perfect breeding ground for the biting midge.

As the piles of hulls grew higher, the midge population grew too. And as the midge population increased, so did an individual human's chances of being bitten by a midge that carried the virus for oropouche.

In the current scenario being played out in New Mexico and nearby states, the thinking is that what made this new disease suddenly appear, apparently out of thin air, is this year's blooming of the pinon tree.

The pinon tree usually blooms just once in a lifetime, producing sweet flowering nuts that attract rodents. This year was one of those rare mass bloomings, so there seem to be far more rodents than usual living near people's homes across the massive Navajo reservation.

The rodents probably are carrying the same virus they always carry, shedding it in their urine and feces as they always have. But with the increase of rodents in proximity to people, there is now more virus to go around. It can be carried on droplets of air, and if it's inhaled it can lead to fever, muscle aches and cough. These flu-like symptoms can progress quickly to respiratory distress: fluid in the lungs, lung collapse and death from suffocation.

To date, at least 26 people have gotten sick, all of them from New Mexico, Arizona, Utah and Colorado. Most have been Native Americans, especially Navajos; most were teenagers and young adults who were previously quite healthy. Sixteen have died.

This tragedy could be only the beginning. Even if this epidemic is brought under control by rodent control methods--which have been used effectively in Argentina and Bolivia--we can be sure that a new epidemic is just around the corner. In the ceaseless push and pull in the relationship between man and microbe, we will inevitably encounter new emerging viruses.

The most notorious emerging virus is, of course, HIV, the one that causes AIDS.

An emerging virus isn't necessarily a new virus; it's just new to the community that is threatened by it. When a virus mutates spontaneously, or crosses species or geographic borders, it imperils a population that was never before exposed. And it's in the first wave of an emerging virus epidemic--like these past four months in the Southwest--that the most damage is done.

The majority of emerging viruses have generally existed, percolating beneath the surface, for quite some time. Something about the virus then changes, causing it to slide out of its original niche and begin infecting a new population.

Viral emergence usually occurs as a result of one of three things. It may come from an actual mutation in one of the virus's genes, which changes its ability to infect (though such a large mutation happens quite rarely). It may result from changes in the natural environment, including patterns of rainfall and temperature, which interfere with the balance between predators and their prey and give an unchanged virus a new niche in which to thrive (as happened in the Southwest).

Or it may occur because of the things people do--building roads into the rain forest, transporting microbes from one region to another, erecting housing on the edge of woodland--that change man's relationship to the environment and expose new populations to viruses they'd never seen before. This last one, the intrusion of humankind into the natural order of things, is responsible for more and more instances of viral emergence.

Students of viral emergence have been predicting that a new virus would soon appear in the United States. They hadn't expected it to be a hantavirus, though; they were placing their bets on dengue.

Dengue fever and its more severe form, dengue hemorrhagic fever, have been a problem in countries to the south of us, such as Mexico and Cuba, and every year a handful of people already infected with dengue come into the United States. The dengue virus is carried by the

Asian tiger mosquito, which was introduced into this country in 1985 in a shipment of used tires from Japan to Texas. Now the tiger mosquito has expanded its range as far north as Illinois. With the vector in place, and the virus occasionally transported into the United States, many scientists believe it's only a matter of time before dengue fever becomes a real public health menace.

Knowing the history of emerging viruses is probably what helped us explain the current epidemic so quickly. It took only a few weeks after the first cases were reported for state and federal researchers to pinpoint the cause as a rodent-borne hantavirus.

That speed is what one hopes will keep us from a devastating death toll when the next surprise comes along.

Robin Marantz Henig, copyright 1993. This article, which originally appeared in <u>The Washington Post</u> on July 18, 1993, is adapted from <u>A Dancing Matrix: How Science Confronts Emerging Viruses</u> (Vintage, 1994). Henic, a Washington medical writer, is the author of "A Dancing Matrix: Voyages Along the Viral Frontier."

MAY 25, 1995
HANTAVIRUS VACCINE AVAILABLE SOON

An experimental vaccine has been developed against hantavirus infection recently by the U.S. Army Medical Research Institute of Infectious Diseases in Fort Detrick, MD.

Dr. Connie Schmaljohn, a scientist with the Institute, says the vaccine is safe, defending the human body by stimulating the immune system, and will become available within a year for use among military personnel, "if they give informed consent," in South Korea and other threatened areas of the world.

Very often fatal, the hantavirus infection has been reported in 21 states of the U.S. and also a few in Canada and Brazil. But the virus, carried by rodents, occurs chiefly in North and South Korea, China and Russia.

By the end of Nov 1952, the author was at home, but the peace negotiations continued. Shown here, the NKPA and the CCF delegations were adjourning on the first day of the resumed peace talks, April 1953. Photo credit: USMC

APPENDIX 3
MY FRIEND, COLONEL BILL SHANKS USMC (RET)

Following the Korean, war Bill Shanks served as Commanding Officer of Station Operations and Engineering Squadron at MCAS El Toro, California, and later as the Executive Officer of VMF-232 while flying FJ-2 Fury jets at MCAS Kaneohe, Hawaii. In June 1962 he finally received a B.S. degree while attending the University of Nebraska at Omaha under the "College Bootstrap Program." He followed this with a tour as the Commanding Officer of the Marine Air Reserve Training Detachment at NAS Olathe, Kansas, training Reserves in the operation and maintenance of the F4D Skyray.

He attended the Armed Forces Staff College at Norfolk, Virginia, and, after being accredited in 1966 was ordered to serve as the Defense and Naval Attaché to five African nations, while attached to the U.S. Embassy at Dakar, Senegal, in West Africa.

The year 1969 found him in Chu-Lai, Vietnam, where he flew 76 combat missions in the F-4 Phantom while serving as the Executive Officer of Marine Aircraft Group 13. Upon returning to the states, he was assigned to the Joint Operations staff of the Commander-in-Chief of Atlantic Forces at Norfolk, Virginia. Subsequently, he assumed command as the Chief of Staff of the 6th Marine Amphibious Brigade at Camp LeJeune, North Carolina. He also served as the Commanding Officer of the 32nd Marine Amphibious Unit while embarking on amphibious shipping in the Mediterranean. His last assignment while serving in the Marine Corps was as the Commanding Officer of Marine Aircraft Group 31, a fighter group of F-4 Phantom aircraft based at MCAS Beaufort, South Carolina. He retired as a Colonel on July 31, 1974.

As if this long and distinguished career in the Corps were not enough, Bill established residence in Virginia Beach, Virginia, and embarked on a *second* career as the Administrator of the Guaranteed Annual Income Program for the Hampton Roads Maritime Association, located at Norfolk, Virginia. In 1983 he journeyed to Sun City Center, Florida, a retirement community, where he continues to enjoy a much deserved life of leisure, playing golf and participating in various volunteer activities of the community. He and his wife, Rose, make occasional visits to their two children and three grandchildren, who at this writing all happen to live in or near Dallas, Texas.

Marine Corps Historical Foundation

APPENDIX 4
RIDING THE RANGE AT MACH 2.5
By World's fastest--LtCol R.B. Robinson, USMC

All who have flown *Phantom II* have known she could break the 1525.96 mph world speed record held by Air Force F-106. However, with so many other important commitments -- test programs, training, etc., of higher priority--it was not until this fall that a plane could be spared for the attempt.

McDonnell engineers and test pilots worked out the flight plan in detail. The goal was to work out a course and flight profile so that the plane would enter the straight-away headed for the starting gate at entry altitude with full internal fuel, high speed, and room to accelerate to top speed. Of course, it was impossible to have the best of all the variables; the idea was to get the best compromise.

The F4H used for the record attempt, named *Skyburner*, carried full internal fuel plus a centerline 600-gallon drop tank and two 370-gallon wing tanks at take-off.

Getting rid of those at exactly the right time, and in a safe place, was one of the big problems. There are only a few restricted areas where drops are allowed, and they are not ideally situated in relation to the record range.

FAI rules for the 15/25 kilometer speed record require some fairly precise flying. The contest aircraft has to hold altitude within 100 meters from the time it crosses the outer marker inbound until the finish gate, 20 miles one way and 17 miles the other on the Edwards AFB course.

Holding altitude within 100 meters was probably no trick back when the rules were laid down, but at 1650 mph, it is like holding a T-28 to plus or minus 10 feet. The fact that the plane is accelerating all the way though the course doesn't make it any easier to keep on altitude. On the first pass, *Skyburner* was at 2.45 over the

WORLD'S FASTEST--ROBINSON AND F4H

outer marker and had accelerated to 2.57 in the few seconds it took to reach the finish gate.

The rules requiring that acceleration to entry speed be done in level flight. If the contest aircraft ever exceeds 500 meters higher than the altitude it first enters the range, it will be disqualified.

On the morning of the record flight, *Skyburner* was towed out to the take-off end of the runway in order to get airborne with every possible drop of fuel.

NAA stewards were waiting at the end of the runway to go through the required formalities. They sealed the fuel tanks--in order to be able to certify that the contest aircraft did not land and refuel during the attempt; started the barograph--the instrument for verifying flight altitudes throughout the flight; examined my FAI sporting license; and verified that the Robert Robinson on the license was indeed the pilot.

Certificates attesting completion of these procedures become part of the record "dossier" submitted to FAI in Paris to support the application for certifying the attempt as an official record.

With these formalities completed, I fired up, gave her the 100% check, released the brakes and the attempt was underway. After a burner take-off, the first part of the climb was made at 100%--all according to the carefully worked-out plan

Take-off was made to the east, with climb-out to the south toward El Centro. Over Salton Sea, I started an easy left turn back and dropped the empty centerline tank over the Chocolate Mountains gunnery range, altitude 33,000 feet.

I then lit the burner, accelerated to Mach 1.3, and continued climbing toward the north. Still right on plan, and on signal from Edwards space positioning radar, the two wing tanks-- which had just gone empty--were dropped over Bristol Dry Lake range, 90 miles east of the starting gate, at entry altitude of 45,000 feet and Mach 1.3. It was full military power--100% and full burner--from that point to the finish gate on the first pass.

I let the nose drop to help build up speed. When air speed hit Mach 1.8, *Skyburner* was down to 41,000 feet, I eased her back up to altitude, still accelerating. All the while, space positioning radar was coaching on line-up to help put us straight down the middle of the two-mile wide record range.

Once across the finish line the plan called for coming out of burner and back to idle to slow down for the turn-back. A slight left turn put us south of the course, so that we would roll out of the turn on centerline for the second pass.

Abeam Point Mugu, speed had bled off to Mach .9, the speed for

APPENDIX 4 cont'd

the turn, so I put on power and cruised on out to make the turn at 105 miles.

Coming back, without the problem of dropping the tanks, there was more room to accelerate. As a result, speed for the second run was at least 50 mph faster and the first go-through.

We had planned to try for the world record for altitude in sustained horizontal flight on Friday, 24 November, but weather forced us to delay the attempt. Cdr George W. Ellis of Flight Test Division of NATC will set that record later. (Editorial note: Ellis set a mark of 66,448 feet 5 December to beat the official record of 55, 300.9 feet.)

I was scheduled to fly the altitude attempt, but came east instead to be on had for *Enterprise* commissioning ceremonies where the Secretary of the Navy, the Honorable John B. Connally, presented me with the DFC in recognition of *Phantom II's* triumph.

CREDIT: Naval Aviation News Jan 1962

LT COL R.B. ROBINSON, whose big accomplishment came when he set the straight course World's Speed Record at 1606.324 MPH in his F4H Phantom. This was Mach 2.5.

R.B. ROBINSON'S POST KOREAN SERVICE

- AES-12, Quantico, VA, leader of Close Air Support Team, F8F, F7F, F6F, F4U-4
- Amphibious Warfare School, Junior Course--Quantico
- VMF-115, D-3 Pohang, Korea F9F-5
- VMR-252, Cherry Point R4Q-2
- VMCJ-2, Cherry Point F9F-8P, F3D-2Q
- U.S. Naval Test Pilot School, Patuxent River, MD Class XXII, 1959
- Head Fighter Branch, Service Test Division, Patuxent River, MD F4H-1, F8U-2N, FF-4, F3H, AD
- F4H *Phantom II* Class Desk Officer, Bureau of Naval Weapons, Washington, D.C.

Retired November 1, 1963--LtCol USMC

LT COL R.B. ROBINSON receiving his DFC on 25 Nov 1961 aboard the new carrier USS ENTERPRISE CVAN-65. The occasion was the commissioning ceremony, where Secretary of the Navy John Connally made the dedication speech and later pinned the Distinguished Flying Cross on Robinson for setting the new world speed record. The new captain of the ENTERPRISE, Vincent P. DePoix, is shown at the podium. [In 1942 DePoix was a fighter pilot flying F4F Wildcats with VF-6 off the old USS ENTERPRISE CV-6, while the author, B.W. Peterson, was serving as a white hat with VT-3 aboard the same carrier during the Battle of Guadalcanal.]

R. B. ROBINSON AFTER RETIREMENT

*Joined McDonnell Aircraft Company as Experimental Test Pilot (F4H Phantom II) November 1963

- Performed separation and jettison tests for a wide variety of weapons and external tanks
- Performed structural demonstrations in the F4K & F4M (British versions of F4H--Rolls Royce engines), F4J & F4M
- Participated in the J79-17 engine development. Many flights out to 2.4 Mach Number.
- Delivered nine (9) F4Ks and F4Ms to Aldergrove, North Ireland
- Delivered 13 F4Es to Israel

Flight Experience

- 7080 total hours in 45 types and models of prop, turboprop and turbine powered aircraft
- 58 carrier landings--F4U-4, CVE-114, *USS RENDOVA*

Personal Awards

Silver Star, DFC, Air Medal with one star, Letter of Commendation with Combat V

Graduated with B.S. in Business Administration, Washington University, St. Louis, MO 1972 and retired from McDonnell Aircraft Company in 1974. He and Lavonne have one son, Robert B. Robinson III, two grandsons, Kelly 19 and Scott 17. Robby and Lavonne live in Ladue, a suburb of St. Louis, MO, and he is, at this writing, involved in his own business of marketing and selling telecommunication systems equipment.

APPENDIX 5
KOREAN REFUGEES AND RESIDENTS IN THE 1ST MARINE DIVISION SECTOR

We had placed ourselves between the enemy and the Korean civilians. From my observation posts I could observe farmers going about their business, plowing their fields behind their ever present water buffalos. This seemed so incredible, because as I turned 180° and looked to the north, a first class war was going on.

The following restricted document was tucked in my duffel bag for future reference.

RESTRICTED
SECURITY INFORMATION
ENCLOSURE (2)   TO PERIODIC INTELLIGENCE REPORT NO. 685
BRIEF OF POLITICAL ADMINISTRATION

The following brief of the political administration of the civilians in the Division rear areas is presented as a matter of common interest.

Some 111,000 civilians live behind "Line STAYBACK" in the 1st Marine Division sector. An estimated 33,800 of these are refugees, the remainder residents of PAJU-GUN, the principal administrative sub-division in this area. A higher administrative division exists, YONGGI-DO. This DO is an area similar in many respects to a state in our government. The Chief of the DO is appointed by the President of Korea, while his assistant is appointed by the Minister of State. Their tenure of office is for life. They are responsible for their DO and the supervision of the government, controlling the area through GUN and MYON Chiefs, who in turn govern through Ri, Ni and Li Chiefs.

The GUN is administered by a "Soo" or Chief who is appointed by the President to govern an area very similar to a county in the United States. He is appointed for life and is responsible to the DO Chief. The next administrative breakdown is the MYON, similar to a large township and its Chief is appointed by the DO Chief. There is a vice Chief who is appointed by the GUN "Soo." Their appointments, like the others, are for life. They are responsible to the DO Chief for the operation of their MYON and have lesser Chiefs for the RI(s), NI(s) and LI(s) as well as from four to 15 separate department heads to assist in managing the affairs of the MYON or township. The major departments are: Welfare, Social, Financial, Paymaster, Real Estate, Military, General Affairs and Agriculture. General Affairs is something of a catchall for the functions not cared for by the others, as it handles education, elections and the enforcements of MYON orders.

The only elected officer in this hierarchy are the RI, (NI or LI) Chiefs. They are elected by popular vote and manage the affairs of the sub-division of the MYON or RI(s). They serve a two- to four-year term and are aided by appointed clerks. The lowest sub-division is the DONG (TONG) which represents a small area including one village, or a group of houses and the surrounding area. The leader of the DONG is appointed by the RI Chief.

We therefore have four sub-divisions of the DO, each intended to maintain supervisory control over their particular constituents. This breakdown also provides the address for civilians residing in a certain area. For example, the address of the Chief of KIMCHON-NI is: KYOHO-MYON, PAJU-GUN, KYONGGI-DO. By this address it is possible to differentiate between the many KUMCHON-NI(s) in South Korea.

Taxes are levied to a large extent on a sliding scale based upon the ability of the individual to pay. This takes into consideration condition of property and business and payment of the taxes may be either in money or by produce. The latter method is usually used by farmers, who pay 10% of the crop if a tenant farmer and 15% if a land lord.

It seems to have been common practice in Korea to re-distribute the land of large land holders by government purchase of the excess land and reselling it to small farmers and landless people. These people are able to buy the land from the government over a five-year period paying about 6 quarts of rice for less than an acre of land. The land is scaled on a 20-point evaluation and its worth determined by this evaluation. In one of the MYONS in the Division sector about one third of the people own their land, the remainder are tenant farmers.

RESTRICTED

APPENDIX 6
SAFE CONDUCT PASS

Periodically air dropped over Communist troops, this safe conduct pass was spread all along the 38th parallel. Due to the prospective users' difficulty in escaping to our side, however, it proved of very little success. None of those prisoners that I saw were carrying this pass. Ironically, we heard that the pass was being used as toilet paper until the UN decided to change the texture of it to that of waxed paper.

APPENDIX 7
MEMORIAL SERVICE IN THE FIELD--KOREA, 26 OCT 52

MEMORIAL SERVICES

CHURCH CALL	*Bugler*
THE NATIONAL ANTHEM	*Division Band*
THE INVOCATION	*Catholic Chaplain*
	Patrick Adams
INTRODUCTION OF THE COMMANDING GENERAL	*Colonel Walter F. Layer*
THE MEMORIAL ADDRESS	*Major General E. A. Pollock*
THE MARINE HYMN	*Division Band*

*** HONORS ***
ROLL CALL OF THE DEAD

1stBn,	1st Marines	LtCol M. A. LaGrone
2ndBn,	1st Marines	LtCol C. E. Warren
3rdBn,	1st Marines	LtCol S. J. Altman
AT-Co,	1st Marines	1stLt B. C. Kearns
3rdBn,	11th Marines	LtCol C. O. Rogers
"C"Co,	1st Tank Bn	Capt G. M. McCain

MINUTE OF SILENT TRIBUTE	*Assembly*
THE MEMORIAL PRAYER	*Protestant Chaplain*
	Oscar Weber
RIFLE SALUTE	*Honor Guard*
TAPS	*Bugler*
THE BENEDICTION	*Jewish Chaplain*
	Samuel Sobel

* * * * *

THE ROLL OF THE DEAD
26 July 1952 to 12 October 1952

First Battalion, First Marines

Allen G. Stenerson	James D. Baker	Richard H. Eidam	Joe H. Turner
Willie Ray Deason	Gerald Bradley	Donald Baily	Harold E. Upmeyer
Henry B. Machado	Ernest J. Garnier	Jasper V. Russel	Edward W. Baumgard
Ruben Cruz	Robert T. Alilovich	Herbert W. Balboni	Robert J. Carroll
Richard W. Arndt	John P. Borseti	Daniel J. Duggan	Charles W. Parrish
Donald A. Fatica	Ervin Lemaster Jr.	Earl W. Lester	Atnory Laboy-Collazo
Hubert J. LeBlanc	Joseph R. Kennel	Thomas G. Dier	Kenneth J. Jack
Francis P. Soucie	John F. Popp	Amous L. Amey	Mario A. Desantis
Daniel F. Belles	Junior R. Collins	James B. Pickworth	Bennie Bennitt Jr.
James V. Cullen	Richard M. Islas	Gene R. Burkman	Howard F. Chase Jr.
Fred M. Allen	Jimmie D. Young	William K. Baker	Loren E. Anderson
Daniel C. Barcak	Herbert W. Smith	Louis D. Drazey	Charles A. Fjaer
John B. Powe	John F. Bagwell III	Gilbert P. Mantey	Regis E. Krug
Johnny Kilburn	Larry E. Miller	Robert L. Aldridge	Eugene Cota
			Robert J. Betz

Second Battalion, First Marines

Wilfred E. Hall
Robert E. Stafford
Joseph L. Francomano
Billy Seals
Donald A. Sorrentino
Vernon Mahan
Bobby Canterberry
Donald C. Trausch
Olie J. Belt
Arthur G. Choquette
Edward R. Belardi Jr.
G. Cruhigger-Rodriguez
James J. Carlson
Floyd F. Cox
James A. Naour
Robert M. Ellars
Owen A. Norton
Larry D. Turner
Thomas R. Cook

Roy L. Griffin
Merlyn Johnson
French Mounts Jr.
John J. Boyle
Donald D. Miner
Henry V. Camire
Juan B. Cordova
Arnold R. Tobias
Harold E. Reins
Jose M. Linares-Ortiz
David E. Halverson
Alfredo P. Charles
William A. McGinnis
Mason C. Hazard
Kenneth F. Wolf
Bill E. Johnson
Raymond L. Hergert
Phillip N. Hobson Jr.
Alber E. Drummond Jr.

Warren E. Christian
George M. Matthews
E. Pomales-Santiago
Roger L. Desclos
John M. Juilien Jr.
Carl M. Burke
Sidney M. White
James W. Buddenberg
Earl D. Stoll
John J. Dopazo
Alefandro Gonzales
William R. Haralson
George R. King
Edward W. Breutzmann
Donald R. Jackson
Thomas A. Janelle
Harold L. Piesik
James L. Gillam
William W. Lewis

Brian B. Thornton
Donald L. Fish
John T. Hoenes
Edward Schmitt
Frank W. Halley
Floyd Cooper Jr.
Horace Hayes
Edward C. Benfold
Richard C. Willmann
Cecil A. Snodgrass
Gerald L. Haer
Richard W. Kountz
Vincent Calvanico
Henry V. Flores
Raymond C. Chapman
Ernest W. Schooley
Robert F. Miconi
Charles H. Hines

* * * * * * * * * *

Third Battalion, First Marines

Melvin H. Weiss
Frank Harris
Merlin M. McKeever
Cornelius F. Harney
Ray A. McClaskey
Andrew J. Morgan
Earl L. Valentine Jr.
Fredrick W. Miner
Herbert L. Golding

Carol C. Prejean
Allan J. Bouquin
Richard Y. Kono
Robert A. Muth
Freddie L. Bradshaw
Robert L. Epperson
Charles E. Skinner
Leocadio Rivera
Stanley T. O'Banion

Robert King
John J. Hughes
Romolo A. Bucci
Tommy J. Neves
Leo A. Biross
Clarence C. Farrell
Spurgeon Wright
Edward Goodman
Kermit M. Ferrell

John E. Finn
Antonia Jaice
John E. Lammers
Manuel G. Alvarado
Marion Ray King
Daniel L. Blubaugh

* * * * * * * * * *

ATCo First Marines

John C. Holley

John P. Langwell

Third Battalion, Eleventh Marines

Cornelius J. Baker Jr.

"C" Company, First Tank Battalion

John R. Hannigan

Eternal Father, Strong to Save
(Navy Hymn)

Eternal Father, strong to save,
Whose arm has bound the restless wave,
Who bids the mighty ocean deep,
Its own appointed limits keep:
O, hear us when we raise our plea
For those in peril on the sea.

O Christ, the Lord of hill and plain
O'er which our traffic runs amain
By mountain pass or valley low'
Wherever, Lord, your loved ones go,
Protect them by your guarding hand
From every peril on the land.

O Spirit, whom the Father sent
To spread abroad the firmament;
O Wind of heaven, by your might
Save all who dare the eagle's flight,
And keep them by your watchful care from
Every peril on the air.

O Trinity of love and pow'r,
Your children shield in danger's hour;
From rock and tempest, fire and foe,
Protect them where so e'er they go;
And them shall rise with voices free
Glad praise from air and land and sea.
Amen.

APPENDIX 8
VMF-214 MARINE FIGHTER SQUADRON--FIRST IN KOREAN ACTION

Marine fighter squadron VMF-214 aboard USS Sicily *CVE118, off Inchon, Korea, September 1950*

Back Row (L to R): 1stLt Stan Osserman, Capt Bob Maloney, MSgt LeRoy Heimrick, Capt Don Galbraith, 1stLt Frosty Townsend, Maj Bill Lundine, Capt Don Conroy, 1stLt Ray Reider, 1stLt O. S. Mendal, 1stLt George Dodenhoff, Capt John S. Perrin.

2nd Row (L to R): 1stLt Bill Simpson, 1stLt Rolo Heilman, Capt Mickey Finn, Capt Henry Schwindeminn, 1stLt J. V. Hanes, 1stLt Bruce Sumnear, 1stLt Frank McComber, Dr (Navy Lt) Robert King, 1stLt Kenny James, Capt John Ross, MSgt Truman Bunce, 1stLt Andy Androsko, Maj Bob Floeck.

1st Row (L to R): Capt John Scorich, 1stLt Jerry Smith, Capt Joe Keller, 1stLt Jim Dunphy, 1stLt Ted Moore, Capt Bill Longfellow, Maj Bob Keller (Ex O), LtCol H.E. Lischeid (CO), MSgt Mossman, 1stLt Bob Minick, Capt Charley Garber, Maj Kenny Reusser, TSgt I. G. Taylor.

The following are ground officers: 1stLt Bruce Sumnear, Administration; 1stLt Frank McComber, Engineering; 1stLt Kenny James, Ordnance.

The following officers were killed: 1. LtCol H.E. Lisheid (CO), killed over Kimpo three weeks after this photo was taken, 2. 1stLt Bob Minick, killed when he was catapulted from his carrier (cold shot) and the carrier ran over him, 3. Capt John Skorish, killed 1952 in jet crash at El Toro, CA, 4. 1stLt Bill Simpson, killed at Inchon, 5. Maj Robert Floeck, killed at Inchon, 6. Capt Jim English (not in picture), killed earlier, while flying at the Puson Peremeter.

Picture courtesy of LtCol John S. Perrin USMC (Ret).

On 3 Aug 1950, eight VMF-214 Corsairs led by squadron executive officer, Major Robert P. Keller, catapulted from the deck of the USS *Sicily* to launch the first Marine air strikes in the Korean action. My dear friend, John S. Perrin, in photo, was Keller's wingman.

From then until 27 Jul 1953, units of the 1st Marine Aircraft Wing flew 127,496 combat sorties in the Korean War, considerably in excess of the 80,000-odd sorties for all Marine aviation during World War II. Of this Korean number nearly a third, more than 39,500, represented the Marine Corps close air support specialty, even though 1st MAW pilots were heavily engaged in other assignments from Fifth Air Force. These included interdiction, general support, air defense patrols, air rescue operations, photo and armed reconnaissance and related tasks to insure Allied air superiority.

APPENDIX 8   cont'd

With the outbreak of Korean hostilities, Stateside Marine air units were alerted for combat duty by 5 Jul 1950. At Major General Field Harris' 1st MAW headquarters, El Toro, MAG-33 elements were quickly readied for deployment to Japanese bases and thence to Korea. Commanded by Brigadier General Thomas J. Cushman, MAG-33 comprised Headquarters and Service Squadron 33, fighter squadrons VMF-214 and -323, an echelon of nightfighters from VMF(N)-513, two radar units (Marine Ground Control Intercept Squadron 1 and Marine Tactical Air Control Squadron 2), plus the observation squadron, VMO-6. Forward elements were quickly on their way, arriving in Japan on 19 July, while the rear echelon reached the Korean Theater on 31 July. Twenty R5Ds from Marine Transport Squadrons 152 and 352 were already providing logistical support for Pacific lift operations.

After practicing some last minute carrier landing approaches, the fighter pilots got into combat almost at once. Following -214 into combat, VMF-323 started operations on 6 August, flying from USS *Badoeng Strait* in support of the Pusan ground defenders. When the brigade mounted out on 7 August on its drive to Chinju, the two MAG-33 carrier squadrons were there with their 5-inch HVAR rockets, napalm, 100- to 500-pound bombs, and 20mm cannon. VMF(N)-513 began its regularly-scheduled night tours over the Korean perimeter that same date, lashing at enemy supply and transportation centers in the Sachon-Chinju area of southern Korea. VMO-6 had already started evacuating casualties from the Pusan area three days earlier.

Throughout the war the four attack squadrons of MAG-12 (VMAs-212, -251, -121; and -332 at the end of the war) had dumped seemingly endless bomb loads on CCF installations, while MAG-33's two jet-fighter squadrons (VMF-115 and -311) had provided the Marine exchange pilots who scoured the lower side of the Yalu with the Air Force F-86s on fighter sweeps.

During Korea the Marine carrier based CVE/CVL squadrons (VMAs-214, -233, -312, and -251) flew more than 25,000 sorties, experimenting with improved techniques for carrier landings. The carrier qualification program of Marine air units, a regular part of their training, also proved its value in combat. In the earliest days of the war, VMF-214 and -323 had operated from two CVEs based off the south coast of Korea, thereby providing close support to the brigade and other Eighth Army elements at a time when all shore-based aircraft were forced to operate from Japan.

VMF-214 was reassigned in Nov 1951, returning to CONUS (continental United States).
Credit: U.S. Marine Operations in Korea, Vol V, Meid & Yingling.

Marine Fighter Squadron VMF-214 over Korea August 1950. Photo taken by Capt John Skorish (later killed). Flying Number 16, Capt John S. Perrin, who supplied the photo. Major Bob Keller (Ex-O) in the lead plane. Capt A. J. Tosdal in Number 10.

APPENDIX 9
LTCOL BEAUMONT COOLEY, USMCR (RET), EXPLAINS DEATH OF SON'S FATHER 43 YEARS LATER

January 11, 1994

Dr. Michael D. Gooden

Dear Dr. Gooden,

In response to your query to the Marine Corps Aviation Association about the death of your father, Captain David Gooden, USMC, in February 1952, and your telephone conversation about this event today with George Nicoud in Dallas, I wish to introduce myself. George and I served with Dave Gooden in VMO-6.

When the Korean War started George Nicoud and I were members of VMF-112, a Reserve Fighter Squadron at NAS Dallas, Hensley Field. We were called to active duty in January 1951. The members of VMF-112 trained for a while in Dallas, and then transferred to MCAS El Toro and subsequently to Korea.

As a Captain in Korea I flew Corsairs for four and a half months with the Blacksheep Squadron, VMF-214, before being transferred to VMO-6 in late November of 1951. VMO-6, an Observation Squadron, part of the First Marine Air Wing attached to the First Marine Division handling aerial reconnaissance, artillery gunfire spotting and the air direction of close air support missions. Earlier in Korea, with the advent of the helicopter, VMO-6 took on the additional duty of transporting wounded. Most of this duty consisted of bringing non-ambulatory wounded from the front line area to rear area aid stations and hospitals in the Marine Corps and the Korean Marine part of front lines. While I was in VMO-6, the squadron complement was nine L-19/OE-1 aircraft and nine Bell HTL-4 helicopters. These latter machines are the ones of your interest and are identical to the copters in the lead-in of M.A.S.H., the TV program.

Whether or not to go on a night-evac was a volunteer thing and up to the duty pilot. I must say that in the four months I was in VMO-6, I never saw or heard of a duty pilot stand-down a requested night-evac. In fact, I sent one of our Sergeant pilots out on a black-black night when it was snowing so hard that visibility was less than 50 yards. It surprised me that he was even willing to attempt the evacuation--but go he did. He landed on a gravel bar in the river twice on the way up, to wait for visibility to improve so he could continue. I was privileged to write this man up for a Commendation, an award certainly well deserved. Later, we had a bad crash on a night-evac where one wounded man died strapped to the litter and the pilot was badly burned about the hands and face trying to effect his rescue.

I will add that flying at night in a helicopter in Korea in 1951-52 was a dicey duty at best. The copter pilots could not use their cockpit instrument lights as the glare reflected on the inside of the bubble and all but eliminated outside visibility. Most pilots at night held a pencil-flashlight in their teeth which they turned on intermittently to check the engine/rotor rpm gauge--a critical instrument in helicopter flying. But, anecdotes are not to the subject at hand.

At the time Dave Gooden and I served together, VMO-6 was located in the valley of the So-Yan-Gang (river) about a mile east of the Punch Bowl, about ten miles west of the east coast of Korea. We flew from a field designated as X-83, "X" standing for Tenth Corps. Our camp was in the village of Shinchon.

To the north on the front lines the Marines had as their right flank companions the I ROK (Army) division. To the Marines immediate left, along the north rim of the Punch Bowl, were the Korean Marines and still further left of them on the west rim of the Punch Bowl and along an area known earlier as "Heartbreak" Ridge was the US Army's 2nd Inf. Div. The entire region was mountainous averaging about 3000 feet above sea level. The terrain was mostly pine forested, particularly on the south side of hills and peaks. The landscape was festooned with sharp, steep sided hills some as high as 8000 feet, and narrow valleys.

APPENDIX 9 cont'd

      Besides being a fixed wing pilot, I served in VMO-6 as S-4 of the squadron, and on the day of Dave's death I was the Duty Operations Officer. It was my job to handle all telephone traffic into the squadron and assign aircraft and pilots for the scheduled and special request missions. About mid-morning we received a call from Air Operations at First Marine Division requesting a single-man evacuation at Hill 812 (812 meters in elevation). Hill 812 was one of the Marine strong points on the front and was well known to all--on both sides of the conflict. I told Division we were on the way!

      The weather on this day was clear and by Korean standards relatively warm, ie, about 20-25 degrees F. Dave was the next in line for flight and was present in the tent as I took the incoming call. By the time I hung up, Dave was on his feet and at my desk awaiting instructions.

      No more than six or seven minutes after Dave's take off, I received a telephone call from Division to the effect that one of our helicopters had just crashed near Hill 812. They said that details were only now coming in and they would get back as soon as possible.

      Within a few minutes we received word that your father had overflown the landing pad at Hill 812, crossed our line of trenches and swung wide over the fronting valley. Observers reported that as he approached the Korean trench line on the adjacent ridge his helicopter was hit by ground fire. I do not remember at this late date whether the machine exploded in air or whether it simply impacted the ground, but the crash site was only about twenty-five meters in front of the Korean (not Chinese) trench on the back side (to us) of a sleep slope. The wreckage scattered over a radius of thirty to forty meters and Dave was thrown from the helicopter. His body was laying face down in the snow about fifteen meters from the central mass of the wreckage.

      Our immediate concern was whether he was still alive. After a discussion between myself, VMO-6's C.O. and several others, we decided to send a fixed wing plane out with a photographer to make a record of the crash. Our intent was to photograph Dave's body to see if we could detect any sign of movement over a time frame. The photographer used a K-10 aerial camera which made 8X10-inch negatives and provided excellent pictures. All the pictures were shot no more than 100 feet above the enemy ridge, a rather hazardous undertaking at best. During the afternoon three photo planes received damage from small caliber fire, but fortunately no one was injured in these forays.

      The ground Marines on the front were very upset about the downed craft, and we received word that they would attempt a rescue after dark. Under the best of circumstances such an undertaking would have been a very dangerous operation as the wreckage lay on a north facing slope of about 30 degrees in the open within hand grenade throwing distance of the enemy trench.

      By 1600 we had about five or six sets of fine quality, extremely detailed pictures in hand and could detect no movement what so ever in the body. As the afternoon shadows lengthened, by 1500 the crash site was in deep shade with the temperature probably near zero. We felt that had your father survived the crash, by 1500 he certainly would have succumbed to the cold. I do not remember what he was wearing as he went out to fly, but if he was like the rest of us, he was dressed in a pair of Marine green winter service trousers, a Khaki or wool shirt, a light weight aviator's flight jacket and thermal boots. Likely he had on long-johns under this outer clothing. Remember, his mission was only a flight to, but not ahead of, the front lines. It was considered strictly routine, a type of flight that VMO-6 sent out dozens of times almost every day.

      I must say this; although I cannot be sure, I believe your father was killed by gunfire directly or died instantly in the ensuing crash. We received absolutely no evidence that suggests anything otherwise. All those who directed the subsequent reconnaissance operations as well as the over-the-site flyers and the ground Marines, who themselves had an excellent view of the crash site, were of this opinion. By 1600 we officially asked the Marines on the front <u>not</u>, I repeat, <u>not</u> to attempt a rescue.

      The next morning we could see numerous tracks in the snow around the wreck site. From these tracks we could tell that during the night the North Koreans had investigated each piece of the wreckage and had dragged your father's body to their trench.

APPENDIX 9 cont'd

We found later the reason that Dave did not land was as he came out of the very narrow valley leading up to the summit of Hill 812, he found a Sikorsky helicopter from HMR-161 sitting on the pad -- his destination. Apparently this copter just happened by and was radioed from the ground that they needed a wounded pickup. To give the ground folks credit they may not have assumed that the HMR craft was the one coming for the pickup. In any event, when Dave came to the site there was no place to set his machine down. At the 2700-foot level he could not hover in the HTL-4 and had to keep the helicopter moving forward to maintain altitude. Rather than turn sharply and return down the valley, he elected instead to make a wide turn. This decision cost him his life.

HMR-161 people flew a heavy lift copter that ordinarily carried ten people plus two pilots. These choppers were not ordinarily used for wounded evacuation as experience showed it was awkward to on-load and off-load litters through the cargo doors. Instead evacuations were made with the small Bell HTL-4s, such as we had in VMO-6, where litters on the outside of the pilot compartment gave easy ground access to the patients.

As I told you in our telephone conversation, it saddens me, even today after the passage of so many years, to think about your father's death and the death of so many of my other friends and acquaintances. I often wonder what might have been had these people not been taken from our world at so young an age. This is the tragedy of war.

I hope that these words in some small way help close what until now has been an unknown chapter of your life. Although, your father died on a very routine operation, this in no way detracts from the fact that he was a hero in all respects. Look at it this way, what we considered ordinary, I am sure would not have been viewed as ordinary by the man he was to evacuate. No doubt there were countless more heroic incidents in Dave's life, unknown now but to God. We will never know. Take solace in the fact that the helicopter pilots of VMO-6 saved many people who went on to have active and productive lives. There are many who owe these people an eternal debt of gratitude. Your father is among a very select few. He gave his life not in destroying others as happens in war, but in performing deeds that others might live.

Doctor Gooden, after I had written the above, it suddenly occurred to me that this short discussion might be of interest to a friend who I served with in VMF-223 during WWII. This man, Bernard W. Peterson, is currently writing a book on his experiences in Korea. He flew in an Attack Squadron in Korea and later served as a Forward Air Observer with the "Mud" Marines and received a Purple Heart and a Silver Star. I am sending a copy of this letter to him with the request if he uses any part of this letter, he does so only with your concurrence.

As a matter of interest, I call to your attention Pete's first book, <u>Briny to the Blue</u>, a narrative of his adventures during the World War II. Pete began his service career just out of High School in the pre-war Navy as an aviation mechanic and rear seat gunner. He participated in the early Pacific sea battles aboard the carriers USS Enterprise, USS Saratoga *and* USS Yorktown, *in Torpedo Squadron Three (VT-3) and completed his tours in VMF-223 in the Liberation of the Philippine Islands, the Air Defence of Okinawa and the Japanese Homeland Air War as a Corsair pilot. In light of your father's service, I heartily recommend this book to you. Pete did a remarkable job in presenting an exciting journal that I'm sure you would enjoy.*

Semper Fidelis

LtCol Beaumont B. Cooley, USMCR (Ret)
Austin, TX

Author's note: Sections of original letter have been shortened for brevity.

APPENDIX 10
MARINE PILOTS AND ENEMY AIRCRAFT DOWNED IN KOREAN WAR

21 Apr 51		1stLt Harold D. Daigh (VMF-312, F4U-4, USS *BATAAN*)	1 YAK
21 Apr 51		Capt Phillip C. DeLong (VMF-312, F4U-4, USS *BATAAN*)	2 YAKs
30 Jun 51	†	Capt Edwin B. Long (VMF[N]-513, F7F-3N)	1 PO-2
12 Jul 51		Capt Donald L. Fenton (VMF[N]-513, F4U-5NL)	1 PO-2
23 Sep 51		Maj Eugene A. Van Gundy (VMF[N]-513, F7F-3N)	1 PO-2
4 Nov 51	*	Maj William F. Guss (VMF-311)	1 MIG
5 Mar 52	*	Capt Vincent J. Marzello (VMF-311)	1 MIG
16 Mar 52	*	LtCol John S. Payne (1st MAW)	1 MIG
7 Jun 52		1stLt John W. Andre (VMF[N]-513, F4U-5NL)	1 YAK-9
10 Sep 52		Capt Jesse G. Folmar (VMA-312, F4U, USS *SICILY*)	1 MIG
15 Sep 52	*	Maj Alexander J. Gillis (VMF-311)	1 MIG
28 Sep 52	*	Maj Alexander J. Gillis (VMF-311)	2 MIGs
3 Nov 52	‡	Maj William T. Stratton, Jr. (VMF[N]-513, F3D-2)	1 YAK-15
8 Nov 52		Capt Oliver R. Davis (VMF[N]-513, F3D-2)	1 MIG
10 Dec 52	§	1stLt Joseph A. Corvi VMF[N]-513, F3D-2)	1 PO-2
12 Jan 53		Maj Elswin P. Dunn (VMF[N]-513, F3D-2)	1 MIG
20 Jan 53	*	Capt Robert Wade (MAG-33)	1 MIG
28 Jan 53		Capt James R. Weaver (VMF[N]-513, F3D-2)	1 MIG

APPENDIX 10 cont'd

31 Jan 53		LtCol Robert F. Conley (VMF[N]-513, F3D-2)	1 MIG
7 Apr 53	*	Maj Roy L. Reed (VMF-115)	1 MIG
12 Apr 53	*	Maj Roy L. Reed (VMF-115)	1 MIG
16 May 53	*	Maj John F. Bolt (VMF-115)	1 MIG
18 May 53	*	Capt Harvey L. Jensen (VMF-115)	1 MIG
22 Jun 53	*	Maj John F. Bolt (VMF-115)	1 MIG
24 Jun 53	*	Maj John F. Bolt (VMF-115)	1 MIG
30 Jun 53	*	Maj John F. Bolt (VMF-115)	1 MIG
11 Jul 53	*	Maj John F. Bolt (VMF-115)	1 MIG
12 Jul 53	*	Maj John H. Glenn (VMF-311)	1 MIG
19 Jul 53	*	Maj John H. Glenn (VMF-311)	1 MIG
20 Jul 53	*	Maj Thomas M. Sellers (VMF-115)	2 MIGs
22 Jul 53	*	Maj John H. Glenn (VMF-311)	<u>1 MIG</u>

35 TOTAL

(26 MIGs)

*   Marines on temporary exchange duty with Fifth Air Force flying F-86 Sabres.
†   First enemy aircraft destroyed at night by UNC
‡   First enemy jet aircraft destroyed through use of airborne intercept radar equipped fighter.
§   First enemy aircraft destroyed by means of lock-on radar gear.

APPENDIX 11
MARINE CORPS CASUALTIES (GROUND AND AIR)

KOREAN WAR 1950-1953

Date	**KIA	Killed non-Battle	***WIA	Cumulative Total
Aug-Dec 1950	1,526	30	6,229	7,785
Jan-Dec 1951	960	82	7,924	8,966
Jan-Mar 1952	87	19	600	706
Aug 1950-Mar 1952	2,573	131	14,753	17,457
Apr-Dec 1952	960	66	6,815	7,841 *
Jan-Jul 1953	729	47	4,470	5,246
Apr 1952-Jul 1953	1,689	113	11,285	13,087
TOTAL: Aug 1950 to Jul 1953	4,262	244	26,038	30,544

- *   This roughly represents the time period that I was in Korea
- ** Killed in action
- *** Wounded in action

Participation of the 1st MAW (First Marine Air Wing) in the war could also be measured in a different way. On the inevitable red side of the ledger: 258 Air Marines had been killed (including 65 MIA and presumed dead) and 174 WIA. A total of 436 Marine aircraft were also lost in combat or operational accidents.

A few months after returning home I drove over to Davis Monthan Air Force Base in Tucson. As we drove along I counted the old obsolete aircraft parked in seemingly endless row after row waiting to be cut up and melted down. They had over 3,200 fixed wing aircraft and helicopters stored on the 3,000 acres of desert. I was amazed when my count reached 436, the number of planes the Marines alone lost during the Korean War, and the rows continued on. Assuming a normal squadron complement consisted of 24 aircraft, that number would fill out over 18 full squadrons. Using the combined figures for Air Marines killed, missing and wounded, their number would fill every one of those cockpits (432 combined). It makes one contemplate the magnitude of the operation and the dedication. I'm sure the average "Joe Public" has no idea of the sacrifice and determination this struggle represented. I do!

APPENDIX 12
GLOSSARY OF TECHNICAL TERMS AND ABBREVIATIONS

AAA--Antiaircraft Artillery
AA--Antiaircraft
AD--Douglas "Skyraider" Single-Engine Attack Aircraft
ADC--Assistant Division Commander
ANGLICO--Air and Naval Gunfire Liaison Company
AO--Aerial Observer
ASP--Ammunition Supply Point
AT--Antitank
AU--Attack model of Vought F4U "Corsair"
BAR--Browning Automatic Rifle
BLT--Battalion Landing Team
Bn--Battalion
Brig--Brigade
Btry--Battery
CAS--Close Air Support
CCF--Chinese Communist Forces
CG--Commanding General
CinCFE--Commander in Chief, Far East
CinCUNC--Commander in Chief, United Nations Command
CinCPacFlt--Commander in Chief, Pacific Fleet
CMC--Commandant of the Marine Corps
CNO--Chief of Naval Operations
Co--Company
CO--Commanding Officer
ComdD--Command Diary (also called Historical Diary, or War Diary)
ComNavFE--Commander, Naval Forces, Far East
ComServPac--Commander, Service Force, Pacific
CONUS--Continental United States
COP--Combat Outpost
CP--Command Post
CPX--Command Post Exercise
CSG--Combat Service Group
CTE--Commander Task Element
CTF--Commander Task Force
CTG--Commander Task Group
CVE--Escort Aircraft Carrier
CVL--Light Aircraft Carrier
Div--Division
DMZ--Demilitarized Zone
DOW--Died of Wounds
Dtd--Dated
DUKW--Marine Amphibious Truck
ECIDE (U)--East Coast Island Defense Element (Unit)
ECM--Electronic Countermeasures
Engr--Engineer
EUSAK--Eighth United States Army in Korea
F2H-2P--McDonnell "Banshee" Two-Engine Jet Fighter (photo model)
F3D-2--Douglas "Skyknight" Two-Engine Jet Fighter
F4U--Vought "Corsair" Single-Engine Fighter

F7F-3N--Grumman "Tigercat" Twin-Engine Night Fighter
F9F-2,4,5--Grumman "Panther" Single-Engine Jet Fighter
F-80--Air Force "Shooting Star" Fighter Aircraft
F-84--Air Force "Thunderjet" Fighter Aircraft
FAC--Forward Air Controller
FAF--Fifth Air Force
FASRon--Fleet Air Service Squadron
FDC--Fire Direction Center
FEAF--Far East Air Forces
FECOM--Far East Command
FMFLant--Fleet Marine Force, Atlantic
FMFPac--Fleet Marine Force, Pacific
FO--Forward Observer (artillery)
FY--Fiscal Year
HE--High Explosive
Hedron-Headquarters Squadron
H&I--Harassing & Interdiction
HMR--Marine Helicopter Transport Squadron
HO3S-1--Sikorsky Three-Place Observation Helicopter
Hq--Headquarters
HQMC--Headquarters, U.S. Marine Corps
HRS-1--Sikorsky Single-Engine Helicopter
H&S--Headquarters and Service
HTL-4--Bell Two-Place Helicopter
Interv--Interview
JCS--Joint Chiefs of Staff
JOC--Joint Operations Center
KCOMZ--Korean Communication Zone (sometimes KComZ)
KIA--Killed in Action
KMAG--Korean Military Advisory Group
KMC--Korean Marine Corps
KMC/RCT--Korean Marine Corps Regimental Combat Team
KPR--Kimpo Provisional Regiment
KSC--Korean Service Crops
LogCom--Logistical Command
Ltr--Letter
LST--Landing Ship, Tank
LVT--Landing Vehicle, Tracked
M4A3E8-Flame Tank, Medium
M-46--Medium Tank
MAC--Military Armistice Commission
MACG--Marine Air Control Group
MAG--Marine Aircraft Group
Mar--Marine(s)
MARLEX--Marine Landing Exercise
MASRT--Marine Air Support Radar Team
MAW--Marine Aircraft Wing
MBP--Main Battle Position
MDL--Military Demarcation Line

APPENDIX 12 cont'd

MGCIS--Marine Ground Control Intercept Squadron
MIA--Missing in Action
MIG--Russian Single-Seat Jet Fighter-Interceptor
MLR--Main Line of Resistance
MOH--Medal of Honor
MOS--Military Occupation Specialty
Mosquito--Single Engine Plane used as Airborne FAC and for Target Spotting
MP--Military Police
MPQ--Ground Radar-Controlled Bombing
MS--Manuscript
Msg--Message
MSR--Main Supply Route
MTACS--Marine Tactical Air Control Squadron
MT--Motor Transport
NCAS--Night Close Air Support
NCO--Noncommissioned Officer
NGF--Naval Gunfire
NKPA--North Korean People's Army
N.D.--Date not given
NNRC--Neutral Nations Repatriation Commission
NNSC--Neutral Nations Supervisory Commission
N.T.--Title not given
OCMH--Office of the Chief of Military History (USA)
OE-1--Cessna Single-Engine Light Observation Plane
OOB--Order of Battle
OP--Observation Post (Sometimes used to refer to an Outpost)
OPLR--Outpost Line of Resistance
OY--Consolidated-Vultee Light Observation Plane
PIR--Periodic Intelligence Report
PO-2--Russian Trainer Aircraft
POW--Prisoner of War
PPSH--Soviet-made 7.62mm Submachine ("Burp") Gun
Prov--Provisional
PUC--Presidential Unit Citation
R4D--Douglas Twin-Engine Transport (Navy and Marine Corps designation of C-47)
R5D--Douglas Four-Engine Transport (Navy and Marine Corps designation of C-54)
RCT--Regimental Combat Team
ROK--Republic of Korea
SAR--Special Action Report
SecDef--Secretary of Defense
SecNav--Secretary of Navy
Serv--Service
Sig--Signal
SOP--Standing Operating Procedure
TACC--Tactical Air Coordination Center
TADC--Tactical Air Direction Center
TAFC--Turkish Armed Forces Command

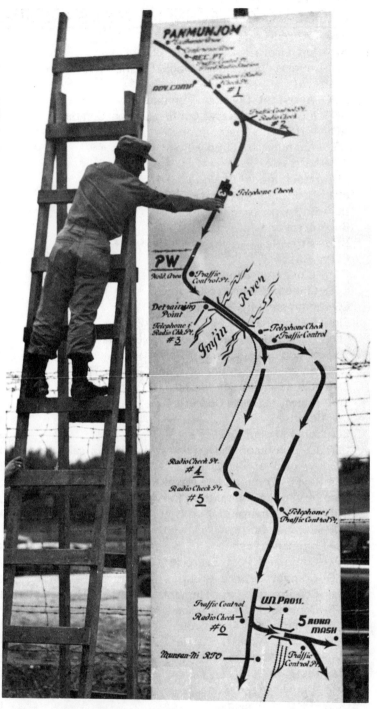

Operation BIG SWITCH—Road map of route taken by repatriated UN prisoners of war as convoy reaches radio check points. Progress of convoy is immediately relayed to Freedom Village and entered on map. Photo credit: USMC
At 1000 hours on 27 July 1953 LtGen William K. Harrison Jr, the senior UN delegate to the armistice negotiations, signed the armistice papers. At the same time the senior enemy delegate, Gen Nam Il, placed his signature on the documents. The armistice went into effect at 2200 hours of the same day.

CHUCKWALLA PUBLISHING Publishes the following books:

SHORT STRAW
Memoirs of Korea by a Fighter Pilot/Forward Air Controller
Captain Bernard W. Peterson USMCR (Ret)
Approximately 565 pages including photos and maps
8 1/2 x 11 inches, $29.95 hardcover
ISBN: 0-9631875-3-8

BRINY to the BLUE:
Memoirs of WWII by a Sailor/Marine Fighter Pilot
Captain Bernard W. Peterson USMCR (Ret)
Approximately 379 pages, 200 photos and maps
8 1/2 x 11 inches, $29.95 hardcover
ISBN: 0-9631875-0-3

AIR FORCE: Official Service Journal of the U.S. ARMY Air Forces
Introduction by Captain Bernard W. Peterson USMCR (Ret)
A facsimile of six months, January through June 1943
272 pages, hundreds of illustrations and photos
8 1/2 x 11 inches, $22.95 softcover
ISBN 0-9631875-1-1
Series Number 1

BOOK ORDER FORM

Please send me the following:

Title	ISBN	Price
A.		$
B.		$
C.		$
	Subtotal	$
	*Plus postage and handling	$
	Subtotal	$
	Add 6.7% sales tax for delivery within AZ	$
	TOTAL AMOUNT ENCLOSED	$
	(Check or Money Order Only)	$

*Postage and handling is:
$3.50 for orders under $30.00 and $4.50 for orders $30.01 or more

MAIL TO: ADD YOUR NAME AND ADDRESS (Please Print):
Customer Service   Name
Chuckwalla Publishing   Street address
27015 N. 92nd St.   City/State/Zip
Scottsdale, AZ 85255